The Rorschach: A Comprehensive System, in two volumes
  by John E. Exner, Jr.
Theory and Practice in Behavior Therapy
  by Aubrey J. Yates
Principles of Psychotherapy
  by Irving B. Weiner
Psychoactive Drugs and Social Judgment: Theory and Research
  edited by Kenneth Hammond and C. R. B. Joyce
Clinical Methods in Psychology
  edited by Irving B. Weiner
Human Resources for Troubled Children
  by Werner I. Halpern and Stanley Kissel
Hyperactivity
  by Dorothea M. Ross and Sheila A. Ross
Heroin Addiction: Theory, Research and Treatment
  by Jerome J. Platt and Christina Labate
Children's Rights and the Mental Health Profession
  edited by Gerald P. Koocher
The Role of the Father in Child Development
  edited by Michael E. Lamb
Handbook of Behavioral Assessment
  edited by Anthony R. Ciminero, Karen S. Calhoun, and Henry E. Adams
Counseling and Psychotherapy: A Behavioral Approach
  by E. Lakin Phillips
Dimensions of Personality
  edited by Harvey London and John E. Exner, Jr.
The Mental Health Industry: A Cultural Phenomenon
  by Peter A. Magaro, Robert Gripp, David McDowell, and Ivan W. Miller III
Nonverbal Communication: The State of the Art
  by Robert G. Harper, Arthur N. Wiens, and Joseph D. Matarazzo
Alcoholism and Treatment
  by David J. Armor, J. Michael Polich, and Harriet B. Stambul
A Biodevelopmental Approach to Clinical Child Psychology: Cognitive Controls and
Cognitive Control Theory
  by Sebastiano Santostefano
Handbook of Infant Development
  edited by Joy D. Osofsky
Understanding the Rape Victim: A Synthesis of Research Findings
  by Sedelle Katz and Mary Ann Mazur
Childhood Pathology and Later Adjustment: The Question of Prediction
  by Loretta K. Cass and Carolyn B. Thomas
Intelligent Testing with the WISC-R
  by Alan S. Kaufman
Adaptation in Schizophrenia: The Theory of Segmental Set
  by David Shakow
Psychotherapy: An Eclectic Approach
  by Sol L. Garfield
Handbook of Minimal Brain Dysfunctions
  edited by Herbert E. Rie and Ellen D. Rie
Handbook of Behavioral Interventions: A Clinical Guide
  edited by Alan Goldstein and Edna B. Foa
Art Psychotherapy
  by Harriet Wadeson
Handbook of Adolescent Psychology
  edited by Joseph Adelson
Psychotherapy Supervision: Theory, Research and Practice
  edited by Allen K. Hess

Continued on back

THE ROLE
OF THE FATHER
IN CHILD DEVELOPMENT

THE ROLE
OF THE FATHER
IN CHILD DEVELOPMENT

Second Edition
Completely Revised and Updated

Edited by

MICHAEL E. LAMB

University of Utah
Salt Lake City, Utah

A WILEY-INTERSCIENCE PUBLICATION

JOHN WILEY & SONS, New York•Chichester•Brisbane•Toronto•Singapore

This publication is designed to provide accurate and
authoritative information in regard to the subject
matter covered. It is sold with the understanding that
the publisher is not engaged in rendering legal, accounting,
or other professional service. If legal advice or other
expert assistance is required, the services of a competent
professsional person should be sought. *From a Declaration
of Principles jointly adopted by a Committee of the
American Bar Association and a Committee of Publishers.*

Library of Congress Cataloging in Publication Data:

The role of the father in child development.

(Wiley series on personality processes, ISSN 0195-4008)
"A Wiley-Interscience publication."
Includes index.
1. Fathers—Addresses, essays, lectures.
2. Father and child—Addresses, essays, lectures.
3. Paternal deprivation—Addresses, essays, lectures.
4. Single-parent family—United States—Addresses, essays, lectures.
5. Child development—United States—Addresses, essays, lectures.
I. Lamb, Michael E., 1953–   . II. Series: Wiley series on personality processes.

HQ756.R64   1981   308.8'7   81-3063
ISBN 0-471-07739-9   AACR2

Printed in the United States of America

10 9 8 7 6 5 4

TO THE MEMORY OF
MY FATHER

Contributors

Henry B. Biller, Department of Psychology, University of Rhode Island, Kingston, Rhode Island

Jonathan Bloom-Feshbach, Yale Bush Center in Child Development and Social Policy, New Haven, Connecticut.

Candice Feiring, Infant Laboratory, Educational Testing Service, Princeton, New Jersey

Martin L. Hoffman, Department of Psychology, University of Michigan, Ann Arbor, Michigan

Mary Maxwell Katz, Laboratory of Human Development, Graduate School of Education, Harvard University, Cambridge, Massachusetts

Melvin J. Konner, Department of Anthropology, Harvard University, Cambridge, Massachusetts

Michael E. Lamb, Department of Psychology, University of Utah, Salt Lake City, Utah

Michael Lewis, Infant Laboratory, Educational Testing Service, Princeton, New Jersey

Veronica J. Mächtlinger, Psychoanalyst in Private Practice, Berlin

Ross D. Parke, Department of Psychology, University of Illinois, Champaign, Illinois

Frank A. Pedersen, National Institute of Child Health and Human Development, Bethesda, Maryland

Norma Radin, School of Social Work, University of Michigan, Ann Arbor, Michigan

William K. Redican, Research Psychologist, Behavioral Medicine Associates, Santa Rosa, California

David M. Taub, Yemassee Primate Center, Yemassee, South Carolina

Barbara R. Tinsley, Department of Psychology, University of Illinois, Champaign, Illinois

Jaan Valsiner, Department of Psychology, University of North Carolina, Chapel Hill, North Carolina

Marsha Weinraub, Department of Psychology, Temple University, Philadelphia, Pennsylvania

Series Preface

This series of books is addressed to behavioral scientists interested in the nature of human personality. Its scope should prove pertinent to personality theorists and researchers as well as to clinicians concerned with applying an understanding of personality processes to the amelioration of emotional difficulties in living. To this end, the series provides a scholarly integration of theoretical formulations, empirical data, and practical recommendations.

Six major aspects of studying and learning about human personality can be designated: personality theory, personality structure and dynamics, personality development, personality assessment, personality change, and personality adjustment. In exploring these aspects of personality, the books in the series discuss a number of distinct but related subject areas: the nature and implications of various theories of personality; personality characteristics that account for consistencies and variations in human behavior; the emergence of personality processes in children and adolescents; the use of interviewing and testing procedures to evaluate individual differences in personality; efforts to modify personality styles through psychotherapy, counseling, behavior therapy, and other methods of influence; and patterns of abnormal personality functioning that impair individual competence.

IRVING B. WEINER

Case Western Reserve University
Cleveland, Ohio

Preface

Since the first edition of *The Role of the Father in Child Development* was published in 1976, the paternal role has elicited a great deal of attention from both theorists and researchers. In fact, the interest has been so great that it has become necessary to prepare a revision of the book. The present volume reflects the manner in which the field is currently approached and the ways in which this has changed in recent years. Let me briefly enumerate those changes that seem most important.

A considerable effort has been made in the last few years to explore and understand the ways in which the father's relationships with various members of the family supplement and interact with one another in mediating both direct and indirect influences on child development. Three of the chapters in this anthology reflect a special sensitivity to the fact that many paternal influences may be indirectly mediated through the husband–wife relationship. Pedersen (Chapter 8) focuses exclusively on the interface between the spousal and parent–child relationships, and Parke and Tinsley (Chapter 12) discuss this interface from the perspective of research on early parent–infant interactions. Lewis, Feiring, and Weinraub (Chapter 7) consider direct and indirect influences more generally. The importance of these considerations is also underscored by the number of references to them in other chapters throughout the book.

A second area of widespread concern today has to do with fathers who play nontraditional roles within the family. Although most fathers continue to see themselves as primary breadwinners and their wives as primary caretakers, a small but increasing number of couples are reversing or sharing breadwinning and caretaking roles. In addition, a substantial number of children spend at least part of their childhood without fathers, and a smaller number are raised by single fathers. Biller (Chapters 9 and 14) reviews the extensive research on the effects of father absence and divorce, and several other contributors discuss findings from studies of nontraditional families. Two other chapters, those by Valsiner (Chapter 5) and Katz and Konner (Chapter 4), provide further reminders that most research has been done on traditional, modern, American families despite the fact that 95 percent of the people in the world are raised in families that differ substantially from this pattern.

Studies of both indirect effects and nontraditional paternal roles have been concerned largely with development in infancy. This tendency is so marked that I have included not just one but two reviews of the research on father–infant relationships. Parke and Tinsley (Chapter 12) emphasize the interactions that occur in the first months of life, whereas Lamb (Chapter 13) emphasizes studies of older infants and their parents.

Advances since 1975 have not been limited to studies of indirect effects, infancy, or nontraditional families. So great has been the interest in father–child relationships, in fact, that all of the chapters in this book have been written especially for this anthology. It is a mark of the field's rapid development that many chapters bear little resemblance to the chapters on the same topics published in the first edition—even when the authors are the same as before. Thanks to the energetic efforts of a coterie of researchers and theorists, we have seen more progress between the publication of the first and second editions than in the preceding decades. We are slowly coming to understand the role of the father in child development.

As before, the book will be of greatest use to professionals, researchers, and graduate students interested in the study of the family and the study of socialization. In addition to the topics already mentioned, the book includes timely syntheses concerned with paternal influences on sex role, moral, and intellectual development, as well as reviews of psychoanalytic theory, paternal behavior among primates, and historical changes in popular portrayals of fathers. The contributors have provided up-to-date summaries of the theories and research findings bearing on their topics. Their integrative reviews are likely to prove invaluable to those planning to enter the area as well as to those who are already active. The heuristic impact of the first edition is demonstrated by the need for a revised edition within several years: there is every reason to expect that the scholarly papers included in the present edition will have a comparable impact.

Finally, I would like to thank Nancy Becker for her fine typing, and Karen Boswell for assistance in the preparation of the index.

MICHAEL E. LAMB

Salt Lake City, Utah
August 1981

Contents

THE ROLE
OF THE FATHER
IN CHILD DEVELOPMENT

CHAPTER 1

Fathers and Child Development: An Integrative Overview

MICHAEL E. LAMB

University of Utah

Taken together, the chapters in this book provide an analysis of current thinking and knowledge concerning paternal contributions to socialization and personality development. Each of the later chapters focuses on a specific perspective or topic; the purpose of this chapter is to provide an integrative review of the entire area. Although I review a variety of diverse perspectives, the resulting synthesis represents my personal views on a sprawling and somewhat undisciplined field of endeavor.

The first edition of this book (Lamb, 1976e) was published at a time of suddenly increased interest in the father–child relationship. This newfound interest was manifest in a flurry of books aimed at the professional and lay markets (e.g., Benson, 1968; Biller, 1971a, 1974d; Biller & Meredith, 1974; Broderick, 1977; Daley, 1978; Dodson, 1974; Gilbert, 1975; Green, 1976; Hamilton, 1977; Lamb, 1976e; Levine, 1976; Lynn, 1974; Pedersen, 1980; Roman & Haddad, 1978; Shedd, 1975; Stafford, 1978; Stevens & Mathews, 1978). Although the spate of activity appears to have died down, the contemporary literature reveals a new maturity: Fathers are now accorded serious attention in textbooks and treatises on socialization; theorists and researchers ponder the patterns of influence within the family rather than independent maternal and paternal "effects"; and parenting manuals are directed to a mixed readership of mothers and fathers. The chapters written for this revised edition reflect the increasing maturity and sophistication of the field.

In the first section of this chapter, I consider possible reasons for the long neglect and deemphasis of father–child relationships and speculate about the source of the renewed interest we are now witnessing. I then turn to the major theoretical frameworks that have guided the interpretation of research findings for several decades (namely, psychoanalysis, attachment theory, Parson's theory, and social learning theory). The section concludes with a critique of these four approaches.

In the third section, the focus shifts from theory to empirical endeavors as I review evidence concerning the father–child relationship:—when does it form? What are its salient characteristics? How does it differ from (or appear similar to) the mother–child relationship?

The bulk of published research has been directed toward the issue discussed in the fourth section: the aspects of personality development that fathers appear to influence. Paternal effects on sex role, moral, and intellectual development have all been studied, as have influences on general personality adjustment. The effects of father absence and marital disharmony are then reviewed in the fifth and sixth sections, respectively. Finally, in a summary section, I survey what we know, what we could do better, and what we have yet to investigate. Since there is much that we do not yet know, I attempt to identify issues toward which further investigation might profitably be directed. I also wish to draw attention to the dangers of overspecialization and the related need to appreciate the interdependencies among aspects of development (e.g., cognitive, emotional, social) and among agents of influence (e.g., mothers, fathers, peers). It is important to recognize that the father's role is defined by, and must be seen in the context of, a network of significant relationships within and outside the family. It is also necessary to see continuity within the life cycle and to recognize that the father–infant, father–child, and father–adolescent relationships represent different stages in the evolution of a developing relationship between two individuals.

FATHERHOOD: DISAPPEARANCE AND REDISCOVERY

Cultural presumptions and cultural change probably account for both the devaluation of the paternal role and the recent ascendant interest in it. The industrialization of western societies brought with it a stricter division of labor and roles within the family than had previously existed. Industry demanded that laborers work long fixed hours at central locations that were often far removed from the workers' homes. At least initially, furthermore, it was brawn and endurance they sought, rather than facility and skill. The preference was thus for male workers, whose wives in turn assumed an increasing responsibility for domestic chores and child-rearing. Fathers became unavailable to their children, and the nature of work was such that they could no longer train their young children to help in the way they had helped in agricultural communities. Roles within the family were strictly differentiated very rapidly; mothers changed from having responsibility for early caretaking to responsibility for childrearing, while fathers changed from influential agents of socialization to economic providers. Katz and Konner (Chapter 4) indicate in their chapter that in nonindustrial cultures fathers retain an important and active role in socialization despite rigidly defined sex roles.

It is interesting that industrialized societies maintained strict distinctions between maternal and paternal roles even after the labor market changed, making it no longer necessary for fathers to work long hours away from home. By this time, fathers had lost their responsibility to train children in the family occupations, be they farming, blacksmithing, or hunting, because the world of work was no longer receptive to (or appropriate for) young apprentices. Within the home, meanwhile, mothers clung to their responsibility for socialization as the number of economically productive tasks they could perform dwindled in the face of urbanization, labor-saving appliances, and consumerism.

Cultural realities alone were not responsible for the emphasis that psychological theorists placed on maternal influences. An influential and disparate group of scholars drawn from anthropology, behavioral biology, comparative psychology, ethology, and a new field, sociobiology, argued that the traditional division of parental roles and responsibilities should not be viewed as accidents of cultural organization. Instead, they argued that these roles were "natural"—that is, they were determined at least in part by biological predispositions and imperatives. The facts that women alone lactate and that males tend to be little involved in childcare throughout mammalian species were viewed as sufficient reason for concluding that women were biologically destined to assume primary responsibility for both caretaking and socialization. Lehrman, a pioneer in research on the biological/hormonal determinants of parental behavior, wrote perceptively that such arguments involved "using what look like scientific considerations to justify our social prejudices" (1974, p. 194). As Lehrman implied, most arguments concerning the biological bases of sex differences in parental behavior drew on evidence concerning the role of hormones in the establishment of maternal behavior in rats (see Lamb, 1975b, for a review); few even acknowledged that the relevance of this evidence was questionable. The variability among rodent species, the stereotypic nature of rodent parenting compared with the complexity of socialization and parenting in humans, the frequent incidence of maternal behavior in nulliparous human males and females, and the absence of data demonstrating that females are biologically designed (lactation excepted) to be exclusive socializers, or indeed that they perform this task more competently (L. Hoffman, 1974; Parke & Sawin, 1977), combine to make the rodent model totally inappropriate (see also Bernal & Richards, 1973). Ford and Beach (1951) pointed out many years ago that the role of hormones in the display of sexual behaviors decreases as one ascends the phylogenetic scale, whereas culturally learned factors increase in importance. There is every reason to believe that, among humans, societal prescriptions are *at least* as important in the regulation of parental as of sexual behavior. There is no reason to believe that a specific constellation of hormones is either necessary or sufficient for the elicitation of human parental behavior.

As I have argued elsewhere (Lamb, 1980b; Lamb & Goldberg, 1982), most biological predispositions are biases or tendencies rather than imperatives. The biological tendencies are such that they would be trivial if not supplemented by social forces; they could be reversed readily if they were contradicted rather than reinforced by cultural influences. In fact, however, societies tend to employ mechanisms that capitalize on and exaggerate biologically based tendencies. The resulting behavior patterns or sex differences are the joint product of biological influences and social learning. As in past eras, unfortunately, social scientists remain rather in awe of biological influences.

Thus the psychologists who began studying socialization themselves lived in societies in which mothers "naturally" assumed primary responsibility for parenting while fathers pursued advancement and money outside the home (see, for example, Briffault, 1927; Demos, 1974; Favez-Boutonier, 1955; Gorer, 1948; MacCalman, 1955; Metraux, 1955; Nash, 1965; Sunley, 1955; Westermarck, 1921). The paternal role was widely devalued (Birdwhistell, 1957; Brenton, 1966; Foster, 1964; Kluckhohn, 1949; Rohrer & Edmondson, 1960). It is not surprising that all the major theories focused on maternal influences; nor is it surprising that when parental attitudes or behaviors were of interest, it was mothers who were interviewed or observed. By the late 1960s, however, things began to change as several social scientists had predicted (Bernhardt, 1957; Christopherson, 1956; Mogey, 1957; Olsen, 1960). There are several apparent reasons for this.

First, the focus on mother–infant and mother–child relationships became so extreme and imbalanced that researchers were forced to ask whether fathers could legitimately be deemed irrelevant entities in socialization. A second reason for the ascendant interest in both fathers and families was that the traditional family structure itself appeared to be in mortal danger of displacement. The rapidity and extensiveness of recent changes in children's rearing environments (Bronfenbrenner, 1975c, 1979) forced social scientists to reevaluate the presumed strengths and weaknesses of the traditional social structure and to consider the likely consequences of the changes taking place. Unfortunately, social scientists found themselves knowing little about family influences or the father–child relationship, even though it was the father–child relationship that was most frequently disrupted (Bronfenbrenner, 1975c; Clausen, 1966; Herzog & Sudia, 1970, 1973; Wynn, 1964).

Third, it is increasingly apparent that modern fathers do not want to be peripheral figures in the lives and socialization of their children. Recent surveys, such as that described by Sheehy (1979), find that the vast majority of young men want to be integrally involved in relationships with their children. The women's movement has raised the consciousness of both men and women and has led women to demand that their husbands play a more active role within the family so that they too can pursue their own aspirations outside the home. National surveys conducted in the 1960s found that the husbands of employed women did not spend more time on household and childcare chores than the husbands of full-time mothers, but more recent data indicate that the husbands of working mothers are now more involved (Pleck, 1977, 1979, in press; Feshbach, 1980; Baruch & Barnett, 1979; Gold & Andres, 1978a, 1978b; Oakley, 1972; Hoffman & Nye, 1974; Lamouse, 1969; Haavio-Mannila, 1971; but see Gold, Andres, & Glorieux, 1979). They still leave primary responsibility to their wives, but the trend to greater participation is undeniable (see also Hoffman, 1977). Levine, Klein, and Owen (1967) reported that modern African fathers were also more affectionate and intimate than traditional fathers.

Fourth, although full-time mothers obviously spend more time with their children than working fathers do, there is a tendency to exaggerate the extent of interaction between mothers and young children. The evidence suggests that even when mother and child are in the same room, interaction can be relatively infrequent (Clarke-Stewart, 1973). Goldberg (1972) and Leiderman and Leiderman (1974, 1975, 1977) note that little social interaction takes place in African cultures even when the infant is being carried almost continually by its mother. Much of the time involved in caretaking is taken up by activities (e.g., laundering, food preparation) that do not involve interpersonal interaction (Fitzsimmons & Rowe, 1971; Stone, 1970).

Fifth, students of both cognitive and social development have come to realize that the amount of time adults spend with children is not linearly related— perhaps not related at all—to the amount of influence they have. Empirical and theoretical considerations indicate that the amount of time spent with the parent is a poor predictor of the quality of the infant's relationship with either mother or father (Feldman, 1973, 1974; Pedersen & Robson, 1969; Schaffer & Emerson, 1964). Perhaps the best evidence of this is the fact that daily separations from mothers such as those demanded by daycare attendance do not appear to disrupt the infant–mother attachment (Belsky & Steinberg, 1978; Bronfenbrenner, 1975a; Caldwell, Wright, Honig, & Tannenbaum, 1970; Doyle, 1975; Doyle & Somers, 1975; Feldman, 1973; Ragozin, 1975; Ramey & Mills, 1975; Ricciuti & Poresky, 1973; Roopnarine & Lamb, 1978; Kagan, Kearsley, & Zelazo, 1978), and there is no reason that the daily separations from a working father need be more disruptive.

The quality of the interaction and of the adult's behavior (Ainsworth et al., 1971, 1974; Bossard & Bell, 1966; Pedersen & Robson, 1969; Schaffer & Emerson, 1964) are far more important than the quantity: A few hours of pleasurable interaction may be much more conducive to the formation of strong and secure attachments than hours of cohabitation with a dissatisfied, harrassed, or ignoring mother (Birnbaum, 1971; Lamb, Chase-Lansdale, & Owen, 1979; Yarrow, Scott, DeLeeuw, & Heinig, 1962). With fathers as with mothers, there is no necessary correlation between the quantity of time together and the quality of interaction. Even though fathers spend relatively little time with their children, therefore, they may still have a significant impact on the children's development. This realization increased the pressure to study fathers, the "forgotten contributors to child development" (Lamb, 1975a).

Further, as several chapters in this book explain, important influences do not have to be direct (see the chapters by Lewis, Feiring, and Weinraub [Chapter 7], Pedersen [Chapter 8], and Parke and Tinsley [Chapter 12], especially). There exists within the family a network of relationships and influences that make it possible for any one individual (e.g., the father) to influence any other (e.g., the child) by way of the former's relationship with and influence on another family member (e.g., the mother). Thus even when a father interacts rarely with his child and has little direct influence on it, he may still exert a significant influence indirectly.

Finally, there has been a revolution in the way in which children—especially infants—are conceptualized. Whereas theorists once portrayed infants and children as the passive recipients of social influences, they now recognize that children play an active role in eliciting and shaping social interactions and in constructing subjective conceptualizations of the social world. This realization has led social scientists, particularly in the study of infant social development, to wonder whether they have underestimated the capacity of infants to establish formatively significant relationships with persons other than their mothers.

MAJOR THEORETICAL PERSPECTIVES

Psychoanalytic Theory[1]

The most influential characterization of the father–child relationship was provided by Sigmund Freud's psychoanalytic theory, which is reviewed more thoroughly by Mächtlinger in Chapter 3. Although Freud acknowledged that infants did become cathected to and identified with both parents (Burlingham, 1973; Freud, 1948, 1950), he stressed that both boys and girls formed their first and most important relationships with their mothers. (This emphasis on the formative significance of the mother–infant relationship represented a late evolution in Freud's thinking. For most of his life, he regarded the Oedipal phase as especially important, and he tended to exaggerate the father's role.)

[1]Although Jung (1949) published a book on the father's role, he consistently placed greater emphasis on the mother and on archetypal representations of the father (Von Der Heydt, 1964). Consequently, little will be said about his theory.

Since Freud's time, theorists of all persuasions have followed his lead in assuming that the mother–infant relationship has a disproportionately significant impact on psychological development (Bijou & Baer, 1961; Bowlby, 1951, 1958, 1969, 1973; Freud, 1940; Kohlberg, 1966; Maccoby & Masters, 1970; Mowrer, 1950; Parsons, 1958; Sears, 1957; Winnicott, 1965). Freud (and later Bowlby) explicitly described the mother–infant relationship as "the prototype of all later love relationships," even though, as Schaffer (1971) wrote: "Whether a child's first relationship is in any way the prototype of all future relationships we do not as yet know; the clinical material bearing on this point is hardly convincing" (p. 151).

Belief in the unique significance of the mother–infant relationship developed from the fact that the mother typically takes on the role of primary caretaker. Although Freud described a complex psychodynamic sequence, his working assumption was that (in the terminology of learning theorists) the first affective relationship developed as a consequence of the continued association of the mother with the positive sensation of need gratification (Dollard & Miller, 1950). This *secondary drive hypothesis,* at least in its traditional form, lost adherents in the general fall from favor of Hull's (1943) drive reduction model of learning and was further weakened by Harlow's demonstration that infant monkeys prefer to cling to and seek comfort from soft terrycloth mother surrogates rather than wire surrogates that fed them (Harlow, 1961; Harlow & Zimmerman, 1959). Consistent with this, Ainsworth (1963, 1967) and Schaffer and Emerson (1964) reported that many infants had strong attachments to persons who had little to do with their caretaking and physical gratification. To the chagrin of psychoanalysts and the social learning theorists they had inspired and influenced, researchers have been unable to find consistent relationships between infantile gratification and later dependency behavior (Caldwell, 1964; Maccoby & Masters, 1970; Sears, Maccoby, & Levin, 1957; Sears, Whiting, Nowlis, & Sears, 1953).

Freud's (1900, 1905) rendition of the Oedipal phase was as follows. At around 3 to 5 years of age, the boy realized that his mother also loved his father, and so he began to see his father as a rival for mother's affections. At roughly the same time, furthermore, the young boy became aware of the anatomical differences between the sexes. Assuming that girls (and his mother) once had penises that had been removed in punishment, the boy feared that his father might castrate his son and rival in retaliation (Mullahy, 1948). To avert this, the boy repressed his affection for his mother and identified with his father (Freud, 1948). By so doing, he hoped to diminish father's aggression ("he would not castrate someone like himself") while ensuring mother's continued affection ("she loves father and thus will love me if I am like father"). According to psychoanalytic theory, this identification played a crucial role in the development of gender role and gender identity and also presaged the formation and internalization of the superego, a prerequisite for the development of morality and moral behavior (Freud, 1963, 1962, 1924).

The young girl, according to Freud, underwent an analogous experience during this period. Since she concluded that castration (by mother) had already taken place, however, the girl lacked the strong motive to identify (castration anxiety) that impelled the boy. As a result, identification and the internalization of the superego were said to be less thoroughgoing and complete in girls than in boys (Freud, 1950). Most psychoanalysts followed Freud in his assumption that girls and women had weaker superegos than boys (e.g., Deutsch, 1944) although this is now seen as an unnecessarily sexist conclusion on Freud's part.

Since 1960 especially, psychoanalytic theorists have devoted most attention to pre-Oedipal relationships between parents and children. Although they have acknowledged that father–infant relationships may exist, the major emphasis has been on the mother–infant relationship (A. Freud, 1965; Brody, 1956; Escalona, 1968; Murphy, 1956; Murphy & Moriarty, 1976). Psychoanalytic accounts of infant development lack systematic considerations of the nature and influence of the father–infant relationship (Ross, 1979), although Mahler's followers are notable exceptions. Mahler and her students, assuming that the mother–infant relationship necessarily develops first, have suggested that the father entices the toddler to break away from a symbiotic relationship with its mother (Abelin, 1971, 1975, in press; Mahler, 1968; Mahler, Pine, & Furer, 1975). This proposition is reminiscent of the arguments made earlier by psychoanalysts (e.g., Meerloo, 1956, 1968; Von Der Heydt, 1964) who stressed that the father symbolically "cut the cord" between mother and child. This notion also presumed the absence of an early father–infant relationship (Sullivan, 1953). Meerloo went so far as to suggest that if an early father–infant relationship involved the father in a feminine style of interaction, the father would be unable to sever the mother–child symbiosis. Other analysts discussed the father's role in shifting the boy's identification from mother to father (Boehm, 1930; Horney, 1924, 1926, 1932, 1933; Kestenberg, 1956, 1968, 1975; Ross, 1975, 1977, 1979; Gurwitt, 1976). In these discussions attempts have been made to emphasize nonhostile elements in pre-Oedipal father–infant relationships (Boehm, 1930; Loewald, 1951; Greenacre, 1971; Van Der Leeuw, 1958).

The study of the Oedipal constellation and its consequences reflects the clearest influence of psychoanalytic theory on research concerning fathers, but Mächtlinger also draws attention to another issue that psychoanalysts have stressed to no apparent avail. Psychoanalysts have long argued that much of the father's importance accrues from his role within the family system. Unfortunately, the need to be concise has led many researchers to present overly simplistic conceptualizations of the father's role. Psychoanalysts have continually stressed both the dangers of oversimplification and the complexity of personality development.

Attachment Theory

Of the several schools of thought that Freud engendered, the object relations theorists such as Fairbairn (1952), Winnicott (1958), and Klein (1957) placed greatest emphasis on the very earliest months of life, and their emphasis on the mother–infant relationship was practically exclusive. One member of this school, John Bowlby (1951, 1958, 1969), was sufficiently moved by his experiences with the effects of institutionalization (Bowlby, 1944, 1951) to propose a revolutionary revision of psychoanalytic theory—a revolution that involved replacing Freud's secondary drive assumptions with a system that was drawn from contemporary evolutionary biology (Hinde, 1970; Lorenz, 1935; Sluckin, 1965). Attachment theorists like Bowlby (1969) and Ainsworth (1967, 1973, 1979) proposed that infants were born with a biologically based tendency to seek protective proximity to and contact with adults. Bowlby then introduced the notion of monotropy: that infants come to focus their proximity seeking behaviors on *a* particular individual, who then becomes the primary attachment figure. Although Bowlby did not deny that other relationships could be formed, it was several years before attachment theorists recognized that many infants formed significant relationships to both parents, even if the caretaker–infant relationship was most important.

According to attachment theorists, individual differences in the quality or security of infant–adult relationships depend on variations in the adult's propensity to respond sensitively and appropriately to the infant's signals (Ainsworth et al., 1974, 1978). Infants who have secure relationships later generalize their cooperativeness and sociability to interactions with others, whereas those with insecure attachments generalize their anger or avoidance (Ainsworth et al., 1978; Main, 1973; Thompson & Lamb, 1981). The security of both mother– and father–infant relationships should affect the infant's social style in the same way, although (presumably) the relationship with the primary attachment figure should be more influential. Attachment theory has dominated recent research on father–infant relations.

Parsons' Theory

Parsons (1954, 1958; Parsons & Bales, 1955), like Mowrer (1950) and Dollard and Miller (1950), proposed a theory of personality development comprising an elaboration of Freud's theory of identification (Bronfenbrenner, 1960, 1961a). In the main, however, this theory has been more influential among sociologists and family social scientists than among psychologists, and it is more frequently referred to in post hoc fashion than as the source of predictions and hypotheses.

Parsons depicted the child's social world as one consisting of only mother and child, but during the period in which Freud located the Oedipal conflict, Parsons suggested that the mother–child subsystem expanded to incorporate the father as well. Before then, Parsons argued, the mother played both expressive (nurturant, empathic) and instrumental (competence–directed, achievement–focused) functions in relation to the child. Thereafter, however, the father was established as the primary representative of the instrumental role and the mother played a more restricted expressive role. The functional dichotomy seen by Parsons reflected basic and universal sex role differences, not just parental role differences (Stephens, 1963; Zelditch, 1955; Barry, Bacon, & Child, 1953). In Parsons' scheme, a power dimension also governed family structure, differentiating parental from child roles.

Empirical research has confirmed the existence of a power dimension along which family members can be arrayed (Emmerich, 1959a, 1959b, 1961). Furthermore, although sex differences along the function dimension do not appear to be as dramatic and widespread as Parsons predicted (Maccoby & Jacklin, 1974; see Hartley, 1964, for a contrary view) this dimension does seem to be useful for differentiating between maternal and paternal roles within the family (Emmerich, 1959b), and consequently it has elicited widespread—if guarded— endorsement (Black, 1961; Slater, 1961; Lamb, 1975a; Stein, 1974; Meerloo, 1968). Others have criticized Parsons' formulations, however (Aranoff & Crano, 1975; Aldous, 1977).

According to Parsons, the father represents to the child an executive, action-oriented approach and serves as the primary link between the family system and the social system beyond the family. The latter was important to Parsons (Parsons & Shils, 1951), who sought parallels, if not "isomorphisms," between the family structure and the general social structure (Baldwin, 1961). From this perspective, fathers are responsible for introducing children to the sex role prescriptions of the wider world, for encouraging the acquisition of competencies necessary for adaptation to the world, and for communicating the values and morals of the society. Unfortunately, although it is possible to relate demonstrated paternal effects to the father's instrumental function (e.g., Lynn, 1974), this is clearly not the only plausible interpretation. Ultimately the theory fails because it is not formulated in a sufficiently precise way to be open to validation or rejection.

Social Learning Theory

Other than the research on infancy, in which an eclectic perspective inspired by ethological attachment theory is dominant, most of the research reviewed in this book has been conducted within the framework of social learning theory. As noted earlier, the failure of secondary drive theory discredited both psychoanalytic and social learning predictions about infant development (Harlow, 1961). The few learning theorists who avoid secondary drive assumptions and deny the predispositions proposed by the ethologists (e.g., Bijou & Baer, 1961; Gewirtz, 1972, 1977) have constructed a theory that is contradicted by the available evidence and has few adherents (see Rajecki, Lamb, & Obmascher, 1978, for a review).

Although the social learning theorists have more disagreements among themselves than are often recognized, most of them believe that behavioral shaping by reinforcement and punishment as well as by identification or imitation are crucial processes in socialization and personality development (Bandura, 1977; Mussen, 1967). As far as learning from reinforcing and punishing contingencies is concerned, it is a commonplace observation that both parents can, and do, attempt to shape their children's behavior in this way. Mothers typically spend more time with their children, particularly in the preschool years, and so they are likely to administer more reinforcements and punishments than fathers do. On the other hand, paternal responses may attain greater salience and effectiveness by virtue of the father's relative novelty and greater punitiveness.

A larger group of social learning theorists (Bandura, 1968, 1977; Bandura & Huston, 1961; Bandura & Walters, 1963; Mussen, 1967) emphasize the importance of the learning that takes place without explicit reinforcement or punishment. They portray observational learning as the crucial process in sex role development, underscoring the importance of the father in providing a model of masculinity and achievement for his son. In his criticism of social learning theory, however, Kohlberg (1966, 1968) argued that the child's recognition of its own sex led it to seek out same-sex models to observe and imitate. These models need not be family members, although if the father is the male with whom the boy has most frequent contact, he is likely to learn more from him than from other males. Lynn (1961, 1962, 1966, 1969) deemphasized the father's role by arguing that boys "identify with the stereotype of the masculine role which the culture in general, not simply the father in particular, spells out for them" (Lynn, 1959, p. 130).

Imitation of the father is obviously not relevant to sex role development in daughters. However, many social learning theorists believe that fathers facilitate the feminine development of girls by rewarding dependent, flirtatious, and other feminine behaviors and by discouraging masculine behavior (Biller, 1971; Lynn, 1974; cf. Deutsch, 1944). In addition, it has been suggested that fathers provide a model of masculine behavior that their daughters learn to complement (e.g., Hetherington, 1972). This "reciprocal role learning" is an idea mentioned also by psychoanalysts like Deutsch (1944) as well as Parsons and Johnson (1963). Nevertheless, since the paternal identification involved in the development of masculinity is deemed more powerful than reciprocal role learning, social learning theorists implicitly believe that fathers have a greater impact on sex role development in boys than in girls. Sex role adoption has attracted the greatest amount of attention, as is discussed in a later section as well as in Chapter 9. Fathers, however, model other behaviors too, and in these respects one would expect boys and girls to imitate both of their parents unless differences in salience, power, or nurturance lead them to imitate one parent preferentially.

Critique

Although I have discussed each of these theoretical approaches separately, it is clear that there is a great deal of overlap and complementarity. Social learning theorists, for example, have tried to understand the processes (e.g., imitation/identification, punishment, and reinforcement) whereby parents influence their children's development. Psychoanalysts and Parsonian role theorists describe patterns of influence rather then mechanisms of psychological influence, whereas attachment theorists provide a perspective on human behavioral predispositions. All three schools assume that identification and behavioral shaping is important, although they do not consider how or why. Each of the approaches thus contributes in some way to our understanding of socialization. However, each theorist assumes the existence of particular constellations within the family. Until recently, these basic assumptions resulted from the theorists' informal observations, because there were no data available concerning the typical patterns of interaction and interrelation within the family. This seriously restricted the ability to shift from the level of general predictions to the level of specific, testable hypotheses, and it explains why descriptive analyses of family relationships are popular and why most of the research that has been conducted appears to be haphazardly atheoretical.

THE FATHER–CHILD RELATIONSHIP

Most of the studies concerning the development of father–child relationships have attempted to determine at what point in infancy or early childhood children form relationships to their fathers and whether they show preferences for either parent over the other. Another goal has been to identify any characteristics that make the father–child relationship distinctive when contrasted with other relationships such as that between mother and child.

When Do Father–Child Relationships Develop?

So strong have been the assumptions concerning the mother's preeminence in infancy that empirical investigations of father–infant relationships have been attempted only in the last few years. In a pioneering study, Schaffer and Emerson (1964) reported that infants protested separation from their mothers more often than from their fathers around 9 months of age, although by 18 months most infants protested separation from either parent. Perhaps because the technique of data collection (maternal reports) biased Schaffer and Emerson's findings, subsequent researchers have found that, when separation protest is the dependent measure, there is no demonstrable preference for either parent in the home or in the laboratory (Cohen & Campos, 1974; Kotelchuck, 1972, 1973, 1976; Kotelchuck, Zelazo, Kagan, & Spelke, 1975; Lamb, 1976c, 1979; Ross, Kagan, Zelazo, & Kotelchuck, 1975; Spelke, Zelazo, Kagan, & Kotelchuck, 1973). Although they did not compare responses to mothers and fathers, Pedersen and Robson (1969) reported from an analysis of positive responses to reunion that most infants appeared to be attached to both parents by 8 months of age. Indeed, one study suggests that the intensity of greeting behavior may imply a preference for fathers (Lamb, 1979).

Measures of attachment other than separation protest and greeting behavior confirm that most infants are attached to both their parents from the second half year of life. In stress-free situations, infants appear to show no preference for either parent (Lamb, 1977a, 1977c); when infants are distressed, they organize their attachment behaviors similarly around whichever parent is present (Lamb, 1976a, 1976g; Feldman & Ingham, 1975; Willemsen, Flaherty, Heaton, & Ritchey, 1974). However, when they are distressed and can choose between the two parents, infants of 10 to 18 months turn to their mothers preferentially (Cohen & Campos, 1974; Lamb, 1976a, 1976g). Eight- and 24-month-olds do not show comparable preferences (Lamb, 1976c, 1976d). Affiliative behaviors (such as smiling and vocalizing) are directed to fathers more than to mothers, largely because fathers are more novel and themselves emit more affiliative behaviors than mothers do (Belsky, 1979; Clarke-Stewart, 1978; Lamb, 1977a, 1977c).

The empirical evidence thus fails to confirm the existence of monotropy (Bowlby, 1969). Infants clearly do become attached to both of their parents at about the same time. However, they appear to prefer their mothers, at least prior to 2 years of age. This supports a modified notion of monotropy. Note, however, that these preferences are not evident unless the infants are distressed. In fact, during the second year of life, boys start to show strong preferences for their fathers on attachment behavior measures (Lamb, 1977a, 1977b). These preferences appear to be caused by fathers' greater interest in sons than in daughters.

The fact that infants typically do become attached to their fathers demonstrates that fathers spend at least enough time with their infants to become attached to them. Estimates of the amount of time involved vary widely. From parental reports, Kotelchuck (1975) determined that the average mother spent 9 waking hours per day in the same house as her infant, whereas the average father spent 3.2 hours. Lewis and Weinraub (1974) reported that fathers averaged only 20 minutes per day. Although they did not quantify paternal availability in terms of hours or minutes, Newson and Newson (1963, 1968) and Gavron (1966) reported that most English fathers were highly accessible to their infants and children during nonworking hours. Estimates of paternal availability probably vary depending on the culture or socioeconomic group studied, historical cohort differences, and whether the researcher defines availability in terms of ''interaction'' or ''accessibility.''

Characteristics of Paternal Behavior

Just because fathers and mothers are attachment figures does not guarantee them psychological significance in children's lives. Since mothers are the preferred and more involved (temporally) parents, fathers could be redundant as far as socialization is concerned (Lamb, 1975a). This does not appear to be the case, however. Rather, fathers and mothers represent different types of interactions and experiences from early in children's lives. From infancy, fathers engage in physically stimulating and playful interactions, whereas mothers engage in conventional play and are primarily responsible for caretaking (Lamb, 1976b, 1977c; Clarke-Stewart, 1978; Yogman et al., 1976, 1977). Even primary caretaking fathers behave like secondary caretaking fathers rather than primary caretaking mothers in many respects (Field, 1978; Lamb, Frodi, Hwang, & Frodi, in press). The association of fathers with play and mothers with caretaking was confirmed by Kotelchuck's (1975) analysis of reported parental time use. Furthermore, from the first year onward, infants and young children appear to prefer playing with their fathers, since they respond more positively to paternal bids; boys choose fathers over mothers as playmates through 4 years of age (Ammons & Ammons, 1949; Clarke-Stewart, 1978; Lamb, 1976b, 1977c; Lynn & Cross, 1974). Girls shift their preferences from fathers to mothers between the ages of 2 and 4 (Lynn & Cross, 1974).

The identification of fathers with play is acknowledged by parents too. Fagot (1974) found that the parents of 2-year-old boys believed that the fathers' functions involved playing with and providing role models for their sons. It is significant that parents of girls did not believe that mothers and fathers needed to play differentiable roles. Because this is compatible with the finding that boys are more consistent in their preference for play with fathers, these studies may reflect a cultural assumption that fathers should play a more active role in the socialization of their sons.

Few attempts have been made to distinguish empirically between maternal and paternal styles in interaction with older children. In one study involving observations of parent–child interaction in the laboratory, Osofsky (Osofsky & O'Connell, 1972; Osofsky & Oldfield, 1971) reported findings consonant with Parsons' theory. In situations designed to elicit dependent and independent task-related behaviors from 5-year-old girls, fathers were consistently more likely to take an action-oriented role, whereas the mothers more often provided emotional support and encouragement. Cunningham (1973) and Krige (1976) have replicated these findings. Girls themselves exhibit "more task specificity with their fathers and more interpersonal interaction with their mothers" (Osofsky & O'Connell, 1972, p. 167).

Other researchers have asked parents how they would behave in a variety of hypothetical situations and have then compared the responses of mothers and fathers (e.g., Atkinson & Endsley, 1976; Lambert, Yackley, & Hein, 1971; Marcus, 1975; Rothbart & Maccoby, 1966), have asked children how they perceive their mothers' and fathers' roles (e.g., Kagan, Hosken, & Watson, 1961; Nadelman, 1976), or have relied upon both parents' and children's reports (Bronfenbrenner, 1961b; Devereux, Bronfenbrenner, & Rodgers, 1969; Devereux, Bronfenbrenner, & Suci, 1962; Devereux, Shouval, Bronfenbrenner, Rodgers, Kav-Venaki, & Kiely, 1974; Kohn, 1959; Radke, 1946). Such studies reveal that mothers retain their association with caretaking and nurturance, whereas fathers, although associated with play and adventure, are perceived as more threatening, rigid, and demanding. It is interesting that children's conceptions about average families are usually more stereotyped than attitudes about their own parents (Nadelman, 1976).

There appear to be interactions between sex of parent and sex of child (Bearison, 1979; Rothbart & Maccoby, 1966; Margolin & Patterson, 1975); however, Bearison (1979) reported that parents were more person-oriented than position-oriented when attempting to control the behavior of same-sex rather than opposite-sex children. Cross-sex leniency has also been reported (Langlois & Downs, 1980; Tasch, 1952; Lansky, 1967; Noller, 1980; Atkinson & Endsley, 1976; Aberle & Naegele, 1952; Rothbart & Maccoby, 1966; cf. Lambert, Yackley, & Hein, 1971).

As in the research on parent–infant relationships, it is consistently found that fathers are more directly involved in the rearing of sons than of daughters (Kemper & Reichler, 1976; Bronfenbrenner, 1961b; Kohn & Carroll, 1960). Fathers believe that mothers should be responsible for the socialization of daughters (Bronfenbrenner, 1961b; Kohn & Carroll, 1960). Fathers are especially unwilling to deal with female sexuality and menstruation (Fox, 1978;

Hipgrave, 1979). In addition, Maxwell (1976) reported that paternal involvement often had a vicarious, distant, character.

Although studies of differences between maternal and paternal roles help to identify their effects on their children's development, one must not lose sight of the similarities nor exaggerate the differences. Even in infancy, for example, mothers usually play more than fathers do, but play represents a greater proportion of the total paternal interaction and so may come to characterize the father–infant relationship (Lamb, 1980a). Furthermore, even if fathers are more concerned than mothers about adherence to conventional sex roles or mores (Kohn, 1969, 1979; Bronfenbrenner, 1961; Fagot, 1978; Sears, Maccoby, & Levin, 1957; Goodenough, 1957; Heilbrun, 1965), both parents obviously affect the sex-role and moral development of their children.

Recent research has pointed to important similarities in the capacity of males and females to be responsive to their infants. Both parents respond positively to childbirth, especially when fathers are present (Fein, 1976; Frank, 1973; Greenberg & Morris, 1974; Parke, 1979). Studies of children, teenagers, and parents found no sex differences on physiological measures of responsiveness to infant signals (Frodi & Lamb, 1978; Frodi, Lamb, Leavitt, & Donovan, 1978; Frodi, Lamb, Leavitt, Donovan, Neff, & Sherry, 1978). On behavioral measures of responsiveness during feeding, Parke and Sawin (1976, 1977) found that mothers and fathers were equally sensitive, although fathers tended to assign responsibility for caretaking to their wives. Although involvement appears not to be affected by childbirth preparation classes (Wente & Crockenberg, 1976), it is affected by special programs for new fathers (Parke, Hymel, Power, & Tinsley, 1980; Lind, 1974; Zelazo, Kotelchuck, Barber, & David, 1977). Involvement also relieves anxious inhibition of further involvement (Fein, 1976). When observed interacting with unfamiliar babies, young fathers were less interested in infants than their wives were (Feldman & Nash, 1977, 1978; Nash & Feldman, 1981). Nevertheless, fathers are obviously sensitive enough when interacting with their own infants to permit attachments to form: the insecure attachments that result from parental insensitivity (Ainsworth et al., 1971, 1974, 1978) are no more common to fathers than to mothers (Lamb, 1978). Like mothers, fathers adjust their patterns of speech when speaking to young children (Gleason, 1975; Golinkoff & Ames, 1979; Kauffman, 1977).

Critique

On the whole, the empirical evidence is consistent with the theoretical predictions. Fathers and mothers both appear to be psychologically salient to their children from the time the children are infants, and they appear to adopt differentiable roles from this point on. Mothers are consistently assigned responsibility for nurturance and physical childcare, whereas fathers tend to be associated with playful interaction as well as with demands that children conform to cultural norms. Fathers do appear to be more demanding and exacting, as social learning theorists, psychoanalysts, and Parsonians assumed. Whether or not they have more influence on them, fathers are more involved in the socialization of sons than of daughters.

Unfortunately, there have been few attempts so far to gather observational data concerning patterns of interaction between parents and children older than infants. Some descriptive information has been gathered by interviewing parents and/or children, but there is always some question about the comparability of various investigators' definitions of "masculinity," "nurturance," "instrumentality," and so forth. Careful, descriptive longitudinal studies are still needed. As I noted several years ago (Lamb, 1975a, 1976f), we must describe the father–child relationship carefully and thoroughly if we wish to understand its effects on child development.

PATERNAL EFFECTS ON CHILD DEVELOPMENT

Sex Role Development

All of the theories reviewed propose that fathers have a major impact on sex role development. Most of the researchers discussed in this section emphasize modeling or identification in this regard, although some note that fathers demand conformity to cultural norms more strictly than mothers do. Unfortunately, despite this consensus and the extensiveness of research in this area, the literature is extraordinarily inconclusive and contradictory.

Fathers are more consistent than mothers in wanting sons (Arnold, Bulatao, Buripakdi, Ching, Fawcett, Iritani, Lee, & Wu, 1975; Coombs & McClelland, 1975) and they show behavioral preferences for sons from their children's earliest infancy (Parke & O'Leary, 1976; Gewirtz & Gewirtz, 1968; Margolin & Patterson, 1975; Weinraub & Frankel, 1977; Rendina & Dickerscheid, 1976; Lamb, 1977a; Kotelchuck, 1976). The preferential treatment of sons becomes more marked in the children's second year of life, when fathers make themselves more salient and attractive to sons than to daughters (Lamb, 1977a, 1977b). In response, boys develop preferences, which have been described as early forms of same-sex identification, for their fathers (Lamb, 1977a, 1977b). Fagot (1974) found that the parents of 2-year-olds already believed that fathers had to provide role models for their sons. These data should be considered in the context of Money's claims (Money & Ehrhardt, 1972; Money, Hampson & Hampson, 1957; Hampson & Hampson, 1961) that gender identity must be acquired by the third year of life; reassignment after this age causes greater difficulty and more socioemotional problems than earlier reassignment does. Others, too, have noted how early sex differences in interpersonal behavior (Brooks & Lewis, 1974; Goldberg & Lewis, 1969; Maccoby & Jacklin, 1973; Messer & Lewis, 1972) and in the preference for sex-typed roles (Greif, 1973; Hartup & Zook, 1960) emerge. Unfortunately, we do not know how significant the fathers' contribution is, since the sex-differentiating behavior of mothers has been studied more systematically than that of fathers (e.g., Goldberg & Lewis, 1969; Lewis, 1972a, 1972b, 1975b; Lewis & Weinraub, 1974; Moss, 1967; Endsley, Garner, Odom, & Martin, 1975). Lewis has suggested that fathers and mothers may contribute in different ways to sex role development (Ban & Lewis, 1974; Lewis & Weinraub, 1974).

Researchers who emphasize identification/modeling believe that there should be behavioral similarities between fathers and sons, especially in crucial areas like masculinity, resulting from children's attempts to be like their same-sex parents (Beier, 1953; Emmerich, 1959a; Gray & Klaus, 1956; Rau, 1960). However, with a few exceptions (Gray, 1959; Hartup, 1962; Heilbrun, 1965; Radin, 1978; Sopchak, 1952, 1958), there is little evidence that masculine fathers have masculine sons. In fact, preadolescent boys are no more similar to their fathers than to their mothers (Hetherington, 1965; Hetherington & Brackbill, 1963; Lazowick, 1955; Lynn & Maaske, 1970; Sears, Rau, & Alpert, 1965) and do not perceive themselves as more similar to fathers than to mothers (Gray & Klaus, 1956; Kagan, Hosken, & Watson, 1961; Middleton & Putney, 1963). The sex role preferences of fathers and sons are not significantly correlated (Angrilli, 1960; Mussen & Rutherford, 1963; Payne & Mussen, 1956). In fact, the most consistent correlate of paternal masculinity is the femininity of daughters (Heilbrun, 1965; Johnson, 1963; Mussen & Rutherford, 1963; Sears, Rau, & Alpert, 1965)—a correlation that supports the notion of complementary role learning. These findings thus appear to support Maccoby and Jacklin's (1974) claim "that modeling plays a minor role in the development of sex-typed behavior" (p. 300).

However, modeling theorists predict that the degree of filial identification varies depending on the fathers' nurturance (Bandura & Walters, 1959; Mussen, 1967). Therefore, warm, accessible, masculine fathers should have masculine sons, as indeed they do (Biller & Borstelmann, 1967; Hetherington, 1967; Reuter & Biller, 1973), whereas less similarity would be expected when the relationship is more distant. Fathers who are warm, nurturant, and involved in childrearing have masculine sons (Anzimi, 1964; Bandura & Walters, 1959; Biller, 1969b; Distler, 1964; Freedheim, 1960; Kaplar, 1970; Moulton et al., 1966; Mussen, 1961; Mussen & Distler, 1959, 1960; Mussen & Rutherford, 1963; Payne & Mussen, 1956; Sears, 1953; Sears et al., 1957; Stoke, 1954) and feminine daughters (Johnson, 1963) regardless of their masculinity or punitiveness. In contrast, when the father–child relationship is stressful, paternal and filial masculinity are negatively correlated (Bronson, 1959). These findings strongly imply that characteristics of the father–child relationship have greater formative significance than the fathers' avowed masculinity or punitiveness. Several studies have shown relationships between the father's role in the family and his son's masculinity. Thus fathers who are seen as heads of their households have more masculine sons (Biller, 1969b; Freedheim, 1960; Hetherington, 1965, 1967; L. Hoffman, 1961; Kagan, 1958; Mussen & Distler, 1959), and the masculinity of sons is lower when the father plays a feminine role at home (Altucher, 1957; Bronfenbrenner, 1958). The greatest father–son similarity (in a variety of areas) has been found in families in which fathers dominate their wives (Biller, 1969b; Hetherington, 1965; Hetherington & Brackbill, 1963; Hetherington & Frankie, 1967). However, in her most recent study, Radin (1978) found that sex role identification was not affected by degree of paternal involvement in childrearing (a "feminine" activity); indeed, highly participative fathers were no more feminine or androgynous than traditional fathers—a finding that contrasts with those of Russell (1978). Brayman and DeFrain (1979) found that children with androgynous parents had more flexible sex role attitudes than the children of nonandrogynous (traditional) parents.

Research assessing the effectiveness of paternal attempts to shape their children's behavior has also been inconclusive. Some basic assumptions have been substantiated, however. Although both parents obviously participate in such training (Biller, 1968) and usually agree on goals regarding their children's sex roles (Emmerich, 1969), several studies have found that fathers are more concerned about sex typing than mothers are and that they have more traditional attitudes (Bronfenbrenner, 1961; Fagot, 1978; Goodenough, 1957; Heilbrun, 1965; Sears, Maccoby, & Levin, 1957; Tasch, 1955). However, fathers—particularly middle class fathers—expect their wives to assume primary responsibility for raising daughters (Bronfenbrenner, 1961b; Kohn & Carroll, 1960). This too would lead one to expect fathers to affect the development of sons more than the development of daughters. In fact, studies have investigated only the relationship between paternal strictness/punitiveness/limit setting and filial masculinity. Three studies found a modest correlation (Altucher, 1957; Lefkowitz, 1962; Moulton, Burnstein, Liberty, & Altucher, 1966) but several others have failed to find any significant relationship (Biller, 1969a; Mussen & Distler, 1959, 1960; Mussen & Rutherford, 1963; Sears et al., 1965). Despite these researcher's predictions, however, there is actually no reason to expect a linear correlation between punitiveness and masculinity (Becker, 1964; Biller, 1971a): other characteristics of the father–child relationship should influence this correlation. Thus, for example, Bandura and Walters (1959) found that paternal punitiveness was correlated with filial masculinity only when the father was also nurturant.

Although male sex roles are defined earlier, more sharply, and more strictly than female sex roles (Brown, 1956, 1957a, 1958b; Cava & Rausch, 1952; Goodenough, 1957; Gray, 1957; Hacker, 1957; Lansky, 1967) and fathers aim to have a greater influence on their sons, there is greater consistency in the results of the few studies investigating feminine development. Deutsch (1944) suggested that fathers enhanced the femininity of their daughters by rewarding "feminine" traits such as passivity and dependence with affection. In accordance with this prediction, several studies have reported significant correlations between paternal masculinity and daughter's femininity (Gardner, 1947; Heilbrun, 1965; Johnson, 1963; Landis, 1960; Mussen & Rutherford, 1963; Sears et al., 1965). As with sons, the quality and warmth of the father–daughter relationship is also crucial (Johnson, 1963).

Moral Development

There is far less consensus among theorists about the father's role in moral development than there is about his role in sex role development. Freud believed that moral development depended on identification following the Oedipal crisis, whereas Parsons saw the father as the representative within the family of the values and standards of the society. Both thus accorded a prominent role to fathers. Social learning theorists have attributed greater importance to mothers than to fathers, since the former have more opportunity to be models for and to shape their children's behavior.

Unfortunately, empirical research has been inconclusive. In an authoritative review, Hoffman (1970b) noted that relationships between maternal behavior and children's morality were more common than relationships between paternal behavior and morality. Subsequently, Holstein (1969) reported significant mother–child similarity in moral judgment but little father–child similarity. However, Hoffman's own research (Hoffman, 1966, 1970a, 1971a, 1971b; Hoffman & Saltzstein, 1967) showed that fathers who felt positively about childrearing had sons who identified with them and displayed an internalized morality. Other studies have reported that nurturant fathers (Rutherford & Mussen, 1968; Speece, 1967) and fathers who are more actively involved in caretaking (Speece, 1967) foster altruism and generosity, although Livson (1966) failed to replicate this finding. Weisbroth (1970) found that moral judgment in males was related to identification with both parents, whereas in females it was related only to identification with fathers. Following his review of the earlier literature, however, Hoffman (1970b) concluded that "identification may have little bearing on moral development" (p. 317).

Although psychoanalysts emphasized the value of paternal punitiveness (e.g., Fenichel, 1945), paternal reliance on love-oriented discipline is associated with filial morality (MacKinnon, 1938; Moulton et al., 1966; Mussen &

Distler, 1960). Further, several studies have shown that delinquent sons often come from homes in which fathers are antisocial, unempathic, and hostile (Andry, 1957, 1960, 1962; Bandura & Walters, 1959; Chinn, 1938; Crane, 1951; Glueck & Glueck, 1950, 1959; McCord, McCord, & Howard, 1961, 1963; Schaefer, 1965; Thrasher, 1927). In fact, Andry found that poor father–child relationships were common antecedents of delinquency, even when there were apparently normal mother–child relationships. Hoffman (1971a) concluded that "the effects of low identification with fathers who are present are quite similar though somewhat less pronounced than the effects of father absence" (p. 404).

Achievement and Intellectual Development

Parsons proposed that fathers were more instrumental than mothers (Peters & Stewart, 1979) and hence that identification with them should enhance achievement motivation and performance. In a series of studies, Radin (1972, 1973; Radin & Epstein, 1975; Jordan, Radin & Epstein, 1975) tested the prediction that boys with nurturant fathers excel in intellectual tasks by virtue of an enhanced paternal identification (Kagen, 1958; Mussen & Rutherford, 1963; Payne & Mussen, 1956; Sears, 1953). Her findings supported the hypothesis among middle class boys but not among lower-class boys. The correlation between paternal nurturance and intellectual competence was evident with boys but not with girls (Jordan et al., 1975). In fact, it appeared that fathers did not facilitate the intellectual performance of girls at all: mixed messages characterized father–daughter interaction, and this seemed to retard intellectual performance (Radin & Epstein, 1975). Paternal attitudes affected daughters indirectly, being mediated through the mothers (Epstein & Radin, 1975; Radin, 1974). In her review Radin (1976) concluded that fathers had little effect on their daughters' cognitive development, although she has since shown that highly involved fathers have an especially marked impact on the cognitive development of daughters (Radin, 1978). These issues are discussed more fully in Chapter 11.

Two other observational studies (Harrington, Block & Block, 1975; Osofsky & O'Connell, 1972) have shown that fathers treat girls in an expressive rather than instrumental fashion; boys get more instrumental support (Harrington et al., 1975). Both parents emphasize achievement and competition in boys more than in girls (Aberle & Naegele, 1952; Barry, Bacon, & Child, 1957; Hoffman, 1977; Block, 1979); we know that paternal encouragement of intellectual performance is related to achievement (Crandall, Dewey, Katkovsky, & Preston, 1964) and that paternal rejection is detrimental to it (Heilbrun, Harrell, & Gillard, 1965; Hurley, 1967). Furthermore, nurturant fathers who deprecate intellectual performance in women can retard the achievement of their daughters (Biller, 1974a, 1974d; Lamb, Owen, & Chase-Lansdale, 1979). Several studies report that successful professional women had especially close relationships with supportive fathers (Braskamp & Flessner, 1971; Barnett & Baruch, 1978; Block, von der Lippe, & Block, 1973; Lozoff, 1974; Oliver, 1975), although others have stressed that when fathers have traditionally low expectations of their daughters very close relationships between fathers and daughters impede achievement (Honzik, 1967; Helson, 1971; Worell & Worell, 1971).

Only Radin, Block and Block, and Osofsky have gathered observational data concerning the father–child relationship; other studies have relied on parental or filial reports and paper-and-pencil measures. A review in 1967 concluded that parental influences on cognitive development were poorly understood (Freeberg & Payne, 1967), and this remains true. There is some evidence (albeit correlational) of paternal influences on intellectual development, however (Brenton, 1966; Lederer, 1964; Radin, 1976). High achievers value their father's companionship more than low achievers do (Mutimer, Loughlin, & Powell, 1966) and they perceive themselves as similar to their fathers (Shaw & White, 1965). Boys whose fathers are accessible to them are more cognitively competent (Blanchard & Biller, 1973; Reis & Gold, 1977). Furthermore, although this may not be true across all social classes (Kahl, 1953), a close father–child relationship and the characterization of the father as both dominant and democratic are associated with high achievement motivation in both boys and girls (Bandura, 1960; Bowerman & Elder, 1964; Elder, 1962; Ellis & Lane, 1963; Gill & Spilka, 1962; L. Hoffman, 1961; Kahl, 1957), particularly boys (Norman, 1966; Werts, 1966). In contrast, underachieving boys have inadequate relationships with their fathers, whom they regard as rejecting or hostile (Grunebaum, Hurwitz, Prentice, & Sperry, 1962; Hurley, 1967; Kimball, 1952). Both Smelser (1963) and Douglas (1964) reported an association between the downward mobility of fathers and the achievement behavior of their sons.

Observed (Solomon, 1969) and reported (Katz, 1967) paternal encouragement are correlated with achievement. Psychologically salient fathers (Dreyer, 1975) and close father–son relationships (Bieri, 1960; Dyk & Witkin, 1965) are both associated with the adoption of a "masculine" (i.e., analytic) cognitive style. Boys are less susceptible than girls to pressure exerted by their mothers (Kagan & Freeman, 1963). However, the dangers inherent in reliance on correlational studies were illustrated recently by Clarke-Stewart (1978, 1980), who suggested that fathers responded to, rather than accounted for, individual differences in infant cognitive capacity.

Elder (1979; Elder & Rockwell, 1979) has recently shown that boys (born in 1928–1929) in the Berkeley Guidance Study were marked by low aspirations when their families had been economically deprived during the Great Depression. In contrast, boys (born in 1920–1921) in the Oakland Growth Study (Elder, 1974) were very highly motivated toward achievement. The difference, argued Elder and Rockwell, resulted from the fact that the fathers of the Berkeley boys became less attractive models at an earlier and more critical stage than did the fathers of the Oakland boys. The harshest effects were suffered by boys in the Berkeley sample whose families were marked by both economic deprivation and parental discord.

The importance of fathers in fostering academic success, particularly in their sons, is clearly relevant to intervention programs aimed at improving the intellectual performance of "deprived" children. Most of these children come from populations in which father absence is particularly frequent (Bronfenbrenner, 1975c; Herzog & Sudia, 1970). It clearly would be desirable to involve fathers in enrichment programs whenever possible (Scheinfeld, 1969), even if this means confronting the stereotypes that hamper these efforts (Kohn & Carroll, 1960; Komarovsky, 1964; Tuck, 1969).

Social Competence and Psychological Adjustment

The warmth and sensitivity of paternal behavior determines the security of father–infant attachment relationships, and, as in the case of mothers, secure relationships foster the ability to relate positively to others (Main & Weston, in press; Lamb, Hwang, Frodi, & Frodi, in preparation). Although observational studies are rare, several studies have reported that the warmth of the father–son relationship is associated with social competence (Cox, 1962; Howells, 1969; Leiderman, 1959; Mussen, Bouterline-Young, Gaddini, & Morante, 1963; Rutherford & Mussen, 1968). Paternal warmth is also associated with self-esteem (Coopersmith, 1967; Medinnus, 1965; Rosenberg, 1965; Sears, 1970) and personality adjustment (Mussen, 1961; Mussen et al., 1963; Reuter & Biller, 1973; Slater, 1962; Warren, 1957) in boys. As far as girls are concerned, paternal nurturance is associated with adjustment (Baumrind & Black, 1967; Fish & Biller, 1973) and happiness in later heterosexual relationships (Fisher, 1973; Lozoff, 1974), whereas distant relationships are associated with maladjustment (Harrison, 1973). Tower (1980) found that fathers' positive self-concepts were associated with measures of their children's (especially their daughters') fantasy life and enthusiasm in the preschool setting. Burke and Weir (1977) reported that although most teenagers were dissatisfied with their father's availability and assistance, those who were satisfied with their fathers appeared in other respects to be better adjusted. Boys from mother-dominated homes reportedly have difficulty in achieving the acceptance of peers (L. Hoffman, 1961).

Disturbed father–child relationships (Becker, 1960; Becker, Peterson, Hellmer, Shoemaker, & Quay, 1959; Peterson, Becker, Hellmer, Shoemaker, & Quay, 1959; Peterson, Becker, Shoemaker, Luria, & Hellmer, 1961; Warren, 1957) and the failure to achieve same-sex identification (Lynn, 1961) may be pathogenic. Some have even suggested that disturbed father–child relationships are precursors of homosexuality (Brown, 1957b, 1958a; Nash, 1965). Nevertheless, it is always important to remember that both parents contribute to psychological adjustment. A recent longitudinal study (Block, 1971; Block, van der Lippe, & Block, 1973) demonstrated that the best adjusted adults were those who, in childhood, had warm relationships with effective mothers and fathers in the context of a happy marital relationship.

Critique

Although most research on the father–child relationship has been focused on the presumed effects, the literature in this area is remarkably inconclusive. A conceptual fallacy is perhaps the major reason for this inconclusiveness. Researchers have tended to focus on a small number of paternal characteristics, often ignoring other relevant factors and the family constellations within which father–child relationships are embedded. This failure to view individual characteristics in context is probably the major reason for inconsistency in the literature, because it has resulted in failures to control for extraneous sources of variance. In addition, researchers may have focused on less significant paternal characteristics. As Mussen and Distler (1959) wrote, "From the child's point of view, the significant factor seems to be the father's salience—his importance in the child's life—rather than the particular technique he uses in dealing with his child" (p. 354). Mussen and Distler also found that salient mother- and father–child relationships had different outcomes, suggesting that the relationships were qualitatively differentiable. They were not able to identify the differences, however.

The focus on a traditional, stereotyped notion of masculinity is also problematic. Many fathers (especially today) are neither "masculine" themselves, nor do they wish their sons to be "masculine" and their daughters "feminine." We need to take the parents' goals and values into account far more seriously than they have been.

Methodological problems have also abounded. Often evidence regarding both the presumed influence (e.g., punitiveness) and the presumed outcome (e.g., masculinity) are obtained from the same individual, thereby guaranteeing nonindependence. Even when several sources of evidence are available, it is still rare for the fathers themselves to be interviewed. Instead, mothers are often asked to describe their spouses' behavior. Finally, the techniques used to assess both outcomes and determinants are of questionable validity and reliability. Bronfenbrenner (1958) criticized research on sex role development several years ago on these grounds, but his suggestions for improvement have yet to be heeded widely. As I concluded earlier, "These studies should be regarded as pilot investigations, preparing the way for methodologically and conceptually superior projects that, regrettably, have never been undertaken'' (1976f, p. 17).

Summary

Despite the large number of studies that have been conducted, the conclusions we can draw with confidence are few. As far as sex role development is concerned, the father's masculinity and his status in the family are correlated with the masculinity of his sons and the femininity of his daughters. However, this association depends on the fathers having sufficient interaction with their children—thus the extent of the father's commitment to childrearing is crucial. One of the best established findings is that the masculinity of sons and femininity of daughters is greatest when fathers are nurturant and participate extensively in childrearing. Therefore, the father's similarity to a caricatured stereotype of masculinity is far less influential than his involvement in what are often portrayed as female activities.

Psychoanalytic theorists have stressed the power and aggressiveness of the father in explaining identification (Fenichel, 1945, but see Jacobson, 1964; Ross, 1979), whereas learning theorists, whether they choose to talk about "identification" or "modeling," predict that a child will be more likely to imitate a model about whom he or she feels positively than one of whom he or she is afraid. In general, the evidence is consistent with the latter hypothesis. The most influential fathers appear to be those who take their role seriously and interact extensively with their children. Only in the context of such relationships does punitiveness seem to be a useful technique. Hence in this respect learning theory depicts identification and sex role adoption better than psychoanalytic theory.

The results of many studies have failed to support the learning theorists' predictions, however. The demonstration that paternal masculinity is often uncorrelated with filial masculinity (methodological problems notwithstanding) fails to validate a learning theory hypothesis that identification should involve behavioral similarity; but it neither supports nor contradicts the Freudian postulate that identification refers to a motive or process. "If the core of the concept of identification is a *motive* to become like another person, the presence of similarity is, at best, only a by-product rather than an essential feature of the phenomenon" (Bronfenbrenner, 1960, p. 29).

Parsons' theory is much more difficult to evaluate empirically because it is not formulated with sufficient precision; its testable predictions typically are also consistent with either the learning theory or psychoanalytic positions. The fact that paternal warmth is crucial suggests that Parsons incorrectly overstresses the instrumental function of the father while underrepresenting the importance of paternal expressiveness. However, Parsons' theory is best able to explain the fact that masculine fathers have feminine daughters (learning a complementary role). It is conceivable that such fathers are more concerned about shaping their daughters' behavior and that role complementarity is irrelevant (see, for instance, Mussen & Rutherford, 1963).

Parsons may have the most parsimonious hypothesis concerning the father's role in moral development, although the inconclusiveness of the research makes it impossible to evaluate the predictive validity of any of the theories in this area. If moral development is a product of early socialization in the family, developmental psychologists have had little success in specifying cause–effect relationships. Their failure could be caused by either the inadequacies of research methodologies or the real unimportance of the family in moral socialization.

As Radin also notes (Chapter 11), there appears to be a correlation between the warmth of the father–child relationship and the child's academic performance. This is consistent with a learning theory prediction that children are more likely to imitate and identify with persons for whom they feel affection. However, there may be tension in the father–daughter relationship, which makes girls less eager to model their fathers. Girls' ambivalence about achievement may be reinforced by explicit disapproval of academic competence. Since female sex roles are currently being reevaluated, uncertainty about their daughters' present and future roles may have rendered the fathers in Radin and Epstein's (1975) study ambivalent. And since fathers are more concerned than mothers about sex typing, the ambivalence and tension is more marked in the father–daughter than in the mother–daughter relationship.

In sum, none of the theories is entirely consistent with the evidence, but all three appear correct in certain respects. It is not clear, moreover, that further research employing currently popular methodologies will ever permit unambiguous refutation or validation of any theory. The greatest problem is that researchers have relied almost exclusively on correlational strategies. Even if the other methodological problems—the nonindependent sources of evidence, the dubious validity of many of the instruments used—were overcome, researchers would still be unable to distinguish among causes, correlates, and effects. In order to determine that specific characteristics of the father–child relationship affect certain aspects of the child's personality, it is necessary to use those correlational strategies that permit causal inferences (such as cross-lagged panel correlations) to supplement experimental and quasi-experimental studies. Unfortunately, these strategies have rarely been employed.

Our efforts would be well served by serious attempts to understand the nature of interaction within the family: "nurturance," "punitiveness," and "masculinity" are concepts that are currently too vague, nonspecific, and subjective to be of predictive utility. To complicate things further, the very definition of the paternal role is being reevaluated, along with the traditional characterization of masculinity. Because of these recent changes in the cultural definitions of role-appropriate behavior, there is little one can say about the effects on children. It is clear, however, that paternal participation in childrearing is not seen as "unmasculine" by children; indeed, children expect their fathers to be as influential and emotionally involved as their mothers, even if the temporal extent of their involvement is substantially less (Hartley & Klein, 1959; Dunn, 1960; Dyer & Urban, 1958; Bowerman & Elder, 1964).

Several studies have shown that fathers are more concerned than mothers about the adoption of cultural values and traditionally defined sex roles. When contemporary fathers favor more egalitarian sex roles, these too should be fostered, particularly if, by their own behavior, these fathers show that nontraditional behavior is compatible with masculine gender identity. There is little reason to expect that paternal influence would be diminished by these developments; indeed, if they increased the involvement of many currently uninvolved fathers, it should maximize the formative significance of the father–child relationship.

FATHER ABSENCE

Instead of attempting to understand paternal influences by studying the effects of variations in paternal characteristics such as masculinity, punitiveness, and nurturance/warmth, many researchers have explored the fathers' role by comparing children raised with and without fathers. Their operational assumption has been that differences between these two groups are attributable to direct paternal effects.

Many of these studies have been focused on sex role development, and most have adopted a very traditional definition of masculinity/femininity, deviations from which are negatively evaluated (Biller, 1971, 1974, 1976, Chapters 9 and 14). Numerous studies report that boys raised without fathers are less masculine (Altus, 1958; Bach, 1946; Biller, 1969b, 1974b; Biller & Bahm, 1971; Burton & Whiting, 1960; Drake & McDougall, 1977; Hetherington, 1966; Leichty, 1960; Lynn & Sawrey, 1959; Santrock, 1970a; P. Sears, 1951; R. Sears, Pintler, & P. Sears, 1946; Stoltz et al., 1954; Winch, 1949) or else exhibit "compensatory" hypermasculinity and aggressiveness (Bartlett & Horrocks, 1958; Lynn & Sawrey, 1959; McCord, McCord, & Thurber, 1962; Pettigrew, 1964; Tiller, 1958, 1961). When the age at father–child separation is considered, studies show that father absence has the greatest effect on the masculinity of boys separated from their fathers in early childhood (Blaine, 1963; Blanchard & Biller, 1971; Carlsmith, 1964; Hetherington, 1966, 1972; Hetherington & Deur, 1971; Holman, 1953; Langner & Michael, 1963; Leichty, 1960; Santrock, 1970b). Perhaps this is because extrafamilial agents of socialization become increasingly important as the child grows older (Mischel, 1970). Furthermore, the presence of a male model other than father (e.g., an older brother) may inhibit the negative effects of father absence (Brim, 1958; Koch, 1956; Rosenberg & Sutton-Smith, 1964; Santrock, 1970a; Sutton-Smith & Rosenberg, 1965; Wohlford, Santrock, Berger & Liberman, 1971), although Biller (1968, 1971a) argues that the father is a superior role model.

In girls, father absence is associated with difficulties in interaction with males (Hetherington, 1972; Jacobson & Ryder, 1969, although Hainline & Feig, 1978, failed to replicate this). Some studies report that girls raised without fathers reject femininity (Jacobson & Ryder, 1969; Landy, Rosenberg, & Sutton-Smith, 1967), but other studies have failed to replicate this (Lynn & Sawrey, 1959; Santrock, 1970a, 1970b). In girls, early father absence appears to be most disadvantageous, even though the effects may remain unobserved until adolescence (Hetherington, 1972). Nevertheless, because they have a same-sex role model present, girls are spared the harsher effects of father absence suffered by boys. One recent study (Oshman, 1975) even reported that girls whose fathers were absent attained higher SAT scores than girls whose fathers were present. Warshak and Santrock (1979) reported that children living with a single parent of the opposite sex were most likely to show ill effects.

Moral development also appears to be affected by father absence. Several researchers have reported that delinquents are more likely to come from father-absent homes (Bacon, Child, & Barry, 1963; Bandura & Walters, 1959; Burton & Whiting, 1961; Glueck & Glueck, 1950, 1956; Gregory, 1965; Miller, 1958; Rohrer & Edmonson, 1960; Scarpitti, Murray, Dinitz, & Reckless, 1960; Siegman, 1966; Stephens, 1961) although father absence apparently has "no discernible effect on the conscience development of girls" (Hoffman, 1971a, p. 405, but see Clausen, 1961).

As far as achievement is concerned, one of the more consistently reported effects of father absence on boys is a deterioration of school performance (Bronfenbrenner, 1967; Deutsch, 1960; Deutsch & Brown, 1964) and intellectual capacity (Blanchard & Biller, 1971; Landy, Rosenberg, & Sutton-Smith, 1969; Lessing, Zagorin & Nelson, 1970; Maxwell, 1961; Santrock, 1972; Sciara, 1975; Sutton-Smith, Rosenberg, & Landy, 1968), although these effects may be spared when mothers assume an instrumental role in the husbands' absence (Hillenbrand, 1976). However, father absence does not have the same impact on achievement motivation in girls (Lessing et al., 1970; Santrock, 1972; Sutton-Smith et al., 1968, but see Sciara, 1975). Father-absent boys from both lower and middle class families also lack masculine (i.e., analytic) cognitive styles (Altus, 1958; Barclay & Cusumano, 1967; Blanchard & Biller, 1971; Carlsmith, 1964, 1973; Deutsch & Brown, 1964; Lessing et al., 1970; Milton, 1957; Nelson & Maccoby, 1966; Santrock, 1972) and they are more field dependent (Barclay & Cusumano, 1967; Goldstein & Peck, 1973; Chapman, 1977). In her earlier review, Radin (1976) concluded that father absence has little or no effect on achievement behavior in advantaged populations.

Paternal presence is associated with greater ease in establishing satisfying peer relationships (Leiderman, 1959; Lynn & Sawrey, 1959; Mitchell & Wilson, 1967; Stoltz et al., 1954; Tiller, 1957, 1958), behavioral adjustment (Ellison, 1979; LeCorgne & Laosa, 1976; Crumley & Blumenthal, 1973), and later success in heterosexual relationships (Barclay, Stilwell, & Barclay, 1972; Hetherington, 1972; Holman, 1959; Palmer, 1960; Seplin, 1952; Winch, 1950), particularly in boys. As might be expected, boys react more negatively to the loss of their fathers in war than girls do (Lifshitz, Berman, Galili, & Gilad, 1977).

Critique

As Herzog and Sudia (1970, 1973), Shinn (1978), and Brandwein, Brown, and Fox (1974) pointed out in their reviews, research on the effects of father absence is characterized by a lack of methodological rigor. Often (especially in studies of the relationship between father absence and delinquency) the children in father-absent and father-present families come from vastly different socioeconomic backgrounds. Fathers are usually absent because of divorce, and the divorce process itself has negative effects on children (Hetherington, Cox, & Cox, 1976, 1978; Wallerstein & Kelly, 1974, 1975, 1976). In addition, many factors not usually controlled in studies of father absence actually affect the outcome substantially. These factors include the timing of paternal departure, the reasons for the fathers' absence—divorce, death, military service (Hetherington, 1972; Illsley & Thompson, 1961; Santrock, 1977; Santrock & Wohlford, 1970), the family composition and structure—that is, the presence of siblings, stepparents, or grandparents (Oshman & Manosevitz, 1976; Chapman, 1971; Santrock, 1972; Wilson, Zurcher, McAdams, & Curtis, 1975), socioeconomic status (Kogelschatz, Adams, & Tucker, 1972; Chilman & Sussman, 1964), ethnic culture (Hunt & Hunt, 1975), the mother's behavior (Biller, 1970; Crain & Stamm, 1965; Hillenbrand, 1976), the mother's reaction to the separation (Biller, 1969a; Biller & Bahm, 1971; Lerner, 1954; Pedersen, 1966; Wylie & Delgado, 1959), and the extent of marital discord prior to the separation. Hess and Camara (1979) reported that the quality of postdivorce relationships with the parents was more predictive of adjustment or maladjustment than was the level of discord between the parents.

There are two reasons why we should not discount the studies of father absence entirely. First, the few methodologically rigorous studies do reveal significant differences between children raised with and without fathers. Second, there is an impressive congruence between these findings and the findings of studies employing other strategies to investigate the father–child relationship. Studies of father absence confirm that fathers influence sex roles, morality, achievement, and psychosocial adjustment. Finally, children whose fathers are psychologically absent (e.g., distant and inaccessible) suffer consequences that are similar to, although not as extreme as, those suffered when fathers are physically absent (e.g., Hoffman, 1971a; Blanchard & Biller, 1971). Boss and her colleagues (Boss, 1977; Boss, McCubbin, & Lester, 1979) have attempted to determine the characteristics of maternal and family response that distinguish between pathogenic and healthy reactions to temporary and prolonged father absence. Nevertheless, it is important to distinguish between the *existence* of effects (e.g., lower masculinity in father-absent boys) and the *evaluation* of these effects (i.e., boys who are less masculine are at a disadvantage). In fact, some of the effects of father absence can be deemed advantageous, disadvantageous, or neutral, depending on one's point of view.

FATHERS IN FAMILY CONTEXT

Although the chapters in this book focus on the father's role in child development, it is obvious that fathers are but one element in the complex and multifaceted process of socialization. Both parents contribute to the psychological development of their offspring, and it is unlikely that their contributions are independent. Dyadic models, although simpler to conceptualize, seriously distort the psychological and sociological realities of the environments in which children develop.

Since children have to be integrated into an extremely complex social system, the process of socialization itself must by complex, flexible, and multifaceted. It should not be surprising that such a process demands the complementary participation of several persons. In Western societies, primary responsibility for socialization traditionally devolves on the family (Bronfenbrenner, 1975c; Clausen, 1966; Parsons & Bales, 1955; Hoffman & Reiss, 1979), although the family itself has been considerably weakened of late by the increasing number of divorces (Bronfenbrenner, 1975b; Bane, 1977) and the rising influence of the peer group (Condry & Siman, 1974). Children are cut off increasingly from the world of work (Bronfenbrenner, 1972, 1974b), and fathers are absorbed by work and are thus drawn away from their families. The effects of these changes are poorly understood, although it seems certain that children raised in single-parent families are "at risk." The absence of a primary socializing agent (usually the father) is likely to have direct effects on the child as well as indirect effects mediated by the emotionally and economically strained (Herzog & Sudia, 1970; Maccoby, 1977) and socially isolated (Hetherington, Cox, & Cox, 1975) single parent. Single fathers may have special difficulty in attempting to raise daughters (e.g., Lamb & Bronson, 1980; Hipgrave, 1979; Warshak & Santrock, 1979), although DeFrain and Eirick (1979) reported that single mothers and fathers faced similar problems and had similar attitudes. O'Brien (1978) found that androgynous and previously involved fathers felt the least unease about single fatherhood.

Intact families comprise numerous reciprocal relationships, role demands, and expectations, and thus the father's role is largely defined by the father's position within the family system (Burgess, 1926; Burgess & Locke, 1953; Handel, 1965). Responsibilities and relationships obviously change over time. Around puberty, for example, boys gain influence in the family—at the expense of their mothers in middle-class families and at the expense of fathers in working-class families (Alexander, 1973; Hill, 1979; Jacob, 1974; Kandel & Lesser, 1972; Steinberg & Hill, 1979). Each member of the family system affects each other member (M. Hoffman, 1960; Yarrow, 1974; Belsky, 1981; Lewis & Weinraub, Chapter 7; Pedersen, Chapter 8) and thus fathers affect child development both directly and indirectly (i.e., through their effects on other family members). Lytton (1979), for example, found that fathers' presence increased the effectiveness of mothers' attempts to control their young children. We must, however, avoid assuming that all paternal effects are indirectly mediated (Feiring, 1976; Feiring & Taylor, 1980; Lewis & Weinraub, 1976); such stances take us back to an earlier era in which fathers were viewed simply as mother substitutes (Corter, 1974; Josselyn, 1956) or as sources of emotional support for mothers (Bartemeier, 1953; Bowlby, 1951; Westley & Epstein, 1960). Further, paternal effects will vary depending on the family constellation. Siblings, for example, not only interact with the target child, thus becoming salient aspects of the social environment (Sutton-Smith & Rosenberg, 1970) but also affect the manner in which the parents interact with and perceive the target child (Elder & Bowerman, 1963; Koch, 1955; Lansky, 1964, 1967).

Several studies attest to the importance of the family system in fostering the psychological development of children (Schaefer, 1974; Martin & Hetherington, 1979). Most common are studies showing the adverse effects of extensive family discord, hostile or rejecting parental attitudes, and disagreements over childrearing and aspirations for the child's future on psychosocial adjustment (Baruch, 1937; Baruch & Wilson, 1944; Block, Block, & Morrison, 1980; Coopersmith, 1967; Cottle, 1968; Elmer, 1967; Farber, 1962; Farber & McHale, 1959; Giovannoni & Billingsley, 1970; Gordon & Gordon, 1959; Graham & Rutter, 1973; M. Hoffman, 1960; Kauffman, 1961; Langner & Michael, 1963; Medinnus, 1963; Medinnus & Johnson, 1970; Power, Ash, Schoenberg, & Sorey, 1974; Nye, 1957; Putney & Middleton, 1960; Rutter, 1971, 1973, 1974, 1979; Rutter, Cox, Tupling, Berger, & Yule, 1975; Rutter & Madge, 1976; Uddenberg, 1976; Van der Veen, 1965; West & Farrington 1973, 1977; Wyer, 1965). The effects of divorce and family discord are greater for boys than for girls (Block et al., 1980; Hetherington et al., 1976; Porter & O'Leary, 1980; Rutter, 1979; Wallerstein & Kelly, 1980). Others have shown the more subtle effects of the temporary absence of one parent on the other parent's attitude toward the child (Marsella, Dubanoski, & Mohs, 1974). Father–son identification is enhanced by positive maternal attitudes about the father (Helper, 1955; Rau, 1960), and children's attitudes toward absent fathers are also related to their mothers' attitudes toward the fathers (Bach, 1946; Biller, 1971b). The father's status in the family influences his children's sex role adoption and their willingness to display responsibility and leadership (Bronfenbrenner, 1961b). Intimate relationships within the family are unlikely to develop unless the mother–father relationship is positive (Westley & Epstein, 1960), and, according to Landis (1960), the perception of closeness to the father is the best indicator of family intimacy and coherence. Heath (1976) found that affectionate and involved fathers reported marital gratification, open communication with their spouses, and psychological well-being, thus illustrating the interrelatedness of different aspects of family functioning.

Such findings underscore the limitations of attempts to specify the fathers' effects without simultaneous consideration of the context in which both father and child exist. Advances will depend on understanding patterns of interrelation within the family system as a whole. This demands a readjustment in the manner in which research on socialization is typically conducted. Having demonstrated *that* fathers affect child development, we now need to determine *how* and *how much*. The new focus should be motivated both by the fruitlessness of many old studies of socialization (Caldwell, 1964; Zigler & Child, 1969; Zigler, Lamb, & Child, in press), and by an appreciation of the complexity and multidimensionality of social development.

CONCLUSION

After decades of attention from researchers, there remains much that we do not yet know about the father's role in child development. At this point, we have some descriptive information about the nature of father–infant interaction, but we know little about the quality of relationships between older children and their fathers. Even in the infancy literature, furthermore, there has been little research on developmental trends and on factors such as socioeconomic status that affect the patterns of interaction. This lack of information about the nature of father–child relationships continues to hamper attempts to understand paternal influences on child development. Most studies of this sort are of a correlational nature, seeking to associate variations in outcome measures with measures of paternal characteristics that are believed to be formatively important. This body of literature has been disappointingly inconclusive, both because researchers have not known which characteristics to focus on and because the measures thereof remain impoverished. Progress depends on three things: the development of valid and reliable measures of personality characteristics; descriptive data permitting researchers to make insightful predictions and tests; and an appreciation of the complex interrelations among the determinants of psychological development. These topics recur continually throughout this volume; two chapters focus exclusively on the ways in which the network of relationships inside and outside the family interrelates to affect child development (Chapters 7 and 8).

An additional limitation is represented by the fact that the available evidence, with minor exceptions, concerns traditional fathers in traditional, two-parent families. A steadily decreasing number of children are raised in such families as a result of secular demographic and economic trends, yet we know little about patterns of interaction and influence within the nontraditional family types now emerging. Where research has been done on nontraditional families (e.g., on father absence and maternal employment), it is plagued by confounded factors, poor measurement, and methodological inadequacy. Processes of development and influence are only now being explored in nontraditional families (Field, 1978; Lamb, in press; Radin, 1978; Russell, 1978).

REFERENCES

Abelin, E. L. The role of the father in the separation–individuation process. In J. B. McDevitt & C. F. Settlage (Eds.), *Separation-Individuation*. New York: International Universities Press, 1971.

Abelin, E. L. Some further observations and comments on the earliest role of the father. *International Journal of Psychoanalysis,* 1975, **56**, 293–302.

Abelin, E. L. *Self-image, gender identity, and the early triangulations.* Manuscript in preparation, 1980.

Aberle, D. F. & Naegele, F. D. Middle-class fathers' occupational role and attitude toward children. *American Journal of Orthopsychiatry,* 1952, **22**, 366–378.

Ainsworth, M. D. S. The development of infant–mother attachment among the Ganda. In B. M. Foss (Ed.), *Determinants of infant behaviour,* Vol. 2. London: Methuen, 1963.

Ainsworth, M. D. S. *Infancy in Uganda: Infant care and the growth of love.* Baltimore: Johns Hopkins Press, 1967.

Ainsworth, M. D. S. The development of infant–mother attachment. In B. M. Caldwell & H. N. Ricciuti (Eds.), *Review of child development research,* Vol. 3. Chicago: University of Chicago Press, 1973.

Ainsworth, M. D. S. Attachment as related to mother–infant interaction. In J. S. Rosenblatt, R. A. Hinde, C. Beer, & M. Busnel (Eds.), *Advances in the study of behavior,* Vol. 9. New York: Academic Press, 1979.

Ainsworth, M. D. S., & Bell, S. M. Attachment, exploration and separation: Illustrated by the behavior of one-year-olds in a strange situation. *Child Development,* 1970, **41,** 49–67.

Ainsworth, M. D. S., Bell, S. M., & Stayton, D. J. Individual differences in strange situation behavior of one-year-olds. In H. R. Schaffer (Ed.), *The origins of human social relations.* London: Academic, 1971.

Ainsworth, M. D. S., Bell, S. M., & Stayton, D. J. Infant–mother attachment and social development: Socialisation as a product of reciprocal responsiveness to signals. In M. P. M. Richards (Ed.), *The integration of a child into a social world.* Cambridge: Cambridge University Press, 1974.

Ainsworth, M. D. S., Blehar, M. C., Waters, E., & Wall, S. N. *Patterns of attachment.* Hillsdale, N.J.: Lawrence Erlbaum Associates, 1978.

Aldous, J. The search for alternatives: Parental behaviors and children's original problem solutions. *Journal of Marriage and the Family,* 1975, **37,** 711–722.

Aldous, J. Family interaction patterns. *Annual Review of Sociology,* 1977, **3,** 105–135.

Alexander, J. F. Defensive and supportive communications in normal and deviant families. *Journal of Consulting and Clinical Psychology,* 1973, **40,** 223–231.

Allen, V. L., & Crutchfield, R. S. Generalization of experimentally–reinforced conformity. *Journal of Abnormal and Social Psychology,* 1963, **67,** 326–333.

Altucher, N. Conflict in sex identification in boys. Unpublished doctoral dissertation, University of Michigan, 1957.

Altus, W. D. The broken home and factors of adjustment. *Psychological Reports,* 1958, **4,** 477–479.

Ammons, R. B., & Ammons, H. S. Parent preference in young children's doll-play interviews. *Journal of Abnormal and Social Psychology,* 1949, **44,** 490–505.

Andry, R. G. Faulty paternal and maternal–child relationships, affection, and delinquency. *British Journal of Delinquency,* 1957, **8,** 34–48.

Andry, R. G. *Delinquency and parental pathology.* London: Methuen, 1960.

Andry, R. G. Paternal and maternal roles and delinquency. In *Deprivation of maternal care: A reassessment of its effects.* Geneva: WHO, 1962.

Angrilli, A. F. The psychosexual identification of pre-school boys. *Journal of Genetic Psychology,* 1960, **97,** 327–340.

Anzimi, C. Masculinity, femininity and perception of warmth and saliency in parent–son relationships. Unpublished doctoral dissertation, Michigan State University, 1964.

Arnold, R., Bulatas, R., Buripakdi, C., Ching, B. J., Fawcett, J. T., Iritani, T., Lee, S. J., & Wu, T. S. *The value of children: Introduction and comparative analyses,* Vol. 1. Honolulu: East–West Population Institute, 1975.

Arnstein, H. The crisis of becoming a father. *Sexual Behavior,* 1972, **2,** 42–48.

Aronoff, J., & Crano, W. D. A reexamination of the cross-cultural principles of task segregation and sex-role differentiation in the family. *American Sociological Review,* 1975, **40,** 12–20.

Atkinson, J., & Endsley, R. C. Influence of sex of child and parent on parental reactions to hypothetical parent–child situations. *Genetic Psychology Monographs,* 1976, **94,** 131–147.

Bach, G. R. Father-fantasies and father-typing in father-separated children. *Child Development,* 1946, **17,** 63–80.

Bacon, M. K., Child, I. L., & Barry, H. A cross-cultural study of correlates of crime. *Journal of Abnormal and Social Psychology,* 1963, **66,** 291–300.

Baldwick, J. O., & Balkwell, J. W. Self-disclosure to same- and opposite-sex parents: An empirical test of insights from role theory. *Sociometry,* 1977, **40,** 282–286.

Baldwin, A. The Parsonian theory of personality. In M. Black (Ed.), *The social theories of Talcott Parsons.* Englewood Cliffs, N.J.: Prentice Hall, 1961.

Ban, P., & Lewis, M. Mothers and fathers, girls and boys: Attachment behavior in the one-year-old. *Merrill-Palmer Quarterly,* 1974, **20,** 195–204.

Bandura, A. Social-learning theory of identificatory process. In D. S. Goslin, & D. C. Glass (Eds.), *Handbook of socialization theory and research.* Chicago: Rand McNally, 1968.

Bandura, A. *Social learning theory.* Englewood Cliffs, N.J.: Prentice-Hall, 1977.

Bandura, A., & Huston, A. C. Identification as a process of incidental learning. *Journal of Abnormal and Social Psychology,* 1961, **63,** 311–318.

Bandura, A., & Walters, R. H. *Adolescent aggression: A study of the influence of child-rearing practices and family interrelationships.* New York: Ronald, 1959.

Bandura, A., & Walters, R. H. *Social learning and personality development.* New York: Holt, Rinehart, & Winston, 1963.

Bane, M. J. *Here to stay: American families in the twentieth century.* New York: Basic Books, 1976.

Barclay, A. G., & Cusumano, D. Father absence, cross-sex identity, and field-dependent behavior in male adolescents. *Child Development,* 1967, **38,** 243–250.

Barclay, J. R., Stilwell, W. E., & Barclay, L. K. The influence of parental occupation on social interaction measures of elementary school children. *Journal of Vocational Behavior,* 1972, **2,** 433–446.

Bardwick, J. M. *Psychology of women.* New York: Harper & Row, 1971.

Barnett, R. C. Parental child-rearing values: Today and yesterday. Unpublished manuscript, Wellesley College, 1979.

Barnett, R. C., & Baruch, G. K. *The competent woman: Perspectives on development.* New York: Irvington, 1978.

Barry, H., Bacon, M. K., & Child, I. L. A cross-cultural survey of some sex differences in socialization. *Journal of Abnormal and Social Psychology*, 1957, **55**, 327–332.

Bartemeier, L. The contribution of the father to the mental health of the family. *American Journal of Psychiatry*, 1953, **110**, 277–280.

Bartlett, C. J., & Horrocks, J. E. A study of the needs status of adolescents from broken homes. *Journal of Genetic Psychology*, 1958, **93**, 153–159.

Baruch, D. A study of reported tension in interparental relationships as coexistent with behavior adjustment in young children. *Journal of Experimental Education*, 1937, **6**, 187–204.

Baruch, D., & Wilcox, A. J. A study of sex differences in preschool children's adjustment coexistent with interparental tensions. *Journal of Genetic Psychology*, 1944, **64**, 281–303.

Baruch, G. K., & Barnett, R. C. Fathers' participation in the care of their preschool children. Unpublished manuscript, Wellesley College, 1979.

Baumrind, D., & Black, A. E. Socialization practices associated with dimensions of competence in preschool boys and girls. *Child Development*, 1967, **38**, 291–327.

Bearison, D. J. Sex-linked patterns of socialization. *Sex Roles*, 1979, **5**, 11–18.

Becker, W. C. The relationship of factors in parental ratings of self and each other to the behavior of kindergarten children. *Journal of Consulting Psychology*, 1960, **24**, 507–527.

Becker, W. C. Consequences of different kinds of parental discipline. In M. L. Hoffman, & L. W. Hoffman (Eds.), *Review of child development research*, Vol. 1. New York: Russell Sage Foundation, 1964.

Becker, W. C., Peterson, D. R., Hellmer, L. A., Shoemaker, D. J., & Quay, H. C. Factors in parental behavior and personality as related to problem behavior in children. *Journal of Consulting Psychology*, 1959, **23**, 107–118.

Beier, E. G. The parental identification of male and female college students. *Journal of Abnormal and Social Psychology*, 1953, **48**, 569–572.

Bell, R. Q. A reinterpretation of the direction of effects in studies of socialization. *Psychological Review*, 1968, **75**, 81–95.

Bell, R. Q. Stimulus control of parent or caretaker behavior by offspring. *Developmental Psychology*, 1971, **4**, 63–72.

Belsky, J. Mother–father–infant interaction: A naturalistic observational study. *Developmental Psychology*, 1979, **15**, 601–607.

Belsky, J. Early human experience: A family perspective. *Developmental Psychology*, 1981, **17**, 3–23.

Belsky, J. & Steinberg, L. D. The effects of day care: A critical review. *Child Development*, 1978, **49**, 929–949.

Benson, L. *Fatherhood: A sociological perspective*. New York: Random House, 1968.

Bernal, J. F., & Richards, M. P. M. What can the zoologist tell us about human development? In S. A. Barnett (Ed.), *Ethology and development*. London: Heinemann, 1973.

Bernhardt, K. S. The father in the family. *Bulletin of the Institute for Child Study*, 1957, **19**, 2–4.

Bieri, J. Parental identification, acceptability, and authority, and within-sex differences in cognitive behavior. *Journal of Abnormal and Social Psychology*, 1960, **60**, 76–79.

Bijou, S. W., & Baer, D. M. *Child development I. A systematic and empirical theory.* New York: Appleton-Century-Crofts, 1961.

Biller, H. B. A multiaspect investigation of masculine development in kindergarten-age boys. *Genetic Psychology Monographs*, 1968, **76**, 89–139.

Biller, H. B. Father-absence, maternal encouragement, and sex-role development in kindergarten age boys. *Child Development*, 1969, **40**, 539–546(a).

Biller, H. B. Father dominance and sex role development in kindergarten age boys. *Developmental Psychology*, 1969, **1**, 87–94(b).

Biller, H. B. Father absence and the personality development of the male child. *Developmental Psychology*, 1970, **2**, 181–201.

Biller, H. B. *Father, child, and sex role.* Lexington, Mass.: Heath, 1971(a).

Biller, H. B. The mother-child relationship and the father-absent boy's personality development. *Merrill-Palmer Quarterly*, 1971, **17**, 227–241(b).

Biller, H. B. Paternal and sex-role factors in cognitive and academic functioning. In J. K. Cole & R. Dienstbier (Eds.), *Nebraska symposium on motivation*. Lincoln: University of Nebraska Press, 1974(a).

Biller, H. B. Paternal deprivation, cognitive functioning, and the feminized classroom. In A. Davids (Ed.), *Child personality and psychopathology: Current topics*. New York: Wiley, 1974(b).

Biller, H. B. *Paternal deprivation: Family, school, sexuality and society.* Lexington, Mass.: Heath, 1974(c).

Biller, H. B., & Bahm, R. M. Father absence, perceived maternal behavior, and masculinity of self-control among junior high school boys. *Developmental Psychology*, 1971, **4**, 178–181.

Biller, H. B., & Borstelmann, L. J. Masculine development: An integrative review. *Merrill-Palmer Quarterly*, 1967, **13**, 253–294.

Biller, H. B., & Meredith, D. L. *Father power.* New York: David McKay, 1974.

Biller, H. B., & Weiss, S. D. The father-daughter relationship and the personality development of the female. *Journal of Genetic Psychology*, 1970, **116**, 79–93.

Birdwhistell, R. L. Is there an ideal father? *Child Study*, 1957, **34**, 29–33.

Birnbaum, J. A. Life patterns, personality style, and self esteem in gifted family oriented and career committed women. Unpublished doctoral dissertation, University of Michigan, 1971.

Black, M. (Ed.) *The social theories of Talcott Parsons.* Englewood Cliffs, N.J.: Prentice-Hall, 1961.

Blaine, G. B. The children of divorce. *The Atlantic,* 1963 (March), 98–101.

Blanchard, R. W., & Biller, H. B. Father availability and academic performance among third grade boys. *Developmental Psychology,* 1971, **4,** 301–305.

Blehar, M. C. Anxious attachment and defensive reactions associated with day care. *Child Development,* 1974, **45,** 683–692.

Block, J. *Lives through time.* Berkeley: Bancroft, 1971.

Block, J., van der Lippe, A., & Block, J. H. Sex role and socialization: Some personality concomitants and environmental antecedents. *Journal of Consulting and Clinical Psychology,* 1973, **41,** 321–341.

Block, J. H. Another look at sex differentiation in the socialization behaviors of mothers and fathers. In F. Denmark (Ed.), *Psychology of women: Future directions of research.* New York: Psychological Dimensions, 1979.

Block, J. H., Block, J., & Morrison, A. Parental agreement–disagreement on child-rearing orientations and gender-related personality correlates in children. Unpublished manuscript, University of California, Berkeley, 1980.

Boehm, F. The femininity complex in men. *International Journal of Psychoanalysis,* 1930, **11,** 444–469.

Bordua, D. J. Educational aspirations and parental stress on college. *Social Forces,* 1960, **38,** 262–269.

Boss, P. G. A clarification of the concept of psychological father presence in families experiencing ambiguity of boundary. *Journal of Marriage and the Family,* 1977, **39,** 141–151.

Boss, P. G., McCubbin, H. I. & Lester, G. The corporate executive wife's coping patterns in response to routine husband–father absence. *Family Process,* 1979, **18,** 79–86.

Bossard, J. H., & Bell, E. S. *The sociology of child development.* New York: Harper & Row, 1966.

Bowerman, C. E. & Elder, G. H. Variations in adolescent perception of family power structure. *American Sociological Review,* 1964, **29,** 551–567.

Bowlby, J. Forty-four juvenile thieves: Their characters and home life. *International Journal of Psychoanalysis,* 1944, **25,** 107–128.

Bowlby, J. *Maternal care and mental health.* Geneva: WHO, 1951.

Bowlby, J. The nature of the child's tie to his mother. *International Journal of Psychoanalysis,* 1958, **39,** 350–375.

Bowlby, J. *Attachment and Loss,* Vol. 1. *Attachment.* New York: Basic Books, 1969.

Bowlby, J. *Attachment and Loss,* Vol. 2. *Separation: Anxiety and anger.* New York: Basic Books, 1973.

Brandwein, R. A., Brown, C. A., & Fox, E. M. Women and children last: The social situation of divorced mothers and their families. *Journal of Marriage and the Family,* 1974, **36,** 498–514.

Braskamp, L. A., & Flessner, D. The congruency between parental and entering freshman expectations. *Journal óf College Student Personnel,* 1971, **12,** 179–185.

Brayman, R., & DeFrain, J. Sex role attitudes and behaviors of children reared by androgynous parents. Paper presented to the Groves Conference on Marriage and the Family, Washington D. C., April 1979.

Brenton, M. *The American male.* New York: Howard-McCann, Inc., 1966.

Briffault, R. *The mothers.* New York: Macmillan, 1927.

Brim, O. G. Family structure and sex role learning by children. *Sociometry,* 1958, **21,** 1–16.

Broderick, G. B. Fathers. *Family Coordinator,* 1977, **26,** 269–275.

Brody, S. *Patterns of mothering.* New York: International Universities Press, 1956.

Brody, S., & Axelrad, S. *Mothers, fathers, and children.* New York: International Universities Press, 1978.

Bronfenbrenner, U. The study of identification through interpersonal perception. In R. Tagiuri & L. Petrullo (Eds.), *Person perception and interpersonal behavior.* Stanford: Stanford University Press, 1958.

Bronfenbrenner, U. Freudian theories of identification and their derivatives. *Child Development,* 1960, **31,** 15–40.

Bronfenbrenner, U. Parsons' theory of identification. In M. Black (Ed.), *The social theories of Talcott Parsons.* Englewood Cliffs, N.J.: Prentice Hall, 1961(a).

Bronfenbrenner, U. Some familial antecedents of responsibility and leadership in adolescents. In L. Petrullo & B. M. Bass (Eds.), *Leadership and interpersonal behavior.* New York: Holt, Rinehart, & Winston, 1961(b).

Bronfenbrenner, U. The changing American child. *Journal of Social Issues,* 1961, **17,** 6–18(c).

Bronfenbrenner, U. The psychological costs of quality and inequality in education. *Child Development,* 1967, **38,** 909–925.

Bronfenbrenner, U. The roots of alienation. In U. Bronfenbrenner (Ed.), *Influences on human development.* Hinsdale, Ill.: Dryden, 1972.

Bronfenbrenner, U. Who cares for America's children? In F. Rebelsky & L. Dorman (Eds.), *Child development and behavior,* 2nd ed. New York: Knopf, 1973.

Bronfenbrenner, U. *Is early intervention effective?* Washington, D.C.: Department of Health, Education, & Welfare, Office of Child Development, 1974(a).

Bronfenbrenner, U. The origins of alienation. *Scientific American,* 1974, **23,** 53–61(b).

Bronfenbrenner, U. Research on the effects of day care. Unpublished manuscript, Cornell University, 1975(a).

Bronfenbrenner, U. Social change: The challenge to research and policy. Paper presented to the Society for Research in Child Development, Denver, April 1975(b).

Bronfenbrenner, U. Who cares for America's children? Unpublished manuscript, Cornell University, 1975(c).

Bronfenbrenner, U. *The ecology of human development.* Cambridge, Mass.: Harvard University Press, 1979.

Bronson, W. C. Dimensions of ego and infantile identification. *Journal of Personality*, 1959, **27**, 532–545.

Brooks, J., & Lewis, M. Attachment behavior in thirteen-month-old, opposite sex twins. *Child Development*, 1974, **45**, 243–247.

Brown, D. G. Sex role preference in young children. *Psychological Monographs*, 1956, **70**, 1–19.

Brown, D. G. Masculinity-femininity development in children. *Journal of Consulting Psychology*, 1957, **21**, 197–203(a).

Brown, D. G. The development of sex role inversion and homosexuality. *Journal of Pediatrics*, 1957, **50**, 613–619(b).

Brown, D. G. Inversion and homosexuality. *American Journal of Orthopsychiatry*, 1958, **28**, 424–429(a).

Brown, D. G. Sex role development in a changing culture. *Psychological Bulletin*, 1958, **55**, 232–242.

Burgess, E. S. The family as a unity of interacting personalities. *The Family*, 1926, **7**, 3–9.

Burgess, E. W., & Locke, H. J. *The family*. New York: American Book Co., 1953.

Burke, R. J., & Weir, T. Working men as fathers of adolescents. Unpublished manuscript, York University, 1977.

Burlingham, D. The pre-oedipal infant-father relationship. *Psychoanalytic Study of the Child*, 1973, **28**, 23–47.

Burton, R. W., & Whiting, J. W. M. The absent father: Effects on the developing child. Paper presented to the American Psychological Association, Chicago, September 1960.

Burton, R. W., & Whiting, J. W. M. The absent father and cross-sex identity. *Merrill-Palmer Quarterly*, 1961, **7**, 85–95.

Caldwell, B. M. The effects of infant care. In M. L. Hoffman & L. W. Hoffman (Eds.), *Review of child development research*, Vol. 1. New York: Russell Sage Foundation, 1964.

Caldwell, B. M., Wright, C. M., Honig, A. S., & Tannenbaum, J. Infant day care and attachment. *American Journal of Orthopsychiatry*, 1970, **40**, 397–412.

Caplan, G. *Concepts of mental health and consultation*. Washington, D.C.: U.S. Department of Health, Education and Welfare, 1959.

Carlsmith, L. Effect of early father-absence on scholastic aptitude. *Harvard Educational Review*, 1964, **34**, 3–21.

Carlsmith, L. Some personality characteristics of boys separated from their fathers during World War II. *Ethos*, 1973, **1**, 466–477.

Cava, E. L., & Rausch, H. L. Identification and the adolescent boy's perception of his father. *Journal of Abnormal and Social Psychology*, 1952, **47**, 855–856.

Chapman, M. Father absence, stepfathers, and the cognitive performance of college students. *Child Development*, 1977, **48**, 1155–1158.

Chilman, L., & Sussman, M. B. Poverty in the United States in the mid-sixties. *Journal of Marriage and the Family,* 1964, **26,** 391–395.

Chinn, W. L. A brief survey of nearly 1000 juvenile delinquents. *British Journal of Educational Psychology,* 1938, **8,** 78–85.

Christopherson, V. A. An investigation of patriarchal authority in the Mormon family. *Marriage and Family Living,* 1956, **18,** 328–333.

Clarke-Stewart, K. A. Interactions between mothers and their young children: Characteristics and consequences. *Monographs of the Society for Research in Child Development,* 1973, **38,** serial number 153.

Clarke-Stewart, K. A. And daddy makes three: The father's impact on mother and young child. *Child Development,* 1978, **49,** 466–478.

Clarke-Stewart, K. A. The father's contribution to children's cognitive and social development in early childhood. In F. A. Pedersen (Ed.), *The father–infant relationship: Observational studies in a family setting.* New York: Praeger Special Publications, 1980.

Clausen, J. A. Drug addiction. In R. K. Merton, & R. A. Nisbet (Eds.), *Contemporary social problems.* New York: Harcourt, Brace, & World, 1961.

Clausen, J. A. Family structure, socialization, and personality. In L. W. Hoffman, & M. L. Hoffman (Eds.), *Review of child development research,* Vol. 2. New York: Russell Sage Foundation, 1966.

Cohen, L. J., & Campos, J. J. Father, mother, and stranger as elicitors of attachment behaviors in infancy. *Developmental Psychology,* 1974, **10,** 146–154.

Condry, J. C., & Siman, M. A. Characteristics of peer- and adult-oriented children. *Journal of Marriage and the Family,* 1974, **36,** 543–554.

Coombs, C. H., Coombs, L. C., & McClelland, G. H. Preference scales for number and sex of children. *Population Studies,* 1975, **29,** 273–298.

Coopersmith, S. *The antecedents of self-esteem.* San Francisco: Freeman, 1967.

Corter, C. Infant attachments. In B. M. Foss (Ed.), *New perspectives in child development.* Harmondsworth: Penguin, 1974.

Cottle, T. J. Father perceptions, sex role identity, and the prediction of school performance. *Education and Psychological Measurement,* 1968, **28,** 861–886.

Cox, F. N. An assessment of children's attitudes towards parent figures. *Child Development,* 1962, **33,** 821–830.

Crain, A. J., & Stamm, C. S. Intermittent absence of fathers and children's perceptions of parents. *Journal of Marriage and the Family,* 1965, **27,** 344–347.

Crandall, V. J., Dewey, R., Katkovsky, W., & Preston, A. Parents' attitudes and behaviors and grade school children's academic achievements. *Journal of Genetic Psychology,* 1964, **104,** 53–56.

Crane, A. R. A note on preadolescent gangs. *Australian Journal of Psychology,* 1951, **3,** 43–46.

Cronenwett, L. R., & Newmark, L. L. Fathers' responses to childbirth. *Nursing Research,* 1974, **23,** 210–217.

Crumley, F. E., & Blumenthal, R. S. Children's reactions to temporary loss of the father. *American Journal of Psychiatry,* 1973, **130,** 778–782.

Cunningham, J. L. A comparison of the didactic interactions of mothers and fathers with their preschool children. Unpublished doctoral dissertation, Michigan State University, 1973.

Daley, E. *Father feelings.* New York: William Morrow, 1978.

DeFrain, J., & Eirick, R. Coping as divorced single parents: A comparative study of fathers and mothers. Paper presented to the American Psychological Association, New York, September 1979.

Demos, J. The American family in past time. *American Scholar,* 1974, **43,** 422–446.

Deutsch, H. *The psychology of women,* Vol. 1. New York: Grune & Stratton, 1944.

Deutsch, M. Minority group and class status as related to social and personality factors in scholastic achievement. *Monographs of the Society for Applied Anthropology,* 1960, **2,** 1–32.

Deutsch, M., & Brown, B. Social influences in Negro–white intelligence differences. *Journal of Social Issues,* 1964, **20,** 24–35.

Devereux, E. C., Bronfenbrenner, U., & Rodgers, R. R. Child-rearing in England and the United States: A cross-cultural comparison. *Journal of Marriage and the Family,* 1969, **32,** 257–270.

Devereux, E. C., Bronfenbrenner, U., & Suci, G. Patterns of parent behavior in the United States of America and the Federal Republic of Germany: A cross-cultural comparison. *International Social Science Journal,* 1962, **14,** 488–506.

Devereux, E. C., Shouval, R., Bronfenbrenner, U., Rodgers, R. R., Kav-Venaki, S., & Kiely, E. Socialization practises of parents, teachers, and peers in Israel: The kibbutz versus the city. *Child Development,* 1974, **45,** 269–282.

Distler, L. S. Patterns of parental identification: An examination of three theories. Unpublished doctoral dissertation, University of California, Berkeley, 1964.

Dodson, F. *How to father.* Los Angeles: Nash, 1974.

Dollard, J., & Miller, N. E. *Personality and psychotherapy.* New York: McGraw-Hill, 1950.

Douglas, J. W. B. *The home and the school.* London: MacGibbon & Kee, 1964.

Douvan, E. Independence and identity in adolescence. *Children,* 1957, **4,** 180–190.

Douvan, E. Sex differences in adolescent character processes. *Merrill-Palmer Quarterly,* 1960, **6,** 203–211.

Doyle, A.-B. Infant development in day care. *Developmental Psychology,* 1975, **11,** 655–656.

Doyle, A.-B. & Somers, K. The effect of group and individual day care on infant development. Paper presented to the Canadian Psychological Association, Quebec, June 1975.

Drake, C. T., & McDougall, D. Effects of the absence of a father and other male models on the development of boys' sex roles. *Developmental Psychology,* 1977, **13,** 537–538.

Dreyer, A. S. Family interaction: Situational and cross-sex effects. Paper presented to the Society for Research in Child Development, Denver, April 1975.

Dunn, M. S. Marriage role expectations of adolescents. *Marriage and Family Living,* 1960, **22,** 99–104.

Dyer, W. G., & Urban, D. The institutionalization of equalitarian family norms. *Marriage and Family Living,* 1958, **20,** 53–58.

Dyk, R. B., & Witkin, H. A. Family experiences related to the development of differentiation in children. *Child Development,* 1965, **36,** 21–55.

Elder, G. H. *Adolescent achievement and mobility aspirations.* Chapel Hill. N.C.: University of North Carolina, 1962.

Elder, G. H. Historical change in life-patterns and personality. In P. B. Baltes, & O. G. Brim (Eds.), *Life-span development and behavior,* Vol. 2. New York: Academic, 1979.

Elder, G. H. *Children of the Great Depression.* Chicago: University of Chicago Press, 1974.

Elder, G. H., & Bowerman, C. E. Family structure and child-rearing patterns: The effect of family size and sex composition. *American Sociological Review,* 1963, **28,** 891–905.

Elder, G. H., & Rockwell, P. C. Economic depression and postwar opportunity: A study of life patterns and health. In P. A. Simmons (Ed.), *Research in community and mental health.* Greenwich, Conn.: JAI Press, 1978.

Ellis, R. A., & Lane, W. C. Structural supports for upward mobility. *American Sociological Review,* 1963, **28,** 743–756.

Ellison, E. Classroom behavior and psychosocial adjustment of single and two-parent children. Paper presented to the Society for Research in Child Development, San Francisco, March 1979.

Elmer, E. *Children in jeopardy: A study of abused minors and their families.* Pittsburgh: University of Pittsburgh Press, 1967.

Emmerich, W. Parental identification in young children. *Genetic Psychology Monographs,* 1959, **60,** 257–308(a).

Emmerich, W. Young children's discrimination of parent and child roles. *Child Development,* 1959, **30,** 403–419(b).

Emmerich, W. Family role concepts of children aged six to ten. *Child Development,* 1961, **32,** 609–624.

Emmerich, W. The parental role: A functional cognitive approach. *Monographs of the Society for Research in Child Development,* 1969, **34,** serial number 132.

Endsley, R. C., Garner, A. R., Odom, A. H., & Martin, M. J. Interrelationships among selected maternal behaviors and preschool children's verbal and nonverbal curiosity behavior. Paper presented to the Society for Research in Child Development, Denver, April 1975.

Epstein, A. S., & Radin, N. Paternal questionnaire data, observational data, and child performance. Unpublished manuscript, University of Michigan, 1975.

Eron, L. D., Banta, T. J., Valder, L. D., & Laulicht, J. H. Comparison of data obtained from mothers and fathers on child rearing practices and their relation to child aggression. *Child Development,* 1961, **32,** 457–472.

Escalona, S. K. *The roots of individuality.* Chicago: Aldine, 1968.

Fagot, B. I. Sex differences in toddler's behavior and parental reaction. *Developmental Psychology,* 1974, **10,** 554–558.

Fagot, B. I. The influence of sex of child on parental reactions to toddler children. *Child Development,* 1978, **49,** 459–465.

Fairbairn, W. R. D. *Psychoanalytic studies of the personality.* London: Routledge, 1952.

Farber, B. Marital integration as a factor in parent-child relations. *Child Development,* 1962, **33,** 1–14.

Farber, B., & McHale, J. L. Marital integration and parent's agreement on satisfaction with their child's behavior. *Marriage and Family Living,* 1959, **21,** 65–69.

Favez-Boutonier, J. Child development patterns in France. In K. Soddy (Ed.), *Mental health and infant development,* Vol. 1. London: Routledge & Kegan Paul, 1955.

Fein, R. A. Men's entrance to parenthood. *Family Coordinator,* 1976, **25,** 341–348.

Feiring, C. The preliminary development of a social systems model of early infant–mother attachment. Paper presented to the Eastern Psychological Association, New York, March 1976.

Feiring, C., & Taylor, J. The influence of the infant and secondary parent on maternal behavior: Toward a social systems view. Unpublished manuscript, Educational Testing Service, 1980.

Feldman, S. S. Some possible antecedents of attachment behavior in two-year-old children. Unpublished manuscript, Stanford University, 1973.

Feldman, S. S. The impact of day care on one aspect of children's social-emotional behavior. Paper presented to the American Association for the Advancement of Science, San Francisco, February 1974.

Feldman, S. S., & Ingram, M. E. Attachment behavior: A validation study in two age groups. *Child Development,* 1975, **46,** 319–330.

Feldman, S. S., & Nash, S. C. The effect of family formation on sex-stereotypic behavior: A study of responsiveness to babies. In W. Miller, & L. Newman (Eds.), *The first child and family formation.* Chapel Hill: University of North Carolina Press, 1977.

Feldman, S. S., & Nash, S. C. Interest in babies during young adulthood. *Child Development,* 1978, **49,** 617–622.

Fenichel, O. *The psychoanalytic theory of neurosis.* New York: Norton, 1945.

Feshbach, J. B. The beginnings of fatherhood. Unpublished manuscript, Yale University, 1980.

Field, T. Interaction behaviors of primary versus secondary caretaker fathers. *Developmental Psychology,* 1978, **14,** 183–184.

Fish, K. D., & Biller, H. B. Perceived childhood paternal relationships and college females' personal adjustment. *Adolescence,* 1973, **8,** 415–420.

Fisher, S. F. *The female orgasm: Psychology, physiology, fantasy.* New York: Basic Books, 1973.

Fitzsimmons, J. J., & Rowe, M. P. *A study in child care, 1970–1971.* Cambridge, Mass.: ABT Associates, 1971.

Ford, C., & Beach, F. A. *Patterns of sexual behavior.* New York: Harper, 1951.

Foster, J. E. Father images: Television and ideal. *Journal of Marriage and the Family,* 1964, **26,** 353–355.

Fox, G. L. Mothers and their teenaged daughters. Unpublished manuscript, Merrill-Palmer Institute, Detroit, 1979.

Frank, S. T. The effect of husband's presence at delivery and childbirth preparation classes on the experience of childbirth. Unpublished doctoral dissertation, Michigan State University, 1973.

Freeberg, N. E., & Payne, D. T. Parental influence on cognitive development in early childhood: A review. *Child Development,* 1967, **38,** 65–87.

Freedheim, D. K. An investigation of masculinity and parental role patterns. Unpublished doctoral dissertation, Duke University, 1960.

Freud, A. *Normality and pathology in childhood: Assessments of development.* New York: International Universities Press, 1965.

Freud, S. The interpretation of dreams (1900). *The Standard Edition,* Vol. 4. London: Hogarth, 1964.

Freud, S. *Three essays on the theory of sexuality* (1905). New York: Avon, 1962.

Freud, S. Analysis of a phobia in a five-year-old boy (1909). In *The sexual enlightenment of children.* New York: Collier, 1963.

Freud, S. *The ego and the id* (1923). New York: Norton, 1962.

Freud, S. The passing of the Oedipus Complex. In *Collected Papers,* Vol. 2. London: Hogarth, 1924.

Freud, S. Moses and monotheism (1939). *The Standard Edition,* Vol. 23. London: Hogarth, 1964.

Freud, S. *An outline of psychoanalysis* (1940). New York: Norton, 1940.

Freud, S. *Group psychology and the analysis of the ego* (1905). London: Hogarth, 1948.

Freud, S. Some psychological consequences of the anatomical distinction between the sexes (1939). In *Collected Papers,* Vol. 5. London: Hogarth, 1950.

Frodi, A. M. & Lamb, M. E. Sex differences in responsiveness to infants: A developmental study of psychophysiological and behavioral responses. *Child Development,* 1978, **49,** 1182–1188.

Frodi, A. M., Lamb, M. E., Leavitt, L. A., & Donovan, W. L. Fathers' and mothers' responses to infant smiles and cries. *Infant Behavior and Development,* 1978, **1,** 187–198.

Frodi, A. M., Lamb, M. E., Leavitt, L. A., Donovan, W. L., Neff, C., & Sherry, D. Fathers' and mothers' responses to the faces and cries of normal and premature infants. *Developmental Psychology,* 1978, **14,** 490–498.

Gardner, L. P. An analysis of children's attitudes towards fathers. *Journal of Genetic Psychology,* 1947, **70,** 3–28.

Gavron, H. *The captive wife: Conflicts of housebound mothers.* London: Routledge & Kegan Paul, 1966.

Getzels, J. W., & Walsh, J. J. The method of paired direct and projective question-naires in the study of attitude structure and socialization. *Psychological Monographs,* 1958, **72,** Whole No. 454.

Gewirtz, H. B., & Gewirtz, J. L. Visiting and caretaking patterns for kibbutz infants: Age and sex trends. *American Journal of Orthopsychiatry,* 1968, **38,** 427–447.

Gewirtz, J. L. Attachment, dependency, and a distinction in terms of stimulus control. In J. L. Gewirtz (Ed.), *Attachment and dependency.* Washington, D.C.: Winston, 1972.

Gilbert, S. D. *What's a father for?* New York: Parents' Magazine Press, 1975.

Gill, L. J., & Spilka, B. Some nonintellectual correlates of academic achievement among Mexican-American secondary school students. *Journal of Educational Psychology,* 1962, **53,** 144–149.

Giovannoni, J. M., & Billingsley, A. Child neglect among the poor: A study of paren-tal adequacy in three ethnic groups. *Child Welfare,* 1970, **49,** 196–204.

Gleason, J. B. Fathers and other strangers: Men's speech to young children. In D. P. Dato (Ed.), *Language and linguistics.* Washington, D.C.: Georgetown University Press, 1975.

Glueck, S., & Glueck, E. *Unraveling juvenile delinquency.* New York: Commonwealth Fund, 1950.

Glueck, S., & Glueck, E. T. *Physique and delinquency.* New York: Harper, 1956.

Glueck, S., & Glueck, E. *Predicting delinquency and crime.* Cambridge, Mass.: Harvard University Press, 1959.

Gold, D., & Andres, D. Relations between maternal employment and development of nursery school children. *Canadian Journal of Behavioural Science,* 1978, **10,** 116–129(a).

Gold, D., & Andres, D. Comparisons of adolescent children with employed and nonemployed mothers. *Merrill-Palmer Quarterly,* 1978, **24,** 243–254(b).

Gold, D., Andres, D., & Glorieux, J. The development of Francophone nursery school children with employed and nonemployed mothers. *Canadian Journal of Behavioural Science,* 1979, **11,** 169–173.

Goldberg, S. Infant care and growth in urban Zambia. *Human Development,* 1972, **15,** 77–89.

Goldberg, S., & Lewis, M. Play behavior in the year-old infant: Early sex differences. *Child Development,* 1969, **40,** 21–31.

Goldstein, H. W., & Peck, R. Maternal differentiation, father absence, and cognitive differentiation in children. *Archives of General Psychiatry*, 1973, **29**, 370–373.

Golinkoff, R. M. & Ames, G. J. A comparison of fathers' and mothers' speech with their young children. *Child Development*, 1979, **50**, 28–32.

Goodenough, E. W. Interest in persons as an aspect of sex difference in the early years. *Genetic Psychology Monographs*, 1957, **55**, 287–323.

Gordon, R. S., & Gordon, K. Social factors in the prediction and treatment of emotional disorders of pregnancy. *American Journal of Obstetrics and Gynecology*, 1959, **77**, 1074–1083.

Gorer, G. *The American people: A study of national character.* New York: Norton, 1948.

Graham, P., & Rutter, M. Psychiatric disorder in the young adolescent: A follow-up study. *Proceedings of the Royal Society of Medicine*, 1973, **66**, 1226–1229.

Gray, S. Masculinity–femininity in relation to anxiety and social acceptance. *Child Development*, 1957, **28**, 203–214.

Gray, S. Perceived similarity to parents and adjustment. *Child Development*, 1959, **30**, 91–107.

Gray, S. W., & Klaus, R. The assessment of parental identification. *Genetic Psychology Monographs*, 1956, **54**, 81–114.

Green, M. *Fathering.* New York: McGraw-Hill, 1976.

Greenacre, P. *Emotional growth.* New York: International Universities Press, 1971.

Greenberg, M., & Morris, N. Engrossment: The newborn's impact upon the father. *American Journal of Orthopsychiatry*, 1974, **44**, 520–531.

Gregory, I. Anterospective data following childhood loss of a parent. I. Delinquency and high school dropout. *Archives of General Psychiatry*, 1965, **13**, 99–109.

Greif, E. B. A study of role-playing in preschool children. Unpublished doctoral dissertation, Johns Hopkins University, 1973.

Grunebaum, M. G., Hurwitz, I., Prentice, N. M., & Sperry, B. M. Fathers of sons with primary neurotic learning inhibition. *American Journal of Orthopsychiatry*, 1962, **32**, 462–473.

Gurwitt, A. R. Aspects of prospective fatherhood. *Psychoanalytic Study of the Child*, 1976, **31**, 237–271.

Haavio-Mannila, E. Convergences between east and west: Traditions and modernity in Sweden, Finland, and the Soviet Union. *Acta Sociologica*, 1971, **14**, 114–125.

Hacker, H. M. The new burdens of masculinity. *Marriage and Family Living*, 1957, **19**, 226–233.

Hainline, L., & Feig, E. The correlates of childhood father absence in college-aged women. *Child Development*, 1978, **49**, 37–42.

Hamilton, M. L. *Father's influences on children.* Chicago: Nelson-Hall, 1977.

Hampson, J. L., & Hampson, J. G. The ontogensis of sexual behavior in man. In W. C. Young (Ed.), *Sex and internal secretions*, 3rd ed. Baltimore: Williams & Wilkins, 1961.

Handel, G. Psychological study of whole families. *Psychological Bulletin*, 1965, **63**, 19–41.

Harlow, H. F. The development of affectional patterns in infant monkeys. In B. M. Foss (Ed.), *Determinants of infant behaviour*, Vol. 1. London: Methuen, 1961.

Harlow, H. F., & Zimmerman, R. R. Affectional responses in the infant monkey. *Science*, 1959, **130**, 421.

Harper, L. W. The young as a source of stimuli controlling caretaking behavior. *Developmental Psychology*, 1971, **4**, 73–85.

Harrison, D. M. The relationship between perceived paternal attitude toward the daughter during childhood and subsequent tendency toward emotional disorders in the daughter. Unpublished doctoral dissertation, University of Maryland, 1973.

Hartley, R. E. Sex role identification: A symposium. A developmental view of female sex role definition and identification. *Merrill-Palmer Quarterly*, 1964, **10**, 3–16.

Hartley, R. E., & Klein, A. Sex role concepts among elementary school-age girls. *Marriage and Family Living*, 1959, **21**, 59–64.

Hartup, W. W. Some correlates of parental imitation in young children. *Child Development*, 1962, **33**, 85–97.

Hartup, W. W., & Zook, E. A. Sex role preferences in three- and four-year old children. *Journal of Consulting Psychology*, 1960, **24**, 420–426.

Heath, D. H. Competent fathers: Their personalities and marriages. *Human Development*, 1976, **19**, 26–39.

Heilbrun, A. B. An empirical test of the modelling theory of sex-role learning. *Child Development*, 1965, **36**, 789–799.

Heilbrun, A. B. Parent identification and filial sex-role behavior: The importance of biological context. In J. K. Cole & R. Dienstbier (Eds.), *Nebraska symposium on motivation*. Lincoln: University of Nebraska Press, 1974.

Heilbrun, A. B., Harrell, S. N., & Gillard, B. J. Perceived identification of late adolescents and level of adjustment: The importance of parent-model attributes, ordinal position, and sex of child. *Journal of Genetic Psychology*, 1965, **107**, 49–59.

Helper, M. M. Learning theory and the self-concept. *Journal of Abnormal and Social Psychology*, 1955, **51**, 184–194.

Helson, R. Women mathematicians and the creative personality. *Journal of Consulting and Clinical Psychology*, 1971, **36**, 210–220.

Herzog, E., & Sudia, C. *Boys in fatherless families*. Washington, D.C.: Department of Health, Education and Welfare, 1970.

Herzog, E., & Sudia, C. Children in fatherless families. In B. M. Caldwell & H. N. Ricciuti (Eds.), *Review of child development research*, Vol. 3. Chicago: University of Chicago Press, 1973.

Hess, R. D., & Camara, K. A. Post-divorce family relationships as mediating factors in the consequences of divorce for children. *Journal of Social Issues*, 1979, **35**, 79–96.

Hetherington, E. M. A developmental study of the effects of sex of the dominant parent on sex-role preference, identification, and imitation in children. *Journal of Personality and Social Psychology*, 1965, **2**, 188–194.

Hetherington, E. M. Effects of paternal absence on sex-typed behaviors in Negro and white preadolescent males. *Journal of Personality and Social Psychology*, 1966, **4**, 87–91.

Hetherington, E. M. The effects of familial variables on sex typing, on parent-child similarity, and on imitation in children. In J. P. Hill (Ed.), *Minnesota symposia on child psychology*, Vol. 1. Minneapolis: University of Minnesota Press, 1967.

Hetherington, E. M. Effects of father-absence on personality development in adolescent daughters. *Developmental Psychology*, 1972, **7**, 313–326.

Hetherington, E. M., Cox, M., & Cox, R. Beyond father absence: Conceptualization of effects of divorce. Paper presented to the Society for Research in Child Development, Denver, April 1975.

Hetherington, E. M., Cox, M., & Cox, R. Divorced fathers. *Family Coordinator*, 1976, **25**, 417–428.

Hetherington, E. M., Cox, M., & Cox, R. The aftermath of divorce. In J. H. Stevens & M. Matthews (Ed.), *Mother/child, father/child relationships*. Washington, D.C.: National Association for the Education of Young Children, 1978.

Hetherington, E. M., & Deur, J. L. The effects of father absence on child development. *Young Children*, 1971, **26**, 233–248.

Hetherington, E. M., & Frankie, G. Effects of parental dominance, warmth, and conflict on imitation in children. *Journal of Personality and Social Psychology*, 1967, **6**, 119–125.

Hetherington, E. M., & Martin, B. Family interaction. In H. C. Quay & J. S. Werry (Eds.), *Psychopathological disorders of childhood*. New York: Wiley, 1979.

Hill, J. P. The early adolescent and the family. In *Seventy-Ninth Yearbook of the National Society for the Study of Education*. Chicago: University of Chicago Press, 1980.

Hillenbrand, E. D. Father absence in military families. *Family Coordinator*, 1976, **25**, 451–458.

Hinde, R. A. *Animal behavior: A·synthesis of ethology and comparative psychology*. New York: McGraw-Hill, 1970.

Hines, J. D. Father: The forgotten man. *Nursing Forum*, 1971, **10**, 176–200.

Hipgrave, T. When the mother is gone: The position of the lone father. Unpublished manuscript, University of Leicester, 1979.

Hoffman, L. W. The father's role in the family and the child's peer-group adjustment. *Merrill-Palmer Quarterly*, 1961, **7**, 97–105.

Hoffman, L. W. Effects of maternal employment on the child: A review of the research. *Developmental Psychology*, 1974, **10**, 204–228.

Hoffman, L. W. Changes in family roles, socialization, and sex differences. *American Psychologist*, 1977, **32**, 644–657.

Hoffman, L. W., & Lippitt, R. The measurement of family life variables. In P. H. Mussen (Ed.), *Handbook of research method in child development.* New York: Wiley, 1960.

Hoffman, L. W., & Nye, F. I. *Working mothers.* San Francisco: Jossey-Bass, 1974.

Hoffman, M. L. Power assertion by the parent and its impact on the child. *Child Development,* 1960, **31,** 129–143.

Hoffman, M. L. Paternal practices and the development of internal social control. Paper presented to the Society for Research in Child Development, Bowling Green, Ohio, March 1966.

Hoffman, M. L. Conscience, personality, and socialization technique. *Human Development,* 1970, **13,** 90–126(a).

Hoffman, M. L. Moral development. In P. H. Mussen (Ed.), *Carmichael's manual of child psychology,* Vol. 2. 3rd ed., New York: Wiley, 1970(b).

Hoffman, M. L. Father absence and conscience development. *Developmental Psychology,* 1971, **4,** 400–406(a).

Hoffman, M. L. Identification and conscience development. *Child Development,* 1971, **42,** 1071–1082(b).

Hoffman, M. L., & Saltzstein, H. D. Parent discipline and the child's moral development. *Journal of Personality and Social Psychology,* 1967, **5,** 45–57.

Holman, P. Some factors in the etiology of maladjustment in children. *Journal of Mental Science,* 1953, **99,** 654–688.

Holman, P. The etiology of maladjustment in children. *Journal of Mental Science,* 1959, **99,** 654–688.

Holstein, C. G. Parental consensus and interaction in relation to the child's moral development. Unpublished doctoral dissertation. University of California, Berkeley, 1969.

Honzik, M. P. A sex difference in the age of onset of the parent–child resemblance in intelligence. *Journal of Educational Psychology,* 1963, **54,** 231–237.

Horney, K. On the genesis of the castration complex in women. *International Journal of Psychoanalysis,* 1924, **5,** 50–65.

Horney, K. The flight from womanhood. *International Journal of Psychoanalysis,* 1926, **7,** 324–339.

Horney, K. The dread of women. *International Journal of Psychoanalysis,* 1932, **13,** 348–360.

Horney, K. The denial of the vagina. *International Journal of Psychoanalysis,* 1933, **14,** 57–70.

Howells, J. G. Fathering. In J. G. Howells (Eds.), *Modern perspectives in international child psychiatry.* Edinburgh: Oliver & Boyd, 1969.

Hull, C. L. *Principles of behavior.* New York: Appleton-Century-Crofts, 1943.

Hunt, L. L., & Hunt, J. B. Race and the father–son connection. *Social Problems,* 1975, **23,** 35–51.

Hurley, J. R. Parental malevolence and children's intelligence. *Journal of Consulting Psychology,* 1967, **31,** 199–204.

Illsley, R., & Thompson, B. Women from broken homes. *Sociological Review,* 1961, **9,** 27–54.

Jacob, T. Patterns of family conflict and dominance as a function of child age and social class. *Developmental Psychology,* 1974, **10,** 1–12.

Jacobson, E. *The self and the object world.* New York: International Universities Press, 1964.

Jacobson, G., & Ryder R. G. Parental loss and some characteristics of the early marriage relationship. *American Journal of Orthopsychiatry,* 1969, **39,** 779–787.

Johnson, M. M. Sex role learning in the nuclear family. *Child Development,* 1963, **34,** 315–333.

Jordan, B. E., Radin, N., & Epstein, A. Paternal behavior and intellectual functioning in preschool boys and girls. *Developmental Psychology,* 1975, **11,** 407–408.

Josselyn, I. M. Cultural forces, motherliness, and fatherliness. *American Journal of Orthopsychiatry,* 1956, **26,** 264–271.

Jung, C. G. *The significance of the father in the destiny of the individual.* Zurich: Rascher, 1949.

Kagan, J. The concept of identification. *Psychological Review,* 1958, **65,** 295–305.

Kagan, J. Acquisition and significance of sex-typing and sex-role identity. In M. L. Hoffman & L. W. Hoffman (Eds.), *Review of child development research,* Vol. 1. New York: Russell Sage Foundation, 1964.

Kagan, J., & Freeman, M. Relation of childhood intelligence, maternal behaviors, and social class to behavior during adolescence. *Child Development,* 1963, **34,** 899–911.

Kagan, J., Hosken, B., & Watson, S. Child's symbolic conceptualization of parents. *Child Development,* 1961, **32,** 625–636.

Kagan, J., Kearsley, P., & Zelazo, P. *Infancy: Its place in human development.* Cambridge, Mass.: Harvard University Press, 1978.

Kahl, J. A. Educational and occupational aspirations of ''common man'' boys. *American Educational Review,* 1953, **23,** 186–203.

Kahl, J. A. *The American class structure.* New York: Holt, Rinehart, & Winston, 1957.

Kandel, D., & Lesser, G. S. *Youth in two worlds.* San Francisco: Jossey-Bass, 1972.

Kanin, E. T. Male aggression in dating–courtship relations. *American Journal of Sociology,* 1957, **63,** 197–204.

Kaplar, J. E. Creativity, sex-role preference, and perception of parents in fifth-grade boys. Unpublished doctoral dissertation, University of Massachusetts, 1970.

Katz, I. Socialization of academic motivation in minority group children. In D. Levine (Ed.), *Nebraska symposium on motivation.* Lincoln: University of Nebraska Press, 1967.

Kauffman, A. L. Mothers' and fathers' verbal interactions with children learning language. Paper presented to the Eastern Psychological Association, Boston, April 1977.

Kauffman, J. H. Interpersonal relations in traditional and emergent families among midwest Mennonites. *Marriage and Family Living*, 1961, **23**, 247–252.

Kemper, T. D., & Reichler, M. L. Father's work integration and types and frequencies of rewards and punishments administered by fathers and mothers to adolescent sons and daughters. *Journal of Genetic Psychology, 1976,* **129**, 207–219.

Kestenberg, J. Vicissitudes of female sexuality. *Journal of the American Psychoanalytic Association*, 1956, **4**, 453–476.

Kestenberg, J. Outside and inside, male and female. *Journal of the American Psychoanalytic Association*, 1968, **16**, 459–520.

Kestenberg, J. *Children and parents*. New York: Aronson, 1975.

Kimball, B. The Sentence Completion Technique in a study of scholastic underachievement. *Journal of Consulting Psychology*, 1952, **16**, 353–358.

Klein, M. *Envy and gratitude*. London: Tavistock, 1957.

Kluckhorn, C. *Mirror for man*. New York: McGraw-Hill, 1949.

Koch, H. L. Some personality correlates of sex, sibling position and sex of siblings among five- and six-year-old children. *Genetic Psychology Monographs*, 1955, **52**, 3–50.

Koch, H. L. Sissiness and tomboyishness in relation to sibling characteristics. *Journal of Genetic Psychology*, 1956, **88**, 231–244.

Kogelschatz, J. L., Adams, P. L., & Tucker, D. McK. Family styles of fatherless households. *Journal of the American Academy of Child Psychiatry*, 1972, **11**, 365–383.

Kohlberg, L. Moral development and identification. In H. W. Stevenson (Ed.), *Child psychology*. Chicago: University of Chicago Press, 1963.

Kohlberg, L. The development of moral character and ideology. In M. L. Hoffman & L. W. Hoffman (Eds.), *Review of child development research,* Vol. 1. New York: Russell Sage Foundation, 1964.

Kohlberg, L. Stage and sequence: The developmental approach to moralization. In M. L. Hoffman (Ed.), *Moral processes*. Chicago: Aldine, 1966.

Kohlberg, L. Stage and sequence: The cognitive–developmental approach to socialization. In D. A. Goslin (Ed.), *Handbook of socialization theory and research*. Chicago: Rand McNally, 1969.

Kohn, M. L. Social class and the exercise of parental authority. *American Sociological Review*, 1959, **24**, 352–366.

Kohn, M. L. *Class and conformity: A study in values*. Homewood, Ill.: Dorsey, 1969.

Kohn, M. L. The effects of social class on parental values and practices. In D. Reiss & H. A. Hoffman (Eds.), *The American family: Dying or developing*. New York: Plenum, 1979.

Kohn, M. L., & Carroll, E. E. Social class and the allocation of parental responsibilities. *Sociometry,* 1960, **23,** 372–392.

Komarovsky, M. *Blue-collar marriage.* New York: Random House, 1964.

Kotelchuck, M. The nature of the child's tie to his father. Unpublished doctoral dissertation, Harvard University, 1972.

Kotelchuck, M. The nature of the child's tie to his father. Paper presented to the Society for Research in Child Development, Philadelphia, April 1973.

Kotelchuck, M. Father caretaking characteristics and their influence on infant-father interaction. Paper presented to the American Psychological Association, Chicago, September 1975.

Kotelchuck, M. The infant's relationship to the father: Experimental evidence. In M. E. Lamb (Ed.), *The role of the father in child development.* New York: Wiley, 1976.

Kotelchuck, M., Zelazo, P., Kagan, J., & Spelke, E. Infant reaction to parental separations when left with familiar and unfamiliar adults. *Journal of Genetic Psychology,* 1975, **126,** 255–262.

Krige, P. Patterns of interaction in family triads with high-achieving and low-achieving children. *Psychological Reports,* 1976, **39,** 1291–1299.

Lamb, M. E. Fathers: Forgotten contributors to child development. *Human Development,* 1975, **18,** 245–266(a).

Lamb, M. E. Physiological mechanisms in the control of maternal behavior in rats: A review. *Psychological Bulletin,* 1975, **82,** 104–119(b).

Lamb, M. E. Effects of stress and cohort on mother- and father-infant interaction. *Developmental Psychology,* 1976, **12,** 435–443(a).

Lamb, M. E. Interactions between eight-month-old children and their fathers and mothers. In M. E. Lamb (Ed.), *The role of the father in child development.* New York: Wiley, 1976(b).

Lamb, M. E. Interactions between two-year-olds and their mothers and fathers. *Psychological Reports,* 1976, **38,** 447–450(c).

Lamb, M. E. Parent-infant interaction in eight-month-olds. *Child Psychiatry & Human Development,* 1976, **7,** 56–63(d).

Lamb, M. E. (Ed.) *The role of the father in child development.* New York: Wiley, 1976(e).

Lamb, M. E. The role of the father: An overview. In M. E. Lamb (Ed.), *The role of the father in child development.* New York: Wiley, 1976(f).

Lamb, M. E. Twelve-month-olds and their parents: Interaction in a laboratory playroom. *Developmental Psychology,* 1976, **12,** 237–244(g).

Lamb, M. E. The development of mother–infant and father–infant attachments in the second year of life. *Developmental Psychology,* 1977, **13,** 637–648(a).

Lamb, M. E. The development of parental preferences in the first two years of life. *Sex Roles,* 1977, **3,** 495–497(b).

Lamb, M. E. Father–infant and mother–infant interaction in the first year of life. *Child Development,* 1977, **48,** 167–181(c).

Lamb, M. E. Qualitative aspects of mother– and father–infant attachments. *Infant Behavior and Development*, 1978, **1**, 265–275.

Lamb, M. E. Separation and reunion behaviors as criteria of attachment to mothers and fathers. *Early Human Development*, 1979, **3/4**, 329–339.

Lamb, M. E. On the origins and implications of sex differences in human sexuality. *Behavioral & Brain Sciences*, 1980, **3**, 192–193.

Lamb, M. E. The development of social expectations in the first year of life. In M. E. Lamb & L. R. Sherrod (Eds.), *Infant social cognition: Empirical and theoretical considerations*. Hillsdale, N.J.: Lawrence Erlbaum Associates, 1981.

Lamb, M. E. (Ed.) *Nontraditional families: Parenting and child development*. Hillsdale, N.J.: Lawrence Erlbaum Associates, in press.

Lamb, M. E., & Bronson, S. K. Fathers in the context of family influences: Past, present, and future. *School Psychology Review*, 1980, **9**, 336–353.

Lamb, M. E., Chase-Lansdale, L., & Owen, M. The changing American family and its implications for infant social development: The sample case of maternal employment. In M. Lewis, & L. A. Rosenblum (Eds.), *The child and its family*. New York: Plenum, 1979.

Lamb, M. E., Frodi, A. M., Hwang, C. P., & Frodi, M. Varying degrees of paternal involvement in infant care: Attitudinal and behavioral correlates. In M. E. Lamb (Ed.), *Nontraditional families: Parenting and child development*. Hillsdale, N.J.: Lawrence Erlbaum Associates, in press.

Lamb, M. E., & Goldberg, W. A. The father–child relationship: A synthesis of biological, evolutionary and social perspectives. In R. Gandelman & L. W. Hoffman (Eds.), *Perspectives on parental behavior*. Hillsdale, N.J.: Lawrence Erlbaum Associates, in press.

Lamb, M. E., Owen, M., & Chase-Lansdale, L. The father–daughter relationship: Past, present, and future. In C. B. Kopp (Ed.), *Becoming female: Perspectives on development*. New York: Plenum, 1979.

LaMouse, A. Family roles of women: A German example. *Journal of Marriage and the Family*, 1969, **31**, 145–152.

Lambert, W. E., Yackley, A., & Hein, R. M. Child training values of English Canadian and French Canadian parents. *Canadian Journal of Behavioural Science*, 1971, **3**, 217–236.

Landis, P. H. Research on teen-age dating. *Marriage and Family Living*, 1960, **22**, 266–267.

Landy, F., Rosenberg, B. G., & Sutton-Smith, B. The effect of limited father-absence on the cognitive and emotional development of children. Paper presented to the Mid-Western Psychological Association, Chicago, May 1967.

Landy, F., Rosenberg, B. G., & Sutton-Smith, B. The effect of limited father-absence on cognitive development. *Child Development*, 1969, **40**, 941–944.

Langer, T. S., & Michael, S. T. *Life stress and mental health*. New York: Free Press, 1963.

Langlois, J. H. & Downs, A. C. Mothers, fathers, and peers as socialization agents of sex-typed play behaviors in young children. *Child Development,* 1980, **51,** 1237–1247.

Lansky, L. M. The family structure also affects the model: Sex-role identification in parents of preschool children. *Merrill-Palmer Quarterly,* 1964, **10,** 39–40.

Lansky, L. M. The family structure also affects the model: Sex-role attitudes in parents of preschool children. *Merrill-Palmer Quarterly,* 1967, **13,** 139–150.

Layman, E. M. Discussion of Symposium: Father influence in the family. *Merrill-Palmer Quarterly,* 1961, **7,** 107–111.

Lazowick, L. M. On the nature of identification. *Journal of Abnormal and Social Psychology,* 1955, **51,** 175–183.

LeCorgne, L. L., & Laosa, L. M. Father absence in low-income Mexican-American families: Children's social adjustment and conceptual differentiation of sex role attributes. *Developmental Psychology,* 1976, **12,** 470–471.

Lederer, W. Dragons, delinquents, and destiny. *Psychological Issues,* 1964, **4,** Whole No. 3.

Lefkowitz, M. Some relationships between sex role preference of children and other parent and child variables. *Psychological Reports,* 1962, **10,** 43–53.

Lehrman, D. S. Can psychiatrists use ethology? In N. F. White (Ed.). *Ethology and psychiatry.* Toronto: University of Toronto Press, 1974.

Leichty, M. The absence of the father during early childhood and its effect upon the Oedipal situation as reflected in young adults. *Merrill-Palmer Quarterly,* 1960, **6,** 212–217.

Leiderman, G. F. Effect of parental relationships and child-training practices on boy's interactions with peers. *Acta Psychologica,* 1959, **15,** 469.

Leiderman, P. H., & Leiderman, G. F. Familial influences on infant development in an Eastern African agricultural community. In E. J. Anthony & C. Koupernik (Eds.), *The child in his family: Children at psychiatric risk.* New York: Wiley, 1974.

Leiderman, P. H., & Leiderman, G. F. Affective and cognitive consequences of polymatric infant care in the East African Highlands. In A. D. Pick (Ed.), *Minnesota symposia on child psychology,* Vol. 8. Minneapolis: University of Minnesota Press, 1975.

Leiderman, P. H., & Leiderman, G. F. Economic change and infant care in an East African agricultural community. In P. H. Leiderman, S. R. Tulkin, & A. Rosenfeld (Eds.), *Culture and infancy.* New York: Academic Press, 1977.

Leifer, A. D., Leiderman, P. H., Barnett, C. R., & Williams, J. A. Effects of mother–infant separation on maternal attachment behavior. *Child Development,* 1972, **43,** 1203–1218.

LeMasters, E. E. Parenthood as crisis. *Marriage and Family Living,* 1957, **19,** 352–355.

Lerner, S. H. Effects of desertion on family life. *Social Casework,* 1954, **35,** 3–8.

Lessing, E. E., Zagorin, S. W., & Nelson, D. WISC subtest and IQ score correlates of father absence. *Journal of Genetic Psychology,* 1970, **67,** 181–195.

Levine, J. *And who will raise the children? New options for fathers and mothers.* Philadelphia: Lippincott, 1976.

Levine, R. A., Klein, W. H., & Owen, C. R. Father–child relationships and changing life styles in Ibadan, Nigeria. In H. Minor (Ed.), *The city in modern Africa.* New York: Praeger, 1967.

Lewis, M. Parents and children: Sex role development. *School Review,* 1972, **80,** 229–240(a).

Lewis, M. State as an infant–environment interaction: An analysis of mother–infant behavior as a function of sex. *Merrill-Palmer Quarterly,* 1972, **18,** 95–121(b).

Lewis, M., & Rosenblum, L. A. (Eds.), *The effect of the infant on its caregiver.* New York: Wiley, 1974.

Lewis, M., & Weinraub, M. Sex of parent x sex of child: Socioemotional development. In R. C. Friedman, R. M. Richart, & R. L. Vande Wiele (Eds.), *Sex differences in behavior.* New York: Wiley, 1974.

Lewis, M., & Weinraub, M. The father's role in the infant's social network. In M. E. Lamb (Ed.), *The role of the father in child development.* New York: Wiley, 1976.

Liebenberg, B. Expectant fathers. *American Journal of Orthopsychiatry,* 1967, **37,** 358–359.

Lifshitz, M., Berman, D., Galili, A., & Gilad, D. Bereaved children: The effect of mother's perception and social system organization on their short-range adjustment. *Journal of the American Academy of Child Psychiatry,* 1977, **16,** 272–284.

Lind, R. Observations after delivery of communications between mother–infant–father. Paper presented to the International Congress of Pediatrics, Buenos Aires, 1974.

Livson, N. Parental behavior and children's involvement with their parents. *Journal of Genetic Psychology,* 1966, **109,** 173–194.

Loeb, R. C. Concomitants of boy's locus of control examined in parent–child interactions. *Developmental Psychology,* 1975, **11,** 353–358.

Loewald, H. Ego and reality. *International Journal of Psychoanalysis,* 1951, **32,** 10–18.

Lorenz, K. Companions as factors in the bird's environment (1935). In *Studies in animal and human behavior.* Cambridge, Mass: Harvard University Press, 1970.

Lozoff, M. M. Fathers and autonomy in women. In R. B. Kundsin (Ed.), *Women and success.* New York: Morrow, 1974.

Lynn, D. B. A note on sex differences in the development of masculine and feminine identification. *Psychological Review,* 1959, **66,** 126–135.

Lynn, D. B. Sex differences in identification development. *Sociometry,* 1961, **24,** 372–383.

Lynn, D. B. Sex role and parental identification. *Child Development,* 1962, **33,** 555–564.

Lynn, D. B. The process of learning parental and sex-role identification. *Journal of Marriage and the Family,* 1966, **28,** 466–470.

Lynn, D. B. *Parental and sex-role identification: A theoretical formulation.* Berkeley: McCutcheon, 1969.

Lynn, D. B. *The father: His role in child development.* Monterey, Calif.: Brooks/Cole, 1974.

Lynn, D. B., & Cross, A. R. Parent preferences of preschool children. *Journal of Marriage and the Family,* 1974, **36,** 555–559.

Lynn, D. B., & Maaske, M. Imitation versus similarity: Child to parent. Paper presented to the Western Psychological Association, Los Angeles, April 1970.

Lynn, D. B., & Sawrey, W. L. The effects of father-absence on Norwegian boys and girls. *Journal of Abnormal and Social Psychology,* 1959, **59,** 258–262.

Lytton, H. The socialization of two-year-old boys: Ecological findings. *Journal of Child Psychology and Psychiatry,* 1976, **17,** 287–304.

Lytton, H. Disciplinary encounters between young boys and their mothers and fathers: Is there a contingency system? *Developmental Psychology,* 1979, **15,** 256–268.

MacCalman, D. R. Background to child development patterns in the United Kingdom. In K. Soddy (Ed.), *Mental health and infant development,* Vol. 1. London: Routledge & Kegan Paul, 1955.

Maccoby, E. E. Current changes in the family and their impact upon the socialization of children. Paper presented to the American Sociological Association, Chicago, September 1977.

Maccoby, E. E., & Jacklin, C. N. Stress, activity, and proximity seeking: Sex differences in the year-old child. *Child Development,* 1973, **44,** 34–42.

Maccoby, E. E., & Jacklin, C. N. *The psychology of sex differences.* Stanford: Stanford University Press, 1974.

Maccoby, E. E., & Masters, J. C. Attachment and dependency. In P. H. Mussen (Ed.), *Carmichael's manual of child psychology,* (3rd ed.), Vol. 2. New York: Wiley, 1970.

MacKinnon, D. W. Violations of prohibitions. In H. A. Murray (Ed.), *Explorations in personality.* New York: Oxford University Press, 1938.

Mahler, M. S. *On human symbiosis and the vicissitudes of individuation.* New York: International Universities Press, 1968.

Mahler, M. S., Pine F., & Bergman, A. *The psychological birth of the human infant.* New York: Basic Books, 1975.

Main, M. Exploration, play, and level of cognitive functioning as related to child–mother attachment. Unpublished doctoral dissertation, Johns Hopkins University, 1973.

Marcus, R. F. The child as elicitor of parental sanctions for independent and dependent behavior: A simulation of parent–child interaction. *Developmental Psychology,* 1975, **11,** 443–452.

Margolin, G., & Patterson, G. Differential consequences provided by mothers and fathers for their sons and daughters. *Developmental Psychology*, 1975, **11**, 537–538.

Marsella, A. J., Dubanoski, R. A., & Mohs, K. The effects of father presence and absence upon maternal attitudes. *Journal of Genetic Psychology*, 1974, **125**, 257–263.

Maxwell, A. E. Discrepancies between the pattern of abilities for normal and neurotic children. *Journal of Mental Science*, 1961, **107**, 300–307.

Maxwell, J. W. The keeping fathers of America. *Family Coordinator*, 1976, **25**, 387–392.

McCord, W., McCord, J., & Howard, A. Familial correlates of aggression in nondelinquent male children. *Journal of Abnormal and Social Psychology*, 1961, **62**, 79–93.

McCord, W., McCord, J., & Howard, A. Family interaction as antecedent to the direction of male aggressiveness. *Journal of Abnormal and Social Psychology*, 1963, **66**, 239–242.

McCord, J., McCord, W., & Thurber, E. Some effects of paternal absence on male children. *Journal of Abnormal and Social Psychology*, 1962, **64**, 361–369.

McGuire, C. Sex role and community-variability in test performances. *Journal of Educational Psychology*, 1961, **52**, 61–73.

Mead, M. *Sex and temperament in three primitive societies*. New York: Morrow, 1935.

Mead, M. *Male and female*. New York: Morrow, 1949.

Mead, M. A cultural anthropologist's approach to maternal deprivation. In *Deprivation of maternal care: A reassessment of its effects*. Geneva: WHO, 1962.

Medinnus, G. N. The relation between inter-parent agreement and several child measures. *Journal of Genetic Psychology*, 1963, **102**, 139–144.

Medinnus, G. N. Delinquents' perceptions of their parents. *Journal of Consulting Psychology*, 1965, **29**, 5–19.

Medinnus, G. N., & Johnson, T. M. Parental perceptions of kindergarten children. *Journal of Educational Research*, 1970, **63**, 370–381.

Meerloo, J. A. M. The father cuts the cord. *American Journal of Psychotherapy*, 1956, **10**, 471–480.

Meerloo, J. A. M. The psychological role of the father: The father cuts the cord. *Child and Family*, 1968, 102–114.

Messer, S. B., & Lewis, M. Social class and sex differences in the attachment and play behavior of the one-year-old infant. *Merrill-Palmer Quarterly*, 1972, **18**, 295–306.

Metraux, R. Parents and children: An analysis of contemporary German child-care and youth guidance literature. In M. Mead & M. Wolfenstein (Eds.), *Childhood in contemporary culture*. Chicago: University of Chicago Press, 1955.

Middleton, R., & Putney, S. Political expression of adolescent rebellion. *American Journal of Sociology*, 1963, **68**, 527–535.

Miller, D. R., & Swanson, G. E. *The changing American parent*. New York: Wiley, 1958.

Miller, W. B. Lower class culture as a generating milieu of gang delinquency. *Journal of Social Issues*, 1958, **14**, 5–19.

Milton, G. A. The effects of sex-role identification upon problem solving skills. *Journal of Abnormal and Social Psychology*, 1957, **55**, 208–212.

Mischel, W. Sex typing and socialization. In P. H. Mussen (Ed.), *Carmichael's manual of child psychology*, (3rd ed.), Vol. 2. New York: Wiley, 1970.

Mitchell, D., & Wilson, W. Relationship of father-absence to masculinity and popularity of delinquent boys. *Psychological Reports*, 1967, **20**, 1173–1174.

Mogey, J. M. A century of declining paternal authority. *Marriage and Family Living*, 1957, **19**, 234–239.

Money, J., & Ehrhardt, A. A. *Man and woman: Boy and girl*. Baltimore: Johns Hopkins University Press, 1972.

Money, J., Hampson, J. G., & Hampson, J.L. Imprinting and the establishment of gender role. *Archives of Neurology and Psychiatry*, 1957, **77**, 333–336.

Money, J., & Tucker, P. *Sexual signatures*. Boston: Little, Brown, 1975.

Moss, H. A. Sex, age, and state as determinants of mother-infant interaction. *Merrill-Palmer Quarterly*, 1967, **13**, 19–36.

Moulton, P. W., Burstein, E., Liberty, D., & Altucher, N. The patterning of parental affection and dominance as a determinant of guilt and sex-typing. *Journal of Personality and Social Psychology*, 1966, **4**, 363–365.

Mowrer, W. H. Identification: A link between learning theory and psychotherapy. In *Learning theory and personality dynamics*. New York: Ronald, 1950.

Mullahy, G. A. Sex differences in patterns of self-disclosure among adolescents: A developmental perspective. *Journal of Youth and Adolescence*, 1973, **2**, 343–356.

Mullahy, P. *Oedipus: Myth and complex*. New York: Hermitage, 1948.

Murphy, L. B. *Personality in young children*. New York: Basic Books, 1956.

Murphy, L. B., & Moriarty, A. E. *Vulnerability, coping and growth*. New Haven: Yale University Press, 1976.

Murrell, S. A., & Stachowiak, J. G. The family group: Development, structure and therapy. *Journal of Marriage and the Family*, 1965, **27**, 13–18.

Mussen, P. H. Early socialization: Learning and identification. In T. M. Newcomb (Ed.), *New directions in psychology*, Vol. 3. New York: Holt, Rinehart, & Winston, 1967.

Mussen, P. H. Some antecedents and consequences of masculine sex-typing in adolescent boys. *Psychological Monographs*, 1971, **75,** Whole No. 506.

Mussen, P. H. *The psychological development of the child*. Englewood Cliffs, N.J.: Prentice-Hall, 1973.

Mussen, P. H., Bouterline-Young, H., Gaddini, R., & Morante, L. The influence of father–son relationships on adolescent personality and attitudes. *Journal of Child Psychology and Psychiatry*, 1963, **4**, 3–16.

Mussen, P. H., & Distler, L. Masculinity, identification, and father–son relationships. *Journal of Abnormal and Social Psychology*, 1959, **59,** 350–356.

Mussen, P. H., & Distler, L. Child rearing antecedents of masculine identification in kindergarten boys. *Child Development,* 1960, **31,** 89–100.

Mussen, P. H., & Parker, A. L. Mother nurturance and the girl's incidental imitative learning. *Journal of Personality and Social Psychology,* 1965, **2,** 94–97.

Mussen, P. H., & Rutherford, E. Parent–child relations and parental personality in relation to young children's sex-role preferences. *Child Development,* 1963, **34,** 589–607.

Mussen, P. H. Rutherford, E., Harris, S., & Keasey, C. B. Honesty and altruism among preadolescents. *Development Psychology,* 1970, **3,** 169–194.

Mutimer, E., Loughlin, L., & Powell, M. Some differences in the family relationships of achieving and underachieving readers. *Journal of Genetic Psychology,* 1966, **109,** 67–74.

Nadelman, L. Perception of parents by London five-year-olds. Paper presented to the American Psychological Association, Washington D. C., September 1976.

Nash, J. Critical periods in human development. *Bulletin of the Maritime Psychological Association,* 1954, 18–22.

Nash, J. The father in contemporary culture and current psychological literature. *Child Development,* 1965, **36,** 261–297.

Nash, S. C., & Feldman, S. S. Sex role and sex-related attributions: Constancy and change across the family life cycle. In M. E. Lamb, & A. L. Brown (Eds.), *Advances in developmental psychology,* Vol. 1. Hillsdale, N. J.: Lawrence Erlbaum Associates, 1981.

Nelsen, E. A., & Maccoby, E. E. The relationship between social development and differential abilities on the scholastic aptitude test. *Merrill-Palmer Quarterly,* 1966, **12,** 269–289.

Newson, J., & Newson, E. *Infant care in an urban community.* London: Allen & Unwin, 1963.

Newson, J., & Newson, E. *Four years old in an urban community.* London: Allen & Unwin, 1968.

Noller, P. Cross gender effects in two-child families. *Developmental Psychology,* 1980, **16,** 159–160.

Norman, C. D. The interpersonal values of parents of achieving and nonachieving gifted children. *Journal of Psychology,* 1966, **64,** 49–57.

Nowlis, V. The search for significant concepts in a study of parent–child relationships. *American Journal of Orthopsychiatry,* 1952, **22,** 286–299.

Nye, F. I. Child adjustment in broken and unbroken homes. *Marriage and Family Living,* 1957, **19,** 356–361.

O'Brien, M. Father role and male sex role after marital separation: Men coping with single parenthood. Paper presented to the British Psychological Society Social Psychology Conference, Cardiff (Wales), September 1978.

Oakley, A. Are husbands good housewives? *New Society,* 1972, **19,** 337–340.

Oliver, L. W. The relationship of parental attitudes and parent identification to career and homemaking orientation in college women. *Journal of Vocational Behavior,* 1975, **7,** 1–12.

Olsen, M. E. Distribution of family responsibilities and social stratification. *Marriage and Family Living,* 1960, **22,** 60–65.

Osgood, C., Suci, G., & Tannenbaum, P. H. *The measurement of meaning.* Urbana: University of Illinois Press, 1957.

Oshman, H. P., & Manosevitz, N. Father absence: Effects of stepfathers upon psychosocial development in males. *Development Psychology,* 1976, **12,** 479–480.

Osofsky, J. D. Neonatal characteristics and directional effects in mother–infant interaction. Paper presented to the Society for Research in Child Development, Denver, April 1975.

Osofsky, J. D., & O'Connell, E. J. Parent–child interaction: Daughters' effects upon mothers' and fathers' behaviors. *Developmental Psychology,* 1972, **7,** 157–168.

Osofsky, J. D., & Oldfield, S. Children's effects upon parental behavior: Mothers' and fathers' responses to dependent and independent child behaviors. Paper presented to the American Psychological Association, Washington, D.C., August 1971.

Owen, M. T., Chase-Lansdale, L., & Lamb, M. E. The relationship between mother–infant and father–infant attachment. Unpublished manuscript, University of Michigan, 1980.

Pakizegi, B. The interaction of mothers and fathers with their sons. *Child Development,* 1978, **49,** 479–482.

Palmer, R. C. Behavior problems of children in Navy officers' families. *Social Casework,* 1960, **41,** 177–184.

Parke, R. D. Perspectives of father–infant interaction. In J. D. Osofsky (Ed.), *Handbook of infant development.* New York: Wiley, 1979.

Parke, R. D., Hymel, S., Power, T., & Tinsley, B. Fathers and risk: A hospital-based model of intervention. In D. B. Sawin & R. C. Hawkins (Eds.), *Psychosocial risks during pregnancy and early infancy.* New York: Brunner/Mazel, in press.

Parke, R. D., & O'Leary, S. Father–mother–infant interaction in the newbord period: Some findings, some observations, and some unresolved issues. In K. F. Riegel & J. Meacham (Eds.), *The developing individual in a changing world,* Vol. 2. *Social and environmental issues.* The Hague: Mouton, 1976.

Parke, R. D., O'Leary, S., & West, S. Mother–father–newborn interaction: Effects of maternal medication, labor, and sex of infant. *Proceedings of the 80th Annual Convention of the American Psychological Association,* 1972, 85–86.

Parke, R. D., & Sawin, D. B. The father's role in infancy: A reevaluation. *Family Coordinator,* 1976, **25,** 365–371.

Parke, R. D., & Sawin, D. B. The family in early infancy: Social interactional and attitudinal analyses. Paper presented to the Society for Research in Child Development, New Orleans, March 1977.

Parke, R. D., & Sawin, D. B. The family in early infancy: Social interactional and attitudinal analyses. In F. A. Pedersen (Ed.), *The father–infant relationship: Observational studies in the family setting.* New York: Praeger Special Publications, 1980.

Parsons, T. The father symbol: An appraisal in the light of psychoanalytic and sociological theory. In L. Bryson, L. Finkelstein, R. M. MacIver, & R. McKeon (Eds.), *Symbols and values.* New York: Harper & Row, 1954.

Parsons, T. Social structure and the development of personality: Freud's contribution to the integration of psychology and sociology. *Psychiatry,* 1958, **21,** 321–340.

Parsons, T., & Bales, R. F. *Family, socialization, and interaction process.* Glencoe, Ill.: Free Press, 1955.

Parsons, T., & Shils, E. A. (Eds.) *Towards a general theory of action.* Cambridge, Mass.: Harvard University Press, 1951.

Payne, D. E., & Mussen, P. H. Parent–child relations and father identification among adolescent boys. *Journal of Abnormal and Social Psychology,* 1956, **52,** 358–362.

Pedersen, F. A. Relationship between father absence and emotional disturbance in male military dependents. *Merrill-Palmer Quarterly,* 1966, **12,** 321–333.

Pedersen, F. A. Does research on children reared in father–absent families yield information on father influences. *Family Coordinator,* 1976, **25,** 457–464.

Pedersen, F. A. (Ed.) *The father-infant relationship: Observational studies in the family setting.* New York: Praeger Special Publications, 1980.

Pedersen, F. A., & Robson, K. S. Father participation in infancy. *American Journal of Orthopsychiatry,* 1969, **39,** 466–472.

Peters, D. L., & Stewart, R. B. Father–child interactions in a shopping mall: A naturalistic study of father role behavior. Paper presented to the Society of Research in Child Development, San Francisco, March 1979.

Peterson, D. R., Becker, W. C., Hellmer, L. A., Shoemaker, D. J., & Quay, H. C. Parental attitudes and child development. *Child Development,* 1959, **30,** 119–130.

Peterson, D. R., Becker, W. C., Shoemaker, D. J., Luria, Z., & Hellmer, L. A. Child behavior problems and parental attitudes. *Child Development,* 1961, **32,** 131–162.

Pettigrew, T. F. *A profile of the Negro American.* Princeton, N.J.: Van Nostrand, 1964.

Piaget, J. *The moral judgment of the child.* New York: Harcourt, Brace, 1932.

Pleck, J. The work–family role system. *Social Problems,* 1977, **24,** 417–427.

Pleck, J. Men's new roles in the family: Housework and childcare. In C. Safilios-Rothschild (Ed.), *Family and Sex Roles,* in press.

Pleck, J. H. Father's childcare, families, and public policy. Paper presented to the American Psychological Association, New York, August 1979.

Porter, G., & O'Leary, O. K. Marital discord and child behavior problems. *Journal of Abnormal Child Psychology,* in press.

Power, M. J., Ash, P. M., Schoenberg, E., & Sorey, E. C. Delinquency and the Family. *British Journal of Social Work,* 1974, **4,** 13–38.

Putney, S., & Middleton, R. Effect of husband wife interaction on the strictness of attitudes towards child rearing. *Marriage and Family Living,* 1960, **22,** 171–173.

Radin, N. Father–child interaction and the intellectual functioning of four-year-old boys. *Developmental Psychology,* 1972, **6,** 353–361.

Radin, N. Observed paternal behaviors as antecedents of intellectual functioning in young boys. *Developmental Psychology,* 1973, **8,** 369–376.

Radin, N. Observed maternal behavior with four-year-old boys and girls in lower class families. *Child Development,* 1974, **45,** 1126–1131.

Radin, N. The role of the father in cognitive, academic and intellectual development. In M. E. Lamb (Ed.), *The role of the father in child development,* New York: Wiley, 1976.

Radin, N. Childrearing fathers in intact families with preschoolers. Paper presented to the American Psychological Association, Toronto, September 1978.

Radin, N., & Epstein, A. Observed paternal behavior and the intellectual functioning of preschool boys and girls. Paper presented to the Society for Research in Child Development, Denver, April 1975.

Radke, M. J. The relation of parental authority to children's behavior and attitudes. *University of Minnesota Institute of Child Welfare Monograph,* 1946, No. 22.

Ragozin, A. Attachment in day care children: Field and laboratory findings. Paper presented to the Society for Research in Child Development, Denver, April 1975.

Rajecki, D. W., Lamb, M. E., & Obmascher, P. Toward a general theory of infantile attachment: A comparative review of aspects of the social bond. *Behavioral and Brain Sciences,* 1978, **1,** 417–464.

Ramey, C. T., & Mills, P. J. Mother–infant interaction patterns as a function of rearing conditions. Paper presented to the Society for Research in Child Development, Denver, April 1975.

Rau, L. Parental antecedents of identification. *Merrill-Palmer Quarterly,* 1960, **6,** 77–82.

Rebelsky, F. G., Allinsmith, W. A., & Grinder, R. Sex differences in children's use of fantasy confession and their relation to temptation. *Child Development,* 1963, **34,** 955–962.

Reis, M., & Gold, D. Relation of paternal availability to problem solving and sex-role orientation in young boys. *Psychological Reports,* 1977, **40,** 823–829.

Reiss, D., & Hoffman, H. A. (Eds.), *The American family: Dying or developing.* New York: Plenum, 1979.

Rendina, I., & Dickerscheid, J. D. Father involvement with first-born infants. *Family Coordinator,* 1976, **25,** 373–378.

Reuter, M. W., & Biller, H. B. Perceived paternal nurturance–availability and personality adjustment among college males. *Journal of Consulting and Clinical Psychology*, 1973, **40**, 339–342.

Ricciuti, H. N., & Poresky, R. H. Development of attachment to caregivers in an infant nursery during the first year of life. Paper presented to the Society for Research in Child Development, Philadelphia, March 1973.

Rivenbark, W. H. Self-disclosure patterns among adolescents. *Psychological Reports*, 1971, **28**, 35–42.

Rohrer, J. H., & Edmonson, M. S. (Eds.) *The eighth generation*. New York: Harper, 1960.

Roman, M., & Haddad, W. *The disposable parent*. New York: Holt, Rinehart, & Winston, 1978.

Roopnarine, J. L., & Lamb, M. E. The effects of day care on attachment and exploratory behavior in a strange situation. *Merrill-Palmer Quarterly*, 1978, **24**, 85–95.

Rosenberg, B. G., & Sutton-Smith, B. Ordinal position and sex role identification. *Genetic Psychology Monographs*, 1964, **70**, 297–328.

Rosenberg, M. *Society and the adolescent self-image*. Princeton: Princeton University Press, 1965.

Ross, G., Kagan, J., Zelazo, P., & Kotelchuck, M. Separation protest in infants in home and laboratory. *Developmental Psychology*, 1975, **11**, 256–257.

Ross, J. M. The development of paternal identity: A critical review of the literature on nurturance and generativity in boys and men. *Journal of the American Psychoanalytic Association*, 1975, **23**, 783–817.

Ross, J. M. Toward fatherhood: The epigenesis of paternal identity during a boy's first decade. *International Review of Psychoanalysis*, 1977, **4**, 327–348.

Ross, J. M. Fathering: A review of some psychoanalytic contributions on paternity. *International Journal of Psychoanalysis*, 1979, **60**, 317–327.

Rothbart, M. K., & Maccoby, E. E. Parent's differential reactions to sons and daughters. *Journal of Personality and Social Psychology*, 1966, **4**, 237–243.

Russell, G. The father role and its relation to masculinity, femininity, and androgyny. *Child Development*, 1978, **49**, 1174–1181.

Rutherford, E. E., & Mussen, P. H. Generosity in nursery school boys. *Child Development*, 1968, **39**, 755–765.

Rutter, M. Parent–child separation: Psychological effects on the children. *Journal of Child Psychology and Psychiatry*, 1971, **12**, 233–260.

Rutter, M. Why are London children so disturbed? *Proceedings of the Royal Society of Medicine*, 1973, **66**, 1221–1225.

Rutter, M. Epidemiological strategies and psychiatric concepts in research on the vulnerable child. In E. J. Anthony & C. Koupernik (Eds.), *The child in his family: Children at psychiatric risk*, Vol. 3. New York: Wiley, 1974.

Rutter, M. Maternal deprivation, 1972-1978: New findings, new concepts, new approaches. *Child Development,* 1979, **50,** 283–305.

Rutter, M., Cox, A., Tupling, C., Berger, M., & Yule, W. Attainment and adjustment in two geographic areas, I: The prevalence of psychiatric disorder. *British Journal of Psychiatry,* 1975, **126,** 493–509.

Rutter, M., & Madge, N. *Cycles of disadvantage: A review of research.* London: Heinemann, 1976.

Santrock, J. W. Effects of father absence on sex-typed behaviors in male children: Reason for the absence and age of onset of the absence. *Journal of Genetic Psychology,* 1977, **130,** 3–10.

Santrock, J. W. Paternal absence, sex typing, and identification. *Developmental Psychology,* 1970, **2,** 264–272(a).

Santrock, J. W. Influence of onset and type of paternal absence on the first four Eriksonian developmental crises. *Developmental Psychology,* 1970, **3,** 273–274(b).

Santrock, J. W. Relation of type and onset of father-absence to cognitive development. *Child Development,* 1972, **43,** 455–469.

Santrock, J. W., & Wohlford, P. Effects of father absence: Influence of the reason for and the onset of the absence. Paper presented to the American Psychological Association, August 1970.

Scarpitti, F. R., Murray, E., Dinitz, S., & Reckless, W. C. The "good" boy in a high delinquency area: Four years later. *American Sociological Review,* 1960, **25,** 555–558.

Schaefer, E. S. Children's reports of parental behavior: An inventory. *Child Development,* 1965, **36,** 413–424.

Schaefer, E. S. The ecology of child development: Implications for research and the professions. Paper presented to the American Psychological Association, New Orleans, August 1971.

Schaffer, H. R. *The growth of sociability.* Harmondsworth: Penguin, 1971.

Schaffer, H. R., & Emerson, P. E. The development of social attachments in infancy. *Monographs of the Society for Research in Child Development,* 1964, **29,** Serial No. 94.

Scheinfeld, D. R. On developing developmental families. Paper presented at Head Start Research Seminar 5, Washington, D.C., January 1969.

Sciara, F. J. Effects of father absence on the educational achievement of urban black children. *Child Study Journal,* 1975, **5,** 45–55.

Sears, P. S. Doll play aggression in normal young children: Influence of sex, age, sibling status, father's absence. *Psychological Monographs,* 1951, **65,** No. 6.

Sears, P. S. Childrearing factors related to the playing of sex-typed roles. *American Psychologist,* 1953, **8,** 431 (Abstract).

Sears, R. R. Identification as a form of behavioral development. In D. R. Harris (Ed.), *The concept of development*. Minneapolis: University of Minnesota Press, 1957.

Sears, R. R. Relation of early socialization experiences to self-concepts and gender role in middle childhood. *Child Development*, 1970, **41**, 267–289.

Sears, R. R., Maccoby, E. E., & Levin, H. *Patterns of child rearing*. Evanston, Ill.: Row Peterson, 1957.

Sears, R. R., Pintler, M. H., & Sears, P. S. The effect of father separation on preschool children's doll play aggression. *Child Development*, 1946, **17**, 219–243.

Sears, R. R., Rau, L., & Alpert, R. *Identification and child rearing*. Stanford: Stanford University Press, 1965.

Sears, R. R., Whiting, J. W. M., Nowlis, V., & Sears, P. S. Some child-rearing antecedents of aggression and dependency in young children. *Genetic Psychology Monographs*, 1953, **47**, 135–236.

Sedler, J. A. The origin of differences in extent of independence in children: Developmental factors in perceptual field dependence. Unpublished bachelor's thesis, Radcliffe College, 1957.

Seplin, C. D. A study of the influence of the father's absence for military service. *Smith College Studies in Social Work*, 1952, **22**, 123–124.

Shaw, M. C., & White, D. L. The relationship between child-parent identification and academic underachievement. *Journal of Clinical Psychology*, 1965, **21**, 10–13.

Shedd, C. *Smart dads I know*. New York: Sheed & Ward, 1975.

Sheehy, G. Introducing the postponing generation. *Esquire*, 1979, **92**(4), 25–33.

Shinn, M. Father absence and children's cognitive development. *Psychological Bulletin*, 1978, **85**, 295–324.

Siegman, A. W. Father-absence during childhood and antisocial behavior. *Journal of Abnormal Psychology*, 1966, **71**, 71–74.

Slater, P. E. Parental role differentiation. *American Journal of Sociology*, 1961, **67**, 296–311.

Slater, P. E. Parental behavior and the personality of the child. *Journal of Genetic Psychology*, 1962, **101**, 53–68.

Sluckin, W. *Imprinting and early learning*. London: Methuen, 1965.

Smelser, W. T. Adolescent and adult occupational choice as a function of family socio-economic history. *Sociometry*, 1963, **26**, 393–409.

Solomon, D. The generality of children's achievement-related behavior. *Journal of Genetic Psychology*, 1969, **114**, 109–125.

Sopchak, A. L. Parental identification and tendencies toward disorders as measured by the MMPI. *Journal of Abnormal and Social Psychology*, 1952, **47**, 159–165.

Sopchak, A. L. Spearman correlations between MMPI scores of college students and their parents. *Journal of Consulting Psychology*, 1958, **22**, 207–209.

Spelke, E., Zelazo, P., Kagan, J., & Kotelchuck, M. Father interaction and separation protest. *Developmental Psychology*, 1973, **9**, 83–90.

Stafford, L. M. *One man's family*. New York: Random House, 1978.

Stein, E. V. Fathering: Fact or fable? *Journal of Pastoral Care*, 1974, **28**, 23–25.

Steinberg, L. D., & Hill, J. P. Patterns of family interaction as a function of age, the onset of puberty, and formal thinking. *Developmental Psychology*, 1978, **14**, 683–684.

Speece, B. A. Altruism in the elementary school. Unpublished doctoral dissertation, University of Nebraska Teachers College, 1967.

Stephens, W. N. Judgement by social workers on boys and mothers in fatherless families. *Journal of Genetic Psychology*, 1961, **99**, 59–64.

Stephens, W. N. *The family in cross-cultural perspective*. New York: Holt, Rinehart, & Winston, 1963.

Stevens, J. H., & Mathews, M. (Eds.) *Mother/child, father/child relations*. Washington, D.C.: National Association for the Education of Young Children, 1978.

Stoke, S. M. An inquiry into the concept of identification. In W. E. Martin & C. B. Stendler (Eds.), *Readings in child development*. New York: Harcourt, Brace, & World, 1954.

Stoltz, L. M., et al. *Father relations of war-born children*. Stanford: Stanford University Press, 1954.

Stone, P. J. Child care in 12 countries. Paper delivered at the World Congress of Sociology, Varna, Bulgaria, 1970.

Sullivan, H. S. *The interpersonal theory of psychiatry*. New York: Norton, 1953.

Sunley, R. Early nineteenth-century American literature on child rearing. In M. Mead & M. Wolfenstein (Eds.), *Childhood in contemporary cultures*. Chicago: University of Chicago Press, 1955.

Sutton-Smith, B., & Rosenberg, B. G. Age changes in the effects of ordinal position on sex-role identification. *Journal of Genetic Psychology*, 1965, **107**, 61–73.

Sutton-Smith, B., & Rosenberg, B. G. *The sibling*. New York: Holt, Rinehart, & Winston, 1970.

Sutton-Smith, B., Rosenberg, B. G., & Landy, F. Father-absence effects in families of different sibling compositions. *Child Development*, 1968, **38**, 1213–1221.

Tallman, I. Spousal role differentiation and the socialization of severely retarded children. *Journal of Marriage and the Family*, 1965, **27**, 37–42.

Tasch, R. J. The role of the father in the family. *Journal of Experimental Education*, 1952, **20**, 319–361.

Tasch, R. J. Interpersonal perceptions of fathers and mothers. *Journal of Genetic Psychology*, 1955, **87**, 59–65.

Thompson, R. A. & Lamb, M. E. Quality of attachment and stranger sociability in infancy. Unpublished manuscript, University of Michigan, 1981.

Thrasher, F. M. *The gang*. Chicago: University of Chicago Press, 1927.

Tiller, P. O. Father absence and personality development of children in sailor families: Part II. In N. Anderson (Ed.), *Studies of the family*, Vol. 2. Gottingen: Vandenhoeck & Ruprecht, 1957.

Tiller, P. O. Father-absence and personality development of children in sailor families. *Nordisk Psyckologi's Monograph Series*, 1958, **9**, 1–48.

Tiller, P. O. *Father separation and adolescence*. Oslo: Institute for Social Research, 1961.

Tower, R. B. Parents' self-concepts and preschool children's behaviors. *Journal of Personality and Social Psychology*, 1980, **39**, 710–718.

Tuck, S. A model for working with black fathers. *Institute for Juvenile Research: Research Report*, 1969, **6**, Whole No. 11.

Uddenberg, N. Mother–father and daughter–male relationships: A comparison. *Archives of Sexual Behavior*, 1976, **5**, 69–79.

Van Der Leeuw, P. J. The preoedipal phase of the male. *Psychoanalytic Study of the Child*, 1958, **13**, 352–374.

Van der Veen, F. The parent's concept of the family unit and child adjustment. *Journal of Counseling Psychology*, 1965, **12**, 196–200.

Von Der Heydt, V. The role of the father in early mental development. *British Journal of Medical Psychology*, 1964, **37**, 123–131.

Wallerstein, J., & Kelly, J. The effects of parental divorce: The adolescent experience. In E. J. Anthony & C. Koupernik (Eds.), *The child in his family: Children at psychiatric risk*, Vol. 3. New York: Wiley, 1974.

Wallerstein, J., & Kelly, J. The effects of parental divorce: Experiences of the preschool child. *Journal of the American Academy of Child Psychiatry*, 1975, **14**, 600–616.

Wallerstein, J., & Kelly, J. The effects of parental divorce: Experiences of the child in later latency. *American Journal of Orthopsychiatry*, 1976, **46**, 256–269.

Wallerstein, J., & Kelly, J. *Surviving the breakup*. New York: Basic Books, 1980.

Warren, W. Conduct disorders in children. *British Journal of Delinquency*, 1957, **1**, 164.

Warshak, R., & Santrock, J. W. The effects of father and mother custody on children's social development. Paper presented to the Society for Research in Child Development, San Francisco, March 1979.

Weerts, C. E. Social class and initial career choice of college freshman. *Sociology of Education*, 1966, **39**, 74–85.

Weinraub, M., & Frankel, J. Sex differences in parent-infant interaction during free play, departure, and separation. *Child Development*, 1977, **48**, 1240–1249.

Weisbroth, S. P. Moral judgement, sex, and parental identification in adults. *Developmental Psychology*, 1970, **2**, 396–402.

Wente, A. S., & Crockenberg, S. B. Transition to fatherhood: Lamaze preparation, adjustment difficulty and the husband–wife relationship. *Family Coordinator,* 1976, **25,** 351–357.

West, L. W. Sex differences in the exercise of circumspection in self-disclosure among adolescents. *Psychological Reports,* 1970, **26,** 226.

Westermarck, E. A. *The history of human marriage.* New York: Macmillan, 1921.

Westley, W. A., & Epstein, N. G. Parental interaction as related to the emotional health of children. *Social Problems,* 1960, **8,** 87–92.

Willemsen, E., Flaherty, D., Heaton, C., & Ritchey, G. Attachment behavior of one-year-olds as a function of mother vs. father, sex of child, session, and toys. *Genetic Psychology Monographs,* 1974, **90,** 305–324.

Williams, R. M. *American society* (2nd ed.). New York: Knopf, 1965.

Wilson, K. L., Zurcher, L. A., McAdams, D. C., & Curtis, R. L. Stepfathers and stepchildren: An exploratory analysis from two national surveys. *Journal of Marriage and the Family,* 1975, **37,** 526–536.

Winch, R. F. The relation between the loss of a parent and progress in courtship. *Journal of Social Psychology,* 1949, **29,** 51–56.

Winch, R. F. Some data bearing on the Oedipal hypothesis. *Journal of Abnormal and Social Psychology,* 1950, **45,** 481–489.

Winnicott, D. W. *Collected Papers.* London: Tavistock, 1958.

Winnicott, D. W. *The maturational process and the facilitating environment.* London: Hogarth, 1965.

Wohlford, P., & Liberman, D. Effect of father absence on personal time, field independence, and anxiety. Paper presented to the American Psychological Association, August 1970.

Wohlford, P., Santrock, J. W., Berger, S. E., & Liberman, D. Older brother's influence on sex-typed, aggressive, and dependent behavior in father-absent children. *Developmental Psychology,* 1971, **4,** 124–134.

Wyer, R. S. Effect of child-rearing attitudes and behavior on children's responses to hypothetical social situations. *Journal of Personality and Social Psychology,* 1965, **2,** 480–486.

Wylie, H. L., & Delgado, R. A. Pattern of mother–son relationship involving the absence of the father. *American Journal of Orthopsychiatry,* 1959, **29,** 644–649.

Wynn, M. *Fatherless families.* London: Michael Joseph, 1964.

Yarrow, M. R., Scott, P., DeLeeuw, L., & Heinig, C. Child rearing in families of working and non-working mothers. *Sociometry,* 1962, **25,** 122–140.

Yarrow, M. R., Waxler, C. Z., & Scott, P. M. Child effects on adult behavior. *Developmental Psychology,* 1971, **5,** 300–311.

Yogman, M. W., Dixon, S., Tronick, E., Adamson, L., Als, H., & Brazelton, T. B. Development of infant social interaction with fathers. Paper presented to the Eastern Psychological Association, New York, April 1976.

Yogman, M. W., Dixon, S., Tronick, E., Als, H., Adamson, L., Lester, B., & Brazelton, T. B. The goals and structure of face-to-face interaction between infants and fathers. Paper presented to the Society for Research in Child Development, New Orleans, March 1977.

Zelazo, P. R., Kotelchuck, M., Barber, L., & David, J. Fathers and sons: An experimental facilitation of attachment behaviors. Paper presented to the Society for Research in Child Development, New Orleans, March 1977.

Zelditch, M. Role differentiation in the nuclear family: A comparative study. In T. Parsons & R. F. Bales (Eds.), *Family, socialization, and interactional processes.* Glencoe, Ill.: Free Press, 1955.

Zigler, E., & Child, I. L. Socialization. In G. Lindzey & E. Aronson (Eds.), *Handbook of social psychology* (2nd ed.). Reading, Mass.: Addison-Wesley, 1969.

Zigler, E., Lamb, M. E., & Child, I. L. *Socialization and personality development.* New York: Oxford University Press, in press.

CHAPTER 2

Historical Perspectives on the Father's Role

JONATHAN BLOOM-FESHBACH

Yale Bush Center in Child Development and Social Policy

There has been a virtual explosion of interest in fathers during the last decade. Social scientists have "discovered" the importance of fathers in child development and in family functioning (e.g., Lamb, 1976; Parke & Sawin, 1976). The public has been presented with an array of father-related articles in newspapers such as the *New York Times,* in magazines such as *Ladies' Home Journal,* and in popular books such as Biller and Meredith's (1974) *Father Power.* The movie of the year in 1980—*Kramer vs. Kramer*—illustrates how single-parent fathers have emerged as a new familial structure. Divorce and custody settlements increasingly take into consideration the father's interest in maintaining contact with his children. Hospitals now frequently encourage fathers to accompany their wives through the delivery process.

But how widespread and significant are such changes? Are new family structures in the making, or are the "new fathers" a vocal minority? If changes in family roles have reached the mainstream, will this new direction endure? These and many other questions are complicated and not readily answered without the benefit of hindsight. Perhaps in several generations the nature of change in the current era can be evaluated more accurately. But one strategy that may augment our understanding of present-day directions is the examination of our past. A historical view of what has preceded us may afford some insight into the salience, meaning, and potential of current trends in the father's family role.

The purpose of this chapter is to review some of the historical changes in the father's role, from the beginnings of human evolution to the twentieth century. To accommodate the breadth of this topic, the lens of analysis used will vary with proximity to the present: a brief look at distant events and a more detailed analysis of modern patterns. The lens will be narrowed further by its focus on Western European history and, in particular, on change in the United States. Deciding what constitutes historical change also depends on the level of analysis. For example, in an examination of four generations of seventeenth century Puritans, Grevin (1970) found that father–son relationships changed with shifting property ownership patterns. Thus within one century differences in paternal functions and father–son interactions emerged. However, when one looks over a broader time span, viewing the father's role in, for example, agricultural versus urban modes of adaptation, subtle generational changes diminish in importance. For our purposes, microanalyses such as Grevin's research will serve primarily as illustrations that help illuminate large-scale historical trends. Further, major societal shifts in patterns of adaptation do not follow the same chronology in different geographical areas. Therefore, the discussion necessarily will be limited to typical patterns and can only sample the immense span of human history.

The recent upsurge of interest in studying adult development (Gould, 1972; Levinson, 1978; Sears, 1977; Vaillant, 1977) has influenced the burgeoning field of social history (e.g., Elder, 1979; Hareven, 1978). New historical emphases on quantitative data, demographic patterns and social processes now include a recognition that people change markedly *throughout* the life course. Marital relationships, for example, are affected by the birth of children (Bloom-Feshbach, 1980a; Hoffman & Manis, 1978; Lamb, 1978), by the child's departure from home (Lewis, Freneau, & Roberts, 1979), and by the continued development of both marital partners. In considering fatherhood, the life span perspective suggests that the paternal role may vary as a function of the father's developmental stage, the status of his wife's development, and the ages of his children.

Another complicating factor is the impact of era-specific events on a cohort; the course of adult development is shaped profoundly by historically unique, formative events. Elder and Rockwell (1979) have demonstrated this effect, finding significant cohort differences in adult development patterns, depending on the age at which the Great Depression was experienced. Rossi (personal communication) raises similar issues with Levinson's (1978) failure to consider the impact of World War II military service in shaping patterns of adult development. However, neither the changes in paternal behavior over the life span nor the influence of unique historical events can be systematically addressed in this chapter. These complexities will receive less emphasis in the search for generalizations about historical change in paternal function.

It may be useful to outline briefly the sequence of major historical transformations in family roles presented here. After an overview section, the patterns of human evolution that spawned the phenomenon of social fatherhood are considered. The purpose of this brief foray into evolutionary times is to high-light the origins of family functions transmitted thereafter as a cultural heri-tage. The examination of family roles in the hunting and gathering mode of adaptation is followed by a discussion of family life in agricultural society. The social stratification created by the sedentary nature of agricultural econo-my necessitates looking at how family roles shift with socioeconomic status. To emphasize the historical roots of Western civilization, ancient Hebrew and Roman family patterns are discussed briefly. The focus then turns to the Mid-dle Ages in Western Europe when, as Ariès (1962) has claimed, the concep-tion of "childhood" slowly came into being. Next the Industrial Revolution is discussed. At that time major economic and demographic changes contributed to the rise of industrial urban culture, and significant shifts occurred in fathers' roles. Finally, in our current "postindustrial" era, several sources of data sug-gest that something new in family structure is again underway. In order to achieve a better understanding of these emerging trends, several interpretations of recent historical patterns are compared and the influential characteristics unique to current times are considered.[1]

OVERVIEW OF FAMILY FUNCTIONS

Before beginning the historical review, it may be useful to consider several basic dimensions of family functioning. The family is defined here as "a mar-ried couple or other group of adult kinsfolk who cooperate economically and in the upbringing of children, and all or most of whom share a common dwell-ing" (Gough, 1971, p. 760). One classical distinction regarding family roles is the instrumental versus expressive dichotomy originally suggested by Parsons and Bales (1955). In this conceptualization of the functioning of social groups, one or more individuals in any social group are considered primarily responsi-ble for the practical tasks required to maintain the group—the instrumental

[1]It should be noted that I am not a historian by training. Though I have a background in adult development, in research on fathers, and in clinical psychology, the historical approach required for this chapter has been a new direction. In conceptualizing the interdisciplinary skills necessary for historical studies of the family, Hareven (1971) has emphasized that a broad social science background may be as much a prerequisite as the typical tools of the historian. I hope the inade-quacies of this chapter on historical grounds are balanced by the particular blend of clinical and research perspectives brought to the task. Many disputes currently characterize the relatively new field of family history; the interpretations I have selected or offered reflect a particular view of human nature developed through both academic study and the clinical interview. In advance, I would like to credit the work of social historians who have pioneered this new and exciting field and who are responsible for many of the ideas presented here. Among these are: P. Ariès, L. deMause, J. Demos, J. Donzelot, G. Elder, C. Fairchilds, K. Gough, T. Hareven, D. Hunt, W. Kenkel, C. Lasch, C. Ross, F. Shorter, and L. Tilly.

function. Other group members are allocated the responsibility of sustaining the social–emotional life of the system—the expressive function. In the Parsonian family, the father's role is predominantly instrumental (providing economic resources), whereas the mother's role is predominantly expressive (providing love and nurturance). This conception has been criticized on theoretical grounds (Slater, 1961), given that instrumental and expressive roles need not be distributed to particular individuals but can be distributed throughout an entire system. From this perspective, both fathers and mothers may fulfill practical and emotional functions. The instrumental/expressive dimension also has been criticized on empirical grounds. Crano and Aronoff's (1978) recent examination of family role complementarity yielded cross-cultural evidence contradicting the view that instrumental functions are served universally by husbands and expressive functions by wives. It also should be noted, however, that Crano and Aronoff's examination of 186 societies fails to consider a second crucial dimension: *system boundaries*. The instrumental/expressive polarity has validity only when this additional dimension is considered as well.

The "system boundary" factor requires assessing the proximity of instrumental and expressive tasks to the family center—the household. For example, in the hunting and gathering family (the earliest family structure) fathers predominantly perform instrumental tasks outside the family system (hunting, defense, tribal governance) while mothers perform instrumental tasks more proximal to the family center (gathering food, caring for children, tending the shelter). In this situation, both parents also fulfill expressive functions. The maternal role governs emotional transactions within the family system (nurturance for children, marital affection), and the paternal role is specialized for social–emotional tasks outside the family (relations with other men, social interaction in religious functions). Thus hunting and gathering fathers serve more instrumental and expressive functions at the boundary or beyond the perimeters of the family system. By including the "system boundary" dimension, the instrumental/expressive framework becomes a useful and valid way of organizing family roles.

As is well-known in organizational theory, the leader of any group is that individual who manages the external boundaries of a system (e.g., Newton & Levinson, 1973). Whether the leader is the principal of a school, the president of a nation, the chief of a tribe, or the head of a family, the leader's role is to protect the existence of his or her group or organization by governing interactions with outside people or groups. This regulation of intersystem relationships simultaneously confers authority over intrasystem functioning. Hence the father's location at the outside boundary of the family system inherently has facilitated a dominance over family members.

In summary, the three basic dimensions that best characterize parental roles include: (1) the instrumental versus the expressive nature of family functions;

(2) the boundary location of these tasks (distant from versus proximal to the family center); and (3) the varying degrees of authority assumed by family members. By examining historical fluctuations in these three dimensions of family life, the significance of current changes in the father's role can be examined.

ORIGINS OF THE FAMILY: NONCLASS SOCIETY

Very little is known about the origin of the family: did the family unit develop at one point in time and spread through diffusion, or did it evolve from multiple sources? Infrahuman species do not form family units, although paternal nurturance and sharing of food resources have been noted among animals (see Chapter 6). It is generally accepted that the evolution of Homo sapiens is intertwined with the emergence of family structure—in fact, families are universally found in *all* human cultures. Even when social families are disrupted, as they were in slave groups in America, cohesion of the family unit remains a strong goal. Along with marriage and a cooperative division of labor, the evolution of family structure included the phenomenon of *social* fatherhood. Although the nature of the father's role is variable, all human societies recognize a special bond between a child and one or more "fathers" who serve particular social and often religious functions. This relationship exists even in cultures that do not understand the father's biological role in procreation, in cultures in which the "father" has no physiological relation to the child, in polyandrous societies in which women have several mates, and in matrilineal societies in which group membership and property pass through women (Schneider & Gough, 1961).

A brief look at some aspects of human evolution will highlight basic characteristics of the family existing throughout history, albeit in modified forms. A common reconstruction of evolutionary events emphasizes climatic change during the Miocene period (before 12 million years ago) in which subtropical forests had dwindled, forcing apes (probably in Africa) to leave tree habitats and develop terrestrial niches. Through the processes of natural selection over million of years, ancestral hominids and finally the modern Homo sapiens evolved. During this process, human beings developed an upright body posture, an opposable thumb, and feet specialized for walking. Such change freed the hands for grasping, using tools, and carrying infants. An expanded brain capacity, an increased period of infantile dependence, and the development of new linguistic and cognitive capacities were intimately linked to these biological changes, with reciprocal influences among biological, mental, and behavioral factors.

As the forests continued to recede and indigestible grasses spread on the open savannahs, the ground-dwelling ancestors of modern humans became active hunters. Using tools, cooperating in bands, and communicating and planning in symbolic forms marked a distinctively human mentality. The increased range of hunting territory (several miles, compared to primate daily distances of several thousand feet) encouraged division of labor. Women tended to care for the young and forage for food, and men specialized in hunting and group protection. The household center, with a fire in a hearth, further shaped the beginnings of "home life." The use of fire in cookery was common in Neanderthal man some 150,000 to 100,000 years ago in the Acheulean and Mousterian cultures.

Various theories have been proposed to explain the introduction of the incest taboo, a central feature of human family structure. These include Freudian notions about psychosexuality, evolutionary perspectives on genetic variability, and ecological views about social cohesion and group survival. Murdock (1957) has suggested that a range of factors brought about the incest restriction. The ban on sexual relations among close kinfolk helped preserve the cooperative nature of the family unit by avoiding competition for mates. Reduced sexual competition strengthened the bonds between families and brought more order to the tribal group as a whole. With marital and filial loyalty, the father could venture confidently farther from "home" on hunting expeditions. Evolutionary events thus encouraged mothers to be the prime agents of childrearing and cast fathers in the "provider" and "defender" roles.

The hunting and gathering societies studied by anthropologists during the last three centuries are thought to be technologically similar to those cultures common to the Mesolithic period, between 15,000 and 10,000 years ago. Though family structure probably passed through various stages prior to this point, for our purposes of establishing basic principles of the father's role it is useful to consider the hunting and gathering culture as representative of the "original family." Traditional division of labor in hunting and gathering societies tends to be consistent. In analyzing 175 of these cultures, Murdock (1957, 1967) found that 97 percent confined hunting to men; when fishing was an economic base, it was solely or mainly men's work in 93 percent of the cultures studied. In 60 percent of these societies only women gathered food. As a rule, the male domain included fighting, protecting the tribe, and maintaining religious functions, whereas the female domain consisted of childcare, tending of shelters, and cooking, processing, and storing food (Gough, 1971). Tribal decision making was generally controlled by men, although women in such cultures exerted an important though generally less formal influence on "public policy" (Berndt & Berndt, 1969).

While childrearing fell primarily within the province of women and grandparents, the hunting and gathering father still was involved with his children, especially in educating his sons about hunting and religious customs (Berndt & Berndt, 1969). In a study of pygmies in the Belgian Congo, Turnbull (1962) notes how fathers train their sons, reporting that "a fond father will make a tiny bow for his son, and arrows of soft wood with blunt points. He may also give him a strip of hunting net" (p. 128). Aborigine fathers also are known to train their sons in hunting and religious customs (Berndt & Berndt, 1969). In subsistence cultures, even in those that utilize some agriculture, fathers are very involved in childrearing. Reporting on Malinowski's (1962) classic accounts of life in the Trobriand Islands, Kenkel (1966, p. 86) pointed out how "the father has a considerable share in the care of young children. He bathes the baby, feeds it mashed vegetables, and will carry it about for hours at a time. He is genuinely fond of children and a close companion to them while they are young." This involvement occurs despite the Trobriander notion that fathers have *no* biological relationship to children. Paternal rights, privileges, and duties in the family derive from a man's role as husband to the children's mother.

Thus the social relationship of the father to his children and to the family unit is established clearly in the many nonclass hunting and gathering societies that predominated through 800 B.C. Despite sharp divisions in parental roles, with men on the outside and women on the inside of the family system, fathers did participate in some social aspects of childrearing.

Paternal authority over decision making tends to predominate in the nonclass society. In fact, compared to other societal structures, women in subsistence-oriented cultures achieve relatively greater equality. The communal value system and the economic interdependence between husband and wife foster a more balanced distribution of power. Frequent male absence from the home base to pursue hunting activities can leave a power vacuum in day-to-day affairs, offering an opportunity for female control over home-centered functions.

THE AGRICULTURAL ADAPTATION AND THE DEVELOPMENT OF CLASS SOCIETIES

The second major mode of human adaptation[2] was agricultural—the domestication of animals and plants. This profound change in the economic basis of human life brought equally far-reaching influences on human social structure. The development of agricultural techniques permitted the acquisition of surplus

[2]For purposes of simplicity, the nomadic adaptation, in which the tribal group wanders, has been omitted from discussion. This pattern is generally considered an alternative ecological niche to the hunting and gathering society, or, because of livestock domestication, as a transition to a more sedentary agricultural life style.

wealth, which when unequally distributed led to the first class societies. The favored position obtained by males in class society fostered significant inequality and greater differentiation of sex roles within the family. Because a class structure includes different social groups (ruler and ruled), multiple patterns of family structure may coexist within the larger culture. This multiplicity contrasts sharply with the comparative homogeneity of family life within hunting and gathering societies.

An important change that emerged with the agricultural habitat was the village setting. Although hunters and gatherers were not constantly nomadic, their home bases were relatively temporary, whereas farming life required a more sedentary existence. The earliest evidence for domestication in villages dates from about 7000 B.C. in the Old World (Mesopotamia and the highlands of Iran) and from about 3500 B.C. in the New World (South and Meso-America).

The very different timing of the introduction of agricultural techniques in the New and Old Worlds points to the asynchrony in the evolution of human societies. Some hunting and gathering cultures rapidly acquired knowledge of domestication; others never shifted in their patterns. Thus some agricultural societies eventually differentiated into highly sedentary, trade-oriented urban states; Mesopotamia in 3000 B.C., and later Greek, Hebrew, and Roman cultures are good examples. Other agricultural societies remained relatively stable in population and did not experience the shift to urban life or the rise and fall of major political/military empires. As with any other type of societal organization, the full range of cultural and historical variations in agricultural societies is difficult to address. It is more instructive to consider different types of characteristic family patterns in qualitatively different social/economic organizations (hunting and gathering, agricultural, and industrial/urban), illustrating these with a suggestive sample of actual cultures. In this manner, overall trends and principles of the father's family role best can be delineated. With this strategy in mind, we will consider briefly the consequences for the family of the shift from a hunting and gathering subsistence economy to an agricultural style of life. For this discussion, our progression through a historical, chronological sequence is suspended temporarily.

Economy, Psychology, and Family Roles

One of the first thinkers to outline clearly the impact of economic factors on family structure was Friedrich Engels (1894). Although some of Engels' ideas about the origins of the family now generally are rejected (e.g., the existence of early matriarchal societies; see Bamburger, 1974), some of his propositions have stood the test of time or have brought issues into focus for debate (Sacks,

1974). Engels was especially concerned with the importance of private property ownership in shaping social relationships. Property for Engels did not include the kind of goods possessed by hunting and gathering peoples. Although property existed in such societies, its' purpose was for living, not accumulation. Frequently, when an individual perished in a hunting and gathering society, his or her things were distributed among all members of the tribe, reflecting an underlying communal attitude toward wealth. In a similar manner, when an animal was hunted successfully, the spoils were shared widely.

In contrast, the domestication of nature in agricultural societies yielded property that could be accumulated, and this led to asymmetrical power relations between adults. Storing grains, tending herds, and trading for goods created the first class structure. Engels made it clear that he did not attribute male control over wealth to a malignant motivation for power. Rather, Engels considered male domination attributable to serendipity. He speculated that the domestication of livestock preceded the development of agricultural techniques. The greater physical strength of men as well as their freedom from the reproductive task of childbirth led to greater involvement in tending animals. Since livestock was the first "capital" to be accumulated, and men controlled it, women were rendered powerless.

Engels' views are instructive in the suggestion that "macrostructural" variables—factors relating to the overall socioeconomic structure—shape the intimate, "micro" interactions within the family system. Thus as men achieved economic power, their family roles became more patriarchal, with greater control over decision making, less involvement in childrearing, and greater segregation of household tasks. In agricultural societies where women played more important roles in the economy, their political status increased and childrearing functions were distributed more equally. For example, among the Iroquois male involvement in war and trading activities fostered female control over agricultural production (Noon, 1949). Anthropologists think that such economic power was responsible for the Iroquois women's influence on tribal policies (Sanday, 1974). Sanday (1974) cites data that Samoan and Yoruba women have achieved greater authority and public status through more active participation in the economic process. Sacks (1974) has tested Engels' hypothesis that women are more subordinate in societies with increased ownership of private property. Focusing especially on both domestic and public status, she compared four African societies that vary along a continuum from egalitarian to class societies—Mbuti, Lovedu, Pondo, and Ganda:

Among Mbuti, Lovedu, and Pondo, women's productive activities are social, and women have an adult social status. But in Ganda, where women's productive activities are domestic, the status of women is that of wife and ward only—despite the fact that women produce the bulk of the food. This suggests that Engels is right in seeing public or social labor as the basis for social adulthood.

But a more detailed look shows that women do not have to be characterized as *either* social adults *or* wifely wards. Rather, the data suggest that women can be both simultaneously. Women's status in a marital relationship seems to vary independently of their status in the larger society. But Engels seems correct in seeing the status of wife relative to husband as dependent on their relationships to the property of the household; that is, the spouse who owns the property rules the household. (p. 214)

In contrast, Somali women have played an important and visible role in their economy but have not achieved commensurate social or domestic status. Somali men have subordinated their women by threat and have, for example, "regarded female children as stock" (Sanday, 1974). Thus economic factors are important but are only one set of variables in a wide net of other influences.

Lewis (1976) and Chodorow (1977), among others, have emphasized the male's psychological need to dominate the female. An insecurity about sexual performance and achievement and a need to keep feelings under control are considered among the sources of male assertion of dominance. Chodorow suggests that young boys develop early identifications with mothers that must be suppressed before a masculine identity can develop. She hypothesizes that defending against an underlying feminine identification renders males psychologically insecure and vulnerable, spawning a "macho" attitude and fostering a distancing from affective experience. For men, feeling deeply may run the risk of expressing a deep feminine part of the self, which can threaten the male self-concept. The male degradation of women among the Somali illustrates the need for men to be powerful and macho when their manhood is in question. Poverty, limited resources, and female participation in the economic sector (even performing heavy agricultural labor) can threaten the masculine self-concept of strength and power and lead to destructive modes of establishing self-efficacy. Hence societies in which mothers dominate early childrearing may create strong feminine identifications in males and foster more authoritarian expressions of power in adult men—a cycle that would lead to further paternal reluctance to engage in nurturant parenting behavior. As an overall perspective, it is important to note that the influence of the economic niche *interacts* with psychological factors to determine adult sexual behavior and family interaction patterns.

As the body of cross-cultural research on field dependence reveals, adaptation to a particular ecological niche helps shape family communication and childhood socialization practices (Witkin, 1978; Witkin & Berry, 1975). An individual's degree of field dependence reflects an enduring tendency to be either autonomous from the environmental surround (field independent) or more sensitive to environmental cues (field dependent). This field dependence dimension cross-cuts all levels of psychological functioning and reflects the amount of psychological differentiation in perceptual, cognitive, affective, and personality domains (Witkin, Dyk, Faterson, Goodenough, & Karp, 1974); it is even linked to neuropsychological parameters (Bloom-Feshbach, 1980b; Witkin, Goodenough, & Oltman, 1977). Field independent individuals are more autonomous, less subject to social influence and tend to use isolation of affect and intellectualization as defenses. Field dependent persons are more sensitive, linked to social cues, have better memory for faces, are better at conflict resolution, are more conforming, and utilize repression and denial as typical psychological defenses (e.g., Schimek, 1968; Witkin et al., 1974). Because field dependence can be measured by nonverbal techniques, it has proved to be a useful avenue for the study of how personality styles emerge from the childrearing practices characteristic of different cultures. For our purposes, such cross-cultural analyses provide a window into historical patterns because they reflect the complexity of development among human societies. Thus variations in present-day cultures may illustrate important divergences among societies of earlier historical epochs.

Witkin's (1978) review indicates that cultural differences in degree of field dependence are linked consistently to the ecological demands exerted by the economic/social structure. In comparing agriculturally based nonliterate societies with hunting and gathering subsistence cultures, it is clear that as a whole, hunters and gatherers are more field independent. They are required to range over larger territories, must depend on the cooperation of the community for survival, and yet must be able to function in an autonomous way. Hunting frequently demands learning new routes and responding to novel contingencies. Gathering food in changing environments also requires greater differentiation about particular locations, a capacity to separate figure (food) from ground, and skill in developing new appraisals of the relationship between self and environment. In contrast, a farming existence more typically depends on established routines, a stable location, and a family as opposed to a tribal working unit. In this social constellation, family relationships tend to be closer, and the father becomes a patriarch, the ruler of the household. His power is supported by an outdoor (system boundary) task location, a physical capacity to tend livestock and fields, and an economic organization that makes his household a self-governing unit. These structural/economic variables are ' reinforced by the psychological need of fathers to assert manhood in a world with few channels for aggressive/competitive expression. In simplified fashion, it might be said that the hunter dominates his prey, whereas the farmer governs his family. Consistent with this view, Kohn has found that men's occupational experiences shape their childrearing practices: being powerless at work fosters domination in the home (Kohn, 1969; Kohn & Schooler, 1973).

Just as the distribution of tasks between men and women is more differentiated and inequitable in the farming context, so too are family childrearing tasks segregated. The mother's place in the home receives greater emphasis, as does her nurturant relationship with the children. The father becomes the disciplinarian, exerting an authoritarian mode of control that breeds conformity and successful adaptation to farming life. The agricultural father is less available for playful, nonwork interactions with children, but rather sets and enforces standards of behavior.[3]

Another contrast between hunting and gathering and farming groups is the amount of time absorbed by work; in the former society, 20 hours of work a week might be sufficient, while in the latter, 7 full days of work might be necessary each week. There is simply less time available for the farmer father to participate in story telling, rituals, and community affairs that characterize the life of the hunter–gatherer. Again individual differences must be emphasized, within and across cultures. In some hunting and gathering societies, there is not enough nourishment to subsist on, and nearly all of the time may be spent seeking food. Some farming communities have long indoor winters, enriching the social life of the family for half of the year. Nevertheless, it is clear that the economic base of the society, in combination with the psychological needs of the individuals within it, creates social structures and patterns of communication, which in turn shape the behavior of mothers and fathers, and hence the behavior of their children. Lamb (1978) has pointed out how psychologists studying development typically have ignored the influence of these macrostructural variables on socialization and family communication. Family roles, socioeconomic status, and cultural norms—typically the province of sociologists and anthropologists—must be blended with the rigorous research methodologies of the psychologist to produce a more complete and meaningful analysis of the father's role and the father–child relationship (Lamb, 1978).

THE ANCIENT HEBREW FAMILY

Historical information about ancient Hebrew civilization is drawn from the Old Testament. These writings are a compendium of many documents written from about 1400 through 400 B.C. Granting the many limitations of this historical source, including problems of translation and quality of manuscripts as well as uncertainties about whether family references are prescriptions, observations, myths, or narrative accounts, we can still capture something of the spirit of the ancient Hebrew family. The pattern of family life was transmitted over the centuries to later Jewish households. It is more important, however, that the ancient Hebrew tradition, through its influence on Christianity, has affected family structure significantly in Western culture on the whole.

---

[3]Alan Wheelis' description of the father–son relationship on a farm aptly and vividly illustrates this stereotype (Wheelis, 1973).

By the twelfth century B.C., the Israelites in Canaan were agriculturists, and their family system was patriarchal. Kenkel (1966, pp. 40–41) describes the ancient Hebrews.

Here they raised a variety of crops including wheat, barley, grapes, figs, and olives. As villages grew, a host of new occupations developed. We read of plasterers, carpenters with their rules and compasses, and later of potters and various metalsmiths. The change from a nomadic pastoral life brought a lessening of kinship ties. Village communities became important and, within them, the large family consisting of the male head, his wife, and married or unmarried children. Later we find great cities and the development of commerce and industry... Throughout the periods described above, the culture of the Hebrews prescribed a patriarchal extended family. By *patriarchal* we mean that power was vested in the male head of the household. We use the expression *extended* to indicate that the usual family group is more inclusive than the conjugal pair and their offspring... The extended structure of the Hebrew family had much to do, of course with the roles assigned to family members. To the male head, as we have said, was given great authority. He could choose wives for his sons and could sell his daughters into slavery, albeit not to a foreigner. Needless to say, the man had considerable control over his wife, even as Eve was told that her husband would "rule over" her (Genesis 3:16). So great was the authority of the patriarch that he could invalidate even a solemn vow to the Lord made by his wife or unmarried daughter (Numbers 30:2–16).

The Bible thus indicates that the father was a powerful and central figure in the ancient Jewish family. Along with power and authority came the tremendous responsibilities of a leader:

He was the leader of what could be a sizable group, the manager of a great herding or farming enterprise, the overseer of the camp, the religious functionary, the interpreter of justice, and the public relations expert who maintained the harmony of the group. (Kenkel, 1966, pp. 41–42)

The ancient Hebrew father served both instrumental and expressive functions in the service of maintaining a healthy family system. As is evident from these brief descriptions, the location of paternal family tasks was at the boundary of the family's structure; the father was the governing helm of the whole unit. The Hebrew father controlled family decision making, even filial marital choices, and it is likely that he developed harsh, less nurturant relationships with his children. Hebrew women were clearly subordinate and had definite responsibilities and duties, including childbearing (to assure that a husband's "name be not put out of Israel"), childrearing, and homemaking.

Harsh discipline was prescribed for misbehaving children, who were commanded to "Honor thy father and thy mother." Although tales of parental care and kindness indicate that the Jewish child was also socialized through love and loyalties—beyond the threat of discipline—the Proverbs taught that "He that spareth the rod hateth his son"(13:24).

The biblical image of Abraham submitting to God's request to sacrifice his son Isaac reveals a great deal about the Hebrew father's role and the broader cultural significance of paternal authority. God was a Father, omnipotent, demanding (as Job understood), often inscrutable, yet also caring and illuminating (speaking to Moses through the holy light of the burning bush; leading the Israelites out of bondage). But God also could be cruel or punitive, as demonstrated in the plagues with which he beset the Egyptians. And God could demand loyalty beyond personal need or sense of righteousness, as Abraham's willingness to sacrifice Isaac illustrates; it was a willingness based simply on the need to obey an authority beyond himself. God the Father demanded complete obedience from his flock, just as the father of a family expected unquestioned authority. As God was loving as well as demanding, so too was the Hebrew husband; he was more than a disciplinarian and was dictated by the Bible to be a man of love (Genesis 2:18). Upon marriage the new bridegroom could not go off to war or trade, "but he shall be free at home for one year, and shall cheer up his wife which he hath taken" (Deuteronomy 24:5).

The ancient Hebrew father's role as the religious head of the family strengthened and legitimized his pervasive authority. This paternalistic Judaic tradition, modified and recast in Christian terms, influenced the nature of Western family life even to the present. Today, as adherence to religious custom wanes, so too the father's authority diminishes. The modern cries and rebuttals that God or the family is dead reflect fractures both in the foundation of modern religious belief and in the basis of current paternal family authority.

THE ANCIENT ROMAN FAMILY

Roman history can be divided roughly into two periods. The first begins prior to the founding of the Republic about 500 B.C., and continues until the Punic Wars from about 267 to 202 B.C. The second period dates from the wars with Carthage and continues until the fourth century A.D. Like the Hebrews, the Romans had patriarchal extended families, and Roman sons could not as a rule establish their own households until the male head—the "paterfamilias"—passed away. Such close families, constituting economic–educational–religious units, were more characteristic of the early period:

During the nearly 1000 years that you can designate as the Ancient Roman Period, the family in Rome underwent significant change. In the early years we find large, closely knit families caring for most of the needs of family members, and worshiping their household gods together; marriage and the continuation of the family line are important values in these early times. At a later period marriage is taken lightly, childlessness abounds, and adultery and prostitution are rampant. (Kenkel, 1966, p. 63)

The rapid infusion of vast quantities of wealth into Rome after the Carthaginian wars usually is considered the central cause of the decline of traditional Roman social structure and the parallel decline of paternal authority (Davis, 1960; Kenkel, 1966). As long as land was the economic base, the *patria protestas* (authority of the father) was almost unlimited. The Roman father possessed the right of corporal punishment and the power of life and death over his children. The rigid boundaries of this family-based society broke down as the influx of wealth permitted women and sons to acquire independent sources of power. Growing wealth also fostered a generally hedonistic orientation, with gluttonous banquets, lavish sex, and gambling. The culture-wide breakdown in values and familial patterns even extended to the common person who had less access to extreme wealth.

The fragmentation in Roman family structure was sufficiently alarming to spur a wave of legislative efforts designed to counter such trends. The decline was reflected in increasing childlessness, less emphasis on faithful marriages, and rising infanticide and abandonment. Unlike the Jews, who permitted polygamy and concubines (Epstein,1942), the early Romans had been monogamous. This more restrictive Roman tradition had fallen to the wayside, when by A.D. 40, the emperor Caligula granted greater freedom to prostitutes (Bardis, 1963), who were even "well within the reach of the common man" (Kenkel, 1966, p. 78).

The first laws aimed at strengthening the family were introduced by Augustus in 18 B.C. Not until A.D. 3 were the first of the *Lex Julia et Papia Poppaea* enacted, with increased rewards for married persons and parents, and penalties for the celibate and/or childless. For example, a married candidate for public office was given preference, and one with children even greater preference. Special fines and taxes were exacted on unmarried men and women. Other laws were designed to curb excessive divorce and marital infidelity. A husband was compelled to divorce an adulterous wife; failure to do so constituted a crime. A man guilty of adultery could lose half of his property. Despite these and other laws in a similar vein, sexual permissiveness continued, and this early attempt to alter social behavior through legislation cannot be deemed successful in terms of immediate change. However, the precedent for governmental intervention in the affairs of the family was established in the beginning of the Christian era.

Child Abuse

The uninformed reader will be horrified to learn of the physical, emotional, and sexual abuse heaped on children, which continued even until the more recent past. Much behavior that we currently deem abusive was accepted as the norm in ancient Rome. Indeed, Roman society provides an illustration of the terrible plight of children in historical times. In the first century A.D., the Roman writer Petronius, for example, enjoyed portraying adults touching the "immature little tool" of young boys. He describes the rape of a 7-year-old girl, with adult women standing around the bed clapping. The reader should note, however, that sexual abuse of small children was not unique to the Romans. Aeschines quotes Athenian laws aimed at limiting sexual abuse of school children by teachers. Further, deMause (1975, p. 44) notes:

> Aeschines, when prosecuting Timarchus for having hired himself out as a boy prostitute, put several men on the stand who admitted having paid to sodomize Timarchus. Aeschines admitted that many, including himself, were used sexually when they were children, but not for pay, which would have made it illegal.

The Jews as well, who had strict laws against adult homosexuality, were more lenient regarding copulation with young children. The penalty for sodomy with children older than 9 years was death by stoning, and whipping was prescribed as punishment for sodomy with children under age 9 (deMause, 1975). In Imperial Rome, the preferred sexual usage of children was for anal intercourse. Castration frequently was ordered for infants and young boys as these "voluptates" were a favorite in the brothels.

There are many similar historical references to sexual and other forms of abuse of children by adults, summarized in detail in deMause's (1975) edited volume on the history of childhood. However, it is likely that deMause's emphasis on the historical cruelty toward children is overstated. Certainly many nonliterate people and probably many individuals in past Western societies were intuitively sensitive—possibly because of biological factors (Rossi, 1977)—to the tasks of childrearing. Though deMause reports evidence indicating general physical retardation in historical times (e. g., walking at late ages), if the abuse he reports were as rampant as he claims, children might not have been able to thrive at all. DeMause criticizes Ariès (1962) for underplaying parental harshness, yet Hunt (1970) even criticizes Ariès' view of medieval parental "indifference" to children, noting that "children are weak and immature both physically and cognitively . . . if parents were truly indifferent, their children would die"(Hunt, 1970, p. 49). The true degree of parental indifference or insensitivity has ebbed and flowed through history, depending on local norms, religious customs, economic stability, and so forth. However, the thrust of deMause's argument appears valid—that we have underestimated the extent of past abuse of children. A greater sensitivity toward the lives and special needs of children—especially in ideology—is one sign of progressive movement in Western history.

THE DEVELOPMENT OF A NURTURANT IDEOLOGY:
A.D. 200-1750

The current public clamor surrounding changes in parental roles includes a call for more nurturant fathering. In addition, men are being urged to become more emotionally expressive in marital relationships and in their lives in general. These modern shifts toward greater emotional sensitivity on the part of males may be better understood within the context of the gradual development of a nurturant ideology in Western culture from the time of ancient Rome (A.D. 200) until the Industrial Revolution (around 1750). Slowly but steadily, the notion of sensitive, empathic, emotional relations between people became a popular ideal, first for mothers, and eventually for fathers as well.

An important stage in the development of this attitude emerged between the fourth and eighth centuries. Although it was a full millennium before nurturance became a popular goal, it is significant that a small ray of light for children emerged during an otherwise bleak and dark age.

> The gains for children in this period [A.D. 200 to 800] appear mainly theoretical, and only dimly perceived by most parents. Folk-customs are deep-seated, and repeated prohibitions by civil and religious authorities seemed to avail little against even such grim acts as infanticide, abortion, sale of children, and abandonment. The most substantial change suggested herein is in the nurturant role of the mother. The gap remains wide between the mothers appearing in Ausonius's poetry and those mentioned in Augustine's theology, but by the 7th century many pagan motifs seemed to have faded, and parental love is often described as natural and forthcoming. The continued need for legislation, as well as other scattered evidence, suggests, however, that the distance between ideals and actuality had closed rather little in half a millennium. (Lyman, 1975, p. 95)

Thus by A.D. 800 to 900 the more elite ideal of nurturant maternal love appeared. Nevertheless, this progression was slow, and the nurturant mother was not a widely noted phenomenon in the general populace.

One striking example of parental insensitivity to children's needs for stability and consistency was the institutionally sanctioned practice of abandoning children. Child sale was the most extreme and oldest form of abandonment. In the seventh century, Theodore, Archbishop of Canterbury, finally issued an edict that a father could not sell his son as a slave past the age of 7. The English sold their children to the Irish for slaves through the twelfth century, and child sale was not outlawed in Russia until the nineteenth century (deMause, 1975). One thinks in contrast of the modern parental expression "I wouldn't take a million dollars for my child."

Even within the family system, the amount and quality of time parents spent with children was limited. The practice of placing children in the care of wet nurses was common even among less wealthy groups, for nursing frequently was considered repulsive:

> Contrary to the assumptions of most historians, the custom of not breastfeeding infants at all reaches back in many areas of Europe at least as far as the 15th century. (deMause, 1975, p. 34)

The fairly universal practice of swaddling infants—tying them up tightly for hours so that they could not move—may have reflected a general incapacity to recognize the needs of the developing child. Although swaddling has been defended by some modern researchers (Lipton, Steinschneider, & Richmond, 1965), it seems to have functioned as a means of discipline for the crying infant, as did feeding them opium and liquors.

By the time of the Renaissance, the nurturant mother–child motif (exemplified in Michelangelo's *Pieta*) was common in art and sculputure. It has been suggested that these creative visions were compensatory, reflecting idealized wishes for care and love that had not been provided for the artists themselves during their early years (deMause, 1975). Nevertheless, the prevalence of the nurturant ideal is significant. It contrasted with the generally harsh socialization practices of preindustrial Europe. There are many references, for example, to children brought on school field trips to see hangings, and to parents whipping them on returning home to make them remember what they had seen (deMause, 1975, note 60, has nine references to this practice; also cited is evidence on how disturbed children became after witnessing executions). Beating children was widespread, and it was noted even by humanist educators that drawing blood from a whipping was appropriate, although killing the child was not. Finally, by 1693, John Locke advised that "Whipping will work but an imperfect Cure . . . Frequent *Beating* . . . is therefore carefully *to be avoided*" (Kessen, 1965, p. 63).

The capacity for true empathy for a child—essential in healthy parenting (e.g., Benedek, 1970; Feshbach, 1980)—is considered a relatively new historical development. During the preindustrial era, the modal style of parent–child interaction was characterized by parental projection of primitive, unconscious fantasies. For example, children were identified with their excrement. Newborns have been called "ecrême," and the French "merdeux" (little child) derives from the Latin "merda" (feces). As David Hunt (1970, pp. 144–145) notes:

> The fact that the child's excrement looked and smelled unpleasant meant that the child himself was somewhere deep down inside badly disposed . . . the excrement . . . was regarded as the insulting message of an inner demon.

Children throughout the ages also have been the object of mutilations. The Huns cut the cheeks of male children, and in Italy during the Renaissance, it was common practice for parents to burn the newborn child's neck with a hot iron of burning wax to prevent "falling sickness."

Because of the scanty nature of historical evidence and the tendency to emphasize upper class experience along with the unusual or bizarre, skepticism about the degree and prevalence of brutality and perversity toward children is understandable. Philippe Ariès argues, for example, that the traditional child during the late Middle Ages was happier because of greater freedom to interact with a variety of age groups and socioeconomic classes, that "a special condition known as childhood was 'invented' in the early modern period, resulting in a tyrannical concept of the family which destroyed friendship and sociability and deprived children of freedom" (deMause, 1975, p. 5). But even Ariès notes ample evidence of destructive behavior toward children, documenting, for example, so much open sexual molestation of children that "playing with children's private parts formed part of a widespread tradition" (Ariès, 1962, p. 203).

Ariès' theory about the relatively recent invention of childhood probably has been one of the most oft-cited and uncritically accepted notions in the history of childhood and in historical studies of the family. There is, however, considerable evidence countering this thesis, demonstrating that artists in antiquity and in the Medieval era were able to depict children realistically rather than paint them as miniature adults (e.g., for the Medieval period, see Lasarelf, 1938, pp. 26–65, cited in deMause, 1975). Further, the notion that the concept of "childhood" was unknown until the Middle Ages is disputed by etymological evidence. Finally, the Ariès view that the early modern family inflicted harsher punishment on the child than the family in the Middle Ages does not mesh with the bulk of the evidence.

Although Rousseau (in the eighteenth century) has been cited as the first to challenge "the idea of the child as miniature adult" (Nash, 1976, p. 67), it might be more accurate to view Rousseau as marking one transformation in a series of evolving stages in popular conceptions of childhood. It is true that the eighteenth century was characterized by significant shifts in the parent–child relationship; these include great reductions in the projection of parental anxiety on the child, less severe modes of punishment (hitting as opposed to whipping), an increase in nursing, a general rise in parental openness to the tasks of childrearing, and the beginnings of true empathy. The relationship between husband and wife during this period also changed, paralleling the transformation in parent–child interactions. The "companionate" marriage came into being, in which the affective bond between husband and wife was as important as their functional ties. These new patterns of parent–child and marital relationships reflected a new historical stage in family and social life, intertwined with a cluster of major sociocultural changes, including the Industrial Revolution, the urbanization of Western Europe, the emergence of new (capitalistic) economic patterns, and shifts in basic demographic variables such as birthrate and age of marriage. The discovery of the child's needs and the realization of a wife's emotional needs emerged along with a decline in the dictatorial power of the father's family role, ushering in the modern era.

MODERN PERIOD: EIGHTEENTH, NINETEENTH, AND EARLY TWENTIETH CENTURIES

Prior to 1750, European and, to a lesser degree, American family structure was patriarchal and extended. Common folk lived in multipurpose rooms in large groups with little opportunity for privacy and intimacy. The nuclear unit, along with other kin such as grandparents and even unrelated hired workers, would eat, work and sleep in the same cramped space. Functional, instrumental ties bound the group. Economic solvency, reproduction, and the transmission of property and the family name were central tasks. Marriages tended to be affectionless, and social life was pursued outside the family in male club organizations or female groups (Shorter, 1975). As family patriarch, the father was the local authority in a feudal political hierarchy. For twentieth century individualistic Americans, it may be hard to imagine the widespread lack of differentiation between one member of a family and his or her kin. During the thirteenth century, for example, a whole extended family (and its descendants) would be held accountable for a crime committed by one relative (Tuchman, 1979). The range of kinship ties deemed responsible for one relative's misdeed diminished gradually, until the legal system and informal censure focused on the guilty party alone, as is done today. To have a principal government leader with a relative in prison—as U.S. President Jimmy Carter had—would have been unthinkable.

Preindustrial women and children, clearly subordinate, were devalued. Shorter (1975) notes that the death of a cow often was considered far more calamitous than that of a wife or child. The community was a major socializing force, with the church, "town fathers," guilds, and youth organizations supervising births, marriages, and deaths. Courtship rituals were public and chaperoned. Women alone handled childrearing, and, as already discussed, babies were typically farmed out to understaffed and inadequate wet-nursing facilities.

By the late eighteenth century community ties began to break down and were replaced by an individualistic orientation. This attitude was particularly manifest in new emphases on privacy, personal expression, romantic love, and more empathic modes of childrearing. Ariès (1962) suggests that this shift toward intimate privacy was obtained at the expense of sociability, and historians in general agree that a major transformation in social and family relations occurred at this time. However, ongoing debates leave unanswered such questions as (1) whether changes in family structure began initially with the lower or the middle class (Shorter, 1975); (2) what factors brought about these changes (Fairchilds, 1978; Tilly, Scott, & Cohen, 1976); (3) what is valid evidence about the status of women (e.g., Tilly et al., 1976); and (4) can changes in family structure (as a dependent variable) also lead to further sociocultural change? (See Hareven, 1971, for a discussion of Family Structure as an independent variable.)

There is consensus, however, that modernization brought a significant reduction in family and informal community functions, along with a decline in the authority and responsibility of the father. "The history of the family has been a history of contraction and withdrawal . . . the gradual surrender to other institutions of functions that once lay very much within the realm of family responsibility" (Demos, 1970, p. 183). Hareven (1971, p. 409) similarly notes that "modernization of the family is the story of the loss of its functions as school, church, correctional institution, hospital, and workshop." Thus in Parsonian terms, the multipurpose, preindustiral family structure became archaic and gave way to a differentiated set of organizations that could cope more effectively with new historical circumstances (Smelser, 1959).

Gender distinctions increased with industrialization. The dress as male attire was confined to infants, the use of male wigs declined, and female concern with a thin and feminine body increased (Stearns, 1979). This apparent need to accentuate concrete dimensions of gender differentiation may have reflected the uncertainty that accompanied widespread changes in sex roles. In addition, with the advent of greater awareness of children's needs came an emphasis on motherhood.

It is ironic that, as the nuclear, intensive, inward-turning modern family developed, the father became less involved in childrearing, especially among the working classes. "Working away from home, the father was an intermittent boss and authority model at best" (Stearns, 1979, p. 49). This phenomenon—working away from home—was one of the most significant influences of the Industrial Revolution is shaping the modern father's "provider" role (Benson, 1968). However, the modern father's authority was not commensurate with his economic function in the family. As noted in the discussion of the Roman Empire, the shift from an agrarian, land-based economy to a dependence on capital diminishes paternal control, as sons, and even women, can independently enter the labor force. The rise of modern capitalist economy reshaped society in manifold ways. Women's work in the home (e.g., clothing manufacture) became men's work in the factory. Young adults could earn a personal income and achieve individual power and status—and they could become alienated as individuals as well. Increased population led to insufficient land resources, which, in combination with economic opportunities in cities, fostered geographical mobility from the countryside. This population shift loosened kinship ties and encouraged sex in and outside of marriage. A bourgeois class emerged, with an emphasis on satisfying marital social–emotional needs within the nuclear family. Education replaced apprenticeship and promoted vocational choices automonous from family tradition and paternal dictate. As the father's authority declined, so did religious tradition, and with the diminution of both modes of control came the waning of sexual restrictions based on religious belief.

In this tumultuous period of social change, so challenging for historians to understand, certain indisputable facts remain the subject of conflicting interpretations (Fairchilds, 1978; Shorter, 1975; Tilly et al., 1967; Wells, 1977). Illegitimate fertility rates soared between 1750 and 1850 all over Europe, from modest figures of 1 to 3 percent of all baptisms, to 10 to 15 percent. Between 1815 and 1848, over one-third of all children born in Paris were born to unwed mothers (Fairchilds, 1978). More recently it has been discovered that legitimate fertility among women also rose during the late eighteenth century and that both legitimate and illegitimate fertility declined during the late nineteenth century (Shorter, 1973). There was thus a dramatic upsurge in the number of births beginning around 1750 and a decline toward the end of the nineteenth century. Without attempting to pinpoint all the factors responsible for these demographic shifts or to establish the causal directions of interweaving influence, it is possible to conclude that (1) the fertility rise reflects a greater frequency of sexual relations, both in and outside of marriage, and (2) the drop in fertility reflects a burgeoning awareness of birth control techniques—primarily coitus interruptus and abortion.

Shorter (1975) thinks that the capitalist/industrial economy facilitated financial and familial autonomy. He suggests that a new spirit of independence made individualism and personal fulfillment an overall value, leading to feminine emancipation in the sexual domain. Other historians (e.g., Fairchilds) agree with the notion that romantic love and courtship rituals emerged during this time, but they assign different causal factors. In any event, all over eighteenth century Europe men grew more sensitive to women's sexual experience ("From an Unfortunate Necessity to a Cult of Mutual Orgasm," Gordon, 1971), and women were motivated, either out of interest (Shorter, 1975), or out of economic or social circumstance (Fairchilds, 1978; Tilly et al., 1976), to pursue sexual relations prior to marriage. With the continued rise in female domestic power, men became aware of and began to use birth control techniques, even if this meant some sacrifice in personal pleasure. Male willingness to use coitus interruptus reflected an increased female authority to set limits on childrearing and allowed women to reserve personal lives apart from their responsibilities as mothers. It also signified recognition on the part of men and women that limiting the *costs* of childrearing would add to their mutual benefit. Further, the use of birth control could occur only within relationships that valued the mutuality of need satisfaction. Such mutuality reflects a higher degree of ego development, suggesting that psychological growth in societal consciousness was shaped by, and in turn shaped, socioeconomic events, bringing new dimensions to the marital relationship and to childrearing.

Social change during the eighteenth and nineteenth centuries took a somewhat different course in the United States and Europe and created different family patterns in the working and middle classes as well. Shorter (1975) notes that sexual expressiveness and female emancipation first occurred with the working classes in Europe but were introduced by middle-class women in the United States. This difference in pathway toward a similar outcome suggests that the divergence in interpretations of demographic and family change during the early modern era may reflect the multifactored nature of the phenomenon. These two class-linked family structures have remained essentially intact through the twentieth century. Pleck (1979) has labeled these patterns of male adulthood "traditional" (working class) and "modern" (middle class).

In the traditional or working-class family, functional ties outweigh expressive ones—especially for the father. Husband and wife have an institututional marriage (Burgess & Locke, 1945), and men satisfy their affiliative needs in friendships with other men. For entertainment and social life in the nineteenth century, "working men focused on the neighborhood tavern that was rigorously masculine, where men could talk and play cards or darts without distraction" (Stearns, 1979, p. 75). To this day, the traditional man tends to derive social satisfaction outside the home. He participates rather little in childrearing, and in general suffers a loss of parental authority in contrast to his peasant predecessors who possessed some amount of property and hence authority over a domain.

Working-class jobs, particularly in the industrial world, can be conceptually dull and characterized by low autonomy, a combination that shapes nonrational, authoritarian childrearing practices (Kohn, 1969). Statistical designs that establish causality have demonstrated that with increasing time spent in jobs with such low satisfaction, paternal behavior is shaped in the direction of using more assertion of will in childrearing (Kohn & Schooler, 1973). It has been suggested that the working-class man has few avenues in which to express or establish a sense of masculinity, self-efficacy, and autonomy (Rubin, 1976). The frustration of vocational subordination may lead to irrational expressions of familial authority.

Further isolating the traditional father was the switch in the nineteenth century to the female network of relatives. In previous European village society, brides went to live with husbands' relatives on their property. Since urban men lacked property and women's childrearing tasks received increasing emphasis, newlyweds tended to organize their lives around the wife's kin. When economics demanded it, the new marrieds often would live with the wife's parents, further eroding the young father's authority and sense of personal worth. As Stearns (1979, p. 49) notes, "A survey of literary autobiographies (from about 1750 to 1900) traces growing hostility to fathers (and attachment to mothers) throughout this crucial period. Too many fathers were asserting authority that they no longer really possessed." It is no wonder that recent studies of working-class families reveal widespread suffering and a sense of impotence experienced by working-class men (Rubin, 1976; Sennett & Cobb, 1973).

The middle-class or modern male role placed less emphasis on concrete expressions of masculinity and focused instead on success and achievement. Social–emotional satisfaction characteristically was derived from family interaction in the new bourgeois class that forms the basis of today's "modern" male role. Pleck (1979, p. 402) notes:

The characteristic patterns of emotional and interpersonal life also differ in the two roles. In the traditional male role, interpersonal and emotional skills are relatively undeveloped, and feelings of tenderness and vulnerability are especially prohibited. Anger and impulsive behavior are encouraged, especially with other males, and are often experienced as particularly validating of masculinity. By contrast, in the modern male role, interpersonal skills are expected, especially insofar as these promote smooth collaboration with others toward achievement, as in management. Capacity for tenderness and emotional intimacy are also encouraged, but closely restricted to romantic heterosexual relationships and excluded elsewhere. Staying emotionally "cool" is a major value, and anger and impulsive behavior are particularly prohibited.

The "modern" or middle-class male is freed by the capitalist system to pursue education and a variety of vocational options. Parsons and Bales (1955) view the nuclear, private, modern family as an adaptation to modern life, whereas Sennett (1964) suggests it is a maladaptive refuge from it. Perhaps the nuclear unit is more or less advantageous depending on socioeconomic class, or whether its liberating or alienating features are emphasized. Elder's (1974) study of the impact of a single, major historical event on development—the Great Depression—indicates how economic deprivation influences the father's family orientation.

Men and women who had grown up in depression-marred homes were most likely to anchor their lives around family and children, perhaps reflecting the notion of home as a refuge in an unpredictable world. They ranked family activities and parenthood higher in their scheme of values than did sons and daughters of more affluent parents. (Elder & Rockwell, 1979, p. 97)

Thus Sennett's view that the modern family serves a "refuge" function has validity, as does the Parsonian view that this stance is adaptive.

It is important to stress the "companionate" nature of middle-class marriages. The concept of romantic love was first introduced by troubadors in the twelfth century, as they traveled throughout Europe singing songs of love. Although some historians have viewed the troubadors as merely wandering minstrels, Idries Shah (1971) presents evidence that the troubadors were heavily influenced by the mystical works of St. Francis of Assisi and by the Sufi tradition. The introduction of romantic love to the West reflected troubador contact with the Middle East, where romantic love had been introduced earlier by Sufi mystics like Omar Khayyam and Saadi. These and other Persian and Arabic writers produced poetic analogies between marital love and love of God (Shah, 1971). The Puritans similarly considered marriage the highest form of mortal union (Morgan, 1966), and the Protestant notion of a *contract* with God paved the way for a contractual view of the relationship between husband and wife. The Protestant source of companionate marriage in America may account for the earlier middle-class origin of female emancipation in the United States. The repressive nature of American working-class sexuality and even middle-class sexuality (compared to Continental patterns) may be linked to the relatively democratic but affectively sterile Protestant ethos.

Middle-class or modern mothers increasingly had fewer household tasks (facilitated by technological innovations) and were freed from working outside the home to supplement family income. Thus they could focus the whole of their efforts on the task of childrearing. In consequence, as prosperity increased in America during the postdepression, postwar years, family roles became increasingly segregated, with middle-class fathers more involved in work activities and middle-class mothers in childrearing. As the "importance of motherhood steadily increased," there was a tendency for "the implicit downgrading of the paternal role. Many fathers began to serve essentially as disciplinarians of last resort . . . 'Wait till your father comes home' " (Stearns, 1979, p. 98). Thus the nuclear, modern family originally served to draw husband and wife closer together emotionally, but as family roles became more differentiated, even the middle-class father frequently grew estranged from his home life.

The modern father is usually less authoritarian than his working-class counterpart; middle-class jobs tend to encourage the use of reason and granting of autonomy in childrearing (Kohn, 1969). The middle-class father also has more realistic sources of power in his reasonable income, property ownership, and ability to finance children's professional training. These visible signs of economic success raise the esteem and perceived authority of the father, as studies of depression families illustrate (Furstenberg, 1974).

Yet, as already noted, there were many sources of discontent for twentieth century middle-class fathers. Friendships beyond the work place were rarely pursued (Lewis, 1978), and the modern father had only a secondary role in household maintenance and childrearing. These factors helped foster a sense of alienation. Such emotional and social isolation, along with pressure to achieve, has victimized the modern male with "provider stress." Research has demonstrated a greater incidence of heart disease and other characteristically "type A" (competitive, achievement-oriented) illness among contemporary men (Waldron, 1976, 1978).

Thus the outstanding development during the 200 years from 1750 to 1950 was the emergence of traditional and modern male/paternal roles. The coalescing of these distinct styles was a gradual process, with considerable variation and overlap between individuals, within a man's life cycle, and among ethnic groups.

As the twentieth century has progressed, the simple equation between working-class and traditional, and middle-class and modern, has broken down. It is partly for this reason that Pleck uses the traditional–modern nomenclature. Many working-class men today fit the modern family pattern, and many middle-class men drink "with the boys," are emotionally distant from their wives, and experience low vocational satisfaction. These stereotypes are primarily meant to classify overall group tendencies rather than "diagnose" the individual case.

In addition, there are parallels between the decline of traditional family patterns in ancient Rome and family changes in the two centuries after the Industrial Revolution. In both contexts, the father's role as governor (as local gendarme for the state, enforcing discipline and controlling behavior) eroded as society grew increasingly differentiated and as the extended family system gave way to the nuclear family unit. In ancient Rome, institutionalized religion became the proponent of family values, eventually reviving the emphasis on family stability and offering a new, more nurturant ideology. In the modern era, the decline of both religious and paternal authority left a gap filled by the professional–scientific–medical establishment. This new authority structure has emerged as a mediator between family and government (Donzelot, 1979). The impact of this relatively novel historical force—the professional—is considered in greater detail in the following discussion of contemporary life.

CONTEMPORARY TIMES

When Benjamin Spock published the first edition of *Baby and Child Care* in 1946, he advised, "It doesn't make sense to have mothers go to work and have them pay other people to do a poorer job of bringing up their children"

(Norris & Miller, 1979, p. 13). By 1976, Spock reversed himself: "Both parents have an equal right to a career if they want one . . . and an equal obligation to share in the care of their children" (Norris & Miller, 1979, p. 13). What happened during this 30-year period that encouraged Dr. Spock—the parental advisor par excellence—to change his views? It is obvious that the factors are many, but one that is undeniably important is the rapid and steady increase of women in the paid labor force. This pattern is not attributable to feminist ideology but rather reflects decades of economic pressures inducing women to enter the marketplace. Table 1 illustrates how the percentage of mothers in the labor force has climbed steadily since 1940.

Table 1. Labor Force Participation Rates of Mothers with Children under 18, 1940–1978

Year	Percentage	Year	Percentage
1978	53.0	1960	30.4
1976	48.9	1958	29.5
1974	45.7	1956	27.5
1972	42.9	1954	25.6
1970	42.0	1952	23.8
1968	39.4	1950	21.0
1966	35.8	1948	20.2
1964	34.5	1946	18.2
1962	32.9	1940	8.6

Source: National Academy of Sciences Summary Proceedings of Ad Hoc Meeting on Work, Family, and the Community, 1980.

This dramatic increase in maternal employment outside the home is only one demographic statistic signaling social change in this century. Since 1900, the divorce rate in America has increased nearly 700 percent (Keniston, 1977), to the point where four out of every 10 children born in the 1970s will spend part of their childhood in a one-parent family. A large upsurge in the number of unwed mothers also contributes to this trend. These statistics about broken homes and fatherless families characterize all races and socioeconomic classes in the United States. Currently, "the traditional nuclear family, composed of father as breadwinner, mother as homemaker, and one or more children, has declined to less than one third of all families with children" (Hayes, 1980, p. 1.)

Urie Bronfenbrenner has compiled similar statistics illustrating contemporary change in family structure and has reported national data suggesting that these trends are hurting the quality of children's lives. Over the last several decades there have been increasing rates of infant mortality, decreasing levels of student achievement, rising rates of children killed by homicide and suicide, and increasing cases of juvenile delinquency (Bronfenbrenner, 1975). Our "post-modern" era appears to create stress on family life that negatively affects the well-being of many children. Why?

Of the many possible reasons, certainly the Western, growth-oriented cap-italist economy and value system is an important influence. The push to-ward upward mobility, material acquisition, and competitive standing among peers has encouraged the entry of women into the paid labor force. In addi-tion to the difficult enough task of financially supporting everyday needs, families experience hunger for possessions stimulated by the advertisement industry and the media. Children in every small town across the country are aware of the latest toys, and their parents are exposed to constant images of new fashions, motor vehicles, and services. Many families depend on two incomes for mere survival. The growth of a corporate economy has pro-duced multinational conglomerates, creating greater distance between peo-ple's needs and the profit-based survival needs of big business. Geographic mobility further lessens community and familial ties, encouraging the nucle-ar—and part-nuclear—family unit.

It has been suggested that the decline in the number of adults in the Ameri-can household is detrimental to the mental health of children. In healthy fami-lies, the father assumes a very important role in decision making and problem solving (Westley & Epstein, 1969). The mother's behavior itself is affected by the presence of the father. For example, mothers are more interested in the nursing and care of newborns when fathers are emotionally supportive (Peter-son, Anderson, & Cain, 1980). Women experience less guilt and stress about working when their husbands approve of their employment (Carew, 1978). Fi-nally, longitudinal studies show that when a mother is the only adult in a fami-ly, the family's children will be at greater risk for social maladaptation and psychological disorder (Kellam, Ensminger, & Turner, 1977). The absence of the father has been shown to be less critical than the "aloneness of the mother in relation to risk . . . the presence of certain second adults serves an important ameliorative function . . . mother/grandmother families being nearly as effec-tive as mother/father families" (Kellam et al., 1977, p. 1012). This finding is consistent with recent views that certain crucial parental functions need to be fulfilled regardless of which parent meets a given responsibility (Bloom-Feshbach, Bloom-Feshbach, & Gaughran, 1980). However, the father plays a unique and critical role in a child's achievement of gender identity (see Chap-ter 9). Because psychological absence may be functionally equivalent to physi-cal absence (Blanchard & Biller, 1971), the father's active participation in the family is crucial.

Apart from the child's psychological need for multiple sources of identifica-tion, the tasks of childrearing and economic support of a household are fre-quently simply too much for one person to shoulder, especially for women who face salary discrimination in the marketplace (Barrett, 1979). The incidence of single-parent, father-headed households has climbed over the last 10 years (a 33 percent increase); in absolute numbers, the shift was from .75 million in 1970, to almost 1 million such families in 1979. During this same period, mother-only households increased from 7.5 million to over 10.5 million families. By 1979, among blacks, the single-mother family numbered 42 percent of all families (statistics from the U.S. Bureau of the Census, Current Population Reports, cited in Glick, 1980).

Behind these dry statistics lie the realities of changing family patterns. One cause of the rising incidence of adolescent pregnancy and the increasing rate of divorce is the significant loosening of sexual mores in the last few decades (Shorter, 1975). Although the high remarriage rate (tripled since 1930) indicates that marriage is not out of style (Glick & Norton, 1973), the high rates of divorce and unwed births suggest that personal fulfillment and sexual expression are not necessarily linked to the stable "one person for life" marriage of the past. During this era of rapid technological and social change, one remarkable development has been adolescent indifference to family values (not opposition, but indifference: Keniston, 1960; Lasch, 1979; Shorter, 1975). The present-day adolescent often is socialized by peers rather than by parents. One root of this phenomenon is the steady erosion of paternal authority and the father's family significance. For the contemporary father, work life is removed from home life, both physically and psychologically. Children today frequently cannot understand their father's work. Stockbrokering, computer programming, and many other modern jobs are not easily explainable in the concrete terms a child comprehends. Whereas many fathers in the past were removed from the task of childrearing, the additional father–child distance caused by the abstractness of modern vocations heightens the father's alienation from the family.

Television competes with paternal authority. When a youngster watches television excessively, the socialization process is diluted, just as political authority is diminished when a half-hour Presidential address is followed by twice as much media commentary. Many of these propositions might be addressed by research: How is the father–child relationship influenced by the father's occupational world? How does the quality and quantity of television viewing affect a child's image of father and mother? What factors predict a child's perception of legitimate paternal authority?

The decline in paternal family significance since the Industrial Revolution has been seen in psychological as well as environmental and economic terms. In *The Wish to Be Free: Society, Psyche, and Value Change,* Weinstein and Platt (1969) emphasize the emotional need of children to react against paternal authority. The desire for emancipation is an important aspect of the adolescent's identity strivings (e.g., Erikson, 1963), and is fostered by the capitalist emphasis on individualism. Psychoanalytic theory suggests that sons, in particular, seize opportunities to devalue, triumph over, and rebel against the father in the normal course of development (Freud, 1923). However, unchecked Oedipal rebellion leads to massive guilt and self-hatred. Father absence fosters a fantasy that the child is responsible for removing the father. Such feelings may underlie depression, which itself may be masked by aggressive acts or attempts at self-medication, evident in the high incidence of drug use among youth. Some authorities believe that this latter phenomenon has reached epidemic proportions in modern society.

The multidetermined influence of increased paternal family involvement might foster less conflictual Oedipal development and provide much needed discipline and limit setting for growing children. Involved fathers also would serve as the role models for identification that children require. Further, the father's impact is felt through his support of the mother, facilitating problem solving and conflict resolution in the family, as well as offering a balance or alternative to maternal perspectives. These many factors suggest that a "systems" view of the father's role is necessary to explain his full significance (Bloom-Feshbach et al., 1980; Garbarino, 1976; Westley & Epstein, 1969). One important avenue for future research in an era of large-scale funding for drug abuse studies might be investigating how the father's family participation (reflected in both marital and father–child relationships) affects the child's proclivity toward substance abuse. Exploring how community networks and other kinship ties mediate paternal–maternal influence would be of interest as well. If social science knowledge is to encompass an understanding of real-life phenomena, research designs must accommodate the multilevel complexity that affects human behavior (Bronfenbrenner, 1977).

The Role of Social Science

Recent studies of family history since the Industrial Revolution have focused on the link between the emergence of the modern family and the development of the medical–psychiatric–social science establishment. Since 1950, the volume of professional activity has increased exponentially, and myriads of experts advise us on almost every aspect of family life, including sexual relations, childrearing, and marital satisfaction. Lasch (1979) has pointed out how "professional advice" has intruded on the lives of families. Further, such expert views are often contradictory (witness Benjamin Spock's reversal on parenting roles) and foster parental guilt and uncertainty over childrearing behavior. Lasch notes that the current fragmentation in the family in part has been created by "professional" influence aimed at counteracting such fragmentation. Like Lasch, Donzelot (1979) observes how the social scientific–medical–psychiatric professions have assumed influence over the family as father and church once did—experts serve a paternal function for our society. However, Donzelot views the decline in paternal authority from a slightly different perspective. He attaches less responsibility or blame to the professional influence on current fragmentation in family life and instead emphasizes the interdependent roles of all factors; as the family has contracted and the father's authority has diminished, a societal institution inevitably emerged in order to link the state and the family. The new socializing agent—the professional establishment—was thus a natural outgrowth of and spur to the family's decline.

In my view, Donzelot, like Lasch, falls into the trap of casting judgment, of blaming the professions. Although my identity as a clinical professional clearly creates its own bias, I believe that the social science–medical–psychiatric professions require more patience. Professional mistakes of the past do not mean that the future will follow the same course, nor do the negative effects of the professions completely outweigh their beneficial influence. The challenge for research and clinical care in the future will be to incorporate the recognition that "well-intended" interventions in family life can injure the well-being of the family. By addressing more macroscopic, indirect influences on family life—such as economic security or the strength of neighborhood and local services—some iatrogenic trends may be mitigated.

In addition, there may be a tendency for social critics to mythologize the family of the past. Lasch, for example, seems to yearn for a cohesive, historic family that may never have existed. Historical studies may help dispel the notion than an ideal, nurturant family existed in preindustrial times. Although the family is clearly under stress today and may, according to statistics, continue to change in the direction of fragmentation, the comparative prevalence of parental nurturance and the widespread recognition of the importance of child development suggest that positive changes are also in the making. Marital instability, loss of paternal authority, and children's difficulties all serve to increase societal concern for the family. This concern is more than a professional awareness, but is reflected in changes in societal attitudes and behaviors. It is not my intention to minimize the complexity and difficulty of contemporary life, but to underline the possibility that new, more adaptive societal patterns also may be evolving.

The parallel with ancient Rome is again suggested. One of the positive effects of the overall societal decline of the Roman Empire was recognition of the importance of family welfare. This realization was itself stirred by the breakdown in family structure. By the fourth century, the concept of maternal *nurturance* first emerged. Infanticide was first outlawed in A.D. 374. It may be, as Lao Tse and Hegel have suggested, that opposite consequences result from any given antecedent condition. Thus Roman decadence and the abandonment of family well-being as a primary goal spawned the first laws and statements aimed at protecting the family. Similarly, the current historical era is both destructive to families—in producing fragmentation—and growth-promoting—in facilitating new and more adaptive family patterns. Traditional societies operate through conformity and external restriction, be it religious, paternal, or political authority. As traditions break down and expressions of individual need increase, the variety that results may be regressive in part (more impulsive and self-centered), and in other respects more differentiated (other-centered). Thus our society has been hailed as a "Culture of Narcissism" (Lasch, 1980), and yet at the same time manifests signs of heightened sensitivity to the needs of the less powerful (the rights of Blacks, women, children, the aged, and the handicapped). In today's social policy arena there is intense debate between proponents of government interventions designed to aid children and families and opponents of any government/professional programs. It remains to be seen what new patterns will result from these conflicting ideological stances. It is clear, however, that all agree on the undesirability of the continued incidence of child abuse and neglect as well as other forms of domestic violence; at issue is how to cope with these acknowledged problems.

Fathers and Changes in Sex Roles

Until recently, the scientific community, as Lamb (1975) noted, fostered the view that fathers were comparatively unimportant in family functioning and childrearing. The first edition of this volume was a pioneering effort to systematically compile psychological evidence of the father's influence on almost every aspect of child development (Lamb, 1976). Although the father's importance to the growing child had been suggested long ago by Freud (eg, 1923; 1926), paternal salience ironically has declined in psychoanalytic thought, and only recently have social scientists recognized that fathers can serve as attachment figures (Schaffer & Emerson, 1964). Not until the 1970s was there clear empirical research demonstrating the significance of the father's role as early as infancy (e.g., Cohen & Campos, 1974; Kotelchuck, 1976; Lamb, 1977; Parke & Sawin, 1976).

Direct paternal involvement in childrearing—particularly in the care of infants—reflects a radical departure from nearly all previous patterns of family structure. Not only does biology favor the new mother's sensitivity to the child (Rossi, 1977), but the entire course of human history vitiates against paternal participation in childrearing. The current possibility that fathers might begin to assume more instrumental and expressive tasks inside the boundaries of the family system signals the cultural development of a new family structure, labeled "postmodern" (Pleck, 1979), "emergent" (Fein, 1978), or "androgynous." The androgynous individual is someone whose personality and behavior reflect both stereotypic masculinity and femininity. Similarly, in the androgynous family, men and women function both in the home and in the marketplace. Sandra Bem (1974, 1975) and Janet Spence (Spence, Helmreich, & Stapp, 1975), among others, have popularized this new perspective on sex roles. They consider masculinity and femininity as separate dimensions rather than poles of one continuum; hence those individuals who have high scores on both sex role dimensions are deemed androgynous. The androgynous orientation is consistent with Werner's (1957) general theory of development, which postulates that organisms become increasingly differentiated and hierarchically integrated through development. Since the Industrial Revolution, the traditional family structure has undergone a heightened degree of role segregation. The modern family reflects a developmental progression toward an increased degree of integration of function; modern men are more affectively oriented when involved in family relations, formerly the sole province of women. The androgynous family reflects a greater degree of integration occurring at higher states of differentiation. Thus androgynous men and women are sensitive and forceful, capable of task *and* affective orientations.

Although the evidence is still scanty, it has been suggested that an androgynous sex role is more adaptive than conventional sex roles, permitting flexible behavioral response to a broad range of environmental contingencies (Kaplan & Bean, 1976). Russell (1978) has studied the interaction of sex role and parental behavior, finding that "fathers classified as androgynous were . . . more involved in day-to-day care activities and play than those classified as masculine" (p. 1174). However, this investigation did not address the direct link between androgynous parenting and child development. Some research has shown that androgynous parents produce androgynous children (Block, 1973), suggesting that the frequency of androgyny will continue to increase in our society.

But how common are egalitarian parents and family structures? As women increasingly enter the paid labor force, extending beyond the family boundaries, to what extent are men willing to (and women willing to let them) increase their family commitments?

Table 2.   Attitudes Toward Women's Status

Year	Favor	Oppose	Not Sure
1970	42%	41%	17%
1971	48%	36%	16%
1975	59%	28%	13%
1977	64%	27%	9%
1978	64%	25%	11%

Source: Surveys by Louis Harris and Associates from 1970 through 1978.

Surveys of national opinion provide one index of change in societal attitudes. The Louis Harris poll asked a representative national sample of Americans at five intervals throughout the 1970s the following question: "There has been much talk recently about changing women's status in society today. On the whole, do you favor or oppose most of the efforts to strengthen and change women's status in society today?"

Thus nearly two-thirds of Americans favor current changes in women's status, although one-quarter oppose this trend.

The Gallup organization provides a 40 year comparison of national opinion on the question, "If your party nominated a woman for President, would you vote for her if she were qualified for the job?" The answers provide an indirect index of how women's entry into the public world is perceived by men and women.

Table 3.   Attitudes Toward Female Leadership

| Year | Would Vote for Woman President | | |
	National	Women	Men
1937	34%	41%	27%
1949	50%	53%	47%
1955	54%	59%	49%
1963	57%	53%	61%
1976	76%	74%	78%
1978	80%	81%	80%

Note: Slight variatrion of question wording over the years.
Source: Surveys by American Institute of Public Opinion (Gallup) from 1937 through 1978.

The data in Table 3 suggest that men are open to accepting women's authority in the public sphere. However, in the domestic sphere, men's needs remain dominant. In 1977, a CBS News/New York Times survey asked whether a family should move if a wife was promoted to a job in another city when both husband and wife work. Only 12 percent of the sample suggested moving, and 66 percent unequivocally indicated the family should not move. Another 1977 national survey (conducted by the General Mills Consumer Center) found that mothers retain primary responsibility for household chores. Only 20 to 30 percent of the sample even suggested that fathers should prepare meals or shop for children's clothes. However, fathers were viewed as equal contributors to the discipline of the children.

These opinion surveys are, of course, vulnerable to the distortion and bias of subjectivity. Behavioral estimates of childrearing and household task performance ("family work") indicate that husbands spend much less time than their wives on such activities (Pleck, 1977). Pleck and Lang's (1978) research along with their review of "time budget" studies indicate that housewives may do six times as much family work as their husbands, while employed wives do between two and four times as much family work. Until 1977, no study had shown that husbands of empolyed wives performed more family work than husbands of nonemployed wives (when such work was measured in absolute rather than proportional terms). For the first time, a national representative sample (Pleck & Lang, 1978), as well as a small-scale study (Bloom-Feshbach, 1980a), found that husbands of employed wives spend more absolute time in childcare and household task performance than husbands whose wives are not employed outside the home. The figures, though small, are meaningful indicators of a nationwide trend toward greater male participation in family work. As larger numbers of women join the paid labor force, continued increases in male household support will be essential facilitators of their adjustment (Carew, 1978).

Table 4. Mother Versus Father Roles. Question: Who is Responsible?

	Mother	Father	Both (Volunteered)
Prepare the meals	77%	1%	22%
Stay home when children are sick	72%	1%	26%
Shop for children's clothes	66%	1%	32%
Clean the house	65%	1%	33%
Take children for checkups	63%	1%	35%
Go to Open School Week	22%	1%	76%
Help the children with homework	20%	5%	72%
Speak to teachers if children are in trouble	20%	8%	71%
Decide on children's allowances	9%	20%	67%
Discipline the children	7%	9%	83%
Teach the children sports and how to ride bikes	4%	36%	57%

Note: Not sures, neithers, not shown.
Source: "Raising Children in a Changing Society," General Mills Consumer Center, P.O. Box 1133, Minneapolis, MN 55440.

It should also be noted, contrary to popular stereotype, that the majority of men in this country derive more satisfaction from family life than from their work. Pleck and Lang (1978) report that "the family role is the most significant role in men's lives, although they spend less time in it than in their paid work, and positive experience in this role has greater consequences than does any other for men's overall well-being" (pp. 29–30). However, Bloom-Feshbach (1980a) found that for new fathers, higher levels of family work participation were accompanied by heightened enjoyment of parenthood *and* by more stress and difficulty during the transition to the new role. This finding suggests that strengthening the paternal family role may create new sources of satisfaction in men's lives as well as adding further burdens. Thus it may be prudent to observe and study emerging trends before pursuing policy options or interventions.

FUTURE PERSPECTIVES

The publication of the revised edition of this book itself signifies the continuing maturation of social science knowledge about the father's role. Evidence suggests that new patterns of family structure are emerging, although the androgynous family is probably only an avant garde development. The single-father household portrayed in *Kramer vs. Kramer* is increasing in number (Gersick, 1979), but it is not yet a large-scale phenomenon. Current child custody disputes still tend to favor the mother in many jurisdictions (e.g., Kerpelman, 1980).

Future research may be most productive if the multiple systems and relationships in which the father is embedded are studied along with dyadic interactions within the family. Human ecology involves a range of environmental variables and a spectrum of internal psychological factors. We know that paternal behavior is influenced by age or stage of adult development (Bloom-Feshbach, 1980a), by historical events and cohort groups (Elder, 1974), by generational differences (Greven, 1970), and by culture (Demos, 1970). Economic status, sex of the child, personality (Bloom-Feshbach, 1980a), and the wife's employment status (Pleck & Lang, 1978) are other factors affecting paternal family behavior. Because such an extensive array of factors shapes the father's role, many issues remain to be explored in future research. A historical perspective of paternal family involvement may provide a helpful context in which to view these questions.

REFERENCES

Ariès, P. *Centuries of childhood: A social history of family life* (R. Baldick, trans.). New York: Vintage, 1962.

Bamburger, J. The myth of matriarchy: Why men rule in primitive society. In M. Z. Rosaldo & L. Lamphere (Eds.), *Woman, culture and society*. Stanford: Stanford University Press, 1974.

Bardis, P. D. Main features of the ancient Roman family. *Social Science*, 1963, **38**, 225–240.

Barrett, N. S. *The coming decade: American women and human resources policies and programs*. Statement presented to Committee on Human Resources, U.S. Senate, February 1979.

Bem, S. L. The measurement of psychological androgyny. *Journal of Consulting and Clinical Psychology*, 1974, **42**, 155–162.

Bem, S. L. Sex role adaptability: One consequence of psychological androgyny. *Journal of Personality and Social Psychology*, 1975, **31**, 634–643.

Benedek, T. The family as a psychologic field. In E. J. Anthony & T. Benedek (Eds.), *Parenthood: Its psychology and psychopathology.* Boston: Little, Brown, 1970.

Benson, L. *Fatherhood: A sociological perspective.* New York: Random House, 1968.

Berndt, R. M., & Berndt, C. H. *The first Australians.* Sydney: Walkabout, 1969.

Biller, H., & Meredith, D. *Father power.* New York: McKay, 1974.

Blanchard, R., & Biller, H. Father availability and academic performance among third grade boys. *Developmental Psychology,* 1971, **5,** 301–305.

Block, J. H. Conceptions of sex role: Some cross-cultural and longitudinal perspectives. *American Psychologist,* 1973, **28,** 512–526.

Bloom-Feshbach, J. The beginnings of fatherhood. *Dissertation Abstracts International,* 1979, **41B,** (6), 2307(b).

Bloom-Feshbach, J. Differentiation: Field dependence, spatial ability, and hemispheric specialization. *Journal of Personality,* 1980, **48,** 135–148 (b).

Bloom-Feshbach, S., Bloom-Feshbach, J., & Gaughran, J. The child's tie to both parents: Separation patterns and nursery school adjustment. *American Journal of Orthopsychiatry,* 1980, **50,** 505–521.

Bronfenbrenner, U. Ecology of child development. *Proceedings of the American Philosophical Society,* 1975, **119,** 439–469.

Bronfenbrenner, U. Toward an experimental ecology of human development. *American Psychologist,* 1977, **32,** 513–531.

Burgess, E. W., & Locke, H. J. *The family: From institution to companionship.* New York: American Book Company, 1945.

Carew, M. C. *Employment and mothers' emotional states: A psychological study of women reentering the work force.* Unpublished doctoral dissertation, Yale University, 1978.

Chodorow, N. *The reproduction of mothering: Family structure and feminine personality.* Berkeley: University of California Press, 1977.

Cohen, L. J., & Campos, J. J. Father, mother, and stranger as elicitors of attachment behaviors in infancy. *Developmental Psychology,* 1974, **10,** 146–154.

Crano, W. D., & Aronoff, J. A cross-cultural study of expressive and instrumental role complementarity in the family. *American Sociological Review,* 1978, **43,** 463–471.

Davis, W. S. *The influence of wealth in Imperial Rome.* New York: Macmillan, 1910.

deMause, L. *The history of childhood.* New York: Harper, 1975.

Demos, J. *A little commonwealth: Family life in Plymouth Colony.* New York: Oxford Press, 1970.

Donzelot, J. *The policing of families.* New York: Pantheon Books, 1979.

Elder, G. *Children of the Great Depression.* Chicago: University of Chicago Press, 1974.

Elder, G. Historical change in life patterns and personality. In P. Baltes & O. Brim, Jr. (Eds.), *Life-span development and behavior,* Vol. 2. New York: Academic Press, 1979.

Elder, G. H., & Rockwell, R. C. The depression experience in men's lives. In A. J. Lichtman & J. R. Challinor (Eds.), *Kin and communities: Families in America*. Washington, D.C.: Smithsonian Press, 1979.

Engels, F. *The origin of the family, private property and the state*, 4th ed.. St. Petersburg: Viatz Khanova, 1894.

Epstein, L. M. *Marriage laws in the Bible and the Talmud*. Cambridge, Mass.: Harvard University Press, 1942.

Erikson, E. *Childhood and society*, 2nd ed. New York: Norton, 1963.

Fairchilds, C. Female sexual attitudes and the rise of illegitimacy. *Journal of Interdisciplinary History*, 1978, **4**, 627–667.

Fein, R. Research on fathering: Social policy and an emergent perspective. *Journal of Social Issues*, 1978, **34**, 122–135.

Feshbach, N. D. The psychology of empathy, and the empathy of psychology. Paper presented at the meeting of the Western Psychological Association, Honolulu, May 1980.

Freud, S. The ego and the id (1923). *Standard Edition*, Vol. 19. London: Hogarth, 1961.

Freud, S. Inhibitions, symptoms and anxiety (1926). *Standard Edition*, Vol. 20. London: Hogarth, 1961.

Furstenberg, F. F., Jr. Work experience and family life. In J. O'Toole (Ed.), *Work and the quality of life*. Cambridge: MIT Press, 1974.

Garbarino, J. A preliminary study of some ecological correlates of child abuse: The impact of socioeconomic stress on mothers. *Child Development*, 1976, **47**, 178–185.

Gersick, K. E. Fathers by choice: Divorced men who receive custody of their children. In G. Levinger & O. C. Moles (Eds.), *Divorce and separation: Context, causes and consequences*. New York: Basic Books, 1979.

Glick, P. C. Demographic shifts: Changes in family structure. In C. D. Hayes (Ed.), *Work, family and community: Summary proceedings of an ad hoc meeting*. Washington, D.C.: National Academy of Sciences, 1980.

Glick, P. C., & Norton, A. J. Perspectives on the recent upturn in divorce and remarriage. *Demography*, 1973, **10**, 301–314.

Gordon, M. From an unfortunate necessity to a cult of mutual orgasm: Sex in American marital educational literature, *1830–1840*. In J. Henslin (Ed.), *Studies in the sociology of sex*. New York, New York: Appleton-Century-Crofts, 1971.

Gough, K. The origin of the family. *Journal of Marriage and the Family*, 1971, **33**, 760–771.

Gould, R. The phases of adult life: A study in developmental psychology. *American Journal of Psychiatry*, 1972, **129**, 521–31.

Greven, P. J. *Four generations: Population, land, and family in colonial Andover, Massachusetts*. Ithaca, N.Y.: Cornell University Press, 1970.

Hareven, T. The history of the family as an interdisciplinary field. *Journal of Interdisciplinary History,* 1971, **2,** 399–414.

Hareven, T. (Ed.). *Transitions: The family and the life course in historical perspective.* New York: Academic Press, 1978.

Hayes, C. D. (Ed.). *Work, family, and community: Summary proceedings of an ad hoc meeting.* Washington, D.C.: National Academy of Sciences, 1980.

Hoffman, L. W., & Manis, J. D. Influences of children on marital interaction and parental satisfactions and dissatisfactions. In R. M. Lerner & G. B. Spanier (Eds.), *Child influences on marital and family interaction: A life-span perspective.* New York: Academic Press, 1978.

Hunt, D. *Parents and children in history: The psychology of family life in early modern France.* New York: Basic Books, 1970.

Kaplan, A., & Bean, J. *Beyond sex-role stereotypes: Readings toward a psychology of androgyny.* Boston: Little, Brown, 1976.

Kellam, S. G., Ensminger, M. E., & Turner, R. J. Family structure and the mental health of children. *Archives of General Psychiatry,* 1977, **34,** 1012–1022.

Keniston, K. *The uncommitted: Alienated youth in American society.* New York: Harcourt, Brace & World, 1960.

Keniston, K. *All our children: The American family under pressure.* New York: Harcourt Brace Jovanovich, 1977.

Kenkel, W. F. *The family in perspective.* New York: Appleton-Century-Crofts, 1966.

Kerpelman, L. J. Child custody best decided by jury. *New Haven Register,* April 1980, p. 11.

Kessen, W. *The child.* New York: Wiley, 1965.

Kohn, M. *Class and conformity: A study in values.* Homewood, Ill.: Dorsey, 1969.

Kohn, M. L., & Schooler, C. Occupational experience and psychological functioning: An assessment of reciprocal effects. *American Sociological Review,* 1973, **38,** 97–118.

Kotelchuck, M. The infant's relationship to the father: Experimental evidence. In M. E. Lamb (Ed.), *The role of the father in child development.* New York: Wiley, 1976.

Lamb, M. E. Fathers: Forgotten contributors to child development. *Human Development,* 1975, **18,** 245–266.

Lamb, M. E. *The role of the father in child development.* New York: Wiley, 1976.

Lamb, M. E. Father–infant and mother–infant interaction in the first year of life. *Child Development,* 1977, **48,** 167–181.

Lamb, M. E. Influence of the child on marital quality and family interaction during the prenatal, perinatal, and infancy periods. In R. M. Lerner & G. B. Spanier (Eds.), *Child influences on marital and family interaction: A life-span perspective.* New York: Academic Press, 1978.

Lasch, C. *Haven in a heartless world: The family besieged.* New York: Basic Books, 1979.

Lasch, C. *The culture of narcissism.* New York: Warner, 1980.

Levinson, D. *The seasons of a man's life*. New York: Knopf, 1978.

Lewis, H. B. *Psychic war in men and women*. New York: New York University Press, 1976.

Lewis, R. A. Emotional intimacy among men. *Journal of Social Issues*, 1978, **34**, 108–121.

Lewis, R. A., Freneau, P. J., & Roberts, C. L. Fathers and the post-parental transition. *Family Coordinator*, 1979, **28**, 514–520.

Lyman, R. B. Barbarism and religion: Late Roman and early medieval childhood. In L. deMause (Ed.), *The history of childhood*. New York: Harper, 1975.

Malinowski, B. *The sexual life of savages*. New York: Harcourt, Brace & World, 1962.

Morgan, E. S. *The Puritan family*. New York: Harper & Row, 1966.

Murdock, G. World ethnographic sample. *American Anthropologist*, 1957.

Murdock, G. *Ethnographic atlas*. Pittsburgh: University of Pittsburgh Press, 1967.

Nash, J. Historical and social changes in the perception of the role of the father. In M. E. Lamb (Ed.), *The role of the father in child development*. New York: Wiley, 1976.

Newton, P., & Levinson, D. The work group within the organization: A sociopsychological approach. *Psychiatry*, 1973, **36**, 115–142.

Noon, J. A. *Law and government of the Grand River Iroquois*. New York: Viking Fund Publications in Anthropology, 1949, No. 12.

Norris, G., & Miller, J. *The working mother's complete handbook*. New York: Dutton, 1979.

Parke, R. D., & Sawin, D. B. The father's role in infancy: A reevaluation. *Family Coordinator*, 1976, **25**, 365–371.

Parsons, T., & Bales, R. F. *Family socialization and interaction process*. Glencoe, Ill.: Free Press, 1955.

Pedersen, F. A., Anderson, B. J., & Cain, R. L. An approach to understanding linkages between the parent-infant and spouse relationships. In F. A. Pedersen (Ed.), *The father-infant relationship: Observational studies in a family context*. New York: Praeger Special Publications, 1980.

Pleck, J. The work-family role system. *Social Problems*, 1977, **24**, 417–427.

Pleck, J. The male sex role: Definitions, problems, and sources of change. In J. H. Williams (Ed.), *Psychology of women: Selected readings*. New York: Norton, 1979.

Pleck, J., & Lang, L. *Men's family role: Its nature and consequences*. Wellesley, Mass.: Wellesley College Center for Research on Women, 1978.

Rossi, A. A biosocial perspective on parenting. *Daedalus*, 1977, **106**, 1–31.

Rossi, A. Personal communication, November 1979.

Rubin, L. B. *Worlds of pain: Life in the working-class family*. New York: Basic Books, 1976.

Sacks, K. Engels revisited: Women, the organization of production, and private property. In M. Z. Rosaldo, & L. Lamphere (Eds.), *Woman, culture, and society*. Stanford: Stanford University Press, 1974.

Sanday, P. R. Female status in the public domain. In M. Z. Rosaldo, & L. Lamphere (Eds.), *Woman, culture, and society*. Stanford: Stanford University Press, 1974.

Schaffer, H. R., & Emerson, P. E. The development of social attachments in infancy. *Monographs of the Society for Research in Child Development*, 1964, **29** (Serial No. 94).

Schimek, J. G. Cognitive style and defenses: A longitudinal study of intellectualization and field independence. *Journal of Abnormal Psychology*, 1968, **73**, 575–580.

Schneider, D., & Gough, K. *Matrilineal kinship*. Berkeley: University of California Press, 1961.

Sears, R. Sources of life satisfactions of the Terman gifted men. *American Psychologist*, 1977, **32**, 119–128.

Sennett, R. *Families against the city*. Cambridge, Mass.: Harvard University Press, 1964.

Sennett, R., & Cobb, J. *The hidden injuries of class*. New York: Vintage Books, 1973.

Shah, I. *The Sufis*. Garden City, N.Y.: Anchor Books, 1971.

Shorter, E. Female emancipation, birth control, and fertility in European history. *American Historical Review*, 1973, **78**, 605–640.

Shorter, E. *The making of the modern family*. New York: Basic Books, 1975.

Slater, P. Parental role differentiation. *American Journal of Sociology*, 1961, **67**, 296–311.

Smelser, N. *Social change in the Industrial Revolution*. London: Routledge & Kegan Paul, 1959.

Spence, J. T., Helmreich, R., & Stapp, J. Ratings of self and peers on sex-role attributes and their relation to self-esteem and conceptions of masculinity and femininity. *Journal of Personality and Social Psychology*, 1975, **32**, 29–39.

Stearns, P. N. *Be a man! Males in modern society*. New York: Holmes and Meier, 1979.

Tilly, L., Scott, J., & Cohen, M. Women's work and European fertility patterns. *Journal of Interdisciplinary History*, 1976, **3**, 447–456.

Tuchman, B. *A distant mirror: The calamitous 14th century*. New York: Ballantine, 1979.

Turnbull, C. *The forest people*. New York: Clarion, 1962.

Vaillant, G. E. *Adaptation to life*. Boston: Little, Brown, 1977.

Waldron, I. Why do women live longer than men? *Journal of Human Stress*, 1976 (March), 2–14.

Waldron, I. Type A behavior pattern and coronary heart disease in men and women. *Social Science and Medicine*, 1978, **12**, 167–171.

Werner, H. *Comparative psychology of mental development*. New York: International Universities Press, 1957.

Weinstein, F., & Platt, G. M. *The wish to be free: Society, psyche, and value change.* Berkeley: University of California Press, 1969.

Wells, R. V. Review of "The making of the modern family" by E. Shorter. *Journal of Social History,* 1977, **10,** 361–364.

Westley, W. A., & Epstein, N. B. *The silent majority.* San Francisco: Jossey-Bass, 1969.

Wheelis, A. *How people change.* New York: Harper & Row, 1973.

Witkin, H. Cognitive styles in personal and cultural adaptation. *The 1977 Heinz Werner Lectures.* Worcester, Mass.: Clark University Press, 1978.

Witkin, H., & Berry, J. Psychological differentiation in cross-cultural perspective. *Journal of Cross-Cultural Psychology,* 1975, **6,** 4–87.

Witkin, H. A., Dyk, R. B., Faterson, H. F., Goodenough, D. R., & Karp, S. A. *Psychological differentiation: Studies of development.* New York: Wiley, 1974.

Witkin, H. A., Goodenough, D. R., & Oltman, P. K. Psychological differentiation: Current status. *Research Bulletin of the Educational Testing Service,* Princeton, N.J., 1977.

CHAPTER 3

The Father in Psychoanalytic Theory

VERONICA J. MÄCHTLINGER

Berlin

Since the first edition of this book (Lamb, 1976) the increased interest in the father and his place and functions in the life of the child has also been reflected in psychoanalytic writings. In this chapter I emphasize those analytic speculations about the father and his importance that have been further developed between 1975 and 1980. However, in reviewing specific lines of thought, earlier contributions are considered where necessary.

For a detailed examination of analytic thinking about the father until 1975, with special reference to the pre-Oedipal and Oedipal phases of development, the reader is referred to my earlier chapter (Mächtlinger, 1976). In this chapter I summarize the main conclusions of the previous chapter and discuss present analytic efforts to understand the role and functions of the father, as well as the developmental process of becoming a father—a process that provides a basis for understanding individual differences in the ways in which fathers relate to their children.

A SUMMARY OF EARLIER PSYCHOANALYTIC VIEWS CONCERNING THE FATHER

Any discussion of psychoanalytic theories about the father takes place against the background of Freud's thinking on the subject. Freud allotted the father a place of considerable importance in his theory of infantile psychosexual development. Indeed, at first he thought that the father–child relationship was more important than the mother–child relationship—a view he later modified. Freud emphasized three aspects of the father–child relationship:

1. Feelings of love and admiration for the father during the pre-Oedipal years of development were considered vitally important (especially for boys) as a source of positive identifications. In speaking about identification in 1921, Freud pointed out that children identify with those they are tied to emotionally. "It plays a part in the early history of the Oedipus complex. A little boy will exhibit a special interest in his father; he would like to grow like him and be like him and take his place everywhere. We may say simply that he takes his father as his ideal. This behaviour has nothing to do with a passive or feminine attitude towards his father (and towards males in general); it is on the contrary typically masculine" (Freud, 1921, p. 105). These positive and loving feelings toward the father also lay the foundations for the conflicts that make up the Oedipus complex.

2. A strong need for protection by somebody he or she loves arises out of the child's smallness and helplessness. In his discussion of the origins of religious feelings, Freud linked this need to be protected particularly to the relationship with the father and thought it to be one of the strongest needs of childhood. "As we already know, the terrifying impression of helplessness in childhood aroused the need for protection—for protection through love—which was provided by the father" (Freud, 1927, p. 30).

3. The small child also regards the father as an authority, as someone from whom punishment can be expected. This aspect of the father–child relationship becomes greatly intensified and reaches a peak in the fears and fantasies that shape the boy's image of the "Oedipal" father during the phallic–Oedipal phase of development (i.e., in the image of the threatening, punishing, and castrating father). For the girl, the "Oedipal" father has become her main love object toward whom her Oedipal–phallic sexual wishes are directed during the "positive" Oedipal conflict.

Freud considered the Oedipus complex to be the culmination of infantile sexual development, after which the child enters the latency phase. The Oedipus complex was the name Freud gave to the conflicts of the phallic–Oedipal phase, which, if unresolved or unsatisfactorily resolved, later resulted in neurotic symptoms:

> In the very earliest years of childhood (approximately between the ages of two and five) a convergency of the sexual impulses occurs of which, in the case of boys, the object is the mother. This choice of an object, in conjunction with a corresponding attitude of rivalry and hostility towards the father provides the content of what is known as the *Oedipus complex* which in every human being is of the greatest importance in determining the final shape of his erotic life. It has been found to be characteristic of the normal individual that he learns to master his Oedipus complex, whereas the neurotic subject remains involved in it. (Freud, 1923, pp. 245–246)

This connection between the fate of the Oedipal conflicts and later neurotic symptomatology led the first generation of analysts to concentrate their attention on the conflicts of the phallic–Oedipal phase. However, this emphasis gradually shifted to the so-called pre-Oedipal developmental stages and the processes and events in them, which prepared the intrapsychic ground for the later emergence of the Oedipus complex and its conflicts. In this sense, the presence of the Oedipus complex has come to be regarded as evidence that the child's personality has attained a given degree of organization, structure, and integration—not to be found in those children in whom various developmental delays, disturbances and arrests have seriously interfered with the development and function of the ego as well as object relationships (A. Freud, 1965).

Freud at first described the Oedipus complex as it develops in boys and assumed that a parallel process took place in girls. In the face of negative clinical evidence, however—obtained mainly from work with adult female patients—he abandoned the theory of an analogous process occurring in girls (Freud, 1919). It was also clinical work with women patients that drew analysts' attention to the intensity and duration of the pre-Oedipal attachment to the mother. The concept of bisexuality, together with the idea that children of both sexes take as their love objects parents of both sexes, led to the theory of the "positive" and "negative" forms of the complex (i.e., that every Oedipal relationship is in fact a fourfold one, with boys and girls developing affectionate and hostile impulses toward both parents).

The boy enters the phallic phase of his libidinal development with a strong existing pre-Oedipal attachment to his mother (his first love object) as well as the pre-Oedipal identifications based on his love and admiration for his father. For a time these two relationships coexist without giving rise to conflict. When the boy's phallic–Oedipal sexual wishes toward his mother become intense, however, the father is perceived as an obstacle or rival to their fulfillment, and the simple *positive Oedipus complex* develops (i.e., the boy's feeling for his father becomes ambivalent rather than hostile and changes into a wish to get rid of him and take his place with the mother). Under the impact of this conflict, however, and as an expression of the boy's own bisexuality and latent feminine identifications, he may retreat (regress) to the *negative* Oedipal position, showing an affectionate attitude toward his father and a corresponding hostility and jealousy toward his mother. The negative Oedipal position in the boy can therefore also be a regressive attempt to escape from the conflicts of the Oedipal situation, an attempt, through identification with the mother, to retain the love of the father. However, both positive and negative forms of the Oedipus complex arouse castration fears in the boy. In the positive form he believes (fantasizes) that he might lose his penis as a punishment for his sexual wishes toward his mother and his hostility toward his father; in the negative form, the loss of his penis is seen as a precondition to being loved, as a woman, by the father.

Under normal conditions, this fantasized threat of castration results in the destruction, or dissolution, of the Oedipus complex in boys. The boy renounces his sexual (phallic–Oedipal) love for his mother, bows to the demands of reality, and identifies instead with the moral demands of the father. These identifications, which involve a renunciation of sexual wishes, are what Freud called the "heirs" to the Oedipus complex. He thought them crucial for the establishment, consolidation, and stabilization of the superego. "The object cathexes are given up and replaced by identifications. The authority of the father or the parents is introjected into the ego, and there it forms the nucleus of the superego, which takes over the severity of the father" (Freud, 1924, pp. 176–177).

In the girl, the Oedipus complex takes a different course. In 1919 Freud changed his earlier view that a process parallel to that in boys also takes place in girls, but as late as 1924 he still thought that the Oedipus complex in girls was a relatively simple matter, consisting of the wish to take the mother's place and the adoption of a feminine attitude to the father. Later, however, Freud came to regard the Oedipus complex and its conflicts as presenting more difficult and complicated problems for the girl to overcome than for the boy. First, the boy, unlike the girl, does not have to change his primary love object, the mother. The girl, who also enters the phallic Oedipal phase with a strong (albeit ambivalent) preexisting pre-Oedipal attachment to the mother, must free herself from her mother and take the father as her primary love object—a process that seldom occurs without difficulties. Freud also thought that the girl faced an additional problem of having to change her leading genital zone as well—from the clitoris to the vagina. Freud saw clearly that a disappointing or disinterested Oedipal father could have a devastating effect on the ongoing sexual development of his daughter, causing her to fall back into her pre-Oedipal relationship with her mother (1931, pp. 241). It is the girl's close pre-Oedipal attachment to the mother, which at the beginning of the phallic stage becomes linked with sexual strivings directed toward her, that Freud designates as the "negative" Oedipus complex in girls. It precedes the positive complex and may be defensively and regressively retreated to in the face of Oedipal conflicts.

The shift from the negative to the positive Oedipus complex in the girl (i.e., the shift from the mother to the father as the primary love object) was considered by Freud to be caused by the meaning that the girl attaches to the anatomical difference between the sexes. The girl, in the phallic–Oedipal phase, interprets her lack of a penis as a castration for which she blames her mother. Out of her disappointment with the mother and according to the mental equation *penis*=*child*, the girl now directs her sexual wishes toward her father, and her Oedipal fantasies are concerned with having a child by him. In the girl, then, the positive Oedipal position is brought about by her imagined castration. Turning away from her mother in anger and disappointment, she seeks to take her father as her love object, and the mother becomes the object of hostility and jealousy. Because the fantasized threat of castration does not exist in the same form in girls as it does in boys, Freud thought that the resulting internalizations in girls of the moral authority of the parents did not attain the same status and stability as those found in boys. Fear of loss of love was thought by Freud to play an important role in the girl's renunciation of her Oedipal wishes, together with disappointment of these wishes.

In Freud's view, bisexuality (i.e., the relative strength on the masculine and feminine sexual dispositions) as well as the early identifications with both parents decisively influences the course and outcome of Oedipal conflicts. This outcome will be decided by a great variety of individual factors, dispositional, maturational, internal, and external, and this makes a simple description of the "normal" resolution of the Oedipal complex extremely difficult.

There seems to be a tendency in the more recent psychoanalytic literature to maintain that Freud's emphasis was on the punishing, frightening, and castrating aspects of the fantasized Oedipal father and that analysts after Freud have continued to reflect this bias. I do not share this view, at least with regard to Freud himself. It may well be that analysts dealing with the Oedipal father (as he comes to be seen from behind the couch) have tended to place their emphasis on these aspects of the father. Analysts who deal with children, faced as they are with the child's relationship to the "real" father as well as with the fantasized father, might be less prone to such a one-sided view. Freud himself, from the very beginnings of psychoanalysis, continually referred to and stressed the loving and admiring aspects of the child's view of the father, and he considered them very important for essential pre-Oedipal identifications. An example of this is to be found in the case of Little Hans (Freud, 1909), the 5-year-old boy whose phobia was the first infantile neurosis dealt with psychoanalytically. In this case, the boy's positive and loving relationship with his father forms the very basis of the analytical work with the child. There are many references to Hans' great love for his father, and it is only when his phallic–Oedipal wishes become pressing that he begins "to notice that his love for his father was wrestling with his hostility towards him in his capacity of rival with his mother" (p. 44), and then: "But this same father whom he could not help hating as a rival, was *the same father whom he had always loved and was bound to go on loving, who had been his model, who had been his first playmate, and who had looked after him from his earliest infancy: and this it was that gave rise to the first conflict.*" (p. 134, italics added).

The case history of Little Hans also illustrates another aspect of the psychoanalytic approach that must be borne in mind when considering psychoanalytic theories. Although in this case study both Hans' mother and father are clearly characterized as individuals, it is not their actual personalities or the interaction between their own and the child's personality that constitute the primary focus of attention. The parents are mainly seen as agents of the stimuli to which Hans reacts. Freud concentrated on the sequence of these reactions and on their dynamic interrelations with the child's other experiences. It is only when questions of identification with the parental figures are discussed that the parents are considered in terms of their own personalities, as Kris (1950) points out.

Psychoanalysts are concerned with the "internalized representation" of the father—that is, with the feelings, fantasies, and wishes that the child has come to attach to the father and which might or might not reflect the real father. Anna Freud and Dorothy Burlingham (1944), for example, describe a little girl (separated from her father between the ages of 2½ and 5½ years) who used "almost abnormal" terms of endearment when referring to her father—a man who was considered by others to be "elderly and morose" and "rather strict and uncompromising" with his large family.

With the growth of interest in the infantile pre-Oedipal developmental phases and with the development of "genetic developmental psychoanalysis" (see Hartmann, 1950; Hartmann & Kris, 1945; A. Freud, 1950), observations of infants and toddlers in the preverbal period came to be considered by some analysts as a legitimate field of study and as able to make important contributions to basic theoretical knowledge about the early developmental years. In this way, the behavior of the infant and small child, observed from the outside, came to be scrutinized in detail (e.g., Spitz, 1965). It is nevertheless the workings of the "mental apparatus" and the fantasies and meanings that the child attaches to perceptions and experiences during the course of development, that continue to be the focus of psychoanalytic attention.

Theoretical speculations in which observations of behavior are combined with inferences about internal structures and their functions (ego, id, and superego), drive components, and specific fantasy content, present a special problem. Once a child can verbalize his fantasies or even give clues to them in play, this difficulty is lessened, although controversies can and do arise about the status and meaning of children's statements and analysts' observations. In the pre-verbal stages, observations of and inferences from behavior are often difficult to differentiate. This is true of much of the work done on the early relationship to the father, where observations of the actual observable relationship between father and child and speculations about internal processes within the child are not always clearly distinguished from one another in the psychoanalytic literature.

Although in clinical work with patients the father had always been granted his place and importance, no extensive or systematic attempts were made in the early years after Freud to specify his role and functions in more detail. At first this neglect was no doubt caused by the increasing attention paid to the early mother–infant relationship in psychoanalytic theorizing. In 1944, however, Anna Freud and Dorothy Burlingham called attention to the neglect of the father's importance to the child and stated, "The infant's emotional relationship to his father begins later in life than that to his mother, but certainly from the second year onward it is an integral part of his emotional life and a necessary ingredient in the complex forces which work towards the formation of his character and personality" (p. 638).

Other analysts, such as Mahler and Gosliner (1955), Winnicott (1960), Greenacre (1960, 1966), Neubauer (1960), and Leonard (1966), had similarly called attention to the importance of the early father–child relationship. The growing dissatisfaction with the lack of adequate theoretical attempts to understand the father's role was strongly expressed in 1973 by Burlingham in her paper on the pre-Oedipal relationship. Burlingham felt that the neglect of the father had led to distortions in thinking about the nature of the mother–infant relationship. Specifically, she proposed that the father assists the child in individuating from the mother. Loewald (1951) had already suggested that the father had an important role to play in aiding processes of ego development, individuation, and differentiation in the pre-Oedipal period. In describing the Oedipus complex as a process in which the child must come to terms with the demands of reality and give up infantile wishes, Loewald suggests that for the child the very concept of reality is represented by the father—that is, reality is experienced as an external force, typically represented by the paternal figure. Loewald also stresses the fact that the child's pre-Oedipal relationship to the mother is an ambivalent one, consisting of both the positive infantile sense of unity with her as well as the dread of "sinking back into the original unstructured state of identity with her" (p. 16). He proposes a specific role for the father: to help the child's ego achieve greater organization, differentiation, and integration, in order to free himself of the mother. In Loewald's view, the "dread of re-engulfment" by the mother, in both boys and girls, works hand in hand with the threat of paternal castration in boys as a stimulus toward greater differentiation of the ego and subsequent structuralization of reality.

Mahler and Gosliner (1955) also postulated that the early tie to the father plays an essential role in helping the child to free himself of the early symbiotic tie with the mother and to develop autonomy in ego functions. The father, according to these authors, represents for the child an "uncontaminated" (by ambivalence), "other-than-mother" world. Abelin (1971) put forward a similar view and, within the framework of Mahler's separation–individuation theory, stressed that the small child's specific attachment to the father in the practicing subphase plays a decisive role in aiding differentiation and individuation processes.

An examination (Mächtlinger, 1976) of clinical and observational studies showed that the richness and complexity of early father–infant and father–child interactions had not been overlooked. Weissman (1963) and Burlingham (1973), using analytic material from adult patients (who became fathers during their analyses), paid particular attention to the effect of the fathers' personalities on their children (especially sons). Kolansky and Moore (1966) and Sprince (1972) also pointed out this effect in accounts of simultaneous analyses of father and son pairs. A pathological father–daughter relationship had been described by Moore (1974), in which the father's failure (through disinterest) to help his daughter free herself from her negative Oedipal tie to the mother was crucial to her pathology. Leonard (1966) similarly stressed the essential role of fathers in helping their daughters successfully negotiate Oedipal conflicts. She concluded that a father who is present and participates in his daughter's upbringing from the pre-Oedipal stages onward is essential to her normal sexual development.

A simultaneous analysis of a father and his daughter in a family observed from the child's birth as part of the Yale longitudinal research program (Ritvo et al., 1963) showed how misleading it is to isolate the effect of one parent on the development of the child. In this case, as in other cases of simultaneous analyses, it was clear that the combined effects of the total family situation and interactions, as well as the particular mental and physical characteristics of the child herself, all contributed to the final clinical picture. To isolate the father's role in the life of this child from all her other relationships and interactions could only lead to an oversimplified and distorted statement.

The absent father also received a good deal of attention from psychoanalysts before 1976. Anna Freud and Dorothy Burlingham (1944) as well as Peter Neubauer (1960) stressed the importance of the fantasies that children develop about their absent fathers—fantasies that often have a profound effect on the mental life and development of the child and, because of the absence of the father, are not subject to correction through experience with a real, concrete, living, and present father. The problems children have in freeing themselves from the pre-Oedipal attachment to the mother are also correspondingly greater when the father is absent. Clinical evidence has shown that the father's presence contributes to the resolution of Oedipal conflicts. An absent father does not present the same fantasized castration threat to the boy as the father who is actively present does. Nor can a girl develop a strong pre-Oedipal attachment to a father who is not physically or emotionally available to her, and so deprives her of a basis from which she can redirect her positive Oedipal wishes in the Oedipal phase.

Finally, Anna Freud and Dorothy Burlingham's (1944) account of the progressive development of a fantasy father in an illegitimate child who had never known a father is especially striking. This child could mold his fantasy father according to his developmental needs, and his successive father "images" reflected his own developmental progress.

PSYCHOANALYTIC VIEWS ON THE FATHER SINCE 1975

This section considers the more recent contributions to the literature on the role of the father, and the discussion is divided among the following topics:

1. Those theories that deal with the father's functions and importance during the pre-Oedipal and Oedipal stages of development.
2. Theories primarily concerned with the father's role in the development of the child's sexuality and gender identity.
3. Psychoanalytic views of fathering as an ongoing developmental process, having its roots in the childhood of the father.
4. A brief consideration of available psychoanalytic views on the role of the father during latency and adolescence.

Recent Psychoanalytic Views on the Father in the Pre-Oedipal and Oedipal Years

Among the views of the pre-Oedipal and Oedipal father that have formed the basis for psychoanalytic discussion since 1975, the "early triangulation" model of Ernest L. Abelin has probably received the most widespread attention. An earlier form of these speculations, called the *general early triangulation model,* was concerned with the process thought to be involved in the internalization of the child's self as a concept—processes considered by Piaget to occur around 18 months of age. In the later, so-called *tripartite model of early triangulation,* Abelin adds a specific gender component to the hypothesized internalized self-concept at this age. The psychoanalytic framework within which Abelin works is provided by the separation–individuation theory ("the psychological birth of the infant") of Margaret Mahler (Mahler, Pine, & Bergman, 1975). His thinking, however, leans heavily on Piaget's concepts of intellectual development—a theoretical allegiance that poses a number of problems in discussing his ideas from a psychoanalytic point of view.

Another problem in discussing Abelin involves the wide variety of observations, concepts, and even systems of thinking that he uses in constructing his model. The significance of the widely different meanings attached to the same terms as they are used in various theoretical approaches as well as the different levels of observation and inference involved are not explicitly mentioned, and no attempt appears to have been made to reconcile such differences. Abelin (1980) says that his speculations are buttressed by "large clusters of data . . .

(pertaining) to such disparate fields as biological and psychological gender differences and their origins, ethology, social affinities of infants, the corticalization of the extrapyramidal system, the early genital stage, early language development, self-recognition in the mirror, Piaget's findings, psychoanalytic reconstruction, family dynamics, or systems theory'' (p. 161). Comment on all these aspects of Abelin's model is both outside my competence and not possible within the framework of this chapter. I can only describe the evolution of Abelin's thinking from the earlier to the later, expanded version of the model and then point to some of the problems that arise in trying to relate these concepts to developmental psychoanalytic views. A brief summary of Mahler's separation–individuation theory which forms the background to Abelin's thinking, will be given where necessary.

Abelin developed his "early triangulation" model, in which the father was thought to fulfill an important function in the pre-Oedipal years, in the process of studying schizophrenic children and their families. He took as a starting point the idea that schizophrenia is characterized by a breakdown both of symbolic mental functioning and of the mental image of the self, and he agreed with Piaget that both these intellectual achievements normally appear around 18 months of age. He then asked how the child at this age forms a mental self-image and in what way this achievement is related to the emergence of symbolic mental functioning. Using the family dynamics of schizophrenia as a basis for his speculations, he hypothesized that both achievements must depend not only on the child having a satisfactory relationship with each parent, but also on the existence of a satisfactory relationship *between* the parents. This suggested to him that "in normal development, *some kind of internalization* of the relationship between the parents takes place around 18 months," leading to the following hypothesis: "This internalization *somehow* leads to the formation of the self-image and of symbolic mental representations in general" (Abelin, 1980, p. 152, italics added).

Abelin's argument is based on Piaget's account of the inner world and experience of the toddler living in a sensorimotor world—a world that Piaget describes as egocentric, yet without an ego. He means by this that children before 18 months experience themselves as being at the center of their world but without any *self*-awareness (i.e., without a *concept* of self as a subject or object). This is the stage in which relationships to objects (and Piaget is talking about inanimate objects) are of a one-to-one kind, based on imitation and mirroring. Abelin adopts this Piagetian view of the inner world of the 18-month-old child, adding, however, that the main focus of the child's attention at this age is usually the "libidinal attachment object"—that is, the mother. (Here is one example of a shift of conceptual framework in which the psychoanalytic concept of the "libidinal object" is, by implication at least, equated with the Piagetian "object.")

Abelin similarly shares Piaget's views on motivation. The child is thought not to experience or perceive wishes and desires as emanating from inside the self but as being situated in the outside world. The wished-for object is seen to *be* desirable—desirability is perceived as a quality of the object. The child's imitations of objects are taken as evidence that a relatively stable image (mental representation) of that object now exists in the mind of the child, and that the image is independent of actions performed on the object. Piaget dates this achievement of internalized images (the concept of object permanence) at about 18 months and suggests that actions, through imitation, become "transmuted into symbolic mental images" in this way. Thus mental images arise when the imitation of an object has been carried out previously. This theory of the origin of mental images naturally raises the question of how the mental image of the *self* arises, since children cannot imitate themselves. Abelin's argument is that children cannot construct "true" images of themselves until they can recognize *their own wish* for the object. "Selfhood is the acknowledgement of one's core wish" (Abelin, 1980, p. 153), and the wished-for object is always the libidinal object. This basic wish for the object can only be recognized as emanating from the self when it is seen and imitated (and thus internalized) in a triangular situation in which the toddler perceives one libidinally cathected object desiring another (i.e., the father desiring the mother). This painful experience of exclusion, of being "left out" with no one to relate to and no one to mirror (in Piaget's sense), leaves the toddler no alternative but to imagine actively being in the place of the rival—"indeed, as *a* being like his rival . . . There must be an I, like him, wanting her" and thus "early triangulation is this identification with the rival" (Abelin, 1980, p. 153). The parents, relating to one another to the exclusion of the child, function as a kind of double mirror in which, according to Abelin, the child *sees himself* for the first time. "Suspended as he is between two patterns of interacting he can do nothing but recognize his own frustrated wish in the action of the rival" (Abelin, 1975, p. 294). Abelin regards this first mental representation of the self as being the "first symbolic image" and thus forming the "bridge between sensorimotor and symbolic functioning" (Abelin, 1980, p. 153).

In his original model, Abelin assumed that the prototypical rival in the early triangulation experience was the father—hence the specific function proposed for the father of being crucial to the formation of the internalized images of the self as well as the wished-for object, the mother. This triangulation situation, consisting of mother, father, and child, was called the *primal constellation*. It is also important to note that although Abelin talks about the internalization of a triangular situation, the father is thought to act only as a kind of catalyst, sparking off the internalization of the self-image and the image of the wished-for object. The mental image of the rival father (i.e., the third image in the triangle) is not thought to be included in these first self– and object–images existing in symbolic relation to one another. According to Abelin, a further extension of symbolic functioning to include this third image of the rival occurs later during the classical Oedipal triangle. This model assumes that the father should have become an important libidinal object for the child before the age of 18 months. This has been confirmed by many investigators (see Chapter 13)—a fact that Abelin regards as confirmation of the predictive value of his model.

The nature of this specific early relationship to the father is discussed and described by Abelin in terms of Mahler's separation–individuation theory and concepts (Mahler, 1979). Mahler's theory is concerned with the gradual development in the infant and small child of a sense of separateness from and relation to what the child comes to perceive as the outside world—the world of external reality. The main representative of this world for the child, to begin with, is the primary caretaker, usually the mother, who also gradually becomes the primary love object (A. Freud, 1954). Psychoanalysts assume that the child at birth (and immediately thereafter) exists in a state of biological unity with the mother—a stage that Mahler calls "autistic." According to Mahler, this stage is followed by a "symbiotic" stage—a state of fusion, of undifferentiation, in which the infant makes no distinctions between itself and the mother (between I and not-I). This is the so called preobject stage or need-satisfying (anaclitic) relationship, in which the infant is absolutely dependent on the symbiotic partner. Out of this symbiotic fusion with the mother, a growing awareness of separateness (together with the corresponding intrapsychic representations of objects in the external world and of the bodily self) develops.

For those not familiar with psychoanalytic thinking it is perhaps necessary to point out that, although it is obvious that there is a real interaction between a mother and her child (i.e., that they relate to one another as objects), it is quite a different matter when it comes to making assumptions about the existence of intrapsychic differentiations in the child's mind between self- and object representations. The ability to differentiate between self and object is a necessary prerequisite for such intrapsychic differentiation and both processes are thought to go hand-in-hand with the maturation, growth, and development of ego functions (see Spitz, 1954). When these mental images or representations of objects come to be cathected with libido, psychoanalysts refer to a "libidinal object" and "object relations." In watching a mother–child interaction, the external observer can only guess what the child's *experience* of this interaction might be and the level of intrapsychic differentiation and discrimination that might be involved.

There are considerable differences in psychoanalytic views concerning the possible processes involved in the first months of development. Mahler (1979) emphasizes the development of object relations and describes four consecutive but overlapping subphases in the process of separation–individuation, which, she stresses, is not just the achievement of physical independence from the mother but also an intrapsychic independence in the sense defined above. The next two phases are *differentiation* (5 to 9 months): a period in which the total bodily dependence on the mother begins to decrease, and the first beginnings of a primitive internal differentiation between body and object images are though to develop; and *practicing* (9 to 14 months): a period in which the child actively and physically moves away from the mother to explore the environment. Mahler and others suggest that it is in this stage that the relationship with the father becomes especially important. The father relationship, unlike that with the mother, does not have its origins in the state of symbiotic fusion; rather, the father has an exciting "other-than-mother" quality—he belongs to the new and exciting "outside" world. The fourth phase *rapprochement* (15 to 24 months), is thought to involve a rediscovery of the mother after the movement away from her in the practicing phase. The mother is, however, now perceived and experienced as a separate individual. The child's corresponding awareness of his or her separateness and consequent vulnerability (as well as the loss of the narcissistic feelings of omnipotence that are thought to form part of the symbiotic union), leads to the so-called rapprochement crisis, in which an ambivalent conflict between the wish to be one with the mother again and at the same time the wish to retain the newfound intrapsychic independence, leads to temper tantrums, intense separation reactions, and a depressively tinged mood.

Mahler considers this last phase and its attendant conflicts of crucial developmental importance (see Lax, Bach, & Burland, 1980). Whether and how the child resolves these rapprochement conflicts around internal independence are thought to be highly significant for later development—indeed "it may set an unfavourable fixation point interfering with later oedipal development, or at best add to the difficulty of the resolution of the oedipal conflict" (Mahler, 1972, in Mahler, 1979). The final phase in the separation–individuation process is an open-ended one in which (in normal development) a consolidation of individuality and emotional object constancy is achieved. This means that relatively stable object and self-representations have been established in the sense that the maternal image has now become intrapsychically available to the child in the same way that the actual mother has been libidinally available up to this point: as a provider of comfort and love.

Abelin too (1971) describes the child's early relationship to the father in the practicing and rapprochement subphases that Mahler does. The father, coming from outside the state of symbiotic fusion between child and mother, is experienced by the child as someone new and exciting. The relationship with him is less burdened by ambivalence than that with the mother—indeed, the relationship with the father is thought to have a vital function in helping the child resolve the ambivalent relationship to the mother and thus separate and individuate. During the rapprochement subphase and its upheavals, Abelin suggests, the father offers the child "a stable island of practicing reality" (Abelin, 1980, p. 153). To the extent that the rapprochement crisis arises out of the child's ambivalent reaction to the growing sense of separateness, the early triangulations thought to give rise to these earliest self-images are considered by Abelin to form the mechanism underlying the rapprochement phenomena.

In further studies, however, Abelin found that it was not only the father to whom the child formed specific, early, other-than-mother attachments. Siblings, grandparents, and familiar adults also become important libidinal objects for the child. Indeed, he found that contrary to his theoretical expectations, the first situations in which children showed "sensitivity to triangular rivalry" were those involving not the father but other children. This led him to postulate an earlier triangular situation ("more universal and archaic") than the primal constellation—the so-called Madonna constellation—in which a rival baby, rather than the father, is resented and envied in competition for the mother. The internalized self-images, thought to arise out of this early triangulation (i.e., its "resulting identifications"?) are twofold: an identification with the (passive) rival baby and an identification with the (active) nurturing mother. It remains unclear whether Abelin means to imply that identification is conceptually the same thing as a self-image. The terms, at any rate, are used interchangeably.

A later investigation of sexual differences in early triangular situations led to the latest version of Abelin's views—the tripartite model of early triangulation (1980). Here the process of self-image internalization is thought to involve three separate steps, only the last of which is said to differ in boys and girls. The new model does not invalidate the older one, but rather adds to the internalized self-image a specific content relating to gender identity. This model is based on observations of a brother–sister pair and speculations on the differences in the relationships that boys and girls are thought to have with their fathers and mothers (Abelin, 1975; Panel, 1977). Girls are said to show a greater degree of reinvolvement with the mother, greater ambivalence, and a more depressive basic mood than boys do during the rapprochement subphase. Boys, in contrast to girls, are said to form a closer attachment to and to identify earlier with their fathers, and it is this shift (before rapprochement) from a primary attachment to the mother that is thought to be important in aiding the beginnings of specific gender identity.

The incorporation of gender information into the girl's self-image is thought to occur only in the Oedipal phase (i.e., in the Oedipal triangular situation). Before rapprochement, the father is thought to remain a "peripheral if exciting" object for the girl. Her primary attachment figure (libidinal object) remains the mother. Abelin thus maintains that in the boy a self-image that includes gender information arises as a result of the primal constellation (which is therefore also considered to be a "sexual triangulation") and its corresponding identification with the rival father. In girls, however, a self-image containing only generational information (bigger/smaller, older/younger) in terms of rank order and based on the identifications inherent in the Madonna constellation is established at this time. The first basic rapprochement wish, "I want Mommy" (also thought to be the first longing of the separate self), is the same in boys as in girls. In boys, however, the wished-for object is of a different sex and does not mirror his own body. The boy's "basic wish" thus takes the form, "I (male) want Mommy (female/nonmale)." In this sense the boy's wish is thought to be gender specific, although in fact Abelin offers no evidence here that the boy wishes for his mother *as a female*—she just happens to be female. In girls, however, the wished-for object in the primal constellation, the mother, is of the same sex, and the girl's "core rapprochement wish" consequently does not contain the same reference to gender as that of the boy.

The explanation offered for this hypothesized difference is that girls remain caught in the identifications of the Madonna constellation (i.e., with the passive baby and with the active mother). These identifications, according to Abelin, are only implicitly feminine. The self-image based on them is not "genuinely" feminine as it would presumably be if the object of the wish were a member of the opposite sex. (This conclusion leads Abelin to state that the presence of the father in the pre-Oedipal stages is less important for the development of gender identity in girls than in boys—a statement with which I profoundly disagree.) On the basis of these considerations, Abelin concludes that gender identity emerges "more readily" in boys than in girls. Abelin uses Greenson's concept of "dis-identifying" with the mother in discussing the shift of attachment from mother to father, which is the important foundation stone on which the boy's self-image, inclusive of gender identity, is thought to be based. Greenson (1968) describes the necessity for the boy to "dis-identify" with the mother (i.e., to give up his primary early identification with her) and to identify with the father in order to develop a satisfactory male gender identity. The term dis-identify, as I understand Greenson, is a purely descriptive one and says nothing about the manner in which such a switch of identifications is thought to occur, or even what it means in metapsychological[1] terms

---

[1] I use the term "metapsychological" in the sense defined by Anna Freud (1968): "Psychoanalytic thinking, in classical terms, implied the specific demand that every clinical fact should be approached from four aspects: *genetically,* as to its origin; *dynamically,* as to the interplay of forces of which is the result; *economically,* with regard to its energy discharge; *topographically* (later *structurally*), concerning its localization within the mental apparatus. It was the psychology based on this view of mental functioning which was singled out by the name of *metapsychology* (p. 153; see also Brenner, 1980). This viewpoint is being challenged increasingly in psychoanalysis (Klein,

(see Greenson, 1968 in 1978, p. 132, in which he himself raises these questions and says that they must remain at present unanswered). Abelin also uses the term in this descriptive sense, although the implication is that it has explanatory value. He does not, at any rate, discuss the fate of the primary identifications with the mother and what a "dis-identification" involves in terms of inner processes. What is important for Abelin is that the boy must have made this switch from the mother to the father before the primal constellation occurs—that is, before the father is experienced as a rival for the mother's affection.

A brief summary of the triangulation model may well be useful at this point. In boys and girls, early triangulation is thought of as the process through which the child internalizes his or her first mental representation of the self (i.e., the first "core self-image"). This process is thought to take place in three stages, each involving the identification with a rival in a triangular situation. This is a traumatic experience for the child and leads to some kind of internal representation of the self. The first such triangular situation is the Madonna constellation, consisting of the mother–baby–self triangle. This is said to be experienced similarly by both sexes and gives rise to self- and object images based on rank order (generational identity). The second early triangulation situation, the primal constellation (also a sexual triangulation for the boy) involving the mother–father–child, results in the internalization of self- and wished-for object images. These two mental images are thought to exist in symbolic relationship to one another and contain the "core rapprochement wish." Although the primal constellation triangulation is said to be the same for both sexes, the boy is thought to develop a "core self-image" that includes gender identity, whereas the girl's self-image still contains only "generational" information, based on rank order and not on basic gender differences. According to Abelin, a "true" self-image in girls, including gender identity, only arises in the Oedipal triangular situation (the third stage of the tripartite triangulation process). In both boys and girls, the mental image of the rival, in symbolic relation to the images of the self and the wished-for object, finally becomes internalized in the Oedipal triangular situation.

Abelin's model diverges profoundly from traditional psychoanalytical views (and by this I mean those presented within the classical metapsychological framework) concerning the gradual differentiation, development, and delineation of self- and object images and representations thought to form part of the

1976; Kohut, 1971; Schafer, 1976). Volume 27, No. 2, of the *Journal of the American Psychoanalytic Association,* 1979, lists the papers presented on the topic in a Panel on Object Relations held in 1977. Such theoretical controversies are probably of little interest to nonpsychoanalysts and have little to do with the father and his role. They must, however, be mentioned, since my own theoretical position naturally shapes my discussion of theoretical issues, and this viewpoint cannot be regarded as being generally accepted in psychoanalysis.

child's subjective, inner (representational) world. This divergence arises largely out of Abelin's adoption of Piaget's view that the toddler in the sensorimotor stage *has* no inner world in the sense in which psychoanalysts use that term. Abelin defines the child's interaction with the environment as Piaget does, in terms of action schemata (all mental activity exists only in action) and states specifically that the toddler "relates sometimes with father and sometimes with mother, with no self-concept and no evocative memory and no inner images" (Panel discussion, 1977, p. 155).

Evocative memory (as contrasted with recognitive memory) in Piaget's view is linked indissolubly with the development of the object concept (Piaget, 1937). There can be no "object concept" without "mental representation" and no "mental representation" without an "object concept." Both achievements involve mental operations on a symbolic level. Piaget maintains that he sees no compelling reason to assume the existence of mental images of any kind before the age of 16 to 18 months. This viewpoint contrasts strongly with psychoanalytic views in which the gradual structuring of the child's inner (and outer) world is related to the growth and maturity of psychic structure and function (especially the ego), drive components, and object relations. In this view, the child's inner world is thought to be one in which initial differentiations arising out of a primary undifferentiated state are made between experiences of pleasure and unpleasure. This is the basis from which the infant begins very gradually to distinguish an inner from an outer world, his own body boundaries (and thus a primitive self from not-self), and self from object.

The different meanings attached to the words "object permanence" by Piaget and by psychoanalysts must also be taken into account. Piaget's studies are concerned with inanimate physical objects. Psychoanalysts are concerned with the infant's and child's relationship to highly cathected animate (human) objects. The question arises whether the child's relationship to the two different kinds of object can be regarded as the same. Psychoanalysts would decisively reject such a view. Piaget himself recognized that a human object was for the child "the most interesting cognitive object, the most alive, the most unexpected . . . an object which implies a multitude of exchanges in which cognitive as well as affective factors play a role" (Piaget, 1954, p. 66, Gouin-Décarie, 1965, p. 211). Gouin-Décarie, in her study of "object permanence" of libidinally cathected human objects, says,

Let us note that the attempt to verify psychoanalytic data by means of Piagetian data and vice versa requires extreme caution. One must remember that the objectivation of the human being, and thus at the same time the representation of that person, *precedes* (even according to Piaget) the objectivation of the inanimate object. It does so not only because the human being forms the emotional object *par excellence* but also because, strictly from the point of view of intelligence, persons are at the crosspoint of numerous assimilatory and accomodatory schemata (Gouin-Décarie, 1965, p. 210, italics added).

These and other essential differences between Piaget's views and those of psychoanalysts (which make it difficult to graft one theory simply on the other) have been excellently and extensively discussed by several authors, notably by Wolff (1960), and Gouin-Décarie (1965). Selma Fraiberg (1969) has suggested one way of trying to resolve the differences but has also clearly spelled out the problems involved. She points out that much of the confusion and many of the disagreements among psychoanalysts about the possible ages at which mental representations are thought to arise are based on semantic confusion and differences in terminology. A great difficulty in discussing Abelin's model is that he does not mention these problems, so that one does not know what he means by his attempt to "span the gap between psychology and psychoanalysis" (Abelin, 1980, p. 166).

The psychoanalytic view of the development of the self-image and later the self-concept is of a gradually developing process (Fenichel, 1945; Jacobson, 1964) in which many body and self-images come to be organized in the course of time into a self-representation (Sandler & Rosenblatt, 1962). Many psychoanalytic authors make a distinction between the "experiential" and the "conceptual" self (Noy, 1979). According to Noy, any inner representation of the self must include both aspects, the self perceived from within (self-feeling or experience) and from without. From the developmental point of view, the experiential aspects of the self will always precede the conceptual aspects. In Abelin's model, there seems to be no room for such early experiential aspects of the self, arising as they do from the inner world, which is thought by Piaget and Abelin not to exist.

Whatever differences exist among psychoanalysts about the timing of these inner processes and events, the terms that they use are usually defined within a specific theoretical framework, which makes it possible to know what they mean. Abelin, using terms drawn from a metapsychological framework (e.g., the terms libidinal object and identification) within the framework of another theory (Piaget), makes it difficult to know precisely what he means. Terms that are defined are *redefined* in Piagetian terms (e.g., "libidinal cathexis" is defined as "an added feature of some recognitive schemata"). The term thus loses its psychoanalytic meaning—that is, the investment of the mental image/representation of an object with a particular form of drive energy. Abelin's use of the term identification is also unclear. It is used interchangably with self-image, but a problem arises in trying to imagine what the identifications of the Madonna constellation consist of, because these are supposed to occur at a time when no mental images exist. Thus the psychoanalytic definition of the term cannot apply. Similar problems arise when one attempts to understand the terms "true" or "core" self-image. They simply are not defined.

In psychoanalytic theory, a triadic situation is not thought to be essential for the development of the self-concept. Abelin's insistence on the triangular basis for the development of the self-concept comes from Piaget's idea that all mental images, at this stage of development, arise out of imitation. Children must therefore *see* themselves in the wishes of the others—that is, experience themselves through another person in triadic constellations. (Abelin's emphasis on the visual aspects of the triangular situation raise questions about the development of the self-concept in blind children (see Fraiberg & Freedman, 1964; Burlingham, 1972). It has also been stressed by Greenacre (1958) and Jacobson (1964) that situations involving comparisons between the self and rival sharpen and aid the development of feelings of *identity* (which must obviously be related in some way to a self-concept). However, both authors appear to be talking about later stages of development.

Several questions also arise about the content of Abelin's model. The Madonna constellation is described largely from the point of view of the girl. The boy's identifications with the nurturing mother in this early triangle are brushed aside as being of no great importance because of the rapid shift thought to take place in the primary attachment from the mother to the father before the primal constellation. Abelin seems to underestimate the strength and importance of these early identifications with the mother. Such identifications are by no means incompatible with strong masculine identifications and wishes—a clinical observation of which "Little Hans" (Freud, 1909) again provides an excellent example. (See also Ross, 1971; Gurwitt, 1979; and the discussion in this chapter on fathering as a developmental process.)

In contrast to the discussion of the Madonna constellation, the primal constellation is considered largely from the point of view of the boy in Abelin's model, and the corresponding processes in the girl remain obscure. What does it mean to say that the boy's identification with the father in the primal constellation is a "full-blown" identification, whereas that of the girl with the father in the same situation is not? Is the implication that the boy identifies with the father's *person* (and therefore gender) and the girl only with the father's *wish* for the mother (without reference to gender)?

Another problem to which I have already referred emerges in the conclusions Abelin draws concerning the importance of the father for the development of gender identity in girls. He maintains that the father only becomes important for gender identity during the girl's Oedipal phase. Clinical evidence, however, suggests that the opposite is true. The fact that the girl's self-image is implicitly feminine (through her primary identification with her mother) does not mean that the little girl does not need continuous pre-Oedipal interaction with a male person (usually the father) in order to *define* her gender identity (Kleeman, 1967, 1973). It is my contention that it is precisely such continuous and affectionate interaction with a father (or father substitute) that makes it possible for her to direct her Oedipal wishes toward him in the Oedipal situation. There is much clinical evidence that little girls who have had little regular contact with males in their pre-Oedipal years (or who have fathers who are libidinally unavailable) have great difficulties in entering the Oedipal phase, even when a male becomes emotionally available. It is perhaps significant that Abelin quotes only psychological and not psychoanalytic (i.e., clinical) evidence to support his argument on this point.

In commenting on Abelin's model, Rotmann (1978, 1980) takes a different point of view—one that shows dissatisfaction with Abelin's understanding of the nature of the infant's affective world. Rotmann questions the contention that the infant and toddler are only capable of having purely one-to-one relationships to objects. He refers to Winnicott's descriptions of a 7-month-old infant's growing ability to relate to two things (and two people) at the same time. "This step in the infant's development, by which he becomes able to manage his relationship to two people who are important to him (which fundamentally means to both his parents), at one and the same time, is a very important one . . . According to my observations this important step is first taken within the first year of life" (Winnicott, 1941, p. 65). Rotmann argues that the infant born into a world where both mother and father are present develops from the very beginning in a family constellation in which the basic patterning of relationships is at least triadic (and may be even more complex). The child probably becomes aware of this fact very soon after developing beyond the symbiotic phase. He considers that the small child both registers and internalizes this perception in some way within the first year and that this process also forms the basis of the early identifications with both parents.

This basic triangular ground plan or framework of relationships within the average family prepares the way intrapsychically for the development of later triangular situations involving envy and jealousy and thus for the Oedipal triangular situation. Above all, Rotmann thinks that the infant is a much more social being than Abelin would have us believe. He proposes that what Abelin calls "early triangulation" is the inherent basic patterning of relationships within the average family that forms the inevitable background to normal development and thus should not be experienced suddenly as a conflict situation. Rotmann also quotes Winnicott's remark that "there is no such thing as an infant." Winnicott means, of course, that one can never consider the infant without considering the attendant parental care. "Father, mother and infant, all three living together" (Winnicott, 1965, p. 43).

Rotmann agrees with Loewald (1951), Mahler and Gosliner (1955), Abelin (1971), and Burlingham (1973) that the father is of the utmost importance in helping the child to differentiate and individuate from the mother, but he adds the observation that the father, through his relationship with the mother, may also function as a living demonstration for the child that it is possible to have an intimate relationship with her and nevertheless retain one's autonomy. This means that the parental relationship (when it is a reasonably good and communicative one) can serve as a reassurance to the child that fears of "reengulfment" are unfounded (see also Loch & Jappe, 1974). Individuality need not mean disloyalty to the mother—she "permits" the father to be separate from her, and nevertheless continues to value him.

In essence, therefore, Rotmann disagrees with Abelin's views regarding the nature of the child's interactions with his or her world in the first 15 months of life. He quotes the work of developmental psychologists who have shown and emphasized that infants are far more active in their interactions with the environment than was formerly thought to be the case. In particular, the infant's capacity to make and respond to fine discriminations, considered together with the small child's special responsiveness in social situations, leads Rotmann to regard it as likely that some kind of internalization of triangular situations and interactions (involving important libidinal objects) takes place long before 16 to 18 months of age and that this occurs as part of the normal developmental process.

James Herzog (1979) attempts to particularize the more specific contributions of the father to the psychological development of the child in the pre-Oedipal years by looking at the fantasy, play, and dreams of children at different developmental stages, whose fathers were either completely or partially absent because of divorce. At all stages a predominant feature of this material is its aggressive content—an observation that applies particularly to boys between 18 and 60 months of age. In girls a similar preponderance of and preoccupation with aggression and aggressive themes was found at a later age and developmental stage—from 60 to 84 months.

On the basis of such observations, Herzog speculates that the father functions (from the viewpoint and experience of child) as a modulator of aggressive drive and fantasy. A corollary to this is that the father's absence during early phases of development may have specific long-term consequences, affecting the ego's capacity to deal with and control aggressive feelings and impulses. The observed age differences between expressions of aggression in boys and girls also suggest a specific vulnerability on the part of boys to such an early father loss. It is clear from the material and from the examples that Herzog quotes that the small boy experiences the loss of the father as a disruption of *his own* control of his aggressive drives. (From the clinical material cited, this is not true of girls.) Herzog reports on a group of over 70 children, referred to a children's clinic because of symptoms (sleep disturbances, anxiety states, depressive withdrawal reactions) they developed in the weeks and months following the separation and/or divorce of the parents. He was able to distinguish clearly three groups based on age and sex, and demonstrated strikingly the special sensitivity and susceptibility of the small boy to the partial or total loss of his father. All of the 12 children who were between the age of 12 and 28 months were boys. Of the 30 children between the ages of 36 and 60 months, 28 were boys, and of the 30 in the oldest group—60 to 84 months of age—16 were boys and 14 were girls.

From Herzog's clinical material (some of the children were seen in psychotherapy), it is the boys who were the more outspoken in expressing the need for the father as a controller of the child's own aggression. All the children were preoccupied with the disruption of the family unit—an external disruption that severely disrupted the inner life of the child. Although Herzog believes that the attendant family stress may have produced some of the children's problems, the loss of the father is specifically linked in the child's experience with the emergence of aggressive feelings, fantasies, and impulses, and the father's return is considered by the child to be restitutive. The emotional state of the mother, also left by her husband and feeling to some extent bereft and overtaxed by her situation, probably plays a part in the child's feeling that the return of the father will restore the family to normal. This cannot be the only reason, however, since Herzog observed that these reactions occurred in children of mothers who were competent, proficient, and perhaps even relieved by the dissolution of the marriage.

Turning his attention to the question of why boys should be more vulnerable to the loss of the father at these ages and developmental stages, Herzog postulates that boys have a greater aggressive endowment at birth than girls do and consequently a greater subsequent need for help in its management—help in the form of greater external control. The fact of gender similarity is clearly important as well. From the point of view of the boy's experience, it is his "sameness" with the father that he stresses and that makes it impossible for the mother to replace the father. Boys expressed the need to manage a mutual concern with the father as well as the need to "be shown how" (which Herzog considers to be an important aspect of the child's pre-Oedipal relationship with the father). One boy maintained that only the return of his father could help him with his problems because "he is like the boy. He can, 'cause he knows the boy. He is not a Mommy." It seems that girls, whatever their need for the father at this age and stage may be, do not need him in this particular sense at this particular time.

In another investigation into the sleep disturbances (night terrors) of 18 to 28-month-old boys drawn from the youngest group in the study just mentioned Herzog (1980) shows that it is the child's fear of something *inside* himself that threatens to overwhelm him and get out of control that leads to the specific longing for the father that Herzog calls "father hunger." The mother's attempts to comfort the boy, because of the "dread of reengulfment" in the ongoing struggle for individuation at this age, may make things worse and add to the boy's feeling that only the presence of the father can protect him from inner and outer dangers. In the one 6½-year-old girl whose clinical material is presented, the child's reaction to her parents' divorce is depressive in nature with a marked tendency to blame herself for events. Such material shows that in the girl too the basic conflicts are concerned with aggressive drives and impulses, but they are dealt with in a different way—in this case directed inward.

It is Herzog's thesis that in a normally functioning marriage in which the parents relate in an adequate way to one another, the bond between the parents (which provides an outlet for affects and impulses on an adult–adult basis) acts as a protective shield for the child who might otherwise become (as often happens in unhappy or unsatisfactory marriages) the recipient of affects normally absorbed by the marriage partner.

Such affects are potentially dangerous to the child when expressed in a parent–child interaction. When they are discharged in adult–adult interaction, the parents are usually able to perform their care-taking functions and protect the child from traumatic exposure to the adult world. When this protective shield breaks down in a divorce (or long before this in a disintegrating relationship), the child may be confronted too early and disruptively with an adult reality. When the one parent does leave, the remaining parent may also experience the loss of this protective shield and be more likely to focus inappropriate libidinal and aggressive impulses and their derivatives on the children (Anthony, 1974). Such interactions could be another source of the children's pervasive anxiety about control and the lack of it, especially control of aggressive fantasies and impulses. In all the children, Herzog found evidence that the father was seen as the modulator of aggression and that his absence produced an "unmodulated" state of affairs. Herzog points out that although his clinical material may well be interpreted differently by different investigators, the fact that the children themselves make intrapsychic associations between the loss of the father and "aggressive discontrol" presents us with the child's "intrapsychic truth" deserving consideration. In any case, analysts deal with such examples of "intrapsychic causality" most of the time.

The Role of the Father in Psychoanalytic Speculations Concerning the Development of Gender Identity

Sexual identity, when considered from the psychological rather than biological point of view, consists of the concept of the self as being male or female. This concept is made up of the child's genital experiences and their extensions in relationships with others. The question of how such a gender concept comes into being, how early it is established, and when it reaches a relatively stable form has preoccupied psychoanalysts (see Ross, 1979b). It is generally agreed that bodily experiences involving genital sensations contribute to a gradually developing awareness of sexual identity (Kestenburg, 1975). In addition,

Grossman (1976) suggests that the child's awareness of genital differences acts as an important organizer of genital experience. Roiphe (1968), Kleeman (1965, 1966, 1977), and Galenson and Roiphe (1977, 1979) have all demonstrated the existence of an early (pre-Oedipal) genital phase thought to organize early genital experience. Within the first year of life, boys and girls begin to stimulate themselves genitally in what is thought to be at first part of a general bodily exploration. Galenson and Roiphe (1979) consider this early genital play to be significant in the developing sense of sexual identity. A second phase of genital stimulation, characterized by greater intensity and what appears to be a more focused pleasure, develops during the second year and overlaps with what the authors call an anal phase and urinary organization of behavior arising independently of the initiation of toilet training. Intense curiosity about urinary and anal behavior in others is one hallmark of this behavior, which contributes to the discovery and awareness of genital differences. The perception of genital difference may lead, especially in girls (but also in boys with a disturbed developmental history), to severe castration anxiety (Edgcumbe & Burgner, 1975).

Such reactions may have a specially damaging effect on the girl's developing relationship to her father during the second year and in this way contribute to disturbances in her growing gender identity. Girls showing less severe castration anxiety developed a new, intense, and erotically tinged relationship with the father. Those manifesting severe reactions, however, clung ambivalently to the mother, were unable to separate, and developed a fear of strangers. Here the shift of erotic attachment to the father did not take place. Galenson and Roiphe (1979) consider that these early genital experiences are influenced by conscious and unconscious parental attitudes, but they state that it is exceedingly difficult to demonstrate how such factors shape the infant's self-concept as male or female.

Psychoanalytic investigations of sexual deviations and so-called gender disorders have concerned themselves with the contribution made by conscious and unconscious parental attitudes and behavior to profound disturbances of gender identity. A detailed description of various clinical conditions and hypotheses concerning the parents' (especially the father's) role would be too extensive here and not directly relevant. Readers are referred to the review volumes by Rosen (1979) and Karasu and Socarides (1979) in which various theoretical positions are presented and discussed. Here it is sufficient to state that all investigators agree on the importance of the parents' pathological influence on the child, whereby the unconscious factors in the very early mother–child interaction are thought by some to be crucial (Stoller, 1975). However, all psychoanalytic investigators stress the role and position of the father in the total family constellation. This consideration avoids the mistake of looking at mother–child and father–child interaction in isolation. The nature of the mother–father relationship is considered a critical factor in the parent–child interaction. In most descriptions of such families, the father, usually as a result of his own pathology, is thought to fail in his function of protecting the child against the mother's pathological influence (Stoller, 1975; Rosen, 1979; Socarides, 1968; Volkan, 1979). Attempts made so far to isolate highly specific family constellations and unconscious attitudes (e.g., in transsexual conditions,) have not been successful (see Volkan, 1979, for a review). It is perhaps important to mention that although the work discussed has been carried out by psychoanalysts, the clinical evidence they consider is not drawn from analytic work with patients but from interview material. A common finding is that fathers who are especially passive (and thus presumably insecure in their own gender identity) fail both as models of masculine identification for their male children and as protectors of children of both sexes against the mother's pathology.

This touches on a point made by Greenson (1968). He notes that the majority of gender disorders are found among men and suggests that this may reflect a general "uneasiness" about gender in males resulting from the male child's difficult developmental task of resolving his primary identification with his mother. Whether the male child can give up his primary libidinal tie (and its resulting identifications) with the mother and identify with his father will depend partly on the personality and behavior of both parents. Anna Freud (1965) points out that the mother's attitude to the father is also important to the child—she can facilitate her son's identification with his father by admiring his developing masculinity. Greenson's (1966) account of his treatment of a transvestite boy provides an interesting clinical example of some of these problems.

An observation of Anna Freud (1951) might serve as a cautionary reminder that not all of a boy's masculine behavior can be explained fully in terms of identificatory processes. In describing the behavior of boys in the Hampstead nurseries at the time of the transition from the anal to the phallic developmental stages, she reports on a "puzzling change" in their attitude and behavior toward their nursery "mothers";

They developed masculine qualities and a protective, often overbearing, sometimes indulgently affectionate attitude toward the woman—an attitude which under normal conditions would invariably have been classified as a close imitation of the father and an identification with him. These children lived without fathers, and, in the cases referred to here, had had no opportunity to watch their fathers' attitude toward the mother.

She suggests that such behavior may be regarded as a "manifestation of the phallic trends, with or without identification with the father" (p. 161), although she adds that outside stimulation in the form of the occasional presence of men or other fathers cannot be ruled out completely. If such behavior were indeed the result of occasional, chance observations of men with whom the children had no strong emotional tie, it would tend to reinforce Anna Freud's speculation that there are some forms of behavior that seem not to originate in but be "merely stimulated and developed, by life experience." This viewpoint—a familiar one to psychoanalysts—suggests that in some of the more extreme gender disorders a specific drive component (a constitutional factor) is collaborating with the early environmental influences already mentioned.

The nature of female sexual development is currently a vigorously disputed topic within psychoanalysis (Blum, 1977; Edgcumbe, 1976; Fast, 1978, 1979) There is a clearly discernible tendency to question earlier assumptions about the conflictful origins of femininity, and several authors postulate a state of "primary femininity" (Stoller, 1977; Kleeman, 1977), a "primary, constitutional feminine disposition" (Edgcumbe & Burgner, 1975), a "first genital" or "proto-genital phase" (Parens et al., 1977), or a "primary female genital organization" (Fast, 1979). Such suggestions show an unwillingness to regard the small girl's feminine wishes and attitudes as being only reactive to pre-Oedipal and Oedipal disappointments. Fast states, "When the girl becomes aware of sex difference she develops a complex sense of femininity and herself as feminine in relation to a concurrently developing sense of masculinity attributed to males and experienced in relation to them" (Fast, 1979, p. 443). In such a view, disturbances in the development of female gender identity are no longer considered to be an inherent part of female sexual development but rather as secondary phenomena arising out of family constellations in which the father is either absent or unresponsive, and/or the mother is a poor object for feminine identification.

McDougall (1979) discusses female homosexuals in psychoanalytic treatment. All these women have profoundly disturbed relationships with their fathers as well as with their mothers. McDougall shows that the consciously detested and denigrated father representation in such patients is a defensive structure behind which lies "the image of the father who has *failed in his specific parental role"* —that is, he has failed to protect her from a "devouring or controlling, omnipotent maternal image" (p. 215). "Behind the conscious wish to eliminate or denigrate the father, all of my homosexual patients revealed narcissistic wounds linked to this image of the *indifferent* father" (p. 217), and later, "The father has become lost as a love object, and equally lost as a representative of security and strength, which bars the way to future genital relations" (p. 218; see also Socarides, 1968). The mother is thought to contribute as well, through her attitude to the father, to his destruction as an inner authority figure for the girl.

Such evidence supports the view that for a healthy female gender identity to develop, more is needed than an identification with the mother. True gender identity can be experienced only by the child in relationships with the opposite sex. This means that the sense of female gender must become extended to include wishes, fantasies and impulses directed toward boys and men (see also Blum's remarks in Clower, 1970). In my opinion this vital extension of the experience of being feminine is probably only fully possible on the basis of a secure, loving, and reasonably continuous relationship with a father throughout the pre-Oedipal phases. The suggestion by various psychoanalysts (Stoller, 1975; Abelin 1977; Greenson, 1968) that a pre-Oedipal relationship with the father is less important for girls than for boys is questionable. It may be that in emphasizing the boy's need to identify with the father at this time, these authors overlook the rather different needs of the girl during these developmental phases (i.e., her need for a loving tie to a responsive father who can act as a foil to her emerging femininity). This would be ideally a relationship in which the girl would "discover" and experience the first extensions of her femininity in a "safe" relationship with an admiring and responsive father. I also feel that such a relationship prepares the way for the development of the positive Oedipus complex and its attendant wishes directed toward the father. It is difficult to conceive of a girl developing a healthy and secure gender identity without such a gradually developing awareness of what her femininity is and means to her. Fast (1979) in her discussion of gender differentiation expresses a similar point of view. She suggests that as the little girl establishes her gender identity she begins to relate to each parent in specifically gender terms—to her mother as a same-sex person with whom she can identify as a woman and to her father as specifically male in relation to herself as specifically female. "These new orientations provide contexts within which she practises and elaborates the differentiated notions of femininity and masculinity she is developing" (p. 451).

Fathering, Fatherhood, and the Developmental Process of Becoming a Father

Paul (1970) begins his essay on parental empathy with the letter that Kafka wrote to his father at the age of 36. The painful feelings aroused in the reader by this description of the "frightening gulf between father and son," the missed opportunities, and the failure of empathy and understanding no doubt reflect the universality of such experiences. Paul believes that one reason for the ubiquity of this lack of understanding between parents and their children lies in the "insufficient attention parents give to their own emotional histories" (pp. 343).

Psychoanalysts have turned their attention increasingly since 1960 to the developmental aspect of becoming and being a parent (Benedek, 1959, 1970; Anthony & Benedek, 1970; Kestenberg, 1975). More recently, as part of the growing interest in the father, attempts have been made to trace and understand the specific developmental processes involved in fathering and fatherhood (Benedek, 1970; Ross, 1975, 1977, 1979a, 1979b; Gurwitt 1976; Herzog, 1979). Benedek (1970) points out that the emotional relationship a father has with his child contains at least two identifications that complement one another: an identification with the child (on the basis of the father's own childhood), which ideally facilitates empathy, and an identification with his own father, which also reflects the culturally established norms for fathers raising their children. Benedek emphasizes that beneath the father's mature "role" within his family, "there is a flow of repressed memories and emotions of the father's developmental experiences which may become mobilized in response to the child's development" (p. 173). The boy's development toward sexual maturity and his full male gender identity is shown not only in the acquisition of a secure heterosexuality that remains unthreatened by the awareness and expression of nurturing needs, but also in an acceptance of its consequences: by becoming a father. This extension of male gender identity to include paternal identity, to accept responsibility as a child's protector and provider, and to function with empathic "fatherliness" is considered a process with a long developmental history having its roots in the father's own childhood (Ross, 1979b).

Considerations of the factors held to be important in the male's psychological preparation for becoming a father usually begin with the well-known psychoanalytic observations of the small boy's wish to have and *to bear* children. ("Little Hans" is again a good example of this; Freud, 1909.) A bisexual constitution and developmental events and processes reaching back to pre-Oedipal stages are thought to give rise to this wish (Boehm, 1930; Jacobson, 1950; Van der Leeuw, 1958). Such wishes are doomed to be disappointed and, in many men, their frustration results in an intense (if often denied) envy of women's active procreative functions. (See Ross, 1977, and Jaffe, 1977, for extensive reviews of this literature.) Ross (1975) suggests that a boy's disapointment at his "barrenness" may be appeased to some extent and his generative and creative urges partly expressed by his identification with a father perceived as nurturing and procreative. *An assumption of the father's role in reproduction and relation to caretaking helps an adult man come to terms with his hitherto repressed and disquieting "maternal desires"* (p. 797; italics in original). Ross also points out that the earlier tendency to regard the boy's wish to have and to take care of children only as a manifestation of the wishes of the negative Oedipus complex has given way to a recognition of the active and progressive aspects of these procreative strivings. This can be seen in the organizing role these wishes have in the evolution of male identity.

Ross (1977), using Anna Freud's concept of developmental lines, attempts to trace such a line of generative and procreative development in boys—a line that will result in a sense of paternal identity (see also Ross, 1979b). He particularly stresses the fluidity of the child's pre-Oedipal attitudes. The boy moves from wishes and concepts of being a baby to having a baby, from being cared for by a parent to being a parent. Such fantasies, verbalized or acted out in play, sooner or later come into conflict with the boy's growing awareness of his gender identity and his identification with his father. Throughout middle childhood, however, such nurturing behavior may remain important for the boy and be expressed in the care of plants and animals. In this phase the father is experienced as a "mentor." Ross stresses that a good relationship with a father through latency is important in helping the boy discover his skills and talents and explore and experiment with the world. This relationship is especially valuable for the boy after the conflicts of the Oedipal phase and can help the child engender a male identity that is caring and fatherly and not dominated by aggressive features. Although adolescent sons and daughters, in their attempts to free themselves psychologically from their parents, tend to repudiate them, Ross thinks that it is important that the parents do not withdraw from communication (see also Anthony, 1970). Parents provide their adolescent children with a foil on which they can try out their newfound sense of identity. More recently, Ross (1979a, 1979b) has focused on the adult crisis in paternity and the father's role in the development and consolidation of his child's gender identity.

Several analysts, among them Benedek (1959), Kestenberg (1975), Anthony (1970), and Ross (1979a), regard the process of becoming a parent, mother or father, as a developmental phase or task, often involving a "developmental crisis." Parenthood confronts mothers and fathers with many internal and external adjustments and adaptations, and as Herzog (1979) points out, men approach fatherhood with very different attitudes and degrees of involvement in the process. He thinks that the fact that fathers are "once-removed" from pregnancy, compared with the "psychobiological" involvement of the mother, gives them an element of choice (which mothers do not have) as to the intensity of their participation in the pregnancy process. In his study of the fathers of prematurely born infants, Herzog (1978) distinguished three groups of fathers according to their degree of participation in their wives' pregnancy. Such emotional participation correlated (not surprisingly) with the degree to which the men were involved in an ongoing empathic relationship with their wives. In addition, however, the degree of contact they had with their own feelings and fantasies also correlated with their involvement. Herzog's study is "psychoanalytically oriented" rather than psychoanalytic. However, he feels that under the impact of the emotions aroused by the birth of premature infants, many fathers were able to reveal aspects of their fantasy lives that otherwise might not have become visible in situations of this kind. In the "most attuned" group, Herzog observed a powerful incentive on the part of the fathers during their wives' pregnancies to seek solutions to the conflicts in their relationships with their own fathers. Such attempts were not always successful, and the fathers who had failed "to make peace" with their own fathers showed the greatest internal difficulties in the latter half of the pregnancy. One father expressed it this way: "The way I hook up with my old man determines how the kid will hook up with me." The belief that to be a good father one must have had a good father revived efforts to establish contact with the old "good" pre-Oedipal father, the "guide and mentor" of the latency years, the father who helped the boy see "what a man is and what he does."

In those fathers who were "least attuned" to their own feelings or to their wives, fatherhood seemed "irrelevant or accidental" and there was no sense of an unbroken, caretaking, developmental line from childhood. These fathers were all "father hungry"—that is, they had all suffered the lack of a father. Herzog states that if one is always searching for a father, it interferes with the ability to be one.

Gurwitt's (1976) account of the analytical treatment of a young man whose wife became pregnant and delivered a baby girl while he was in analysis provides detailed analytical material about the way in which the pregnancy was experienced and worked through as a "developmental challenge." Gurwitt doubts that there is enough clinical evidence to support the contention that parenthood is a "developmental phase" in the usual sense of that term. On the basis of his analytic material, however, he is able to show several "stages" in his patient's intrapsychic reactions to his wife's pregnancy, indicating that it could be regarded as a period of preparation for fatherhood. Gurwitt divides his patient's reactions in the roughly 12-month period prior to the birth of his daughter into the stages of getting ready, conception, bridging and the early months, mid-pregnancy, and coming to term(s). The *fact* of pregnancy mobilized in this young man a preoccupation with his relation to his own parents and *their* role for him as models of parenting. He stated, "I am not yet through being a son, let alone ready to become a father" (p. 255). He could later begin to work on his relationship to his father in his analysis, and in the final phase of the pregnancy he was able to talk to his ailing father about themselves and their relationship.

Gurwitt's clear and detailed account shows that the relationship of a father to his child begins long before birth. Impregnation and pregnancy constituted a developmental challenge for the prospective father that resulted in internal upheavals and change, the outcome of which was critical to the whole family. It seems that a state of adult equilibrium—shown in the choices already made regarding sexual identity, career, and marital partner—may be severely shaken by the prospect of becoming a father. Gurwitt compares the internal upheaval in his patient to the developmental crisis of early adolescence (Ritvo, 1971) and describes the pregnancy and the child-to-be as "new organizing foci" for his patient. The patient's "preparation for the pregnancy and the pregnancy itself initiated a major reworking of the past and current relationships with his mother, father, siblings and wife, as well as a shift and resynthesis of his sense of self. All of these coalesced to color the psychological atmosphere into which his daughter was born" (p. 263).

The result was a father who, at the birth of his infant, was intrapsychically ready to enter into a relationship with her and to offer himself as an important libidinal object from the very beginning of the child's life. The gender of the child was very important to this father. He wanted a girl and was relieved when a daughter was born. Benedek too (1970) makes the point that Gurwitt makes in this connection: the patient did not want to have a boy because having a son might reactivate the old conflicts he had had with his father. Gurwitt emphasizes that more such information, obtainable only from the analytic method, is needed to assess these aspects of fathering and fatherhood. In this particular patient, the period of prospective fatherhood coincided with the terminal phase of his analysis and the mental and physical deterioration of his own father—mutually influencing factors that no doubt colored the working through of themes described, in a special way, in this analysis. Gurwitt concludes, "Whatever the reasons for the past silence on fathers may have been, it appears that we are at last beginning to recognize the significance of the early role of the father. To gain a better understanding of that role, we must turn our attention to the early developmental process involved in becoming a father. Prospective fatherhood is a critical stage in that development" (p. 268).

Fathers in Latency and Adolescence

Kestenberg (1970) describes latency as "the period of part-time parenthood." She is referring to the fact that the child's world in latency begins to be extended beyond the immediate family. A normal child of 6 or 7 years has reached a level of intrapsychic organization, physical and emotional maturity, and independence, which permits a relative degree of autonomy. The conflicts of the Oedipal phase and their partial resolutions (Blos, 1962), together with the profound reorganization of psychic structure to which they give rise, are followed by a period in which the child is less troubled by drives and less engrossed in inner conflicts. The latency child is often described as being "desexualized." New cognitive abilities and a predominance of secondary process over primary process thinking and functioning enable him or her to adapt to the demands made in school. Nevertheless, the latency child is still young enough to be very dependent on parents for emotional support and nurturance.

As Anthony and Benedek (1970) point out, parenthood is a process of progressive adaptation. Latency tests the parents' capacity to adapt to the widening world of the child, to share their influence with teachers and others, and thus help the child develop an increasing sense of personal identity and adapt to an environment outside the home and family. Kestenberg (1970) points out how difficult it is to conceptualize the "tasks" of parenthood in latency and adolescence, compared with earlier developmental stages. She thinks that this is because parents are no longer responding to the relatively clean-cut libidinal phases of early childhood but to an increasingly complex evolving personality organization. She thinks that parents' memories of their own latency phase and adolescence lead to their responding with reaction formations built on their own experiences instead of responding to their individual child.

Benedek (1970) makes the point that when children go to school many parents become apprehensive. School means that the child's behavior and performance in work and play will be exposed to a comparative scrutiny that makes some parents feel exposed. Their own self-esteem may be threatened. Clinical experience shows how the child's self-esteem can also be drastically affected during latency by a nagging and fault-finding mother or an overcritical father—parents who feel personally exposed by the imperfections of their children. Latency, however, is also the age of the "family romance" (Burlingham, 1945)—those daydreams that reveal children's progressive disillusionment with their parents—especially fathers—when they begin to compare them with admired people in the outside world. Children begin to correct their earlier overestimation of their parents and begin to see them in a more reasonable and realistic light. It seems important that the latency father should react tolerantly to the child's growing detachment, objectivity, and reality testing. To my knowledge there are no analytic contributions that examine this aspect of the latency father–child relationship from the point of view of the father's reactions and their consequences.

A striking observation in examining the scattered literature on parents in latency is the amalgamation of the "mothers" and "fathers" of the preceding developmental phases into the "parents," as though the desexualization of the latency child has resulted in the merging of the gender-differentiated mother and father into desexualized parents (a process that is again reversed in adolescence, when mothers and fathers are again described as responding, in differing ways, to the emerging sexuality of their pubertal children). Specific statements about latency fathers (or mothers for that matter) are relatively rare. One exception to this is the attention given the role of the father in encouraging and promoting his son's interest in sport and the development of bodily skills. Such statements usually refer to the father–son relationship, although we know that such a relationship between father and daughter can also be extremely important in latency and is frequently observed. Similarly close contact between fathers and sons and fathers and daughters may arise from a sharing of intellectual interests or hobbies. In my experience, it is important for the father to convey to his daughter that such interests are by no means incompatible with her developing feminine identity. Many investigators comment on the "guide and mentor" aspect of the father–child relationship in latency—a relationship that can only exist meaningfully when the latency father spends time with and shows interest in his children. One aspect of latency that also seems important is the question of the child's contact with the father's work. This is an area that has not been extensively considered, although some commentators mention that few children have direct contact with their fathers' work. How the child's attitudes about work are influenced by the father and what he conveys about what he does has not been investigated.

Anna Freud (1965) points out that the child's superego requires external support from the parents throughout latency and adolescence in order to reinforce the still insufficiently consolidated inner controls. Bettelheim's (1976) discussion of the fairy tale "The Frog King" gives a good example of this function performed by the father during late latency. The princess, who makes promises that she does not take seriously and later does not want to keep, is made to keep them by her father. He thus helps her to take a step toward an acceptance of moral responsibility, which leads into adolescence and the adult (sexual) world.

The advent of puberty "resexualizes" the child's image for the parents who usually (at least in our Western culture) react to the impending signs of adolescence with a certain amount of apprehension. Both parents show a preoccupation with the child's sexual life. Fathers are thought to maintain a greater distance from their childrens' bodies during latency, and this attitude tends to persist into adolescence. Anthony (1970) regards it as essential that parents respond to their adolescent children as individuals and not on the basis of "adolescent stereotypes." In his view, adolescence can be seen as a learning process in which the adolescent is constantly practicing the adult role under the experienced eye of a friendly and encouraging adult. Fathers and mothers should try to retain a relationship that the adolescent experiences as basically helpful and trustworthy. This means that fathers in particular should temper their reactions to what Anna Freud (1958) has described as the "uncompromising adolescent" and Peter Blos (1962) as "adolescent totalism." The father's own maturity will obviously play an important part in such reactions. Analytic literature contains many references to fathers' reactions that are considered potentially dangerous to the adolescent (e.g., fathers who are overcritical, jealous, and interfering in the relationships that their daughters have with young men—in some cases to the point that normal heterosexual friendships are sabotaged; fathers who become overcompetitive and critical of their sons and who react with hostility to a son's growing maturity, virility and occupational success).

Anthony (1970) points out that one way to retain a relationship with an adolescent (and with the child who is lost to the parents in adolescence) is to help the adolescent process of separation and individuation to its culmination in the adolescent's entry into the adult world. Ideally, this enables parents and their children to achieve a relationship in which they take a mature pleasure in each other as people. For the parent, this constitutes a "rediscovery" of the child as an adult object—a satisfaction only "earned" by parents to have "gracefully relinquished" the child during the adolescent process.

It is obvious that a great deal of work needs to be done analytically to try to understand the father, his place, and functions in the life of latency and adolescent children. The analyses of fathers with children at these ages and stages would provide more information about how the father himself sees his role. Studies in late latency and adolescence of children of divorced parents (Wallerstein & Kelly, 1974; Anthony, 1974) are useful in showing, through the children's disappointment, how they would ideally like their fathers to *be*. Certainly from all the available evidence, the *active* presence of the father throughout latency and adolescence is experienced by the children as essential for their well-being. One analyst working with adolescents and their families also regards the presence of the father as crucial for the mother—to step in and protect her against the often very aggressive attacks of adolescent sons and daughters (Sheila Mason, personal communication).

Finally, Benedek (1970) has a word to say about the father of the adult who has emerged from the child. She describes how the wheel turns full circle. The father, faced with the conflicts arising out of his own declining powers, may need a son's or daughter's generous and loving attitude to maintain his self-esteem, just as his children earlier were helped in their development through the father's love. In this way the father may ultimately come to feel dependent on his children. Benedek discusses how an economic dependency, in addition to an emotional one, can increase a father's need for respect and his sensitivity to real or imagined slights. She also points out how difficult it is, especially for a son, to empathize with the emotions of his once powerful father, who in his decline is dependent on his love, respect, and admiration. Benedek regards this process as demonstrating the significance of parenthood in the identity of the parent.

SUMMARY

This review examines the psychoanalytic literature from 1975-1980 in detail, following a brief statement of Freud's and earlier psychoanalytic views on the meaning and functions of the father.

The more recent psychoanalytic theories stress the importance of the father in aiding the process of psychic differentiation and individuation in the child. Early identifications with the father, based on the child's early (pre-Oedipal) love and admiration for him (as described by Freud), are thought to strengthen ego development and reality testing and help the child to separate (individuate) from the mother. During the toddler's struggle for psychic independence the father is thought to offer the child a relationship that is less ambivalent than that to the mother. Psychoanalysts therefore consider the presence of *both* parents to be essential for promoting healthy personality growth. The absence of one parent increases the likelihood that the child may become the target of affects which belong more appropriately in an adult–adult relationship.

Several theories pay attention to a specific aspect of the individuation process—the development of gender identity. The controversial "tripartite model of early triangulation" which links the development of a self-concept to that of gender identity, is described and discussed in detail. The tendency in psychoanalytic writings to emphasize the importance of the pre-Oedipal relationship to the father in the boy's developing gender identity and the relative neglect of the father's equally important function in promoting the girl's femininity, is commented upon. Successful gender identity in girls seems not to depend only upon a successful identification with the mother. Clinical studies suggest that women with problems of gender identity have experienced their *fathers* as having failed to protect them against their mothers. It is suggested here that a close pre-Oedipal relationship between father and daughter facilitates the switch to the father as the Oedipal love object. In addition, a loving interaction between father and daughter provides the girl with a masculine foil for her growing femininity.

Considerable attention has also been paid in the past 5 years to the developmental process of becoming a father. Such psychoanalytic studies attempt to trace the "developmental lines" through which a small boy's wishes to bear and nurture children (based in part on his identification with the mother) become integrated into his growing personality by way of a satisfying relationship with the father into and through latency, finally taking the form of wishing to be a father (i.e., paternal identity becomes included into a masculine gender identity). Studies suggest that it is difficult to be a good father if one has not had a good experience of being fathered. A detailed analytic study of a "prospective" father indicates that pregnancy may be experienced by the father as a "developmental challenge"—one important aspect of which concerns the wish to come to terms with his own father.

Fathers in latency and adolescence have received less concentrated attention from psychoanalysts than earlier developmental stages. The available literature is discussed from the point of view of behavior and attitudes that are regarded as desirable or undesirable at these ages. Such conclusions are drawn from clinical work with children and adolescents in which the damaging effects of specific behavior and attitudes on the part of the father have played their part in the final pathological picture.

REFERENCES

Abelin, E. L. The role of the father in the separation–individuation process. In J. B. McDevitt, & C. F. Settlage (Eds.), *Separation–individuation*. New York: International Universities Press, 1971.

Abelin, E. L. Some further observations and comments on the earliest role of the father. *International Journal of Psychoanalysis,* 1975, **56,** 293–302.

Abelin, E. L. The role of the father in core gender identity and in psychosexual differentiation. Presented at the Annual Meeting of the American Psychoanalytic Association, April 1977. Panel discussion reported by Robert C. Prall, *Journal of the American Psychoanalytic Association,* 1977, **26,** 143–161.

Abelin, E. L. Triangulation, the role of the father and the origins of core gender identity during the rapprochement subphase. In R. Lax, S. Bach, & A. Burland (Eds.), *Rapprochement.* New York: Jason Aronson, 1980.

Anthony, E. J. The reactions of parents to adolescents and to their behavior. In E. J. Anthony, & T. Benedek (Eds.), *Parenthood.* Boston: Little, Brown, 1970.

Anthony, E. J. Children at risk from divorce: A review. In E. J. Anthony, & C. Koupernick (Eds.), *The child in his family: Children at psychiatric risk,* Vol. 3. New York: Wiley, 1974.

Bell, S. The development of the concept of object as related to infant–mother attachment. *Child Development,* 1970, **41,** 291–311.

Benedek, T. Parenthood as a developmental phase. *Journal of the American Psychoanalytic Association,* 1959, **7,** 389–417.

Benedek, T. Fatherhood and providing. In E. J. Anthony, & T. Benedek (Eds.), *Parenthood.* Boston: Little, Brown, 1970.

Benedek, T. Parenthood during the life cycle. In E. J. Anthony, & T. Benedek (Eds.), *Parenthood.* Boston: Little, Brown, 1970.

Bettelheim, B. *The uses of enchantment: The meaning and importance of fairytales.* New York: Knopf, 1976.

Blos, P. *On adolescence.* New York: Free Press, 1962.

Blum, H. (Ed.) *Female psychology: Contemporary psychoanalytic views.* New York: International Universities Press, 1977.

Boehm, F. The femininity complex in men. *The International Journal of Psychoanalysis,* 1930, **11,** 444–469.

Brenner, C. Metapsychology and psychoanalytic theory. *The Psychoanalytic Quarterly,* 1980, **49,** 189–214.

Burlingham, D. The fantasy of having a twin. *Psychoanalytic Study of the Child,* 1945, **1,** 205–210.

Burlingham, D. Some problems of ego development in blind children. In *Psychoanalytic studies of the sighted and the blind.* New York: International Universities Press, 1972.

Burlingham, D. The pre-oedipal infant–father relationship. *Psychoanalytic Study of the Child*, 1973, **28**, 23–47.

Clower, V. The development of the child's sense of his sexual identity: Panel Report. *Journal of the American Psychoanalytic Association*, 1970, **18**, 165–176.

Edgecumbe, R. & Burgner, M. The phallic-narcissistic phase: The differentiation between pre-oedipal and oedipal aspects of development. *Psychoanalytic Study of the Child*, 1975, **30**, 161–180.

Edgecumbe, R., et al. Some comments on the concept of the negative oedipal phase in girls. *Psychoanalytic Study of the Child*, 1976, **31**, 35–61.

Fast, I. Developments in gender identity: The original matrix. *International Review of Psychoanalysis*, 1978, **5**, 265–273.

Fast, I. Developments in gender identity: Gender differentiation in girls. *International Journal of Psychoanalysis*, 1979, **60**, 443–453.

Fenichel, O. *The psychoanalytic theory of neurosis*. London: Routledge and Kegan Paul, 1945.

Fraiberg, S., & Freedman, D. Studies in the ego development of the congenitally blind child. *Psychoanalytic Study of the Child*, 1964, **19**, 113–157.

Fraiberg, S. Libidinal object constancy and mental representation. *Psychoanalytic Study of the Child*, 1969, **24**, 9–47.

Frankel, S. A., & Sherick, I. Observations of the emerging sexual identity of three to four-year-old children: With emphasis on female sexual identity. *International Review of Psychoanalysis*, 1979, **6**, 297–309.

Freud, A. The contributions of psychoanalysis to genetic psychology (1950). In *The writings of Anna Freud*, Vol. 4. London: Hogarth, 1969.

Freud, A. Observations on child development (1951). In *The Writings of Anna Freud*, Vol. 4. London: Hogarth, 1969.

Freud, A. Problems of infantile neurosis: Contributions to the discussion (1954). In *The writings of Anna Freud*, Vol. 4. London: Hogarth, 1969.

Freud, A. Adolescence. *Psychoanalytic Study of the Child*, 1958, **13**, 255–278.

Freud, A. *Normality and pathology in childhood*. New York: International Universities Press, 1965.

Freud, A. Difficulties in the path of psychoanalysis: A confrontation of past with present viewpoints (1968). In *The writings of Anna Freud*, Vol. 7. New York: International Universities Press, 1971.

Freud, A. A discussion with René Spitz (1970). In *The writings of Anna Freud*, Vol. 7. New York: International Universities Press, 1971.

Freud, A., & Burlingham, D. *Infants without families* (1944). In *The writings of Anna Freud*, Vol. 3. New York: International Universities Press, 1973.

Freud, S. Analysis of a phobia in a five-year-old boy (1909). *Standard Edition*, Vol. 10. London: Hogarth, 1955.

Freud, S. A child is being beaten: A contribution to the study of the origins of sexual perversions (1919). *Standard Edition*, Vol. 17. London: Hogarth, 1955.

Freud, S. Group psychology and the analysis of the ego (1921). *Standard Edition,* Vol. 18. London: Hogarth, 1955.

Freud, S. Two encyclopedia articles (1923). *The Standard Edition,* Vol. 18. London: Hogarth, 1955.

Freud, S. The dissolution of the Oedipus Complex (1924). *Standard Edition,* Vol. 19. London: Hogarth, 1961.

Freud, S. The future of an illusion (1927). *Standard Edition,* Vol. 21. London: Hogarth, 1961.

Freud, S. Female sexuality (1931). *Standard Edition,* Vol. 21. London: Hogarth, 1961.

Galenson, E., & Roiphe, H. Some suggested revisions concerning early female development. In H. Blum (Ed.), *Female psychology.* New York: International Universities Press, 1977.

Galenson, E., & Roiphe, H. The development of sexual identity: Discoveries and implications. In T. B. Karasu & C. W. Socarides (Eds.), *On sexuality: Psychoanalytic observations.* New York: International Universities Press, 1979.

Gouin-Décarie, T. *Intelligence and affectivity in early childhood.* New York: International Universities Press, 1965.

Greenacre, P. Early physical determinants in the development of the sense of identity. *Journal of the American Psychoanalytic Association,* 1958, **6,** 612–627.

Greenacre, P. Considerations regarding the parent–infant relationship. *International Journal of Psychoanalysis,* 1960, **41,** 571–584.

Greenacre, P. Problems of overidealization of the analyst and of analysis. *Psychoanalytic Study of the Child,* 1966, **21,** 193–212.

Greenson, R. A transsexual boy and an hypothesis (1966). In *Explorations in psychoanalysis.* New York: International Universities Press, 1978.

Greenson, R. Disidentifying from mother: Its special importance for the boy (1968). In *Explorations in psychoanalysis.* New York: International Universities Press, 1978.

Grossman, W. I. Discussion of Freud and female sexuality. *International Journal of Psychoanalysis,* 1976, **57,** 301–305.

Gurwitt, A. R. Aspects of prospective fatherhood. *Psychoanalytic Study of the Child,* 1976, **31,** 237–270.

Hartmann, H. Psychoanalysis and developmental psychology. *Psychoanalytic Study of the Child,* 1950, **5,** 5–17.

Hartmann, H., & Kris, E. The genetic approach in psychoanalysis. *Psychoanalytic Study of the Child,* 1945, **1,** 11–29.

Herzog, J. Attachment, attunement and abuse: An occurrence in certain premature infant-parent dyads and triads. Unpublished manuscript, 1978.

Herzog, J. The father's role in the modulation of aggressive drive and fantasy. Paper presented at the fall meeting of the American Psychoanalytic Association, New York City, December, 1979.

Herzog J. Sleep disturbance and father hunger in 18–28 month old boys: The Erlkönig syndrome. *Psychoanalytic Study of the Child,* 1980, **35,** 219–233.

Jacobson, E. Development of the wish for a child in boys. *Psychoanalytic Study of the Child*, 1950, **5**, 139–152.

Jacobson, E. *The self and the object world*. New York: International Universities Press, 1964.

Jaffe, D. S. The masculine envy of woman's procreative function. In H. Blum (Ed.), *Female psychology: Contemporary psychoanalytic views*. New York: International Universities Press, 1977.

Karasu, T. B., & Socarides, C. W. (Eds.) *On sexuality: Psychoanalytic observations*. New York: International Universities Press, 1979.

Kestenberg, J. The effect on parents of the child's transition into and out of latency. In E. J. Anthony, & T. Benedek (Eds.), *Parenthood*. Boston: Little, Brown, 1970.

Kestenberg, J. *Children and parents*. New York: Jason Aronson, 1975.

Kleeman, J. A boy discovers his penis. *Psychoanalytic Study of the Child*, 1965, **20**, 239–266.

Kleeman, J. Genital discovery during a boy's second year: A follow-up. *Psychoanalytic Study of the Child*, 1966, **21**, 358–392.

Kleeman, J. The peek-a-boo game. Part 1: Its origins, meanings and related phenomena in the first year. *Psychoanalytic Study of the Child*, 1967, **22**, 239–273.

Kleeman, J. Freud's views on early female sexuality in the light of direct child observation. In H. Blum (Ed.), *Female sexuality: Contemporary psychoanalytic views*. New York: International Universities Press, 1977.

Klein, G. *Psychoanalytic theory*. New York: International Universities Press, 1976.

Kohut, H. *The analysis of the self*. New York: International Universities Press, 1971.

Kolansky, H., & Moore, W. T. Some comments on the simultaneous analysis of a father and his adolescent son. *Psychoanalytic Study of the Child*, 1966, **21**, 237–268.

Lamb, M. E. (Ed.) *The role of the father in child development*. New York: Wiley, 1976.

Lax, R. F., Bach, S., & Burland, A. (Eds.) *Rapprochement: The critical subphase of separation–individuation*. New York: Jason Aronson, 1980.

Leonard, M. Fathers and daughters. *International Journal of Psychoanalysis*, 1966, **47**, 325–334.

Loch, W., & Jappe, G. Die Konstruktion der Wirklichkeit und die Phantasien. *Psyche*, 1974, **28**, 1–31.

Loewald, H. Ego and reality. *International Journal of Psychoanalysis*, 1951, **32**, 10–18.

Mächtlinger, V. Psychoanalytic theory: Preoedipal and oedipal phases with special reference to the father. In M. E. Lamb (Ed.), *The role of the father in child development*. New York: Wiley, 1976.

Mahler, M. Rapprochement: Subphase of the separation–individuation process (1972). In *The selected papers of Margaret S. Mahler*, Vol. 2. New York: Jason Aronson, 1979.

Mahler, M. & Gosliner, R. On symbiotic child psychosis: Genetic, dynamic and restitutive aspects. *Psychoanalytic Study of the Child*, 1955, **10**, 195–212.

McDougall, J. The homosexual dilemma: A clinical and theoretical study of female
homosexuality. In I. Rosen (Ed.), *Sexual deviation* (2nd ed.). New York: Oxford
University Press, 1979.

Moore, W. T. Promiscuity in a thirteen year old girl. *Psychoanalytic Study of the
Child*, 1974, **29**, 301–318.

Neubauer, P. The one-parent child and his oedipal development. *Psychoanalytic Study
of the Child*, 1960, **15**, 286–309.

Noy, P. The psychoanalytic theory of cognitive development. *Psychoanalytic Study of
the Child*, 1979, **34**, 169–216.

Parens, H., Pollock, L., Stern, J., & Kramer, S. On the girl's entry into the Oedipus
complex. In H. Blum (Ed.), *Female psychology: Contemporary psychoanalytic
views*. New York: International Universities Press, 1977.

Paul, N. L. Parental empathy. In E. J. Anthony, & T. Benedek (Eds.), *Parenthood*.
Boston: Little, Brown, 1970.

Ritvo, S., McCollum, A. T., Omwake, E., Provence, S., & Solnit, A. J. Some relations of constitution, environment and personality as observed in a longitudinal
study of child development. In A. J. Solnit, & S. Provence (Eds.), *Modern perspectives in child development*. New York: International Universities Press, 1963.

Ritvo, S. Late adolescence. *Psychoanalytic Study of the Child*, 1971, **26**, 241–263.

Roiphe, H. On an early genital phase. *Psychoanalytic Study of the Child*, 1968, **23**,
348–365.

Rosen, I. The general psychoanalytic theory of perversion: A critical and clinical review. In I. Rosen (Ed.), *Sexual deviation* (2nd ed.). New York: Oxford University
Press, 1979.

Ross, J. M. The development of paternal identity. A critical review of the literature on
nurturance and generativity in boys and men. *Journal of the American Psychoanalytic Association*, 1975, **23**, 783–817.

Ross, J. M. Toward fatherhood: The epigenesis of paternal identity during a boy's first
decade. *International Review of Psychoanalysis*, 1977, **4**, 327–347.

Ross, J. M. Fathering: A review of some psychoanalytic contributions on paternity.
International Journal of Psychoanalysis, 1979, **60**, 317 (a).

Ross, J. M. Paternal identity: The equation of fatherhood and manhood. In T. B.
Karasu, & C. W. Socarides (Eds.), *On sexuality: Psychoanalytic observations*.
New York: International Universities Press, 1979 (b).

Rotmann, M. Über die Bedeutung des Vaters in der "Wiederannäherungs-Phase."
Psyche, 1978, **32**, 1105–1147.

Rotmann, M. Der Vater der frühen Kindheit—ein strukturbildendes drittes Objekt. Un-
published manuscript of a lecture presented at the Psychoanalytic Seminar, Basel,
November 1979 and at a meeting of the German Psychoanalytic Association in
Stuttgart, November 1979.

Sandler, J., & Rosenblatt, B. The concept of the representational world. *Psychoanalytic Study of the Child,* 1962, **17,** 128–145.

Schafer, R. *A new language for psychoanalysis.* New Haven: Yale University Press, 1976.

Socarides, C. W. *The overt homosexual.* New York: Grune and Stratton, 1968.

Spitz, R. *The first year of life.* New York: International Universities Press, 1965.

Sprince, M. The development of a pre-oedipal partnership between an adolescent girl and her mother. *Psychoanalytic Study of the Child,* 1962, **17,** 418–424.

Stoller, R. *The transsexual experiment: Sex and gender,* Vol. 2. London: Hogarth, 1975.

Stoller, R. Primary femininity. In H. Blum (Ed.), *Female psychology: Contemporary psychoanalytic views.* New York: International Universities Press, 1977.

Van der Leeuw, P. J. The pre-oedipal phase of the male. *Psychoanalytic Study of the Child,* 1958, **13,** 352–374.

Volkan, V. D. Transsexualism: As examined from the viewpoint of internalized object relations. In T. B. Karasu, & C. W. Socarides (Eds.), *On sexuality: Psychoanalytic observations.* New York: International Universities Press, 1979.

Wallerstein, J. S., & Kelly, J. B. The effects of parental divorce: The adolescent experience. In E. J. Anthony, & C. Koupernick (Eds.), *The child in his family: Children at psychiatric risk,* Vol. 3. New York: Wiley, 1974.

Weissman, P. The effects of pre-oedipal attitudes on development and character. *International Journal of Psychoanalysis,* 1963, **44,** 121–131.

Wolff, P. H. *The developmental psychologies of Jean Piaget and psychoanalysis.* New York: International Universities Press, 1960.

Winnicott, D. W. The observation of infants in a set situation (1941). In *Through paediatrics to psychoanalysis.* London: Hogarth, 1975.

Winnicott, D. W. The theory of the parent–infant relationship. *International Journal of Psychoanalysis,* 1960, **41,** 585–595.

Winnicott, D. W. *The maturational processes and the facilitating environment.* London: Hogarth, 1965.

CHAPTER 4

The Role of the Father:
An Anthropological Perspective

MARY MAXWELL KATZ

Harvard University

MELVIN J. KONNER

Harvard University

A current anthropological perspective on the role of the father must include several levels of analysis. The broadest are evolutionary theory and the comparative study of male parental behavior in vertebrate species and mammals in particular. When we shift to the comparative study of human societies, we add several new levels to our discussion, because of the more complex psychological and communicative aspects of our behavior. From a cross-cultural perspective, the role of the father is deeply embedded in the patterns of social relationships associated with diverse family and community structures and in general cultural definitions of male and female.

In this chapter, therefore, our discussion follows several steps. The first section employs a cross-phylogenetic perspective in describing human male parental behavior at the species level. The basic characteristics of the human family are compared with the range of bonding and male parental behavior found in animal species, and the relationship of male parental behavior to ecology and social organization in two mammalian orders is reviewed. Evidence for the plasticity of male parental behavior within species is also discussed. This section suggests that male parental behavior is subject to the influence of species, ecological, and social factors.

We are indebted to Nancy Nicolson, Martin Etter, and Irven DeVore for their help in preparing this first revision. For the original edition, we remain grateful to John Whiting, Beatrice Whiting, Sarah Blaffer Hrdy, John Sodergren, Martin Etter, Irven DeVore, Robert Trivers, and Steven Stepak.

The second section presents cross-cultural data illustrating the dimensions of the human father's role and relates variations to social and ecological differences among human societies. Several types of data are utilized: (1) descriptive data from individual ethnographic monographs; (2) quantitative data from a cross-cultural survey; and (3) quantitative data on parent–offspring relations among the !Kung San, a foraging people representing one variant of the sociocultural adaptation that existed for most of human and protohuman history. Ending this section is a characterization of the American middle-class periurban family in cross-cultural perspective and a corresponding interpretation of recent psychological research on fathers' roles in infancy.

At the present time, as at the time of the publication of the first edition of this volume in 1976, few studies exist of non-Western fathers and their young children using the quantity and detail of empirical measurement that psychologists have used on Western samples. This is true for several reasons. Fathers in some non-Western societies spend relatively little time in proximity to their children or in social interaction with them, so that in studies using time sampling of naturally occurring behavior, the quantity of data on fathers may be small. This problem, for example, prevented separate analysis of father–child interaction in the Whitings' 1975 six-culture study (B. Whiting, personal communication), the most comprehensive cross-cultural study of children's social behavior to date.

In addition, more controlled studies of non-Western fathers are rare. Because the contexts and meanings of social behaviors differ cross-culturally, anthropologists hesitate to apply the particular questions or methods defined by Western psychology unless the research includes a large ethnographic component. Without this, the results of experimental procedures may be subject to culture-biased misinterpretation, or, at the least, the researcher may overlook important cultural elements in attending narrowly to predefined questions. More broad-based research is very expensive and time-consuming and therefore not often undertaken. Three prominent recent examples of such comprehensive studies are the !Kung San study directed by I. DeVore and R. Lee in the late 1960s and 1970s, of which the data on father–infant relations collected by the second author are summarized in this chapter; and the recent studies of child development in the Gusii and Ngecha communities of Kenya, directed by R. LeVine and B. and J. Whiting, respectively. In the latter two studies, fathers are relatively scarce in the environment of young children and are not a focus of the empirical data. Finally, the rich qualitative data produced by ethnographic work remain one of the most significant and unique contributions of cross-cultural research.

The anthropological perspective presented here remains the same as it was in 1976: the consideration of the bases for male parental behavior given by the phylogenetic perspective and evolutionary theory, and the description of social relationships associated with diverse family and community types as reported in ethnographic literature.

NATURAL SELECTION AND PARENTAL BEHAVIOR

Male Parental Investment

Recent theory in evolutionary biology considers that the predominant behavior patterns of a species are those that have maximized individual reproductive success. This is because the genes of those individuals who respond to any situation in a way that is reproductively advantageous to them are present in a higher frequency in subsequent generations. Thus differences in parental behavior between species (or any separately breeding populations) represent different patterns that have maximized individual reproductive success in the separate populations. Furthermore, where there is variation in parental care pattern *within* a species, we expect that it is related to different environmental conditions and that the various strategies function to maximize reproductive success in particular ecological settings. In these species, therefore, a flexible program for parental behavior is available and is used adaptively.

The concept of "parental investment" has been formulated by Trivers (1972) to summarize the action of natural selection on the parental behaviors of a species. According to this theory, natural selection causes the varying amounts of parental investment of males and females in a species in terms of courtship and mating patterns, patterns of competition, adult sex differences, and sex ratio. While the care of offspring is a major form of parental investment, the concept includes other parental behaviors as well as the metabolic energy invested by each parent in the production of the original gamete cells. Parental investment is theoretically defined as "any investment that enhances the offspring's chances of survival at the cost of the parent's ability to invest in another offspring" (p.139).

Trivers points out that in species in which the female must give major effort to the care of offspring, (lactating species), the female is more limited than the male in the number of offspring that can be produced over their lifetimes. In many of these species a polygynous pattern has evolved; the male acquires higher reproductive success if he is able to mate with several females. This pattern can also be associated with adult sex differences such as greater size and strength among males, with competition between males, and even with special adaptations for competition among males, such as long canine teeth or other weaponry. In other species, male and female parental investment appear about equal, and this pattern is associated with a monogamous mating system. In monogamous bird species, for example, the male may find and defend a nesting place, help build the nest and brood the eggs, defend the female and provide for her during the nesting period, and help feed and protect the young. In group-living species, for instance, many of the primates, defense of the group in general may also be a form of male parental investment. Ridley (1978) has recently reviewed the species in which *only* the male gives parental care. Although nonexistent among mammals because of female lactation, and rare in birds and amphibians, exclusively paternal care of young occurs among many fish species. It is associated with external fertilization of the ova and with a mating system combining slight male polygyny with sequential polyandry among females. An additional contribution to parental investment theory has been made by Maynard-Smith (1977), who has clarified the necessarily prospective means by which natural selection governs ongoing breeding behavior.

Table 1 depicts an idealized continuum of four major variables considered in Trivers' formulation and gives examples illustrating several points. The differences from left to right are merely ordinal and do not represent an interval scale. While Ridley's review indicates that the right side of this table is oversimplified, this outline presents the basic form of the theory and is sufficient for our purposes. According to this phylogenetic perspective, the human species occupies a roughly middle position in the full range that can be described. Some species represent more fully monogamous examples, especially certain birds. Across human societies, monogamy with some incidence of polygyny is the most common form of marriage. Even where monogamy is the cultural norm, pair bonding in our species is less permanent than in many monogamous birds. In many human societies, cultural norms permit men to have secondary spouses but impose harsh sanctions against this on women. While polyandry does occur in human societies, it is rare. On a world sample of nonindustrial cultures (Murdock & White, 1969), forms of marriage are distributed as follows: 1 percent polyandry, 17 percent monogamy, 51 percent occasional polygyny, and 31 percent common polygyny. Adult sex differences in humans are in keeping with a middle placement on the continuum: human males are slightly larger and heavier than females and have a higher metabolic rate and higher mortality.

Although this viewpoint places our species in a broad phylogenetic perspective, we must turn to other studies to describe the range of behavioral variations in different contexts and to consider the question of the behavioral limitations or plasticity available to us as a species.

Attempts have been made to apply these formulations of evolutionary theory to more exact predictions of human behavior under the rubric of "human sociobiology" (e.g., Alexander, 1979; Daly & Wilson, 1978; Wilson, 1978), and related views of human sexuality have also emerged (Symons, 1979), but the best empirical support still resides in invertebrate studies. In discussing the behavior of higher species, this approach is vulnerable to misapplication and partisan overinterpretation. Even without refering to the larger issues that have been raised in intellectual debate (e.g., Gregory, Silvers, & Sutch, 1978), there is the problem of measurement. In measuring parental investment, for example, how do we determine whether feeding the young represents more investment than defending the troop, especially if defense activities are frequent or the male risks his life? And even where applicable, a good portion of variance is left unexplained, giving room for ecological, cultural, and psychological approaches to increase our understanding of human societies.

Table 1. Continuum of Parental Investment and Related Variables

	Elephant Seals, Baboons, Macaques	Monogamous Birds, Humans, Marmosets	Polyandrous Birds
Parenting	Male parental investment lower than female parental investment	Male and female parental investment about equal	Female parental investment lower than male parental investment
Mating system	Polygyny	Monogamy	Polyandry
Courtship	Male–male competition for females, female choice	Low intrasex competition	Female–female competition for males, male choice
Adult sex differences	Males larger, higher metabolic rate, perhaps more brightly colored, etc.	Low sexual dimorphism	Females larger, etc.

Male Parental Behavior, Social Organization, and Ecology

In comparing paternal behavior across species, we find that direct paternal care of the young is unusual among vertebrates, especially among mammals. Whereas there are 8000 species of monogamous birds and some polyandrous species, among mammals both long-term pair bonding and significant male care of young are rare. In mammals the female is uniquely adapted to care for the young, and the male is not necessarily joined to the mother–offspring unit. In most mammals the parents do not remain together after copulation, and the male contributes no parental investment except the sperm. The best mammalian examples of high male parental investment are certain species of wild canids and nonhuman primates. Among wild canids both sexes feed the young by regurgitation after the hunt, a pattern resembling that of pair-bonding birds. The female is provisioned if she is unable to hunt, as are other "babysitters" or other nonhunting individuals (Fox, 1975; van Lawick & van Lawick-Goodall, 1971). In several species of New World monkeys the male is reported to carry the young the majority of the time and to provision them in some cases

(Epple, 1975; Mason, 1966; Mitchell & Brandt, 1972; Starin, 1978). The amount of direct care of offspring by human fathers is much less than in these species of canids or New World monkeys, but the human father also provides for and defends the female and offspring. Provision of resources and defense are the most important forms of male parental investment in human beings. We examine the variance in human paternal behavior in detail in the next section.

Why has the role of males become more prominent in these species? They have in common the need to care for slow-developing ("altricial") young (Eisenberg, 1966, p. 68). But there are many altricial species in which the father does not have a large role. The extensive carrying of young by male marmosets simply may be related to twinning; nursing two slow-developing primate young is such a burden for the female that other care devolves upon the male. Jolly (1972, p. 212) speculates that the selective advantages of the human pairbonded family may be related to scarcity of resources on the savannah (the probable environment of most of human evolution), to a need to protect females and young; and to long infant dependency. Recent experimental research by Dudley (1974a, 1974b) on the California mouse, *Peromyscus californicus,* which usually lives in isolated pairs and exhibits high amounts of male parental care, shows that the male's presence significantly increases the pups' chances of survival and their weight gain, especially under conditions of the sporadic presence of the mother or of early weaning. (Under natural conditions foraging requires the mother to be frequently absent—more so if there are scare resources.) A field study of marmots in two different settings (Barash, 1975) shows that males interacted with their young more in the less populated setting. Here they lived in the same burrows with the mother and offspring, but in the more populated setting they made separate burrows and interacted less frequently with their offspring and more frequently in vigilant and defensive encounters with other adult males.

These studies indicate that ecological factors affect the male's proximity to the mother–offspring unit and the forms of male parental investment he gives. If defense or male–male competition are required, he may be distant *or* close; if caretaking is required, he must remain close. Since there is also variation in the relationships of human fathers to their children across cultures that can be described in terms of basic "proximity," these studies suggest that we should consider ecological factors in our cross-cultural analyses of humans as well.

Ecological factors have been discussed by comparative zoologists who study differences in social organization across groups of related species (e.g., Crook, 1970; Eisenberg, 1966; Fox, 1975). It is probably impossible to draw conclusions that would apply *cross-phylogenetically* about specific ecological determinants of male parental investment. But relationships between male parental investment and social organization can be distinguished, and ecology is the final framework within which both of these must be considered.

Gradients of social organization are found within both canids and nonhuman primates. Some species are asocial, some live in isolated pairs with offspring, and some live in larger groups. The longest pair bonds occur where the pair lives separately, as in coyote and golden jackal pairs, who remain together beyond the breeding and rearing season. In pack-living canids, the bond between a mated pair persists during the rearing period and may persist subsequently in the wolf, but this is not fully verified (Fox, 1975, p. 445). Although data on male parental investment in the three types of social organization are not complete, it appears to be highest in those species living in isolated pairs. In observations of dingos, an asocial species, the adult male visited the den regularly and was greeted affectionately but was not seen to provide food (Corbett & Newson, 1975). Among coyotes, however, who form isolated pairs, the male provides food for his mate in late pregnancy when she does not hunt and to the pups when they begin to eat solid food (Gier, 1975). In the pack-living African wild dogs, all pack members share in the feeding and protection of the young (Estes & Goddard, 1967), suggesting that the contribution of the father to his own offspring exclusively may be less than in the coyote. Since packs are extended family units (Fox, 1975), the sharing of caretaking is probably an example of kin-directed altruism (Hamilton, 1964). Fox (1975) relates the three types of social organization to ecological factors—mode of hunting and size of prey, food availability and dispersion, and predation pressure.

Adult male–infant relations are reviewed in this volume by Redican and Taub in Chapter 6, and the reader is referred to this chapter for a complete review of the literature. Redican's and other's reviews present evidence that different *forms* of male parental investment—especially "care" versus "protection"—accompany different forms of social organization and ecological conditions. Male care of infants does not follow phylogenetic trends and may be more related to ecology (Jolly, 1972). The siamang, a lesser ape of Southeast Asia, and the several New World monkeys that exhibit the most caretaking are arboreal and live in isolated pairs or extended families. These include the marmosets, tamarins, calimico, night monkey, and titi. In marmosets, for example, the male may assist at birth, receiving and washing the infants, and he assumes the major responsibility for carrying and grooming the infants until they become physically independent. The extent of provisioning of food is less well understood, but male and female parents share food and allow the young to take food from them. The female has priority access to food after parturition (Snyder, 1972). Provision of food to infants by the male titi monkey in the wild is documented by Starin (1978).

Males among Old World monkeys, gorillas, and chimpanzees do not give continuous care to infants but often protect, retrieve, and defend them as well as the troop as a whole. Males respond rapidly to infants' distress cries. In some species play is found, and in most there are distal associations such as orienting to or traveling beside an infant. Babysitting and adoptions occasionally occur. These species are all group-living and at least partly terrestrial, and they engage in polygynous bonds, brief consortships, or promiscuous mating. Precise assessment of male parental investment is difficult because paternity is sometimes not known.

The function of adult male–infant relationships in Old World troops is at present difficult to formulate. Packer (1980), in observations of olive baboons, reported that male associations with infants consisted of both caretaking and exploitative relationships. By carrying infants during encounters with other males, adult males decreased the probability of being threatened and increased their relative dominance. Infants were sometimes injured or killed in these encounters. Males also groomed infants and defended them against both chimpanzee predation and conspecific aggressors. Both exploitation and caretaking were restricted to males who were potentially fathers of the infants and were highest in males who had resided in the troop the longest. Nicolson (personal communication) reports from recent observations of a savannah baboon troop that adult males were seen to groom, protect, and carry infants. About half of the 26 infants observed over a 2-year period had a close adult male associate, but in many cases it was known that the male associate could not have been the father. Hamadryas baboon males attend to female infants who will later become sexual partners for them in their "harems" (Kummer, 1967). Crook and Goss-Costard (1972) note that male care of young in Japanese macaques may permit a rise in the social rank of the male if the infant receiving attention is kin to higher-ranking animals. Ransom and Rowell (1972) report that mature male baboons sought contact and interaction with high-ranking females but rarely with low-ranking females. Blaffer Hrdy (1976) has reviewed adult male–infant relations in primates from the perspective of the enhancement of individual reproductive success.

Of Old World species, the Barbary macaque shows a high degree of male care of infants. In the one-male troops observed by Burton (1972), the adult male is described as having a definite role in socializing infants into appropriate behavior sequences. Still, it appears that in Old World monkeys generally, protection and distal associations between males and infants are the rule, and these are related to the social structure of the troop.

A comparison of the three mammalian cases in which long-term pair bonding occurs shows that there are important differences in several features (Table 2). In canids the male's importance lies in providing food resources, which for these carnivorous species requires continuous hunting. In omnivorous humans there is less extreme reliance on hunting, but the male is an important provider of various resources. The number of young and way of locating them also differ. The three cases represent three quite different phylogenetic adaptations, but they have in common long-term pair bonding and significant association between male and female parents and offspring.

Table 2. Comparison of Mammalian Species with Relatively Long Pair Bonds

	Coyote, Golden Jackal	New World Monkeys	Humans
Number of young	Several	Twins	Single
Location of young	Cached	Carried	Carried
Role of male in provisioning female and young	High	Low	High
Importance of meat in diet	High	Low	Medium
Female sexual receptivity	Noncontinuous	Noncontinuous	Continuous
Relationship of pair to other conspecifics	Isolated	Isolated	In group

Plasticity in Male Parental Behavior

Our discussion of natural selection and parental behavior emphasizes differences among species in forms of male parental behavior, but examination of variability *within* species shows considerable plasticity and points to the importance of environmental factors. The most dramatic demonstrations of this are the results of experimental pairing of adult male rhesus monkeys with infants (Gomber & Mitchell, 1974; Redican & Mitchell, 1973). Rhesus males in the wild show indifference to infants. When paired in the laboratory, adult males and infants developed many attachment behaviors and engaged in high levels of physical contact and interaction. The male in the first experiment responded strongly to distress cries of the infant on maternal separation and to the infant's assuming a depressed posture in the cage. The "nurturance" or "attachment" that developed may spring from the protective response found throughout baboons and macaques in the wild.

Plasticity in more natural conditions can also be demonstrated. In an anubis baboon case observed in the field by Ransom and Ransom (1971) where the mother gave abnormally low amounts of care to an infant, an adult male gave more and more attention to the infant. Adult male langurs in the wild pay no attention to infants, usually avoiding the mothers and young, but in the captive colony they are interested in the young and nuzzle and inspect them (Dohlinow, 1975). The study of marmots by Barash (1975) described earlier shows different amounts of male attention to the young in populated and isolated settings. All these studies point to plasticity in the behavioral capabilities of males that is subject to environmental influences. Quantitative data sometimes also show marked individual differences within settings—for example, the amount of carrying done by male tamarins in Epple's (1975) laboratory study. Experimental studies, such as Dudley's (1975b) on the California mouse, that manipulate environmental conditions and measure both parental behavior and development in the offspring are extremely helpful in understanding relations between ecological factors and parental behavior. In humans, the cross-cultural data we will examine show some sociocultural correlates of different forms and levels of male parental investment.

There is, however, some evidence for limits to the plasticity of these behaviors in the neural and endocrine systems. It is well known that testosterone administered experimentally acts to reduce nurturant behavior of various mammalian females. Male mice are more likely than female mice to kill strange young presented to them, and the tendency of females to kill pups is increased by administration of testosterone as a function of dosage (Davis & Gandleman, 1972). Administration of testosterone during the last 12 days of gestation in the rabbit results in postnatal scattering of young, cannibalism of young, failure to nurse, and depressed nest building activity (Fuller, Zarrow, Anderson, & Denenberg, 1970). In a semi free-ranging troop of rhesus monkeys, the only male seen to exhibit substantial amounts of nurturance toward infants was one who had been castrated (Breuggeman, 1973).

Other evidence suggests that physiological differences between the sexes underlying the differences in parental behavior extend beyond hormone levels. Preadolescent male rhesus monkeys who have been raised in total social ioslation are more aggressive and less nurturant toward infants presented to them for the first time than preadolescent females raised under the same deprived conditions are (Chamove, Harlow, & Mitchell, 1967). This means there is a residue of gender differentiation in parental behavior in monkeys that have had no social experience that could influence gender-specific behavior. Furthermore, the test is performed before adolescence, when dramatic sex differences in hormone levels appear.

Experiments with other species on the "fetal androgenization" phenomenon may help explain this difference. Many experiments have demonstrated that administration of male sex hormones to female mammals at or near the time of birth acts to change the adult behavior of the females in a "masculinizing" direction. For example, in a study that measured retrieval, licking, crouching over, and nursing of strange pups, adult female rats that had received injections of androgen at 4 days of age behaved less maternally (and more like normal males) than nonandrogenized females did (Quadagno & Rockwell, 1972). In the same study males castrated at birth but not males castrated at 25 days of age showed more nurturant behavior than intact males, suggesting a possible sensitive period for the effects of androgens on nervous system circuits governing nurturant behavior in these animals. In bird species in which males play a role in the care of offspring similar to or exceeding that of females, it is clear that the males have elaborate neural and endocrine adaptations that suit them to these behaviors (Lehrman, 1955), and such adaptations do not appear to be present in males of species in which parental investment is overwhelmingly female. What, if any, special physiologic adaptations may characterize males of primate or candid species with high male parental investment, such as marmosets, is not known, but this would be a suitable avenue for investigation.

For human beings the data are obviously more difficult to interpret. In the best extant cross-cultural study of child behavior (Whiting & Whiting, 1975a) girls in six widely separated cultures were found to be more likely to be with infants and to show more nurturance (offer more help and support) generally than boys the same age, and this sex difference increases from age 3 to ·11. Previous work (Barry, Bacon, & Child, 1957), however, has shown that virtually all cultures studied had socialization practices that would tend to produce such sex differences, and so the uniform sex difference in child behavior cannot be taken as a biologically based lack of plasticity. Furthermore, cultures vary in socializing sex differences, and this factor is related to accumulation of resources (Barry, Child, & Bacon, 1959).

However, there is evidence that fetal androgenization contributes to sex differences in the nurturant behavior of human beings. This evidence comes from the leading laboratory working on gender anomalies in human infants, members of which for some years defended the concept of "psychosexual neutrality" in human beings at birth. This position has been jeopardized by the study of 10-year-old girls who for one reason or another had high levels of circulating androgen during the latter part of fetal life, and in whom this condition was corrected at the time of birth (Money & Ehrhardt, 1972). Interviews with these girls and with their mothers showed that they played less with dolls, were more "tomboyish," and were less likely to be looking forward to marriage and motherhood than a comparable sample of nonandrogenized girls were. This finding may be taken as initial evidence that circulating androgens effect changes in the human male during fetal life that dispose him less to develop nurturant behaviors than human females.

Still the evidence from studies such as Mitchell's (cited above) is compelling. It demonstrates that the male and female nervous systems are not so different as might be inferred from studies of naturalistic behavior and that under certain conditions the male nervous system can produce behaviors usually almost exclusively female at something approximating the same order of magnitude or level of incidence. Although the conditions of the experiment are very special—they are protected from competition, are not required to forage, are in social isolation, have no sexual opportunities, and are presented with infants whose behavior is probably abnormal because they have just been removed from their own mothers—the finding that there are conditions in which males can be induced to show fully "maternal" forms of nuturant behavior shows the importance of environment in molding parental behavior.

THE ROLE OF THE FATHER IN CROSS-CULTURAL PERSPECTIVE

In our comparative study of human societies, two empirical studies are presented—one on the socioecological correlates of the father's role in non-Western societies and the other on father–infant interaction among the !Kung people of southern Africa, a foraging people who represent one variant of the subsistence adaptation that characterized most of human and protohuman history (Lee & DeVore, 1968). We then consider the additional levels of analysis derived from the psychological and communicative aspect of our behavior as a species, expressed in diverse family and community contexts.

To allow any empirical analysis of the father's role across a large sample of cultures, we must sacrifice psychological complexity and accept some simple measures to describe his role and other selected variables on an appropriate worldwide sample. This type of data is available in the work of G. P. Murdock and his associates (Murdock, 1967; Murdock & White, 1969; Murdock & Wilson, 1972), who have over the years attempted to classify and code the basic characteristics of hundreds of cultures described in the ethnographic literature. We have used this data to perform a socioecological analysis of the father's role in 80 nonindustrial societies. The socioecological variables chosen are subsistence adptation, family organization, and division of labor. These are the analogs, in the adaptation of human societies to their environment, to the elements of ecology and social organization considered above in nonhuman species.

The cultures in our sample are a subsample of Murdock and White's (1969) Standard Cross-Cultural Sample, a world sample of historically and linguistically independent societies. The subsample was determined to be those cultures rated by Barry and Paxson (1971) at their highest degree of confidence on the nature of the father's relationship with infants and young children. The sample and scales are described further in the appendix.

To illustrate the variation found within the sample, we first present ethnographic sketches of five of these societies, which also represent different major subsistence adaptations. These sketches show differences in the basic proximity of fathers to young children and in the degree to which they participate in childcare, as well as in fathers' economic, protective, and didactic roles. Also apparent, although not developed here, are differences in the psychological characteristics of family life in these different settings.

Fathers' Roles in Five Major Subsistence Adaptations

!Kung San (Bushmen), in Northwestern Botswana in 1970. Source: Konner (fieldwork). The !Kung are typical warm-climate gatherers and hunters living in a semiarid region of northwestern Botswana. Subsistence derives 60 to 80 percent from vegetable foods collected and prepared by women. Meat hunted by men supplies the remaining 20 to 40 percent. Each sex works about half the days in the week, allowing much leisure. The family is usually monogamous with a small (5 or less) percentage of polygynous marriages, in the context of a seminomadic band of about 30 people representing the extended families of either or both spouses.

Indulgence of infants and young children is as high as has ever been described for a human population, and older children are given much freedom and few responsibilities. Women carry infants more than half the waking hours, sleep with them, and nurse them several times an hour. Almost no restrictions are placed on premarital sex, but traditional marriage occurs at early adolescence for girls and young adulthood for men.

Since fathers are not occupied in subsistence activities for half the days of the week and are often available for parts of the remaining days, their potential contact with infants and children is high. They often hold and fondle even the youngest infants, though they return them to the mother whenever they cry and for all forms of routine care. Young children frequently go to them, touch them, talk to them, and request food from them, and such approaches are almost never rebuffed. Boys are not expected to become involved in hunting activity until early adolescence at the soonest and then follow their fathers and uncles on hunts for years before being able to conduct hunts themselves. Information transfer on such hunts has an "observational learning" rather than a "teaching" character. The same may be said about the transfer of spiritual medicine, though this is rarely acquired from the young man's own father. Traditional male initiation rites involve making boys dance in the cold for a few days, frightening them in the dark, and making small cuts on their foreheads to signify their accession to manhood. Homicidal violence occurs in this society, but wars were apparently very rare historically, and no wars had occurred for many decades at the time of the study. Preparation for fighting did not occupy the men in any way, and learning to fight was not considered an important skill for boys.

Lesu Village in New Ireland, Melanesia, in 1930. Source: Powdermaker (1933). Lesu is typical of many cultures in the Pacific islands in which the primary mode of subsistence is small-scale gardening in combination with fishing. Fishing, done mainly by men, and taro gardening, done mainly by women, are equally important, each providing 40 percent of subsistence. The household is usually a monogamous, nuclear family, although a few men have two wives, each with separate houses. The sexes keep separate in public life, and men's houses exist where older boys, unmarried men, and men whose wives are pregnant or nursing sleep at night. But in family life the sexes are affectionate and intimate, and the family is described as a close-knit unit. The husband quite frequently takes care of the baby while his wife is busy in the garden or with her cooking.

He will sit in the compound in front of the house, or on the beach, with the infant, playing with him, fondling and petting him . . . The father and mother are equally tender towards their child, as are also other male and female relatives. A man plays with his child for hours at a time, talking pure foolishness to the baby . . . Whenever there is a group of natives together . . . or men idling on the sand, the child is tossed about from one to the other, fondled, patted, jumped up and down, and kissed . . . Or they may croon one of the dance songs to the infant.

Children from 3 to 6 years old are rarely left alone; they are either with their parents in the village, or, if the latter are away in the gardens or fishing, they are with their older brothers or sisters.

When the parents are in the village, the little child follows them about. They are present at all the adult activities, dance rehearsals, rites, communal preparations of food, etc . . . thus their education is begun in the observance of those activities in which they will later participate . . . At all rites, and in social life, the boys are with the men and the little girls are with their mothers.

As children grow older, there is a gradual increase in their participation in the village life, but girls are kept busier than boys.

[The boys] watch the adult male activities but do not participate as actively as the girls do in the women's work. When the men are fishing the boys are present, eagerly watching it all, but they do not participate.

At age 9 to 11, elaborate initiation rites mark a boy's entrance into adult society. They endure for many months and involve much feasting and dancing. At the height of the rites, the adult men and women engage in a spirited fight, hurling stones and coconut shells and exchanging jeering talk. The men enter a specially built enclosure, where the boys are circumcised while the women dance in sympathy for them. The father holds his son steady while another man does the cutting. The boys are then secluded from women for several weeks while they are instructed by the older men. Finally they are ritually returned to society.

Although fighting between villages occurred in the past, it appears to have been on a small scale.

Koreans of Sondup'o village, Kanghwa Island, in 1950. Source: Osgood (1951). This community represents advanced agriculture—that is, plow agriculture with intensive rather than extensive land use. Advanced agriculture differs from the small-scale agriculture of Lesu and Thonga in that men are in charge of it, the use of the plow makes a larger scale possible, and it comes to dominate any other subsistence activities of the culture. Analysis of a large sample (presented below) shows that in advanced agriculture there is greater variance in the father's closeness to the family than in other subsistence types. But on the average they are midway between the harshness of the Thonga and Rwala and the warmth of !Kung and Lesu fathers.

The family is monogamous and usually extended, with patrilocal residence and patrilineal inheritance. The oldest son inherits all the father's property. The father is described as "stern and somewhat distant" from his children.

The father is likely to be tolerantly affectionate to the little [daughter] but becomes more removed as she grows up . . . The relationship between father and son has an ambivalent quality . . . it is not a union of familiarity and demonstrable affection . . . The father becomes the symbol of the disciplinarian and is apt to be a strict one in practice . . . The son must show utter respect regardless of how he really feels . . . [The children] run to their mothers for relief and she is known as the "kind parent," he as the "stern" one.

Young children are cared for by the mother and older siblings; older children go to school. The mother works some in the fields, but most of her work is domestic. The father is separated from his children during the day because he works in the fields, and children only occasionally help with this. The state provides police and defense.

Thonga of the Ronga subtribe, east coast of South Africa, in 1895. Source Junod (1927). The Thonga represent simple field agriculture—small-scale grain and vegetable agriculture done mainly by women—which is here found in combination with herding, done mainly by men. As in Lesu, the women's gardening is a substantial direct contribution to subsistence, but here polygyny is more common, and the men do herding instead of fishing. The family is the extended polygynous family, each wife having her own hut within the large family compound. The man's ideal is to acquire several wives who bear him many children, and large herds of cattle, with which he can acquire wives for his sons.

Relations between fathers and infants are dramatically different from those in Lesu. The men do not relate to infants and young children except in occasional ritual events. Taboos prevent the father from almost any contact with infants younger than 3 months. Babies are cared for by the mother and older siblings, and upon weaning, toddlers go to live with the grandparents for a few years. The distance between fathers and young children does not seem to be caused by lack of free time, since the ethnographer specifically comments on this:

> Their life is far from being as active as that of the women . . . their duties only require of them isolated effort from time to time . . . a great part of their time is devoted to paying visits . . . we can fairly estimate at three months the time required for the work which they have to do for the village and for the community. The remaining months are devoted to pastimes and pleasures.

When slightly older, the girls help their mothers and the boys tend goats.

> If they are negligent, the father will thrash the boys when they come back. . . . The [father] relationship implies respect and even fear. The father, though he does not take much trouble with his children, is nevertheless their instructor, the one who scolds and punishes. Absolute obedience is due him on the part of his sons and daughters.

Though no data are given on the frequency of fueding or warfare, there are elaborate war costumes and weapons and an army numbering about 2000.

Rwala Bedouin, North Arabian desert, in 1913. Source: Musil (1928). Although the Rwala Bedouin are a seminomadic people like the !Kung, their subsistence depends on the management of herds of camels and horses. These animals form the central focus of their lives, providing food, transportation, and trade resources.

The Rwala Bedouin are one of the fiercest peoples described in the ethnographic literature, engaging in frequent warfare and raiding among their clans. The management of these activities is the province of the adult men, while the work of women is associated with the domestic sphere.

In family life, the separation of males and females is as extreme as can be found anywhere in the literature. This separation is both ideological and physical. The dwelling tent is divided into separate compartments for men and women; men also eat separately from women and children.

In early years, children are physically separated from their fathers; until age 7, it is said they "go to their father only for an occasional talk." A boy is circumcised with a knife by his own father between the ages of 3 and 7, in the course of ceremonies lasting several days.

In later years the father trains his male children for obedience and bravery. Younger children are punished with a stick by father or mother; older boys are punished for disobedience by their father with a saber or dagger.

> By cutting or stabbing them the father not merely punishes the boys but hardens them for their future life. In the opinion of the Bedouin the son who disobeys is guilty of rebellion, for which the proper punishment is the saber.

Older boys spend more time with their fathers and other adult men, attending to the horses, bringing food and water to the men's quarters, and learning the techniques of warfare by mid-adolescence.

This Bedouin tribe, plus two African cultures—the Masai and Dodoth—are societies in this sample that depend on animal husbandry for their *primary* mode of subsistence. Many more cultures combine animal husbandry with agriculture—notably the Bantu peoples of sub-Saharan Africa; the family relations described among these herding peoples are remarkably similar.

From these and other ethnographies it is possible to distinguish several dimensions of the human father's role: progenitor; caregiver; playmate; instructor or model of adult skills and values; authority figure (head of household, disciplinarian); figure in ritual events concerning his children; provider of resources; defender and protector. Cultural ideologies variously emphasize one or another of these aspects. In his classic ethnography on the African Azande, Evans-Pritchard (1932) states that among this polygynous people, the function of fatherhood is defined as the original act of procreation rather than any consequent service that a father may perform.

Another classic ethnography of the same era on the Trobriand Islands people in the southwestern Pacific reports that the father's duty towards his wife's children is, in their phrase, "to receive them into his arms" (Malinowski, 1927). Malinowski depicts the Trobriand father as plying the favor and attention of his children in a matrilineal family in which he is a somewhat marginal member. Describing father–child relationships, he notes:

He has to carry them about when on the march the mother is tired, and he has to assist in the nursing at home. He tends them in their natural needs, and cleanses them, and there are many stereotyped expressions in the native language referring to fatherhood and its hardships, and to the duty of filial gratitude towards him. A typical Trobriand father is a hard-working and conscientious nurse and in this he obeys the call of duty, expressed in social tradition. The fact is, however, that the father is always interested in the children, sometimes passionately so, and performs all his duties eagerly and fondly. (pp. 23–24)

A Socioecological Study of the Father's Role in Infancy

In our examination of fathers' roles cross-culturally in relation to socioecological variables, we have used a measure of father–child "proximity" developed by Barry and Paxson (1971). It is based on typical descriptions of family life available in the ethnographic literature and is available for two age periods, 0 to 2 years and 2 to 5 years. Since ethnographies vary considerably in the level of detail offered on this topic, it has not been possible for cross-cultural researchers to develop a measure of actual paternal care on a large sample. Barry and Paxson were able to rate "proximity" (see Table 3 for scale definition) with a high degree of confidence for 80 historically and linguistically independent cultures for the infancy period and 86 cultures for the early childhood period. A review of the sources used suggests that this scale is a global measure of the father–child relationship in terms of both emotional warmth and physical proximity. Also, there is evidence that it reflects at least some degree of paternal nurturance or dependency. Father–infant proximity is correlated with their additional measures of "Nonmaternal Relationships" ($r = .36$, $p < .01$), and "Earliness of Child Autonomy," defined as independence from earlier caretakers ($r = -.48$, $p < .01$).

Proximity of Fathers and Mothers to Young Children. How much variation is there cross-culturally in the extent of fathers' and mothers' relationships to infants and young children? Although the nature and qualities of parent–child relationships differ greatly across cultures, it is useful to begin our discussion with a very simple quantitative description of cross-cultural differences. Barry and Paxson's scales are useful for this purpose (Table 3). The distributions on these scales show that in 90 percent of the sample societies the mother was the "principal" or "almost exclusive' caretaker of infants. By early childhood (ages 2 to 5), in 27 percent of the sample cultures the child spent more than half of the time in the care of the mother. In only 4 percent of sample cultures was a "regular close relationship" apparent between fathers and infants, and in only 9 percent between fathers and young children. At the other extreme, in 57 percent of cultures the father had only occasional or less frequent proximity to infants. In early childhood, in 39 percent of cultures the father was only occasionally or less frequently in proximity, but in only 2 percent was the child away from the mother "practically all of the time."

Subsistence Adaptation and Family Organization. What conditions predict father–infant proximity in our sample? Using Murdock and Wilson's (1972) codes, we find that father–infant proximity is greatest where either gathering or "horticulture" (small-scale vegetable gardening and fruit growing as practiced throughout the Pacific Islands) is the primary mode of subsistence and where combinations of polygny, patrilocal residence, the extended family, or patridominant division of labor are absent. These variables are interrelated but, at least in this sample, are not highly correlated with each other. It is combinations of these conditions, or their absence, that predict father–child proximity. The findings also suggest that the need for males to engage in warfare and the degree to which women provide subsistence resources are important underlying factors.

The relation of father–infant proximity to primary mode of subsistence is shown in Table 4. Dichotomizing the father–infant scale, fathers are most likely to be "close" in two of seven nonindustrial subsistence adaptions— "gathering" (as in !Kung) and "horticulture" (as in Lesu). Cultures with *extreme* dependence on hunting, such as the three in this sample, are probably not typical of most of human evolution. These findings are basically consistent with Whiting and Whiting's (1975b) finding on a larger sample that husband–wife intimacy is greater among cultures without accumulated resources or capital investments that must be defended. "Horticulturalists" are an exception in both our sample and theirs, but the Whitings note that these cultures are mainly in the Pacific islands and that insularity may provide a degree of protection. The Whitings pose a two-level interpretation of their findings on subsistence: husbands and wives are distant (in terms of sleeping arrangements) where warriors are needed to protect property, and distance between husbands and wives has the psychological effect of producing hyperaggressive males.

Table 3. Percent of Cultures with Various Degrees of Proximity Between Parents and Children (scales from Barry and Paxson, 1971)

Infancy (age 0-2)

Role of father (*n* = 80)		Role of mother (*n* = 104)	
No close proximity	5	0	Practically all care is by others
Rare proximity	15	0	Most care except nursing by others
Occasional proximity	37	2	Mother's role is significant but . . .
Frequent proximity	39	8	Mother provides half or less of care
Regular close relationship	4	44	Principally mother, others important
		43	Principally mother, others minor
		3	Almost exclusively the mother

Early Childhood (age 2-5)

Role of father (*n* = 86)		Role of mother (*n* = 82)	
No close proximity	1	2	Practically all time away from mother
Rare proximity	11	33	Majority of time away from mother
Occasional proximity	19	39	Half or less time with mother
Frequent proximity	60	27	Principally mother, others important
Regular close relationship	9	0	Almost exclusively mother

Other cross-cultural research has shown an association between relative father absence and violent or hypermasculine behavior. In the Whiting six-culture study, more cases of assault and homicide occur in the two father-distant cultures. There is also a notably different preoccupation with and attitude toward violence and strife (B. Whiting, 1965). Bacon, Child, and Barry (1963) show that the frequency of theft and personal crime is higher in societies with mother–child households. J. Whiting (1972) reports that, in another large sample, pursuit of military glory is associated with exclusive mother–son sleeping arrangements (ϕ=.40). These findings are interpreted according to the "protest masculinity" hypothesis: where the mother dominates the infant's and young child's world but men dominate the adult world, protest masculinity develops in boys as a defense mechanism against cross-sex identity conflict. In many of these cultures, boys undergo severe initiation rites at adolescence (Burton & Whiting, 1961; Whiting, Kluckhohn, & Anthony, 1958). Whereas the association between father absence and aggressive behavior may hold across cultures of different types, it may not apply within cultures.

Table 4. Father–Infant Proximity and Primary Mode of Subsistence in 80 Nonindustrial Cultures

Primary Mode of Subsistence	Father–Infant Proximity	
	Distant	Close
Gathering	1	7
Hunting	3	0
Fishing	6	4
Herding	4	1
Simple agriculture	12	6
Horticulture	3	10 $\chi^2 = 17.9$
Advanced agriculture	16	6 $p < .01$

Findings on family organization are shown in Table 5. None of the elements alone predicts father–infant proximity above the .05 level, but when two or more are combined, they do ($\chi^2=7.67$, $\phi=.31$, $p<.01$). Of the few cultures with strictly monogamous and nuclear families—the typical form in our own culture—all have close fathers ($n=6$). In extended families, monogamy or very low polygyny predicts "close" fathering only if residence is not patrilocal.

Warfare is suggested as a factor, since both polygyny and patrilocal residence are associated with internal warfare and feuding (Otterbein, 1968; Otterbein & Otterbein, 1965; van Velson & van Weterling, 1960). In many patrilocal or polygynous cultures, warfare and raiding are means of acquiring resources, including women. Bride theft and raiding for wives are found in polygynous cultures (Ayres, 1974), and even where women are not kidnapped, the communities that are at war with each other are often the same ones that intermarry. Patrilocal residence is related to warfare in that it enables father and sons to remain together when the sons marry. When these families accumulate, patrilocal clans are formed that act as small military organizations to defend the interests of the group when necessary. Paige and Paige (1973) discuss the conditions necessary for the development of these clans (or "fraternal interest groups") and propose that they exist in large part to assert paternity rights.

The division of labor—the degree to which women versus men provide subsistence resources—is suggested as a factor since, in both gathering and horticulture (the "close" fathers), women make a high contribution to subsistence.

Where the mother is especially busy and provides essential resources, we would expect that the father could be called on to help with childcare. This hypothesis is not supported when Murdock's (1967) Atlas scale on contribution of men and women to subsistence is used but is supported if all subsistence types in which women typically make a high contribution—gathering, horticulture, shifting agriculture—are considered (χ^2=6.6, ϕ=.31, p=.011).

Table 5. Father–Infant Proximity and Family Organization[a]

	Percent of Cultures with Distant Fathers
Polygyny (n=24)	75%
Patrilocal or avunculocal residence (n=51)	65%
Extended family (n=43)	65%
Distant fathers in entire sample	57%

	Family Organization	
Father–infant proximity	Two or More of the Above	One or None of the Above
Distant	31	15
Close	11	21
	χ^2=7.67, ϕ=.31, p<.01	

[a]These results are based on the Murdock and Wilson (1972) codes, which use the same ethnographic date as the Barry and Paxson (1971) ratings. Stronger results are obtained if Murdock's (1967) codes are used, but in some cases these are based on an earlier ethnographic date (father proximity and form of marriage, ϕ=.25; father proximity and patrilocal residence, ϕ=.28). It may be that traditional family organization continues to influence father–child proximity when family structure has changed recently.

In simple field agriculture, women labor long hours and provide important resources, but polygyny is common and fathers are mostly distant. It is interesting that in these cultures babies are often cared for by siblings, and toddlers will often go to live with their grandparents for a while. This suggests a model for predicting nonmaternal caretakers. Where the male's role includes polygyny and/or military activities, he does not contribute to childcare, regardless of women's contribution to subsistence. When these are absent, he contributes if the mother is busy with subsistence activities especially if the family is not extended. When the father is absent and the mother's workload is high, grandparents and siblings help with childcare. At present there are no really adequate scales on women's contribution to subsistence or on warfare, and so the model cannot be properly tested.

We did test a rough version of this model that supported it (Table 6). We examined father–infant proximity interacting with form of marriage, division of labor, and family type. The scale on division of labor is the one described—

it simply lumps subsistence types in which the contribution of women to subsistence is typically high (gathering, horticulture, and simple agriculture). The interactions of the four variables were assessed by use of the ECTA program from multidimensional contingency tables written by D. Oliver (Harvard University) for the method originally described by Goodman (1970). The testing of various models of interaction showed that the four variables are not independent ($\chi^2 = 39.97$, $p = .003$) but that the entire table can be explained by three separate two-variable interactions: fathering and marriage, fathering and women's contribution, marriage and women's contribution. Extendedness of family was not critical in the four-dimensional table. The table shows that the high contribution of women increases father participation unless his other roles prevent it: where the contribution of women is high, fathers are "close" unless there is polygyny. Fathering in cultures with low polygyny shifts according to the contribution of women: where it is high they are "close," where it is low they are "distant."

Table 6.   Father–Infant Proximity in Relation to Form of Marriage, Division of Labor, and Family Type (Number of Cultures with Distant Fathers/Close Fathers)

Form of Marriage:		Monogamy		Low Polygyny		High Polygyny	
Family Type:		Ext.	Nucl.	Ext.	Nucl.	Ext.	Nucl.
Women's contribution	High	1/2	0/2	2/6	5/12	4/1	4/1
to subsistence:	Low	6/1	0/5	12/3	7/1	3/1	2/0

In conclusion, variation existing across nonindustrial cultures in the father–infant relationship, described in terms of basic physical and emotional "proximity," is correlated with socioecological factors. The form of marriage, isolation of the parental pair, division of labor, and requirements for male participation in defense activities are related to father–infant proximity. The data suggest that some subsistence adaptations present conditions in which competition and polygyny separate the father physically and psychologically from young children. The significant associations found among the variables, while weak, are meaningful given the level of measurement error unavoidably present in scales describing family relationships over large cross-cultural samples. Further research should seek improved definitions and scales for these variables.

Father–Infant Interactions Among !Kung Hunter–Gatherers

Father–infant relationships among the !Kung San people of Botswana are of special interest for two reasons. First, they are a warm-climate gathering and hunting people who represent one variant of the mode of subsistence that characterized 98 to 99 percent of human and protohuman history (Lee & DeVore, 1968). Thus the forces of natural selection operating on human fathers and their relationships with their children during the time when the basic nature of such relations were being formed are in evidence in this context. Second, the !Kung are classified by Barry and Paxson as "high" on the scale of closeness of fathers to infants and young children in the sample of nonindustrial societies surveyed in the previous section. They thus represent the upper end of the range of direct male care of offspring seen in the ethnographic record and, by inference, in the human past. Quantitative data collected by Konner on the behavior of fathers toward infants and toward 2- to 6-year old children are summarized here, and the reader is refered to the original edition for the full report of the data.

Observations of 43 infants during daylight hours over all days of the year, begun only when the infant was within 15 feet of the mother, showed that fathers interacted with infants under 2 years of age 14 percent of the time. They interacted with infant boys less than 26 weeks of age 12 percent of the time and at age 27–99 weeks, 22 percent of the time. They interacted less often with infant girls, 3 percent and 11 percent respectively (sex differences at older age is significant). The mother is estimated to interact with her infant in nearly 100 percent of randomly distributed time samples.

Although the discrepancy between mothers and fathers in amount of interaction with infants is wide, the breakdown of type of proximity with the infant when either is primary caretaker is similar. Physical contact occurs 80 to 85 percent of the time that either parent is primary caretaker of younger infants, and 60 percent of the time for older infants. As primary caretakers, mothers or fathers were face-to-face with young infants about 10 percent of the time, not touching but within 2 feet about 5 percent of the time, and almost never more than 2 feet away. In older infants, time face-to-face with mothers or fathers decreased to about 3 percent. Time more than 2 feet away also increased, to 7 to 9 percent.

The father was present in 30 percent of observations on children aged 2 to 6, also made throughout daylight hours and on all days of the week. This contrasts with 19 percent on similar observations made by Konner in London for a comparative study (Blurton Jones & Konner, 1973). On observations of 3- to 11-year-old children in six different cultures including a New England community in the United States, father presence ranged from 3 to 14 percent of the time, with 9 percent in the small-town New England community (Whiting & Whiting, 1975b). Although these figures refer to children in slightly different age ranges, !Kung fathers appear to be present in the social environment of children more often than fathers in at least six other cultures including our own industrial society.

Family Relations in Cross-Cultural Perspective

Our review of the father's role across species and across human societies suggests that economic conditions, the division of labor, family organization, and isolation of the parental pair are major factors affecting family roles and relationships. Given that these conditions are changing now in our own culture, it is not surprising that our ideology is also undergoing change. Our popular and scientific literature repeatedly attests to our uncertainty about the nature and roles of mothers and fathers. We are presently studying the competency of human males to care for and respond to infants—the role that our culture has most strongly associated with the mother in our past conceptions. In addition, we seek to document the existing noncaretaking roles of the father. At this point we have good descriptive data for at least one segment of our population—the middleclass educated families who are the subjects of most of the recent research.

Studies of mother–infant and father–infant interaction in families where the mother is the primary caretaker have found many similarities between mothers and fathers in the nature of their responses to infants. This finding is consonant with a view of the relative helplessness and immature status of the infant as the main determinant of the nature of adult responses. In cross-cultural research, the powerful effect of infants in determining the nature of interactions to them across the sexes and also across ages has been demonstrated in the six-culture data of Whiting and Whiting (1975a). In recent American research, a number of subtle and interesting differences have also been reported. These are reviewed at length in the other chapters in this volume. (We refer especially to the father's role as a playmate of infants, as one who may introduce the child to the outside world and to the particular quality or style of paternal play—characterized by more physical stimulation, rough and tumble activity, praise for the child, and social–physical rather than intellectual stimulation.) While there are at present no studies of father–infant interaction in non-Western populations using the detailed level of observational data found in the American research, even more gross observational data are sufficient to suggest that the American findings are not valid across cultures.

This possibility is suggested by a simple example from the first author's recent fieldwork in the outer Fiji Islands, located at the juncture of Melanesia and Polynesia in the southwest Pacific Ocean. The fieldsite is an isolated area, 8 to 12 hours by boat from any town, and accessible irregularly every 1 to 3 weeks in unpredictable and often dangerous weather. Living in small villages, the people subsist by farming and fishing and earning a little cash from processing copra. A great deal of cooperation and interdependence is required between individuals, between families, and between villages.

The young child grows up in a small village of clustered households, with the father's and often the mother's parents and siblings living in the same village or a neighboring one. These relatives constantly visit each other's houses, and they greet and interact with young children when they do. In randomly scheduled "spot observations" (method described by Rogoff, 1978), which the first author made over a 15-month period on the 14 children aged 6 to 42 months in one village, the mother was the caretaker in 51 percent of the observations of infants aged 6 to 12 months, and in 39 percent of the observations of infants aged 13 to 20 months. Her main helper was an adolescent or school-age girl. Fathers were found to hold, carry, cuddle, or "keep an eye on" infants from time to time; they were present in 18 percent of the observations of children aged 6 to 30 months, but were the caretaker in charge in only 8 percent. They rarely fed or cleaned infants and were never observed to change an infant's diaper. These activities were strictly the task of women and were culturally defined as such.

But the style of interaction between adult males and infants or toddlers could reveal a tender attitude and manner of behavior quite different from that typically seen between males and infants in our own culture. Rough or vigorous play, which may be a masculine style of interaction with infants in our culture, did not characterize the interactions of Fijian fathers or other males with infants. The game of tossing babies in the air, for example, was never seen. Both men *and* women engaged in a certain kind of vigorous sensory stimulation of infants—greeting and talking to the baby in a dramatic voice, giving sharp playful slaps or vigorous jiggling. However, these interactions were not usually offered by either the mother *or* father, but by the baby's *other* significant relatives. The father's interactions with his young children were in general more reserved. The most remarkable feature of interactions of males with infants was the possibility of relaxed and passive relations with infants. Thus an adult male might sit quietly and engage in a long visual regard of the child, fan the flies off a sleeping infant, or merely sit quietly with an infant in a tender and protective attitude. This could characterize the father's interactions, but even more so the grandfather's or mother's brother's interactions. In contrast, the fathers in our American research seem to engage in more *active* playful exchanges.

This simple example should warn us against considering the father's roles, during infancy or later, in any unidimensional sense. At least three elements emerge: (1) the patterns of social behavior that may result from long periods of caretaking responsibility; (2) cultural differences in the social network of the infant, in the roles that persons in this network play, and in the kinds of stimulation they provide to the infant or child; and (3) cultural differences in the acceptable male and female styles of behavior and their origin. The last has been the topic of a large literature in the field of psychological anthropology, led by J. Whiting's work cited earlier and Mead's (1935) debunking of our sex role stereotypes in *Sex and Temperament in Three Primitive Societies*.

Finally, it may be helpful to provide a very broad characterization of American periurban family life in cross-cultural perspective. As one member of a team conducting field studies in non-Western cultures under the direction of Beatrice and John Whiting, the first author has shared observations on family life with fieldworkers recently returned from rural East and West Africa, Micronesia, Mexico, Israel, urban Hong Kong, and Iran. Especially impressive in this perspective are the following characteristics of the middle-class periurban American family: (1) the relative lack of preparation of both mothers and fathers for parenthood; (2) the isolation of nonemployed mothers from a congenial adult context; and (3) their high degree of dependency on the spouse for emotional and material support.

As noted in the ethnographic examples, in many non-Western societies women make very significant contributions to the subsistence resources of the family. They often engage in foraging, agriculture, fishing, or marketing activities, which draw them outside of any definable domestic sphere and also bring them into contact with other adult women. In contrast, the productive work settings provided by our society are less compatible with child rearing, and there are fewer sources of help in child care available to the mother. In addition, our culture tends to devalue domestic work, and its devaluation is dramatized perhaps by the wide range of work specializations and discrepancies in work compensation that exist.

Finally, we notice that the sexes are integrated in our cultural ideology, in striking contrast to the separately defined spheres of male and female found in many agricultural societies. In these societies, the peer group of adult men and women is their same sex group, whereas in our society men and women interact and even compete against each other within one sphere. Related to our ideology is the expectation that the husband–wife relationship is outstanding among all other social relationships. Among women observed in rural Fiji, for example, a wife's interactions with her husband were be a minor portion of her social interactions in general; most of her interactions were be with other women, her children, and other children. Such differences in social context probably influence the patterns of father–infant interaction and stimulation observed in the different cultures.

The general point here is that reports on the role of fathers in the American research should not be over generalized but considered as data describing particular types of families. In other contexts, we would expect that the role of the father and his relationship to his children would be quite different.

SUMMARY

A model derived from natural selection theory relating parental behavior to mating patterns, competition, and sex differences is presented, and species with different forms and levels of parental behavior are compared. In a broad phylogenetic perspective, our species shows more male parental behavior than some species but less than others. A review of mammals, and primates in particular, shows that male care of young is associated with monogamy. In some species it also accompanies a long period of infant dependency, and occurs when the parents are relatively isolated from other conspecifics and one adult alone cannot provide the necessary food resources or protection. Variations *within* species in the level and forms of male parental behavior are also found, and they are related to environmental conditions. Some hormonal correlates of nurturant behavior are absent in human males; but there is no evidence that, in spite of these hormonal differences, human males cannot be fully adequate caretakers.

In cross-cultural perspective, fathers in nonindustrial subsistence adaptations are found to have a very small role in the actual care of young children compared to mothers. But variation is evident in the degree to which the father takes on a nurturant or affiliative role, as well as in his economic, protective, and didactic roles. Using a scale of father–infant "proximity," variations found in a sample of 80 nonindustrial societies are related to family and community organization and to economic adaptation. Fathers are more likely to be in proximity to their infants in monogamous, nuclear-family, and nonpatrilocal cultures and in subsistence adaptations in which the mother makes a large contribution to the resources of the family. On this scale, fathers are relatively "close" among foragers, who represent the sociocultural adaptation that existed for 99 percent of human history.

The results of recent American research on the roles of fathers should be considered in relation to the particular types of families that are the subjects of the research. Diverse family and community structures found across human societies provide a context for variations in the roles and interpersonal relationships among family members. In a broad cross-cultural perspective, for example, the American middle-class educated periurban family is one in which both mothers and fathers are relatively unprepared for parenthood, and in which mothers of young children are often isolated from a congenial adult social context and highly dependent on the spouse for material and emotional support. By comparing the social contexts and work demands on parents in different cultural contexts, we may better inform our psychological research on family roles and relationships and their effects on child development.

REFERENCES

Alexander, R. D. *Darwinism and human affairs*. Seattle: University of Washington Press, 1979.

Ayres, B. Bride theft and raiding for wives in cross-cultural perspective. *Anthropological Quarterly*, 1974, **47**, 238–252.

Bacon, M. K., Child, I. L., & Barry, H. A cross-cultural study of correlates of crime. *Journal of Abnormal and Social Psychology*, 1963, **66**, 241–300.

Barash, D. P. Ecology of parental behavior in the hoary marmot *(Marmota caligata):* An evolutionary interpretation. *Journal of Mammalogy*, 1975, **56**, 613–618.

Barry, H., Bacon, M. K., & Child, I. L. A cross-cultural survey of some sex differences in socialization. *Journal of Abnormal and Social Psychology*, 1957, **55**, 327–332.

Barry, H., Child, I. L., & Bacon, M. K. Relation of child training to subsistence economy. *American Anthropologist*, 1959, **61**, 51–63.

Barry, H., & Paxson, L. M. Infancy and early childhood: Cross-cultural codes. *Ethnology*, 1971, **10**, 467–508.

Blaffer Hrdy, S. The care and exploitation of nonhuman primate infants by conspecifics other than the mother. In J. Rosenblatt, R. Hinde, & C. Beer (Eds.), *Advances in the study of behavior*, Vol. 6. New York: Academic Press, 1976.

Blurton Jones, N. G., & Konner, M. J. Sex differences in behavior of two- to- five-year-olds in London and among the Kalahari Desert Bushmen. In R. P. Michael, & J. H. Crook (Eds.), *Comparative ecology and behavior of primates*. London: Academic Press, 1973.

Breuggeman, L. A. Parental care in a group of free-ranging rhesus monkeys *(Macaca mulatta)*. *Folia Primatologica*, 1973, **20**, 178–210.

Burton, F. D. The integration of biology and behavior in the socialization of *Macaca sylvana* of Gibraltar. In F. E. Poirier (Ed.), *Primate socialization*. New York: Random House, 1972.

Burton, R. V., & Whiting, J. W. M. The absent father and cross-sex identity. *Merrill-Palmer Quarterly*, 1961, **7**, 85–95.

Chamove, A., Harlow, H., & Mitchell, G. Sex differences in the infant-directed behavior of pre-adolescent rhesus monkeys. *Child Development*, 1967, **38**, 329–335.

Corbett, L., & Newson, A Dingo society and its maintenance: A preliminary analysis. In M. W. Fox (Ed.), *The Wild Canids*. New York: Van Nostrand Reinhold, 1975.

Crook, J. L. The socioecology of primates. In J. H. Crook (Ed.), *Social behavior in birds and mammals*. New York: Academic Press, 1970.

Crook, J. L., & Goss-Custard, J. D. Social ethology. *Annual Review of Psychology*, 1972, **23**, 277–312.

Daly, M., & Wilson, M. *Sex, evolution and behavior*. North Scituate, Mass.: Duxbury Press, 1978.

Davis, P. G., & Gandleman, P. Pup-killing produced by the administration of testosterone propionate to adult female mice. *Hormones and Behavior,* 1972, **3,** 169–173.

Dohlinow, P. J. Lecture delivered at Institute on Evolution and the Development of Behavior, Institute of Child Development, University of Minnesota, 1975.

Dudley, D. Contributions of paternal care to the growth and development of the young in *Peromyscus californicus. Behavioral Biology,* 1974, **11,** 155–166 (a).

Dudley, D. Paternal behavior in the California mouse, *Peromyscus californicus. Behavioral Biology,* 1974, **11,** 247–252 (b).

Eisenberg, J. F. The social organizations of mammals. *Handbuch der Zoologie,* 1966, **8,** 1–92.

Epple, G. Parental behavior in *Saguinus fuscicollis* spp. *(Callithricidae). Folia Primatologica,* 1975, **24,** 221–238.

Estes, R. D., & Goddard, J. Prey selection and hunting behavior of the African wild dog. *Journal of Wildlife Management,* 1967, **31,** 52–70.

Evans-Pritchard, E. E. Heredity and gestation, as the Zande see them. *Sociologus,* 1932, **8,** 400–414.

Fox, M. W. Evolution of social behavior in canids. In M. W. Fox (Ed.), *The wild canids.* New York: Van Nostrand Reinhold, 1975.

Fuller, G. B., Zarrow, M. X., Anderson, C. O., & Denenberg, V. H. Testosterone propionate during gestation in the rabbit: Effect on subsequent maternal behavior. *Journal of Reproduction and Fertility,* 1970, **23,** 285–290.

Gier, H. T. Ecology and social behavior of the coyote. In M. W. Fox (Ed.), *The wild canids.* New York: Van Nostrand Reinhold, 1975.

Gomber, J., & Mitchell, G. Preliminary report on adult male isolation-reared rhesus monkeys caged with infants. *Developmental Psychology,* 1974, **10,** 298.

Goodman, L. A. The multivariate analysis of qualitative data: Interactions among multiple classifications. *Journal of the American Statistical Association,* 1970, **65,** 226–256.

Gregory, M., Silvers, A., & Sutch, D. *Sociobiology and human nature.* San Francisco: Jossey-Bass, 1978.

Hamilton, W. D. The genetical theory of social behavior, I, II. *Journal of Theoretical Biology,* 1964, **7,** 1–52.

Jolly, A. *The evolution of primate behavior.* New York: Macmillan, 1972.

Junod, H. A. *The life of a South African tribe* (2nd ed., 2 vols.). London: Macmillan, 1927.

Kummer, H. Tripartite relations in hamadryas baboons. In S.A. Altmann (Ed.), *Social communication among primates.* Chicago: University of Chicago Press, 1967.

Lee, R. B., & DeVore, I. (Eds.), *Man the hunter.* Chicago: Aldine, 1968.

Lehrman, D. S. The physiological basis of parental feeding behavior in the ring dove. *Behavior,* 1955, **7,** 241–286.

Malinowski, B. *Sex and repression in savage society.* New York: Harcourt, Brace, 1927.

Mason, W. A. Social organization of the South American monkey, *Callicebus moloch:* A preliminary report. *Tulane Studies in Zoology,* 1966, **13**, 23–28.

Maynard-Smith, J. Parental investment: A prospective analysis. *Animal Behaviour,* 1977, **25**, 1–9

Mead, M. *Sex and temperament in three primitive societies.* New York: Morrow, 1935.

Mitchell, G., & Brandt, E. M. Paternal behavior in primates. In F. E. Poirier (Ed.), *Primate socialization.* New York: Random House, 1972.

Money, J., & Ehrhardt, A. A. *Man and woman, boy and girl.* Baltimore: Johns Hopkins University Press, 1972.

Murdock, G. P. Ethnographic atlas. *Ethnology,* 1967, **6**, 109–236.

Murdock, G. P., & White, D. R. Standard cross-cultural sample. *Ethnology,* 1969, **8**, 329–369.

Murdock, G. P., & Wilson, S. F. Settlement patterns and community organization. *Ethnology,* 1972, **11**, 254–269.

Musil, A. *The manner and customs of the Rwala Bedouin.* New York: The American Geographical Society, 1928.

Nicolson, N. Personal communication, June 4, 1980.

Osgood, C. *The Koreans and their culture.* New York: Ronald, 1951.

Otterbein, K. F. Internal war: A cross-cultural study. *American Anthropologist,* 1968, **70**, 277–289.

Otterbein, K. F., & Otterbein, C. S. An eye for an eye, a tooth for a tooth: A cross-cultural study of feuding. *American Anthropologist,* 1965, **67**, 1470–1482.

Packer, C. Male care and exploitation of infants in *Papio anubis. Animal Behaviour,* 1980, **28**, 512–520.

Paige, K. E., & Paige, J. M. The politics of birth practices: A strategic analysis. *American Sociological Review,* 1973, **38**, 663–677.

Powdermaker, H. *Life in Lesu.* New York: Norton, 1933.

Quadagno, P. M., & Rockwell, J. The effect of gonadal hormones in infancy on maternal behavior in the adult rat. *Hormones and Behavior,* 1972, **3**, 55–62.

Ransom, T. W., & Ransom, B. S. Adult male-infant relations among baboons *(Papio anubis). Folia Primatologica,* 1971, **16**, 179–195.

Ransom, T. W., & Rowell, T. E. Early social development of feral baboons. In F. E. Poirier (Ed.), *Primate socialization.* New York: Random House, 1972.

Redican, W. K., & Mitchell, G. A longitudinal study of parental behavior in adult male rhesus monkeys: I. Observations on the first dyad. *Developmental Psychology,* 1973, **8**, 135–136.

Ridley, M. Paternal care. *Animal Behaviour,* 1978, **26**, 904–932.

Rogoff, B. Spot observation: An introduction and examination. *Quarterly Newsletter of the Institute for Comparative Human Development,* 1978, **2**, 21–26.

Snyder, P. A. Behavior of *Leontopithecus rosalia* (The Golden Lion Marmoset) and related species: A Review. In D. D. Bridgewater (Ed.), *Saving the lion marmoset*. Wheeling, W. Va.: The Wild Animal Propagation Trust, 1972.

Starin, E.D. Food transfer by wild titi monkeys (*Callicebus torquatus torquatus*). *Folia Primatologica*, 1978, **30**, 145–151.

Symons, D. *The evolution of human sexuality*. New York: Oxford University Press, 1979.

Trivers, R. L. Parental investment and sexual selection. In B. Campbell (Ed.), *Sexual selection and the descent of man 1871–1971*. Chicago: Aldine, 1972.

van Lawick, H., & van Lawick-Goodall, J. *Innocent killers*. Boston: Houghton Mifflin, 1971.

van Velsen, H. H. E. T., & Van Weterling, W. Residence, power groups and intra-society aggression. *International Archives of Ethnology*, 1960, **49**, 169–200.

Whiting, B. B. Sex identity conflict and physical violence: A comparative study. *American Anthropologist*, 1965, **67**, 123–140.

Whiting, B. B. Personal communication, June 1974.

Whiting, B. B., & Whiting, J. W. M. *Children of six cultures: A psychocultural analysis*. Cambridge, Mass.: Harvard University Press, 1975 (a).

Whiting, J. W. M., & Whiting, B. B. Aloofness and intimacy of husbands and wives: A cross-cultural study. *Ethos*, 1975, **3**, 183–207 (b).

Whiting, J. W. M. The place of aggression in social interaction. In J. F. Short, Jr., & M. E. Wolfgang (Eds.), *Collective violence*. Chicago: Aldine-Atherton, 1972.

Whiting, J. W. M., Kluckhorn, R., & Anthony, S. A. The function of male initiation ceremonies at puberty. In E. E. Maccoby, T. Newcomb, & E. Hartley (Eds.), *Readings in social psychology*. New York: Holt, 1958.

Wilson, E. O. *On human nature*. Cambridge, Mass.: Harvard University Press, 1978.

Appendix

SAMPLE AND SCALES FOR ANALYSES ON FATHER–INFANT PROXIMITY

Sample

The sample is a subsample of 80 from Murdock and White's (1969) Standard Cross-cultural Sample, a world sample of historically and linguistically independent cultures. Cultures were selected that were rated by Barry and Paxson (1971) on the father–infant proximity scale at their highest confidence level. The resultant sample includes all subsistence types except industrialized societies and is geographically distributed as follows:

Africa	12	Oceania	19
Europe and Circum-Mediterranean	10	North America	17
Asia	10	South America	12

Scales

Father–Infant Proximity (Tables 5–8)	Barry and Paxson (1971)
Father–Child Proximity (Table 5)	Barry and Paxson (1971)
Nonmaternal Relationships (Table 5)	Barry and Paxson (1971)
Earliness of Autonomy	Barry and Paxson (1971)
Dependency Satisfaction Potential	Whiting and Child (1953)
Primary Mode of Subsistence (Table 6, 8)	Murdock and White (1969)
Polygyny (dichotomized) (Table 7) (P/MN)	Murdock and Wilson (1972) (p. 260, col. 8)
Polygyny (trichotomized) (Table 8) (QS/NPR/M)	Murdock (1967) (p. 155, col. 14)
Extended/Nuclear Family (Table 7) (EFS/MNPQ)	Murdock and Wilson (1972) (p. 260, col. 8)
Extended/Nuclear Family (Table 8) (EFS/MNOPQRS)	Murdock (1967) (p. 155, col. 14)
Patrilocal-Avunculocal Residence (Table 7) (PA/BMN)	Murdock and Wilson (1972) (p. 261, col. 9)

CHAPTER 5

The Father's Role in the
Social Network of a Soviet Child:
The Nationalization of the Family

JAAN VALSINER

University of North Carolina

The human tendency to assign roles to mothers and fathers and to expect them to behave according to the general social norms of a particular culture is an interesting area for psychological study and speculation. Since assigning roles is a phenomenon of culture rather than a simple expression of biological realities, it is subject to various kinds of societal–political influences (e.g., women's emancipation and men's liberation movements). Of course, this link with highly politicized issues does not improve the clarity of scientific discussions on the subject.

The roles of parents have received unequal treatment from the social scientists. Both historically and in the extent of research efforts, mothers have received more attention than fathers. This tendency toward overconcern with mothers' roles recently seems to have given way to some interest in the role of fathers. Since both parents constitute the most important part of the social network of children (especially in modern urbanized societies with low birth rates), the widening of interest to include research on fathers' roles presents the childrearing process in a more balanced framework. Attempts to analyze the social networks of the child rather than the roles of the mother and the father separately have been undertaken (see Chapters 1, 7, 8 and 12) and it has been emphasized that the influence of fathers (who in the majority of cultures have been less connected to immediate childrearing problems than mothers) may be *indirect* rather than direct (see Chapters 1, 7, 12, and 13). Because of the great intracultural variability in the ways that the influences of the father on the child are implemented, it is difficult to present a clear-cut picture of them—even on the basis of empirical data. It is easier to characterize the social network of the child on the basis of cultural role prescriptions and texts and viewpoints inside a culture dealing with that question.

The close relationship of parental roles to the biological reproductive act is interesting. In empirical case analyses it is easy to observe the roles of the parents of a child. At the same time, the roles that are taken are provided by the culture. Therefore, it is interesting to study three different but interwoven aspects of fathers' roles in children's (and mothers') social networks:

1. The comparative psychological aspect of father's roles as a possible basis of human universals in the role requirements of the fathers.

2. The cross-cultural aspect: To what extent are roles of the father similar or different in different cultures?

3. the environmental–psychological aspect: To what extent is the cross-cultural variability in fathers' role caused by the physical, economic, and social constraints on family existence in the particular culture?

West and Konner (1976) have revealed that at least some of the cross-cultural variation in fathers' contributions to the care of offspring is attributable to the ecological conditions of the particular culture. The European, monogamous, male–female relationship as a model of the family (with a relatively small number of offspring and a lot of fuss about the ways in which to bring them up) is an exception, not the rule. West and Konner have shown that the role behavior of the father in different cultures is dependent on: (1) the forms of marriage, (2) women's contribution to the subsistence of the family, (3) the extendedness of the family, and (4) the tendency toward warlike behavior within the particular culture.

This chapter is concerned with the analysis of the father's role in families in the Soviet Union. Attempts by the Soviet system to introduce changes into traditional patterns have been considered highly original and have been referred to as "the Soviet experiment" (Lynn, 1974, pp. 45–50). This analysis of the developments in the father's role in the Soviet Union is from a society-based, cross-cultural point of view. Unfortunately, because of the lack of empirical data, this presentation remains partly speculative.

THE MULTIPLICITY AND PATTERNS OF CULTURE IN THE SOVIET UNION

One of the frequent misconceptions about the Soviet Union is the idea of cultural uniformity inside the state. This understanding probably is caused by the lack of information about what people and life are like in the Soviet Union. The Russian people historically have had little contact with people from other countries. Additionally, it has been the aim of the official Soviet authorities who create the public image of one sixth of the world's population to depict the cultures within the state as uniformly "Soviet." In reality, the variety of cultures in that country is as noteworthy as in any other comparably large landmass on the globe. The cultures of national minorities differ in their ecological conditions and in their religions. They also differ in their relative independence from U.S.S.R. cultural expansionism. The "creation of Soviet culture" advertised by the regime constitutes an attempt to change traditional patterns of national minority cultures and make them assimilate Russian cultural patterns. Since the governing Soviet administration is able to introduce economic constraints on the conditions of existence of national minorities as well as introduce administrative organs according to Russian principles, the development of the high variability of nationally unique cultures has been influenced to some extent by Russian cultural patterns. This influence has been greater in urbanized areas and in places where Russians mix with the local nationalities. In rural areas the Russian influence is less effective—especially in the national republics of the Soviet Union. Resisting or assisting the process of change is also dependent on the internal patterns of the respective cultures. For example, Georgians and Armenians as well as Estonians, Latvians, and Lithuanians resist such intrusions, but at the same time a number of minor non-Russian cultures in the Russian Federation are open to these influences.

To understand the attempts made by the Soviet administration to change family patterns after 1917, a brief account of Russian cultural patterns is necessary. It must be stressed that these cultural patterns, furnished by Soviet ideology, are practically the essence of the "Soviet culture" as it is called officially in the Soviet Union. The patterns of Russian culture, like those of any culture, began a number of centuries ago and are based on the historical and economical development of the nation. On the pages that follow are described some of the basic patterns of Russian culture. These patterns are presented without any attempt at cross-cultural comparison, nor are they evaluative in any sense. The aim is to give the reader a quick and not very detailed outline of the basic principles that have governed Russian culture (and the Russian empire) for a number of centuries with little difference between the pre-1917 and post-1917 eras.

Basic Principles of Russian Culture

Group Sharing and Control. Traditionally, the overwhelming majority of resources (material and nonmaterial) any community has are shared among the members of the community. However, the community leadership has control over individual members, both through the distribution of the resources and the conformist behavior of the members of that particular community. The Russian village community *(obstshina)* traditionally has been the basis of this cultural pattern.

This principle is also effective in less complex individual relationships. A person may be extremely helpful to another, sharing (without profit) almost anything he or she has, and sometimes expecting the other person to behave in ways considered "right" in his or her norms. This is usually done in some generalized way, rather than by saying "I do this—you must do that."

Deep Religious and Moralistic Reasoning. Popular and influential ideas in the culture are moral–emotional rather than rational–pragmatic. "Finding the truth" is the ultimate goal and method of argumentation in pursuing any ideas in the culture. This can be observed at all levels of society—from inter-individual encounters devoted to finding out which is the "right way" (="true way") to lead one's life to the contents of state propaganda messages and the rituals of governmental actions. Based on this characteristic, religion has always been part and parcel of Russian culture (at least during the last five or more centuries). This religiousness has very often been either covertly or openly militant toward anybody who does not conform to its standards.

The common understanding that religion has been forced out of the scene and that atheism prevails in post-1917 Russia is not contradictory to the present principle—practically all the official ideologies in modern Russia function along the same principles as Russian orthodox religion did before 1917: as the religion of the state. In the process of replacing one type of religion by another (the latter usually utilizing the very same methods to assert its influence on people, from icons to obligations and force), it is no wonder that the old religion comes under fierce attack. However, more than 60 years of "militant atheism" in the Soviet Union has not been very successful; so for people inside the country there is a choice available between officially sanctioned atheistic communism and officially disliked religion of any form. It has been customary in Russia for centuries not to like (and often to persecute) dissident thinkers and people with nonconformist behavior.

Subjectively Evaluative, Clear-Cut "Good-Bad" Logic. The Russian way of argumentation is heavily dependent on two-valent logic, which is highly emotionally (and moralistically) flavored. Practically the first thing in any argument in Russian culture is to label phenomena along the criteria good and bad, and then to pursue subjective argumentation in favor of the good phenomena as opposed to the bad. Some phenomena are often labelled implicitly good (e.g., everything that is Russian is good, whereas everything that is alien—that is, non Russian or not pro-Russian, is bad).

The exact argumentation around some phenomena may change dramatically in time, especially when the labeling is redefined in some instances (e.g., Soviet propaganda dealing with China over the decades). However, the method of argumentation remains the same—irrespective of the contents.

Intervention Tendencies and "We-They" Contraposition. Russian culture is highly interventionistic. It is also furnished by the "insider–outsider" distinction ("we belong together and are facing "them"") that functions hierarchically at any level of society, from referent groups of individual people (with high sentiments of belonging to the group) to the maximum abstract referent group advertised as the "Soviet society." Thus the intrusion of the state into the lives of individuals who do not conform to the norms of "Soviet society," with no respect to their individual personalities and plans is simply a traditional cultural pattern quite different from Western ideas about relationships between individuals and society.

Hierarchical Organization of Social Institutions. In the Russian culture of fierce, emotionally-furnished intergroup fights of different kinds and at different levels, it is not surprising that the society usually has been organized by a totalitarian hierarchical system of social institutions. This hierarchical system makes it advantageous for anybody to become an official (*tschinovnik*) of at least one level above other people.

Relevance of Word Magic and Clear-Cut Taboos in the Culture. Malinowski (1927) has discussed the pragmatic role of words as magic in the Trobriand culture. Words are extensively used to change phenomena in Russian culture. For example, it is customary for the officials in the Soviet Union to deliver highly emphatic speeches about the excellent results of the "socialist economic system" when in reality there is more than average trouble with economic management. This word magic naturally does not bring with it any changes in reality but is influential on people, dissociating them from any attempts to understand the reality. It is effective, working through people's faith in the government (i.e. the Tsar) and the conformism that allows them to believe in the official viewpoints advocated by the huge administrative institutions.

In addition to using word magic, the culture also blocks some areas from being extensively dealt with by the people—the culture has clear-cut moral-based Taboo areas. Perhaps the most important of these is the suppression (not only institutional, but also interindividual) of problem orientation in the culture. The Soviet society has been advocated as a society with no problems (or with minor, quickly soluble problems that are efficiently dealt with by the authorities). The areas of social problems and sexual relationships are taboo fields. These social taboo areas complement the word magic—the former keep the people generally ignorant thus simplifying the effects of the latter.

Varying Openness to Influences from Other Cultures. Although in its essence Russian culture is self-confined and highly traditional and closed to influences from other cultures, there have been periods in history of relative openness to other influences. However, these periods (particularly of openness to European cultural traditions) have been only episodic, ending in closure of the cultural ties and relabeling the absorbed elements ''Russian.''

Display of ''Potyomkin Villages'' to Outsiders. The high self-evaluation of the Russian culture leads to the custom showing off the facades (sometimes these are just specially designed for such display, having no other functions) of some aspects of the culture, while making other sides of the phenomenon in question a taboo area. This tendency to show off is present in the relationship of the Soviet culture with other cultures as well as within the culture itself (especially well-advanced between the hierarchical levels of the administration). The economic results going upward in the government and state hierarchy provide a good example: every new (higher) level of the hierarchy tends to show itself in a more favorable manner to its superior level (and even fake data), so when the information reaches the top it is greatly changed.

THE NATIONALIZATION OF THE FAMILY

The patterns of family interaction and fathers' roles in families have been changed a great deal in the Soviet Union (Lynn, 1974). Contrary to old traditions of strong patriarchal families, the immediate post-1917 reforms encouraged women's emancipation. However, in liberating women from the authoritarian rule of the men and changing the ways that men and women interact in families, the ruling authorities were concerned with the transfer of the authoritarian, almighty role of the individual fathers to the state which assumed governing and controlling functions applicable to all families. This was done under the pretext of building up ''a new, socialist type of a family,'' but should be viewed in the context of the nationalization of the entire economy and as an extension of this to include family life.

The resulting liberation of women from the exclusive wife–mother role in the traditional family system created a woman who is free to work in industry, agriculture, and so forth, without any control from the husband, but under strict state control. The image of the Soviet woman as an ''active participant in society'' (under state control) and not as a feminine figure devoted to the care of children has prevailed in the official contemplation of women's roles since the inception of the Soviet state.[1] Feminine character-

---

[1]Problems related to sex differences in the Soviet Union have not been considered worth studying by the state officials who control psychological research. In the 1960s, when a psychologist from one of the Baltic republics went to Moscow to present data on the psychological differences between men and women, the psychologists there were very sympathetic to him because he came from a backward Soviet province where these ''capitalist remnants'' of male/female psychological differences have not disappeared yet.

istics and functions are not emphasized except in terms of mothering responsibilities (giving birth to children is considered essential—but by no means
most important—because this is the way to acquire new active members of
the society). Instead, the ability of women to take jobs traditionally performed by men is emphasized and positively evaluated by state authorities.
Thus the important change in fathers' roles in the Soviet Union is based on
the transfer of his primary control over wife and children to the Soviet state
institutions. Whereas traditional Russian state hierarchy has executed control
over children and their mothers through fathers (one level higher than wom-
en), this pattern has changed (see Figure 1). It has been replaced by level-
ing the status differences between fathers and mothers and introducing a

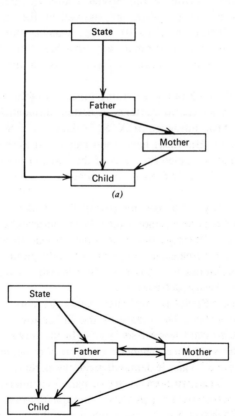

Figure 1. The nationalization of family roles in the Soviet Union. (*a*) Traditional role system.
(*b*) Soviet role system.

new direct channel of control over the life of the family. The direct control of mothers by the state has become the leading mechanism in governing children as well as fathers. Consciously or nonconsciously, the anonymous architects of Soviet totalitarian society have made great use of the natural emergence of women's liberation movements to control the behavior of fathers. The majority of housekeeping and childrearing activities is realized by mothers rather than fathers in the Soviet Union (as in the majority of other cultures), irrespective of the advertised "equality" between the sexes. However, in planning strategies and making decisions about careers, political activity, and so forth, women have gained far greater influence than before. By introducing the direct state → mother influence channel in the society, the state has been able to introduce one more control into the life of Russian families. The reality of life in the Soviet Union including economic, social–moral and bureaucratic constraints, as well as the effects of "socialist upbringing" (Bronfenbrenner, 1970) makes women more loyal "agents" within the family. They can eliminate any possible "misbehaviors" of children and fathers in their embryonic form, working through interpersonal pressures.

The transfer of the controlling/providing functions in the family from fathers to the state can be followed in the texts of certain influential Soviet writers on educational topics. The influence of A. S. Makarenko in Soviet education has prevailed for decades. His ideas have been canonized as the basis of "Soviet pedagogics." He has presented his ideas of the "Soviet family" explicitly (see Bronfenbrenner, 1970, p. 3, for an exact citation):

1. The Soviet family is "an organic part of Soviet society and every attempt to build up its own experience independently of the moral demands of society is bound to result in disproportion, discordant as an alarm bell" (i.e., any attempt to preserve or create an independent family group not subservient to state control is not tolerated by this first characteristic of the "Soviet family" as opposed to the "bourgeois family").

2. Parents in the "Soviet family" have authority only in the reflection of the authority of the state. The "duty of the father toward his children is a particular form of his duty toward society." (In the Soviet Union, "society" equals "state".) The state has "handed over" to the parents "a certain measure of social authority," and it demands from the parents "correct upbringing of future citizens." Here, two points are of particular interest. First, the handing over of state functions to the parents, consequently making them responsible, is a common Soviet turn of phrase when introducing central state control in different fields. Second, the rules for bringing up children are set by the state, and parents who do not conform to these principles are punished, in one way or another.

The basic (ideal, for the Soviets) society (and the family within it), functions according to centrally settled principles. These principles should be internalized so well that the "Soviet family" functions on the basis of them alone. This has been demonstrated in a study by Bronfenbrenner (1970, pp. 76–81), in which he reveals a tendency among Soviet schoolchildren of Russian origin to try to correct "misbehaviors" of other children themselves, without reporting to adults. These kinds of "corrections" at interpersonal levels are paired by the requirements to report occurrences of "misbehaviors" to the relevant authorities. Thus the *Intervene Yourself* (IY) rule (which is the most optimal way for the state to govern in a totalitarian society) is paralleled by the *Report-On-Others* (ROA) rule. Thus the state executes control without much effort and has all the necessary information about what is going on in the society. These two rules are applied at all levels of society and in every age group. An example of how these rules work is the very widely publicized case of Pavel Morozov, a Russian schoolboy of the post-1917 decades. His actions—attempting to persuade his father to behave in a "loyal" way (to give his grain to the state), and upon his father's refusal reporting him to the authorities—are widely advertised as examples of "right behavior" in children. Although there is considerable variability in living according to the rules of IY and ROA because of the great heterogeneity of the society, these rules nevertheless are the essence of the organization of Soviet society. Parental roles are mostly executed on the mother–father level with an occasional required information exchange on child behavior with the state's representatives (teachers). In these exchanges, the father's role is supposed to be the same as that of the mother since both of them are considered servants of the state in educational matters. Nevertheless, the traditional patriarchal father role of great disciplinary authority still prevails, although in milder forms. The father's role in Soviet society has indeed undergone certain changes. However, it has been in the form of transferring the traditional role to the state, rather than creating any new father role. This change has been paralleled by changes in the mother's role, so that both roles have become increasingly similar. These role changes tend to develop families with no sex-role differences that function to create additional citizens of that particular society—a goal widely advertised by the Soviet official media.

ECONOMIC CONSTRAINTS ON FAMILY LIFE IN THE SOVIET UNION

Despite intense claims to the contrary by USSR propaganda, the economic conditions of Soviet families is by no means easy. Salaries (although equal for men and women) are low, and it is economically impossible for a wife to stay at home to be a housewife. The housing shortage is a serious problem for families, and dissatisfaction with present housing conditions is noteworthy even among families who have relatively modern apartments. There is still too little space for different activities (Kruusvall & Heidmets, 1979). Low wages and limited facilities, especially housing and childcare,[2] are additional factors in breaking down the traditional father–mother roles and substituting the state as provider–caretaker, not only for the child but also for the parents. Fathers and mothers must show their "active loyalty" to the state, usually in the form of consenting to take on some "societal functions"—work that is not paid for but is taken into consideration in the granting of places for children in kindergartens and car-purchasing permits, distribution and redistribution of housing facilities, and so forth. The people who demonstrate their willingness to do extra work can sometimes receive the necessary benefits to improve their families' functioning. As an alternative, it is possible to obtain the necessary facilities through a framework of acquaintances among the people who control these facilities. This has become increasingly popular—especially since it is a more efficient way to cope with economic problems and inflationary influences.

Economic survival is most difficult for people who are neither engaged in any way in the state hierarchy nor have sufficient acquaintances in the "black economy" network. If these people belong to the lower-income category (young specialists with university education, teachers, secretaries, nurses, shop assistants, etc.), it is possible for them to survive either by severe restrictions in consumption or with the help of their parents. Parental help constitutes a special kind of social welfare system that is not connected to the state but is organized by its own kinship-based principle, and it helps young families deal with financial and other difficulties. Its informality makes it difficult to analyze further without special data. However, the housing and economic crises make it a common practice for young families to live with their parents or parents-in-law. These three- (and sometimes four-) generation extensions of the family create greater kinship groups that share the problems of coping with economic difficulties. Since this way of communal living is customary in Russian cultural tradition (as sharing of resources is), it constitutes a natural way of survival in the totalitarian society.

CROSS-CULTURAL VARIABILITY IN FATHERS' ROLES

The vast majority of cultures in the Soviet Union can be divided into general subgroups on the basis the religious roots of their existence. Despite certain

---

[2]Although the number of places available in nurseries is growing from year to year, there are still not enough to meet the demands of the people. Parents who cannot place their child in a nursery have to hire a nanny (which is very expensive) or use their own parents for the purpose.

frictions among Russians, Ukrainians, and Byelorussians, their common religion (Russian Orthodox Church) has provided them with relatively similar cultural patterns. The most numerous single religion-based group of cultures in the Soviet Union pursuing independent cultural traditions is the Islamic group of cultures in Central Asia and around the Caucasus mountains. The basic cultural traditions of these nations have long been influenced by Muslim religious patterns. Among the different subgroups the influence has varied in intensity. For example, the Kirghiz are not governed intensely by Islamic rules, whereas the Islamic influence among Uzbeks, Tadjiks, and Turkmens is prominent. Partly because of the relatively short period of time since Central Asia was captured by Russian colonial troops in the nineteenth century (Carrère d'Encausse, 1967) and partly because of the inherent nature of Islam, Muslim cultural traditions are highly resistant to assimilating other cultural patterns.

The migration of Russians and other nationalities culturally closely related to them has been noteworthy—their number in Central Asia is constantly growing—and increased Russian presence in urban areas includes various state government bodies. The influx of non-Muslim nationalities into rural areas has not been noteworthy. Evidently, the main cause for this Russian inability to mix with Central Asian people in rural areas is the strong pressure of the local population on the new settlers to accept the cultural patterns of their region. However, the Muslim traditions in Central Asia have changed during the post-1917 government's handling of affairs. Some religious practices (the long Ramadan feast, religious pilgrimages, strict observance of Friday's rest, polygamy, and the wearing of veils among women) have disappeared (Ryvkin, 1975). However, the relationships between men and women and the role prescriptions in family life have remained under strong (albeit covert) Islamic influence. The Soviet establishment tried to introduce changes into these traditional family-role relationships in their usual campaignlike way in the 1920s. They attempted to change women's roles in Central Asia in order to nationalize the family in these regions. However, this created serious turmoil and resistance among the people, so the state-imposed campaign had to be toned down (Massell, 1975).

It is curious that the Islamic cultures and Soviet Russian cultural patterns are fairly similar in their totalitarianism (Ryvkin, 1975). However, whereas in the Islamic case the totalitarian society is based on the personal authoritarianism of a (usually older) male, the Soviet totalitarianism is the more anonymous type of state authoritarianism. The Islamic family roles give the father almost total power over the wife and the children. Male children are highly valued by the parents, and this attitude is well evidenced in the very high birth rate in all the Central Asian territories. The father traditionally does not take part in the education of his children or in their rearing (except for punishing them), and the social distance between fathers and children is great. The traditional Muslim upbringing of females has developed intense feelings of subservience to men.

Thus it is clear why early attempts by the U.S.S.R. government to "liberate" women and change family life in Central Asia were not successful. The Soviets were expecting intensive support from women for this action, which in Central Asia was highly contrary to the cultural norms of the women as well as the men. The importance of individuals in these cultures grows as men (and women) become older. The "old wise men" (*aksakals*) are the people whose word counts in decisions. To speak of the father's role in child development in these Islamic cultures in terms of *direct* influences on the child is a projection of the European way of thinking on a totally different way of life. However the *indirect* influences of the father (e.g., in leading the household) is enormous, even if the father says not a word per day to his child. One can argue that the mere presence of the authoritarian figure of the father in the family creates the framework of role-specific child development. This role-specific development is also sex-specific. Boys and girls internalize different norms and roles. Since these social norms dictate absolute subservience of younger to older, of every member of the family to the father, and of women to men, equality of the sexes and nonauthoritarian interpersonal relationships cannot emerge when the children grow up unless the children are later influenced by non-Islamic social norms. This possibility is minimized by the militant character of Islam against other cultures. Thus the Soviet state has influenced change in many external signs of Islamic life (veils, feasts, etc.), but the internal structure of Islamic culture has not been affected[3]), and family life has remained traditional. The role of the father is still the cornerstone of the existence of the family and the socialization of children.

It is noteworthy that the cultures different from the Russian culture that have survived in their essence despite the Soviet policy of gradual reduction of the cultural differences (i.e., gradual intervention of Russian culture) are situated geographically on the borders of the Soviet Union. These nations have been incorporated into the Soviet Union as a result of the centuries-old policy of Russian governments to annex new (and strategically important) territories. Central Asia is one example. The three Baltic states—Estonia, Latvia, and Lithuania—constitute another. The first of the three, Estonia, was annexed first in 1710 as a result of Russian–Swedish war. The cultural influences of Russian rule were meager until the 1880s, when the Russian government tried to introduce a program of Russian culture (the traditional culture was related to Germany and Scandinavia). In 1920 Estonia gained independence. Then, in

---

[3]Some aspects of Russian and Central Asian Islamic cultures have become integrated, creating some very interesting conditions. For example, the Islamic authoritarian principle of personalized leadership has been closely integrated with Russian Soviet leadership principles. The natural result of this is that one can find the Soviet administration in Central Asia working even more autocratically than in Russia itself.

1940, Estonia was occupied by the Soviet Union. From 1941 to 1944 it was occupied by Germany, and from 1945 on it has again been annexed by the Soviet Union.

The Estonian culture is very interesting in itself. It has been influenced mainly by Scandinavian and German cultural patterns; the influence of Russian patterns has always been minimal. Some aspects of this culture follow:

1. The Estonian culture has never operated on the principle of group sharing and control. On the contrary, individual and independent control of environment and resources has been the norm in Estonia.

2. The Estonian culture is not highly religious, although most Estonians are Lutherans. The Estonians have been very pragmatic in using religious ideas for their own benefit and this pragmatism also applies to the newly introduced U.S.S.R. "religion". Without faith in it, the majority of Estonians try to make the most of it.

3. Instead of subjective–evaluative, good–bad logic common to the Russian culture, the Estonians base their decisions on established norms, although also using two-valence logic. This approach is rational, not emotional, and to a great extent is closely connected to German patterns.

4. The Estonians are highly individualistic—any intervention into private life is fiercely opposed by individuals. The ingroup–outgroup distinction is not elaborate in comparison with the Russian analog.

5. The hierarchy of organization in Estonia has never been very elaborate. The culture is not obsessed by hierarchy or by social mobility as a goal *per se*.

6. Labeling is uncommon in traditional Estonian culture. The Estonians introduce changes into their life through hard labor rather than word magic.

7. The Estonian culture, as a young sociopsychological structure, is constantly open to the influences of other cultures. However, it takes a long time before other cultural influences are absorbed into Estonian patterns. This may be connected to agricultural practices. The Estonians, first and foremost, have been peasants who have had to fight climatic and other conditions to ensure their harvest. The control of the influx of patterns from other cultural backgrounds is affected by slow strategies rather than quick enthusiastic introduction.

As one can see from this comparison of cultural patterns, the differences between Estonian and Russian cultures are very great. Of course, as in the case of Central Asia, some Estonian cultural patterns have been used by the Soviet Union to impose control over the nation.[4]

---

[4]There are some interesting integrations of Estonian and Soviet Russian cultural patterns in the ways in which Soviet directives are implemented in Estonia. The Estonian way of carrying out

The family in Estonia traditionally has been a separate unit not connected closely to any bigger community. The roles of father and mother have been strictly separated, perhaps because all of the adults in the peasant household had to work on similar jobs. Therefore, the father's role in Estonian families has never been autocratic—greatly different from traditional Russian (pre-1917) and Islamic cultures. However, childrearing has always been women's work in the Estonian culture, as indeed in most European cultures. Nevertheless, the father is interested in his children, and this probably stems from traditional peasant households, in which children constituted an important addition to the labor force. The distribution of childrearing in younger-generation Estonian mothers and fathers is highly democratic and equal. However, the children are not as highly valued in contemporary Estonia as they formerly were (evidently because of economic constraints), and the wish to have children is less explicit in Estonia than it is in Russia and Central Asia.

The Estonian cultural patterns and the father's role in Estonian families are similar to those in Latvia and Lithuania. As we noted earlier, the numerous Islamic cultures in Central Asia are also relatively similar to each other. Thus the two general cultural groups, the Islamic from the Asian regions and European from the Baltic regions, provide challenges to the attempts of the Soviet government to undertake "experiments" in the field of culture-bound life practices. It is important to realize that there is no such thing as a "Soviet family" in the sense of some new cultural entity. The families living in the Soviet Union belong to a great many ethnic groups of different cultural backgrounds, and the attempts to change these traditional role structures in family life have not been utterly successful—contrary to the announcements of official U.S.S.R. media.

CONCLUSIONS

The "Soviet experiment" is not at all an experiment in creating new role requirements of fathers and mothers, but is the taking over of the old role functions by the state. Of course, this has influenced the role of fathers and mothers in the Soviet Union: they are made equally subservient to the totalitarian state. The more subtle effects of these changes in roles need further study. In any case, parental sex roles are diminished in the state-owned family, and there is greater equality in the amount of childcare by fathers and mothers. In general, this seems to comply with the principle of greater maternal participa-

---

these directives is very exact, whereas the directives themselves are meant for the Russians, who do not adhere to them with great orderliness. Thus problems frequently arise when Russian directives are implemented by local Estonian leaders with German-type orderliness.

tion is subsistence activities and fathers' increased contribution to childrearing (West & Konner, 1976). However, the causes of this increase in maternal subsistence activities evidently differ between the cultures studied by West and Konner and the general Soviet society. The Soviet Union is engaged in the totalitarian concentration of control of leadership functions in society, and, to that end, the patriarchial father's role has been transferred to the state.

There is greater heterogeneity in family (and father's) roles among the many cultures inhabiting the territory of the Soviet Union. It is an inexact procedure to subsume all the heterogeneity of multi-cultural patterns under the label of "Soviet" culture. Although the totalitarian state tries to impose traditional Russian cultural patterns on those of the national minorities, it has not been very effective. It is not possible to speak of a homogeneous picture of the role of the Russian father that is more than an abstraction. This chapter is more concerned with the high variability of cultural patterns and the ways in which the Soviet state attempts to reduce this variability than it is with general tendencies in real developments within the family.

REFERENCES

Austin, P.M. The development of modern literary Uzbek: Some historical analogies. *Canadian Slavonic Papers,* 1975, **17**, 510–523.

Bronfenbrenner, U. *Two worlds of childhood.* New York: Sage, 1970.

Carrère d'Encausse, H. Systematic conquest, 1865 to 1884. In E. Allworth (Ed.), *Central Asia: A century of Russian rule.* New York: Columbia University Press, 1967.

Kruusvall, J., & Heidmets, M. Family and apartment in new microregion. In *Man, Environment and Space.* Tartu, 1979, pp. 43–82 (In Russian).

Lynn D. B. *The father: His role in child development.* Monterey, Calif.: Brooks/Cole, 1974.

Malinowski, B. *Sex and repression in savage society.* New York: Harcourt, Brace, 1927.

Massell, G. J. Family law and social mobilization in Soviet Central Asia: Some comparisons with communist China. *Canadian Slavonic Papers,* 1975, **17**, 374–403.

Rywkin, M. Religion, modern nationalism and political power in Soviet Central Asia. *Canadian Slavonic Papers,* 1975, **17**, 271–285.

West, M. M., & Konner, M. The role of the father: An anthropological perspective. In M. Lamb (Ed.), *The role of the father in child development.* New York: Wiley, 1976.

CHAPTER 6

Male Parental Care in Monkeys and Apes

WILLIAM K. REDICAN

Behavioral Medicine Associates

DAVID M. TAUB

Yemassee Primate Center

Recent years have witnessed a significant growth of interest in the role of the male in the development of immature nonhuman primates. Several contributing factors might be pointed out. First, there is a considerable interest in the association between caretaking and other cooperative or altruistic behavior on the one hand and genetic relatedness on the other. Under untampered circumstances, an offspring can be assured of bearing a one-half complement of genes from its mother. But the likelihood that a given infant and adult male are genetically related varies widely according to the nature of a species' mating system and group organization—ranging from monogamous to promiscuous systems. Thus the male nonhuman primate has come under closer scrutiny in recent years to test some currently vital theories of social behavior that have sprung from evolutionary biology.

Second, it is probably correct to say that investigators of nonhuman primates have followed the lead of their colleagues in the human social sciences and trends in societies at large. That is, there has been a progressive shift away from viewing the female as the exclusive caretaker—indeed this book demonstrates this. These trends have encouraged a similar modification of thinking about nonhuman primate social systems.

Third, there has been a growing accumulation of data from field and laboratory sources on the behavior of our relatives in the primate order. It is easy to forget that primatology is a relatively neonatal discipline, having coalesced only in the past few decades. In recent years there has been an opportunity to examine a broader range of questions than had been possible with earlier methods and conceptual orientations. The understanding of the male's role has benefited greatly from this development.

The objectives of this chapter are to present a broad overview of patterns of male parental caretaking in monkeys and apes. It is intended for readers who might be unfamiliar with much of the literature in primatology, but we are confident that primatologists will avail themselves of it as well. It differs from the same undertaking (Redican, 1976) in the first edition of this book in the following ways: sections on two taxa have been added (the stumptail macaque and the squirrel monkey); important new data have been incorporated into several sections (notably those on marmosets and tamarins, the Barbary macque, and cynocephalus baboons); and the discussion and conclusion sections have been revamped. Most important, a collaboration has been enjoined between a laboratory psychologist (Redican) and a field anthropologist (Taub) to provide an enhanced perspective on the area. For a more extensive assesment of the issues treated here, the reader is referred to *Primate Paternalism: An Evolutionary and Comparative View of Male Investment* edited by Taub. It will include a review by the editor of this volume, Michael Lamb, on the role of the human father in child development—the mirror image of the present undertaking. One can only hope that a true interdisciplinary synthesis is emerging from such interchanges.

For those readers with limited acquaintance with primate taxonomy and group organization, a brief survey of the principal features may be helpful. There are two major divisions (suborders) of the primate order: prosimians ("before apes") and anthropoids ("like human beings"). Prosimians are small, nocturnal, and predominantly arboreal forms found in Asia and Africa. They have retained the sensory characteristics of "primitive" mammals, such as a prominent sense of smell, scent glands, and claws and paws (instead of nails and hands) in some cases. Since information on prosimian behavior is still fragmentary, and they are only distantly related to *Homo sapiens,* they will not be included in this survey.

The remaining suborder, Anthropoidea, consists of three superfamilies: (1) New World monkeys, (2) Old World monkeys, and (3) apes and humans. New World monkeys are found only in South and Central America, where they have evolved from New World prosimians independently of other monkeys since the Eocene. New World monkeys are thus not ancestral to Old World monkeys, and any similarities between the two groups came about through parallel evolution. New World monkeys are all strictly arboreal and only one genus is nocturnal. Old World monkeys are found in Asia, Africa, and Europe (where a captive colony of Barbary macaques is maintained by the British on Gibraltar). They are a large and diverse group, occupying an extreme diversity of habitats (ranging from the foothills of the Himalayas to Ethiopian semideserts). Most are semiterrestrial. There are four principal groups of apes: gibbons and closely related siamangs, orang utans, gorillas, and chimpanzees. All are tailless, relatively large forms found in Asia and Africa. Their considerable cognitive capacities are well known. Forms of social organization of apes encompass a predominantly solitary one (orang utans), monogamous family units (gibbons and siamangs), and mixed groups (gorillas and chimpanzees). For more detailed information, the reader is referred to works by Chance and C. J. Jolly (1970), Eisenberg, Muckenhirn, and Rudran (1972), A. Jolly (1972), and Napier and Napier (1967), as well as the integrative work by Daly and Wilson (1978).

The previous edition of this review contained a minute scrutiny of terminology that might be applied to the variety of male–infant interactions. It is a problematic issue, since it is often impossible to establish geneological relationships with confidence in nonhuman primates, and therefore terms like "father" must generally be avoided. As in the previous review, the terms *male care* or *male parental care* are adopted in most cases in this chapter since they are free of geneological connotations, they have wide applicability, they are likely to be acceptable to researchers in various disciplines, and a set of corresponding terms (e.g., *female care* or *female parental care*) is available. These terms are here considered to be subsets of the class of behaviors referred to as "parental investment," defined by Trivers (1972) in his landmark contribution as "any investment by the parent in an individual offspring that increases the offspring's chance of surviving (and hence reproductive success) at the cost of the parent's ability to invest in other offspring" (p. 139). As such, parental investment includes the metabolic investment in producing sex cells and any behavioral investment that benefits the young. It excludes efforts to find a mate or to compete with others for access to a mate.

A useful concept in approaching the relationship between mating systems (e.g., monogamy) and parental investment (e.g., male care) is kinship selection. Mating systems in general can be categorized as follows. Monogamy ("one mate") is a situation in which one male and one female form a pair bond for varying intervals of time (a mating season to a lifetime). Polygamy ("many mates") is a generic term implying more than one mate in a single breeding season. Subcategories of polygamy are: (1) polygyny ("many women"), in which a given male mates with more than one female in a single breeding season; (2) polyandry ("many men"), in which a given female mates with more than one male in a single breeding season; and (3) promiscuity ("thoroughly mixed") or polybrachygamy ("many brief matings"; Selander, 1972, p. 194), in which an individual mates with more than one other during a breeding period (i.e., both males and females have more than one mate). There are variations on these themes, to be sure. For example, Peter Scott (cited in Evans, 1974) reported that a male goose can form a lifetime monogamous bond with another male, but one of them may occasionally mate with a female. This ménage is apparently more successful in rearing offspring than male–female pairs, since the two males both protect the offspring. In the case of human beings, there is evidence of both monogamous and polygamous mating systems.

Tipping the scales in favor of monogamy is the transparent observation that pair bonds (marriages) are evident in many societies, and in a few they are regulated by mortal legal sanctions. Monogamous males and females are more nearly equal in size than polygamous animals, since they have relatively comparable social roles, and in the case of human beings, size dimorphism is no greater than that of many monogamous creatures. Neither are human males particularly more brightly colored than females, as is typically the case for polygynous and promiscuous species (see the discussion of polygamy, below).

Many societies, however, have institutionalized polygynous mating systems [e.g., harems (from Arabic *harama,* "he prohibited")]. Moreover, human males are ubiquitously reported to be more aggressive than females (Maccoby & Jacklin, 1974), a characteristic often seen in polygynous males competing with each other. In our society, at least, the advertisement of resources (e.g., hot rod/hot tub/penthouse apartment/etchings) by males competing with each other for females can be likened to nonhuman mating systems in which male courtship displays precede polygynous copulation. Furthermore, although undecorated human males are not more conspicuously colored than females, as in the case of polygynous and promiscuous species, the presence of facial hair may function in intra-sexual aggressive displays much like bright coloration (see Hamilton, 1973). So *Homo sapiens* defies a facile categorization, which should surprise no one. More important than a nominal categorization, however, is the possibility that principles of behavior pertaining to both monogamous and polygamous systems can be applied to the human condition and questions derived therefrom.

The advent of evolutionary theory has brought forth the formulation that, because it involves a far greater expenditure of energy to produce an ovum than a sperm, female gametes are the more limiting resource (i.e., in shorter supply), and a given female mammal is more likely to mate than a given male mammal. It is to a male's evolutionary advantage to try to inseminate as many females as possible, since the expenditure of sperm involves such a relatively slight investment. A consequence of these contingencies is that animals are fundamentally polygamous (more specifically, polygynous), and hence monogamy is a more recent or derived state (Wilson, 1975, p. 327).

A central concept proposed by evolutionary biologists that pertains to parental caretaking (male or otherwise) is kin selection. The concept of kin selection was first proposed by Darwin in *On the Origin of Species* (1859). As it is understood today, chiefly interpreted by Hamilton's (1964) important contributions, the concept suggests that the extent to which one animal is related to another is an important variable affecting the degree to which one will act to enhance the likelihood of survival of the other. In the long run individuals will take greater risks that increase the fitness of another if the latter is a close rather than distant relative. By behaving in such a way (e.g., protection) that the chances for survival of an offspring, for example, are increased, the individual is probably lowering its own fitness. This agent has, however, a genetic investment in the offspring, and if the shared genetic fitness of the agent plus offspring is increased in the next generation because of actions of the benefactor such behavior will be selected for and flourish. In other words genes are selected that perpetuate themselves or are perpetuated, and organisms are thus selected that aid closely related individuals. [For a helpful discussion of these and other concepts, the reader is referred to Wilson (1975), Dawkins (1976), Barash (1977), Kurland (1977), and Daly and Wilson (1978).]

When this concept is applied to monogamous primates, it is evident that young animals that a male protects and cares for are likely to be his own kin—a system that does not necessarily involve *recognition* of relatedness. Investments by the male in caretaking activity tend to increase the probability that his genes would be propagated in subsequent generations. The involvement of both parents in caretaking activities probably makes twinning feasible in monogamous groups. In promiscuous groups adult males and immature animals vary in the extent of kinship relationships, and an investment in parental care may be of no evolutionary value to the adult male. One would thus expect to find less male parental investment in groups with promiscous or polygynous mating systems. This is indeed the pattern that has been observed, but we are getting ahead of ourselves. Let us rather turn to data on specific groups of monkeys and apes in three principal clusters: monogamous, multimale/multifemale, and one-male/multifemale social systems.

MONOGAMOUS GROUPS

A relatively small number of nonhuman primates live in monogamous social units. These units are composed of an adult male and female mated for life (as opposed to seasonally), plus infants, juveniles, and only occasionally a small number of other (probably nonreproductive) adults. All monogamous nonhuman primates are arboreal, all defend territories, and most rear twin or triplet offspring (the only primates to do so regularly) except the gibbons and siamangs. Although the intensity of the process varies from species to species, offspring nearing sexual maturity are chased to the periphery of territories and establish their own family units.

Marmosets and Tamarins

These animals are small New World monkeys—about the size of tree squirrels—found in the tropical rainforests of the Amazon and in other forests of South and Central America. Because of difficult conditions for observation, existing field data are limited. There appear to be only slight differences in the social organization of the two taxa, and both are known to be organized in monogamous family units. They are very similar physically and together they constitute a taxon (subfamily) by the name of Callithricinae or callithricids (from Homeric Greek for "beautiful fur").

Male care of infants is seen in marmosets and tamarins to the greatest known extent among nonhuman primates. Male marmosets *(Callithrix jacchus)* have been known to assist during the births of infants and to hold and lick stillborn neonates. They may even chew solid food for infants during the first month, which is noteworthy, since food-sharing—even between parents and offspring—is rare in nonhuman primates. Adult males may carry infants on their backs throughout the day, with the exception of nursing episodes every 2 to 3 hours, for the first two months, and they may continue to carry the young even after weaning (Lucas, Hume & Henderson Smith, 1927, 1937; Fitzgerald, 1935; Stellar, 1960; Langford, 1963; Mallinson, 1971a; Ingram, 1975).

A major factor in accounting for patterns of parental care in callithricids is the evolution of a complementary system making possible the production and rearing of a relatively large number of offspring. All marmoset and tamarin mothers characteristically give birth to twins or triplets. The female marmoset, for example, bears multiple offspring every 5 to 6 months and regularly has triplets when maintained on the relatively rich diet of most laboratories. As proposed by Ingram (1975, p. 204), in her landmark study of marmoset development:

> The most plausible hypothesis for the involvement of the father in the care of young is related to the freeing of maternal energy for milk production. . . . [A marmoset mother] must product twice as much milk as a primate only feeding one infant, thus her energy requirements to be met by foraging for food to support milk production will be high. In addition to this, she may conceive again during her post-partum oestrous, and so two weeks after she has given birth to one pair of twins she could be supporting another pair "in utero." It seems unlikely that this high reproductive level could be maintained without the assistance of the male in transporting the rapidly growing infants, whose combined weight by the age of four weeks is about one third that of an adult.

As to why marmosets and tamarins bear twins instead of singletons, Leutenegger (1973) persuasively argued that since the body size of marmosets has reduced progressively in the evolutionary past (presumably in response to the demands of the habitat), it became increasingly difficult to give birth to a fetus whose cranial size was so large relative to the mother's pelvis. If the total fetal weight were divided by two (twins) or three (triplets), cranial diameter would be reduced accordingly and so would unsuccessful deliveries. Therefore, the proposed selective shift was toward multiple births.

The important point advanced by Ingram is that to make this system work after the birth of offspring, increased demands for caretaking must be met. The mother has "traded" a less difficult birth for enhanced postnatal care. But the virtually incessant gestation of infants places demands on the mother than can be met only by assistance from the male and other caretakers. This interpretation also helps account for observations that marmoset fathers are *more* likely to share food with offspring than are mothers, and the latter are more aggressive toward group members in feeding situations.

However involved the callithricid father and mother may be in caretaking, the clear majority of recent reports indicate that they are not the only active caretakers in such groups. All marmoset and tamarin family members old enough to do so have been seen to assist in carrying and other caretaking activities (e.g., Fitzgerald, 1935; Lucas et al., 1937; Gruner & Krause, 1963; Epple, 1967; Rothe, 1973; and Ingram, 1975 on marmosets; Hampton, 1964; Hampton, Hampton & Landwehr, 1966; Epple, 1967; Thorington, 1970; Mallinson, 1971b; and Epple, 1975 on tamarins). The first set of marmoset infants is transported and otherwise cared for by the parents; the second and especially subsequent sets are cared for largely by their older siblings (Hearn & Lunn, 1975). Of all available siblings, 10- to 15-month-old subadults are most involved in caretaking, being physically more capable than younger siblings and having had some prior experience in handling the last set of offspring (Ingram, 1975). Thus with successive sets of offspring, the role of the adult male marmoset in infant caretaking is diminished (Box, 1975).

The marmoset caretaking system is a fascinating one for evolutionary biologists, since it offers an opportunity to understand whether an investment of such energy by siblings represents an altruistic act. If siblings derived no benefit from their caretaking activity, it would pose a great difficulty for conventional formulations of kin-selection theory, since animals are caring for individuals who are not their own offspring. An important point that has emerged since 1970 is that the investment in caretaking by siblings is beneficial to the young caretakers in the long run. Thus it is not an exclusively altruistic act. The evidence is as follows.

The opportunity for premature marmoset offspring to participate in the care of younger siblings is a crucial factor in producing parents who will successfully care for their own offspring (Hampton, Hampton, & Levy, 1972; Epple, 1975; Hearn & Lunn, 1975; Coimbra-Filho & Mittermeier, 1976; Hoage,

1977). Early attempts to breed marmosets in captivity were utterly unsuccessful because juveniles were removed from the nest to establish new reproductive units before they had a chance to interact with younger siblings. If left in the nest long enough to do so, marmosets mature to be prolific breeders in captivity.

To illustrate the potential generality of such a behavioral system, let us briefly turn to a pertinent study of birds. Woolfenden (1975) studied the mating of Florida scrub jays, which, like marmosets, are long-lived, perennially monogamous, and permanently territorial. About half the breeding birds studied by Woolfenden lived as simple pairs. The rest lived in larger groups with "helpers at the nest." These nonbreeding helpers defended territory and nest, mobbed predators, and participated in caretaking of the reproductive pair's young (e.g., by feeding nestlings and fledglings). Breeding pairs with helpers produced significantly more offspring than those without helpers, thus demonstrating that the nest-helper system significantly enhances the reproductive success of the breeding pair. An important finding was that the helpers were, in all but a few cases, *offspring of the breeding pair*. Helpers acted to enhance the reproductive efforts of breeders who were almost invariably their close relatives. Thus the "helper" system of marmosets takes the caretaking system of birds one step further: Not only are helpers relatives of the breeding pair, but such early caretaking confers a critical advantage to the helpers in terms of their own future reproductive success.

Perhaps we can be bold enough to pose a question about the human condition from these observations. If we borrow terminology from the human social sciences, we might say that adult marmosets deprived of an early opportunity to care for infants subsequently display child abuse or child neglect, insofar as they are incapable of successfully rearing their own offspring. Data on marmosets prove nothing about human beings or any other species, but they do propose a potentially valuable question for further research on humans: Might not an opportunity for human children to care for younger siblings or playmates reduce the likelihood that they will be abusive or neglectful parents? A simple prediction generated by this question is that children reared without younger siblings would be less effective parents than those reared with appreciably younger siblings whom they cared for.

Gibbons and Siamangs

The smallest of the apes, the gibbon *(Hylobates)* and siamang *(Symphalangus),* are arboreal, monogamous, and territorial (see Carpenter, 1940; Chivers, 1971, 1972; Ellefson, 1968; McCann, 1933; McClure, 1964; Teneza & Hamilton, 1971). Although they range over a different continent from the monogamous New World monkeys, male investment in caretaking is extensive. These apes are not diminutive enough to have evolved multiple births, and the interbirth interval is longer than for the other monogamous primates. Therefore, the involvement of the male in caretaking is less than in the case of the callithricids.

Adult male gibbons in the wild have been observed to inspect and to groom neonates, and a male in a captive group of gibbons was seen to carry a small juvenile for the greater part of the day (Carpenter, 1940). As infant gibbons mature, they become more independent of their mothers and interact more frequently with their fathers (Berkson, 1966). As offspring near sexual maturity, however, they are threatened and aggressed by one or both parents until they eventually become peripheral to the natal group, and thus eventually establish additional monogamous units (Carpenter, 1940; Ellefson, 1968). This is also the case in callithricids.

There is extensive male–infant contact among siamangs. Chivers (1971, 1972) reported that infant siamangs are dependent on the mother for the first 12 to 16 months of life, but from that point on they are carried by the father until independence is attained during the third year of life. Siamang fathers groom and also sleep with juveniles, whereas mothers groom and sleep with infants. Maturing siamang offspring are also peripheralized from the natal group, but the process appears to be less severe than in the case of the gibbon (Chivers, 1971, 1972; Fox, 1972, 1974)

There are thus striking parallels between the groups of monogamous primates examined in this review: In addition to being monogamous, all are also territorial, exhibit relatively frequent male parental care, and engage in some degree of peripheralization of offspring nearing sexual maturity. Degree of male involvement varies according to the reproductive burden on the mother: Male callithricids may be involved from birth, assuming a major role in infant transport and engaging in intensive caretaking activities such as food sharing. In contrast, monogamous male apes become involved later in infancy and appear not to engage in specialized caretaking behaviors. The reproductive burden is correspondingly much greater on callithricid mothers.

In a very brief way, we have accounted for the relationship between relatively enhanced caretaking by males and monogamous mating systems. A question that remains is why territoriality is so often associated with these patterns. For an answer we first look to the birds, which as a group have been studied far more extensively than nonhuman primates. Male birds' involvement in the care of young is generally more extensive than male mammals' (Crook & Goss-Custard, 1972). As succinctly put by Orians (1969), "The physiology of mammalian reproduction dictates a minor role of the male in the care of the offspring, whereas among birds the only activity for which males are not equally adept as females is egg laying" (p. 596). Male birds collect food and nest material, find and defend a place for the female to lay eggs and to raise young, defend females, hatch eggs, protect young, and provide learning opportunities for offspring (Trivers, 1972).

More than 90 percent of bird species are monogamous (most for a breeding season—some for life), and most monogamous species eat animal matter (e.g., insects) that is difficult for young to obtain themselves (Lack, 1968). The evolution of monogamy is favored in those circumstances in which there is a relatively stable supply of food during mating seasons and where territories are defended. Territories ensure a food supply that is undisturbed and not chronically competed over for both defendants and offspring. Where food is relatively low in nutrients (e.g., seeds, pulpy fruit, and nectar) and only present in seasonal abundance, mothers and offspring fend for themselves, males have little involvement in caretaking, and territories are not defended (Crook, 1964, 1965; Crook & Goss-Custard, 1972; Orians, 1969). As Horn (1968) demonstrated in his study of Brewer's blackbirds, when food is uniformly distributed in space and continually renewed in time, it is to a bird's advantage to defend whatever area that can be efficiently managed. In contrast, if food is unevenly distributed and sporadically renewed, the best strategy is to nest as a colony and forage in groups. Colonial grouping also provides enhanced protection against predators.

It would be shortsighted to suggest that the origins of mating systems and spatial behavior can be reduced simply to patterns of available resources. Other factors, such as predation, are of major importance. A male bird is unlikely to deliver food to mothers and/or offspring if predation pressure is great (Orians, 1969). He could conceivably attract predators to the nest, let alone risk his own life. As Wilson (1975) has suggested, "the territorial strategy evolved is the one that maximizes the increment of fitness due to extraction of energy from the defended area as compared with the loss of fitness due to the effort and perils of defense" (p. 269).

Parallels are evident in other groups of animals. Among mammals monogamy is most prevalent in terrestrial carnivores, for whom capturing high-energy food is a difficult task (Orians, 1969). Since many of them are thus at the top of the food chain, the need for wide dispersal is great, and one way of accomplishing this is through territoriality (Eisenberg, 1966, p. 52). In terms of parental caretaking, very complex forms of behavior have been observed in carnivores such as coyotes, wolves, jackals, hunting dogs, and foxes. Males have been seen to bring food to pregnant females, to regurgitate food for young, to protect young and distract predators away from them, to play with and transport young, and the fox has even been seen to teach the litter to hunt (Eisenberg, 1966).

Available data are not as complete, but there is evidence that the patterns observed in birds and carnivores may also apply to primates. In particular, Gartlan and Brain (1968) reported that vervet monkeys in an area with abun-

dant food resources had smaller, more clearly defined, and more strongly defended territories relative to conspecific groups in poor habitats.

MULTIMALE/MULTIFEMALE GROUPS

A far more common form of social organization in nonhuman primates is one
in which more than one mature female, together with immature offspring,
comprise the group. Most monkeys are organized in this pattern, and most are
promiscuous.

Before examining specific taxa with this form of group organization, some
consideration of the concept of sexual selection would be helpful. In 1871
Darwin described traits that offered no apparent survival benefits to individuals
(e.g., colorful plumage, postures, and many displays). They did, however,
confer advantages in terms of success in acquiring mates. Sexual selection is
defined as a subset of natural selection and is described in terms of two components: (1) competition with one sex (usually the male) for access to mates of
the opposite sex and (2) choice by members of one sex (usually female) of
mates of the opposite sex. Sexual selection pressures brought about the evolution of secondary sexual characteristics such as horns, antlers, relatively large
size, and aggressiveness that come into play during competition with members
of one's own sex. In addition, plumage characteristics and elaborate displays
evolved to serve as means of attracting mates of the opposite sex.

As a consequence of sexual selection, therefore, many promiscuous
monkeys in multimale/multifemale groups show pronounced sexual dimorphism in size, generally high levels of aggressiveness in males, and highly
developed weaponry (e.g., canine teeth) in males. In general, relative to monogamous groups, there is a more pronounced differentiation of roles between
males and females. Males are more energetic in activities such as vigilance,
leadership, and protection; females are more active in direct caretaking of offspring. In nonhuman primates, at least, the monogamous groups are without
exception found in aboreal habitats and polygamous ones in either arboreal,
semiterrestrial, or terrestrial habitats.

Let us now consider several groups of Old World monkeys and apes, and
one New World monkey. An emphasis is placed on macaques and baboons,
about which most information is available.

Rhesus Macaques

If one were to characterize adult males by their relations with infants in free-
ranging rhesus groups, one would describe them as generally indifferent,

somewhat sensitive to approach and contact, occasionally aggressive, and rarely affiliative. Adult rhesus males in North India, for example, were described as "neutral or indifferent" toward infants and juveniles (Southwick, Beg, & Siddiqi, 1965). Adult males frequently attack but only rarely associate peacefully with infants (Lindburg, 1971; Southwick et al., 1965). A male, especially while feeding, may pick up, bite, and throw an infant to the ground. In the field study by Southwick et al. involving 762 hours of observation, on only three occasions were infants seen to play and associate peacefully with adult males for substantial lengths of time. Lindburg (1971) only twice saw males carry immature animals during 900 hours of observation. On only two occasions did he see play between adult males and infants. Lindburg did note that males occasionally defended infants from attack and males threatened nearby animals while sitting close to infants.

In Kaufmann's (1966) study of free-ranging rhesus monkeys in the island colony of Cayo Santiago, very similar types of interactions were observed. Adult males were never seen to approach infants. Infants several weeks of age, however, occasionally approached, contacted, and even climbed on males. On 76 percent of such occasions the males' response was to ignore, withdraw from, threaten, hit, or grab the infants. On the remaining 24 percent of those occasions, Kaufmann reported that the males held the infants gently in their arms.

Breuggeman (1973), who also studied the Cayo Santiago colony, found that age of caretaker and frequency of parental care were positively related. However, 3-year-old males also exhibited high levels of caretaking activity relative to other age groups of males. Males exhibited more frequent caretaking during the mating season than during the birth season. In addition, males showed more frequent care toward male than female young, a finding that has occurred in several different studies.

Captive group-living adult males also tend to show relatively little interest in neonates (Rowell, Hindle, & Spencer-Booth, 1964). In a study of four species of captive macaques, Brandt, Irons, and Mitchell (1970) found that rhesus males showed the lowest total frequency of huddling, proximity, and passive contact with infants. Unlike Breuggeman's (1973) findings, in the studies of both Spencer-Booth (1968) and Brandt et al. (1970), younger males showed more interest in infants than fully mature adult males did. Therefore, the issue of age-related variables relative to male caretaking needs substantial clarification, especially when data for other species are taken into account.

In Spencer-Booth and Hinde's (1967) colony of rhesus macaques in Cambridge, England, when several mothers were removed from the group there was an enhanced degree of male–infant interaction: One adult male frequently played with these infants, and other males sat with and carried them in a ventral–ventral position. (The ventrum is an animal's chest or stomach.) When Bucher (1970) removed the temporal neocortex of rhesus mothers in captive groups, caretaking behaviors such as retrieval were found to be impaired. The adult males in the groups became active in carrying, grooming, and playing with infants—a finding quite similar to Spencer-Booth and Hinde's. These and other observations lend credence to the importance of viewing male caretaking within the context of the social system at large—particularly insofar as the mother's regulation of infant access is concerned.

Male care by adult rhesus males in a laboratory setting has received increased attention in recent years. Redican (1975, 1978; Redican & Mitchell, 1974) chose to study male–infant interaction in a situation in which males were allowed unrestricted access to infants, the goal being an exploration of the dormant or unexpressed caretaking potential of creatures who are typically hostile or indifferent toward infants (see Figure 1). Accordingly, longitudinal data were gathered on four pairs of adult male and infant monkeys housed in the absence of mothers and peers. Comparable data for mother–infant dyads were available (Baysinger et al., 1972; Brandt et al., 1972). All adults were fully mature at the beginning of data collection and were born in the wild. Two infants of each gender were in each rearing condition.

One of the fundamental differences between mother–infant and male–infant pairs was the pattern of physical contact. In general, adult males were less likely than mothers to maintain contact with infants, but this difference was primarily evident in the early months. Several measures are indicative of this pattern. First, the duration of physical contact was generally greater in mother–infant pairs than in male–pairs, with the most pronounced differences during the first and second months. What primarily accounted for the group differences was the time spent in ventral–ventral contact: Adult males spent virtually no time in ventral contact with infants, whereas mothers did so for prolonged periods early in the infant's life.

The generally lower level of contact in male–infant pairs was reflected in patterns of establishing and breaking contact. Over the seven months, mothers as well as their infants broke contact as often as they regained it. In contrast, adult males consistently broke contact more often, and their infants regained contact more often.

Hinde's group (e.g., Hinde Spencer-Booth, 1967; Hinde, 1969; Hinde & White, 1974) has suggested that age changes in such measures as proximity and ventral–ventral contact are due primarily to the mother and not the infant. Putting aside, for the present, the important issue of interactive changes within dyads, according to this form of analysis the principal agents of change in Redican's male–infant dyads were adult males for certain behavioral measures, but infants for other measures. Mothers changed more over time than did adult males, and their role in effecting that change may also have been greater.

Hinde's group also reported that changes over time in mother–infant groups were due to increasingly negative reponses by the mother (e.g., increasingly frequent rejections of the infant). In the case of Redican's male–infant pairs, such behavioral indices were increasingly positive over time. Criteria of attachment thus appear to increase over time in rhesus male–infant pairs, whereas in mother–infant pairs they decrease. In this study, close interaction between mothers and infants took place primarily in the early part of the infants' lives, whereas adult males engaged infants more so in later months.

Figure 1.   An adult male rhesus monkey grooming a male infant. In the absence of mothers who actively restrict contact between infants and other animals, adult males and infants in dyads developed close filial attachments (Redican, 1975).

From the rhesus infant's point of view, perhaps the primary index of whether adult males and adult females are equally suitable objects of attachment is the infant's response to temporary loss or separation. In terms of measures such as vocalizations, approach, locomotion, and self-directed behavior, responses to separation and reunion were similar in mother-reared and adult male-reared infants. This is at least one indication that attributes of rhesus mothers and adult males are sufficiently similar to enable emotional attachments to develop toward both by infants.

In Western societies, human fathers vary their caretaking behaviors according to the sex of the child to a greater extent than do human mothers, and fathers are particularly concerned with sex-typed behaviors in their sons (Lamb, 1976). A similar pattern emerged in Redican's study. First, sex differences were consistently greater in adult-male infant pairs than in mother–infant pairs. Second, mothers interacted only slightly more positively with female infants, whereas adult males clearly did so with male infants. It appears that to the extent that adult males interact with infants, they may affect the direction of socialization toward greater sex differentiation.

In general, Redican interpreted the results of the longitudinal and separation studies as indicating a significant potential both for adult males to form attachments with infants and for infants to form attachments with adult males. Clearly the dimensions of parental caretaking reflected the opportunities available to the individual. In the absence of restrictive mothers, adult males were often seen to interact with infants in a highly affiliative manner very rarely observed in groups in the wild. If such an aggressive and inflexible creature as the rhesus monkey male is capable of such positive interactions with infants, there is reason to expect at least comparable potential in less sexually dimorphic, relatively monogamous, more flexible creatures such as *Homo sapiens*.

In an extensive series of investigations, the Primate Laboratory at the University of Wisconsin has established triadic or "nuclear family" social groups, each composed of a father, mother, and infant (Harlow, 1971; Suomi, 1977, 1979; Suomi et al., 1973). Infants but not adults were allowed access to members of other triads. In social preference tests (Suomi et al., 1973), infants raised in triads preferred their mothers to other adult females, their fathers to other adult males, and their mothers to their fathers. Fathers initiated few play sessions but responded to most of the infants' initiations, playing with male infants more frequently than with female infants. However, infants spent less than 5 percent of their time interacting with all adult males, including their fathers. This was at a rate only slightly higher than that reported for free-ranging animals.

Suomi (1977) reported that adult males showed quite stable behavioral profiles over the 37-month period of this study, in strong contrast to those of adult females and infants. During the relatively limited time males spent interacting with infants, the clear majority of interactions were play. Play and defense were the only categories in which adult males interacted more often with offspring than with other available monkeys. Patterns of sex differences were complex: Males defended male and female infants equally often, but they invited play and responded to invitations more often with male infants. "Major differences in form and frequency of interactions with male versus female infants older than 4 months of age were shown by adult males. Data on mother–infant interactions, in contrast, suggest that son–daughter differences at these ages are present but hardly overwhelming" (p. 1268). Thus, in keeping with several other studies of human and nonhuman primates, males differentially responded to infants on the basis of gender to a greater extent than did females. Moreover, at least until adolescence, this gender disparity increased with adult males and decreased with adult females as the infants grew older (Suomi, 1979). Parke and Suomi (in press) cite preliminary data that infants reared in social groups with adult males show behavioral sex differences earlier than those reared in groups without adult males—a finding that demonstrates the developmental consequences of males' differential treatment of infants according to gender.

Pigtail Macaques

Observations on male care of infants in pigtail macaques *(Macaca arctoides)* remain very limited. Kaufman and Rosenblum (1969) did not observe holding, carrying, or cradling of infants by adult males under any circumstances in any of their laboratory groups. However, when mothers were removed from one group, the adult male threatened animals that aggressed the infants and interposed himself between the infants and antagonists. So defense of infants— what might be termed the least common denominator of male responsiveness vis-à-vis infants—is exhibited by pigtail males although they demonstrate little affiliative care.

Bonnet Macaques

Observations of captive and wild bonnet macaques *(Macaca radiata)* suggest that adult males interact relatively frequently with immature troop members in an affiliative manner. In a laboratory colony in which the mothers had been experimentally removed, adult males became solicitous toward infants and cradled, carried, and held them on a number of occasions (Kaufman & Rosenblum, 1969).

In the groups studied in the wild by Simonds (1965, 1974) and Sugiyama (1971), play emerged as a prominent feature of social activity. Adult males played not only with infants and juveniles but with adults as well. Protection of infants was again an aspect of male–infant relations:

> When the troop crossed the road or open land, one or several babies were sometimes left behind, as they were absorbed in play. Usually, on hearing the high-pitched screams of the babies, a mother or mothers went back to pick them up, but on a few occasions even mothers hesitated to go back from fear of passing close to the observers. On such occasions, young adult males . . . by themselves or leading the mothers, went back to the other side and returned to the troop carrying the babies on their backs or running with them. (Sugiyama. 1971, p. 261)

In general, positive interactions between adult males and juveniles were more often observed than between adult males and infants. Sugiyama (1971) noted that juveniles gathered around adult males when the troop rested, and "Sometimes an adult male pulls a juvenile male close to him and holds him in his arms, and at other times juvenile males come to an adult male and cling to and embrace him" (p. 258). These types of interactions were not reported for infants. Simonds (1974) recently found that adult males consistently avoided contact with young infants with the coat color characteristic of neonates. Adult males interacted more frequently with infants as the latter's color changed, until by the infants' sixth week of age adult males and infants established regular contact. Juvenile females remained in close contact with their mothers and nearby females, whereas juvenile males turned toward play groups of older juveniles, sub-adults, and occasionally adult males.

Japanese Macaques

One of the earliest instances in which attention was drawn to male care among Old World monkeys was Itani's (1959) study of Japanese monkeys (*Macaca fuscata*) at Takasakiyama. Observed male care of infants was described as similar to maternal care, except for a lack of suckling.

> Males hug the infants, carry them on their loins, or accompany them when walking. They keep them from wandering away, and, when sitting, take them to their bosom or make them lie down just in front of their feet and groom them, or sometimes play with them for hours. (p. 62)

Males also displayed the common characteristic of defense of threatened infants. As Alexander (1970) found in a captive troop of this species, "Whenever a neonate has been handled by a human being . . . the dominant males have reacted with an intense rage and have attempted repeatedly to attack the human kidnapper" (p. 284). The extent of potential attachment between adult males and infants is illustrated by Kawai's (1960) observation that infants gathered around and played near the body of a troop leader for several days after the male's death.

Itani observed males caring almost exclusively for 1- and 2-year-old invididuals (not neonates): Yearlings accounted for 74 percent of such interactions with adult males. Intensive male caretaking was seen only during the birth season—when the yearlings were supplanted from maternal care by the arrival of newborns—and only by fully mature males. "In the society of the wild Japanese Monkey [male care] . . . begins like the breaking of a dam" (Itani, 1959, p. 73). The burden of caretaking was thus shifted from mothers to fully mature males at a crucial time from the standpoint of infant survival, an admirably complementary behavioral system. Subsequent observations on this seasonality have confirmed Itani's findings (Alexander, 1970; Hasegawa & Hiraiwa, 1980).

A recent study of orphaned infants in free-ranging Japanese macaques once again points to the significant role of the male—not so much as a constant caretaker but rather as a critical and flexible resource in reserve. Hasegawa and Hiraiwa (1980) found that adult males were the primary caretakers of orphaned infants, surpassing both siblings, other relatives, nonkin peers, and nonkin adult females. Moreover, orphaned infants themselves were seen to prefer adult males to immature kin. Adult males carried, groomed, and defended the orphans. In the case of grooming, the primary caretakers of orphans "seem to substitute fully for the real mother" (p. 152). Indeed:

In general, adult females are indifferent to the offspring of other females and rarely care for them like the adult males of the troop. This holds true even when a female does not have an infant to raise. . . . Adult females do, at times, embrace and groom orphans, but they do not protect them from attacks, as the adult males do. (p. 147)

According to theories of evolutionary biology, such a pattern can make sense: It is to a reproductive female's evolutionary advantage to produce another viable young bearing her genes, and in consequence she (1) turns her attention from her yearling to her newborn and (2) invests little caretaking energy in offspring not bearing her genetic complement (i.e., orphans). In primate taxa, such as the langur, in which adult females do adopt other females' infants (Jay, 1963; Blaffer Hrdy, 1976), it is predicted that such females are much more closely related than those in nonadopting species—indeed, virtually sisters. There are at least two considerations when asking why a Japanese macaque male would adopt a potentially distantly related orphan. First, they may not be so distantly related after all, because there are scattered reports in several species that males may be more likely to care for infants of mothers with whom they had consorted (see Ransom & Ransom, 1971, Altmann, 1980, Packer, 1980, Estrada & Sandoval, 1977). Second, adult males may derive a more proximate gain from caring for infants. Both Itani (1959) and

Hasegawa and Hiraiwa (1980) noted that males can become more fully integrated into the troop as a consequence of interacting with infants. It is very clear, however, that considerable data are needed to clarify the proximate and ultimate gains from male parental investment in a promiscuous species such as the Japanese macaque.

Stumptail Macaques

Early work with stumptail macaques (*Macaca arctoides*) suggested that males were not particularly involved with or interested in infants. For instance, Bertrand (1969) reported that males were tolerant and protective of infants in their group, but were otherwise not actively drawn toward them. Other early reports (Bernstein, 1970; Jones & Trollope, 1968; Brandt et al., 1970) described stumptail macaque male–infant interactions involving contact—males being "very aware" of infants, and, conversely, infants actively seeking proximity to males.

More recent investigations suggest that among polgynous multimale/multifemale groups of Old World monkeys, the stumptail macaque ranks second only to the Barbary macaque in the extent of its interactions with infants. Gouzoules (1975), reporting on a study of a corral group at the Yerkes Primate Center, noted that adult males "showed interest in, and interacted with infants almost as much as females did" (p. 413). Social rank of both the males and the mothers of the infants appeared to be important in influencing the patterns of male–infant interactions in this group. Interestingly, Gouzoules found that subadult males were actively involved with infants, a finding at variance with those reported by Brandt et al. (1970), but very similar to the Barbary macaque pattern.

Hendy-Neely and Rhine (1977) reported on 14 categories of male–infant contact during the early infancy of nine infants living in two social groups; there were two adult males in each group. Momentary touching of infants by males occurred earlier and more often than other behaviors, such as grooming and clinging, most frequently associated with maternal attachment. There was a wide variation among the nine infants in the amount of male attention received. These differences were attributed to differences in the affiliative patterns of the adult group members; that is, important variables were the male's and mother's dominance rank and whether the mother was "permissive" or "restrictive" (i.e., whether they readily allowed males access to the infant). In a later report on these animals (Rhine & Hendy-Neely, 1978), it was noted that males and infants interacted with one another in ways characteristic of mothers and infants and that they interacted significantly more often than in all types of dyads except the mother–infant.

Among the members of a captive colony at the Yerkes Primate Center containing six adult males, Peffer-Smith and Smith (in press) observed extensive interactions between these males and immatures (from birth to 2 years of age). In their study, over 17 percent of all social interactions of the immatures were with adult males. General social and affiliative behavior accounted for 75 percent and 18 percent of the total social interactions, respectively. Immatures initiated most interactions: 65 percent of the affiliative behavior, 73 percent of the general social interactions, and 73 percent of play. These behaviors constituted over 90 percent of all male–infant interactions. The authors concluded that adult males served as important social foci for immatures. Adult male social rank, but not age, had a significant effect on the rate of male–infant interactions. Geneologically related males and immatures were found to interact at a higher rate than nonrelated individuals.

A free-ranging, island colony of stumptail macaques has been studied extensively by Estrada and his colleagues (Estrada et al., 1977; Estrada & Sandoval, 1977). They reported on 16 different caretaking behaviors between males and infants, including carrying, "bridging"[1], huddling, protecting, grooming, and proximity. Infants less than 6 months old received significantly more care from males than older infants. Moreover, there were differences between these two age groups in the type or quality of male care received: Younger infants received more tactile stimulation from males than did the older infants, with whom play predominated. Age correlated weakest with the contact categories of male behavior. Again, there was also a clear-cut preference by males for interactions with male rather than female infants (independent of infant age). Although there were two male and five female infants, male infants received 76 percent of all contact behavior and 88 percent of the proximity and vocalization scores. Not surprisingly, there were sex differences in the type of care the infants received: "While males were touched, their genitals were manipulated, and they were bridged, females interacted more in play, were touched and their genitals were manipulated in this order" (pp. 802–803). Dominance rank of the infant did not correlate with the amount of male care received.

In summarizing the male caretaking system of stumptail macaques, Estrada and Sandoval (1977, pp. 811–812) remark:

The comparison with studies of captive arctoides groups indicate that despite the differences in environmental and social conditions between our study group and those of others, male-care behavior is a recurrent behavioral feature. This could be taken as indicative of the existence of what Kummer (1967) refers to as "phylogenetic adaptation." The variability (or contrasts) observed between our data and that of others (on the same species) can be interpreted as "adaptive modification" (Kummer, 1967); i.e.,

---

[1]Bridging is defined as moving between one animal to the next while touching both.

they are the result of differences in (a) social organization, (b) group traditions, and (c) environmental conditions (Physical).

Barbary Macaques

Among those species of Old World monkey studied in sufficient detail, the Barbary macaque (*Macaca sylvanus*)—the only non-Asian macaque (see Taub, 1977)—clearly shows the greatest degree of male caretaking activity. Studying a zoo group, Lahiri and Southwick (1966) were the first to report extensive involvement between Barbary macaque males and infants.

Detailed observations of male care have been made on the colony of Barbary macaques maintained by the British army at Gibraltar. Each Gibraltar group contains only one adult male, unlike the multimale groups at large in North Africa. First MacRoberts (1970) and later Burton (1972) and Burton and Bick (1972) chronicled extensive male–infant behavioral interactions in this colony. MacRoberts described retrieval and play, and Burton and Bick (1972, p. 37) noted that leader and subadult males regularly held infants for "periods much exceeding 15 minutes."

Burton (1972) furnished detailed observations of the socialization process in the Gibraltar colony and distinguished four major roles of adult males in the socialization process of immatures. In light of the dearth of information on the adult male's role in the socialization process, we cite her observations at some length. Of particular importance are her findings on the impact of male involvement on motor development of offspring:

1. Adult males "encourage the infant to develop motor abilities that permit social interaction" (p. 55). For example, Burton observed the following extraordinary sequences:

> On four occasions, the . . . head male was the initiator of the infant's beginning to walk: he placed the animal on the ground, moving backward away from it to a distance of approximately two feet, lowering his head, looking at the infant and chattering to it. The infant would return the chatter and make crawling motions toward him. . . . As the infant approached within six inches to a foot, and if no other animal except the mother was nearby, the head male would again move away and repeat the chatter. If other animals began to close in, he would pick up the infant, and move away from the crowd, making a mild threat gesture to them. (p. 35)

These interactions occurred during the infant's first week of life, before it had developed skilled motor coordination. Infants maturing in the troop in which these interactions took place were more skilled at locomotor activities at 1½ months of age than were infants of another troop in which the adult males did not engage infants in these activities. It is also instructive to note that infants in the latter troop'' began to walk largely on their own initiative, undoubtedly largely because their mothers often removed them from contact with [the leader male]'' (p. 55).

2. Adult males reorient maturing young infants away from themselves and toward other troop members. For example, a leader male might return an infant to its mother after it had approached the male. Eventually the infant shifts its patterns of association away from adult and subadult males toward peer groups.

3. Adult males "reinforce socially acceptable behaviors appropriate to the age group by not interfering, or by giving positive reward (chatter, embrace, and so on)'' (p.55). An example is the shaping of the infant's sucking movements until the teeth-chattering facial expression emerges: each time the infant makes a sucking movement, both mother and father chatter to it and eventually the infant returns a facial chatter expression.

4. Adult males "extinguish or negate inappropriate behaviors by punishment (threat, chase, and so forth)'' (p. 55). For example, aggressive interactions were disrupted by adult males.

These observations by Burton are invaluable since they document behaviors that involve not only highly affiliative male–infant contact but also interactions that are virtually didactic as well (surprisingly rarely observed among nonhuman primates). Moreover, the role of the mother in regulating the extent of male–infant proximity and contact is illustrated helpfully.

Observations on a semifree-ranging, provisioned colony (i.e., one fed by humans) in France—La Montagne des Singes or "Monkey Mountain"—have also shown that males of this species are characterized by a strong interest in and extensive involvement with infants, even to the extent that adult males will carry dead infants for prolonged periods (Merz, 1978).

When this species was first studied systematically in its natural habitat a decade ago, Deag and Crook (1971) were immediately struck with the magnitude, intensity, and diversity of male–infant relationships. They demonstrated that extensive male caretaking in this species was not an artifact of captivity or provisioning. Taub's subsequent study of wild Barbary macaques in Morocco (1978, 1980) confirmed Deag and Crook's observations, firmly establishing that intensive and elaborate interactions between males and infants are typical and characteristic of this macaque.

Deag and Crook (1971) distinguished two types of male–infant interactions in Barbary macaques: male care and agonistic buffering. The former included all forms of dyadic interactions involving a single male and a single infant. Thus male care subsumed such traditionally "maternal" behaviors as holding, carrying, retrieving, protecting, huddling, and grooming.

The second category of male–infant involvement they described was *agonistic buffering*—a term used for behavioral sequences in which one adult male interacts with another via an infant (Deag & Crook, 1971; Deag, 1974). For example, "it was not unusual to see a male running on three legs holding a baby under him with one hand for as much as 30 to 40 m and taking it straight to another male to which it was then 'presented' " (Deag & Crook, 1971, p. 191). The function of this form of interaction was said to be a means of enabling a subordinate male to approach and remain near a dominant male with a reduced likelihood of attack (i.e., "buffered" by the presence of the infant) (Deag, 1974, p. 341).

Recently, Taub (1980) reexamined the agonistic buffering hypothesis in light of data from his field study, and he found cause both to reject the dichotomy between male care and agonistic buffering and to reevaluate the function of triadic interactions. Social rank did correlate in some general ways with the pattern of triadic interactions, but for the most part the data could not adequately accommodate the earlier hypothesis that agonistic buffering serves to regulate dominance/subordinance relationships among males. Males did not choose other males equally often to interact with, but rather each male had a different set of three other males (out of 11 possible) that he preferred for a triadic interaction. Each male showed striking preferences for certain infants in triadic encounters, and these infants were the same ones preferred by that male in caretaking activities. Finally, males that preferred each other for a triadic interaction showed a mutual preference for the same infants. Taub concluded that "males choose to participate in 'agonistic buffering' [a term Taub prefers to avoid] because, and by means of, a shared, common, and special caretaking relationship with the same infant" (1980, p. 187). Thus Taub shifted the focus of interpretation of triadic relationships away from social status regulation to a shared caretaking network. Furthermore, the categorical split between male caretaking and buffering now seems not to be helpful, particularly in light of the fact that "caretaking" behaviors such as holding, grooming, and carrying clearly take place during "buffering" sequences (see Figures 2 and 3). Once again, the understandable allure of placing behaviors in discrete categories seems to have backfired.

The most salient features of male–infant caretaking among wild Barbary macaques demonstrated by Taub's field study (1975, 1978, in press) were the following:

1. Males interacted regularly with infants in a wide variety of behavioral activities, including carrying, holding, grooming, soliciting approaches, playing, monitoring, retrieving, and protecting. In their review of primate "paternalism," Mitchell and Brandt (1972) described eight levels of interactions that

(a) One male carried the infant on his back to the second male, and here both males sit in a characteristic ventral–ventral posture, grasping the infant, bending over it, and giving an affiliative teeth-chattering facial expression (often directed at the penis or anogenital area of the infant).

(b) Teeth chattering and manipulation of the infant by both males continues for about 15 seconds.

(c) The infant begins to transfer from one male to the other.

(d) Both males sit quietly next each other as the infant climbs explores.

Figure 2. An "agonistic buffering" sequence in Barbary macaques. Two subadult males inter through a male 9- to 10-month-old infant. Taub found that this form of male–infant interaction common among Barbary macaques, although there is variation in its components, depending social context and the identity of participants. (Photographs by David M. Taub.)

(e) The infant manipulates and sucks the penis of one male.

(f) The sequence terminates as one male walks off, leaving the infant with the other male.

Figure 3. An adult male Barbary macaque sitting with a young infant in the Middle Atlas Mountains of Morocco. The male assumes a posture that Taub considered structurally identical to that of a mother, with legs and arms forming a protective "bowl" around the infant. (Photograph by David M. Taub.)

227

may exist between males and infants. Barbary macaques regularly and predictably showed at least seven and possibly all eight (adoption?) of these levels.

2. Particular infants received significantly different amounts of attention from males, and, conversely, some males were more extensively involved with infants than were others. Subadult males, as an age/sex class, were the most extensively involved. There was little correlation between individual social status and a male's frequency of association with infants.

3. Males were highly discriminating in their choice of specific infants to interact with, and they tended to restrict their attention to one or two infants. Therefore, each infant received caretaking from several different males.

4. The only case of infant mortality occurred in an infant that received no male care from adults or subadults.

Taub speculated that the basis of the Barbary macaque's male–infant interactional system was the network of kinship ties, but this could not be verified during his study. The proximate and ultimate factors responsible for the male's ability to make highly discriminating choices of infants to interact with remains unknown.

Cynocephalus Baboons

As with macaques, since field data have expanded in recent years there have been increasingly frequent reports of significant interactions between males and infants in baboon species with a multimale/multifemale social organization. Data are available primarily for yellow, anubis, and chacma baboons— for the sake of convenience here included under the common heading cynocephalus ("dog-headed") baboons. All occupy savannah and forests south of the Sahara. The quality, frequency, and function of cynocephalus baboon male–infant associations overlap considerably with those of the closely related macaques, but they also differ in significant ways.

Interest in infants by anubis and yellow baboon males was documented in an early field study by DeVore (1963), who stated that "the relationship of the infant to the adult males is important at every stage of the infant's maturation" (p. 322). An outline of that relationship follows; again it is presented in considerable detail because it should be of interest to many students of behavioral development.

1. *Month 1–4.* Mature dominant males frequently approach mother–infant dyads. During the first month the infant rarely leaves its mother, but by the third month infants crawl on males, leap on their shoulders, and sit upright on their backs. Interest in infants by adult males appears to peak from month 2½

to 4. [Rowell (cited in Hinde, 1971) estimated this period to be month 1½ to 3½.]

2. *Month 5–6.* Interest in the infant by the adult females declines rapidly during this period, and by the time the infant is solid brown, is negligible. Jealous protection by the adult males continues unabated, however, and the older infants and young juveniles increase their efforts to entice the young infants into a play group. (p. 320)

3. *Month 8.* It is the oldest males of the central hierarchy, who have been near the infants since birth, who are the most active males in breaking up . . . squabbles and protecting the infants. The mother continues to intercede for her infant until it is 2 years old, that is, until her next infant is born, but males usually protect infants well into the infants' third year. (p. 321)

4. *Month 10.* Infants now associate most frequently with peers but run to adult males for protection.

5. *Month 30.* At approximately this period the individual is no longer tolerantly protected, and it has entered into dominance–subordination relationships with other animals.

The relationship between the age of the male and investment in caretaking remains to be clarified. DeVore (1963) reported that juvenile and young adult males showed little interest in infants. Fully mature males of the central dominance hierarchy, in contrast, frequently approached and manipulated infants. This stands in opposition to most of the age-related data for macaques as well as to observations in an extensive field study by Ransom and Ransom (1971) of anubis baboons. They reported that young males (4 to 10 years old) do take an interest in infants—in this case the offspring of low-ranking females. Of particular value is their observation that

An important factor in this type of relationship seemed to be the availability of the infant. Young mothers were more likely than older ones to allow the males to take their infants, probably for reasons which included inexperience as mothers and a comparative lack of well-established pair and subgroup bonds. (p. 186)

Protective responses toward infants are very prominent among all species of baboon. All the adult males of a troop respond to infant distress vocalizations and will attack intensely a human being who comes between an infant and the rest of the troop (DeVore, 1963). Adult males have been seen to carry off an infant after the sudden appearance of a human being, and play groups often form around dominant males (Tayler & Saayman, 1972). They also intervene in conspecific interactions:

Any sign of fear or frustration by the black infant causes an adult male to stare toward the play group, sometimes grunting softly, and the offending juvenile releases the infant immediately. Should the black infant cry out, the adult males leap to their feet and the juveniles scatter in terror while the young infant returns to its mother. (DeVore, 1963, p. 319)

Ransom & Ransom (1971) and Packer (1980) reported enhanced protection and vigilance by males in the presence of predatory chimpanzees. Altmann and Altmann (1970) observed an infant run to an adult male and be carried ventrally by him after a strong earthquake. Other protective relationships are reflected in the observations that females with young tend to associate closely with adult males during troop movements (Rhine & Owens, 1972; Tayler & Saayman, 1972).

There have been several reported cases of adoption of infants by adult males. Bolwig (1959) suggested that two chacma baboon infants had been adopted by adult males. Two large male infants in Nairobi National Park were also seen in constant association with two adult males (Dolhinow & Bishop, 1970). One 6- to 12-month-old infant, whose mother had died, was a constant associate of the second-ranking adult male: The infant groomed the male and walked next to him during troop movements in the day and slept next to him at night (DeVore, 1963).

More recently, Popp (1978) described a phenomenon of "kidnapping" among the baboons of Masai Mara reserve in Kenya, wherein adult and subadult males take infants during agonistic encounters with other males. Popp found that the kidnapper is less likely to be the father of the kidnapped infant than is the opponent. [Contrast this with the opposite situation that Hamilton and Busse (in press) report for South African chacma baboons.] Therefore, the user appears to gain advantage by placing an infant between himself and an opponent who is probably related to the infant. Mostly large, high-ranking males were kidnappers, but they only kidnapped vis-à-vis the few even larger, more dominant males in their troop. This sort of interaction is neither frequent nor regular (39 cases in 341 observation hours, mean duration 47 seconds with a range of 4 to 269 seconds), but it appears to be a form of "agonistic buffering," in the sense that infants are objects that are exploited when needed to achieve a particular end, rather than a form of male caretaking *per se* as reported for other baboons (e.g., Packer, 1980).

Strum and Manzolillo (in press) describe male–infant interactions among the baboons of Gilgil, Kenya, in situations of tension with other males. They suggest that, in such circumstances, males exploit social interactions with infants for their own benefit. They distinguish two types of male–infant interaction that they label "agonistic buffering" and "passports": "In agonistic buffering, the effect of the infant's presence has been interpreted to be the result of an innate releasing mechanism[2] that prevents the aggression of the antagonist

---

[2]An important term in classical ethology, a releasing mechanism is defined as "a special afferent mechanism that removes . . . [CNS] inhibitions at the biologically appropriate moment. This

and results in *increased* distance between the two males. In the second type of infant use (i.e., passports), the presence of the infant appears to allow its caretaker to approach the other male, *decreasing* the distance between them'' (emphasis added). In data collected over a 7-year period, they found that the effective use of infants by males depended on a prior affiliative relationship between the infant and the male. This relationship was sometimes of a close biological kinship, and only affiliated infants cooperated with the male's attempt to use them. Without this infant cooperation the effectiveness of infant use for the male was negated.

In a report on male–infant relations among free-ranging anubis baboons, Ransom and Ransom (1971) and Ransom and Rowell (1972) reported four major types of male–infant associations. The first type derived from a widening of a special bond or attachment between the male and the infant's mother to include the female's infant at birth. The second type was an "intensification of the male's protective role in response to circumstances within his major subgroup" (p. 185), and this type was independent of any bonding relationships between the male and the infants being protected. The third type of male–infant relationship involved young males who took a particular interest in the infants of young, low-ranking females. The fourth was a feature of the dominance relationships among adult males: "This type of relationship appeared to be based on the adult male's ability to increase his effectiveness in interactions with other males insofar as close contact with an infant seemed to inhibit aggressive behavior from them" (p. 187). The three highest-ranking adult males were the most frequently involved in this type of male–infant interaction.

In a recent systematic study of male–infant interactions among anubis baboons, Packer (1980) reports both male care and "exploitation" of infants by males. Packer describes exploitative interactions in which males often carried infants during encounters with other males. During such interactions, the males carrying the infants were said to benefit both by reducing the probability that they would be threatened by other males and by increasing their dominance relative to other males. Caretaking interactions included protecting and rescuing infants from predators (mainly chimpanzees), enhanced vigilance when predators were nearby, and defense of infants against conspecifics of all age/sex classes. Resident males were especially active in defending infants against new males immigrating into the troop, and infants frequently reacted very negatively toward new males entering their troop. Finally, males groomed

---

neurosensory innate releasing mechanism (IRM) allows the central impulses to proceed to the effectors only when certain key stimuli are encountered" (Eibl-Eibesfeldt, 1970, p. 60). In this instance, the stimuli referred to are infantile characteristics such as small size, coat color, high-pitched voice, facial features, and possibly odor.

infants, although the majority of grooming bouts occurred when carrying the infant in triadic interactions with other males.

In considering several variables relating to the basis on which males chose particular infants, Packer found that the age of the infant was the strongest correlate of preference, with males prefering younger infants. Males resident in the troop at the time of possible conception (i.e., potential "fathers") were predominantly more likely to engage infants in this sort of interaction. Moreover, infants spent significantly more time with males present in their troop at their birth. Males that most frequently "exploited" infants in their relations with other males were also those most frequently involved in the caretaking behavior of infants. [Recall that Taub (1978) found a similar pattern among Barbary macaques.] Packer interpreted the system of male caretaking and exploitation among anubis baboons as a case of "mutualism" or "delayed return altruism," in which both the male giving the care and the infant receiving the care ultimately benefit more or less equally.

It should be noted that while anubis baboons exhibit a moderately well-defined system of male–infant interactions, it is quantitatively (and probably qualitatively also) much attenuated from that reported for macaques. For example, in a 2-year period, Packer observed 26 male–male dyads (involving 17 different males) where one carried an infant to the other. Among Barbary macaques, one male might be involved in that number of triadic interactions within a 2-day time span (Taub, 1975, 1978).

J. Altmann (1980) found that individual males showed a wide variance in the degree of interest expressed in infants. As with Ransom, but in contrast to Packer, Altmann found that "for males more than for females, interest depended strongly on the identity of the mother" (p. 109). For example, particular males had clear preferences for associating with certain females, and by extension these males often associated with the infants of these preferred females (p. 74), increasing the likelihood that these males may have been caretaking their own progeny (p. 86). These special male–female–infant relationships usually involved only fully mature males who tended to come from the upper half of the dominance hierarchy.

In an intensive study on male–infant interactions among anubis baboons, Stein's (1980) data address highly pertinent issues:

> The clearest benefits that adult males provide for infants are food-sharing and protection from other baboons in the same group. The carriage of infants by adult males is, surprisingly, an affiliative interaction with the infants playing an active cooperative role. Adult males preferentially carry the infants most likely to be related to them and the infants with whom they have the most affiliative relationships by other criteria. Although adult males seldom groom infants in general, they groom infants often when inter-male tension is high, apparently as a way of keeping the infants nearby.

Once again, the geneological relatedness of infants to males seems to be an important variable in determining patterns of association at the "micro" level of the social group, as well as the "macro" level of the overall mating system (i.e., monogamous versus polygamous).

Hamilton and Busse (in press) found that among some groups of chacma baboons a unique form of male–infant interaction occurred. Infant baboons were carried by resident males vis-à-vis dominant recent immigrants (94 percent of all observations). These recent immigrants could not have fathered the infants carried by the resident males, who in all likelihood were themselves the sires of the infants and were usually the highest-ranking males *at the time of the infant's conception*. Hamilton and Busse argued that instead of using the infants to "buffer" their relations with other males, the observed male–infant behavior is rather a mechanism whereby the probable fathers protect their offspring against injury or possible infanticide by unrelated male immigrants.

Taking into account the diversity of reports on baboon male–infant interaction, it is evident that caretaking does take place in males of several species. Relative to other primates, however, it occurs rather infrequently and as a consequence of a special relationship between the male and the infant's mother—both features being consistent with predictions derived from kinship theory. The primary characteristic of most male–infant interactions appears to be a modulation of relations with the troop members. That is, the focus of attention is less the infant (as it is in some macaque species) than the other animal with whom the male is interacting. Infants, because of their highly effective features that subvert intragroup aggression, appear to play a central role in ameliorating relations among more mature group members. It is not doubted that infants may indeed derive proximate and ultimate benefit from such "exploitative" contact, but the primary relationship for the male does not appear to focus on the infant as an object for the investment of care essential for survival.

Squirrel Monkeys

Every species considered so far in this section on multimale/multifemale groups was an Old World monkey, and most were primarily terrestrial. Let us now turn to an exclusively arboreal species from the New World—the squirrel monkey, *Saimiri sciureus*.

Compared with the monogamous Old World monkeys considered above, male–infant interactions in polygamous squirrel monkeys are infrequent and much attenuated. Typically, these interactions are described as indifferent or negative. In their study of feral squirrel monkeys in Panama, Baldwin and Baldwin (1972) found that when an adult male approached a lone infant, a juvenile, or a subadult male, the latter usually vocalized in distress or fled.

The adult males did not noticeably respond to these behaviors; the Baldwins concluded that "probably [adult males] . . . were indifferent to these younger animals" (p. 175). On other occasions, however, infants (Baldwin, 1969) and juveniles (Baldwin & Baldwin, 1972) were seen to follow and "threaten" adult males, who typically withdrew unaggressively. Apparently, young animals are highly excited by the close proximity of active, boisterous animals such as adult males; they vocalize intensely, which often precipitates the withdrawal of the adult males. Extremely vocal infants were occasionally threatened in return (Baldwin, 1969). Sometimes, when a solitary juvenile approached an adult male, the latter lunged aggressively toward the juvenile, who would then "shriek, run off, and remain at larger distances" (Baldwin & Baldwin, 1973, p. 376).

Observations on adult males and infants in captivity point to a similar pattern. Hopf (1971) found that throughout infancy, young squirrel monkeys rarely interact with adult males at close distances, but they frequently look at adult males. In the second year of life, at approximately the age of final weaning, several of the male juveniles observed by Hopf played with adult males and joined their sleeping group. In the third year, however, subadult males were often grasped and threatened by adult males, and their copulations were interrupted by adult males. Observations by Baldwin (1969) of squirrel monkeys in a large outdoor enclosure concur: Fully mature males chased young adult males whenever they were detected, and several young adult males were seriously wounded in fights with fully mature males.

The lack of contact between adult males and infants was also illustrated in a laboratory study by Rosenblum (1972). Solitary infants were presented to established groups of eight to 30 squirrel monkeys of varying age/sex categories. Overall, males and females did not differ in the frequency of approach or exploration of the infant. Adult males contacted the infant less often than adult females did, but the scores of immature males and females were not significantly different. Somewhat more pronounced differences were seen in retrieval responses: None of the males displayed a complete retrieval pattern (i.e., retrieval plus at least 60 seconds of carrying), whereas 16.7 percent of the females did. Immature females and those in late pregnancy were particularly likely to retrieve infants fully. Only 29.6 percent of the males partially retrieved infants (i.e., for less than 60 seconds), whereas 48.2 percent of the females did.

An important factor to consider in accounting for the general lack of adult male–infant interaction in this species is its unusual pattern of social organization. Squirrel monkeys have been regularly observed to form unisexual subgroups in which mature males and females remain spatially segregated for most of the year except for the breeding season (e.g., Baldwin, 1968, 1971; DuMond, 1968; Mason & Epple, 1968; Thorington, 1968; Mason, 1971; Coe

& Rosenblum, 1974; Fairbanks, 1974). This segregation is maintained largely by adult females, who, together with their young, form a cohesive central core. The permeability of this core to adult males is regulated by adult females. Baldwin (1968) reported that adult males were not involved in most of the troop's activities: Their mere presence "excited and frightened many of the animals until they were chased away from the troop by the adult females" (p. 287). During the birth season, adult males occasionally traveled near the female subgroup apparently without being noticed, but yearlings who detected them typically vocalized and displayed toward them: "The males usually quietly drifted away from such excited yearlings, perhaps because the yearlings' alarms often attracted nearby adult females and the females threatened and chased the males if they were still in the area" (Baldwin, 1968, p. 288). Thus not only do females chase males away from the central subgroup (in which immature individuals are found), but the sight of an infant or juvenile may serve as a cue to males of an imminent attack by females. These and other observations lead to the hypothesis that a significant factor contributing to the relatively infrequent contact between adult male squirrel monkeys and immature conspecifics is an active inhibitory role of mothers and other adult females in the group. Further supportive evidence for this hypothesis is provided by Baldwin's (1969) observation:

When a mother threatened and chased an adult male, her infant usually joined her and threatened and chased, too. Even when the mother was not near the infant, the infant would threaten and chase a nearby adult male. . . .The adult male usually ran away if an infant started to chase him, *but this was probably to avoid attracting the mother*. (p. 55, emphasis added)

This hypothesis is also supported by a recent study by Strayer, Taylor, and Yanciw (1975). They demonstrated that adult females with young avoided adult males more than nulliparous females did. Nulliparae were often observed in close proximity to adult males, but mothers with infants spent almost all of their time in the female subgroup, out of range of the adult males. Their study once again points to the role of mothers in regulating access of adult males to neonates.

Although male–infant interaction in squirrel monkeys is relatively infrequent, in certain circumstances male responsiveness is elicited to an impressive degree. For example, Baldwin (1968, p. 309) reported the following incident in the large group he observed:

On one occasion when an infant was trapped and giving distress calls, the most dominant male returned to visually investigate the trapped infant, then approached closer and closer to the infant, attempted to retrieve it, and finally threatened me (as I stood twenty feet away).

The above report is instructive, since apparently none of the females in the troop, who greatly outnumbered the males, came forward to assist the infant. Baldwin (1968) suggested that adult males may play a "special role of investigating the source of . . . alarm" (p. 309). Support for this conclusion is found in many such episodes in nonhuman primate literature in which males defended, rescued, or retrieved distressed infants while females withdrew from the source of threat.

Chimpanzees

There are only scattered references to male–infant interaction in chimpanzees *(Pan)*. Infant chimpanzees are in virtually unbroken contact with their mothers until 3½ to 5½ months, and it is thus not surprising that early male–infant contact is rarely observed in this promiscuous genus (van Lawick-Goodall, 1967, 1968). Adult males were said to be tolerant of infants while copulating with their mothers (van Lawick-Goodall, 1967), but under the circumstances that is not surprising. Adult male chimpanzees have also been seen to be quite aggressive toward infants. Hamburg (cited in Maccoby & Jacklin, 1974, p. 372) observed an adult male smash an infant against a rock. Afterward he severely aggressed the mother, who was trying to protect it. Indeed, Suzuki (1971) has even documented an instance in which several mature adult males in the Budongo Forest ate a newborn chimpanzee!

ONE-MALE/MULTIFEMALE GROUPS

The remaining major classification of group organization considered here is the one in which a single mature male is present, together with females and young. Additional males close to maturity are excluded from the primary group and either live solitarily or form all-male "bachelor" groups. Since the degree of kinship between the single adult male and the offspring in the group is greater than that between adult males and infants in multimale/multifemale promiscuous groups, and yet lower than that in monogamous groups[3], one would expect to find that the extent of male involvement in caretaking in one-

---

[3]The degree of male–infant kinship would be identical in one-male and monogamous groups if the male in the former were to sire all group infants. We assume that generally not to be the case, because in one-male groups both the male and females may transfer from group to group. Moreover, we assume that females copulate with extraneous males more often in one-male than in monogamous groups, the latter being characterized by more pronounced spatial (territorial) segregation.

male groups is intermediate between the other two types. Although it is difficult to put such a diffuse hypothesis to a rigorous test, evidence suggests that it is a reasonably viable one.

There are relatively few nonhuman primate groups with a one-male/multifemale organization. Most species considered in this section are Old World monkeys, and most are semiterrestrial. Whether one-male groups have evolved from multimale groups (e.g., Crook & Gartlan, 1966; Kummer, 1971, p. 94) or, conversely, have given rise to them (Eisenberg et al., 1972) is a question beyond the scope of this undertaking. It seems reasonable, however, that one-male reproductive groups are economical in the arid, impoverished habitats typical of these species (Gartlan & Brain, 1968). As stated by Crook and Gartlan (1966), "less food per reproductive unit goes to individuals not involved in rearing young" (p. 1202). More specifically Kummer (1971, p. 70) has suggested that, in areas where there is an extreme seasonal variability of food resources such that a population must depend on a high reproductive potential of adults to replace seasonal losses, the number of females relative to males will be at a maximum. Sexual dimorphism is extremely pronounced in these species, presumably reflecting a high degree of sexual selection.

Hamadryas Baboons

Undoubtedly the best-known primate species exhibiting this form of group organization is the hamadryas baboon *(Papio hamadryas)*. Sexual dimorphism in this species is considerable. Males are at least twice as large as females and have a spectacular cape of fur.

The behavior of this species has been documented primarily through the intensive efforts of Hans Kummer, who has studied hamadryas baboons since 1955 (see Kummer, 1968, 1971). Hamadryas form stable and cohesive units usually composed of one adult male, a "harem" of approximately four adult or subadult females, and several infants. The male tirelessly maintains the cohesion of the unit by threatening, neckbiting, or aggressively clasping females who either stray too far away or associate too closely with strangers. Approximately 20 percent of adult males in the troop as a whole do not form a harem, and instead typically associate in all-male groups.

A variety of male–infant interactions has been documented. Adult males frequently carry infants on their back while traveling. In addition (Kummer, 1971, pp. 80–82),

During rest periods, infants actively seek out certain young adult males who then hug and fondle them. Males, too, can adopt an infant. A motherless hamadryas infant is usually taken over by a young adult male that as yet owns no females. He then carries it en route . . . , allows it to sleep huddled against his belly at night, and prevents it from moving too far away.

The key to understanding these sorts of interaction is the process of harem formation. Yearling baboons often play near a subadult or young adult male, out of sight of mothers. Frightened infants or young juveniles occasionally run to the arms of the male, who threatens the antagonist in much the same way as a mother might. The infant or young juvenile gradually establishes a protégé relationship with the older male. As they mature, female infants appear to transfer filial attachment from the mother to a subadult or adult male. Attraction to the male may be enhanced by the appearance of the male's cape of fur, possibly a "supernormal stimulus" for the infant (Jolly, 1963; Kummer, 1967). The process of male–infant attraction is actively supported by the male, of course, through the "adoption" behaviors described above. Such behaviors were not observed in females (exclusive of mothers), and they abruptly ended in males once they had formed a harem (Kummer, 1967). The use of infants by subadults in agonistic interactions could also conceivably enhance the attraction of males to young.

Gelada Monkeys

Gelada monkeys *(Theropithecus gelada),* which are more closely related to macaques than to baboons (e.g., Rowell, 1972, p. 56), are also organized in one-male/multifemale groups similar in many ways to those of hamadryas baboons. Harem units, all-male groups, and loose aggregations of juveniles are evident in free-ranging troops in their arid, mountainous Ethiopian habitat (Crook, 1966). Gelada females are not, however, strictly herded by males and are more likely to disperse throughout the troop. Moreover, one-male groups are formed and/or maintained not only by the male but also by the females (Crook, 1966; Kummer, 1971, p. 109).

Male–infant interaction has not been extensively documented in this genus. However, Bernstein (1975) reported observations of a captive group of geladas that reveal an interesting parallel with hamadryas baboons. He found that the bachelor male, but not the leaders of one-male groups, carried infants ventrally and dorsally (on the back), played with infants, and was the center of their play activities until he became leader of his own group of females. Moreover, on the day following his removal as group leader, an adult male was seen to carry and play with infants, apparently for the first time since becoming leader. Bachelor males aided immature individuals in distress, even during weaning struggles with the mother. This association between rank and male caretaking was confirmed more recently by Mori (1979a,b) in his study of free-ranging geladas. Mobile infants older than 6 months were often cared for by a second-ranking or bachelor male, the males and infants forming specific pairs. Almost all such infants were male, so once again a same-sex preference emerges in male parental care (Mori, 1979a). And just as adults showed interest in infants, the converse applied as well (Mori, 1979b, p. 106):

The male infants also took a strong interest in the second [-ranking] males. If the second male was threatened by the leader and uttered a defensive sound, his steady male infant companion would come into his arms crying an appeasable sound. The second males utilized the consequences of this act and never missed the opportunity to parry the leader's threat by grooming the infant. Such cooperation . . . played a role in the leader's toleration of [the second male]. Further, only male infants gave earnest cooperation to the second male.

It will be recalled that, in Kummer's hamadryas baboons, close affiliative interactions between adult males and infants abruptly terminated when the former formed a harem. It seems likely, therefore, that male–infant affiliative interactions in species with a harem type of social organization are closely or almost exclusively related to the formation of one-male reproductive units.

Patas Monkeys

Patas monkeys *(Erythrocebus patas)* also live in an arid habitat (sub-Saharan Africa), are primarily terrestrial, and show marked sexual dimorphism. Surplus adult males are solitary or form all-male bands. The number of adult females in the reproductive unit is, however, greater than that of geladas and hamadryas, ranging from four to 12. Moreover, males show relatively little aggressiveness toward females, probably because groups are widely dispersed and there is little likelihood of females' straying to another group (Hall, 1965).

The role of the adult male in patas groups is unique among primates in certain respects. Hall (1965) repeatedly observed instances in which adult males engaged in conspicuously watchful and diversionary behavior relative to potential antagonists or predators. For example, as Hall approached a group, the adult male descended noisily to the ground from a tree, crashed around in the brush, and ran off in the opposite direction from the group. During such diversionary tactics, the females and young often lie flat in the grass and hide, running at great speed from predators only as a last resort (Hall, 1965; Kummer, 1971, p. 53).

Hall found that the adult male often stays near the periphery of the group, and mothers with young infants were rarely close to the adult male at all. Kummer (1971, p. 55), however, reported an incident in which a patas male chased a jackal that was carrying an infant patas in its jaws. Such direct protective behavior is apparently rare, and adult males in patas groups benefit infants chiefly through their watchful and diversionary roles.

Langurs

We have considered interactions between males and infants that have been basically of two types: those involving parental investment and those in which
the infant is in some way used or exploited in the amelioration of relationships
between two or more males. We now consider a third: the occurrence of infanticide by conspecifics, which has been reported among some primates—in particular the Asian colobine monkeys. Although infanticide is obviously an
extreme form of male–infant interaction, it seems worthwhile to look more
closely at the celebrated example of the langur monkey.

Troops of the common Indian or hanuman langur *(Presbytis entellus)* are
organized in both one-male and multimale patterns. Factors associated with
these differences offer support for the correlation between habitat and group
organization discussed earlier. Where hanuman langurs are found in dry decid-
uous forest with severe summer conditions and a high population density, they
tend to form one-male/multifemale groups with many extraneous males or all-
male "bachelor" groups. In more temperate, less densely populated areas they
are organized in more homogeneous multimale/multifemale groups (Hrdy,
1974; Jay, 1965; Sugiyama, 1967; Yoshiba, 1968).

While the social organization of langurs tends to be organized loosely
around a hierarchy of males, females, and their offspring, the troop structure
in the southern part of the species' range appears to be even more fluid. Several investigators have reported that all-male bachelor groups may invade troops
containing one dominant adult male and drive him out, whereupon one of the
invading bachelors takes residence in the troop (Sugiyama 1965, 1966, 1967;
Mohnot, 1971; Hrdy, 1974; Blaffer Hrdy, 1977; see also reviews by Blaffer
Hrdy, 1979, and McKenna, in press). Among some of these langur groups, the
bachelor male, having deposed the previous resident male, systematically and
deliberately kills all dependent infants. (A comparable phenomenon is probably operative in another langur species as well—the purple-faced langur, *P.
senex* [Rudran, 1973]). Invading hanuman males either ignore infants or are
hostile to them (Hrdy, 1974); however, established troop leaders are tolerant of
infants (Yoshiba, 1968), actively defend the troop in general and infants in
particular (Hrdy, 1974; Yoshiba, 1968), and have even been observed to engage infants in play (Yoshiba, 1968).

The exact mechanisms influencing this process are the subject of a major
controversy in primatology at the present time. Blaffer Hrdy (1974, 1977,
1979) has argued convincingly that such infanticidal behavior by males is a
reproductive strategy that maximizes the invading male's reproductive success,
since the loss of the infant causes a female to come into estrus (sexual recep-
tivity) and therefore enhances the new male's probability of siring offspring.
Curtin and Dolhinow (1978) and Curtin (1977) have proposed an alternative

explanation, arguing that such infanticidal male behavior is an abnormal, pathological, or nonadaptive response to ecological conditions, especially high population density.

Is there evidence that a comparable behavioral system is operative in other animals? Indeed, although it is not a frequent phenomenon, infanticide among animals is widespread, having been found in such diverse groups as ground squirrels, hyenas, lions, and primates (see reviews by Blaffer Hrdy, 1979, and Fox, 1975). In an excellent recent review of infanticide among animals, Blaffer Hrdy (1979) classified the diversity of infanticide into five explanatory categories: exploitation, resource competition, parental manipulation, sexual selection, and social pathology. "Predicted attributes of the perpetrators (such as sex and degree of relatedness to the infant), attributes of the victim (i.e., age and vulnerability), as well as schedule of gain, vary for each class" (p. 13). Nevertheless, in all cases of infanticide except social pathology, there is some benefit accrued to the perpetrator. "In those cases where infanticide does on the average increase fitness, selection pressures favoring it have arisen as a result of the extensive and time-consuming investment involved in production of young, and the extreme vulnerability that characterizes infancy in many animals" (p. 13). While infanticide is an extreme form of negative male–infant interaction, it must be recognized that all instances of male–infant killing among primates cannot be regarded as examples of nonadaptive social pathology.

Gorillas

The ongoing field study of free-ranging mountain gorillas by Diane Fossey (1976, personal communication) has provided particularly interesting information on male–infant interactions in this species. The group structure of mountain gorillas diverges from those of other species considered in this section insofar as more than one sexually mature male is typically present in a group. However, only the highest-ranking silverback male in each group is reproductively active. Thus the mating system of gorillas may be functionally similar to the one-male, multifemale groups typical of other species.

A striking parallel between langur and gorilla groups was documented by Fossey. In June of 1971, an adult female transferred from Group 4 to Group 8. Almost three years later, the highest-ranking silverback male of Group 8 died, leaving the group with no effective leader male. The transferred female had given birth to an infant 8 months previously. Shortly after the death of Group 8's leader male, the males of Group 4 began following Group 8 closely, and the highest-ranking silverback of Group 4 killed the infant. Its mother returned to Group 4 and subsequently gave birth to an infant sired by Group 4's leader. Once again we see one male eliminating genes of another male and ultimately caring for his own genetic investment. Two other infanticides were documented by Fossey, and in at least one case it is possible that a similar outcome will develop.

Happily, most male–infant interactions among gorillas are far from deadly. The same male that killed the infant of Group 8 had earlier adopted and reared an infant female. After her mother's death, the 3-year-old female made pitiful attempts at constructing nests next to the leading silverback male. On the 2nd or 3rd night, the male took the infant into his sleeping nest. Thereafter the infant traveled behind him constantly, but she walked, as he never carried her. The male groomed her more than a mother would typically groom her infant, and he remained in contact with her during rest periods. He was very protective of the infant, to the extent of not even allowing others to play with her.

Typically, very young individuals have little contact with silverback males. Mature and experienced mothers keep away from silverback males, and mothers with newborns stay on the periphery of the group. Only siblings are allowed nearby for 1–2 weeks, and the last to be allowed in close proximity are the silverback males (when infants are a few months old). Infants begin to approach silverback males by 2–3 years of age, and favorite play sites are the males' nests. Silverback males are typically very tolerant of infants, and low-intensity play sessions have been occasionally observed (e.g., a silverback walks up to an infant and pats it). This is generally responded to favorably by infants, since attention from silverbacks appears to be constantly sought.

SUMMARY AND DISCUSSION

The range of behaviors directed toward immature conspecifics by nonhuman primate males is impressive. They have been observed to assist during the births of neonates; to premasticate food for infants; to carry, sleep with, groom, and especially play with young; to defend young virtually without exception; to provide a refuge during periods of high emotional arousal; to interact with young in a quasi-didactic fashion; to promote motor development; to interrupt potentially destructive agonistic interactions among young; to become primary caretakers of orphaned infants; and to use infants in triadic interactions with other males. They may ultimately contribute to the infant's welfare less directly by defending a territory, the troop, or the mother from predators and conspecifics, and their frequent role as troop leaders may enhance the likelihood of infant survival in the long run. At the opposite extreme they may also threaten, attack, kill, and eat infants, but the more severe of these behaviors have been documented relatively rarely. Moreover, we do not yet have an accurate appraisal of the relative frequency of these potentially destructive behaviors in males versus nulliparous females.

As diverse as this behavioral range is, the primary caretaker in most primate—and mammalian—social systems remains the mother. Indeed, the class of animals in which we find ourselves—Mammalia—is named in honor of one of her life-giving functions. As stated recently by Ridley (1978, p. 904), the work of parental investment "tends to be distributed asymmetrically between the sexes. If one parent cares, it is generally the female: this is familiar for mammals and is also the rule for many other vertebrates and invertebrates." To be more specific, male parental care is rare in mammals, invertebrates, and reptiles, but common in fishes, amphibians, and birds (Werren, Gross, & Shine, 1980).

The relatively high likelihood of female parental care in mammals is consonant with at least two major biological considerations. First, the female's small number of large gametes as well as supportive tissue for the fetus (placenta, lactating tissue) both represent a much more extensive investment than the male's abundant number of small gametes. Second, it is a virtual certainty that the female's offspring bears the mother's genes. Together these two compelling and fundamental principles predict a high degree of parental investment by females in their offspring. As we have seen in the literature reviewed above, the extent of the male's parental care is highly and positively correlated with his genetic relatedness to offspring—in particular, males in polygamous systems are far less solicitous of young than those in monogamous systems.

If the mother's role is preeminent in mammalian parental investment, what then can we say about the male's? A considerable amount, it seems. The emerging picture of the male nonhuman primate in this regard is that of a behavioral resource characterized by a relatively high degree of plasticity. Under certain circumstances the male can come to play a prominent caretaking role—such as in monogamous callithricids, among whom the reproductive burden on the mother is great. There is also considerable potential in polygamous males such as the rhesus macaque if they are allowed regular access to infants in the absence of restrictive group members.

Turning to other mammals for supportive evidence, we find that marmots, for example (Rodentia: *Marmota caligata*), typically live in large colonies in which adult males display little parental care. But in the same species, isolated family units were also observed that consisted of a breeding pair plus offspring. Adult males in these family units directed extensive attention toward infants, engaging in such behavior as reciprocal grooming and rough-and-tumble play. Barash (1977, p. 196) drew the conclusion that "the basic pattern suggested here is one of facultative paternal behavior (capable of being adaptively varied) contrasting with obligatory maternal responsibilities. This seems to be a general pattern among mammals." (One must certainly use caution in applying "obligatory" to a social system in which cultural adaptation is so pervasive—as in the case of *Homo sapiens*—but Barash's conclusion seems to pertain well to observed or unmodified mammalian social systems.)

In birds, it was found that male marsh wrens (*Telmatodytes palustris*) mate polygynously and do not help feed offspring early in the breeding season. Later in the season, when all available females have mated, males show extensive caretaking and help to provision the young (Verner, 1964).

In humans, Davids (1972, p. 219) alluded to the plasticity of male caretaking in human Western societies: "Fatherhood, within the home, means that where the mother is not able to . . . meet particular needs which exceed those of routine daily care, the father, being 'in reserve,' enters the situation as a resource called upon to meet the extraordinary needs." In summary, therefore, these diverse observations depict the mother's role in many social systems as relatively stable, dependable, or consistent, and the male's as relatively variable, potential, or plastic.

An exquisite balance of variables impinges on the social system to affect the expression of the male's caretaking potential. Among them are the abundance and seasonality of food supply; predation; sexual selection (male competition and female choice); and the relatedness of adult caretakers and infants and of the caretakers themselves (e.g., whether troop females are closely related). Factors that may be at a derived or secondary level—that is, resulting from the foregoing primary ones—include the reproductive burden on the mother, the extent of maternal restrictiveness of infants, and the degree to which infants' survival is endangered if male caretaking is not called into play. It is a supremely difficult task—indeed, possibly a futile one—to sort out antecedent and consequent variables. Rather, we would do well to observe the intimate fit between a species' behavioral systems and the environmental demands that are exerted at many levels. To recapitulate:

1. *Monogamous systems* have evolved in habitats in which there is a relatively stable supply of food and predation pressure is not great. Male caretaking is often extensive and territoriality is common.

2. *One-male/multifemale systems* have evolved in habitats in which food resources are seasonally in short supply, so it is advantageous for the ratio of females to reproductive males to be at a maximum. Male caretaking is generally limited to the male's own offspring, and the male may kill the offspring of other males.

3. *Multimale/multifemale systems* have evolved in habitats in which food is relatively low in nutrients, difficult to obtain, or both. Predation pressure may be considerable. Male care is relatively attenuated.

There is evidence that some of the environmental contingencies described above apply also to human societies. On the basis of a sample of 80 cultures,

West and Konner (1976) determined that all cultures with strictly monogamous and nuclear families are characterized by close father–infant relations. In particular:

> Fathers are closest where gathering or horticulture (small-scale vegetable and fruit growing as in the Pacific Islands) is the primary mode of subsistence and where combinations of polygyny, patrilocal residence, the extended family, or patridominant division of labor are absent. (pp. 202–203)

Close father–infant relations are found when a great proportion of time is not spent gathering or defending resources; but where accumulated resources must be defended (especially through warfare), or a considerable amount of time is spent acquiring or defending resources necessary to obtain and maintain multiple wives, distant father–infant relations are typically found (Paige & Paige, 1973; Whiting & Whiting, 1975; West & Konner, 1976). Facile generalizations cannot be made between distant taxa, but it is difficult not to be struck by the parallel models proposed for birds, canids, nonhuman primates, and human primates. That is, extensive male care is seen where a great deal of time is not devoted to acquiring resources, and the extent of parental investment by males is positively correlated with genetic relatedness.

Several variables affecting male parental investment can also be considered at a more proximate level. Foremost among them, perhaps, as proposed in the earlier version of this chapter (Redican, 1976), is the extent to which mothers and possibly also other adult females restrict contact between adult males and infants. It was argued that the extent of male parental investment in a variety of species is positively correlated with relaxed, permissive mother–infant relations. Very simply, if the infant is not available it can hardly be the recipient of male caretaking; the hypothesis teeters perilously on a tautology. Nevertheless, it may be a helpful tautology if it merely demonstrates that the larger social system must be taken into consideration when approaching a topic such as male parental investment. A complex social system does not divide with surgical precision into elegant subsections of dyadic character. That lesson has been learned many times; it is still good to remind ourselves of it. In review, the supportive evidence for this hypothesis derives from an impressively wide range of sources:

1. Baboon mothers of different ages regulate the availability of infants to males by tolerating male–infant contact to varying degrees (Ransom & Ransom, 1971).

2. Barbary macaque mothers in one troop allowed more extensive early male–infant contact than those in another troop, with tangible consequences in the infants' psychomotor development thereby ensuing (Burton, 1972).

3. Permissiveness of mothers was found to be an important variable affecting male access to infants in stumptail macaques (Hendy-Neely & Rhine, 1977).

4. Squirrel monkey females actively repel adult males from close contact with the core of the troop, in which infants reside (Baldwin, 1968, 1969).

5. Squirrel monkey mothers with infants maintain a greater distance from adult males than those without infants (Strayer et al., 1975).

6. Adult male squirrel monkeys were observed to flee from threatening immatures, "probably to avoid attracting the mother" (Baldwin, 1969, p. 53).

7. Male–infant contact in rhesus and bonnet macaque groups increased after removal of the mother (Spencer-Booth & Hinde, 1967; Kaufman & Rosenblum, 1969).

8. Experimental cortical impairment of rhesus mothers was followed by an enhanced degree of male caretaking (Bucher, 1970).

9. Rhesus infants reared by adult males in the absence of mothers developed extensive attachments to the males (Redican, 1975).

10. An ordinal ranking of several macaque and baboon species showed a positive correlation between male parental investment and maternal permissiveness (Redican, 1976).

This hypothesis is vulnerable to criticism if species such as the langur are considered (see Redican, 1976, p. 370n). Langur infants are handed from mother to mother with great abandon, and yet there is little male parental investment. It may well be that the hypothesis holds only for multimale/multifemale social systems, from which all of the supporting data derive. A much more finely-tuned analysis is needed for monogamous systems, but it is not at all unlikely that Freudian theories involving the Oedipal dynamic might shed some light on that domain. And in defense of the hypothesis as it pertains to one-male/multifemale groups, it appears that group females are often very closely related—perhaps as full sisters, something like a superorganism. If so, one must scrutinize the hypothesis in terms of access between the female/infant subgroup and the resident male. As yet, sufficient data are not known by the present authors to make a coherent assessment of that point possible.

Another proximate variable affecting male parental investment in nonhuman primates is the gender of the infant. A variety of data points to a greater involvement of adult males with male infants. Mothers appear to discriminate less on the basis of gender, but if they do, the greater investment is toward female infants. This pattern is in close accord with data for many human societies (e.g., Goodenough, 1957; Johnson, 1963; Maccoby & Jacklin, 1974; Mackey, 1976, 1979).

Of particular concern to developmentalists is the proximate variable of age as it relates to parental investment—in this case, the age not only of the infant but of the adult male as well. There is some indication that older infants or young juveniles are more likely to be recipients of male care than are neonates. The glaring exception is the case of monogamous species in which the male is virtually the primary caretaker; there the male may be involved during the very birth of the infant. Where the mother is the primary caretaker, as in most polygamous systems, there is often a shift in parental investment from mothers to adult males as the infant matures. The male forms something of a bridge from maternal care to the infant's eventual involvement with the social group at large.

In terms of the relationship between age of the adult male and extent of parental care, the situation is more confusing. Male care is restricted to fully mature males in the Japanese macaque, for example, but there are reports that young or subadult males of other macaque species are the principal male caretakers. There are also conflicting reports for the same species. Clearly there is a need for further data, and it should not be overlooked that the available data are in conflict. An important consideration may prove to be the use of infants by males in agonistic interactions with other males, thus distinguishing between "exploitation" of infants by males to enhance their dominance status and parental caretaking in a strict sense.

As every primatologist well knows, the question enduringly poised on the lips of every nonprimatologist is something like, "What do monkeys *really* have to do with human beings?" The query is usually delivered with a glint in the eye, as though the inquirer had an exposé in mind. Sarcasm aside, it is an important concern and one that we have largely left alone in this paper. [There exists an entire volume devoted to the issue, if the reader is interested: von Cranach's *Methods of inference from animal to human behavior* (1976).] Our evasion here is deliberate; we hope that the inferences to be drawn about the human condition might emerge of their own accord. We believe that the wide sweep of species and topics in this survey can help promote such inference. But the reader may understandably be troubled by the very diversity encountered. After all, if there is such variability among monkeys, how much more difficult the task might be to make the inferential bridge from monkey to human. The very same species of monkey has even been known to have a different group organization on opposite sides of a mountain!

In part these concerns can be soothed by forsaking a search for *the* monkey—the representative species. There isn't one, just as there is no representative *Homo sapiens*. To paraphrase one of the most respected of our teachers, William A. Mason, one might survey the diversity of animal behavior and throw one's hands up, saying, "Isn't Nature wonderful!" or one can try to make sense of the systematic patterns one beholds. As he taught his students many times, one way to make sense of it is to ask questions and to learn to ask the right questions. And those questions transcend species. They are addressed to the fundamental issues of how behavior works.

We have examined a small portion of the remarkable and supremely efficient fit between behavior and the demands on a species at a variety of levels. Answering questions about how that fit comes about can, indeed, illuminate more fully the human condition or at least point us more accurately in the right direction toward asking more productive questions about being human. Biology is not destiny, but it can remind us of the limits of our destinies. It can show us the probable boundaries of behaviorial change open to us and the likelihood of fulfillment or nourishment in pursuing the abundance of opportunities available to us as heirs to the human condition.

REFERENCES

Alexander, B. K. Parental behavior of adult male Japanese monkeys. *Behaviour,* 1970, **36,** 270–285.

Altmann, J. *Baboon mothers and infants.* Cambridge, Mass.: Harvard University Press, 1980.

Altmann, S. A., & Altmann, J. Baboon ecology: African field research. *Bibliotheca Primatologica,* 1970, No. 12, pp. 1–220.

Baldwin, J. D. The social behavior of adult male squirrel monkeys *(Saimiri sciureus)* in a seminatural environment. *Folia Primatologica,* 1968, **9,** 281–314.

Baldwin, J. D. The ontogeny of social behaviour of squirrel monkeys *(Saimiri sciureus)* in a seminatural environment. *Folia Primatologica,* 1969, **11,** 35–79.

Baldwin, J. D. The social organization of a semifree-ranging troop of squirrel monkeys *(Saimiri sciureus). Folis Primatologica,* 1971, **14,** 23–50.

Baldwin, J. D., & Baldwin, J. The ecology and behavior of squirrel monkeys *(Saimiri oerstedi)* in a natural forest in western Panama. *Folia Primatologica,* 1972, **18,** 161–184.

Baldwin, J. D., & Baldwin, J. I. The role of play in social organization: Comparative observations on squirrel monkeys *(Saimiri). Primates,* 1973, **14,** 369–381.

Barash, D. P. *Sociobiology and behavior.* New York: Elsevier, 1977.

Baysinger, C. M., Brandt, E. M., & Mitchell, G. Development of infant social isolate monkeys *(Macaca mulatta)* in their isolation environments. *Primates,* 1972, **13,** 257–270.

Berkson, G. Development of an infant in a captive gibbon group. *Journal of Genetic Psychology,* 1966, **108,** 311–325.

Bernstein, I. S. "Paternal" behavior in nonhuman primates. *American Zoologist,* 1970, **10,** 480.

Bernstein, I. S. Activity patterns in a gelada monkey group. *Folia Primatologica*, 1975, **23**, 50–71.

Bertrand, M. The behavioral repertoire of the stumptail macaque. *Bibliotheca Primatologica*, 1969, No. 11.

Blaffer Hrdy, S. Care and exploitation of nonhuman primate infants by conspecifics other than the mother. In J. S Rosenblatt, R. A. Hinde, E. Shaw, & C. Beer (Eds.), *Advances in the study of behavior*, Vol. 6. New York: Academic Press, 1976.

Blaffer Hrdy, S. *The langurs of Abu: Female and male strategies of reproduction.* Cambridge, Mass.: Harvard University Press, 1977.

Blaffer Hrdy, S. Infanticide among animals: A review, classification, and examination of the implications for the reproductive strategies of females. *Ethology & Sociobiology*, 1979, **1**, 13–40.

Bolwig, N. A study of the behaviour of the chacma baboon, *Papio ursinus. Behaviour*, 1959, **14**, 136–163.

Box, H. O. A social developmental study of young monkeys *(Callithrix jacchus)* within a captive family group. *Primates*, 1975, **16**, 419–435.

Brandt, E. M., Baysinger, C., & Mitchell, G. Separation from rearing environment in mother-reared and isolation-reared rhesus monkeys *(Macaca mulatta). International Journal of Psychobiology*, 1972, **2**, 193–204.

Brandt, E. M., Irons, R., & Mitchell, G. Paternalistic behavior in four species of macaques. *Brain, Behavior, and Evolution*, 1970, **3**, 415–420.

Breuggeman, J. A. Parental care in a group of free-ranging rhesus monkeys *(Macaca mulatta). Folia Primatologica*, 1973, **20**, 178–210.

Bucher, K. L. Temporal lobe neocortex and maternal behavior in rhesus monkeys. Doctoral dissertation, The Johns Hopkins University, Baltimore, 1970.

Burton, F. D. The integration of biology and behavior in the socialization of *Macaca sylvana* of Gibraltar. In F. E. Poirier (Ed.), *Primate socialization.* New York: Random House, 1972.

Burton, F. D., & Bick, M. J. A. A drift in time can define a deme: The implications of tradition drift in primate societies for hominid evolution. *Journal of Human Evolution*, 1972, **1**, 53–59.

Carpenter, C. R. A field study in Siam of the behavior and social relations of the gibbon *(Hylobates lar). Comparative Psychology Monographs*, 1940, **16**, 1–212.

Chance, M. R. A., & Jolly, C. J. *Social groups of monkeys, apes, and men.* London: Jonathan Cape, 1970.

Chivers, D. J. Spatial relations within the siamang group. *Proceedings of the Third International Congress of Primatology.* Basel: S. Karger, 1971.

Chivers, D. J. The siamang and the gibbon in the Malay Peninsula. *Gibbon and Siamang*, 1972, **1**, 103–135.

Coe, C. L., & Rosenblum, L. A. Sexual segregation and its ontogeny in squirrel monkey social structure. *Journal of Human Evolution*, 1974, **3**, 551–561.

Coimbra-Filho, A. F., & Mittermeier, R. A. Hybridization in the genus *Leontopithecus, L. r. rosalia* (Linnaeus, 1766) × *L. r. chrysomelas* (Kuhl, 1820) (Callithrichidae, Primates). *Revista Brasileira de Biologia*, 1976, **36**, 129–137.

Crook, J. H. The evolution of social organisation and visual communication in the weaver birds *(Ploceinae)*. *Behaviour*, 1964, Supplement 10, pp. 1–178.

Crook, J. H. The adaptive significance of avian social organizations. *Symposia of the Zoological Society of London*, 1965, **14**, 181–218.

Crook, J. H. Gelada baboon herd structure and movement: A comparative report. *Symposia of the Zoological Society of London*, 1966, **18**, 237–258.

Crook, J. H., & Gartlan, J. S. Evolution of primate societies. *Nature*, 1966, **210**, 1200–1203.

Crook, J. H., & Goss-Custard, J. D. Social ethology. *Annual Review of Psychology*, 1972, **23**, 277–312.

Curtin, R. Langur social behavior and infant mortality. *Berkeley Papers in Physical Anthropology*, 1977, No. 50, pp. 22–27.

Curtin, R., & Dolhinow, P. Primate behavior in a changing world. *American Scientist*, 1978, **66**, 468–475.

Daly, M., & Wilson, M. *Sex, evolution, and behavior*. North Scituate, Mass.: Duxbury Press, 1978.

Darwin, C. [*On the origin of species by means of natural selection, or the preservation of favoured races in the struggle for life.*] Facsimile reproduction of 1st ed. edited by E. Mayr. New York: Atheneum, 1967. (Originally published, 1859.)

Darwin, C. [*The descent of man, and selection in relation to sex.*] (2 vols.). New York: International Publications Service, 1969. (Originally published, 1871.)

Davids, L. Fatherhood and comparative social research. *International Journal of Comparative Sociology*, 1972, **13**, 217–222.

Dawkins, R. *The selfish gene*. New York: Oxford University Press, 1976.

Deag, J. M. A study of the social behaviour and ecology of the wild Barbary macaque, *Macaca sylvanus* L. Doctoral dissertation, University of Bristol, 1974.

Deag, J. M. & Crook, J. H. Social behavior and "agonistic buffering" in the wild barbary macaque *Macaca sylvana* L. *Folia Primatologica*, 1971, **15**, 183–200.

DeVore, I. Mother–infant relations in free-ranging baboons. In H. L. Rheingold (Ed.), *Maternal behavior in mammals*. New York: Wiley, 1963.

Dolhinow, P. J., & Bishop, N. The development of motor skills and social relationships among primates through play. In J. P. Hill (Ed.), *Minnesota symposia on child psychology*, Vol. 4. Minneapolis: University of Minnesota Press, 1970.

DuMond, F. V. The squirrel monkey in a seminatural environment. In L. A. Rosenblum & R. W. Cooper (Ed.), *The squirrel monkey*. New York: Academic Press, 1968.

Eibl-Eibesfeldt, I. *Ethology: The biology of behavior*. New York: Holt, Rinehart, & Winston, 1970.

References 251

Eisenberg, J. F. The social organizations of mammals. *Handbuch der Zoologie: Eine Naturgeschichte der Stamme des Tierreiches,* 1966, **8**(39), 1–92.

Eisenberg, J. F., Muckenhirn, N. A., & Rudran, R. The relation between ecology and social structure in primates. *Science,* 1972, **176,** 863–874.

Ellefson, J. O. Territorial behavior in the common white-handed gibbon, *Hylobates lar* Linn. In P. C. Jay (Ed.), *Primates: Studies in adaptation and variability.* New York: Holt, 1968.

Epple, G. Vergleichende Untersuchungen uber Sexual- und Sozialverhalten der Krallenaffen *(Hapalidae). Folia Primatologica,* 1967, **7,** 37–65.

Epple, G. Parental behavior in *Saguinus fuscicollis* spp. *(Callithricidae). Folia Primatologica,* 1975, **24,** 221–238.

Estrada, A., Estrada, R., & Ervin, F. Establishment of a free-ranging colony of stumptail macaques *(Macaca arctoides):* Social relations I. *Primates,* 1977, **18,** 647–676.

Estrada, A., & Sandoval, J. M. Social relations in a free-ranging troop of stumptail macaques *(Macaca arctoides):* Male-care behavior I. *Primates,* 1977, **18,** 793–813.

Evans, R. I. A conversation with Konrad Lorenz. *Psychology Today,* 1974, **8**(6), 82–93.

Fairbanks, L. An analysis of subgroup structure and process in a captive squirrel monkey *(Saimiri sciureus)* colony. *Folia Primatologica,* 1974, **21,** 209–224.

Fitzgerald, A. Rearing marmosets in captivity. *Journal of Mammalogy,* 1935, **16,** 181–188.

Forbes, H. O. *A handbook to the primates.* London: Edward Arnold, 1897.

Fossey, D. The behavior of mountain gorillas. Lecture presented at Stanford University, May 11, 1976.

Fossey, D. Personal communication, May 14, 1976.

Fox, G. J. Some comparisons between siamang and gibbon behaviour. *Folia Primatologica,* 1972, **18,** 122–139.

Fox, G. J. Peripheralization behavior in a captive siamang family. *American Journal of Physical Anthropology,* 1974, **41,** 479.

Fox, L. R. Cannibalism in natural populations. *Annual Review of Ecology and Systematics,* 1975, **6,** 87–106.

Gartlan, J. S., & Brain, C. K. Ecology and social variability in *Cercopithecus aethiops* and *C. mitis.* In P. C. Jay (Ed.), *Primates: Studies in adaptation and variability.* New York: Holt, 1968.

Goodenough, E. W. Interest in persons as an aspect of sex differences in the early years. *Genetic Psychology Monographs,* 1957, **55,** 287–323.

Gouzoules, H. Maternal rank and early social interactions of stumptail macaques, *Macaca arctoides. Primates,* 1975, **16,** 405–418.

Grüner, M., & Krause, P. Biologische Beobachtungen an Weissspinseläffchen, *Hapale jacchus* (L. 1758) im Berliner Tierpark. *Zoologische Garten,* 1963, **28,** 108–114.

Hall, K. R. L. Behaviour and ecology of the wild patas monkey, *Erythrocebus patas,* in Uganda. *Journal of Zoology,* 1965, **148,** 15–87.

Hamilton, W. D. The genetical evolution of social behaviour. I, II. *Journal of Theoretical Biology,* 1974, **7,** 1–52.

Hamilton, W. J., III. *Life's color code.* New York: McGraw-Hill, 1973.

Hamilton, W. J., III, & Busse, C. Adult male "exploitation" or "investment" in infants among wild chacma baboons. In D. M. Taub (Ed.), *Primate paternalism: An evolutionary and comparative view of male investment.* New York: Van Nostrand-Reinhold, in press.

Hampton, J. K. Laboratory requirements and observations of *Oedipomidas oedipus. American Journal of Physical Anthropology,* 1964, **22,** 239–244.

Hampton, J. K., Hampton, S. H., & Landwehr, B. J. Observations on a successful breeding colony of the marmoset *Oedipomidas oedipus. Folia Primatologica,* 1966, **4,** 265–287.

Hampton, S. H., Hampton, J. K., & Levy, B. M. Husbandry of rare marmoset species. In D. D. Bridgwater (Ed.), *Saving the lion marmoset.* Wheeling, W.V.: The Wild Animal Propagation Trust, 1972.

Harlow, M. K. Nuclear family apparatus. *Behavior Research Methods and Instrumentation,* 1971, **3,** 301–304.

Hasegawa, T., & Hiraiwa, M. Social interactions of orphans observed in a free-ranging troop of Japanese monkeys. *Folia Primatologica,* 1980, **33,** 129–158.

Hendy-Neely, H., & Rhine, R. R. Social development of stumptail macaques *(Macaca arctoides):* Momentary touching and other interactions with adult males during the infants' first 60 days of life. *Primates,* 1977, **18,** 589–600.

Hearn, J. P., & Lunn, S. F. The reproductive biology of the marmoset monkey, *Callithrix jacchus. Laboratory Animal Handbooks,* 1975, **6,** 191–204.

Hinde, R. A. Analyzing the roles of the partners in a behavorial interaction—Mother–infant relations in the rhesus monkey. *Annals of The New York Academy of Sciences,* 1969, **159,** 651–667.

Hinde, R. A. Development of social behavior. In A. M. Schrier & F. Stollnitz (Eds.), *Behavior of nonhuman primates,* Vol. 3. New York: Academic Press, 1971.

Hinde, R. A., & Spencer-Booth, Y. The behaviour of socially living rhesus monkeys in their first two and a half years. *Animal Behaviour,* 1967, **15,** 161–196.

Hinde, R. A., & White, L. E. Dynamics of a relationship: Rhesus mother–infant ventro–ventral contact. *Journal of Comparative and Physiological Psychology,* 1974, **86,** 8–23.

Hoage, R. Parental care in *Leontopithecus r. rosalia:* Carrying behavior. In D. G. Kleiman (Ed.), *The biology and conservation of the Callitrichidae.* Washington, D.C.: Smithsonian Institution Press, 1977.

Hopf, S. New findings on the ontogeny of social behaviour in the squirrel monkey. *Psychiatria, Neurologia, Neurochirurgia,* 1971, **74,** 21–34.

Horn, H. S. The adaptive significance of colonial nesting in the Brewer's blackbird *(Euphagus cyanocephalus)*. *Ecology*, 1968, **49**, 682–694.

Hrdy, S. B. Male–male competition and infanticide among the langurs *(Presbytis entellus)* of Abu, Rajasthan. *Folia Primatologica*, 1974, **22**, 19–58.

Hrdy, S. B. See also Blaffer Hrdy, S.

Ingram, J. Parent–infant interactions in the common marmoset *(Callithrix jacchus)* and the development of young. Doctoral dissertation, University of Bristol, 1975.

Itani, J. Paternal care in the wild Japanese monkey, *Macaca fuscata fuscata*. *Primates*, 1959, **2**, 61–93.

Jay, P. Mother–infant relations in langurs. In H. L. Rheingold (Ed.), *Maternal behavior in mammals*. New York: Wiley, 1963.

Jay, P. C. The common langur of North India. In I. DeVore (Ed.), *Primate behavior: Field studies of monkeys and apes*. New York: Holt, 1965.

Johnson, M. M. Sex-role learning in the nuclear family. *Child Development*, 1963, **34**, 319–333.

Jolly, A. *The evolution of primate behavior*. New York: Macmillan, 1972.

Jolly, C. A suggested case of evolution by sexual selection in Primates. *Man*, 1963, **63**, 177–178.

Jones, N. G. B., & Trollope, J. Social behaviour of stump-tailed macaques in captivity. *Primates*, 1968, **9**, 365–394.

Kaufman, I. C., & Rosenblum, L. A. The waning of the mother–infant bond in two species of macaque. In B. M. Foss (Ed.), *Determinants of infant behaviour*, Vol. 4. London: Methuen, 1969.

Kaufmann, J. H. Behavior of infant rhesus monkeys and their mothers in a free-ranging band. *Zoologica*, 1966, **51**, 17–27.

Kawai, M. A field experiment in the process of group formation in the Japanese monkey *(Macaca fuscata)* and the releasing of the group at Chirayama. *Primates*, 1960, **2**, 181–253.

Kummer, H. Tripartite relations in hamadryas baboons. In S. A. Altmann (Ed.), *Social communication among primates*. Chicago: University of Chicago Press, 1967.

Kummer, H. Social organization of hamadryas baboons. *Bibliotheca Primatologica*, 1968, No. 6, pp. 1–189.

Kummer, H. *Primate societies*. Chicago: Aldine-Atherton, 1971.

Lack, D. *Ecological adaptations for breeding in birds*. London: Methuen, 1968.

Lahiri, R. K., & Southwick, C. H. Parental care in *Macaca sylvana*. *Folia Primatologica*, 1966, **4**, 257–264.

Lamb, M. E. (Ed.) *The role of the father in child development*. New York: Wiley, 1976.

Langford, J. B. Breeding behavior of *Hapale jacchus* (Common marmoset). *South African Journal of Science*, 1963, **59**, 299–300.

Leutenegger, W. Maternal–fetal weight relationships in primates. *Folia Primatologica*, 1973, **20**, 280–293.

Lindburg, D. G. The rhesus monkey in North India: An ecological and behavioral study. In L. A. Rosenblum (Ed.), *Primate behavior: Developments in field and laboratory research*, Vol. 2. New York: Academic Press, 1971.

Lucas, N. S., Hume, E. M., & Henderson Smith, H. On the breeding of the common marmoset (*Hapale jacchus* Linn.) in captivity when irradiated with ultra-violet rays. *Proceedings of the Zoological Society of London*, 1927, **30**, 447–451.

Lucas, N. S., Hume, E. M., & Henderson Smith, H. On the breeding of the common marmoset (*Hapale jacchus* Linn.) in captivity when irradiated with ultra-violet rays. II. A ten years' family history. *Proceedings of the Zoological Society of London*, Series A, 1937, **107**, 205–211.

Maccoby, E. E., & Jacklin, C. N. *The psychology of sex differences*. Stanford, Calif.: Stanford University Press, 1974.

Mackey, W. C. The adult male–child bond: An example of convergent evolution. *Journal of Anthropological Research*, 1976, **32**, 58–73.

Mackey, W. C. Parameters of the adult-male–child bond. *Ethology and Sociobiology*, 1979, **1**, 59–76.

MacRoberts, M. H. The social organization of Barbary apes (*Macaca sylvana*) on Gibraltar. *American Journal of Physical Anthropology*, 1970, **33**, 83–99.

Mallinson, J. J. C. The breeding and maintenance of marmosets at Jersey Zoo. *International Zoo Yearbook*, 1971, **11**, 79–83 (a).

Mallinson, J. J. C. Observations on the breeding of Red-handed Tamarin, *Saguinus* (=Tamarin) *midas* (Linnaeus, 1758) with comparative notes on other species of Callithricidae (=Hapalidae) breeding in captivity. *Annual Review of the Jersey Wildlife Preservation Trust*, 1971, **8**, 19–31 (b).

Mason, W. A. Field and laboratory studies of social organization in *Saimiri* and *Callicebus*. In L. A. Rosenblum (Ed.), *Primate behavior: Developments in field and laboratory research*, Vol. 2. New York: Academic Press, 1971.

Mason, W. A., & Epple, G. Social organization in experimental groups of *Saimiri* and *Callicebus*. *Proceedings of the Second International Congress of Primatology*, Vol. 1. Basel: Karger, 1969.

McCann, C. Notes on the colouration and habits of the white-browed gibbon or hoolock (*Hylobates hoolock* Harl.) *Journal of the Bombay Natural History Society*, 1933, **36**, 395–405.

McClure, H. E. Some observations of primates in climax diptocarp forest near Kuala Lumpur, Malaya. *Primates*, 1964, **3–4**, 39–58.

McKenna, J. J. Primate infant caregiving behavior. Origins, consequences, and variability with emphasis on the common Indian langur monkey. In D. Gubernick & P. Klopfer (Eds.), *Parental care in mammals*. New York: Plenum, in press.

Merz, E. Male–male interactions with dead infants in *Macaca sylvanus*. *Primates*, 1978, **19**, 749–754.

Mitchell, G., & Brandt, E. M. Paternal behavior in primates. In F. Poirier (Ed.), *Primate socialization*. New York: Random House, 1972.

Mohnot, S. M. Some aspects of social changes and infant-killing in the hanuman langur, *Presbytis entellus* (Primates: Cercopithecidae) in Western India. *Mammalia,* 1971, **35,** 175–198.

Mori, U. Development of sociability and social status. In M. Kawai (Ed.), *Contributions to primatology,* Vol. 16. *Ecological and sociological studies of gelada baboons.* Basel: Karger, 1979(a).

Mori, U. Individual relationships within a unit. In M. Kawai (Ed.), *Contributions to primatology,* Vol. 16. *Ecological and sociological studies of geleda baboons.* Basel: Karger, 1979(b).

Moynihan, M. Some behavior patterns of Platyrrhine monkeys. II. *Saguinus geoffroyi* and some other tamarins. *Smithsonian Contributions to Zoology,* 1970, No. 28.

Napier, J. R., & Napier, P. H. *A handbook of living primates.* New York: Academic Press, 1967.

Orians, G. H. On the evolution of mating systems in birds and mammals. *The American Naturalist,* 1969, **103,** 589–603.

Packer, C. Male care and exploitation of infants in *Papio anubis. Animal Behaviour,* 1980, **28,** 512–520.

Paige, K. E., & Paige, J. M. The politics of birth practices: A strategic analysis. *American Sociological Review,* 1973, **38,** 663–677.

Parke, R. D., & Suomi, S. J. Adult male–infant relationships: Human and nonhuman primate evidence. In K. Immelmann et. al. (Eds.), *Early development in animals and man.* New York: Cambridge University Press, in press.

Peffer-Smith, P. G., & Smith, E. O. Adult male–immature interactions in a captive stumptail macaque *(Macaca arctoides)* group. In D. M. Taub (Ed.), *Primate paternalism: An evolutionary and comparative view of male investment.* New York: Van Nostrand-Reinhold, in press.

Popp, J. L. Kidnapping among male anubis baboons in Masai Mara Reserve. Paper presented at the Conference of the Wenner-Gren Foundation for Anthropological Research, 1978.

Ransom, T. W., & Ransom, B. S. Adult male–infant relations among baboons *(Papio anubis). Folia Primatologica,* 1971, **16,** 179–195.

Ransom, T. W., & Rowell, T. E. Early social development of feral baboons. In F. Poirier (Ed.), *Primate socialization.* New York: Random House, 1972.

Redican, W. K. A longitudinal study of behavioral interactions between adult male and infant rhesus monkeys *(Macaca mulatta).* Doctoral dissertation, University of California, Davis, 1975.

Redican, W. K. Adult male–infant interactions in nonhuman primates. In M. E. Lamb (Ed.), *The role of the father in child development.* New York: Wiley, 1976.

Redican, W. K. Adult male–infant relations in captive rhesus monkeys. In D. J. Chivers & J. Herbert (Eds.), *Recent advances in primatology,* Vol. 1. *Behaviour.* New York: Academic Press, 1978.

Redican, W. K., & Mitchell, G. Play between adult male and infant rhesus monkeys. *American Zoologist*, 1974, **14**, 295–302.

Rhine, R. J., & Hendy-Neely, H. Social development of stumptail macaques *(Macaca arctoides):* Momentary touching, play, and other interactions with aunts and immatures during the infants' first 60 days of life. *Primates*, 1978, **19**, 115–123.

Rhine, R. J., & Owens, N. W. The order of movement of adult male and black infant baboons *(Papio anubis)* entering and leaving a potentially dangerous clearing. *Folia Primatologica*, 1972, **18**, 276–283.

Ridley, M. Paternal care. *Animal Behaviour*, 1978, **26**, 904–932.

Rosenblum, L. A. Sex and age differences in response to infant squirrel monkeys. *Brain, Behavior and Evolution*, 1972, **5**, 30–40.

Rothe, H. Beobachtungen zur Geburt beim Weissbüscheläffchen *(Callithrix jacchus* Erxleben, 1977). *Folia Primatologica*, 1973, **19**, 257–285.

Rowell, T. *The social behaviour of monkeys.* Baltimore: Penguin, 1972.

Rowell, T. E., Hinde, R. A., & Spencer-Booth, Y. "Aunt"–infant interaction in captive rhesus monkeys. *Animal Behaviour*, 1964, **12**, 219–226.

Rudran, R. The reproductive cycles of two subspecies of purple-faced langurs *(Presbytis senex)* with relation to environmental factors. *Folia Primatologica*, 1973, **19**, 41–60.

Selander, R. K. Sexual selection and dimorphism in birds. In B. G. Campbell (Ed.), *Sexual selection and the descent of man: 1871–1971.* Chicago: Aldine, 1972.

Simonds, P. E. The bonnet macaque in South India. In I. DeVore (Ed.), *Primate behavior: Field studies of monkeys and apes.* New York: Holt, 1965.

Simonds, P. E. Sex differences in bonnet macaque networks and social structure. *Archives of Sexual Behavior*, 1974, **3**, 151–166.

Snyder, P. A. Behavior of *Leontopithecus rosalia* (Golden-lion marmoset) and related species: A review. *Journal of Human Evolution*, 1974, **3**, 109–122.

Southwick, C. H., Beg, M. A., & Siddiqi, M. R. Rhesus monkeys in North India. In I. DeVore (Ed.), *Primate behavior.* New York: Holt, 1965.

Spencer-Booth, Y. The behaviour of group companions towards rhesus monkey infants. *Animal Behaviour*, 1968, **16**, 541–557.

Spencer-Booth, Y. The relationship between mammalian young and conspecifics other than mothers and peers: A review. In D. S. Lehrman, R. A. Hinde, & E. Shaw (Eds.), *Advances in the study of behavior*, Vol. 3. New York: Academic Press, 1970.

Spencer-Booth, Y., & Hinde, R. A. The effects of separating rhesus monkey infants from their mothers for six days. *Journal of Child Psychology and Psychiatry and Allied Disciplines*, 1967, **7**, 179–197.

Stein, D. M. Adult male baboons' affiliative relations with infants. Paper presented at the third annual meeting of the American Society of Primatologists, Winston-Salem, N.C., June 1980.

Stellar, E. The marmoset as a laboratory animal. Maintenance, general observations of behavior, and simple learning. *Journal of Comparative and Physiological Psychology,* 1960, **53,** 1–10.

Strayer, F. F., Taylor, M., & Yanciw, P. Group composition effects on social behaviour of captive squirrel monkeys *(Saimiri sciureus). Primates,* 1975, **16,** 253–260.

Strum, S. C., & Manzolillo, D. L. A field study of male–infant associations in wild baboons. In D. M. Taub (Ed.), *Primate paternalism: An evolutionary and comparative view of male investment.* New York: Van Nostrand-Reinhold, in press.

Sugiyama, Y. On the social change of hanuman langurs *(Presbytis entellus)* in their natural conditions. *Primates,* 1965, **6,** 381–418.

Sugiyama, Y. An artificial social change in a hanuman langur troop. *Primates,* 1966, **7,** 41–72.

Sugiyama, Y. Social organization of hanuman langurs. In S. A. Altmann (Ed.), *Social communication among primates.* Chicago: University of Chicago Press, 1967.

Sugiyama, Y. Characteristics of the social life of bonnet macaques *(Macaca radiata). Primates,* 1971, **12,** 247–266.

Suomi, S. J. Adult male–infant interactions among monkeys living in nuclear families. *Child Development,* 1977, **48,** 1255–1270.

Suomi, S. J. Differential development of various social relationships by rhesus monkey infants. In M. Lewis & L. A. Rosenblum (Ed.), *The child and its family.* New York: Plenum Press, 1979.

Suomi, S. J., Eisele, C. D., Grady, S. A., & Tripp, R. L. Social preferences of monkeys reared in an enriched laboratory environment. *Child Development,* 1973, **44,** 451–460.

Suzuki, A. Carnivority and cannibalism observed among forest-living chimpanzees. *Journal of the Anthropological Society of Nippon,* 1971, **79,** 30–48.

Taub, D. M. "Paternalism" in free-ranging Barbary macaques, *Macaca sylvanus. American Journal of Physical Anthropology,* 1975, **42,** 333–334.

Taub, D. M. Geographic distribution and habitat diversity of the Barbary macaque, *Macaca sylvanus* L. *Folia Primatologica,* 1977, **27,** 108–133.

Taub, D. M. Aspects of the biology of the wild Barbary macaque (Primates, Cercopithecinae, *Macaca sylvanus* L. 1758): Biogeography, the mating system, and male–infant associations. Doctoral dissertation, University of California, Davis, 1978.

Taub, D. M. Testing the "agonistic buffering" hypothesis. I. The dynamics of participation in the triadic interaction. *Behavorial Ecology and Sociobiology,* 1980, **6,** 187–197.

Taub, D. M. Male care-taking behavior among wild Barbary macaques, *Macaca sylvanus.* In D. M. Taub (Ed.), *Primate paternalism: An evolutionary and comparative view of male investment.* New York: Van Nostrand-Reinhold, in press.

Tayler, C. K., & Saayman, G. S. The social organisation and behaviour of dolphins *(Tursiops aduncus)* and baboons *(Papio anubis):* Some comparisons and assessments. *Annals of the Cape Provincial Museum,* 1972, **9,** 11–49.

Tenaza, R. R., & Hamilton, W. J., III. Preliminary observations of the Mentawai Islands gibbon, *Hylobates klossii. Folia Primatologica,* 1971, **15,** 201–211.

Thorington, R. W., Jr. Observations of squirrel monkeys in a Colombian forest. In L. A. Rosenblum & R. W. Cooper (Eds.), *The squirrel monkey.* New York: Academic Press, 1968.

Trivers, R. L. Parental investment and sexual selection. In B. G. Campbell (Ed.), *Sexual selection and the descent of man: 1871–1971.* Chicago: Aldine, 1972.

van Lawick-Goodall, J. Mother–offspring relationships in free-ranging chimpanzees. In D. Morris (Ed.), *Primate ethology,* Chicago: Aldine, 1967.

van Lawick-Goodall, J. The behaviour of free-living chimpanzees in the Gombe Stream Reserve. *Animal Behaviour Monographs,* 1968, **1,** 161–311.

Verner, J. Evolution of polygamy in the long-billed marsh wren. *Evolution,* 1964, **18,** 252–261.

von Cranach, M. *Methods of inference from animal to human behaviour.* Chicago: Aldine, 1976.

Werren, J. H., Gross, M. R., & Shine, R. Paternity and the evolution of male parental care. *Journal of Theoretical Biology,* 1980, **82,** 619–631.

West, M. M., & Konner, M. J. The role of the father: An anthropological perspective. In M. E. Lamb (Ed.), *The role of the father in child development.* New York: Wiley, 1976.

Whiting, J. W. M., & Whiting, B. B. Aloofness and intimacy of husbands and wives: A cross-cultural study. *Ethos,* 1975, **3,** 183–207.

Wilson, E. O. *Sociobiology: The new synthesis.* Cambridge, Mass.: Belknap Press of Harvard University, 1975.

Woolfenden, G. E. Florida scrub jay helpers at the nest. *The Auk,* 1975, **92,** *i,* 1–15.

Yoshiba, K. Local and intertroop variability in ecology and social behavior of common Indian langurs. In P. C. Jay (Ed.), *Primates: Studies in adaptation and variability.* New York: Holt, 1968.

CHAPTER 7

The Father as a Member of the Child's Social Network

MICHAEL LEWIS

Educational Testing Service

CANDICE FEIRING

Educational Testing Service

MARSHA WEINRAUB

Temple University

In an earlier essay on the role of the father, Lewis and Weinraub (1976) presented the general thesis that to understand the influence of the father on the child's development, it was necessary to understand the nature of the child's larger social network. This thesis, originally proposed in a critical review of attachment theory (Weinraub, Brooks, & Lewis, 1977), has been expanded in several recent papers (Lewis, 1979; Lewis & Feiring, 1978, 1979; Weinraub, 1978). In this essay we continue the development of this theme.

Until recently, it was relatively acceptable to say that as far as most psychologists were concerned, the only important social object in the infant's life was the mother. While this is changing, the research literature is still predominantly concerned with the role of the mother in the child's development. Most studies of children's social development examine the child–mother interaction or relationship. Although no accurate current count of mother–child versus father–child research exists, the number of studies of mothers still outweighs those of fathers or families. Even the language of developmental science continues to reflect the bias of the mother as sole socializer. For example, Snow (1972), in referring to language directed toward young organisms, language

This chapter was supported in part by NICHD Grant No. N01-HD-82849 to the first author and NIMH Grant No. R01-MH-HD32189 to the third author.

characterized in part by high pitched tones, exaggerated speech, and simplified sentence structure, has labeled this adult-to-child speech pattern as "motherese."

The persisting predominance of mother–child studies reflects certain realities. First, although several investigators have argued that the study of social (and cognitive) development requires a broader perspective than exclusive focus on the mother–child dyad (e.g., Lewis & Rosenblum, 1979), relatively little work on such a perspective has been undertaken. Second, despite increases in maternal employment and the increase in the number of very young children found in daycare, homecare, or at babysitters (Bronfenbrenner, 1974), the majority of young children in our culture are still being cared for by their mothers. Because of social and economic factors, even those children who spend time in alternative caregiving environments such as daycare are usually being cared for by someone else's mother.

Finally, despite Parke and O'Leary's demonstration (1975) that fathers are as capable as mothers in caring for and nurturing newborn infants, the inescapable fact remains that competence and performance are not necessarily, or, in the case of fathers and caregiving, frequently related. Despite the feminist movement that began in the 1960s, sex-typed behaviors of children and adults within the family have remained relatively unchanged (Zill, 1979). Given that in general the American prescribed role for the female includes childcare and the male role does not, it is little wonder that mothers, for theoretical, experimental, and practical reasons remain the predominant objects of focus in the child's development.

To understand the power of the theoretical position that holds the mother to be the singular central factor in socialization, it is necessary to review briefly the historical context for this position.

HISTORICAL PERSPECTIVE

The general concern of psychological inquiry can be summarized in the simple question, "Why do organisms behave?" Consideration of such concepts as needs, drives, and motives are all part of the attempt to answer this question. Different theoretical approaches have different terms associated with them. We focus on drives, because much of American psychology was and is concerned with this concept.

Drive theorists (and others) distinguished two major types of drives: basic biological, or primary, drives and secondary, or derived, drives. Primary drives were thought to be those activating and/or directing functions specifically tied to the biological functioning of the organism such as feeding and drinking; secondary or derived drives were thought to be those functions created through the satisfaction of the primary drives. An example of such a derived drive might be dependency, or love.

It was toward such a conceptualization of the biology of humans and theories of motivation that both Harlow's and Bowlby's initial work was directed. In Bowlby's earliest effort (1951), he concluded that the proper care, attention, and love of a caregiver was necessary in order for the young human organism to survive. Without such care the infant would not only fail to thrive but might even die. In effect, by evoking the criteria of survival or failure to thrive, Bowlby was able to argue that the love and care of an adult for the young of the species was not a secondary but a primary drive. If the need for food was primary because the organism could not live without it, so too was the need for love and care. Along with the work of Harlow and Harlow (1965) and Spitz (1945), Bowlby's arguments thrust care and love from its derived and thus nonbiological position back into the arena of biology. Meanwhile, American psychologists such as Sears (Sears, Maccoby, & Levin, 1957) were trying to reformulate psychoanalytic concepts into learning theory. In so doing, they made dependency into a secondary drive derived from the child's need for food.

In his theory of attachment, Bowlby (1969) went one step further than the original demonstration of the primary importance of love for the development of the human infant. In wishing to make love a biological necessity and imperative of development and growth, Bowlby argued for the biological unity of mother and infant. For him, the mother–infant dyad was a biological entity endowed with unique features. It was distinguished from all other relationships and derived from biological and evolutionary necessities.

Following Bowlby's lead, many researchers (e.g., Ainsworth, 1964; Schaffer & Emerson, 1964) became interested in investigating the special features of the mother–child relationship. The resulting research, which became known as the attachment literature, served the important function of focusing our concerns on the infant's early relationship to the caregiver. This relationship has been seen as having a central or primary role in effecting and determining subsequent intellectual as well as social development. However, it has become increasingly obvious that the young child's social, affective, and intellectual development is not determined solely by the mother–infant relationship.

The attachment theories of Bowlby (1969) and Ainsworth (1969) assume an epigenetic model of development (Lewis, 1979). The central premise of the epigenetic model is the assumption that there is a direct relationship from one set of social experiences to the next. According to this model, there is a linear relationship between the infant's primary relationship with the mother and subsequent relationships with others that follow. The model holds that subsequent social relations (peers in particular, but also fathers) are dependent on the initial attachment relationship between mother and infant. Most of the literature arguing this position has dealt with the subsequent development of peer relations from the mother–child relationship (Hartup, 1981; Lewis & Schaeffer, 1980; Matas, Arend, & Sroufe, 1978; Waters, Wippman, & Sroufe, 1979).

We have proposed an alternative model, labeled the *social network model,* which views social development within a broader context than just the mother–infant relationship (Edwards & Lewis, 1979; Lewis, 1979; Lewis & Feiring, 1978, 1979). According to this model, functional social relationships between different systems remain relatively independent. While capable of mutual affect, these systems do not develop linearly from one another. Instead, social relationships are formed simultaneously rather than sequentially, satisfying multiple and differential social needs. An important task in the study of social development is the articulation of the matrix formed by social objects and needs (Edwards & Lewis, 1979; Lewis & Feiring, 1979). Again, in terms of social relationships, the two systems most frequently studied and discussed by proponents of this model are the mother–child and child–peer systems (Harlow & Harlow, 1965; Hartup, 1981; Lewis, 1979; Lewis & Feiring, 1979; Lewis & Schaeffer, 1980; Lewis, Young, Brooks, & Michalson, 1975; Suomi, 1979; Suomi & Harlow, 1975, 1978). However, the conceptualization of the development of the father–infant relationships can be viewed from this model as well.

Within the social network model, the child's social relationships are viewed as centering around the child's needs and the culturally determined method of meeting these needs. For example, some cultures promote the use of multiple caregiving in the form of both mother and older female sibling or friend (Whiting & Whiting, 1975), some cultures support daycare settings with multiple adults, and others support the mother–infant care tradition. The particular goals and values of a culture determine the nature of the social network—the number and nature of the people and their tasks. In a culture where only the mother interacts with the infant for the first 2 or 3 years, it is the mother who is assigned almost all functions. The child's social network in this culture differs from that of the child in another culture in which the mother is the caregiver but peer or paternal experiences are available, and differs still more from the network in a culture in which the older female sibling takes care of the child.

In the predominant U.S. culture, the articulation of the relationship between function and people in the preschool child indicates a separation of function and person; adults are assigned the role of caretaking, older peers that of teaching, and similar-age peers that of play (Edwards & Lewis, 1979). The view that children have multiple needs that are satisfied by a variety of others, not the mother alone, is emphasized by the social network model. Moreover, while one system will affect another, the development of social relationships is not sequential. Thus while the mother–infant attachment may affect the child's peer relationships, these peer relationships may not be determined by the attachment relationship. Lewis and Schaeffer (1980) suggest two ways in which the maternal–infant attachment relationship may cause poor peer relationships, although they do not determine them in the epigenetic sense: (1) lack of experience, and (2) generalized fear. Mothers who are inadequate in terms of "mothering" and who are unable to facilitate an attachment relationship may at the same time prevent the infant from having peer experience. Given that it is the mother who in our culture must facilitate early peer contact, her failure to do so will result in the development of inadequate peer interaction skills. In this case, poor attachment and poor peer relationships are related, but here the failure of the attachment relationship with the mother is not the cause of the poor peer relationships; the cause is lack of experience with peers.

Poor "mothering" resulting in a poor attachment relationship also can produce general fearfulness. This has the effect of inhibiting contact with peers. It is this lack of contact caused by fear that affects peer relationships. This may explain why younger rather than same-age or older peer "therapists" are better able to help depressed children; the younger peer may be less fearful for the "patient" since his or her skills are less advanced (Hartup, 1980). In both cases, it is not the poor interpersonal relationship with the mother in itself that is responsible for poor subsequent relationships, but rather a more indirect effect of the mother that mediates the child's contact with peers and others, for example, the father.

It is within this context that father–child relations can, we think, best be conceptualized. The father–child attachment system may develop from origins similar to those of the mother–child attachment system, and the two systems may be related in a number of ways. However, we believe that the father–child system may not be simply a secondary outgrowth of the mother–child system. Although the data support separate but mutual influencing systems between mother–child and peer–child, the data on mother–child and father–child effects are almost nonexistent. In the following sections, we review the assumptions of the social network model more specifically and then consider aspects of the model with the most relevance for understanding the role of the father in the child's early development.

THE SOCIAL NETWORK MODEL

The child is born into a set of interconnected relationships, including those of adults of varying ages who have relationships to one another. Before we explore the specific nature of the father–child relationship system, we must look at some of the general characteristics of systems and how they interact.

A General Systems Approach

A system is a set of interrelated elements in which each element influences and is influenced by each other element (Monane, 1967; Taylor, 1975; Von Bertalanffy, 1967). Said differently, defining elements are simultaneously the subject and object of influence. A system is usually composed structurally of an interdependent network of subsystems. For example, within the child's social network, the child's relationship with family members can be conceptualized into parent–child, child–sibling, and parent–parent subsystems. Current research illustrates how these child–family member subsystems of the child's social network are characterized by their interdependent nature. Pedersen (1975), for example, demonstrated the ways in which the child–family member subsystems are interdependent—that is, the ways in which the child–parent and parent–parent subsystems mutually influence each other. He found a high interrelationship in the families of boys between the father–infant play and the effect of the father's esteem for the mother as a "mother" as well as the amount of tension and conflict in marriage.

Social systems also possess the quality of nonadditivity. Knowing everything about the subsystems that comprise a system will not tell you everything about the system as it operates as a whole. Any subsystem behaves quite differently within the system from the way it does in isolation. For example, the nature of the interaction in the parent–child subsystem in isolation is different from the nature of the interaction when it is embedded in a larger system. Lamb (1976a, 1977b) reports that infants interact more with either parent in isolated dyads than when the parent–child dyads are embedded in the entire family system of two parents and child. In addition, parents are far less interactive with the child when their spouse is present. Clarke-Stewart (1978, 1980) found that the quality and quantity of the mother-to-child interaction changed when this subsystem was embedded in the mother–child–father triad. The mothers in this study initiated less talk and play with the child (quantity) and were also less engaging, reinforcing, and responsive in their child-directed interactions (quality) when the father was present than when they were alone with the child. Pedersen et al. (1979, 1980) report that while the father/husband frequently divides his behavior between child and spouse in a three person setting, the mother/wife spends much more time in a dyadic interaction with the child. A study by Parke and O'Leary (1975) illustrates both the qualities of interdependence and nonadditivity in the child's social network. When mothers were with their husbands, they were more likely to explore the baby and smile at the baby than when they were alone with the newborn. In addition, when mothers were with fathers, they tended to touch their male children more than their female children; this sex difference in touching was not evident when the mother and the child were alone. Still other research demonstrates the influence of the child on the parent subsystem. Rosenblatt (1974) found that the presence of one or more children reduced the adult–adult touching, talking, and smiling in selected public places such as the zoo, park, and shopping center.

Another important aspect of social systems is that they are characterized by the process of steady states. A steady state is a balance process whereby a system maintains a viable relationship between its elements and its environment. The balance denoted by the term steady state is not the static one implied by the terms homeostasis and equilibrium, which denote a process whereby adjustment maintains a system at a given level. Rather, steady state describes the process whereby a system maintains itself while always changing to some degree. Steady states are characterized by a high degree of complexity and organization and denote an interplay of stability and flexibility in a social system or network. In the social network system, the child functions through his or her lifespan as a member of a social network with ever-changing members and environment. For example, when the first-born child of 2 years acquires a new sibling, the structure of his or her social network changes. The first born must modify his or her mode of functioning with the arrival of a second child. Although the child's goals of learning to adapt to the environment remain the same, the child's actual activities may alter. Research by Dunn and Kendrick (1979) illustrates how children's functioning in their social networks is described by new activities in the service of prior goals. Although independent behavior was encouraged by the mother prior to the birth of the second child and was a child development goal, the amount of and opportunity for independent behavior changed (i.e., increased) as the social network changed to include a new sibling.

Still another aspect of any social system is the environment in which the social system exists. Therefore, stipulation of the child's social network necessitates the examination of the kinds of social, political, and physical environments that characterize the network.

Social Network Propositions

Using a systems approach, it is possible to articulate a set of general propositions from which a model of social development is possible. The set of 10 propositions as explicated in Lewis and Weinraub (1976) follows:

Proposition 1. *People are by nature social and from birth enter into a social network.*

Proposition 2. *The social network is made up of a variety of social objects including mothers, fathers, siblings, other relatives, friends, and self.*

Proposition 3.   *The social network is made up of social objects, functions, and situations.*

Proposition 4.   *Social objects, functions, and situations are only partially related.*

Proposition 5.   *The social network is constructed from a set of networks ranging from the immediate family to the culture at large.*

Proposition 6.   *The child from birth is an active participant in the social network.*

Proposition 7.   *The child's social behavior and the composition of the social network change as a function of developmental status.*

Proposition 8.   *The child has a repertoire of behaviors that are distributed within the social network as befits the object, function, and situation of the specific interaction.*

Proposition 8a.   *Within an individual child's social network, certain objects tend to perform certain functions in certain situations.*

Proposition 8b.   *When more than one object performs the same function, tension is introduced into the system.*

Proposition 9.   *The child acquires knowledge through direct and indirect interaction with the social network.*

Proposition 10.   *The structural aspects of the social network include interactions and relationships that are arranged in a hierarchical order. Interactions and relationships may not directly correspond.*

In this discussion, three propositions as they relate to the father as a member of the social network are considered in detail: first, interactions and relationships are not synonymous; second, the child's world is filled with different social objects and needs; and third, children acquire knowledge through direct and indirect interaction with the social network.

INTERACTIONS AND RELATIONSHIPS ARE NOT SYNONYMOUS

Because mother–child and father–child interactions are different, it has been assumed that their relationships are different. This indeed may be the case, but it is necessary to consider the role of interaction in relationships. Recently, Hinde (1976) has attempted to articulate the meaning of a relationship and has included interaction as only one of the several elements making up such a definition. This exercise alerts us to the possibility that relationships and interactions may not have a high correspondence.

Interactions are specifiable behaviors or sets of behaviors that are observable and measurable. Relationships, on the other hand, are inferred from interactions but are difficult to specify and have proven difficult to measure. Knowledge of the relationship may be helpful in predicting a particular interaction; however, knowing that relationship does not give us any one-to-one correspondence to a single interaction or set of interactions. Conversely, observing the interaction between two individuals does not necessarily specify their relationship. After watching a woman feeding a child, for example, we might infer that the woman is the child's mother, but such a relationship is not necessarily the case (for instance, she could be a wet nurse).

While the father is not distinguished from other male adults, the mother of the child is biologically obvious. In fact, in most primates, the adult female is not monogamous and therefore paternity cannot be determined. Thus neither child nor adult can be certain who is the father. Even within monogamous relationships, knowledge of the relationship between sexual relations and childbirth is required to be able to determine paternity. In contrast, the mother's interactions with the infant clearly distinguish her from all other women. Her biological interaction with the child—through pregnancy and childbirth and nursing—makes known to her and to all other individuals, including the child, that she is "mother."

Not only can the mother be defined through her unique biological relationship, but much of her interactions with the child are likewise defined. The mammalian mother must feed her child by definition, and other interactions naturally follow. For instance, the mother provides satisfaction for the child's needs of warmth, touching and kinesthetics. These early interaction patterns then build into somewhat predictable interactions in most environments. It is not surprising at all that 1-year-old children in general go to their mothers in times of hunger, fatigue, and fear. Thus for mothers, the biological relationship predicts the expected behavioral and cultural mother–child interactions.

Fathers present a different case. Knowing that a man is the father of a child tells us very little about that man's interactions with the child. Fathers have historically served as protectors from predators and helped in the provision of food, warmth, shelter, and stimulation. In todays' American society, however, these functions are not as immediately apparent as the mother's functions are. Moreover, although this kind of paternal role may have helped to perpetuate the species, it is possible that children could have survived even if fathers did not perform their role. It is obvious that this is not the case with mothers' roles. Thus whereas the mother–child relationship is tied to biological dispositions, the father–child relationship is less attached to biology and more free to vary. This lack of predictable, biological, predisposed interaction patterns for fathers not only differentiates the father–infant relationship from that of the mother–infant relationship, but also makes the nature of the father–infant relationship more difficult to discern.

THE SOCIAL NETWORK IS MADE UP OF SOCIAL OBJECTS, FUNCTIONS, AND SITUATIONS

To the degree that the research literature has been extended to include others in the child's life (Dunn & Kendrick, 1979; Lamb, 1976c, 1978; Lewis & Rosenblum, 1979; Zajonc & Marcus, 1975) the notion of a multisocial world to which the young child must adapt has become increasingly more accepted. The task before us, then, is to specify the different ways in which individuals in the child's world behave, what causes these differences, and how these differences affect specific developmental outcomes.

Toward such a goal, Lewis and Feiring (1979) have suggested a model in which a matrix is formed containing a set of social objects (people) and a set of activities, or child needs, which are called functions. This matrix allows the study of the nature and number of the people in the child's life at a given time, the functions performed, and the specification of who is performing what function. From such a descriptive model, it may be possible to articulate the social network of the child—the social processes and structure of the particular network and the consequences on any number of developmental outcomes. For example, ontogenetic constraints on objects, functions, and objects × functions are obvious. Mothers are more likely to play with and feed the infant than older siblings when the infant is 3 months old than when the infant is 9 months old. Family variables such as family size, age of siblings, or the presence or absence of a parent is also likely to affect the matrix. Dunn and Wooding (1977), for example, have shown that first-born children receive more adult attention only until the birth of the next child. Finally, cultural factors also have been shown to affect this matrix. Whiting and Whiting (1975) have shown that in many cultures it is the older female sibling who is responsible for satisfying many of the young child's needs rather than the father or mother.

As a first step toward defining a matrix of people and functions that influence a child, it is necessary to describe some of the differences found in the literature on the qualitative and quantitative behaviors of mothers and fathers. Patterns of mother–child and father–child interactions show both differences and similarities. Given the fact that most mothers are the primary caregivers, it should not be surprising that there are differences in the quantity of parental behavior or, in other words, the frequency of the parents' availability to the child.

Quantity

It is generally agreed that fathers spend very little time interacting with their infants—certainly much less time than mothers. Estimates of the amount of time fathers spend in direct contact with their infants in the first year of life range from less than a minute per day (Rebelsky & Hanks, 1971) to slightly more than an hour per day (Pedersen & Robson, 1969). Although the amount of time fathers spend with their children probably increases as children grow older (Lewis & Weinraub, 1976), the total amount of time fathers spend with their children is limited by the fact that most fathers are empolyed in full-time jobs. Since a larger proportion of women than men hold part-time jobs (U.S. Department of Commerce, 1976), employed mothers are still more likely to have shorter work weeks and more flexible working hours than employed fathers (Weinraub, 1978).

However, differences in the quantity of time fathers and mothers spend with their children do not necessarily imply that mothers and fathers have a differential impact on their children. It is increasingly recognized that the amount of time parents interact with or are available to their children (beyond a minimal amount) has very little effect on the quality of their relationship (Lamb, 1976c). In particular, the amount of time most fathers spend interacting with their children does not appear to predict children's behavior toward their fathers (Ban & Lewis, 1974; Kotelchuck, 1972; Pedersen & Robson, 1969).

In light of the limited amount of time fathers spend with their children, the father's effects on child development may be realized not as a result of the amount of interaction but as a result of the specific quality of his contribution to the child's social network. These effects may be conceptualized as direct effects, resulting from specific activities and behaviors the father engages in when he is with his child, and indirect effects, resulting from the father's membership in and association with other members of the child's social network.

Quality

Considering the limited amount of time fathers engage in interaction with their young children, the father's role in socialization may be studied more fruitfully in terms of the kind, rather than the amount, of interaction.

In their classic discussion of the qualitative differences in mother and father roles in child development, Parsons and Bales (1955) asserted that fathers' and mothers' roles or social functions are divided according to instrumental and expressive functions. The mother's function is viewed as an expressive one and is characterized by a concern with interpersonal relationships, emotional support, nurturance, and caregiving. The father's function is delineated as instrumental and is characterized by a concern with mastery and competence. Observations and interviews with children indicate that mothers are perceived as more affectionate and nurturant, and fathers are seen as more punitive and restrictive (Armentrout & Burger, 1972; Bronfenbrenner, 1961; Emmerich, 1959; Fitzgerald, 1966; Kagan & Lemkin, 1960). Thomas (1968) reports that elementary school children view their fathers as protectors, disciplinarians, and teachers in the home environment. Mothers are more often viewed as supportive and encouraging of their children.

FUNCTION DIFFERENCES BETWEEN FATHERS AND MOTHERS

The nature of activities that characterize the father's interaction with his child may be more notably different in the social functions of sex role teaching, household activities, caregiving, and play. Data collected since 1955 indicate that fathers are more concerned with sex role acquisition than mothers (Aberle & Naegele, 1952; Block, 1973; Goodenough, 1957; Lansky, 1967; Margolin & Patterson, 1975; Sears et al., 1957; Tasch, 1952). Fathers have been demonstrated to be especially opposed to feminine behavior in their young sons. Goodenough (1957) found that fathers were concerned particularly with the appropriate sex role behavior of their sons. Recent studies have reported that fathers are more likely to respond differentially to their children on the basis of gender than mothers (Aldous, 1975; Block, 1973; Fagot, 1974; Margolin & Patterson, 1975).

Information on parental behavior toward young children and children's behavior toward parents makes clear that within the household environment, parents appear to perform different activities. Even today, although there are many working mothers of young children, the distribution of functions appears to remain rather traditional: women remain the primary caregivers of young children, even when men increase their performance of household duties. Although men appear to do more around the home than before (take out garbage, cook, grocery shop, and wash dishes), there are still some activities that men do not perform to any degree, such as cleaning the bathroom, sorting the laundry or cleaning the refrigerator or oven *(Trenton Times,* July 31, 1980). Thus fathers still interact with their young children less than mothers, and mothers are considered the primary child caregivers even though fathers are playing an increasingly active role. This uneven distribution of the amount of time in interaction may hide the differences in parental behaviors, and it may be necessary to take the base level of interaction time into account by observing the proportion of time in various activities as a function of the total time in interaction. Although mothers may engage overall in more functions than fathers, the distribution or proportion of these activities may be the important variable.

The data available on the extent of father–infant caregiving interactions suggest that the fathers interact very infrequently with their infants and take very little responsibility for infant caregiving. Of the 144 fathers with children from 9 to 12 months old that Kotelchuck (1972) interviewed, only 25 percent reported that they had any regular caregiving activity. Lewis and Ban (1977) reported that fathers of 12-month-olds spent only 15 minutes of play a day (this ranged from 0 to 2 hours). Newson and Newson (1968) interviewed mothers of 1- and 4-year-old children and found that although slightly more than 52 percent of the fathers were considered to take an active part in the child's daily life, their activities did not necessarily involve caregiving. In fact, when the remaining fathers of the 1- and 4-year-olds reported they had a "moderate share" in the child's activities, this meant that they did not participate in childcare unless asked or under very special circumstances. Nearly half of these fathers contributed very little to the daily care of their children.

In a recent study (Weinraub, 1980) of fathers and mothers of 2- to 3-year-old, middle-class children in a large metropolitan area, fathers reported spending only 15 percent of their total time caregiving to their children, whereas mothers reportedly spent 25 percent of their total time caregiving. Comparing the *mean* amounts of time that mothers and fathers reported engaging in caregiving, fathers spent an average of 0.8 hour per day caregiving, while mothers spent 2.1 hours per day. Thus fathers spent only about one-third as much time as mothers caring for their children. In this study, there was an interesting sex of child × sex of parent interaction. Fathers spent more time in noncaregiving activities such as watching TV and reading than mothers when the child was a daughter; mothers spent more time than fathers watching TV or reading when the child was a son.

In the area of caregiving, the differences between mothers and fathers appears to be primarily one of performance rather than competence. Parke and O'Leary (1975) observed parents in a hospital room and found that fathers are equally competent as mothers in social interaction with newborns. Although mothers spent more time in caregiving activities in the home, fathers could respond as sensitively and appropriately with newborns in the hospital as mothers.

Mother–father differences are most evident in the balance between play and caregiving activities (Parke & Sawin, 1975, 1980). Lamb (1980) reports that mothers of 15-to-24-month-olds held their children while performing caretaking functions and restricted them more often than fathers, whereas fathers more frequently held their children in order to play. The most consistently reported finding concerning sex of parent and the social function of play is that fathers spend a larger proportion of their time playing with the child than do mothers (Field, 1978; Lamb, 1977a; Trevarthen, 1974; Yogman, Dixon, Tronick, Als, & Brazelton, 1977). In addition, fathers tend to engage in more physical play with their children than do mothers (Lamb, 1977a). In a home-based study, Lamb (1977a) found that fathers played more physical games and engaged in more conventional play activities (i.e., peek-a-boo), reading, and stimulus-centered toy play than mothers. Clarke-Stewart (1978, 1980) found no differences between mothers and fathers in the amount or kind of social play they directed toward their young children at home. However, during laboratory play sessions in which parents were asked to choose an activity to perform with their 15-month-old child, fathers were more likely to select physical and social activities of play with their child, whereas mothers were more likely to choose intellectual and nonsocial activities. Clarke-Stewart's (1978, 1980) research suggested that fathers' play tended to be more arousing and physical in nature in contrast to that of mothers, which appeared relatively more intellectual and didactic. Similarly, Power and Parke (in press) found that when regulating ongoing interaction, mothers used a distal attention-directing approach in contrast to the fathers' use of a more proximal-physical mode. More specifically, fathers spent more time playing with toys and lifting their children while mothers tended to watch their child's activity rather than participate physically in play. Pedersen et al. (1980) reported that when the three family members, mother, father, and child, are together, vigorous tactile–kinesthetic stimulation was higher for fathers than mothers, although this finding did not hold true for father–child dyads observed in isolation.

Table 1.   Family Interactions by Function for Directed Dyads (N = 15)[a]

	Information Seeking	Nurturance	Caregiving
M → C	9.6	4.1	4.3
F → C	9.5	3.3	3.3
C → M	3.5	2.0	.40
C → F	1.9	2.0	.33
M → F	3.2	3.9	1.6
F → M	4.7	2.7	.53

[a]Data are given for mean frequency of interaction over 15 minutes of coded interaction. *Caregiving* is defined as taking care of the physical needs of another, such as offering and serving food, feeding food, cleaning, and assistance with toileting. *Nurturance* is defined as any expression of warmth, whether verbal (such as praise) or nonverbal (such as smiles, kisses, and hugs). *Information Seeking* is defined as any type of question asking and includes "requests for information" (in which information previously unavailable is solicited) as well as "test questions" (in which the answer is already known) and "directive questions" (in which a behavior is requested).

Very little is known about parents' differential performance around functions other than play. In a pilot study of the interaction between 15 3-year-old children and their parents during dinner, an exploration of differences in the functions of mothers, fathers, and children was undertaken (Lewis & Feiring, in press, b).

The mean frequency of interaction for family members of mother (M), father (F), and child (C) by function is given in Table 1. First examining the behavior of parents to the 3-year-old child, we note that both the mother and father direct a similar amount of information seeking and nurturance as well as caregiving to the child. Thus it seems (in our small sample observed over 15 minutes) that both parents perform expressive (nurturance and caregiving) and instrumental (information seeking) functions when dealing with the child. When it comes to the expressive function, mothers performed this role slightly more than fathers, but the difference in parental behavior is very small and not significant. It is also interesting to note that in a dinnertime situation, of those behaviors coded, the most frequent parent activity is not caregiving or nurturance but information seeking. In all functions coded, mothers direct slightly more behavior to the child than fathers do.

Examination of the children's behavior toward their parents reveals that children are more likely to seek information from the mother than from the father even though there are no differences in mother's and father's information-seeking behavior toward the child. This finding suggests that differences in children's behavior toward their parents may not necessarily reflect parental differences in the same domain.

Considering the parents' behavior toward each other, we note that fathers seek information more from mothers, whereas mothers nurture and caregive more to fathers. In the case of the parents' behavior toward each other, it appears that the Parsons and Bales (1955) distinction of roles operates at least to some degree. That is, mothers perform more expressive behaviors toward fathers while fathers perform more instrumental behaviors toward mothers. Thus although parents do not appear to show role differentiation of function toward the child, they do show it toward each other. These findings suggest that the child also may learn about traditional role expectations for male and female behavior through the observation of the parents' interaction. Learning about social behavior through observation rather than participation in interaction is a form of indirect influence that may be a central (and understudied) process of socialization. In general, these findings suggest that even in our small sample, there are differences in the distribution of social function by social objects. In some sense, then, children experience this mother–father difference in two ways: (1) as expressed toward them (the child as object) and (2) as witnessed by them as expressed between their parents (the child as nonparticipant). These different modes of experience may have important implications for the ways in which the child learns about the appropriate ways of behaving in the social world.

Function Differences between Fathers and Mothers as Related to Sex of Child and Social Class

Differences between paternal and maternal behaviors are moderated by the sex of the child. Fathers behave differently depending on whether they are interacting with a son or daughter (Gewirtz & Gewirtz, 1968; Parke & O'Leary, 1975; Rebelsky & Hanks, 1971; Spelke et al., 1973; Weinraub, 1980; Weinraub & Frankel 1977). Parke and O'Leary (1975) found that fathers were more likely to touch and vocalize to first-born sons than to daughters. Gewirtz and Gewirtz (1968) observed that Israeli fathers tended to remain longer in the house with infant sons than with infant daughters. Rebelsky and Hanks (1971) found that fathers were more likely to decrease their vocalization to infant daughters but not to infant sons in the first few months of life. Spelke, Zelazo, Kagan, and Kotelchuck (1973) observed that 1-year-old children tended to vocalize more to the same sex parent than to the opposite sex parent. Weinraub and Frankel (1977) found that, with sons, fathers spend more time sharing play, playing on the floor, and talking to their children than mothers; with daughters, mothers spend more time in these activities than fathers.

Social class appears to be another major moderator of parental behavior. Lynn (1974) suggests that middle-class fathers tend to be more involved in childrearing than lower-class fathers. A study by Freeberg and Payne (1967) indicates that lower-class fathers are more likely to demand conformity and obedience than middle-class fathers. In addition, middle-class fathers are more likely to read to their children, set educational standards, make college plans, and take their children on trips and to the library than are lower-class fathers. Middle-class fathers are more likely to assume a teaching role (Hess & Torney, 1967), to encourage curiosity in their children, and to be concerned with their children's future formal education (Kohn & Carroll, 1960). It is interesting to note that social class differences in father's behavior toward the child seem to indicate that middle-class fathers reflect the instrumental role defined by Parsons and Bales (1955) more clearly than lower-class fathers. In fact, lower-class fathers seem to have much less influence over family life (Benson, 1968) and more middle-class than lower-class children see their fathers as the family boss and disciplinarian (Fitzgerald, 1966).

The work of Pedersen et al. (1980) suggests how the situation, activities, and role may be related in defining the father's relationship to the child. It was found that in families where the father was the primary wage earner, the majority of father–child interaction took place in the three person setting of mother–father–child. In contrast, mother–child interaction more frequently took place when the father was absent. Since allocation of parent-to-child time differs by size of group, it is evident that differences in the social groups in which mothers and fathers more often interact with the child are defining characteristics of parental behavior and role. In the three person setting, unlike the parent–child dyad, parent-to-child behavior decreases as parent–parent interaction occurs. The child still experiences the same amount of net parental attention, but this attention is now distributed between two parents rather than one. In addition, interaction in the husband–wife dyad constrains the kinds of parent–child interaction possible. Pedersen et al. (1980) found adult responses requiring more focused attention to the child such as smiling, vocalizing, and vigorous handling and play were less likely to occur during spouse interaction, whereas holding and rocking the baby was not inhibited by spouse interaction. Thus the proportion of time the father has available for child-focused behavior in a dyadic rather than triadic situation may be an important factor in defining his role.

In summary, fathers, in contrast to mothers, spend much less time in dyadic interaction with their children. They are more concerned with their children's sex role development, and they spend less time than mothers in actual caregiving activities although relatively more time in play. Whereas fathers are perceived by their children as instrumental (controlling and aloof), mothers are seen as expressive (warm and nurturant). It is surprising that few clear-cut differences in specific behaviors engaged in by fathers and mothers with their children have emerged from observational studies. In fact, the similarities may be more striking than the differences. During preschool years and beyond, sex-of-parent differences may depend on the sex of the child and the nature of the child's behavior. Nevertheless, there is no evidence to suggest that fathers are second-class parents. Although they may express their involvement in slightly different styles with some children in some situations, fathers appear to be as sensitive and as concerned with the childrearing process as mothers.

Differences and Similarities in the Child's Behavior Toward Fathers and Mothers

To this point, we have been concerned with differences in the behavior of mothers and fathers toward their children and have not yet examined how children behave differently toward their parents. Whether differences in parental behavior are reflected in differences in child behavior and characteristics is an issue that needs to be addressed. Considering differential behavior on the part of the child toward the parent, the results are mixed. Lewis and Weinraub (1976) found boys and girls showed more touching, staying near, and talking to mothers than fathers in a free play laboratory situation. Boys tended to look more at their fathers than at mothers. Lamb (1976a) reports that in the laboratory infants *under stress* showed preference for the mother over the father. However, under conditions of little or no stress, these same infants showed more affiliative behaviors and slightly more attachment behaviors toward their fathers than mothers. In contrast, Vandell (1976), observing differences in mother–child and father–child contacts at 16, 19, and 22 months, found them to be highly similar. For example, mothers and fathers did not differ in the number of interactions, number of vocal behaviors, or percentage of interactions initiated or terminated.

Weinraub and Frankel (1977) found no differences in 18-month-old children's behavior toward their mothers and fathers in a free-play situation in which parents were free to respond naturally to their children. Likewise, under low-stress conditions Lewis and Weinraub (1976) found no sex differences in 2-year-old children's attachment behaviors toward mothers and fathers.

The research of Clarke-Stewart (1978, 1980) suggests that when differences in the amount of child-affiliative behavior to parents occur, they may be a function of parental behavior rather than of the child's intrinsic preferences. She found that during an assessment of attachment, 20-month-old children were more responsive to play initiated by fathers than mothers although no preference was found when the amount of parental play was held constant. During observation of semistructured play sessions in the home, during which both the mother and father were present, it was found that children were rated more cooperative, interested, and involved in play with the father. Yogman et al. (1977) suggest that infants may elicit different kinds of interaction with their fathers than with their mothers. The 6-month-old infants observed tended to show a reciprocal, contained type of interaction with their mothers, whereas with their fathers they showed a more heightened, alert, playful interaction.

Differences in Parental Behavior and Its Impact on Child Development

As we have suggested, the distribution of functions by objects in the child's social network matrix may be influenced by multiple variables: situations; cultural differences, as exemplified by social class and sex differences; family demographic differences such as birth order and family size; and certainly child characteristics such as ontogenetic factors. Although our information concerning differences in the social object × function relations is increasing, we have almost no information about the potential developmental consequences of these differences. A study by Clarke-Stewart (1978) did examine the relationship between the kinds of functions the parents perform and the child's development. The child's intellectual competence was related to maternal expression of warmth and positive emotion (nurturant function) as well as to maternal verbal stimulation of the child (teaching function). Children's intelligence was also closely associated with the father's engagement of the child in play as well as the father's anticipation of the child's independence.

Belsky (1980) found differences in patterns of maternal and paternal behavior and the child's exploratory competence. Mothers who stimulated and frequently engaged their child in object-mediated and social play had infants who performed competently. However, it was fathers who were verbally responsive, took physical care of the infant, expressed affection, and frequently engaged the child in vigorous motion play who had competently performing infants. Behavior characteristic of mothers such as object-mediated play, was related to infant competence for mothers but not fathers, whereas behavior characteristic of fathers, such as vigorous motion play, was related to infant competence for fathers but not mothers. There were overlapping developmental similarities as well. Fathers and mothers who showed high levels of behaviors (e.g., verbal responsiveness and physical affects and caretaking) had infants who performed competently.

These findings suggest that the ways in which parents differ in their behavior toward the child may be related in part to the child's development. Mothers seem concerned about nurturance and intellectual-verbal stimulation whereas fathers seem more concerned with play and independence, and the concerns of both parents make unique and significant contributions to the child's development.

THE CHILD ACQUIRES KNOWLEDGE THROUGH DIRECT AND INDIRECT INTERACTION WITH THE SOCIAL NETWORK

This proposition suggests that from a systems point of view, information about subsystems in which the child is a member as well as subsystems in which the child is not a member are both important in understanding the child's development. The study of the family interaction at dinnertime previously presented (Lewis & Feiring, in press, b) examines the three subsystems of mother–child, father–child, and mother–father and their possible effects on the child. Not only could children acquire information about how their fathers act when they behave toward them (a direct effect), but they can acquire information about how he acts from watching how he behaves toward his mother (an indirect effect).

Because social behavior and interaction has been studied in the context of a behavioral viewpoint, most theory and empirical findings have centered on the direct effect of one object on another. Thus how much a mother or father talks to a child or how much the parents seek information is related to how much information the child seeks. Indeed, in the study of language acquisition, it is not uncommon to find investigators studying how much the mother vocalizes to the child as it relates to how much the child vocalizes at some future time (e.g., Freedle & Lewis, 1977). However, it might be also the case that behavior not directly involving the child also has important developmental consequences. Such *indirect effects* appear in the literature under a variety of terms including modeling, imitation, or observational learning. Using the dinner table data presented here as an example, from a systems point of view it is possible to inquire whether the child's observation of the parents seeking information from each other has an effect on the child.

Direct effects are defined as those interactions that always involve the target person—for us, the child—as one of the participants. Direct effects, therefore, represent the effect or influence of one person on the behavior of another when both are engaged in mutual interaction. Because direct effects are usually observed in dyadic interactions, the study of direct effects has been restricted to a system of two people. However, it is possible to consider a triad in which mother and father are both interacting with the child at the same time. In this case, the direct effect of the mother and father on the child and the child on the parents can be observed. Unfortunately, measurement systems have not been well developed for social groups larger than two. Because direct effects of parents' behavior toward children and children's behavior toward parents have been discussed earlier under the proposition of social object and social functions, our major focus in this section is on indirect effects.

Indirect effects refer to two general classes of events. One is a set of influences on the target person that occur in the absence of one member of a system. An example is the effect of the mother–father relationship on the mother's behavior toward the child when she and the child are alone.

The other class of indirect effects operates when the interaction among members of the social network occurs in the presence of target person even though the interaction is not directed toward the target person. We have already given an example of this in the situation where the child observes the mother and father seeking information from each other.

The consideration of the indirect effects among members of the social network may take several different forms. In the following discussion, we attend to four different ways that indirect effects are manifested: support, representations, transitivity (or referencing), and modeling.

Support

In the case of the child's nuclear family, it is usually the case that the child has a relationship to each parent and the parents have a relationship to each other as separate from but not independent of the child. The interdependent nature of the child–parent and parent–parent subsystems is a characteristic of the child's social network that engenders the operation of indirect effects. The nature of the parent–parent subsystem in the child's social network can be observed to have an indirect effect on the parent–child subsystem; an important example of this phenomenon is the father's support of the mother as it influences the mother's behavior toward the child.

Within the child's social network, the subsystems that comprise the child's family include child–parent and parent–parent as well as parent–sibling and child–sibling subsystems. Within the young child's nuclear family, the adult–adult subsystem can be conceptualized in terms of two different role relationships, father–mother and husband–wife. In the adults' relationship as husband and wife, their role identities and behaviors may affect the performance of their mother–father roles, which are defined more directly in terms of the child. Barry (1970) suggests that healthy marriages are ones in which the husband is supportive of his wife's efforts in her role as mother. A study conducted by Heath (1976) reported a positive relationship between a mother's perception of marital satisfaction and paternal competence. The woman's perception of her spouse's competence as a husband was related to her perception of her spouse's competence as a father. For the women in Heath's study, a good spouse was a person who had the ability to (1) engender supportive and cooperative relationships between family members (father role); (2) create satisfying adult relationships in such areas as sexual compatability and communication skills for discussing intimate feelings (husband role); and (3) make the wife feel adequate as a mother (father/husband role).

The father's emotional as well as economic support of the mother has an indirect influence on the mother's behavior toward the child. By allaying the mother's anxieties, doubts, and frustrations and by making her feel competent, secure, and self-confident, the husband/father can facilitate the emergence and maintenance of responsive mother-to-child behavior. Several studies have shown that even prior to the child's birth, the husband's support of the wife can be shown to affect the future mother–child relationship. A woman's successful adaptation to pregnancy is associated with the husband's support (Shereshefsky & Yarrow, 1973). Maternal stress during labor and delivery is lessened by the support of the husband (Anderson & Standley, 1976). Mothers who showed postpartum depression characterized their husbands as especially distant and cold—that is, mothers who were despondent and probably less responsive to their infants perceived a lack of support from their husbands (Kaplan & Blackman, 1969). Feiring (1975) studied the relationship between maternal involvement and responsivity to the child and the mother's perception of how much support she received from the father. The results of this study indicated that a strong positive association existed between maternal ratings of support from the father and ratings of maternal involvement and responsivity to the child. Interview data from this study indicated that wives who were involved in their children tended to express a feeling of support from their spouses, although they did not seem to focus on how much support they gave their husbands. Pedersen (1976) demonstrated how the husband–wife subsystem effects the parent–child subsystem. The amount of tension and conflict in the husband–wife subsystem was related negatively to father–infant play as well as mother–infant caregiving. In terms of the issue of support and indirect effects, Pedersen (1975) suggests that the father's warmth and affection may help support the mother and facilitate her performance of effective caregiving activity.

Many of the effects of father absence can be explained by the differences in the mother's behavior toward her children as a result of lack of support, not necessarily the father's absence *per se*. In many cases, mothers whose husbands are absent must provide economic support for the family. Whether or not they want to work, they must. They must also do all the household tasks by themselves with little help from people outside the family. Lynn (1974) reports several studies (e.g., Kriesberg, 1967; Parker & Kleiner, 1966; Tiller, 1958) in which mothers without husbands on a regular or temporary basis described some of the difficulties they experienced. Mothers without husbands felt worse psychologically than and were not as goal oriented as mothers with husbands. They were more concerned about the children's educational achievements than other mothers; they made more inappropriate efforts to help their children; they were more likely to be dissatisfied with the child's level of work and less likely to be involved with the schools or to aspire to a college education for their children. Finally, mothers whose husbands were absent on a regular basis led less active social lives, worked less outside the home, were more overprotective of children, and were more likely to be concerned with their child's obedience and manners rather than happiness and self-actualization. Hoffman (1971) suggests that not having a husband might make a woman feel "busier and more harassed and hence impatient with the child and oriented toward immediate compliance rather than long-range character goals" (p. 405)

Perhaps the global variable of father absence should be replaced by variables that describe the mother's lack of support to explain the effect of the absence on the child's development. Although a subsystems analysis suggests that maternal support of the father should facilitate the father–child relationship, little work has been conducted on this point. If we hold that a loving husband/father facilitates the mother–child relationship, it should also be the case that a loving wife/mother should facilitate the father–child relationship. Any asymmetry in the distribution of support efforts may have important consequences for theories of family interaction. Fathers' perception of what kinds of behaviors constitute support seem to differ from mothers. Expressive kinds of behavior make mothers feel supported while instrumental kinds of behavior make fathers feel supported (Wills, Weiss, & Patterson, 1974). These data suggest that there may be a match between the kind of role a parent performs and the kind of support the parent requires from the spouse in order to fulfill that role.

Representational Modes

Representations of absent social objects can occur (1) when one member tells another about a third, and (2) when one member in the absence of another thinks about that other. In the first condition, the child's knowledge of the father and the child's relationship to the father are created by a third social object. This third social object is most often the mother but must include grandparents, other relatives like uncles/aunts, siblings, and parents' friends. For example, the mother might say, "That's Daddy's briefcase" or, "Daddy's away on a trip but he misses you." A grandparent or friend might say, "You look just like your father." Lewis and Feiring (1978) have suggested that children's varying ability to remember or think about their fathers even in their absence may account for the lack of consistent findings in father-absence studies.

Consider father absence in two cases; in the first, the mother represents the father as "working to obtain money for your education" whereas in the second, "He is out drinking with his friends." In the case of prolonged absence as in death or divorce, these representations may be quite different (Hetherington, 1979). Several studies have shown that children do in fact think about their fathers when they are absent (Bach, 1946; Baker, Fagan, Fischer, Janda, & Cove, 1967; Crain & Stamm, 1965).

The second representational activity involves the re-presenting of an absent object. Most of our behaviorist notions support the view that relationships and their representations are built up and maintained by contact—that is, direct effects. Representations may best be constructed by the child experiencing periods of both direct effects and their absence in some as yet unspecified ratio. The separation of the object from the child that allows for the development of representation has been called "distancing" by Sigel (1970). Distancing requires the child to construct, elaborate, and label the absent one and thus promotes abstraction. Since in the traditional family it is the father who works out of the home, distancing in these families may play a larger role in the father–child relationship than in the mother–child relationship. Given the changing nature of the American family this difference may cease to exist. If indeed leaving the home is responsible for differences in parental representation, we should expect changes, the nature of which can be observed in studies on traditional parental roles.

Unfortunately, there is little research on different representational modes, especially in early childhood. Brooks-Gunn and Lewis (1979) studied the first labels used by infants aged 9 to 36 months. At 15 months, the age of first labeling, 25 percent of the infants labeled pictures of their fathers correctly; no infants labeled pictures of their mothers. By 18 months, all infants labeled pictures of their fathers correctly. Some used the label "daddy" incorrectly, that is, they overgeneralized the label. In contrast, only some of the 18-month-olds used the label "mommy" for their mother and there was very little overgeneralization. Mothers of the 15-month-olds confirmed this mother–father difference in labeling. They reported that "daddy" preceded "mommy" in their children's first speech. This finding has been noted by others (e.g., Jakobson, 1962).

This result is highly counterintuitive but its explanation may be relevant to our discussion. Why should the "daddy" label be acquired before the "mommy" label? Two possible explanations within the representational mode are suggested. These are, in fact, the two modes described earlier. Infants may hear their mothers labeling their fathers more often than the reverse and this experience—knowing about a second social object from a third social object—may account for the phenomenon. In a test of this possibility, Dunn (personal communication) checked the verbal transcripts of 38 different mother–infant pairs seen in their homes for at least 2 hours of observation and recording. The children were 14 months old and the families were all British. Dunn counted 103 "mommy" and 43 "daddy" references in over 5,000 utterances. Thus the frequency of utterances fails to support the differential label use explanation.

The second possibility is provided by the distancing hypothesis. This hypothesis states that representation is acquired best when there is distance between social objects. The failure of sheer numbers of references to account for the phenomenon of differential labeling suggests that this hypothesis may have merit. Further support for the hypothesis comes from two sources. First, the labeling of "mommy" most characteristically took place in Dunn's study during an ongoing activity that the mother was performing. For example, a mother might comment, "Mommy is tying your shoe." Not so for "daddy" labels. These most often took place in discussions of activities not taking place at that time, as in "Daddy will come home early tonight." Thus the "daddy" label may be learned in the absence of the social object, whereas the "mommy" label may be learned in the presence of the social object. A second source of support for the distancing hypothesis comes from an observation by Rosenblum (personal communication) who reports that macaque monkeys reared only with their mothers—never seeing another monkey—have difficulty in finding her (recognizing) when placed in a situation where their mother and other female monkeys are present. Again, the result is counterintuitive if we believe that representation is best built up over repeated experience with the object; the more experience the greater the representation. Representation may be best constructed with the child experiencing both presence (interaction) and absence of the other social object in some as yet unknown ratio.

Although this aspect of knowledge about the father—his label—is just one feature, this example does point out that indirect experience can affect the child's knowledge about social objects. This of course is not restricted to the father. In the Brooks-Gunn and Lewis (1979) study of differential labeling, four mothers worked or left the house more frequently than the others. It was the children of these mothers who used the "mother" label earliest. (This lends support to the view that the changing composition of the work force may effect children's representations.)

In another study, Brooks-Gunn and Lewis (in press) observed the fixation and smiling data of another group of children aged 9 to 36 months when shown slides of pictures of their mothers, fathers, stranger male, and stranger female. At 9 and 12 months, the children showed more differential looking and smiling to pictures of father versus male as compared to mother versus female. These data can only be considered suggestive; however, they may indicate that young children are better able to discriminate (or if not discriminate, show a preference toward) fathers over stranger males as opposed to mothers over stranger females.[1]

One further area of support for the hypothesis that parental representations may be different as a function of separation or distancing appears in the study of ego psychology and Freud's (1953) conceptualization of primary and secondary thought processes. In part, the construction of the ego occurs because of the caregiver's inability to continuously satisfy the child. Representations of missing persons, memory, is one of the first ego processes brought about by the absence of the person. Identification occurs in part because of the missing or absent person. One way in which one can bring back a missing person is through acting like that person. Clinical observation indicates that at the death of one's spouse, the survivor often adopts the mannerisms and behavioral repertoire of the other, and children have been noted to imitate the behavior of siblings who have died (Bowlby, 1980; Weinraub & Frankel, 1977). In fact, this representational phenomenon may explain a rather robust and puzzling finding having to do with the behavior of 1- and 2-year-olds when their mothers were instructed to leave our laboratory playroom. Over 23 percent of the children seen in our laboratory moved to and sat in the chair recently occupied by their mothers even though the chair was not next to the door.

The importance of this type of indirect effect on the members of the social network is broad. First, different social objects may be more or less distant (or absent) from the child. Second, different social functions require different degrees of distancing. Third, the distancing of social objects provokes cognitive capacities such as memory and representation and provides an interface between social and cognitive development.

---

[1]Alternative explanations come readily to mind. For example, if females are associated with nurturance they may be less fearful than males. If this is true, it may be more important for young children to discriminate between males (father versus other) than between females (mother versus other).

Transitivity

An analysis of indirect effect allows for the condition that events of some members or subsystems will have an effect on other members or subsystems. The principle of transitivity takes the following form: A has a relationship to B, B has a relationship to C, therefore A has a relationship to C. The relation between the elements in social transitivity are not bound by the logical constraints of other formal transitivity problems. Nevertheless, there is some evidence that they work similarly (Lewis & Feiring, in press, a). The relation between elements A, B, and C may be positive or negative and may vary in intensity; in any case, A's relationship to C is based in part on A's relationship to B as well as B's relationship to C. Thus even in the absence of a direct relationship between A and C, it is possible for A and C to form a relationship through their mutual relationship to B. Moreover, in the case of a direct relationship between A and C, the indirect relationship formed between A and B and B and C will affect and modify the A–C relationship.

Transitivity relationships are determined by the intensity and sign of the direct relationships. A positive direct relationship is more powerful than a negative indirect one. An A–C direct relationship is greater than an A–C indirect relationship made up of the A–B and B–C relationships. As a systems analysis suggests, A's relationship to C must be affected by A's direct interaction with C as well as A's relationship to B and B's relationship to C.

The child's relationship to the mother and the mother's relationship to the child's father influences the child's relationship to the father in addition to the amount of direct interaction between child and father. Transitivity may operate in all extended social networks. According to this principle, relationships can be created or enhanced by indirect as well as direct relationships. For example, if I love and am loved by my mother and she loves and is loved by my father, then this suggests that I love and am loved by my father, even in the absence of my father's interaction with me. Transitivity is a sophisticated mental process requiring and facilitating knowledge about the self as well as the ability to recognize complex, indirect relationships. This principle can be applied to relationships between child and grandparent. These relationships are mediated through the child's relationship with the parents and the parents' relationship with their parents. Transitivity is very important in influencing children's relationships with their grandparents, especially in cases where the children have little direct interaction with their grandparents because of distance. We have observed that many children express deep feelings for grandparents rarely seen, much more than for a friend of the family whom they see considerably more often. A transitivity explanation takes the following form: A loves B (I love my father), B loves C (my father loves his father), therefore A loves C (I love my grandfather).

Recently Parke, Power, and Gottman (1979) have elaborated on the idea of transitivity as we originally presented it (Lewis & Weinraub, 1976) in regard to father influences. In addition to discussing the general mechanism of transitivity whereby one person mediates the influence of another on a third individual (i.e., for father, mother, and child), Parke et al. specify the causal role position for each person involved in a triadic transitive relationship. In this scheme the central feature of transitive influences is the pivotal role of one person as both the primary recipient and secondary influence source, vis-à-vis the child. For example, transitivity operates when the father is a primary influence source of support to the mother (primary recipient) and the mother is the secondary influence source to the child (secondary recipient of the father's support of the mother).

The literature contains some data on older children that has a bearing on this issue of transitivity. Romm (in Lynn, 1974) has characterized the mother's role as very important in the father–daughter relationship. If the daughter believes that her mother truly cares about her father and loves and respects him, then she can also feel free to develop a close relationship with her father without guilt and resentment toward her mother. Once the girl has experienced a close and warm relationship with her father, she can transfer the same feelings to a man her own age when the time comes. Others have also emphasized the importance of the father in the daughter's acquisition of femininity. According to Hetherington (1979), femininity in girls is related to the father's approval of the mother as a model as well as the father's own masculinity and his reinforcement of the daughter's participation in feminine activities. The mother's femininity, however, was not related to the daughter's femininity.

Although the mother–father–child transitivity has not been studied, Feiring, Lewis, and Starr (in preparation) recently completed a study that examined whether the transitivity effect is a viable concept. Of interest was whether indirect experiences affect the child's behavior toward strangers and whether the child–parent relationship is necessary for the transitivity phenomena to occur. Forty-five 15-month-old children were exposed to one of three situations: in Condition I, the child observed the mother interacting with a stranger[1] in a positive manner consisting of a "good friend" role play; in Condition II, the child observed the stranger[1] interacting with another stranger[2] in a positive manner involving a "good friend" role play; and in Condition III, the stranger[1] entered the room and did not interact with the mother or another stranger but sat and read a magazine. Following exposure to Condition I, II, or III the stranger[1] approached the child to play. It was expected that if the child's relationship to the mother was an essential factor for transitivity to operate, we should observe more positive behavior from child to stranger[1] when the child had observed the mother acting in a positive manner to the stranger[1] (Condition I) compared to the positive interaction between stranger[1] and stranger[2]

(Condition II) or when stranger [1] engaged in no interaction (Condition III). The results indicated that children viewing Condition I showed more toy play with the stranger as well as an increase in their amount of toy play during the play period compared to children in Conditions II and III. The results of this study suggested that transitivity is a possible mechanism in children as young as 15 months.

Modeling

Modeling behavior is an important form of indirect influence. Simple modeling behavior is characterized by the child doing what another does even though the other does not directly interact with the child. Examples of modeling are plentiful (Bandura, 1969) and we need not explore them in any detail. That more learned behavior is not credited to modeling is because of the difficulty in demonstrating this phenomenon within experimental constraints. Most tests of modeling impose a time and behavior constraint so that for the child to model another person it is necessary for the child to behave similarly to this person within a given time period. Unfortunately, the time period may be too short to capture long-term effects, and similarities in behavior may be difficult to define.

CONCLUSION

In 1976, we concluded from our analysis that much work needed to be done to understand the role of the father in the child's development. In particular, we emphasized the need to conceptualize the father as a member of the child's social network. Unfortunately, relatively little work in this area has been undertaken, and therefore it is not inappropriate to repeat much of our previous concern.

The failure to conceptualize adequately the child's social network has done a disservice to the complex fabric of social relationships from which the child is capable of learning. The lack of models of the social network has constrained research efforts not only in the child's relationship to the father but also in the child's relationship to peers, grandparents, uncles, aunts, friends, and so forth. Some propositions that may facilitate study of the social network have been offered. We have focused on the various ways the child has of acquiring knowledge about others. Although most research has emphasized the direct effects of social objects, we have argued for the consideration of additional modes of influence. Members of the social network may affect the child directly or indirectly. These modes of influence affect and are affected by cognitive as well as socioemotional development. Consideration of the father's role in child development has been particularly instructive in alerting us to the importance of indirect influences and effects that go beyond dyadic interaction. Observations of mother, father, and child in dyadic (parent–child) and triadic (mother–father–child) situations indicate that fathers affect the quality as well as the quantity of maternal behavior (Clarke-Stewart, 1978, 1980). As suggested by Pedersen et al. (1980) fathers who work may spend more interaction time with their child in three-person settings than in two-person settings. Settings of three persons or more is a defining characteristic of a situation in which indirect effects occur (Bronfenbrenner, 1977). Since mothers may interact more frequently with the child in dyadic settings (situations correspondent with direct effects), and fathers may more frequently interact with the child in groups larger than two, the father's influence on the child may be more related to indirect processes. Unfortunately, despite the efforts of a few (Clarke-Stewart, 1978; Lamb, 1976b, 1976d, 1979; Lewis & Feiring, 1979; Pedersen et al., 1979, 1980), the problems of measuring the effects of interactions that involve more than two people have continued to inhibit the study of indirect influences (Lamb, Suomi, & Stephenson, 1979). The recent research effort on network systems suggests that only by developing better models and measurement systems of the social network will we come closer to understanding the role of the father in the child's life.

REFERENCES

Aberle, D. F., & Naegele, K. D. Middle-class fathers' occupational roles and attitudes toward children. *American Journal of Orthopsychiatry*, 1952, **22**, 366–378.

Ainsworth, M. D. S. Patterns of attachment behavior shown by the infant in interaction with his mother. *Merrill-Palmer Quarterly*, 1964, **10**, 51–58.

Ainsworth, M. D. S. Object relation, dependency and attachment: A theoretical review of the infant–mother relationship. *Child Development*, 1969, **40**, 969–1026.

Aldous, J. The search for alternatives: Parental behaviors and children's original problem solutions. *Journal of Marriage and the Family*, 1975, **37**, 711–722.

Anderson, B. J., & Standley, K. A methodology for observation of the childbirth environment. Paper presented at the meetings of the American Psychological Association, Washington, D.C., September 1976.

Armentrout, J. A., & Burger, G. K. Children's reports of parental childrearing behavior at five grade levels. *Developmental Psychology*, 1972, **7**, 44–48.

Bach, G. Father fantasies and father typing in father-separated children. *Child Development*, 1946, **17**, 63–80.

Baker, S. L., Fagan, S. A., Fischer, E. G., Janda, E. J., & Cove, L. A. Impact of father absence on personality factors of boys. I. An evaluation of the military family's adjustment. Paper presented at the meeting of the American Orthopsychiatric Association, Washington, D.C., March 1967.

Ban, P., & Lewis, M. Mothers and fathers, girls and boys: Attachment behavior in the one-year-old. *Merrill-Palmer Quarterly*, 1974, **20**, 195–204.

Bandura, A. *Principles of behavior modification*. New York: Holt, Rinehart, & Winston, 1969.

Barry, W. A. Marriage research and conflict: An integrative review. *Psychological Bulletin*, 1970, **73**, 41–54.

Belsky, J. A family analysis of parental influence on infant exploratory competence. In F. A. Pedersen (Ed.), *The father–infant relationship: Observational studies in the family setting*. New York: Praeger, 1980.

Benson, L. *Fatherhood: A sociological perspective*. New York: Random House, 1968.

Block, J. H. Conceptions of sex role: Some cross-cultural and longitudinal perspectives. *American Psychologist*, 1973, **28**, 512–526.

Bowlby, J. *Maternal care and mental health*. Geneva: WHO, 1951.

Bowlby, J. *Attachment and loss,* Vol. 1. *Attachment*. New York: Basic Books, 1969.

Bowlby, J. *Attachment and loss*, Vol. 3. *Loss: Sadness and depression*. New York: Basic Books, 1980.

Bronfenbrenner, U. Some familial antecedents of responsibility and leadership in adolescents. In L. Petrullo & B. M. Bass (Eds.), *Leadership and interpersonal behavior*. New York: Holt, Rinehart, & Winston, 1961.

Bronfenbrenner, U. Developmental research, public policy and the ecology of childhood. *Child Development*, 1974, **45**, 1–5.

Bronfenbrenner, U. Toward an experimental ecology of human development. *American Psychologist*, 1977, **32**, 513–532.

Brooks-Gunn, J., & Lewis, M. "Why Mama and Papa?" The development of social labels. *Child Development*, 1979, **50**, 1203–1206.

Brooks-Gunn, J., & Lewis, M. Infant social perception: Responses to pictures of parents and strangers. *Developmental Psychology*, in press.

Clarke-Stewart, K. A. And daddy makes three: The father's impact on mother and young child. *Child Development*, 1978, **49**, 466–478.

Clarke-Stewart, K. A. The father's contribution to children's cognitive and social development in early childhood. In F. A. Pedersen (Ed.), *The father–infant relationship: Observational studies in the family setting*. New York: Praeger, 1980.

Crain, A. J., & Stamm, C. S. Intermittent absence of fathers and children's perception of parents. *Journal of Marriage and the Family*, 1965, **27**, 344–347.

Dunn, J. Personal communication. October 1975.

Dunn, J., & Kendrick, C. Interaction between young siblings in the context of family relationships. In M. Lewis & L. Rosenblum (Eds.), *The child and its family*. New York: Plenum, 1979.

Dunn, J., & Wooding, C. Play in the home and its implications for learning. In B. Tizard & D. Harvey (Eds.), *The biology of play*. London: Heinemann, 1977.

Edwards, C. P., & Lewis, M. Young children's concepts of social relations: Social functions and social objects. In M. Lewis & L. Rosenblum (Eds.), *The child and its family*. New York: Plenum, 1979.

Emmerich, W. Young children's discrimination of parent and child roles. *Child Development*, 1959, **30**, 403–419.

Fagot, B. I. Sex differences in toddler's behaviors and parental reactions. *Developmental Psychology*, 1974, **10**, 554–558.

Feiring, C. The influence of the child and secondary parent on maternal behavior: Toward a social systems view of early infant-mother attachment. Unpublished doctoral dissertation, University of Pittsburgh, 1975.

Feiring, C., Lewis, M., & Starr, M. Indirect and direct effects of children's reactions to unfamiliar adults. Manuscript in preparation, 1981.

Feldman, S. S. The impact of day care on one aspect of children's social emotional behavior. Paper presented at the meetings of the American Association for Advancement of Science, San Francisco, February 1974.

Field, T. Interaction patterns of primary versus secondary caretaker fathers. *Developmental Psychology*, 1978, **14**, 183–185.

Fitzgerald, M. P. Sex differences in the perception of the parental role for middle and working class adolescents. *Journal of Clinical Psychology*, 1966, **22**, 15–16.

Freeberg, N. E., & Payne, D. T. Dimensions of parental practice concerned with cognitive development in the preschool child. *Journal of Genetic Psychology*, 1967, **111**, 245–261.

Freedle, R., & Lewis, M. Prelinguistic conversations. In M. Lewis & L. Rosenblum (Eds.), *Interaction, conversation, and the development of language*. New York: Wiley, 1977.

Freud, S. Three essays on the theory of sexuality (1905). *Standard Edition*, Vol. 7. London: Hogarth, 1953.

Gewirtz, H. B., & Gewirtz, J. L. Visiting and caretaking patterns for kibbutz infants: Age and sex trends. *American Journal of Orthopsychiatry*, 1968, **38**, 427–443.

Goodenough, E. W. Interest in persons as an aspect of sex difference in the early years. *Genetic Psychology Monographs*, 1957, **55**, 287–323.

Harlow, H. F., & Harlow, M. K. The affectional systems. In A. M. Schrier, H. F. Harlow, & F. Stollnitz (Eds.), *Behavior of nonhuman primates*, Vol. 2. New York: Academic Press, 1965.

Harlow, H. F, & Harlow, M. K. Learning to love. *American Scientist*, 1966, **54**, 244–272.

Hartup, W. Peer play and pathology: Considerations in the growth of social competence. In T. Field (Ed.), *High risk infants and children: Adult and peer interactions*. New York: Academic Press, 1980.

Hartup, W. W. Two social worlds: Family relations and peer relations. In M. Rutter (Ed.), *Scientific foundations of developmental psychiatry*. London: Heineman, 1981.

Heath, D. H. Competent fathers: Their personality and marriages. *Human Development*, 1976, **19**, 26–39.

Hess, R. D., & Torney, J. *The development of political attitudes in children*. Chicago: Aldine, 1967.

Hetherington, E. M. Play and social interaction in children following divorce. *Journal of Social Issues*, 1979, **35**, 26–49.

Hinde, R. A. Interactions, relationships, and social structure. *Man*, 1976, **11**, 1–17.

Hoffman, M. L. Father absence and conscience development. *Developmental Psychology*, 1971, **4**, 400–406.

Jakobson, R. Why "Mama" and "Papa"? In *Selected writings of Roman Jakobson*. The Hague: Mouton, 1962.

Kagan, J., & Lemkin, J. The child's differential perception of parental attitudes. *Journal of Abnormal and Social Psychology*, 1960, **61**, 440–447.

Kaplan, E. H., & Blackman, L. H. The husband's role in psychiatric illness associated with childbearing. *Psychiatric Quarterly*, 1969, **43**, 396–409.

Kohn, M. L., & Carroll, E. E. Social class and the allocation of parental responsibilities. *Sociometry*, 1960, **23**, 372–392.

Kotelchuck, M. The nature of the child's tie to his father. Unpublished doctoral dissertation, Harvard University, 1972.

Kriesberg, L. Rearing children for educational achievement in fatherless families. *Journal of Marriage and the Family*, 1967, **29**, 288–301.

Lamb, M. E. Effects of stress and cohort on mother– and father–infant interaction. *Developmental Psychology*, 1976, **12**, 435–443(a).

Lamb, M. E. Interactions between eight-month-old children and their fathers and mothers. In M. E. Lamb (Ed.), *The role of the father in child development*. New York: Wiley, 1976(b).

Lamb, M. E. The role of the father: An overview. In M. E. Lamb (Ed.), *The role of the father in child development*. New York: Wiley, 1976(c).

Lamb, M. E. Twelve-month-olds and their parents: Interaction in a laboratory playroom. *Developmental Psychology*, 1976, **12**, 237–244(d).

Lamb, M. E. Father–infant and mother–infant interaction in the first year of life. *Child Development*, 1977, **48**, 167–181(a).

Lamb, M. E. The development of mother–infant and father–infant attachments in the second year of life. *Developmental Psychology*, 1977, **13**(6), 637–648(b).

Lamb, M. E. The development of sibling relationships in infancy: A short-term longitudinal study. *Child Development*, 1978, **49**, 1189–1196.

Lamb, M. E. The effects of the social context on dyadic social interaction. In M. E. Lamb, S. J. Suomi, & G. R. Stephenson (Eds.), *Social interaction analysis: Methodological issues*. Madison.: University of Wisconsin Press, 1979.

Lamb, M. E. The development of parent–infant attachments in the first two years of life. In F. A. Pedersen (Ed.), *The father–infant relationship: Observational studies in the family setting*. New York, Praeger, 1980.

Lamb, M. E., Suomi, S. J., & Stephenson, G. R. *Social interaction analysis: Methodological issues*. Madison: University of Wisconsin Press, 1979.

Lansky, L. M. The family structure also affects the model: Sex-role attitudes in parents of preschool children. *Merrill-Palmer Quarterly,* 1967, **13**, 139–150.

Lewis, M. The social network: Toward a theory of social development. Fiftieth anniversary invited address at the meetings of the Eastern Psychological Association, Philadelphia, April 1979.

Lewis, M., & Ban, P. Variance and invariance in the mother–infant interaction: A cross–cultural study. In P. H. Leiderman & S. R. Tulkin and A. Rosenfeld (Eds.), *Cultural and infancy*. New York: Academic, 1977.

Lewis, M., & Feiring, C. The child's social world. In R. M. Lerner & G. D. Spanier (Eds.), *Child influences on marital and family interaction: A life-span perspective*. New York: Academic Press, 1978.

Lewis, M., & Feiring, C. The child's social network: Social object, social functions and their relationship. In M. Lewis, & L. Rosenblum (Eds.), *The child and its family*. New York: Plenum, 1979.

Lewis, M., & Feiring, C. Direct and indirect interactions in social relationships. In L. Lipsitt (Ed.), *Advances in infancy research,* Vol. 1. Norwood, N.J.: Ablex, in press(a).

Lewis, M., & Feiring, C. Some American families at dinner. In L. Laosa, & I. E. Sigel (Eds.), *Families as learning environments for children*. New York: Plenum, in press(b).

Lewis, M., & Rosenblum, L. (Eds.). *The child and its family*. New York: Plenum, 1979.

Lewis, M., & Schaeffer, S. Peer behavior and mother–infant interaction in maltreated children. In M. Lewis, & L. Rosenblum (Eds.), *The uncommon child*. New York: Plenum, 1980.

Lewis, M., & Weinraub, M. The father's role in the infant's social network. In M. E. Lamb (Ed.), *The role of the father in child development*. New York: Wiley, 1976.

Lewis, M., Young, G., Brooks, J., & Michalson, L. The beginning of friendship. In M. Lewis, & L. Rosenblum (Eds.), *Friendship and peer relation*. New York: Wiley, 1975.

Lynn, D. B. *The father: His role in child development*. Monterey, Calif.: Brooks/Cole, 1974.

Margolin, G., & Patterson, G. R. Differential consequences provided by mothers and fathers for their sons and daughters. *Developmental Psychology,* 1975, **11,** 537–538.

Matas, L., Arend, R. A., & Sroufe, L. A. Continuity of adaptation in the second year of life. *Child Development,* 1978, **49,** 547–556.

Monane, J. H. *A sociology of human systems.* New York: Appleton-Century-Crofts, 1967.

Newson, J., & Newson, E. *Four years old in an urban community.* London: Allen & Unwin, 1968.

Parke, R. D. & O'Leary, S. Father–mother–infant interaction in the newborn period: Some findings, some observations, and some unresolved issues. In K. Riegel, & J. Meacham (Eds.), *The developing individual in a changing world: Vol. 2. Social and environmental issues.* The Hague: Mouton, 1975.

Parke, R. D., Power, T. G., & Gottman, J. M. Conceptualizing and quantifying influence patterns in the family triad. In M. E. Lamb, S. J. Suomi, & G. R. Stephenson (Eds.), *Social interaction analysis: Methodological issues.* Wisconsin: University of Wisconsin Press, 1979.

Parke, R. D., & Sawin, D. B. Infant characteristics and behavior as elicitors of maternal and paternal responsiveness in the newborn period. Paper presented at the meetings of the Society for Research in Child Development, Denver, April 1975.

Parke, R. D. & Sawin, D. B. The family in early infancy: Social interactional and attitudinal analyses. In F. A. Pedersen (Ed.), *The father–infant relationship: Observational studies in the family setting.* New York: Praeger, 1980.

Parker, S., & Kleiner, R. J. Characteristics of Negro mothers in single-headed households. *Journal of Marriage and the Family,* 1966, **28,** 507–513.

Parsons, T., & Bales, R. F. *Family, socialization and interaction process.* Glencoe, Ill.: Free Press, 1955.

Pedersen, F. A. Mother, father and infant as an interactive system. Paper presented at the meetings of the American Psychological Association, Chicago, September 1975.

Pedersen, F. A. Does research on children reared in father-absent families yield information on father influences? *The Family Coordinator,* 1976, **25,** 459–464.

Pedersen, F. A. (Ed.) *The father-infant relationship: Observational studies in the family setting.* New York: Praeger, 1980.

Pedersen, F. A., Anderson, B. J., & Cain, R. L., Jr. Parent–infant and husband–wife interactions observed at age five months. In F. A. Pedersen (Ed.), *The father-infant relationship: Observational studies in the family setting.* New York, Praeger, 1980.

Pedersen, F. A., & Robson, K. S. Father participation in infancy. *American Journal of Orthopsychiatry,* 1969, **39,** 466–472.

Pedersen, F. A., Yarrow, L. J., Anderson, B. J., & Cain, R. L. Conceptualization of father influences in the infancy period. In M. Lewis, & L. Rosenblum (Eds.), *The child and its family.* New York: Plenum, 1979.

Power, T. G., & Parke, R. Play as a context for early learning. In L. M. Laosa & I. E. Sigel (Eds.), *Families as learning environments for children.* New York, Plenum, in press.

Rebelsky, F., & Hanks, C. Fathers' verbal interaction with infants in the first three months of life. *Child Development,* 1971, **43**, 63–68.

Rosenblatt, P. C. Behavior in public places: Comparisons of couples accompanied and unaccompanied by children. *Journal of Marriage and the Family,* 1974, **36**, 750–755.

Rosenblum, L. Personal communication. October 1975.

Schaffer, H. R., & Emerson, P. E. The development of social attachment in infancy. *Monographs of the Society for Research in Child Development,* 1964, **29**, Serial No. 94.

Sears, R. R., Maccoby, E. E., & Levin, H. *Patterns of child rearing.* New York: Row, Peterson, 1957.

Shereshefsky, P. M., & Yarrow, L. J. *Psychological aspects of a first pregnancy and early postnatal adaptation.* New York: Raven Press, 1973.

Sigel, I. The distancing hypothesis: A causal hypothesis for the acquisition of representational thought. In M. R. Jones (Ed.), *Miami symposium on the prediction of behavior, 1968: Effect of early experience.* Coral Gables, Fla.: University of Miami Press, 1970.

Snow, C. Mother's speech to children learning language. *Child Development,* 1972, **43**, 549–565.

Spelke, E., Zelazo, P., Kagan, J., & Kotelchuck, M. Father interaction and separation protest. *Developmental Psychology,* 1973, **9**, 83–90.

Spitz, R. A. Hospitalism: An inquiry into the genesis of psychiatric conditions in early childhood. *The psychoanalytic study of the child,* 1945, **1**, 45–67.

Suomi, S. J. Differential development in various social relationships by rhesus monkey infants. In M. Lewis, & L. Rosenblum (Eds.), *The child and its family.* New York: Plenum, 1979.

Suomi, S. J., & Harlow, H. F. The role and reason of peer relationships in rhesus monkeys. In M. Lewis, & L. A. Rosenblum (Eds.), *Friendship and peer relations.* New York: Wiley, 1975.

Suomi, S. J., & Harlow, H. F. Early experience and social development in rhesus monkeys. In M. E. Lamb (Ed.), *Social and personality development.* New York: Holt, Rinehart, & Winston, 1978.

Tasch, R. J. The role of the father in the family. *Journal of Experimental Education,* 1952, **20**, 319–361.

Taylor, J. *Systometrics.* Unpublished manuscript, University of Pittsburgh, 1975.

Thomas, M. M. Children with absent fathers. *Journal of Marriage and the Family,* 1968, **30,** 89–96.

Tiller, P. O. Father absence and personality development of children in sailor families. *Nordisk Psykolgis Monographs,* 1958, **9,** 1–48.

Trevarthen, C. Conversations with a 2-month-old. *New Scientist,* 1974, **2**(5), 230–235.

Vandell, D. L. Mother's and father's social interaction with their toddler sons. Paper presented at the meetings of the Eastern Psychological Association, New York, April 1976.

Von Bertalanffy, L. *Robots, men and minds.* New York: Braziller, 1967.

Waters, E., Wippman, A., & Sroufe, L. A. Attachment, positive affect and cometence in the peer group: Two studies in construct validation. *Child Development,* 1979, **50,** 821–829.

Weinraub, M. Fatherhood: The myth of the second-class parent. In J. H. Stevens, Jr., & M. Mathews (Eds.), *Mother–child, father–child relationships.* Washington, D.C.: National Association for the Education of Young Children, 1978.

Weinraub, M. The changing role of the father: Implication for sex role development in children. Paper presented at the meetings of the American Psychological Association, Montreal, August 1980.

Weinraub, M., Brooks, J., & Lewis, M. The social network: A reconsideration of the concept of attachment. *Human Development,* 1977, **20,** 31–47.

Weinraub, M., & Frankel, J. Sex differences in parent-infant interaction during free play, departure, and separation. *Child Development,* 1977, **48,** 1240–1249.

Whiting, B. B., & Whiting, J. W. M. *Children of six cultures: A psychological analysis.* Cambridge, Mass.: Harvard University Press, 1975.

Wills, T. A., Weiss, R. L., & Patterson, G. R. A behavioral analysis of the determinants of marital satisfaction. *Journal of Consulting and Clinical Psychology,* 1974, **42,** 802–811.

Yogman, M. J., Dixon, S., Tronick, E., Als, H., & Brazelton, T. B. The goals and structure of face-to-face interaction between infants and fathers. Paper presented at the meetings of the Society for Research in Child Development, New Orleans, March 1977.

Zajonc, R. B., & Markus, G. B. Birth order and intellectual development. *Psychological Review,* 1975, **82,** 74–88.

Zill, N. Learning to do things without help: Child and family characteristics associated with the development of practical skills in children of grammar school age. Paper presented at a Conference on the Family as a Learning Environment, Educational Testing Service, Princeton, November/December 1979.

CHAPTER 8

Father Influences Viewed in a Family Context

FRANK A. PEDERSEN

National Institute of Child Health and Human Development

Early research studies of paternal influences utilized primarily a *deficit* paradigm, in which children (usually school age or older) reared in father-absent families were compared with their peers reared in father-present families. When reliable differences emerged between appropriately matched comparison groups, the attribution of reasons for differences was based primarily on speculation and inference. The deficit paradigm yielded meager information on how fathers function within the family, such as the distinctive features of father–child interaction, just as studies of children reared in institutional environments yielded little direct knowledge of the mother–child relationship.

Recently, more research attention has been directed to the behavior of fathers, observed either in the natural home environment or in laboratory settings. The father's behavior, as well as the child's behavior directed to the father, has been compared with data from similar observations conducted with mothers and, in some cases, unfamiliar adults. Qualitative and quantitative differences between maternal and paternal behavior have been noted and emphasized, including differences in preferences for certain styles of playful behavior, interactions involving either verbal or physical stimulus modalities, role specialization in such activities as caregiving, and characteristic affect occurring during interaction. Because the emphasis of this research has been on contrasting one gender category of parent with another, studies of this nature can be called *global descriptive*.

Global descriptive studies have an overwhelming advantage over the deficit paradigm; the psychological processes of interaction—the network of behaviors with which father and child engage one another—are open to scrutiny and evaluation. By comparing paternal and maternal behavior, it is possible to appraise the distinctive experiences that the father contributes at different stages of the child's development as well as to ascertain the possibly equally significant fact that there are areas where maternal and paternal behavior are highly similar. Only behavioral data take one beyond the speculation and inference that are characteristically invoked to explain the effects of father absence.

Although the global discriptive paradigm is a natural early phase of research, there is also a clear need to move on to more complex research questions. *Differential descriptive* research is needed to overcome two major limitations of global descriptive studies: (1) Global descriptive research tends to obscure the variability within a classification category. Comparing fathers with mothers draws attention away from the full range of adaptational possibilities that exist within families today. (2) Global descriptive research tends to ignore the interplay among different family subsystems. For example, the father's behavior vis-à-vis the child—the paternal role—may be influenced by his other roles as husband and wage earner. These role behaviors do not occur in a psychological vacuum but are influenced by the preferences, expectations, and sanctioning behavior of his partner, the wife and mother. Similarly, the mother–child relationship may be influenced by the behavior, values, and attitudes of the husband/father. These pathways of influence within the family are at present poorly understood.

In this chapter, paternal behavior is examined from the perspective of the differential descriptive paradigm. Two major groups of studies are reviewed. One addresses variation, or individual differences, in paternal adaptation patterns, and the second examines the interrelations of different family subsystems. Research conducted within the Child and Family Research Branch, National Institute of Child Health and Human Development (NICHD) is highlighted along with recent findings by other investigators. To keep the scope of the problem within manageable proportions, attention is limited primarily to the infancy period. This is also the developmental period in which there is a paucity of conceptualization of paternal behavior. Because differentiated descriptive studies of father influences appear to be the leading edge of the field, much of what is presented is necessarily tentative or at the level of hypothesis development. By encouraging thinking along these lines, however, this chapter addresses an important goal of sharpening conceptualization of father influences in a family context.

VARIATION IN PATERNAL ADAPTATION PATTERNS

Research studies of the father–infant relationship differ in their sources of data (parental report versus observations), the specificity of the psychological constructs that are appraised ("involvement" versus counts of specific behaviors), the settings in which information is obtained (the home or the laboratory), the structure imposed on participants in the course of data collection, and the background characteristics of the families (their demographic features and life experiences). Methodological variation notwithstanding, the goal of this section is to elucidate how life experience characteristics of fathers may influence their parental adaptation patterns.[1] Such information serves to anchor individual differences in paternal behavior to the larger social context in which they occur. Three background characteristics will be examined that potentially influence the father's behavior: the birth circumstances of the child, the family role organization in regard to income production, and the father's own sex role identification.

Childbirth Circumstances

Since 1970, at least among middle-class sectors of the population, substantial change has occurred in the preparation for childbirth and in the events that transpire when normal childbirth occurs. Often called "natural" childbirth, this change may be more appropriately labeled participative childbirth. Efforts have been made to reduce medical interventions, especially medication that is potentially harmful to the newborn infant. Significant social relationships have been restored in the childbirth setting. Labor and delivery now often occur in the presence of a trained and emotionally supportive person, frequently the husband who participated with the wife in a preparatory program. Rooming-in arrangements in the postdelivery period are vastly more prevalent, and, largely through the influence of pediatricians Marshall Klaus and John Kennell, efforts have been made to minimize the separation between mother and infant that often occurs after hospital deliveries. These changes have occurred in the interest of promoting more optimal infant functioning and a more favorable relationship between mother and infant.

A parallel change has occurred in the father's experiences surrounding childbirth, one that promotes greater supportive involvement with the mother during labor and delivery and increased opportunity for direct experience with the neonate. Research shows that the husband's presence during labor and delivery is associated with a significantly lower probability of the mother receiving medication, and both parents report more positive feelings about the total birth experience (Henneborn & Cogan, 1975). Indeed, some parents describe participative childbirth as a peak emotional experience that strongly reinforces a sense of family commitment (Tanzer & Block, 1972).

[1]This chapter will not address fathers who are primary caregivers in the infancy period, an interesting but statistically infrequent phenomenon. This topic is covered elsewhere; for example, M.E. Lamb (Ed.), *Nontraditional families: Parenting and child development* (Hillsdale, N.J.: Lawrence Erlbaum Associates, in press).

Because the change toward participative childbirth has not occurred uniformly across U.S. society, an important question is whether parental behavior has been selectively affected by departures from traditional hospital practices. For mothers, there is evidence that Lamaze type preparation programs and greater conscious awareness during childbirth are associated with the decision to breast-feed the infant, and to breast-feed for a longer duration. These mothers, moreover, described their initial reactions to their babies in more positive terms (Doering & Entwisle, 1975). In a similar vein, Klaus and Kennell (1976) have summarized evidence that early contact with the infant promotes mother–infant "bonding," which is thought to facilitate nursing, reduce anxiety, and in other ways enhance the development of the mother–infant attachment relationship. Recent research findings dispute the efficacy of early contact *per se* in influencing subsequent mother–infant interaction (Vietze & O'Connor, 1980; Svejda, Campos, & Emde, 1980), but there appears to be widespread acceptance that the larger movement toward participative childbirth has resulted in more positive feelings about the birth experience.

Among fathers, the small amount of available evidence suggests that participative childbirth may have some enhancing effect on subsequent father–infant interaction. The evidence is not strikingly clear-cut, however. In a study that addressed only the immediate postnatal period, Greenberg & Morris (1974) used the term "engrossment" to describe the sense of absorption, preoccupation, and interest that the newborn evokes from fathers. Virtually all fathers showed the powerful impact of first exposure to the infant, whether they experienced first contact at birth (in the delivery room) or only after birth when the infant was shown to them by nursing personnel. Wente and Crockenberg (1976) also found few effects on fathers who had attended Lamaze training and were with their wives at the baby's delivery compared to a control group, but a sizable proportion of the control fathers had attended the birth as well. One study, however, provides stronger evidence that birth-related variables influence later father–infant attachment (Peterson, Mehl, & Leiderman, 1979). Three groups, comparable in background variables, were examined—a hospital group with anesthesia, a hospital group with low levels of anesthesia, and a group that had home deliveries without anesthesia. The father's positive descriptions of the birth experience were strongly related to a composite rating of subsequent father–infant attachment based on both observations and self-reports assessed through the infant's first 6 months postpartum. The index of father attachment was based on many different components, including his caregiving activities, responsiveness to distress cues, playful behaviors, and self-confidence in the paternal role. The investigators also reported that birth-related events were stronger predictors of attachment than data from the pregnancy period were, thus arguing that self-selection factors were not as important as the birth experience itself on subsequent involvement with the baby.

A hypothesis for which there is modest empirical support is that participative childbirth, through preparation for and involvement in the delivery, more positive feelings associated with the birth, and increased opportunity for early contact and interaction with the infant, fosters more frequent father–infant interaction and contributes to the father–infant attachment relationship. Of course, events after the birth—the father's interactions with mother and baby—would undoubtedly be important in determining whether early dispositions endure as visible differences in behavior.

A hypothesis of differential outcome has been proposed by Fein (1976). He suggested that participative childbirth may have a confirming effect on one's role definition as a father but that there are alternative role definitions available to men. He articulated two role patterns. The more traditional he called the *breadwinner* role, which emphasizes the father's provision of economic resources to the family and an emotionally supportive relationship with the mother who, in turn, has the major responsibility for child care. A second adaptational pattern was called a *nontraditional* role, which emphasizes more direct involvement with the infant and equal sharing of childcare responsibilities with the mother during the periods the father is at home. Fein pointed out that, to be effective, either adaptational pattern must be negotiated in terms of the mother's expectations as well. Although factors that predispose either pattern are not articulated, this formulation is intriguing because it draws attention to intervening variables that may mediate alternative outcomes to the same birth experience.

This line of reasoning—that childbirth experience affects subsequent father–infant interaction—raises an important question of what might be the outcome in the case of a delivery complication, such as cesarean childbirth. When there is a cesarean delivery, common medical practice often precludes the father's presence, and the baby is less accessible to both parents because it is often placed in an intensive care nursery for the first 24 hours. Other things being equal, a plausible hypothesis is that cesarean childbirth would not confer the advantages on later parent–infant relationships that are thought to occur with participative childbirth.

There have been several studies of parent–infant interaction subsequent to cesarean delivery. One of the reasons for the interest in this particular childbirth complication is that rates of cesarean delivery have increased at least threefold since 1970 (Bottoms, Rosen, & Sokol, 1980). This increase appears to be primarily a result of changes in the medical response to protracted labor rather than because of evidence that the risk factors have increased substantially. It is ironic that instances of cesarean medical intervention have increased at the same time that more parents have been seeking deliveries at low levels of medication, and psychological preparation for a cesarean delivery has often been minimal.

In a sample of first-born, 5-month-old infants studied by the Child and Family Research Branch, NICHD (Pedersen, Zaslow, Cain, & Anderson, in press), interview measures and home observations of parent–infant interaction were compared for six cesarean-delivered and 17 vaginally delivered infants. Few differences between the groups not specific to the birth itself were found for mothers—that is, cesarean mothers tended to have general anesthesia, had longer hospital stays, and reported greater initial difficulties with the baby. More clear-cut differences in behavior relating to the mode of birth showed up for the fathers. Interview measures indicated more caregiving behavior—feeding, changing diapers, bathing, and dressing—for fathers whose infants were cesarean-delivered, and observational measures pointed in the same direction. Fathers of cesarean-delivered infants were also rated by the observers as significantly more responsive to the infants' distress cues than those in the comparison group. These differences did not appear to generalize to other forms of interaction, however. Measures of purely social stimulation were consistently lower for fathers of cesarean-delivered infants than in the comparison group, and, in particular, there was significantly less positive affect evident in the behavioral exchanges of fathers and cesarean-delivered infants.

Results highly consistent with this were found in a larger, independent sample (17 cesarean- and 58 vaginally delivered infants) studied at age 6 months by another research team at the Child and Family Research Branch (Vietze, MacTurk, McCarthy, Klein, & Yarrow, 1980). In spite of differences in methodologies, fathers of cesarean delivered infants in this sample were observed to engage in more caregiving (especially feeding), to soothe the infant more, but not to show greater overall social interaction than the fathers of vaginally delivered infants. Mothers, moreover, showed few differences related to mode of birth. For the most part, these results tended to fade out by the follow-up period at 12 months. A similar pattern of high paternal involvement has also been identified by Grossman (1980) with 2-month-old cesarean-delivered infants, and she also found that parent–infant interaction was indistinguishable by mode of birth at age 12 months.

To conceptualize these results, it appears that *not* experiencing participative childbirth (i.e., a cesarean delivery) was associated with *greater* amounts of paternal caregiving involvement. The motivating factor likely to draw the father into a more active caregiving relationship following cesarean childbirth is that the mother, in the initial period at home, was recovering from surgery and was possibly more fatigued and "let down" emotionally or even depressed (Bradley, 1977). Although it is reasonable to suppose that the mother's needs in this early period contributed to the father's active caregiving role, there are minimal signs that her behavior with the infant was affected after the first few weeks. Thus the father's greater caregiving involvement with the infant may have persisted longer than did possible changes in the mother's behavior.

These results require one to modify the emphasis that has been placed on the importance of early contact and interaction with the neonate; other factors associated with birth may have a relatively enduring influence as well. This conceptualization implies an indirect influence of the mother on father–infant interaction.

Family Role Organization

In the "traditional" family, the mother characteristically provides a major portion of childcare and has greater household responsibility, whereas the father fulfills the wage-earner role. Virtually all of the global descriptive studies of early father–child interaction were conducted with samples in which this role organization was predominant (Lamb, 1976, 1977; Clarke-Stewart, 1978; Belsky, 1979; Parke & Sawin, 1980; Pedersen, Anderson, & Cain, 1980). Against this sampling practice, there is a clear secular trend toward families with two wage earners, even when there are very young children. Indeed, the rate of increase in employment rates for women is greatest for the group with young children. In the period in which employment rates doubled for mothers with school-age children, there was a threefold increase for mothers with pre-school-age children. In 1979, over 40 percent of U.S. mothers with children under 3 were employed outside the home (U.S. Department of Labor, 1979). An important question is whether families with two wage earners have different styles of interacting with and caring for the young infant than is characteristically found in the traditional single wage earner family.

Hoffman (1977) has summarized several studies that indicate that fathers play a more active part in the rearing of school-age children when the mother is employed. Although the validity of this generalization is disputed (Cook, 1978), it is possible that the more recent trend toward maternal employment when children are very young will ultimately have a strong influence on paternal behavior. In studies of school-age children, the mother more characteristically returned to the work force after the family had experienced several years in which a pattern of maternal specialization in childcare had an opportunity to become solidified. The entry of the mother into the work force at that point may have been accompanied by relatively little change in the father's established pattern in regard to childcare and household participation. When the mother of a very young child works outside the home, paternal sharing in childcare is likely to be encouraged from the outset.

Studies in the infancy period that rely on parental reports of childcare practices tend to support the view that fathers whose wives work outside the home are indeed more actively involved in childcare. Fein's (1976) investigation of 32 couples, which extended from about 4 weeks before to 6 weeks after the birth of the child, indicated that his group of nontraditional fathers—those more deeply involved in the daily care of their babies—tended to come from families in which the mother had relatively well-defined plans to combine mothering with work in the paid labor force or to work toward a professional degree. Because the amount of childcare the father provided was predictable from the prepartum interviews, he suggested that many parents begin to negotiate their allocation of responsibilities even before the birth of the child. Another investigation based on parental report (Young, 1975) found that fathers whose wives were employed spent more time in close proximity to their 1-year-old children and engaged in more caregiving tasks than did the fathers in families where the mother did not work outside the home.

Studies based on observational data do not present as consistent a picture. In a relevant investigation conducted in Sweden (Lamb, Frodi, Hwang, & Frodi, in press), prenatal interviews and observations of parent–infant interaction at age 3 months were obtained. Families were classified as traditional or nontraditional based on the father's prenatal intentions to provide varying amounts of infant care. (Parental leave policies in Sweden provide incentives for parents to distribute childcare between father and mother over the infant's first year.) Note that the classification, traditional versus nontraditional, was not the same as single versus dual wage earner; after the child's first year, the majority of Swedish women are usually in the work force. It was found that the father's prenatally expressed intentions to provide care correlated minimally with the amount of care he had provided in the infant's first 3 months of life. The nontraditional fathers were not significantly more likely than the traditional fathers to have assumed responsibility for the child for a day or more. In the home observations conducted at age 3 months, there were relatively few differences in paternal behavior attributable to traditional or nontraditional attitudes. When the gender of the child was taken into account, however, some differences were found. Traditional families provided boys with more attention and stimulation, whereas nontraditional families treated female children preferentially. Follow-up observations are planned, so it will be possible to determine how stable these patterns are and whether differences in paternal behavior emerge later.

In home observations of 5-month-old U.S. children from either one or two wage earner families (Pedersen, Cain, Zaslow, & Anderson, in press), no differences were found in either parents' *caregiving* behavior that related to role organization. Even though mothers in the work force were less likely to breast-feed their infants, mothers from both types of families spent significantly more time feeding than did the fathers. Differences related to role organization were found in noncaregiving behaviors, however. Mothers who worked outside the home showed a great intensification in rates of verbal interaction with their babies compared to mothers in single wage-earner families. Fathers in two wage-earner families engaged in significantly *less* focused social play with their babies than did their wives, a pattern that was in the reverse direction in single wage-earner families. This finding is especially interesting because previous research on fathers, based almost entirely on single wage-earner families, has emphasized social play as a "specialty" of fathers (Parke, 1979). This generalization does not appear valid in the two wage-earner family. There is one additional finding of note. Looking across *all* categories of parental behavior, the four gender of parent by role organization classifications show a statistically significant pattern in the scores. Mothers in two wage-earner families tended to score highest, fathers from the same families tended to score lowest, and either parent in the single wage-earner family was intermediate. Instead of the two wage-earner family appearing more egalitarian in childcare as suggested by studies based on parental report, our data indicated the reverse!

One interpretation of these findings is that in the American cultural context the mother already in the work force with a 5-month-old infant is somewhat ambivalent about being away from the baby. Higher rates of interaction are probably a combination of the need to engage the baby after spending time away and perhaps a need to compensate for what the child might have missed while receiving substitute care. The father in the two wage-earner family, we speculate, was being "crowded out" by the mother's strong need to interact with the baby. In contrast, in the single wage-earner family, the mother may have been relatively satiated with baby interaction at the time of the observations and may have welcomed a respite during which the father spent time with the baby. This effect might show itself as rather similar overall rates of maternal and paternal behavior.

The difference in results obtained by different methods, observations and parental report, does not necessarily mean that one method is valid and the other invalid. It is perhaps more likely that a research participant's social desirability motive may show itself differently. When *talking* about behavior, the two wage-earner or nontraditional family may stress egalitarian practices; when babies in these families are *observed,* however, the mother may be drawn in to provide higher amounts of stimulation. In addition to the influence of being observed or interviewed, time periods seldom observed (e.g., mornings and weekends) may be weighted in parental report in one direction, and evening observations may provide just the opposite bias. Although the research findings appear inconsistent at this stage of studying the problem, one would expect that as there is greater understanding of how methods affect results there will be greater corroboration.

Sex Role Identification

Just as U.S. society has changed in norms for sex roles away from sharply differentiated patterns (Hoffman, 1977), important change has occurred in the conceptualization of sex roles within social science theory. The traditional theoretical approach to male and female role behavior has been in terms of a unidimensional, bipolar construct in which masculinity–feminity is roughly equated with the instrumental–expressive dimension (Parsons & Bales, 1955). Bakan (1966) similarly conceptualized a dicotomy in which masculinity is associated with an "agentic" orientation, a concern with the individual manifested as self-protection, self-assertion, and self-expansion, and femininity is associated with a "communal" orientation, a sense of being at one with others and concerned about the relationship between oneself and others. As bipolar end points of a single dimension, the perspectives may be called "either/or" theories.

More recent formulations (Bakan, 1966; Bem, 1974; Block, 1973; Heilbrun, 1976; Spence & Helmreich, 1978) may be described as "both/and" theories. The concept of *psychological androgyny* has been proposed to denote the integration in the same individual of both elements of these dichotomized dimensions. Psychological androgyny implies that it is possible for an individual to be both instrumental and expressive, both agentic and communal, depending on behavioral requirements of particular situations. Moreover, in this model personal maturity is associated with greater integration of these behavioral possibilities.

The implication of this changed conceptualization is that more differentiated measurement is possible—that is, high masculinity need not imply low femininity. Using measurement instruments such as the Bem (1974) Sex Role Inventory, individuals may be classified in two independent dimensions of masculinity and femininity. An individual may be either masculine (high in masculinity and low in femininity), feminine (low in masculinity and high in femininity), androgynous (high in both dimensions) or undifferentiated (low in both dimensions). It has been found that many men and women (approximately 30 percent of college student samples) are psychologically androgynous and behave in both masculine and feminine ways. They are more likely to perform cross-sex behavior and are less constrained by sex role stereotypes. In laboratory experiments, androgynous men are as likely as androgynous and feminine women to be nurturant toward a 5-month-old baby, and they display more nurturance than masculine men (Bem & Lenney, 1976; Bem, Martyna, & Watson, 1976).

Russell (1978) investigated the possibility that a father's sex role identification (measured on the Bem scale) is related to the amount of time he spends in either caregiving or social play with young children. He hypothesized that fathers with either an androgynous or feminine identification, in contrast to masculine or undifferentiated fathers, would be more actively involved with children on a day-to-day basis. In his sample of Australian families, and using measures of caregiving and play based on parental report, his hypotheses were indeed confirmed. Androgynous fathers were significantly more involved in both caregiving and play than masculine fathers; androgynous and feminine fathers combined were more involved in caregiving and play than masculine and undifferentiated fathers combined. Mother's scores on the sex role identification scale were not significantly related to their time spent in caregiving and play, which Russell felt was because of the more rigid cultural definitions of the maternal role.

Russell's findings are fascinating because they imply that personality dimensions not perfectly synonymous with biological gender may predispose fathers to alternative but predictable adaptations to parenthood. His results are consistent with Fein's (1976) and Lamb et al.'s (in press) general conceptualizations, even though none classified fathers with precisely the same psychological constructs. There is a basis for encouraging further investigation in the infancy period and making efforts to extend the findings with observational measures.

A review of recent studies of individual differences in paternal behavior indicates more diversity than is suggested in global descriptive studies. The father's psychological relationship with the young infant may be conceptualized in terms of variation in such dimensions as caregiving, social play, and responsiveness to distress cues. There is suggestive evidence that these dimensions are sometimes differentially influenced by the child's birth circumstances, complications in the delivery that affect the mother, the family's role organization in regard to income production, and the father's sex role identification. In spite of contradictory findings, a model in which situational and trait influences interact may emerge. Measures of paternal involvement based on parental report, although often less precise in the behavioral referents, seem to fit a more coherent pattern in spite of psychologists' traditional distrust of this source of data.

INTERRELATIONS AMONG FAMILY SUBSYSTEMS

The expansion of understanding early experience from a dyadic mother-and-infant unit to a mother–father–infant family highlights a major new problem: understanding how interactions between two people influence and are influenced by a third person. Bronfenbrenner (1974) coined the term "second order effects" as a generic concept for these influences, and he appealed for more research on socialization in larger social contexts than merely that of the mother and child. Alternative taxonomic schemes for second order effects have been proposed by Parke, Power, and Gottman (1979) and Lewis and Feiring (in press) to understand the array of psychological influences that occur in social units larger than the dyad. In both systems the number of conceptual categories exceeds the ones that have been examined empirically, but they invite attention to questions that have received either less systematic attention or a different emphasis in the relevant psychological processes.

The consideration of second order effects brings into sharp relief the husband–wife relationship, the unit of the family in which developmental psychology has shown relatively little interest (Aldous, 1977). Evidence of its importance in parenting behavior is available largely in sociological research literature (which rarely includes detailed examination of parent–infant interaction) and in a few investigations that have attempted to bridge disciplinary boundaries. Research methods include both parental report and behavioral observations. Rarely, however, does a study attempt to operationalize a construct such as "marital satisfaction" with objective, behavioral events in the same way that, for example, caregiving activities may be appraised both observationally and by parental report. Thus the types of research questions that have been examined in regard to second order effects appear very different, depending on whether the investigator had a primary committment to observational measures or to eliciting cognitive constructions of experience. Consequently, review of research on the interrelations of different family subsystems may be conveniently divided into two groups: *in situ* behavioral investigations and investigations of the cognitive constructions of experience.

In Situ Behavioral Investigations

An obvious design for appraising the behavioral effects of one parent, such as the father, on the interaction between two others, mother and infant, is to compare behavior directed toward and emitted by the child in groups containing one or both parents. This design ignores the qualitative subtleties of both the husband–wife and parent–child relationships, but asks whether there are structural influences on interaction of the different groups in which a child's socialization occurs. Studies of this nature have been done from the newborn period through toddlerhood, in hospital, laboratory, and home settings, and with experimentally manipulated or naturally occurring changes in group composition. Representative investigations include those of Parke and O'Leary (1976), Lamb (1976, 1978), Clarke-Stewart (1978), Belsky (1979), and Pedersen, Anderson, and Cain (1980). For the most part, there is refreshing consistency in the findings involving infants from 5 months through toddlerhood. In general, rates of interaction between parent and child are consistently *higher* in the dyadic group compared to the three-person group. The influence of group composition appears rather pervasive, being evident in a broad range of behaviors by both parent and child. The presence of either mother or father has virtually the same effect on father–infant or mother–infant interaction respectively. Results in the newborn period (Parke & O'Leary, 1976) in a study conducted in the hospital setting showed findings partly at variance with these generalizations; both mother and father smiled at the baby more when the spouse was present than absent, but other behaviors decreased in the three-person setting.

Although there is a temptation to view consistently replicated findings in psychology as a banality, these have important implications. One is that there should be recognition of the ecological reality in which each parent's interactions with the child characteristically occur. From records kept by parents over a one-week period, striking differences in each parent's social context for child interaction have been documented (Pedersen et al., 1979). In the traditional division of labor in which the father fulfills the wage earner responsibilities, the most characteristic social group involving the infant for the mother is a two-person unit, the mother and infant without the father present. The most characteristic social group involving the infant and the father is a three-person group of mother, father, and infant. This suggests that in the natural environment father–infant interaction is relatively more "diluted" than one would infer from research findings in which each parent's interaction was observed in a comparable size group. Perhaps the proclivity that many fathers have to engage in interludes of robust and activating social play (Lamb, 1977; Clarke-Stewart, 1978) is partly in response to the "pull" toward reduced rates of interaction characteristic of three-person groups.

While the studies noted above focused on changed rates of parent–child interaction in two- and three-person groups, it is important to recognize that the three-person group contains the potential for an additional dyadic relationship: interaction between husband and wife. From time-sampling observations using categories that described husband–wife exchanges in addition to parent and infant behaviors, it was found that the former are every bit as prevalent as the latter (Pedersen et al., 1979). In our sample of families with 5-month-old infants, 51 percent of the observational intervals in which all three people were together in the home included communication between the parents. These observations permitted us to examine the interplay between spousal interactions and behavior directed toward or emitted by the infant. Clarifying some of the linkages between spouse interaction and behavior involving the baby may add to the understanding of ways in which a three-person group of mother, father, and infant is different in content and dynamics than a dyadic unit of parent and infant.

To establish if there was synchrony between husband–wife interaction and behavior involving the infant, observation intervals in which all three family members were together were initially partitioned according to the presence or absence of any spouse communication. Rates of behavior directed toward the infant during units when the parents either were or were not communicating with each other were then compared. Similar analyses were done for both mother and father and for infant behaviors directed to either parent. The results showed a remarkably complex orchestration of behavior in the three-person group.

Findings indicated that behavior requiring relatively great focused attention on the part of the parent—making eye contact, talking, smiling, and playing in various ways with the baby—are inhibited when there is active communication between the parents. These behaviors emerged more strongly in time intervals when there was no communication between the parents. Behaviors that required less focused attention, such as holding the baby, rocking or cuddling, and feeding solids, were not affected by whether the parents were communicating with each other. There was one exception to this overall pattern: nursing or feeding by bottle was *more* prevalent during intervals in which husband and wife interacted with each other. The latter finding suggests one intersection of parent–infant and husband–wife behavior that may be mutually enhancing. Perhaps nursing quiets the activity of the baby directed toward the external environment in such a way that parents are drawn together to talk during these periods.

There were also two significant interactions involving parental gender and the conditions of spouse communication. Rates for talking to the baby and play that involved directing the baby's attention to toys increased significantly more for mothers than fathers when there was no ongoing spouse communication. The findings suggest that, in synchronizing behavior to the infant and spouse communications, in some ways the mother and infant were drawn together a bit more strongly than were the father and infant.

Evaluation of the infant's behavior directed to each parent in relation to communication between the parents showed remarkably parallel results. During periods of no communication between the parents, when focused social interactions with the infant increased, the infant also showed increased rates of socially directed behavior to both mother and father. There was also a significant interaction of gender of parent by spouse communication on the infant looking at the parent's face. An increase in looking toward mothers was greater than toward fathers, a finding that most likely paralleled the statistical interaction associated with maternal verbalizations. These findings go beyond merely showing an accommodation in behavior rates with one or two social partners; they suggest a more complex intermeshing of behavior that is coordinated with the parents' behavior toward each other. The three-person group, which the father's presence typically creates, may thereby provide unique learning opportunities for the infant and contribute to its expanded repertoire of behavior.

One question that observations on marital and parental interaction should address ultimately is whether these relationships either support or perhaps conflict with each other. Inferences may be made from the descriptive findings reported above. In a family with a traditional role organization, the mother may desire an opportunity for adult interaction after extensive periods of providing childcare and performing household tasks; a father may also wish to discuss his personal concerns. One solution to these needs might be to coordinate spouse interaction periods with the infant's feeding, a combination of activities that mixes readily. If one parent desires to engage in more autonomous activities or perform household tasks that require considerable attention, the other parent might find that these are periods well suited for more focused attention to the baby. In either case, they are not periods so readily coordinated with spouse interaction, and attempting such exchanges is likely to introduce competing needs for attention. Another alternative is to recognize that "turn-taking" is possible in directing attention to baby or spouse, and thus the needs of each family member for social interaction can be met without placing one in a competetive position relative to another.

An alternative analytic strategy that places the focus on individual differences in interaction patterns was utilized by Belsky (1979) in his study of families with 15-month-old infants. His observational scheme derived from the one developed by Pedersen et al. (1980), thus permitting simultaneous coding of parent–infant and husband–wife interactions. Communications between husband and wife were differentiated, *inter alia,* into ones relevant to the baby and ones unrelated to the baby, and frequency scores on these categories were then correlated with each parent's interaction rates with the child.

The principal findings were that the *content* of the husband–wife verbal exchanges seemed to influence whether there was an enhancing or conflicting effect on parental behavior. Conversation about the child, emitted by either mother or father, was significantly correlated with several measures of the father's interaction with the child in a positive direction. The frequency of other conversation had negative associations (although rarely significant) with paternal behavior. On the whole, few significant correlations were found for mothers. Belsky interpreted these findings to mean that husband–wife communication, especially concerning their child, has a more enhancing effect on the father–child relationship than on the mother–child relationship. Alternatively, more frequent father–child interaction may stimulate conversation between the parents on matters relating to their child. Similar analyses were performed on observations of 5-month-old infants conducted by Pedersen et al. (1980). The results (unpublished) were generally consistent with Belsky's findings in regard to both directionality of relationships and the differentiation in content of husband–wife interaction. Husband–wife communication about the baby had several significant positive correlations with the father's rates of interacting with the child, whereas associations with mother–child interaction were negative and rarely significant. Taken together, the findings from both investigations draw attention to the possible mediational role that the husband–wife relationship may have on parenting behavior.

Investigations Based on Cognitive Constructions of Experience

Whether based on clinical ratings of observers or self-reports to questionnaires and interviews, variables that describe the marital relationship often are relatively inferential, abstract, and summed across long time intervals. Thus dimensions rich in their psychological implications may be the most difficult to pin down to objective criteria; the eye of the beholder needs to be understood as much as the "reality" it perceives. At the same time, investigations based on the cognitive constructions of experience show sufficient convergence to argue that they do tap a meaningful psychological reality.

Bowlby (1969), the *bête noire* to theorists who have attempted to look at early experience beyond the mother–infant relationship, conceptualized fathers in a way that underscored their second order (or indirect) influences. The primary role of the father, Bowlby said, is to provide emotional and economic support to the mother and thereby enhance the mother–infant relationship. Although Bowlby was not concerned with the effects of *variation* in the father's capacity or willingness to be supportive of the mother, this question is a natural extension of his theoretical framework. Barry (1972) developed this line of reasoning in his review of research studies on factors affecting marital satisfaction or happiness. He highlighted recurring findings that background characteristics of the husband/father (e.g., emotional maturity, a secure sex role identity, and higher educational and occupational attainments) were especially predictive of the wife's marital satisfaction, but similar correlations were less frequently found for background characteristics of the wives themselves. This led him to infer that these aspects of the father were markers of his capacity to be emotionally supportive in the marital relationship. Barry hypothesized that emotional support is most important during periods of role transition, and the transition from wife to wife/mother involves a more pervasive transition than the parallel change for men does.

A variety of studies provides more direct confirmation for the hypothesis that emotional support from the husband and a more satisfying marital relationship have an enhancing effect on the mother's competence and sense of well-being. The husband's emotional support during pregnancy contributes to the wife's more successful adaptation to pregnancy (Shereshefsky & Yarrow, 1973). The presence of the husband throughout labor and delivery is associated with reduced need for pain-relieving medication and a more positive delivery experience (Henneborn & Cogan, 1975). Support and encouragement from the husband is a major factor in the mother's successful breast-feeding (Switzky, Vietze, & Switzky, 1979). Studies of the mother's competence in either breast- or bottle-feeding—her sensitivity and adaptation to the needs of the infant—also suggest the importance of an encouraging and emotionally supportive partner (Price, 1977; Pedersen, 1975). Depressive symptoms in mothers during the postpartum period have been related retrospectively to emotionally cold and distant husbands (Kaplan & Blackman, 1969) and in one prospective investigation, to marriages with a high degree of role segregation (Oakley, 1979).

One especially comprehensive investigation that traced families from the first trimester of pregnancy through the first year postpartum (Grossman, Eichler & Winickoff, 1980) appears to corroborate the overall pattern of marital and parental functioning. Among the many analyses reported, the marital relationship assessed at the first trimester of pregnancy was rather strongly predictive of the mother's psychological adjustment at 2 months postpartum and moderately so at 1 year. The measures were a self-report scale of marital adjustment (Locke-Wallace), ratings from interviews to appraise the mother's emotional well-being, and questionnaire measures for anxiety and depression. Several measures of the woman's treatment of her new infant were linked to aspects of her husband's functioning. His anxiety level, age, and marital satisfaction related to her skills and warmth in handling the baby, as measured by both observation and interview. In general, it appears that the psychological connectedness of these variables throughout the assessment periods was greater for first-time parents than for experienced parents. This suggests that the initial transition to parenthood is more strongly affected by the psychological reactions of both mother and father, whereas adjustment to subsequent children is affected more by external circumstances.

Yet another example of corroboration of the importance of emotional support from the father is seen in Barnard's (1980) longitudinal investigation that studied families from the pregnancy period through the child's fourth year of life. The mother's report of father involvement during the pregnancy—how the father felt about the pregnancy and whether the mother saw him as offering her both emotional and physical support—was consistently correlated with observational measures of the mother's involvement and responsiveness with the child throughout the first 4 years.

Finally, studies of the process of divorce (Hetherington, Cox, & Cox, 1978; Hess & Camara, 1979) indicate that, in the period following separation of the parents, an intensely conflicted relationship between mother and father is strongly associated with disrupted parent–child functioning. Restoration of a more amicable relationship between former spouses appears to lead to more positive parent–child interaction, even though the parents have come to rely on support systems other than the marriage relationship itself.

In spite of the consistent pattern to these findings, one must ask what the psychological ingredients of emotional support are. In part, the answer is seemingly tautological: since researchers often inquire only whether the mother regards the father as supportive, emotional support is whatever a mother conceives it to be. More objective definitions include the father's positive evaluation of the mother's behavior vis-à-vis the child (Pedersen, 1975), agreement between parents on childrearing techniques and goals (Dickie, Schuurmans, & Schang, 1980), and ease of communication between parents on matters relating to the child or their own feelings (Heath, 1976; Painter, 1980). For most families, emotional support is independent of the father's amount of participation in childcare. Three studies converge to show that the psychological relationship between parents is more important than how much the father participates in childcare in determining the mother's responsiveness, involvement, or sense of competence (Dickie et al., 1980; Painter, 1980; Barnard, 1980).

There has been relatively little research on whether a *father* benefits from emotional support from his wife in maintaining an effective parent–infant relationship. Neglect of this question appears to be caused by the pervasive influence of sex role stereotypes that both minimize the importance of the father's direct interaction with a young infant and, while stressing the primacy of the mother–infant relationship, conceive of her as relatively dependent, weak, and more needful of support. Because high involvement of fathers with young infants is contrary to traditional cultural values, however, the case can be made that fathers are *especially* in need of emotional support to maintain their parenting role. The situation may be analogous to maternal employment; departure from a culturally-sanctioned pattern of behavior, to be maintained, requires a support system both within and outside the family (Hoffman & Nye, 1975).

Studies that have examined the supportive relationship of each adult on parent–infant interaction show high congruence in results: both mothers and fathers benefit from the partner's emotional support. Dickie et al. (1980) found equivalent effects for mothers and fathers who provide support to one another on contingent responding, skill and knowledge, and emotional warmth of each parent toward the infant. Fein (1976) stressed the importance of the father's adaptational pattern, whether breadwinner or nontraditional, being negotiated in terms of the values and expectations of the wife and mother. Fathers who reported more difficulty in the postnatal period often were unable to develop a coherent role that was congruent with their partners' expectations. Research on fathers who experienced "blues" in the postnatal period (Zaslow, Pedersen, Kramer, & Cain, 1981) highlighted the importance to fathers of time available to be with their spouse and the quality of this relationship. Thus the pattern of findings that emerges is highly similar to that obtained in regard to emotional support for mothering.

Although discussion has focused on the supportive function of the marital relationship in effective parenting, it should be appreciated that characteristics of the infant and the changing needs of the child at different developmental stages may also impinge upon the marital relationship. For example,

Leiderman and Seashore (1975) reported that in families in which there was a childbirth complication (prematurity) there was a disproportionate stress on the marital relationship. More divorces occurred during the follow-up period in families that experienced a premature birth than in the control group of families with fullterm infants. The implication is that difficulties in coping with the child heightened tension and conflict in the marital relationship. Other findings within the normal range indicate that the perception of the infant as "quiet" (eats well, adapts to routines easily, sleeps through the night, and so on) is less related to of a sense of crisis in the initial stages of parenthood (Russell, 1974). The special needs for nurturing a very young infant may impose one kind of stress on the marital relationship, such as the parents' sense of unavailability to each other, while the older, more exploratory child may present a different kind of stress because of, for example, strong parental disagreements regarding limit setting. Thus a potentially supportive marital relationship may be selectively influenced by problems arising from the child's idiosyncratic characteristics as well as the changing requirements of parenting at different developmental stages.

To complicate this conceptual scheme further, Cook (1979) proposed the possibility of a statistical interaction of infant characteristics and marital satisfaction on parent–infant reciprocity. In her study, infants were classified as either relatively high or low in their behavioral organization, based on the Brazelton Neonatal Assessment Scales; marital satisfaction was measured with the Locke-Wallace questionnaire, and reciprocity in parent–infant interaction was determined in a brief videotaped face-to-face interaction episode at age 1 month. The most positive interaction patterns, regardless of which parent was interacting with the infant, occurred with parents who reported high levels of marital satisfaction and had an organized infant. Couples with high marital satisfaction also showed little variance in their parent–infant interaction scores, suggesting that marital satisfaction can mask the influence of differences in infant organization. Couples with low marital satisfaction, however, appeared more influenced by the kind of infant to which they were adapting. There was a trend, moreover, for fathers to be more influenced than mothers by the organizational level of their infants. The investigation raises interesting hypotheses and is especially noteworthy for its systemic view of parental and marital functioning.

Reviewing examples of the interplay among different family subsystems has highlighted a number of new research questions that the global descriptive strategy tends to ignore. Father influences appear vastly more complex when viewed in the perspective of a family system. Viewing the mother–infant and father–infant relationship in a psychological vacuum is a fiction of convenience that may have been servicable in guiding past research, but it will have to be replaced by more ambitious attempts to conceptualize a broader range of experiences and more complex notions of psychological causation within the family.

REFERENCES

Aldous, J. Family interaction patterns. *Annual Review of Sociology,* 1977, **3,** 105–135.

Bakan, D. *The duality of human existence.* Chicago: Rand McNally, 1966.

Barry, W. A. Marriage research and conflict: An integrative review. *Psychological Bulletin,* 1970, **73,** 41–54.

Belsky, J. Mother–father–infant interaction: A naturalistic observational study. *Developmental Psychology,* 1979, **15,** 601–607.

Belsky, J. The interrelation of parental and spousal behavior during infancy in traditional nuclear families: An exploratory analysis. *Journal of Marriage and the Family,* 1979, **41,** 749–755.

Bem, S. L. The measurement of psychological androgyny. *Journal of Consulting and Clinical Psychology,* 1974, **42,** 155–162.

Bem, S. L., & Lenny, E. Sex typing and the avoidance of cross-sex behaviour. *Journal of Personality and Social Psychology,* 1976, **33,** 48–54.

Bem, S. L., Martyna, W., & Watson, C. Sex typing and androgyny: Further explorations of the expressive domain. *Journal of Personality and Social Psychology,* 1976, **34,** 1016–1023.

Barnard, K. E. Maternal involvement and responsiveness: Definition and developmental course. Paper presented at the Second International Conference on Infant Studies, New Haven, Conn., 1980.

Block, J. H. Conceptions of sex role: Some cross-cultural and longitudinal perspectives. *American Psychologist,* 1973, **28,** 512–526.

Bottoms, S. F., Rosen, M. G., & Sokol, R. J. The increase in the cesarean birth rate. *New England Journal of Medicine,* 1980, **302,** 559–563.

Bowlby, J. *Attachment and loss,* Vol. 1. *Attachment.* New York: Basic Books, 1969.

Bradley, C. The effects of hospital experience on postpartum feelings and attitudes of women. Unpublished doctoral dissertation, University of British Columbia, 1977.

Bronfenbrenner, U. Developmental research, public policy and the ecology of childhood. *Child Development,* 1974, **45,** 1–5.

Clarke-Stewart, K. A. And daddy makes three: The father's impact on mother and young child. *Child Development,* 1978, **49,** 466–478.

Cook, A. H. *The working mother: A survey of problems and programs in nine countries.* Ithaca, N.Y.: Cornell University Press, 1978.

Cook, N. I. An analysis of marital and infant factors in evolving family relationships. Paper presented at the meeting of the Society for Research in Child Development, San Francisco, April 1979.

Dickie, J. R., Schuurmans, S. M., & Schang, B. J. Mothers, fathers, infants—What makes the triad work? Paper presented at the meeting of the American Psychological Association, Montreal, September 1980.

Doering, S. G., & Entwisle, D. R. Preparation during pregnancy and ability to cope with labor and delivery. *American Journal of Orthopsychiatry*, 1975, **45**, 825–837.

Fein, R. A. Men's entrance to parenthood. *Family Coordinator*, 1976, **25**, 341–348.

Greenberg, M., & Morris, N. Engrossment: The newborn's impact upon the father. *American Journal of Orthopsychiatry*, 1974, **44**, 520–531.

Grossman, F. K., Eichler, L. S., & Winickoff, S. A. *Pregnancy, birth and parenthood*. San Francisco: Jossey-Bass, 1980.

Heath, D. H. Competent fathers: Their personalities and marriages. *Human Development*, 1976, **19**, 26–39.

Heilbrun, A. B. Measurement of masculine and feminine sex-role identities as independent dimensions. *Journal of Consulting and Clinical Psychology*, 1976, **44**, 183–190.

Henneborn, W. J., & Cogan, R. The effect of husband participation on reported pain and probability of medication during labor and birth. *Journal of Psychosomatic Research*, 1975, **19**, 215–222.

Hess, R. D., & Camara, K. A. Post-divorce relationships as mediating factors in the consequences of divorce for children. *Journal of Social Issues*, 1979, **35**, 79–96.

Hetherington, E. M., Cox, M., & Cox, R. The aftermath of divorce. In J. H. Stevens, Jr., & M. Mathews (Eds.), *Mother–child, father–child, relationships*. Washington, D.C.: National Association for the Education of Young Children, 1978.

Hoffman, L. W. Changes in family roles, socialization, and sex differences. *American Psychologist*, 1977, **32**, 644–657.

Hoffman, L. W., & Nye, F. I. *Working mothers*. San Francisco: Jossey-Bass, 1975.

Kaplan, E. H., & Blackman, L. H. The husband's role in psychiatric illness associated with childbearing. *Psychiatric Quarterly*, 1969, **43**, 396–409.

Klaus, M. H., & Kennell, J. H. *Parent–infant bonding*. St. Louis: Mosby, 1976.

Lamb, M. E. Effects of stress and cohort on mother– and father–infant interaction. *Developmental Psychology*, 1976, **12**, 435–443.

Lamb, M. E. The development of mother–infant and father–infant attachments in the second year of life. *Developmental Psychology*, 1977, **13**, 637–648.

Lamb, M. E. The effects of the social context on dyadic social interaction. In M. E. Lamb, S. J. Suomi, & G. R. Stephenson (Eds.), *Social interaction analysis: Methodological issues*. Madison: University of Wisconsin Press, 1978.

Lamb, M. E., Frodi, A. M., Hwang, C.-P., & Frodi, M. Varying degrees of paternal involvement in infant care. In M. E. Lamb (Ed.), *Nontraditional families*. Hillsdale, N.J.: Lawrence Erlbaum Associates, in press.

Leiderman, P. H., & Seashore, M. J. Mother–infant separation: Some delayed consequences. *Ciba Foundation Symposia*, 33 (New Series), 1975.

Lewis, M., & Feiring, C. Direct and indirect interactions in social relations. In L. Lipsitt (Ed.), *Advances in infancy research*, Vol. 1. Norwood, N.J.: Ablex, in press.

Oakley, A. *Becoming a mother*. Oxford: Martin Robertson, 1979.

Painter, S. L. Maternal adaptation to parenthood. Unpublished doctoral dissertation, University of British Columbia, 1980.

Parke, R. D. Perspectives on father–infant interaction. In J. Osofsky (Ed.), *Handbook of infant development*. New York: Wiley, 1979.

Parke, R. D., & O'Leary, S. Father–mother–infant interaction in the newborn period: Some findings, some observations, and some unresolved issues. In K. A. Riegel & J. Meacham (Eds.), *The developing individual in a changing world*, Vol. 2. *Social and environment issues*. The Hague: Mouton, 1976.

Parke, R. D., Power, T. G., & Gottman, J. Conceptualizing and quantifying influence patterns in the family triad. In M. E. Lamb, S. J. Suomi, & G. R. Stephenson (Eds.), *Social interactional analysis: Methodological issues*. Madison: University of Wisconsin Press, 1979.

Parke, R. D., & Sawin, D. B. The family in early infancy: Social interactional and attitudinal analyses. In F. Pedersen (Ed.), *The father–infant relationship: Observational studies in the family setting*. New York: Praeger, 1980.

Parsons, T., & Bales, R. F. *Family, socialization, and interaction process*. Glencoe, Ill.: Free Press, 1955.

Pedersen, F. Mother, father and infant as an interactive system. Paper presented at the annual convention of the American Psychological Association, Chicago, 1975.

Pedersen, F. A., Anderson, B. J., & Cain, R. L. Parent–infant and husband–wife interactions observed at age five months. In F. Pedersen (Ed.), *The father–infant relationship: Observational studies in the family setting*. New York: Praeger, 1980.

Pedersen, F. A., Cain, R. L., Zaslow, M. J., & Anderson, B. J. Variation in infant experience associated with alternative family roles. In L. Laosa & I. Sigel (Eds.) *Families as learning environments for children*. New York: Plenum, in press.

Pedersen, F. A., Yarrow, L. J., Anderson, B. J., & Cain, R. L. Conceptualization of father influences in the infancy period. In M. Lewis & L. Rosenblum (Eds.), *The child and its family. New York: Plenum, 1979.*

Pedersen, F. A., Zaslow, M. J., Cain, R. L., & Anderson, B. J. Cesarean childbirth: psychological implications for mothers *and* fathers. *Infant Mental Health Journal*, in press.

Peterson, G. H., Mehl, L. E., & Leiderman, P. H. The role of some birth-related variables in father attachment. *American Journal of Orthopsychiatry,* 1979, **49,** 330–338.

Price, G. Factors influencing reciprocity in early mother–infant interaction. Paper presented at the meeting of the Society for Research in Child Development, New Orleans, March 1977.

Russell, C. Transition to parenthood: Problems and gratification. *Journal of Marriage and the Family,* 1974, **36,** 294–301.

Russell, G. The father role and its relation to masculinity, femininity, and androgyny. *Child Development,* 1978, **49,** 1174–1181.

Shereshefsky, P. M., & Yarrow, L. J. *Psychological aspects of a first pregnancy and early postnatal adaptation.* New York: Raven Press, 1973.

Spence, J. T., & Helmreich, R. L. *Masculinity and femininity.* Austin: University of Texas Press, 1978.

Svejda, M. J., Campos, J. J., & Emde, R. N. Mother–infant "bonding": Failure to generalize. *Child Development,* 1980, **51,** 775–779.

Switzky, L. T., Vietze, P., & Switzky, H. Attitudinal and demographic predictors of breast-feeding and bottle-feeding behavior in mothers of six-week-old infants. *Psychological Reports,* 1979, **45,** 3–14.

Tanzer, C., & Block, J. *Why natural childbirth?* New York: Doubleday, 1972.

U.S. Department of Labor. *Working mothers and their children.* Washington, D.C.: U.S. Government Printing Office, 1979.

Vietze, P. M., MacTurk, R. H., McCarthy, M. E., Klein, R. P., & Yarrow, L. J. Impact of mode of delivery on father– and mother–infant interaction at 6 and 12 months. Paper presented at the International Conference on Infant Studies, New Haven, Conn., March 1980.

Vietze, P. M., & O'Connor, S. Mother-to-infant bonding: A review. In N. Kretchmer & J. Brasel (Eds.), *Biomedical and social bases of pediatrics.* New York: Masson, 1980.

Wente, A. S., & Crockenberg, S. B. Transition to fatherhood: Lamaze preparation, adjustment difficulty and the husband–wife relationship. *The Family Coordinator,* 1976, **25,** 351–357.

Young, S. F. Paternal involvement as related to maternal employment and attachment behavior directed to the father by the one-year-old infant. Unpublished doctoral dissertation, Ohio State University, 1975.

Zaslow, M. J., Pedersen, F. A., Kramer, E. & Cain, R. L. "Postpartum depression" in new fathers. Paper presented at the meeting of the Society for Research in Child Development, Boston, April 1981.

CHAPTER 9

The Father and Sex Role Development

HENRY B. BILLER

University of Rhode Island

A central theme in the study of paternal influence in the family has been the father's impact on children's sex role development and gender identity. In this chapter, data are reviewed indicating that nurturant, competent, and available fathers are important contributors to their sons' and daughters' sex role functioning at various stages of development. This chapter is based on my more extensive discussions of the role of the father in child development (Biller, 1971, 1974c, 1976b).

It must be emphasized at the outset that the study of sex role development has some very controversial issues associated with it (Biller, 1974c, 1977, 1980). There are many researchers who would prefer that definitions of sex role behavior be radically transformed or translated into "nonsexist terms" and/or that sex role concepts be eliminated as relevant topics to investigate. Certainly, traditional definitions of sex role have tended to be limited, restrictive and rigid. Perhaps because of the increasing realization that certain "sex role" expectations can be handicapping, there appeared to be a marked decline in the number of investigations directed at understanding parental influence in the sex role development process during the last decade, although there were numerous attempts to develop less biased sex role measures and to demonstrate the negative implications of traditional definitions of sex role behavior (e.g., Bem, 1979; Kelly & Worrell, 1977; Locksley & Colten, 1979; Spence & Helmreich, 1979).

Despite agreeing with most criticisms of the bias and inadequacy inherent in both conceptual and methodological underpinnings of previous research on sex role functioning, I believe that we can learn much about major dimensions of personality formation by attempting to understand how family interactions influence children's sex role development. For better or worse, sex roles will continue to influence personality development. The father can, of course, have a positive or negative effect on his child's sex role development. The quality

319

of the father-child relationship can be a factor in the learning of either socially desirable or socially undesirable sex role patterns which can affect many areas of the child's emotional, cognitive and interpersonal functioning.

In this chapter the emphasis is, as much as possible, on adaptive dimensions of sex role functioning. Traditional "masculinity" may not be "best" for males and traditional femininity may not be "best" for females but the child who evolves a positive sex role orientation *and* the basic competencies that are associated with his or her sex is more likely to develop a firm self-confidence and a broad range of adaptive qualities that transcend narrowly defined sex role stereotypes. For example, both boys and girls can be independent and assertive as well as nurturant and sensitive to others' feelings; they can learn to be effectively instrumental and expressive. Individuals who develop such a range of abilities are likely to come from families in which there is both a positively involved, competent mother *and* father (Biller, 1974c, 1976b).

The first section of this chapter reviews theoretical concepts and research concerning the father–child relationship and the boy's sex role development. The second section focuses on research data and theoretical views examining the influence of the father–daughter relationship on the girl's sex role development. Variations in paternal influence do not take place in a vacuum. One must consider factors such as the child's constitutional characteristics and developmental status, the quality of the mother–child and father–mother relationships, the family's sociocultural background, and the availability of surrogate models.

MASCULINE DEVELOPMENT

Most of the studies in this section were stimulated by hypotheses derived from theories of identification. These hypotheses center on the significance of the father acting in a certain manner and being perceived by the boy in a particular way if the boy is to identify with him and become masculine (Biller, 1974c). Freudian theory stresses that identification occurs because the father is perceived as punitive and threatening (Fenichel, 1945). Status-envy theory emphasizes that the father needs to be perceived as the primary consumer of resources (Burton & Whiting, 1961). Learning theory underscores the importance of the father being affectionate and rewarding (Sears, 1957). Role theory stresses that the father should be a primary dispenser of both rewards and punishments (Parsons, 1955). Social power theory suggests that the model most likely to be imitated is the person who most controls valued resources (Mussen & Distler, 1959). Identification theorists such as these deal with more than sex role development: They are also concerned with the development of conscience, self-control, and adult role playing. The purpose here however is to discuss only hypotheses relating to sex role development.

Theories of Identification

The Freudian view of the father's role in masculine development is described first, since other identification theory hypotheses are, at least in part, derivatives thereof (Bronfenbrenner, 1960). Freud postulated that the boy desires to have an exclusive relationship with his mother during the Oedipal period when he is 3 to 5 years of age. Freud believed that the boy comes to see his father as a very aggressive competitor for his mother's affection and fears that the father will castrate him. According to Freud, the normal resolution of the Oedipus complex takes place when, in order to cope with his fear of castration, the boy identifies with his father, the aggressor, and represses his desire for his mother. The boy's subsequent strong masculine strivings and desire to be like his father are seen as a byproduct of his identification with his father. In an interesting account of Freud's consideration of the father's role, Burlingham (1973) notes that Freud occasionally alluded to affectionate father–child attachments in pre-Oedipal development. Despite this, in Freudian theory the perception of the father as punitive and threatening, as the "source of decisive frustrations" during the Oedipal period, is seen as a major prerequisite for the boy's masculine development (Fenichel, 1945).

Whiting's status-envy theory of identification is an extension of the Freudian hypothesis of identification with the aggressor (Burton & Whiting, 1961). Whereas the Freudian hypothesis stressed the boy's desire to possess his mother, Whiting emphasized that the child wants to engage in many of the activities of the envied parent. For instance, Whiting argued that the boy will have a masculine identification if he perceives his father having access to more privileges and attractive objects and activities than his mother (Burton & Whiting, 1961). It is assumed that the child is motivated to imitate the behavior of the primary recipient of valued resources and that his identification with that person is much strengthened by fantasy rehearsal of the envied behavior. According to this concept, a young boy will develop a masculine identification only if his father (or father surrogate) is the primary consumer of valued resources. (A young girl will identify with her mother when she perceives her as the primary consumer of valued resources.)

Mowrer (1950) attempted to reformulate Freudian theory in terms of learning theory concepts. He distinguished between defensive and developmental identification. Defensive identification is synonomous with identification with the aggressor, developmental identification with anaclitic identification. Anaclitic identification, a concept used in Freudian theory to explain why girls identify with their mothers and become feminine, is based on fear of loss of love. Although Mowrer acknowledged that identification with the aggressor may be involved in masculine development, he emphasized the importance of *developmental* identification in the sex role development of both boys and girls. The basis for developmental identification is an affectional–emotional link with the parent motivating the child to reproduce "bits of the beloved parent" in order to avoid the feeling of loss of love when the parent witholds rewards or is absent. The identification is supposed to develop out of a nurturant parent–child relationship, and the child becomes dependent on the parent to provide nurturance and affection. Again, as in Freudian theory, the boy's initial identification is viewed as a nonsex-typed one with the mother. As the father becomes more a source of reinforcement (supposedly when the child is around the age of 4) the boy imitates the father and gradually becomes masculine. Similar viewpoints are expressed by other learning theorists (e.g., Sears, 1970).

A view of identification that in certain respects combines the Freudian and learning theory hypotheses has been advanced by some sociologists (e.g., Parsons, 1955). According to Parsons' role theory the boy identifies with the person who is most able to dispense both rewards and punishments to him. Bronfenbrenner (1960) pointed out that the novel concept of role theory as elaborated by Parsons is that "the child identifies not with the parent as a total person, but with the reciprocal role relationship that is functioning for the child at a particular time" (p. 32). Johnson (1963) stressed the importance of fathering in her elaboration of Parsons' theory of identification. The mother has a primarily expressive relationship with both boys and girls. In contrast, the father rewards his male and female children differently, encouraging instrumental behavior in his son and expressive behavior in his daughter. The identification with the father leads to the internalization of a reciprocal role relationship that is crucial for the sex role development of both boys and girls. For example, with his son the father plays roughly and invites aggressive and assertive responses, whereas he is flirtatious and pampering with his daughter, encouraging her to be affectionate and docile.

Social learning (or social power) theorists similarly stress that the model most likely to be imitated is the person who most controls valued resources (e.g., Bandura & Walters, 1963; Mussen & Distler, 1959). These theorists vary somewhat in their specifics, but there is an emphasis on basic learning principles. The degree to which the father is observed to be a decisionmaker and controller of attractive privileges within the family increases the probability that children will imitate him.

A general disadvantage of identification theory hypotheses is that they do not differentiate among different aspects of sex roles. In fact, masculinity is treated generally as a unidimensional concept. These hypotheses consider that the boy begins to become masculine around the age of 3 or 4, when he supposedly begins to make a shift from maternal to paternal identification. However, this is inconsistent with data indicating some degree of masculine sex-typing even in 2-year-old and younger boys and, more importantly, strong father–infant attachments in many families (Biller, 1971, 1974c; Lamb, 1979; Parke, 1979; Pedersen, 1980). From material presented in other chapters of this book, it is clear that father–infant interactions can have an impact on the child's sex role functioning. In Chapter 14 I have summarized many studies that suggest that a lack of fathering during infancy can be disruptive to the child's sex role development.

A Multidimensional Perspective

I have made some beginning steps toward formulating a multidimensional perspective of the father's influence on sex role development (Biller, 1971a, 1974c; Biller & Borstelmann, 1967). This approach emphasizes the complexity of factors involved in the sex role development process. The quality of the father's interaction with his child are seen as very important. However, the father and child usually do not live in isolation from other family members. The quality of the mother–child relationship, the mother–father relationship, and the entire family system (father–mother–child–sibling interactions), as well as various biological and sociocultural factors, all contribute to the father's and son's influences on each other.

The father plays a highly significant role in the development of sex role orientation, even during infancy. For example, it is clear that infants and fathers can become very attached to one another and the boy's perception of himself as a male (and thus more similar to his father than to his mother), is an impetus for him to imitate his father. Parents can, of course, facilitate their son's self-perception by their verbal and behavioral cues. Children generally imitate the behaviors of both parents, and the degree of actual similarity between the father and son can be influenced by genetic and/or constitutional factors, A child may resemble one parent particularly in terms of temperamental and physical characteristics. However, the quality of fathering that the boy receives is generally the most crucial factor in the positive development of his view of himself as a male.

There are many similarities between Kohlberg's (1966) cognitive-developmental conception of sex role development and my formulation: the early learning of orientation, the importance of cognitive factors, the predisposing influence of orientation on later sex role development, the influence of self-concept, and competency motivation. However, the multidimensional formulation is much more inclusive. Kohlberg gave a somewhat circumscribed description of sex role development and generally downplayed the importance of parental factors. He seemed to assume that knowledge of sex role norms is relatively isomorphic with sex role development. Although the ability to discriminate masculine and feminine roles, symbols, and activities is an important factor in sex role development, it does not encompass all of it. There are many individuals who have knowledge of sex role norms but prefer to behave in a manner more characteristic of the other sex. For example, a boy can be aware that he is a male and possess knowledge about sex-typed toys, yet choose to play with girls and engage in feminine sex-typed activities.

The development of an individual's sex role preference and his or her relative desire to adhere to culturally defined sex role guidelines is usually influenced by sex role orientation. But whereas orientation is very much related to discrimination between the specific sex role models of mother and father, preference pertains to discrimination between more general, socially defined symbols and representations of sex roles. Sex role orientation is involved with the individual's self-evaluation; sex role preference is related to the individual's evaluation of certain environmental activities and opportunities. In developing a masculine sex role preference, the boy learns to value certain toys, activities, and interests. Learning experiences are based on more than family interactions; peers and the mass media have become increasingly influential.

Whereas sex role orientation is related to the individuals' views of themselves, sex role adoption pertains to the way in which individuals are perceived by other members in their society. Correlates of sex role adoption are present even in infancy, and sex role adoption continues to evolve in adolescence and adulthood. During this time interpersonal skill development in heterosexual relationships is particularly important. The formation of a masculine sex role adoption, especially in the preschool years, is often related to imitation of the father. A young boy's masculinity is positively related to the degree to which his father is available and behaves in a masculine manner in his interaction with his family. Siblings and peers, of course, also can be quite influential in the development of the child's sex role adoption.

Paternal masculinity is related to what White (1960) has subsumed under the heading of competency. Much of the boy's desire to imitate his father and become masculine can be associated with a desire to master his environment. For example, the boy's ability to solve problems and to build and repair various objects can be much increased if he has the frequent opportunity to observe and imitate his father.

Paternal nurturance facilitates the boy's development of a masculine sex role when the father is relatively masculine. A nurturant father more frequently rewards his son's approach responses than a nonnurturant father, and thus provides more opportunities for his son to observe and imitate his behavior. To put it another way, a nurturant father is a more available model than a nonnurturant father. The nurturant father's behavior is more often associated with affection and praise, and it acquires more reward value. Thus a boy with a nurturant father has more incentive to imitate his father than does a boy with a nonnurturant father. Moreover, a nurturant father is more likely to reinforce his son for imitating him.

If the father is a frequent participant in setting limits for his son, other opportunities for imitation are provided. However, if the father is much more punitive than he is rewarding, his behavior will not have a high incentive value and will be reproduced less. A positive relationship between paternal limit setting and the masculinity of the boy's sex role adoption is predicted only if the father is relatively nurturant. The father's masculinity, nurturance, and limit setting add to his salience. The boy's perception of his father strongly influences his perception of the incentive value of the masculine role and all aspects of his sex role development.

A boy can have a masculine orientation and preference but be limited in the development of a masculine adoption by an inadequate or inappropriate physical status. For example, a boy who is very short or thin may be at a disadvantage in a subculture that strongly associates physical prowess with masculinity. Height and muscle mass seem positively related to masculine sex role adoption. Although a particular type of physique is not sufficient to produce masculine behavior, a boy who is tall and broad or broad though short is better suited for success in many masculine activities than a boy who is tall and thin or short and thin. Parents and others seem to expect more masculine behavior from tall, broad, and/or mesomorphic boys (Biller, 1968a).

The boy's physical status can influence his sex role orientation and sex role preference as well as his sex role adoption. For example, during adolescence boys with especially unmasculine physiques are apt to have insecure self-concepts. Even though they are also likely to be low in masculine sex role adoption, they may express very masculine sex role preferences in an effort to convince themselves and others that they are masculine (Biller & Liebman, 1971).

Children's constitutional predispositions have much to do with their personality development and the way others respond to them. The boy who has a sensory-motor handicap or is intellectually limited can by extremely frustrating to his father. For example, a very sportsminded father might find it difficult to interact with a poorly coordinated son or an intellectually striving father may be uninterested in spending his time with a son who possesses little cognitive ability. However, a boy with a mesomorphic physique, high activity level, superior intelligence, and good coordination is likely to be perceived as masculine and attain much success in many traditionally male activities even if he is paternally deprived (Biller, 1974c).

Methodological Limitations

Some word of caution must be offered about most of the studies that are reviewed in this chapter. Many of the researchers used only a very restricted and
sometimes vague measure of sex role, yet generalized about the effects of a
particular variable on overall sex role development. Much more attention needs
to be given to defining and measuring various aspects and patterns of sex role
functioning. In the great majority of these studies, no account was taken of
certain variables other than parent–child relations that might influence sex role
development. For example, there was no consideration of individual differences among children in intelligence, temperament, or physical appearance.

The bulk of research on father–child relationships and sex role development
can be criticized because of methodological deficiences and/or limited generality. In most investigations the father's behavior is not directly assessed, and
maternal or child reports of paternal behavior are used instead. In many of the
studies the sources of evidence about paternal behavior and the child's behavior are not independent, leading to problems of interpretation. For example,
children are asked to describe both their own and their parents' behavior. More
studies in which there is an assessment of the amount of consistency among
observer ratings of familial interactions and children's and parents' perceptions
of parent–child relationships should be undertaken. In addition, procedures that
allow observers, parents, and children to rate each family member independently should be compared to those in which instructions call for comparative
ratings of family members. One goal of such investigations would be to examine which type or types of measures are most related to specific dimensions
of children's personality functioning.

Most of the studies on the father–child relationship and personality development have been correlational. Often the child's perception of the father or
some report of the father's behavior is linked to a measure of the child's personality development. For instance, when significant correlations are found between the degree to which a boy perceives his father as nurturant and the boy's
masculinity, it is usually assumed that paternal nurturance has been an antecedent of masculine development. But fathers may become nurturant and accepting when their sons are masculine, and rejecting when they are not.
Longitudinal research would be particularly helpful in determining the extent
to which certain paternal behaviors precede or determine particular dimensions
of children's behavior. Careful observations of families in various environmental settings could be especially revealing.

Paternal Masculinity

There are data indicating that the quality of the father–son relationship is a
more important influence than the amount of time the father spends at home on

the boy's masculine development (Biller, 1968a, 1971). A crucial factor in this development is the degree to which the father exhibits masculine behavior in family interactions. Imitation of the father *directly* enhances the boy's masculine development only if the father displays masculine behavior in the presence of his son.

When the father consistently adopts a mother-like role, it is likely that his son will be relatively low in masculinity. Bronfenbrenner (1958), reanalyzing data originally collected by Lansky (1956), found that adolescent boys low in masculine interests often came from homes in which the father played a traditionally feminine role. The fathers of these boys took over activities such as cooking and household chores and generally did not participate in family decision making or limit setting. Bronfenbrenner also described the findings of a study by Altucher (1957) in which adolescent boys with low masculine interests "were likely to come from families in which there was little role differentiation in household activities, and in which the mother, rather than the father, tended to dominate in the setting of limits for the child" (p. 120). What seemed to inhibit the boy's masculine development was not the father's participation in some traditionally feminine activities in the home *per se* (e.g., helping with the housework), but the father's general passivity in family interactions and decision making.

I found a strong relationship between kindergarten-age boys' masculinity and the degree to which they perceived their fathers as making family decisions. On measures of sex role orientation (masculinity–femininity of self-concept), sex role preference (masculinity–femininity of interests and attitudes), and sex role adoption (masculinity–femininity of social and environmental interactions), a high level of perceived decision making by the father was associated with strongly masculine behavior. The boys' perception of their fathers' status in decision making was particularly highly correlated with their sex role orientation, although it was also significantly related to preference and adoption (Biller, 1969a). Other studies have also suggested a positive association between the son's masculinity and his perception of his father's masculinity (Heilbrun, 1965b, 1974; Kagan, 1958; Rychlak & Legerski, 1967).

Even though they consistenly show a relationship between father's and son's masculinity, the studies cited above share a common methodological shortcoming. Measurement of father's and son's masculinity was generally not independent, both assessments usually being deduced from the son's responses. It could be argued that such evidence is not a sufficient basis on which to conclude that father's and son's masculinity are related. For example, an alternative explanation is that masculine sons tend to see their fathers as highly masculine, regardless of their father's actual masculinity. A boy may appear similar to his father and yet have learned his masculine behavior not from him but from his peer group. As Bronfenbrenner (1958) pointed out, the boy's perceived similarity to his father is not necessarily a measure of his identification with his father. Father–son similarity may be just a reflection of exposure to a common social environment.

In a methodologically superior study, Hetherington (1965) evaluated the relative dominance of parents by placing them in an actual decision-making situation. She found that masculinity of preschool-age and preadolescent boys' projective sex role behavior was positively related to paternal dominance. She discovered, moreover, a general tendency for both similarity between father and son and the extent of filial imitation of fathers to be higher in father-dominant than in mother-dominant homes (Hetherington, 1965; Hetherington & Brackbill, 1963; Hetherington & Frankie, 1967).

Using essentially the same parental interaction procedure as Hetherington, I found that father dominance in father–mother interaction was positively related to the masculinity of kindergarten-age boys' sex role orientations, preferences, and adoptions (Biller, 1969a). However, father dominance in parental interaction showed weaker relationships with sex role development than the boy's perception of father dominance did. The boy's behavior seems to be much determined by his particular perception of family interactions, and it may be that his view of the father is the most relevant measure. The boy's perception of his father can also be influenced by his mother's behavior. In father–mother interactions some mothers encouraged their husbands to make decisions, and others appeared to prevent their husbands from serving as adequate models by constantly competing with them for the decision-making role.

Other analyses of the data suggest the complex influences of family interactions on the boy's sex role development. Several of the boys who were low in masculinity had fathers who were dominant in interactions with their wives and generally seemed masculine. However, these fathers also appeared to be controlling and restrictive of their son's behavior. For instance, this type of dominant father punished his son for disagreeing with him. Masculine development is facilitated when the father is a competent masculine model and allows and encourages the boy to be dominant. Such paternal behavior is particularly important in the development of sex role adoption. In families in which the mother and father were competing for the decision-making function, boys were often very restricted. It seems that, in some families, when the mother does not allow her husband to be influential in family decisions, he is more apt to attempt to dominate his son in a restrictive and controlling manner.

It is the father's sex role adoption in family interactions that is crucial and not the degree of masculine behavior he exhibits outside the home. Many fathers have masculine interests and are masculine in their peer and work relationships but are very ineffectual in their interactions with their wives and children. The stereotype of the masculine, hard-working father whose primary activity at home is lying on the couch, watching television, or sleeping is an all too accurate description of many fathers. If the father is not consistently involved in family functioning, it is much harder for his child to learn to be appropriately assertive, independent, and competent. Active parenting can, in turn, have much positive influence on the father's own sex role development and sense of personal maturity (Biller & Meredith, 1974; Heath, 1978; Russell, 1978).

Paternal Nurturance

In general, paternal nurturance refers to the father's affectionate, attentive encouragement of his child. Such behavior may or may not be manifested in the caretaking or protective activities that appear commonly in descriptions of maternal nurturance. From a learning theory perspective, it could be predicted that masculine development is positively related to the degree of warmth and affection the father gives to his son, or, to put it another way, the more love and respect the boy has for his father, the more reinforcing his father's approval will be for him.

In a study of elementary school-age children, Bronson (1959) reported that both the father's masculinity and the quality of the father–son relationship have to be taken into account. The father's behavior and the father–child relationship were assessed from interviews of the fathers and family history data. The masculinity of toy preferences of boys who had chronically stressful relationships with their fathers was negatively associated with the father's masculinity. Boys who had undemonstrative, frustrating, and critcal fathers seemed to reject them as models. In contrast, where the father–son relationship was nonstressful (the father being warm, affectionate, and supportive), the masculinity of boys' toy preferences was positively correlated to fathers' masculinity. Masculine development is facilitated when the father is both masculine and nurturant.

There is other evidence that a warm, affectionate father–son relationship can strengthen the boy's masculine development. In a study by Sears (1953), preschool boys who assumed the father role in doll play activities (that is, used the father doll with high frequency) tended to have warm, affectionate fathers. Mussen and Distler (1959) studied the structured doll play of kindergarten boys. Their results revealed that boys who scored high in masculinity in projective sex role responses perceived fathers as more warm and nurturant than boys with low masculinity scores did. Using the same methodology, Mussen and Rutherford (1963) reported similar findings for first-grade boys. Studying kindergarten-age boys, I found that perceived paternal nurturance was related to a fantasy game measure of sex role orientation (Biller, 1969a).

According to maternal interview data collected by Mussen and Distler (1960), the highly masculine boys described in their earlier (1959) article had more affectionate relationships with their fathers than the less masculine boys did. Interviews with the boys' mothers indicated a trend for the fathers of highly masculine boys to take care of their sons more often, as well as to have more responsibility for family childrearing practices. Many researchers have found evidence suggesting that paternal nurturance is related to older boys' masculinity and/or similarity to their fathers (Bandura & Walters, 1959; Bronson, 1959; Distler, 1964; Mussen, 1961; Payne & Mussen, 1956).

There are data indicating that paternal nurturance is positively related to boys' success in peer relationships: they can model their fathers' positive behaviors in their interactions with peers. For boys, the presence of a masculine and nurturant father, generally sex-appropriate behavior, and popularity with peers are strongly related (Biller, 1974c, 1976b). There is also evidence suggesting that paternal nurturance can be a positive factor in many other facets of the individual's development, including various cognitive abilities and vocational adjustment (Biller, 1974c, 1976).

Paternal Limit Setting

Findings pointing to a relationship between paternal limit setting and masculine development have been presented by several researchers. Lefkowitz's (1962) analyses revealed that third- and fourth-grade boys who made at least some feminine toy choices had fathers who took less part in setting limits for them than fathers of boys who made completely masculine toy choices did. In Altucher's (1957) study, more adolescent boys who scored high in masculine interests than boys who scored low said their fathers set limits for them. Moulton, Burnstein, Liberty, and Altucher (1966) reported a similar association among male college students, but Distler (1964) did not. Other investigators have reported findings linking paternal discipline with various forms of aggressive behavior in boys (Eron, Walder, Tiogo, & Lefkowitz, 1963; Kagan, 1958; Levin & Sears, 1956).

The implication of such data is that boys often learn to be aggressive and masculine by modeling themselves after their fathers, the disciplinary situation being particularly relevant. Other factors may be operating to produce a relationship between paternal limit setting and boys' aggressive behavior. Boys may be aggressive as a function of the frustration engendered by severe paternal punitiveness. Furthermore, global ratings of aggression and other complex personality traits should be viewed with some degree of caution. For example, not all forms of aggression are culturally accepted as appropriate for boys; assertiveness in play and an active physical stance in interactions with peers seem appropriate, but tattling on other children and fighting with younger children seem inappropriate (e.g., Biller & Borstelmann, 1967; Shortell & Biller, 1970).

In any case, findings about the influence of paternal limit setting are inconsistent. In Mussen and Distler's (1959) study, the kindergarten boys who manifested highly masculine projective responses perceived their fathers as somewhat more punitive and threatening in structured doll play situations than boys low in masculinity did. Mussen and Rutherford (1963) found a similar trend for first-grade boys. But in both studies, perceived nurturance of the father was found to be much more closely related to highly masculine preferences. In addition, Mussen and Distler (1960) ascertained nothing to indicate that the fathers of the highly masculine boys actually punished them more than the fathers of the less masculine boys did. In my study with kindergarten-age boys, perceived paternal limit setting was slightly related to a measure of sex role orientation but not to measures of sex role preference or adoption (Biller, 1969a). Sears, Rau, and Alpert (1965) did not find a consistent relationship between interview measures of paternal limit setting and preschool boys' masculinity.

The adolescent boys with highly masculine interests in Mussen's study (1961) described fathers as nonpunitive and nonrestrictive in their TAT (Thematic Apperception Test) stories. The discrepancy between this study and the Mussen and Distler (1959) and Mussen and Rutherford (1963) studies may be explained by age differences. For example, a father who earlier was perceived by his son as threatening because of his "awesome size" may be less threatening when the son becomes similar in size and strength at adolescence. The father is also less likely to use physical means of punishment and more likely to set limits verbally at this stage in his son's life. A related point is that limit setting is not necessarily performed in a punitive context.

When the father plays a significant part in setting limits, the boy's attachment to his father and masculine development are facilitated only if there is an already established affectionate father–son relationship. If the father is not nurturant and is punitive, the boy is likely to display a low level of father imitation. Bandura and Walters (1959) found that adolescent boys who had highly punitive and generally nonnurturant and nonrewarding fathers exhibited relatively low father preference and little perception of themselves as acting and thinking like their fathers.

The emphasis in future research should be on gathering data on paternal participation in limit setting and expectations rather than simply on the relative amount of time that the father is a punishing agent. Firmness and consistency of limit setting relate to clear-cut expectations for the child by the parent and to what Baumrind (1967) terms authoritative childrearing. In this context, it is interesting to note that Coopersmith (1967) reported that fathers of elementary school boys with high self-esteem were more active than fathers of boys with low self-esteem in setting limits.

Paternal Power

Mussen and Distler (1959) found that boys with highly masculine projective sex role behavior perceived their fathers as more "powerful" than boys who were low in masculinity did. When perceived nurturance and perceived punitiveness scores were combined, the difference between the masculine and nonmasculine boys was particularly clear-cut. Mussen and Rutherford (1963) reported similar results for first-grade boys, but the relationship was not as strong. Freedheim's (1960) data suggested that the father's total salience to the child and overall involvement in family decision making is the best predictor of the elementary school boy's masculinity (Freedheim & Borstelmann, 1963). In my study with kindergarten-age boys, the overall amount of perceived father influence was much more important than the perception of the father as dominant in a particular area of family or parent–child functioning (Biller, 1969a).

Hetherington, Cox, and Cox (1978) carried out an especially impressive study that included an analysis of factors related to sex role development of preschool-age children. Their use of measures in dealing with different aspects of sex role functioning is a noteworthy feature of the investigation. In general, they found that fathers were more important than mothers in sex typing. For boys, masculinity on measures of sex role orientation, sex role preference, and sex role adoption was found to be related to paternal warmth, paternal demands for maturity, and paternal dominance and participation in decision making. Boys who seemed to be able to combine a positive masculinity with more generally "androgynous" patterns of social interactions had fathers who were warm, active in decision making and childcare, and emotionally expressive and supportive of the mother–child relationship. Maternal behaviors generally were more influential for the boy's sex role functioning in families where the parents were divorced and the boys were living with their mothers. The Hetherington, Cox, and Cox (1978) data concerning children in divorced families is discussed in Chapter 14.

Parent perception and sex role research with college students have also yielded results that are in line with formulations stressing the importance of the total father–son relationship. Distler (1964) found that college males who described themselves as strongly masculine on an adjective checklist viewed their fathers as high in nurturance, limit setting, and competence—in other words, as very powerful. In a study by Moulton et al. (1966), college males with the most masculine sex role preferences (modified version of Gough's Femininity Scale) reported that their fathers were high in affection and were the dominant disciplinarians in their families.

Bronfenbrenner (1961) found that the development of leadership, responsibility, and social maturity in adolescent males is closely associated with a father–son relationship that not only is nurturant but also includes a strong component of paternal limit setting. A study by Reuter and Biller (1973) also suggests the importance of evaluating both the quality and quantity of paternal behavior. The combination of at least moderate paternal availability with at least moderate nurturance was associated with positive personal adjustment among male college students.

In general, knowledge of the child's overall relationship with the father, including the degree of paternal availability, nurturance, limit setting, competence, and masculinity, is much more predictive of the child's sex role and personality functioning than is information pertaining to just a limited dimension of the father–child relationship.

Family Interaction Patterns

Some of the most intriguing as well as methodologically sound studies have provided observations of family functioning in standardized problem-solving situations. Mishler and Waxler (1968) and Schuham (1970) learned that high paternal involvement in decision making is uncommon in families in which there is a severely disturbed son. In families with nondisturbed sons, the fathers were most often the ascendant figures, and mutually acceptable decisions were much more common (Schuham, 1970).

In his observational study, Alkire (1969) noted that fathers usually dominated in families with normal adolescents, but mothers dominated in families with disturbed adolescents. Other research on interactions in disturbed families has pointed out several subtypes of inappropriate fathering (McPherson, 1970). Paternal hostility toward the child and mother and lack of open communication among families were very common. Leighton, Stollak and Ferguson (1971) found that paternal dominance was more likely and accepted in families with well-functioning children, whereas an ambivalent maternal dominance was common in familes with disturbed children.

Maternal dominance has been associated with a varied array of psychopathological problems, especially among males (Biller, 1974c). Many investigators have, however, found evidence indicating that overly dominant fathers can have just as negative an effect on their child's development as overly dominant mothers can. Researchers have reported much data relating arbitrary paternal power assertion and overcontrol to poor adjustment and psychopathology among children (Biller, 1974c).

The degree of husband versus wife dominance may not be a particularly good indication of the degree of paternal deprivation, except where there is extreme maternal dominance. Extreme paternal dominance, which is indicative of inadequate fathering, squelches the development of independence and competence in the child as much as extreme maternal dominance does.

Adequate personality development seems to be facilitated in families in which the father clearly represents a positive masculine role and the mother a positive feminine one. Kayton and Biller (1971) studied matched groups of nondisturbed, neurotic, paranoid schizophrenic, and nonparanoid schizophrenic adult males. We discovered that the nondisturbed subjects perceived their parents as exhibiting sex-appropriate behaviors to a greater extent than the disturbed subjects did. A smaller proportion of individuals in the disturbed groups viewed their fathers as possessing masculine-instrumental traits, and, particularly among the schizophrenic groups, few viewed their mothers as having feminine-expressive characteristics. Severely disturbed behavior is often associated with difficulties and/or abnormalities in sex role development (e.g., Biller, 1973; Biller & Poey, 1969; Heilbrun, 1974; Kayton & Biller, 1972; McClelland & Watt, 1968).

Block, von der Lippe, and Block (1973) reported longitudinal data that also indicate the complexity of the associations between parental behavior and the child's later personality functioning. They studied a sample of adult males and a sample of adult females from the Berkeley Longitudinal Studies. The sex role and socialization status of the subjects was determined by their scores on the Femininity and Socialization Scales of the California Psychological Inventory. The males and females were separately grouped according to their sex role and socialization patterns. (Data concerning the female groups are discussed in a later section of this chapter.)

Comparisons of the personality characteristics of different groups were done with respect to Q-sort analyses of extensive interview data. The various groups were also compared in terms of observational and interview ratings of the subjects' family backgrounds based on data collected during childhood, and there were also contemporaneous interviewer judgments based on the subjects' retrospective reports of their home environments.

The highly masculine, highly socialized males were perceived as being self-confident, competent, optimistic, and buoyant in affect. Analyses of their family background suggested that their parents had a compatible relationship and that the father was the most important person in their personality development. The fathers of such men granted their sons autonomy and were highly available as models as well as accepting of their sons.

The less masculine, highly socialized males were seen as overcontrolled, conventional, conscientious, and productive. They were viewed as markedly unaggressive yet seemed to be quite responsible and successful. Their fathers were depicted as very positive models in terms of success, ambition, adjustment, and interpersonal relations. The researchers stress that the fathers' capacity for delay of gratification and long-term commitment seems most evident in this group. This group also appeared to have particularly admirable mothers and had been exposed to highly compatible father–mother interactions.

The highly masculine, less socialized males were perceived as hypermasculine in a compensatory manner. They represented a constellation of traits including egotism and lack of impulse control. Family background data clearly indicated that these men had weak, neurotic, and somewhat rejecting fathers. The mother–father relationship was described as very poor and the mothers seemed resentful and dissatisfied with their husbands. In general, the fathers seemed to be very poor models.

The less masculine, less socialized males communicated an attitude of submissiveness, self-doubt, vulnerability, and defensive blame of others. Their fathers appeared to have been relatively uninvolved with their families and yet at the same time produced conflicts. The mothers also appeared inadequate and were described as neurotic, lacking in energy, and rejecting of the maternal role. There was also some evidence indicating that both parents, particularly the fathers, had difficulties in maintaining marriage relationships.

Such data underscore the complexity of family interaction effects on child development. As Belsky (1981) and Pedersen (1980) have so well emphasized, we need to integrate research strategies which help us understand family dynamics and the reciprocal influence of marital interactions and child development.

Sexual Relationships

A positive father–child relationship can greatly facilitate the boy's security in interacting with females. The boy who has developed a positive masculine self-image has much more confidence in heterosexual interactions. There are longitudinal data suggesting that the male who develops a strong sense of masculinity in childhood is likely to be successful in his heterosexual relationships in adulthood (Biller, 1974c; Kagan & Moss, 1962). There is considerable evidence indicating that the male's adjustment to marriage is related to his relationship with his father and his parents' marital relationship (Barry, 1970; Biller, 1974c; Cross & Aron, 1971). Much research indicating that difficulties in forming successful heterosexual relationships are linked to paternal deprivation is reviewed in Chapter 14.

An inadequate father–child relationship often appears to be a major factor in the development of homosexuality among males. West (1967) presented an excellent review of data pertaining to the antecedents of male homosexuality. Males who as children have ineffectual or absent fathers and are involved in intense, close-binding mother–son relationships seem particularly prone to develop a homosexual pattern of behavior. A close-binding mother–son relationship seems more common in homes where the father is relatively uninvolved and may, also with related factors, lessen the probability of the boy's entering into meaningful heterosexual relationships. It is common to find that homosexuals were discouraged by their mothers during childhood from participating in masculine activities and were often reinforced for feminine behavior (e.g., Bieber et al., 1962, Gundlach, 1969).

There is much evidence that male homosexuals do not usually develop strong attachments to their fathers. Chang and Block (1960) compared a group of relatively well-adjusted male homosexuals with a heterosexual control group. They found that the homosexuals reported stronger identification with their mothers and weaker identification with their fathers. A study by Nash and Hayes (1965) suggests that male homosexuals who take a passive, feminine role in sexual affairs have a particularly weak identification with their fathers and a strong one with their mothers.

Both Bieber et al. (1962) and Evans (1969) found that more fathers of homosexuals than fathers of heterosexuals were described as detached and hostile. Mothers of homosexuals were depicted as closely bound with their sons and relatively uninvolved with their husbands. Bené (1965) reported that more male homosexuals than heterosexuals perceived their fathers as weak and were hostile toward them. Similar studies by Apperson and McAdoo (1968) and Saghir and Robbins (1973) suggested a pattern of very negative father–child relations during the childhoods of male homosexuals.

A particularly extensive study of the family backgrounds of homosexuals was conducted by Thompson, Schwartz, McCandless, and Edwards (1973). College-age, well-educated homosexuals were recruited through their friends, and their family backgrounds and childhood activities were compared to those of a control group. Homosexual men described very little interaction with their fathers and a relative lack of acceptance by their fathers during their childhoods. The homosexuals generally viewed their fathers as weak, hostile, and rejecting. In general, Thompson et al. found the classic male homosexual pattern of paternal deprivation coupled with an overintense mother–child relationship and early avoidance of masculine activities.

Heterosexuals as well as homosexuals who avoided masculine activities in childhood reported more distance from both their fathers and men in general. It may be that the major difference between these homosexuals and heterosexuals was their adolescent sexual experiences. For example, opportunities for positive heterosexual relationships may have been more readily available for some of the boys. More homosexuals than heterosexuals described themselves as frail or clumsy during childhood; again there may be mediating constitutional factors in the development of some cases of homosexuality. The data fit well with a hypothesis suggesting that early paternal deprivation makes the individual more vulnerable to certain influences in later development. The particular form of adjustment the paternally deprived male makes is determined by a complex interaction of factors (Biller, 1974c).

Stoller (1968) described the case histories of several boys who felt that they were really females. These boys represented an extreme in terms of the pervasiveness of their femininity. Stoller referred to them as being transsexual. These boys had unusually close physical relationships with their mothers. Mutual mother–child body contact during infancy was especially intense and there was much evidence that the mothers reinforced many forms of feminine behavior. In none of these cases was the father masculine or involved with his child. Stoller's book is replete with references to case studies suggesting that disturbed sex role development in males is associated with an overly intense, relatively exclusive mother–son relationship.

Green (1974) reported a high rate of early paternal deprivation among extremely feminine boys who wished they were girls and preferred to dress like females. These boys had exceedingly strong identifications with their mothers and were very feminine in their sex role orientations, preferences, and adoptions, generally manifesting a transsexual behavior pattern. Of the 38 boys that Green intensively studied, 13 became father-absent prior to age 4. Among the other boys, who were father-present, father–son relationships seemed to have been very limited or distant.

In contrast, the mothers were excessively attached to their sons and had difficulty in perceiving that there was anything deviant in their boys' behavior. Although many of the fathers were upset that their sons continued to behave in a feminine manner by 4 or 5 years of age, they had been generally tolerant and were probably at least indirectly reinforcing of feminine behavior during the boys' infancy and toddler periods. Such data suggest that these fathers were very different from most men who are very uncomfortable when their young children, especially their sons, deviate from culturally expected sex role behavior (Biller, 1971).

Green's work is particularly valuable because he traces the complex interaction of various factors in the development of extremely feminine boys. He discusses how in some cases sibling and peer group reactions as well as parental behavior can strongly reinforce inappropriate sex role behavior. Perhaps the most significant aspect of his research is his suggestion of ways in which the child's characteristics can influence parental behavior. For example, in at least several cases, paternal deprivation was increased because of the young boys' disinclination to participate in masculine activities and seeming inability to relate to their fathers.

It is important to emphasize that constitutional predispositions as well as direct parental influence are often involved in children developing transsexual behavior patterns. Boys who become transsexual are frequently rather "pretty,'' delicate, nonmesomorphic, and resemble their mothers more than their fathers in outward appearance. This is not to say that biological factors cause children to become transsexual, but that constitutional predispositions may increase the likelihood that certain children will develop ''feminine'' behavior patterns. Parents' expectations are very much influenced by their children's appearance and behavior (Bell & Harper, 1977). Furthermore, there are some cases in which biological factors such as genetic anomolies have a relatively more direct impact on the development of transsexualism or other forms of atypical sex role development (Green, 1974; Money & Ehrhardt, 1972).

FEMININE DEVELOPMENT

Unfortunately, much of the theorizing about the father–daughter relationship is marred by negative conceptions of feminine behavior. Freud's theory of identification for girls centers around the Oedipus complex: When the girl discovers that she lacks a penis after being exposed to her brother or male peer, she blames her mother. She then seeks out her father in an attempted retaliation against her mother. Because of her wish to replace her mother, the girl becomes fearful that she will suffer maternal rejection. In an attempt to ward off this fear of loss of love, the girl identifies with her mother. However, according to Freud, the fear of the loss of love is not as strong as the fear of castration, and the girl does not identify completely enough with her mother to resolve the Oedipus complex fully (Fenichel, 1945).

Deutsch (1944) described the traditional psychoanalytic viewpoint in her discussion of Freud's conception of the process of feminine development. According to Deutsch (1944), the father plays an important function in leading the girl to adopt an erotic-passive mode of interacting with males. He showers her with love and tenderness when she acts passive, helpless, and/or femininely seductive, but discourages her masculine and/or aggressive strivings.

The importance of resolving the feminine Oedipal complex successfully was stressed in a somewhat more positive way by Leonard (1966), who suggested the need for a girl to ''establish a desexualized object relationship to her father'' for her to be able ''later to accept the feminine role without guilt or anxiety and to give love to a young man in her peer group'' (p. 332). Adequate fathering is assumed to be an essential requirement for the success of this phase of psychosexual development. Without paternal participation the girl may idealize her father and later, as an adolescent, seek a love object similar to this ideal or maintain a pre-Oedipal narcissistic attitude. Leonard describes such an adolescent as ''unable to give love but rather seeks narcissistic gratification in being loved'' (1966, p. 332). Leonard suggests that a father who ignores or rejects his daughter may contribute to her remaining at a phallic, masculine-identified, phase of development, because in this way the daughter hopes to receive the love of both parents: the mother's love because the daughter is like the father whom the mother loves; the father's love because the daughter has become the boy he once was or the son he wished for.

Some psychoanalytic theorists have emphasized that sex role development begins before the Oedipal period and have pointed to the emergence of the girl's feminine behavior patterns by the time she is 2 or 3 years old (Horney, 1933); Mächtlinger, 1976, Stoller, 1968). In fact, Kleeman (1971a, 1971b) and Green (1974) stressed that the dynamics of the father–daughter relationship can stimulate or disrupt the girl's feminine development even during the first year of her life.

Such learning theorists as Mowrer (1950) and Sears (1957) focused on the importance of parental nurturance in the rewarding of the child's sex-appropriate behaviors. They hypothesized that the child becomes strongly dependent on the parents for supplying nurturance and learns to perform those behaviors that the parents reward. Learning theorists do not generally attach special significance to the father–daughter relationship. However, to the extent that the father has the ability to reward particular behaviors, it can be argued that he is a significant influence on his daughter's personality development. Paternal reinforcement of the girl's attempts to emulate her mother's behavior and the father's general approval of the mother's behavior seem particularly important.

Parsons (1955, 1958) emphasized the role of the father in feminine development. He viewed the mother as very influential in the child's general personality development, but not as significant as the father in a child's sex role functioning. He emphasized that the mother does not vary her role as a function of the sex of the child as much as the father does. The father is supposed to be the principal transmitter of culturally-based conceptions of masculinity and femininity. Johnson (1963) stressed that the mother has a primarily expressive relationship with both boys and girls, whereas the father rewards his male and female children differently, encouraging instrumental behavior in his son and expressive behavior in his daughter. For example, the father's flirtatious and pampering behavior is expected to elicit affection and docility in his daughter.

There has been a marked tendency in the literature to define femininity in negative terms and/or as the opposite of masculinity stressing passivity and dependency (Biller, 1971). Traditional femininity has often been found to be negatively associated with adjustment (Bardwick, 1971; Johnson, 1963). But since a focus of the present discussion is on ways in which the father can facilitate his daughter's sex role competence, it is relevant to analyze the elements of femininity that are related to psychological adjustment rather than maladjustment. It is meaningful to define feminine behavior in positive terms.

For example, femininity in social interaction can be related to skill in interpersonal communication, expressiveness, warmth, and sensitivity to the needs of others (Biller, 1971; Biller & Weiss, 1970).

Femininity, according to the current definition, is based on a positive feeling about being female and a particular patterning of interpersonal behavior. Whether a woman enjoys housework or chooses a career should not be used as the ultimate criterion in assessing her femininity. Women who possess both positive feminine and positive masculine characteristics and secure sex role orientations are most able to actualize their potential. Women who have pride in their femininity and are independent and assertive as well as nurturant and sensitive are likely to achieve interpersonal and creative fulfillment (Biller, 1971, 1974c; Biller & Meredith, 1974).

Paternal Differentiation

The girl's feminine development is greatly influenced by how the father differentiates his "masculine" role from her "feminine" role and what type of behavior he considers appropriate for his daughter. Mussen and Rutherford (1963) found that fathers of highly feminine girls encouraged their daughters more in sex-typed activities than fathers of unfeminine girls did. These investigators suggested that masculine fathers who actively encourage and appreciate femininity in girls are particularly able to facilitate their daughters' sex-role development. In their study with nursery school children, Sears et al. (1965) reported a significant correlation between girls' femininity and their fathers' expectations of their participation in feminine activities.

In an examination of the familial antecedents of sex role behavior, Heilbrun (1965b) concluded that fathers are more proficient than mothers in differentiating between their male and female children. He emphasized that "fathers are more capable of responding expressively than mothers are of acting instrumentally . . . that fathers systematically vary their sex role as they relate to male and female offspring" (p. 796). He found that daughters who perceive themselves as feminine, as well as sons who perceive themselves as masculine, are likely to view their fathers as masculine.

Goodenough's (1957) results support the view that fathers influence their children's sex role development more than mothers do. Focusing on the influence of the parents in determining the social interests of nursery school children, she learned that "the father has a greater interest in sex differences than the mother and hence exerts stronger influence in general sex-typing" (p. 321); for example, there was much more paternal encouragement for girls to develop skills in social interactions. Strong paternal emphasis on sex role differentiation was also noted in a study by Aberle and Naegele (1952). Differences in parent–child interactions are a function of the sex of the child as well as of the sex of the parent (e.g., Bronfenbrenner, 1961; Rothbart & Maccoby, 1966).

Langlois and Downs' (1980) results suggest that fathers are more likely to consistently reward both girls' and boys' play with same sex toys as well as to punish play with cross-sex toys than are mothers. In this carefully planned laboratory analog study with nursery school children, fathers generally seemed to exert more consistent and vigorous pressure for sex-typed play behaviors than either mothers or peers did. As Langlois and Downs noted, previous investigations in which parent–child interactions were observed directly had not, when taken together, provided clearcut evidence for differential parental treatment of sex-typed behaviors (Fagot, 1974, 1978; Margolis & Patterson, 1975; Smith & Daglish, 1977; Tauber, 1979).

Even with infants, fathers appear to be more influenced by the sex of the child than mothers do. They tend to play more with infant sons than with infant daughters, particularly after the first birthday (Lamb 1977). Gentle cuddling is more frequent with infant daughters whereas rough and tumble activities are more common with sons (Biller, 1974c; Lamb, 1976). Some data suggest that fathers are more likely to accept a temperamentally "difficult" male infant but tend to withdraw from a female infant who presents similar problems (Rendina & Dickerchield, 1976). There is also evidence that fathers of preschool and elementary school age children are more likely to be patient and tolerant with highly active sons than with highly active daughters (Buss, 1981).

Tasch (1952, 1955), interviewing the fathers of boys and girls to learn about their conceptions of the paternal role, reported much evidence of paternal differentiation in terms of the sex of the child. Fathers viewed their daughters as more delicate and sensitive than their sons. Fathers used physical punishment more frequently with their sons than with their daughters. Fathers tended to define household tasks in terms of sex-appropriateness. For example, they expected girls to iron and wash clothes and babysit for siblings, whereas boys were expected to be responsible for taking out the garbage and helping their fathers in activities involving mechanical and physical competence. Fathers often have unfortunately rigid sex-role stereotypes, and in their zeal to "feminize" females, they actively discourage the development of intellectual and physical competence in their daughters (Biller & Meredith, 1974).

Hetherington, Cox, and Cox's (1978) data further suggest that in intact families fathers play a more important role in the development of femininity in young girls than mothers do. For example, the fathers of extremely feminine 4-to 6-year-old girls were generally highly masculine in their sex role preferences, liked women, and reinforced feminine behaviors in their daughters. These fathers were nurturant with their daughters and actively involved with them, but also somewhat restrictive and controlling. In contrast, among the maternal variables, only maternal warmth was related to the girls' femininity, the other variables appearing to have no direct impact of the sex-typing of daughters. Girls who displayed a positive "androgyny" in their sex-typed behavior seemed to be influenced by the behavior of both parents: Their fathers were warm, had positive views toward females, and consistently encouraged independence and achievement; their mothers were likely to be working and also encouraged independence. Parental encouragement of independence and achievement and a lack of rigid restrictiveness does seem especially important if young girls are going to develop competence in intellectual and physical endeavors (Biller, 1974c; Biller & Meredith, 1974).

Nevertheless, the child is not merely a passive recipient of familial and sociocultural influences. As stressed in earlier sections of this chapter, the child's constitutional predispositions can play a very important part in influencing parent–child and environmental interactions. For example, the young girl who is temperamentally responsive to social interactions and is very attractive may make it especially easy for her father to encourage her positive feminine development. If a girl facially and physically resembles a highly feminine mother, the father is likely to treat her as female. The girl who is physically large and unattractive, however, may be perceived as unfeminine by her father. The father may reject his daughter if she does not fit his conception of the physical characteristics of femininity. If the father does not have a son and his daughter is particularly vigorous and well-coordinated, he may tend to treat her as if she were a boy (Biller, 1971, 1974c).

Personal and Social Adjustment

When the father is not involved in the family, his daughter is likely to have problems in her sex role and personality development. Hoffman (1961) found that girls from mother-dominant homes had difficulty relating to males and were disliked by boys. Hetherington (1965) did not, however, find a clear-cut association between parental dominance and girl's sex role preferences, although girls with dominant fathers were much more likely to imitate them and to be similar to them than girls with dominant mothers were. Other studies are also consistent with the supposition that paternal dominance is less influential in girls than it is in boys (Biller, 1969b; Hetherington & Frankie, 1967).

My studies suggest that feminine development is facilitated if the mother is seen as a generally salient controller of resources (Biller, 1969b). Kindergarten-age girls perceived their fathers as more competent and more as decision makers, their mothers more as limit setters, and both parents as similar in nurturance. I found a subgroup of girls whose femininity scores were low and who perceived their mothers more as decision makers and limit setters but not particularly nurturant or competent. In most cases at least a moderate level of paternal involvement in decision making seemed important in the girls feminine development.

Zung and Biller (1972) reported data indicating that very strong maternal control and dominance hampers girls' as well as boys' personality development. We noted that high maternal control and intrusiveness was associated with sex role conflict and anxiety among elementary school girls. For girls the optimal level of paternal dominance may be moderate, allowing the mother to be viewed also as a "salient controller of resources" but in a general context of paternal involvement.

An investigation by Fish and Biller (1973) suggests that the father plays a particularly important role in the girl's personality adjustment. College females' perceptions of their relationships with their fathers during childhood were assessed by means of an extensive family background questionnaire. Subjects who perceived their fathers as having been very nurturant and positively interested in them scored high on the Adjective Check List personal adjustment scale. In contrast, subjects who perceived their fathers as having been rejecting scored very low on the personal adjustment measure. Findings from other investigations have also pointed to the influence of positive paternal involvement in girls' interpersonal adjustment (e.g., Baumrind & Black, 1967; Torgoff & Dreyer, 1961).

Block's (1971) analysis of data collected from the Berkeley Longitudinal Study highlights the importance of both the father–daughter and father–mother relationships in the quality of female personality functioning. For example, women who were best adjusted as adults grew up in homes with two positively involved parents. Their mothers were described as affectionate, personable, and resourceful and their fathers as warm, competent, and firm. A second group of relatively well-adjusted females came from homes with extremely bright, capable, and ambitious mothers but rather passive yet warm fathers. In contrast, poorly adjusted females were likely to have been reared in homes where either one or both parents were very inadequate. Even though they represented a wide range of personality adaptations, the poorly adjusted women were likely to have come from homes where there was little opportunity to view a positive father–mother relationship.

Block, von der Lippe, and Block's (1973) study also helps to convey some of the complexity of the associations between parental behavior and later personality functioning. These investigators studied groups of subjects who differed in terms of their femininity and socialization scores on the California Psychological Inventory.

Highly feminine, highly socialized women were described as fitting comfortably into the culturally-expected role for females. They were described as conservative, conventional, dependable, and docile. However, this picture was not completely tranquil, since interviewers frequently perceived vulnerability, indecision, and personal dissatisfaction within the group. The women appeared to come from family-centered environments and have particularly close, warm, and sharing relationships with their mothers. Their mothers seemed to typify a positive adjustment to the stereotypic feminine role. No distinctive picture of the father seemed to emerge from this group. (I would speculate that a relatively passive father who reinforced stereotyped feminine behavior could contribute easily to such overly conforming behavior.)

The highly feminine, less socialized females seemed to resemble the highly masculine, less socialized males in many ways. They were narcissistic and hedonistic. They seemed to have unstable marital relationships similar to their mothers, and they had very inadequate and rejecting mothers. Their relationships with their fathers were stronger but appeared to have been overly seductive and may have prematurely stimulated these females into early sexual experiences. (The investigators noted that this group was particularly attractive. I would emphasize that their appearance may have had a strong impact of their parents. For example, a very attractive daughter can exacerbate an insecure mother's anxiety about herself and increase the probability of seductive behavior on the part of the father.)

The less feminine, highly socialized women conveyed a relaxed, poised, and outgoing appearance and generally seemed to be the most well-adjusted group. They were viewed as conservative and not at all introspective. Their family backgrounds seemed stable, affectionate, and comfortable. Their fathers were described as warm and accepting, and their mothers appeared to be oriented toward rationality, achievement, and intellectual attainment.

The less feminine, less socialized women appeared to be assertive, critical, and rebellious. (As with the highly feminine, less socialized group, they seemed to be unhappy with life, but they expressed their displeasure in a much different manner.) They were aggressively insistent on their autonomy and independence and communicated decisiveness and competence. These women came from very conflicted and inadequate backgrounds. Their mothers appeared to be neurotic, vulnerable, unhappy, and generally interpersonally incompetent. Their fathers were hard driving and status oriented. They were uninvolved with their families, and they tended to reject their daughters.

The most well-adjusted females in the longitudinal study by Block et al. (1973) tended to come from homes in which both parents had been positively involved with them. Their fathers were described as warm and accepting, and their mothers appeared to be oriented toward rationality, achievement, and intellectual attainment. A variety of complex family patterns emerged among the less adjusted females, but it was clear that few if any had family backgrounds marked by a combination of a compatible father–mother relationship and a positively involved father.

Compared to females from father-present homes, females from father-absent homes appear more likely to have difficulties in interacting with males and in forming positive, long-term heterosexual relationships (e.g. Biller, 1974c; Hetherington, 1972). Data concerning the social and sexual relationships of father-absent females is reviewed im Chapter 14.

Marital and Sexual Relationships

Many women choose to pursue a full-time career rather than marriage because of very realistic factors such as self-fulfillment and economic need. The choice of a career, however, is sometimes motivated by a fear of marriage. Unmarried career women often have much underlying sex role conflict (Levin, 1966). In Rushing's (1964) study of adolescents, girls who reported satisfactory relationships with their fathers were less likely to give priority to a career than those who had unsatisfactory relationships with their fathers. When a girl is continually frustrated in her interactions with her father, she may develop a negative attitude toward close relationships with men and marriage. White (1959) compared the self-concepts and familial backgrounds of women whose interests focused on marriage and childrearing with those whose interests revolved around a career. More of the women interested in marriage appeared to have close relationships with both parents and to be comfortable in their self-concepts. More of the women interested in careers came from homes in which the father had died or in which there was inadequate parent–child communication.

Of course, one problem with such studies is that they do not include a group of women interested both in careers and in marriage and childrearing. Women who can comfortably pursue their occupational interests and develop their intellectual competence as well as be successful wives and mothers are more likely to have come from homes in which both parents were positively involved with their children.

Lozoff's (1974) findings, from a study of upper middle class individuals strongly suggest that father–daughter relationships are crucial in the development of women who are successful in both their heterosexual relationships and in their creative, professional endeavors. Such women had brilliant fathers who were personally secure, vital, and achievement-oriented. The fathers treated their children with much respect. They valued their daughters' basic femininity, but at the same time they encouraged and expected them to develop their competencies without any infringement of sex role stereotypes. There was much compatibility between their fathers and mothers and the women developed positive identifications with both parents and comfortable feminine sex role orientations. Other data also indicate that women who have achieved a high level of success in various intellectual and occupational endeavors are very likely to have had a strong relationship with fathers who accepted their femininity but expected them to be persistent and competent (Biller, 1974c). A second group of women that Lozoff described also were autonomous but were in much personal conflict. Their fathers tended to be aloof, perfectionistic and self-disciplined. They had very high expectations for their daughters but did not provide enough emotional support for them to develop a solid self-confidence. A third group of women who were very low in autonomy also came from econonmically privileged but highly sex-typed family situations. The father in such a family seemed to offer his daughter little encouragement for intellectual competence, leaving her socialization mainly up to his wife.

Findings from the Block et al. study (1973) suggest how difficult it is for a female to get the necessary family support to develop into a well-rounded, secure, and competent adult. It is striking that few fathers tended to be adequately involved with their daughters and to encourage both a positive feminine self-concept and instrumental competence. Again, many of these problems seem associated with overly rigid sex typing and a negative definition of feminine behavior. Gradually increasing flexibility in sex roles should lead to more and more women having a positive, feminine self-concept as well as a wide range of competencies and a successful, fulfilling career (Biller & Meredith, 1974).

Other data reveal the long-term consequences that the father–daughter relationship can have on women's marital adjustment. In Winch's (1949, 1950) questionnaire study of college students, females who had long-term romantic attachments reported closer relationships with their fathers than females who did not have serious heterosexual involvements. Luckey (1960) reported that women who were satisfied with their marriages perceived their husbands as more similar to their fathers than women who were not satisfied with their marriages did. The female's ability to have a successful marriage is increased when she has experienced a warm, affectionate relationship with a father who has encouraged her positive feminine development. In questionnaire studies with female students we found a strong association between the students' perceived relationships with their fathers during childhood and their marital adjustments. Divorce, separation, and unhappy marriages were much higher among women reporting that they had had absent fathers or poor or very infrequent interactions with them (Biller, 1974c).

Fisher (1973) presented evidence that paternal deprivation in early childhood is associated with infrequent orgasms among married women. He and his coworkers studied the sexual feelings and fantasies of almost 300 middle-class married women. The women were well-educated volunteers, most of them married to graduate students and in their early and middle 20s. An extensive array of assessment procedures, including interviews, questionnaires, and projective techniques, was used. The limited representatives of Fisher's sample could be questioned, but his results do seem consistent with other data about the father's general impact on the female's sexual development.

A central theme emerging from the low-orgasmic women was that they lacked meaningful relationships with their fathers. There was a high incidence of early loss and of frequent separation from the father among the low-orgasmic group. These women were more preoccupied with fear of loss of control than high-orgasmic women were, and this was associated with their lack of security and lack of trust in their fathers during childhood.

Questionnaire data revealed that the lower a woman's orgasmic capacity, the more likely she was to report that her father treated her in a laissez-faire manner. Low-orgasmic women described uninvolved fathers who did not have well-defined expectations or rules for their daughters. They also recalled much physical and psychological father absence during early childhood. In contrast, high-orgasmic women were more likely to perceive their fathers as having had definite and demanding expectations and a concern for their enforcement. Fisher continually emphasized that his findings revealed that the father is much more important than the mother in the development of orgasmic adequacy in females.

Inappropriate or inadequate fathering seems to be a major factor in the development of homosexuality in females as well as in males. Bené (1965) reported that female homosexuals felt that their fathers were weak and incompetent. The homosexual women were more hostile toward and afraid of their fathers than the heterosexual women were. Kaye et al. (1967), analyzing background data on homosexual women in psychoanalysis, discovered that the fathers of the homosexual women (as compared to the fathers of women in a heterosexual control group) tended to be puritanical, exploitative, and feared by their daughters as well as possessive and infantalizing. They also presented evidence that female homosexuality is associated with rejection of femininity early in life. In another study, lesbians described their fathers as less involved and affectionate than heterosexual women did (Gundlach & Reiss, 1968). In general the lesbians portrayed their fathers as acting like strangers toward them. Other researchers have found that females who feel devalued and rejected by their fathers are more likely to become homosexual than females whose fathers are warm and accepting are (e.g., Hamilton, 1929; West, 1967).

College-age, well-educated female homosexuals were recruited by their friends in a study by Thompson et al. (1973). Compared to a control group of female heterosexuals, the female homosexuals indicated that they were less accepting of their fathers and their femininity during early childhood. There was also some evidence that they perceived their fathers as more detached, weak, and hostile toward them. In general, available research has suggested that inadequate fathering is more of a factor in the development of female homosexuality than inadequate mothering is. Note also the general similarity in negative father–child relations among female and male homosexuals.

Inadequate fathering makes the child more vulnerable to difficulties in sex role and sexual development, but again it is only one of many factors that determine the quality of the individual's adjustment. Other facets of family functioning and the child's constitutional and sociocultural background must be considered if there is to be a better understanding of the influence of the father–child relationship on the sex role development process.

Some interesting preliminary data presented by Green (1978) do not support the notion that homosexual and/or transsexual parents are likely to have children who model their behavior. For instance, a child who has a homosexual parent does not seem particularly likely to become homosexual; however, longitudinal data may indicate that children with homosexual parents are more likely than children with heterosexual parents to develop certain difficulties in sex role and sexual functioning. In any case, it is certainly relevant to note that most homosexuals have heterosexual parents and that the sexual inclination and sexual functioning of the parents *per se* does not appear to be as important in the child's sex role development as the quality of parent–parent and parent–child relationships does.

SUMMARY AND OVERVIEW

Recent findings indicate the need to modify traditional views that the infant's attachment is usually exclusively and primarily with the mother and that the father does not become an important socialization agent for the child until postinfancy. A multidimensional perspective is helpful in understanding ways in which paternal behavior, as well as other family, constitutional, and sociocultural factors, influence the child's sex role development.

It is important to emphasize that the father's contribution to sex role development may not be relevant only in directly understanding individual differences in various aspects of children's masculinity and feminity *per se*, but also in analyzing many dimensions of cognitive, emotional, and social functioning. For example, the impact of the father of the child's sex role orientation, preference, and adoption may influence his or her perceptions of various types of cognitive tasks and social situations. Sex role functioning may mediate the individual's behavior in many different environmental and social interactions. The role of the father as a representative of social reality and a judge of sex-appropriate behavior as well as a companion and playmate can have far-reaching implications for the child's development.

There are data indicating that paternal masculinity, paternal nurturance, and paternal limit setting can be important factors in the masculine development process. However, taken separately, no one of these factors seems sufficient to ensure that the boy will become masculine. A boy can have a masculine father who is not very involved with his family. His father could be nurturant but not a very effective or competent model. The father can be very masculine and set limits but not have developed a basic affectionate relationship with his son.

A warm relationship with a father who is himself secure in his masculinity is an important factor in the boy's masculine development. Boys who have punitive, rejecting fathers or passive, ineffectual fathers generally have less adequate sex role functioning than boys who have interested, nurturant fathers who play a salient and decisive role in family interactions.

Fathers more than mothers vary their behavior as a function of the sex of the child, and fathers appear to play an especially significant role in encouraging their daughters' feminine development. The father's acceptance and reinforcement of his daughter's positive femininity greatly facilitates the development of her self-concept, but a negative or overly rigid view of femininity can hamper her social and sexual development.

Interaction with a masculine and competent father provides a girl with basic experiences that she can generalize in her relationships with other males. Females who have had positive relationships with their fathers are more likely to obtain satisfaction in their heterosexual relationships and to achieve happiness in social and sexual relationships as well as in occupational and career endeavors.

Other facets of family functioning, however, and the child's constitutional and sociocultural background must be considered if a thorough understanding of the influence of the father–child relationship is to be achieved. The father–mother relationship seems to have much impact on the child's personality development. Chronic marital conflict and inappropriate husband–wife interaction can greatly distort the child's view of heterosexual interactions. For example, the girl may learn very unsatisfactory patterns of interacting with males or to avoid close relationships with males. If the father and mother mutually satisfy and value each other, however, the child is much better able to learn effective interpersonal skills.

The optimal situation for the child is to have both an involved mother and involved father. The child is then exposed to a wider degree of adaptive characteristics. Children who are both well-mothered and well-fathered are likely to have positive self-concepts and a comfort about their biological sexuality. They feel good about being male or female and have a pride in their basic sex role orientation. They are comfortable with themselves and their sexuality and are able to be relatively flexible in their interests and responsiveness to others. Security in sex role orientation gives the child more of an opportunity to develop in an actualized way. Children who are paternally deprived, however, are more likely either to take a defensive posture of rigid adherence to cultural sex role standards or to avoid expected gender-related behaviors.

Perhaps the most crucial factor for the child in the intact home is the overall impact of the father–mother model of interaction. The quality of communication, respect, and cooperation between the father and mother has a strong effect on the child's developing conceptions of male–female relationships and the overall quality of his or her sex role functioning. If we are to understand parent–child influences, we have to consider the relative qualities of the parents vis-á-vis one another; we have to grapple with the gestalt of father–mother functioning as it appears to the child. Studying father–child and mother–child relationships in a vacuum may give us only a distorted view of the influence of different parenting styles. Furthermore, we need to consider the impact of different dyadic relationships and other dimensions of family functioning. How is the quality of the father–mother and father–child relationship associated with variations in the mother–child relationship? And, of course, it is important to analyze father–mother–child–sibling relationships. For example, children seem to be particularly influenced by their perceptions of differential parental treatment toward siblings.

A shortcoming of most of the studies discussed in this chapter is that data sources were not independent. In many of the studies both the father–child relationship and the son's or daughter's sex role development were assessed from the child's responses. In other studies, information about the father–child relationship was gathered from maternal reports. Fathers should be included in data assessment. More direct observation of father–mother–child interaction is needed if the father's impact on the child's development is to be better understood. In particular, researchers should take into account the child's characteristics (including appearance, temperament, and cognitive level) in their analyses of family interaction and sex role functioning. A longitudinal perspective considering the impact of various combinations of factors at different stages in the child's life could contribute much to our understanding of sex role and personality development.

REFERENCES

Aberle, D. F., & Naegele, F. D. Middle-class fathers' occupational role and attitude toward children. *American Journal of Orthopsychiatry*, 1952, **22**, 366–378.

Alkire, A. A. Social power and communication within families of disturbed and nondisturbed preadolescents. *Journal of Personality and Social Psychology*, 1969, **13**, 335–349.

Altucher, N. Conflict in sex identification in boys. Unpublished doctoral dissertation, University of Michigan, 1957.

Apperson, L. B., & McAdoo, W. G., Jr. Parental factors in the childhood of homosexuals. *Journal of Abnormal Psychology,* 1968, **73**, 201–206.

Bandura, A. *Principles of behavior modification.* New York: Holt, Rinehart, & Winston, 1969.

Bandura, A., & Walters, R. H. *Adolescent aggression: A study of the influence of child-rearing practices and family interrelationships.* New York: Ronald Press, 1959.

Bardwick, J. M. *Psychology of women.* New York: Harper and Row, 1971.

Barry, W. A. Marriage research and conflict: An integrative review. *Psychological Bulletin,* 1970, **73**, 41–55.

Baumrind, D. Child rearing practices anteceding three patterns of preschool behavior. *Genetic Psychology Monographs,* 1967, **78**, 43–88.

Baumrind, D., & Black, A. E. Socialization practices associated with dimensions of competence in preschool boys and girls. *Child Development,* 1967, **38**, 291–327.

Bell, R. Q., & Harper, L. V. *Child effects on adults.* Hillsdale, N. J.: Erlbaum, 1977.

Belsky, J. Early human experience: A family perspective. *Developmental Psychology,* 1981, **17**, 3–23.

Bem, S. L. Theory and measurement of androgyny: A reply to the Pedhazur-Tetenbaum and Locksley-Colten critiques. *Journal of Personality and Social Psychology,* 1979, **37**, 1047–1054.

Bené, E. On the genesis of female homosexuality. *British Journal of Psychiatry,* 1965, **3**, 815–821.

Benson, L. *Fatherhood: A sociological perspective.* New York: Random House, 1968.

Bieber, I., et al. *Homosexuality: A psychoanalytic study.* New York: Basic Books, 1962.

Biller, H. B. A multiaspect investigation of masculine development in kindergarten boys. *Genetic Psychology Monographs,* 1968, **76**, 89–139.

Biller, H. B. Father dominance and sex-role development in kindergarten-age boys. *Developmental Psychology,* 1969, **1**, 87–94 (a).

Biller, H. B. Maternal salience and feminine development in young girls. *Proceedings of the 77th Annual Convention of the American Psychological Association,* 1969, **4**, 259–260 (b).

Biller, H. B. *Father, child, and sex role.* Lexington, Mass.: Heath, 1971.

Biller, H. B. Sex role uncertainty and psychopathology. *Journal of Individual Psychology,* 1973, **29**, 24–25.

Biller, H. B. Paternal and sex role factors in cognitive and academic functioning. In J. K. Cole, & R. Dienstbier (Eds.), *Nebraska Symposium on Motivation, 1973.* Lincoln: University of Nebraska Press, 1974.

Biller, H. B. Paternal deprivation, cognitive functioning and the feminized classroom. In A. Davids (Ed.), *Child personality and psychopathology: Current Topics,* Vol. 1. New York: Wiley, 1974.

Biller, H. B. *Paternal deprivation,* Lexington, Mass.: Heath, 1974 (c).

Biller, H. B. The father–child relationship: Some crucial issues. In V. Vaughn, & B. Brazelton (Eds.), *The Family—Can it be saved?* Year Book Medical Publishers, 1976, pp. 69–76 (a).

Biller, H. B. The father and personality development: Paternal deprivation and sex role development. In M. E. Lamb (ed.), *The role of the father in child development.* New York: Wiley, 1976.

Biller, H. B. Sex role learning: Some comments and complexities from a multidimensional perspective. In S. Cohen, & T. J. Comiskey (Eds.), *Child development: A study of growth processes.* Ithaca, Ill.: Peackock, 1977.

Biller, H. B. Discussion of methodologic problems in research on psycho-sexual differentiation. In R. Green, & J. Weiner (Eds.), *Methodology in Sex Research.* Rockville, Md: NIMH, 1980.

Biller, H. B., & Barry, W. Sex-role patterns, paternal similarity, and personality adjustment in college males. *Developmental Psychology, 1971,* **4,** 107.

Biller, H. B., & Borstelmann, L. J. Masculine development: An integrative review. *Merrill-Palmer Quarterly,* 1967, **13,** 253–294.

Biller, H. B., & Liebman, D. A. Body build, sex-role preference, and sex-role adoption in junior high school boys. *Journal of Genetic Psychology, 1971,* **118,** 81–86.

Biller, H. B., & Meredith, D. L. The invisible American father. *Sexual Behavior,* 1972, **2** (7), 16–22.

Biller, H. B., & Meredith, D. L. *Father power.* New York: David McKay, 1974.

Biller, H. B., & Poey, K. An exploratory comparison of sex-role related behavior in schizophrenics and nonschizophrenics. *Developmental Psychology,* 1969, **1,** 629.

Biller, H. B., & Weiss, S. The father–daughter relationship and the personality development of the female. *Journal of Genetic Psychology,* 1970, **114,** 79–93.

Biller, H. B., & Zung, B. Perceived maternal control, anxiety, and opposite sex role preference among elementary school girls. *Journal of Psychology,* 1972, **81,** 85–88.

Block, J. *Lives through time,* Berkeley: Bancroft Books, 1971.

Block, J., von der Lippe, A., & Block, J. H. Sex role and socialization: Some personality concomitants and environmental antecedents. *Journal of Consulting and Clinical Psychology,* 1973, **41,** 321–341.

Bronfenbrenner, U. The study of identification through interpersonal perception. In R. Tagiuri & L. Petrullo (Eds.), *Person perception and interpersonal behavior.* Stanford: Stanford University Press, 1958.

Bronfenbrenner, U. Freudian theories of identification and their derivatives. *Child Development,* 1960, **31,** 15–40.

Bronfenbrenner, U. Some familial antecedents of responsibility and leadership in adolescents. In L. Petrullo & B. M. Bass (Eds.), *Leadership and interpersonal behavior.* New York: Holt, Rinehart, & Winston, 1961.

Bronson, W. C. Dimensions of ego and infantile identification. *Journal of Personality,* 1959, **27,** 532–545.

Burton, R. V., & Whiting, J. W. M. The absent father and cross-sex identity. *Merrill-Palmer Quarterly*, 1961, **7**, 85–95.

Buss, D. M. Predicting parent-child interactions from children's activity level. *Developmental Psychology*, 1981, **17**, 59–65.

Chang, J., & Block, J. A study of identification in male homosexuals. *Journal of Consulting Psychology*, 1960, **24**, 307–310.

Coopersmith, S. *The antecedents of self-esteem*. San Francisco: Freeman, 1967.

Distler, L. S. Patterns of parental identification: An examination of three theories. Unpublished doctoral dissertation, University of California, Berkeley, 1964.

Eron, L. D., Walder, L. O., Toigo, R., & Lefkowitz, M. M. Social class, parental punishment for aggression, and child aggression. *Child Development*, 1963, **34**, 849–867.

Evans, R. B. Childhood parental relationships of homosexual men. *Journal of Consulting and Clinical Psychology*, 1969, **33**, 129–135.

Fagot, B. I. Sex differences in toddlers' and parental reaction. *Developmental Psychology*, 1974, **10**, 554–558.

Fagot, B. I. The influence of sex of child on parental reactions to toddler children. *Child Development*, 1978, **49**, 459–465.

Fenichel, O. *The psychoanalytic theory of neurosis*, New York: Norton, 1945.

Ferreira, A. J., Winter, W. D., & Poindexter, E. J. Some interactional variables in normal and abnormal families. *Family Process*, 1966, **5**, 60–75.

Fish, K. D., & Biller, H. B. Perceived childhood paternal relationships and college females' personal adjustment. *Adolescence*, 1973, **8**, 415–420.

Fisher, S. F. *The female orgasm: Psychology, physiology, fantasy*. New York: Basic Books, 1973.

Freedheim, D. K., & Borstelmann, L. J. An investigation of masculinity and parental role-patterns. *American Psychologist*, 1963, **18**, 339 (Abstract).

Gassner, S., & Murray, E. J. Dominance and conflict in the interactions between parents of normal and neurotic children. *Journal of Abnormal Psychology*, 1969, **74**, 33–41.

Goodenough, E. W. Interest in persons as an aspect of sex differences in the early years. *Genetic Psychology Monographs*, 1957, **55**, 287–323.

Gray, S. W. Perceived similarity to parents and adjustment. *Child Development*, 1959, **30**, 91–107.

Green. R. *Sexual identity conflict in children and adults*. New York: Basic Books, 1974.

Green, R. Sexual identity of 37 children raised by homosexual or transsexual parents. *American Journal of Psychiatry*, 1978, **6**, 692–697.

Gundlach, R. H. Childhood parental relationships and the establishment of gender roles of homosexuals. *Journal of Consulting and Clinical Psychology*, 1969, **33**, 136–139.

Gundlach, R. H., & Reiss, B. F. Self and sexual identity in the female: A study of female homosexuals. In B. F. Reiss (Ed.), *New directions in mental health*. New York: Grune and Stratton, 1968.

Hamilton, C. V. *A research in marriage*. New York: Boni, 1929.

Heath, D. What meaning and what effects does fatherhood have on the maturing of professional men? *Merrill-Palmer Quarterly*, 1978, **24**, 265–278.

Heilbrun, A. B. Parental identification and college adjustment. *Psychological Reports*, 1962, **10**, 853–854.

Heilbrun, A. B. The measurement of identification. *Child Development*, 1965, **36**, 111–127(a).

Heilbrun, A. B. An empirical test of the modeling theory of sex-role learning. *Child Development*, 1965, **36**, 789–799 (b).

Heilbrun, A. B. Parent identification and filial sex-role behavior: The importance of biological context. In J. C. Cole, & R. Dienstbier (Eds.), *Nebraska Symposium on Motivation, 1973*. Lincoln: University of Nebraska Press, 1974.

Heilbrun, A. B., & Fromme, D. K. Parental identification of late adolescents and level of adjustment: The importance of parent-model attributes, ordinal position, and sex of child. *Journal of Genetic Psychology*, 1965, **107**, 45–59.

Helper, M. M. Learning theory and the self-concept. *Journal of Abnormal and Social Psychology*, 1955, **51**, 184–194.

Hetherington, E. M. A developmental study of the effects of sex of the dominant parent on sex-role preference, identification, and imitation in children. *Journal of Personality and Social Psychology*, 1965, **2**, 188–194.

Hetherington, E. M. Effects of father-absence on personality development in adolescent daughters. *Developmental Psychology*, 1972, **7**, 313–326.

Hetherington, E. M., & Brackbill, Y. Etiology and covariation of obstinacy, orderliness, and parsimony in young children. *Child Development*, 1963, **34**, 919–943.

Hetherington, E. M., Cox M., & Cox, R. Family interaction and the social, emotional and cognitive development of children following divorce. Paper presented at the Johnson and Johnson Conference on the Family, Washington, D. C., May 1978.

Hetherington, E. M., & Frankie, G. Effects of parental dominance, warmth, and conflict on imitation in children. *Journal of Personality and Social Psychology*, 1967, **6**, 119–125.

Hoffman, L. W. The father's role in the family and the child's peer-group adjustment. *Merrill-Palmer Quarterly*, 1961, **7**, 91–105.

Johnson, M. M. Sex-role learning in the nuclear family. *Child Development*, 1963, **34**, 319-333.

Kagan, J. Socialization of aggression and the perception of parents in fantasy. *Child Development*, 1958, **29**, 311–320.

Kaye, H. E. et al. Homosexuality in women. *Archives of General Psychiatry*, 1967, **17**, 626–634.

Kayton, R., & Biller, H. B. Sex-role development and psychopathology in adult males. *Journal of Consulting and Clinical Psychology,* 1971, **36,** 235–257.

Kelly, J. A., & Worrell, J. New formulations of sex roles and androgyny: A critical review. *Journal of Consulting and Clinical Psychology,* 1977, **45,** 1101–1115.

Kohlberg, L. A cognitive-developmental analysis of children's sex-role concepts and attitudes. In E. Maccoby (Ed.), *The development of sex differences.* Stanford, Cal.: Stanford University Press, 1966.

Lamb, M. E. (Ed.) *The role of the father in child development.* New York: Wiley, 1976.

Lamb, M. E. The development of parental preferences in the first two years of life. *Sex Roles,* 1977, **3,** 495–497.

Lamb, M. E. Paternal influences and the father's role: A personal perspective. *American Psychologist,* 1979, **34,** 938–943.

Lamb, M.E., & Lamb, J. E. The nature and importance of the father–child relationship. *Family Coordinator,* 1976, **25,** 370–386.

Langlois, J. H., & Downs, A. C. Mothers, fathers, and peers as socialization agents of sex-typed play behaviors in young children. *Child Development,* 1980, **51,** 1237–1247.

Lansky, L. M. Patterns of defence against conflict. Unpublished doctoral dissertation, University of Michigan, 1956.

Lazowick, L. M. On the nature of identification. *Journal of Abnormal and Social Psychology,* 1955, **51,** 175–183.

Lefkowitz, M.M. Some relationships between sex-role preference of children and other parent and child variables. *Psychological Reports,* 1962, **10,** 43–53.

Leighton, L. A., Stollak, G. E., & Ferguson, L. R. Patterns of communication in normal and clinic families. *Journal of Consulting and Clinical Psychology,* 1971, **36,** 252–256.

Leonard, M. R. Fathers and daughters. *International Journal of Psychoanalysis,* 1966, **47,** 325–333.

Levin, H., & Sears, R. R. Identification with parents as a determinant of doll play aggression. *Child Development,* 1956, **37,** 135–153.

Levin, R. B. An empirical test of the female castration complex. *Journal of Abnormal Psychology,* 1966, **71,** 181–188.

Locksley, A., & Colten, M. E. Psychological androgyny: A case of mistaken identity? *Journal of Personality and Social Psychology,* 1979, **37,** 1017–1031.

Lozoff, M. M. Fathers and autonomy in women. In R. B. Kundsin (Ed.), *Women and success.* New York: Morrow, 1974.

Luckey, E. B. Marital satisfaction and parental concept. *Journal of Consulting Psychology,* 1960, **24,** 195–204.

Lynn, D. B. *Parental and sex-role identification.* Berkeley: McCutchan, 1969.

Lynn, D. B. *The father: His role in child development.* Belmont, Calif.: Brooks/Cole, 1974.

Mächtlinger, V. Psychoanalytic theory: Preoedipal and oedipal phases with special reference to the father. In M. E. Lamb (Ed.), *The role of the father in child development*. New York: Wiley, 1976.

McClelland, D. C., & Watt, N. F. Sex-role alienation in schizophrenia. *Journal of Abnormal Psychology*, 1968, **73**, 226–239.

Margolin, G., & Patterson, G. R. The differential consequences provided by mothers and fathers for their sons and daughters. *Developmental Psychology*, 1975, **11**, 537–538.

Mishler, E. G., & Waxler, N. E. *Interaction in families*. New York: Wiley, 1968.

Money, J., & Ehrhardt, A. *Man and woman: Boy and girl*. Baltimore: Johns Hopkins University Press, 1972.

Mowrer, O. H. Identification: A link between learning theory and psychotherapy. In O. H. Mowrer (Ed.), *Learning theory and personality dynamics*. New York: Ronald Press, 1950.

Moulton, P. W., Burnstein, E., Liberty, D., & Altucher, N. The patterning of parental affection and dominance as a determinant of guilt and sex-typing. *Journal of Personality and Social Psychology*, 1966, **4**, 363-365.

Mussen, P. H. Some antecedents and consequences of masculine sex-typing in adolescent boys. *Psychological Monographs*, 1961, **75**, Whole No. 506.

Mussen, P. H., & Distler, L. Masculinity, identification, and father-son relationships. *Journal of Abnormal and Social Psychology*, 1959, **59**, 350–356.

Mussen, P. H., & Distler, L. Child-rearing antecedents of masculine identification in kindergarten boys. *Child Development*, 1960, **31**, 89–100.

Mussen, P. H., & Rutherford, E. E. Parent-child relationships and parental personality in relation to young children's sex role preferences. *Child Development*, 1963, **34**, 589–607.

Nash, J. The father in contemporary culture and current psychological literature. *Child Development*, 1965, **36**, 261–297.

Nash, J., & Hayes, T. The parental relationships of male homosexuals: Some theoretical issues and a pilot study. *Australian Journal of Psychology*, 1965, **17**, 35–43.

Parke, R. D. Perspectives on father-infant interaction. In J. D. Osofsky (Ed.), *The handbook of infant development*. New York: Wiley, 1979.

Parsons, T. Family structure and the socialization of the child. In T. Parsons, & R. F. Bales (Eds.), *Family, socialization and interaction process*. Glencoe, Ill.: Free Press, 1955.

Pedersen, F. A. (Ed.) *The father-infant relationship: Observational studies in the family setting*. New York: Praeger, 1980.

Payne, D. E., & Mussen, P. H. Parent-child relations and father-identification among adolescent boys. *Journal of Abnormal and Social Psychology*, 1956, **52**, 358–362.

Rendina, I., & Dickerscheid, J. D. Father involvement with first born infants. *Family Coordinator*, 1976, **25**, 373–379.

Reuter, M. W., & Biller, H. B. Perceived paternal nurturance-availability and personality adjustment among college males. *Journal of Consulting and Clinical Psychology,* 1973, **40,** 339–342.

Rothbart, M. K., & Maccoby, E. E. Parents' differential reactions to sons and daughters. *Journal of Personality and Social Psychology,* 1966, **4,** 237–243.

Rushing, W. A. Adolescent-parent relationships and mobility aspirations. *Social Forces,* 1964, **43,** 157–166.

Russell, G. The father role and its relation to masculinity, femininity, and androgyny. *Child Development,* 1978, **49,** 1174–1181.

Rychlak, J., & Legerski, A. A sociocultural theory of appropriate sexual role identification and level of personality adjustment. *Journal of Personality,* 1967, **35,** 31–49.

Saghir, M. T., & Robbins, F. *Male and female homosexuality.* Baltimore: Williams and Wilkins, 1973.

Schuham, A. I. Power relations in emotionally disturbed and normal family triads. *Journal of Abnormal Psychology,* 1970, **75,** 30–37.

Sears, P. S. Child-rearing factors related to playing of sex-typed roles. *American Psychologist,* 1953, **8,** 431 (Abstract).

Sears, R. R. Relation of early socialization experiences to self-concept and gender role in middle childhood. *Child Development,* 1970, **41,** 267–289.

Sears, R. R., Rau, L., & Alpert, R. *Identification and child rearing.* Stanford: Stanford University Press, 1965.

Shortell, J. R., & Biller, H. B. Aggression in children as a function of sex of subject and sex of opponent. *Developmental Psychology,* 1970, **3,** 143–144.

Slater, P. E. Parental behavior and the personality of the child. *Journal of Genetic Psychology,* 1962, **101,** 53–68.

Smith, P. K., & Daglish, L. Sex differences in parent and infant behavior in the home. *Child Development,* 1977, **48,** 1250–1254.

Spence, J., & Helmreich, R. L. The many faces of androgyny: A reply to Locksley and Colten. *Journal of Personality and Social Psychology,* 1979, **37,** 1032–1046.

Stoller, R. J. *Sex and gender.* New York: Science House, 1968.

Tasch, R. J. The role of the father in the family. *Journal of Experimental Education,* 1952, **20,** 319–361.

Tasch, R. J. Interpersonal perceptions of fathers and mothers. *Journal of Genetic Psychology,* 1955, **87,** 59–65.

Tauber, M. A. Sex differences in parent-child interaction styles during a free-play session. *Child Development,* 1979, **50,** 981–988.

Thompson, N. L., Schwartz, D. M., McCandless, B. R., & Edwards, D. A. Parent-child relationships and sexual identity in male and female homosexuals and heterosexuals. *Journal of Consulting and Clinical Psychology,* 1973, **41,** 120–127.

Torgoff, I., & Dreyer, A. S. Achievement inducing and independence granting synergistic parental role components: Relation to daughter's parental role orientation and level of aspiration. *American Psychologist,* 1961, **16,** 345 (Abstract).

Walters, J. (Ed.), Special issue: Fatherhood. *Family Coordinator,* 1976, **25,** 335–520.

West, D. J. Parental relationships in male homosexuality. *International Journal of Social Psychiatry,* 1959, **5,** 85–97.

West, D. J. *Homosexuality,* Chicago: Aldine, 1967.

White, B. The relationship of self concept and parental identification to women's vocational interests. *Journal of Consulting Psychology,* 1959.

White, R. W. Competence and the psychosexual stages of development. In M. R. Jones (Ed.), *Nebraska symposium on motivation,* Lincoln: University of Nebraska Press, 1959.

Winch, R. F. The relation between loss of a parent and progress in courtship. *Journal of Social Psychology,* 1949, **29,** 51–56.

Winch, R. F. Some data bearing on the Oedipus hypothesis. *Journal of Abnormal and Social Psychology,* 1950, **45,** 481–489.

Wright, B., & Tuska, S. The nature and origin of feeling feminine. *British Journal of Social Psychology,* 1966, **5,** 140–149.

CHAPTER 10

The Role of the Father
in Moral Internalization

MARTIN L. HOFFMAN

University of Michigan

This chapter discusses what is known about the role of the father in the child's internalization of moral norms. The moral norms at issue pertain to how one behaves toward others—for example, considering the feelings of others, telling the truth, keeping a promise, deceiving people, lying, stealing, betraying a trust, or inflicting physical harm. Moral norms are usually considered internalized when the person acts in accord with them even in the absence of any concern about being caught and punished for doing otherwise.

Before we can assess the impact of the father on the child's moral internalization, we need to know something about the dimensions of the father's role as well as the mechanisms by which moral internalization occurs. We can then search for connections between the two.

DIMENSIONS OF THE FATHER'S ROLE

The role of parent, father or mother, has at least four major dimensions, any of which can contribute to the child's moral development. First, by his or her words and actions the parent can serve as a model for the child. Second, the parent disciplines the child—encouraging certain behaviors, discouraging others, and giving explanations. Third, the parent is the major supplier of the child's affectional needs. Fourth, the parent serves as the connecting link between the child and the larger society—in two ways: (1) by bringing the society's demands and expectations into the home and making them real to the child; and (2) by virtue of his or her position in the larger society, conferring a certain status on the child that may be especially important when the child begins to conceive of the outside world and where he or she fits within it.

Regarding the role of fathers in particular, I find the formulation of Parsons and Bales (1955), as elaborated by Johnson (1963), to be a useful heuristic. In this model the mother has the major "expressive" role, which is to supply affection and maintain harmony in the family. The mother is thus the primary caretaker, disciplinarian, and model, especially in the child's early years. She performs this role more or less equally with boys and girls. The father is more likely to be the person who brings the society's larger "instrumental" perspectives and norms into the home, and it is from the father's position in the outside world that the child's social status derives. The father is also viewed as continuing the mother's expressive type of behavior in relation to daughters. With sons, however, the situation is different. The father behaves expressively, to be sure, but as the son gets older, the father not only communicates the outside world's instrumental norms, but he also behaves increasingly in an instrumental manner—for example, he makes rewards more contingent on performance.

The overall effect of this parental division of labor is, of course, to prepare the girl for her adult, expressive role—mother and wife—and to prepare the boy to function both in the instrumental world of work and the expressive role of father and husband. Although obviously devised for traditional society, this model can easily be modified to be in accord with current social change. Insofar as increasing numbers of women are entering the labor force—and indeed it looks as if the working mother is fast becoming the norm—we can anticipate that girls will be increasingly socialized for success in the instrumental as well as the expressive role and that mothers will be instrumental as well as expressive socializers (Hoffman, 1977). And if the male role becomes more expressive, the role of father may include a larger degree of expressive socialization than was formerly the case.

MECHANISMS OF MORAL INTERNALIZATION

Although moral internalization has long been a topic of research interest, only recently has the attempt been made to pull together the various mechanisms that have been advanced to account for it. In my most recent attempt to do this, I suggested four mechanisms, which I now summarize (Hoffman, in press).

Arousal of Deviation Anxiety

During the long period of socialization, in which one has been punished for deviant acts, painful anxiety states may become associated with these acts—that is, with the kinesthetic and perceptual cues produced by the acts as well as the cognitive cues associated with the anticipation of engaging in them. This anxiety over deviation may subsequently be avoided by inhibiting the act, even when no one else is present. The individual may thus appear to behave in an internalized manner, although he or she is actually responding in terms of a subjective fear of external sanctions. The anxiety may, however, become diffuse and detached over time from any conscious fears of detection and punishment. When this happens, the inhibition of the deviant act may be viewed as a primitive form of internalization.

This is the mechanism suggested by some social learning theorists (e.g., Mowrer, 1960; Aronfreed & Reber, 1965). It may also be the mechanism underlying the Freudian process of superego formation. In the Freudian scheme the deviant acts are specified as stemming from hostile and erotic impulses; and because of the anxiety, the child represses these impulses.

Identification

According to Freud, the child, to maintain the repression of hostile and erotic impulses, to offset punishment, and to elicit continuing affection from the parents, identifies with the parents and adopts the rules and prohibitions issued by the parents. To a large degree these reflect the norms of the larger society. Children also adopt the parents' capacity to punish themselves when they violate a prohibition or are tempted to do so—turning the hostility that was originally directed toward the parent inward. This self-punishment is experienced in guilt feelings, which are dreaded because of their intensity and resemblance to the earlier anxieties about punishment and abandonment. Children therefore try to avoid guilt by acting in accordance with incorporated parental prohibitions and erecting various mechanisms of defense against the conscious awareness of impulses to act to the contrary. These basic moral internalization processes are accomplished by about 5 to 6 years of age, and they are then worked through and solidified during the latency period—the remaining, relatively calm years of childhood. Moral internalization, then, occurs early in life, before the child is capable of complex cognitive processing of information. The moral norms consequently become part of a rigid, primarily unconscious, and often severe yet fragile impulse control system.

This process is described in detail for boys, for whom the anxiety in question is castration anxiety and the person with whom the identification takes place is the father. Thus the father is the major moral socialization agent for boys. For girls there are some differences: The anxiety in question is the anxiety over the loss of the mother's love, and the mother is the main identification figure and the main moral socializer. Furthermore, the entire process is more diffuse, and, as a result, girls are typically less morally internalized than boys.

Social learning theorists have attempted to reduce the concept of identification to the more manageable concept of the imitation of models who behave in a moral manner or are punished for behaving in a deviant manner (e.g., Stein,

1967; Walters & Parke, 1964). In the case of exposure to morally behaving models, it is assumed that the child learns by observing the model and consequently tries to behave like the model in similar future situations when the model is not present. When the child is exposed to a deviant model who is punished, it is hypothesized that the child is punished vicariously, or anticipates the same fate as the model and so avoids acting in the deviant manner. It should be noted that the latter case may be irrelevant to moral internalization, since the child may be using the punishment of the model merely as an index of what the external consequences of deviation may be.

Arousal of Empathy and Guilt

I have suggested elsewhere (Hoffman, 1975d, 1977b) that the human capacity for empathy may combine with the cognitive awareness of others and how others are affected by one's behavior, resulting in the arousal of a motive (sympathetic distress, guilt) to consider others' welfare. This motive, unlike deviation anxiety, stems directly from the individual's own internal resources rather than from external concerns about detection and punishment. The major contributing socialization experience suggested by the research (Hoffman, 1977a) is exposure to inductive discipline techniques administered by someone who also provides the child with adequate affection. Inductive discipline under these conditions helps foster the simultaneous experience both of empathy and awareness of harming another person (see especially Hoffman, in press). Reciprocal role taking, especially with peers, may also heighten the child's sensitivity to the inner states aroused in others by one's behavior: Having been in the other's place helps one to know how the other feels.

The reason for stressing the importance of discipline (Hoffman, 1975, in press) is the following. For a moral norm to affect a person's behavior, the norm must not only be internalized, but it must also be able to compete with whatever egoistic, self-serving motive is evoked in the situation. This means that the moral norm must also have motive force. The central moral conflict, then, is between the person's egoistic desire and the dictates of the moral norm—between an egoistic motive and a moral motive. The developmental question is: What past experiences result in the activation of such a moral norm? The most reasonable answer, I submit, is the child's past experiences of being faced with a similar conflict—that between personal desires and the requirements of the norm. The norm at the time was of course external to the child, embedded in some of the discipline techniques used by the parent. Although the information pertinent to moral norms may also be communicated to children by the parents' words and actions outside discipline encounters, it is only in discipline encounters that the connection is made between the moral norm, the child's egoistic desires, and the child's ongoing behavior. And it is

in discipline encounters that children have the earliest experience of being expected to control deviant actions for reasons deriving from their own active
consideration of the norm (Hoffman, in press).

Cognitive Moral Conflict and Equilibration

People may cognitively process information that is at variance with their preexisting moral conceptions and construct new views that resolve the contradiction. When they do this, they will very likely feel a special commitment to
(and in this sense internalize) the moral concepts they have been actively involved in constructing. This mechanism is assumed in Kohlberg's (1969) cognitive-developmental theory of moral development. Kohlberg, however, also
makes the additional assumptions that the contradiction is between "structural" elements of the person's moral scheme and that the person's resulting new
perspective fits into an invariant sequence. Neither assumption has support
from research. It seems to me more plausible to assume that the cognitive
process in question is instigated not by structural conflict but conflict between
the person's moral belief and the newly perceived social reality. The conflict
between morality and reality is assumed by several writers to provide the trig-
ger for moral growth in adolescence (see review by Hoffman, 1980). Erikson
(1970), for example, suggests that the adolescent may, in the face of overwhelming evidence, become disillusioned with the moral beliefs acquired in
childhood. The adolescent may then become strongly motivated to search for a
new moral belief or ideology. To the extent that the child actively constructs
such a moral ideology, feels personally bound to it, and tries to act in accord
with it, the moral ideology can be said to be internalized.

Only one of these mechanisms, identification, is intrinsically tied to a particular parent. In terms of the contribution of identification to moral internalization, fathers should be expected to be especially important for sons, far less so
for daughters. Regarding the formation of associative connections between
anxiety and the child's deviant acts, and between empathy or empathy-based
guilt and the deviant acts, there is nothing intrinsic about these mechanisms
that makes them the province of one or another parent. We know empirically,
however, that fathers do less of the disciplining, especially in the early years,
and this is true for children of both sexes. For this reason we might expect
fathers to be less important than mothers. We have no reason to believe that
either parent is especially likely to provide opportunities for resolving cognitive moral conflicts. Indeed, this mechanism may often operate outside the
home, the mediating socialization agents being peers or teachers rather than
parents. All things considered, our brief analysis of the dimensions of the parent role and the hypothesized mechanisms of moral internalization would lead

to the expectation that mothers would be important for moral internalizaton for children of both sexes and that fathers may have some additional importance for boys.

With these considerations as background, let us look at the data, beginning with those bearing on the effects of the absence of the father.

FATHER ABSENCE

Several studies have been done on the effects of father absence on moral development and aggression but in only two have important variables like social class, age, IQ, and family size been controlled. In one of these (Hoffman, 1971a) the subjects were seventh-grade white children in the Detroit metropolitan area. Several moral indices, each tapping a different aspect of the child's moral structure, were used. Three indices pertain to the degree to which the child's moral orientation is internalized: the intensity of guilt following transgression, the use of moral judgments about others that are based on moral principles rather than on external considerations, such as detection and punishment, and the tendency to accept responsibility for one's misdeeds. The other moral indices pertain to the extent to which the subjects show consideration for others, conform to the rules, express strong support for prosocial moral values, and are physically or verbally aggressive.

Guilt was assessed by responses to story completion items; internal moral judgment by modified Kohlberg-type moral dilemmas; consideration for others by peer ratings. The remaining moral indices were based on the teacher's reports of the extent to which the child engaged in the particular activities in question. The findings were that the boys from homes without fathers obtained lower scores on all the moral indices—significantly lower on internal moral judgment, guilt, acceptance of blame, prosocial moral values, and conformity to the rules. They were also rated by their teachers as significantly more aggressive than the boys who had fathers. No differences between father absence and father presence were obtained for the girls.

In the second study, which was confined to fifth- and sixth-grade boys, a variety of moral indices was also used (Santrock, 1975). Included were story-completion guilt items, Kohlberg-type moral dilemmas (not the same as those in the Hoffman study), and experimental measures of resistance to temptation and sharing. In that study, the only moral index that produced significant findings was the one based on teacher ratings: Boys without fathers were reported by their teachers as less advanced in moral development than boys with fathers. This index was derived from a factor analysis of teacher ratings of variables like guilt, consideration of others, acceptance of blame, self-criticism, self-discipline, and trust. There were no differences on any of the other moral indices.

Santrock suggests that the different findings in the two studies might be caused by cultural differences in the samples (a small West Virginia town versus a large city). I would suggest another reason for the different findings: a major difference in the operational definition of father absence and father presence in the two studies. In the study by Hoffman, the father absent group was defined as having no adult male living in the home for at least 6 months prior to the study. In the Santrock study, father absence was more specifically defined: the father had either died when the boy was 6 to 10 years old or was divorced sometime in the first 10 years of the boy's life. Santrock's father-present group, however, was defined in a far less stringent manner—that is, the father was not "absent from the home more than six months at any time." It may be assumed from this definition that many of these fathers *were* absent a good deal of the time. In Hoffman's father-present group, the father was not only present, but he had always been the subject's father and had always lived at home. Thus many of the boys with fathers in the Santrock study may not have had the kind of stable, intact home and continuing contact with their fathers over as long a period of time as their counterparts in the Hoffman study. The difference between the father-absent and father-present groups in the Santrock study may thus have been less pronounced than the difference in the Hoffman study, which could account for the different results.

Perhaps the difference in the results of the two studies should not be overly stressed. Despite the sample and design differences, the fact is that all the significant findings obtained in both studies were in the expected direction. These findings, furthermore, are buttressed by the findings in the other, less controlled studies to which I alluded earlier. In these studies (reviewed by Hoffman, 1971; Santrock, 1975) father absence was found to be associated with frequent overt aggression in boys. Father absence was not associated with a laboratory measure of resistance to temptation (Mumbauer & Gray, 1970), but that measure is questionable as a moral index (Hoffman, 1976). It seems reasonable to conclude that the absence of a father from the home does appear to have a deleterious effect on the moral development of boys. Boys without fathers are apparently more aggressive and less likely to have an internalized moral perspective than boys with fathers.

To know that the absence of a father from the home is associated with relatively low moral internalization in the child is of course not the same as knowing the process underlying this effect. The finding of low moral internalization in boys who have no fathers may reflect stress or conflict in the home rather than the effects of a missing father. And, in the case of divorce, the stress or conflict may very well have preceded the father's absence. But assuming that at least some of the diminished moral internalization is the result of the father's absence, we may ask what there is about fathers that makes their absence felt in this way. The possible influence of the low intellectual deficit or low socioeconomic status often associated with father absence (e.g., Shinn, 1978) can be ruled out, since these two variables were controlled in the studies just discussed in detail. One explanation that immediately comes to mind is that the loss of the father's influence as a socializing agent is the significant factor. As already noted, the role of the parent as socializer is complex. The parent is model, disciplinarian, and supplier of the child's affectional needs. Each of these might contribute to the child's moral internalization. Let us consider them in detail.

Discipline and Affection

There is an extensive body of research on the effect of discipline and affection on moral internalization, which I have reviewed elsewhere (Hoffman, 1970, 1976). The research indicates that moral internalization and relatively high guilt are most likely to be fostered by the frequent use of inductive discipline and the frequent expression of affection outside the discipline encounter. A moral orientation based on fear of external sanctions and low guilt is most often associated with the frequent use of power-assertive discipline and relatively little affection. These findings are rather clear-cut for mothers. In contrast, very few significant relationships have been obtained for fathers, and there is no apparent pattern among them. There is also evidence that the mother is the main disciplinarian, and it may be that any effects of the father's discipline are transient and overridden in the long run by the mother's discipline and affection pattern. In any case, it does not appear that the effects of father absence are attributable to the absence of the father's role as an administrator of discipline.

Parent Identification

Following the psychoanalytic theorizing about identification summarized earlier, two types of predictions have been made. One is that if moral attributes are acquired through identification, there should be consistency among them (e.g., moral judgments, resistance to temptation, and postransgression responses such as guilt). The other is that if a moral conscience is the product of identification, it should be related to parental discipline techniques in ways predictable from the theory—that is, it should relate positively to love withdrawal. The research is nonsupportive in both cases. The intercorrelations among the moral attributes are generally low (see reviews by Hoffman 1970b and Mischel 1970), and the moral attributes have not been found to relate to love withdrawal in any consistent manner (Hoffman 1970).

Since both types of research assume that identification is a unitary process, that is, the child adopts all parental attributes, the findings would appear to cast doubt on the unitary process notion. It is hard to believe that identification plays no role in moral development, however, since the parent is ever-present in the child's earlier years and provides the major model of social norms to which he or she is exposed. It seems more reasonable to assume that identification does play a role, though perhaps not an all-encompassing one. The investigation of this hypothesis requires independent assessment of the child's motive to identify with the parent and of the different dimensions of the child's moral structure. This has been done in only one study (Hoffman, 1971b).

The general hypotheses of this study is that children are typically motivated to emulate their parents, especially the parent of the same sex. They are also limited in their efforts to do this, however, for several reasons. First, they may lack the requisite cognitive skills, such as ability to classify and correctly infer inner states from another person's overt behavior and put themselves in the other's place. Second, not all parental attributes are communicated equally. Moral values and judgments about others may often be expressed openly, whereas certain inner states may rarely if ever be communicated in the child's presence. With the exception of an occasional apology, for example, parents typically do not evaluate their own behavior critically, not do they express guilt. They therefore do not give the child the necessary information for connecting these feelings with particular acts.

Another important factor is the strength of identification motivation needed to overcome the natural tendency to maximize pleasure and minimize pain. Why should the child, before moral internalization has taken place, adopt parental attributes that call for impulse inhibition and other forms of self-sacrifice or pain. Psychoanalytic theory handles this problem by postulating avoidance of the extremely painful state of anxiety over castration or loss of love as the ultimate motivational base for identification. Since identification is a matter of survival, the child strives to adopt all the parent's attributes, including the capacity for self-criticism and punishment. Such intense motivation seems plausible, especially in the young child, but it also seems likely that it would disrupt cognitive processes and thus interfere with the adoption of the parent's inner states and other attributes that require at least a minimum of cognitive functioning. Although motivated to acquire the parent's pain-producing attributes, the child may not be able to do so. In any case, there is evidence against this view. As noted earlier, the use of love-withdrawing discipline does not relate to the child's moral development. The nonpsychoanalytic theories stress more positive motives for identifying, such as gaining approval or acquiring parental skills and other resources helpful in attaining self-gratification (e.g., Kagan, 1958; Whiting, 1960) and thus seem ill-equipped to explain the adoption of painful states, except perhaps in societies that reward this to a greater degree than our own.

Following this line of reasoning, we expected that children motivated to identify with their parents would acquire only those moral attributes for which a clear model was provided and that did not require complex cognitive operations, pain, or self-denial. It was therefore predicted that identification motives would relate positively to accepting moral values and using them when one was called on to make moral judgments of others, but not in one's own moral encounters as reflected in guilt, self-blame, and confession following transgression. There were no expectations regarding two moral attributes—conformity to rules and consideration for others—which are visible and undemanding cognitively but require some impulse control and self-denial, since our reasoning in these cases led to contradictory predictions.

The subjects were seventh-grade children in the Detroit metropolitan area. Parent identification was measured in terms of a composite score based on the subject's expressed admiration for the parent, desire to emulate the parent, and perception of similarity to the parent. Social class and IQ were controlled. The moral indices were essentially the same as those used in the father-absence study by Hoffman cited earlier. Few significant relations were obtained, but all were positive. Father identification related to internal moral judgment in middle- and lower-class boys, rule conformity in middle-class boys and girls, and moral values in middle-class boys; mother identification related to rule conformity in middle-class boys. Guilt, confession, and acceptance of blame did not relate to identification in any of the subsamples.

It is of special interest here that this study suggests that the father's importance as an identification figure may actually exceed that of the mother, which is in striking contrast to the discipline findings summarized earlier. A similar pattern has been found in two investigations of the correlation between parents and their children, in moral judgment, and in prosocial behavior. In one of these studies (Hoffman, 1975b), the extent to which the fathers expressed prosocial moral values correlated significantly with peer ratings of prosocial behavior by their sons and daughters. For mothers the correlation was significant only in daughters. In the second study (Haan, Langer, & Kohlberg, 1976), the scores on some of Kohlberg's moral dilemmas obtained by young men in three age groups (10 to 15 years, 16 to 20 years, and 21 years and over) were found to correlate significantly with the scores obtained by their fathers. Significant correlations were also obtained between the sons' moral judgment scores and those of their mothers, but only in the two younger age groups. None of the correlations for daughters were significant.

Such correlations, it must be noted, are not necessarily the result of the child's identification with the parent. Some other process may be at work. Parents may teach moral reasoning to their children directly, for example. It is also possible that the parents may have learned from their children, rather than the reverse. This is especially likely in the study by Haan et al., in which the "children" were mainly adolescents and young adults, and many of them, especially in the older age group who demonstrated higher levels of moral reasoning, had fathers and mothers who demonstrated *lower* level reasoning.

Aside from such speculation, when we put together all the findings in the above studies it appears that under certain conditions identification with the father (perhaps to a slightly greater extent than the mother) may contribute to the acquisition of moral attributes that are visible (overt acts, moral judgments) and do not require much self-denial. Some of these attributes may be internalized in the sense that the child uses them rather than external sanctions as the criterion of right and wrong, for example, in judging the behavior of others. The research does not suggest, however, that father (or mother) identification contributes to the use of standards as an evaluative perspective from which to examine one's *own* behavior in the absence of authority—that is, to a truly internalized moral perspective.

It may be instructive to compare the effects of the father's presence or absence with the effects of identifying or not identifying with a father who is present. It was possible to make such a direct comparison in my own research since the subjects in the studies of the effects of father absence and of identification were drawn from the same, large sample. When the comparison is made (Hoffman, 1971a) it is clear that the effects of low identification with fathers who are present are quite similar although somewhat less pronounced than the effects of father absence. The main difference is that father absence is associated with low scores for guilt and acceptance of blame, whereas low father identification is not associated with these variables. Guilt and acceptance of blame, despite their limitations, are very likely the best indexes of moral internalization (which may in essence be defined as the application of standards to one's own behavior without regard to sanctions by authority) used in the study, for the following reasons. First, it seems reasonable to assume that the guilt measure, which was based on story completion responses, reflects the subject's own response to transgression, since a prerequisite for coding guilt was evidence that the subject identified with the story hero. The moral judgment measure, however, pertains to judgments of transgressions of others, and although one may "sincerely," and in that sense internally, hold the beliefs that one applies to the conduct of others, this may not indicate the reaction to one's own transgression. Furthermore, the moral values index pertains to surface acceptance of moral standards and may therefore be irrelevant to internalization. Finally, the scores for aggression and rule conformity are based on teacher ratings of behaviors that have obvious relevance to "social desirability" and may therefore reflect a proauthority orientation rather than an internally based self-control. This is apt to be less true of acceptance of blame, which, although also based on teacher ratings, involves acknowledging to authority that one has behaved in a disapproved fashion.

If our argument is correct, we may tentatively conclude that the extent of the boy's identification with his father influences the degree to which he accepts moral standards, uses them as a basis for judging right and wrong, and behaves in accord with them in the presence of authority. The presence or absence of a father also bears on these matters, but in addition it influences the entent to which the boy applies moral standards to his own behavior even in the absence of authority. These differences suggest that the lack of a paternal model may contribute to the effects of father absence, but it cannot explain why boys without fathers in the home are less likely to admit blame and feel guilty when they violate a moral norm.

What else is operating that can explain the effects of the father's absence? Earlier, I summarized the research suggesting that an internalized moral perspective may be fostered under certain conditions in discipline encounters—that is, in being criticized by another person rather than in identifying with another's self-criticism. I have also suggested that it may only be in discipline encounters that the synthesis between affective and cognitive processes necessary for moral internalization can occur (Hoffman, in press). And, finally, since the mother is the main disciplinarian (e.g., Hoffman, 1970; Lytton, 1976, 1979) and the research summarized earlier demonstrates the effects of maternal discipline, individual differences in internalization may be caused primarily by the child's contact with the mother. If father absence has an effect, then, perhaps it may be an indirect effect. That is, the absence of the father may influence the mother's behavior toward the child, which in turn results in a diminished moral internalization capability in the child.

Effects of Father Absence on Mother's Behavior

One possible factor in father absence is the necessity of the mother's taking over the father's customary role in certain interactions with the child. The father is often the ''heavy'' in discipline encounters. For example, it is well-known that fathers are generally more power-assertive than mothers (e.g., Zussman, 1978). In the absence of a father, the mother may be expected to be more power-assertive. Also contributing to increased power assertion by the mother is the likelihood that without a husband the mother is busier and more harassed, hence impatient with the child and oriented toward immediate compliance rather than long-range character goals. As a result, she may express affection less frequently and in her discipline use more power assertion and less induction—the pattern found in previous research to be associated with weak moral internalization. Furthermore, we might expect this pattern to be more pronounced with boys, who are normally more aggressive and resistant to influence than girls and may even be more so when they have no father. To test this hypothesis, we used available data from the subjects' reports of their mother's expression of affection and the discipline techniques used in several situations. These measures are described in detail elsewhere (Hoffman & Saltzstein, 1967). The findings provide partial support for the hypothesis. Boys without fathers reported that their mothers expressed less affection than boys with fathers did. There was no difference in the type of discipline reported, but is seems reasonable to assume that the paucity of affection would have an adverse effect on the boys' reactions in the discipline encounter.

Other investigators have found evidence that mothers without husbands are more power-assertive. Longabaugh (1973) reports that the mothers are more likely to "deprive their sons of resources" and "autonomy." And Santrock (1975) found that divorced mothers, but not widows, were more power-assertive with their sons than mothers with husbands were. All in all, it seems a plausible hypothesis that a greater proportion of mother–son interactions, when there is no father present in the home, must revolve around discipline encounters. It is also likely that the discipline used is more power-assertive and less inductive. But even if this is not true, the mother is apt to spend less time in affectionate interchange with her son, which may have a negative effect on his response to her discipline attempts. The absence of a father, then, may affect the child's moral internalization adversely in part through its effects on the mother's pattern of discipline and affection.

The situation for girls may be somewhat different. First of all, there is evidence that the impact of father absence in general and divorce in particular on social and emotional development is less pervasive and enduring for girls than for boys (e.g., Biller, 1974; Hetherington, Cox, & Cox, 1978). Furthermore, in our own research the findings were the reverse of those obtained for boys: Girls without fathers reported that their mothers expressed affection *more* frequently. They also report less power assertion and more induction, although these findings are nonsignificant. This pattern of findings suggests that the mother may compensate for the father's absence, but only with girls. Perhaps it is more difficult to do this with boys because of their more abrasive qualities, especially if what the mother wants is ease in running the household. This stands in contrast to the girl who is more likely to help with household chores rather than make additional trouble.

It is also likely that when the reason for the father's absence is divorce the mothers may carry a residue of resentment which is expressed toward their sons. The findings by Santrock mentioned earlier, that divorced women were more power-assertive toward their sons than widows and women with husbands were, suggests that this carry-over effect may occur.

Other Indirect Effects of Fathers

It is not only the father's absence that may effect the mother's behavior toward the child. The father's presence may also have an effect, in different ways. Consider the finding reported some time ago (Hoffman, 1963) in a lower-class Detroit sample, suggesting that women whose husbands frequently assert power toward them are likely to be power-assertive toward their preschool children. By asserting power toward their wives, these men may well have contributed negatively, though indirectly, to moral internalization in their children.

It is also possible that the presence of the father often provides a kind of backup *support* for the mother, giving her a certain amount of creditability that may increase the likelihood of the child's responding constructively to her inductions. Possibly indicative of this effect is Lytton's (1979) report in a study of 2- and 3-year-old children, that the father sometimes openly reinforced the mother's request, and when he did this the child was more apt to comply with the mother. Perhaps of even greater interest is the finding that even if the father said nothing, when he was present the children were more apt to comply in response to their mother's discipline attempts than when he was absent. Compliance, of course, is not the same as moral internalization, and we have no evidence that the discipline techniques used by the mothers in the father's presence were often inductions. So there is a limit to how far we can extrapolate these findings. It does seem plausible, however, to expect that the image of the power and authority vested in the father may increase the likelihood that the child will pay serious attention to the content of the mother's inductions. If so, the absence of this image could be a factor in the adverse effects of father absence.

FATHERS, INSTRUMENTAL ROLE DEMANDS, AND MORAL DEVELOPMENT

The research indicates that mothers are the main moral socializers for children of both sexes. The question this raises is whether this is because of the type of moral norms that have been studied. Most of the moral internalization measures—guilt, for example—pertain to the interpersonal norm against harming others in face-to-face situations, and an interpersonal morality would seem to fit in with the traditional mother's "expressive" role. If mothers, more than fathers, interact with others on the basis of feelings, if they encourage expressions of empathy and guilt, and if they strive for harmony in their relations with others, then they may be automatically socializing their children in a way that fosters the internalization of interpersonal moral norms. Fathers, however, may socialize children in a way that fosters internalization of "instrumental" moral norms. These are norms about the importance of laws, rules, and sanctions against violating them that are applied equally to all people rather than on the basis of kinship and personal sentiment; norms about the importance in institutional settings of operating on the basis of rationality and long-term objectives rather than immediate feelings; norms regarding the allocation of resources to people on the basis of objectively assessed performance rather than friendship and personal feeling.

There is no evidence that fathers socialize their children in a way that encourages them to internalize such norms or even that fathers typically have internalized such norms themselves. In the only study comparing morally internalized behavior of men and women in a noninterpersonal setting, the men were *less* likely than the women to return valuable items found in the street when no witnesses were present (Gross, 1972). Only when others were in the vicinity did the men return the items as often as the women. Perhaps more pertinent to the issue at hand are some findings, reported elsewhere (Hoffman, 1975c), that I will briefly note here. The subjects were the parents of fifth- and seventh-grade children in the Detroit area. There were no sex differences on an internal moral judgment score based on modified Kohlberg-type moral dilemmas. On a story-completion index of guilt intensity, however, the fathers in each of two independent samples obtained significantly lower scores than the mothers. Also, as was expected in view of the expressive–instrumental dichotomy discussed earlier, the fathers rated achievement and success far higher on a scale of human values then the mothers did, and they rated "going out of one's way to help others" significantly lower.

Is achievement a moral value for males? It seems reasonable that it might be, since achievement has often been thought of as part of the Protestant Ethic. If achievement were an internalized moral value, we would expect this to be demonstrated in responses to a story completion item in which the protagonist wins a lot of money in a short story writing contest by plagiarizing rather than through his own efforts. That is, we would expect internalized subjects to produce more responses involving considerable guilt and also, perhaps, responses showing concern for the person who really deserved to win the prize. The findings were that the men showed significantly less guilt and less concern for the true winner than did the women. The men also showed significantly more fear over getting caught and in many instances their responses dwelled on the subtle ways in which the protagonist might be trapped.

Further research is obviously needed, but the findings suggest the tentative conclusion that achievement striving is not only more prevalent in males but may also be more the result of an egoistic motive than an internalized moral norm. This may not be too surprising given phenomena like the Watergate affair suggesting that even men who are trained in the law may bend it toward their own egoistic ends. Consider also the findings in a business survey in which most executives agreed with the statement that businessmen "would violate a code of ethics whenever they thought they could avoid detection" (Baumhart, 1961). And, more recently, the experience of a reporter who posed as an accident victim and went to 13 New York attorneys with a fabricated case that could produce a large legal fee. The reporter found that five of the lawyers "offered. . . to engage in the felony of aiding and abetting perjury." Said one lawyer, "As it stands, you don't have a case. But if you're asking me to help fabricate a story, I can do this. All we have to do is bend the facts a little . . . Everybody lies under oath" (Berentson, 1980).

This is not to say that fathers are by nature any less moral than mothers.[1] But the pressures on males to achieve, compete, and succeed, which increases with age owing largely to traditional work demands and the tendency that still exists in our society to define masculinity largely in terms of success, may often conflict with the moral norms that males may have internalized in childhood. Furthermore, these pressures may often be powerful enough to override the moral norms and dull the edges of one's sensitivity to the needs of others. The instrumental world, in short, may often operate as a corrupting influence on the morality of males. It is important to know if the same thing will happen to women as more of them assume an instrumental role in society and if the same thing does happen, what the implications will be for the moral socialization of children in the future.

To the question, do fathers socialize children to internalize instrumental moral norms, the answer at this point would appear to be "no." Fathers may indeed be especially important in socializing children for achievement—there is some evidence for this (e.g., Block, Block & Harrington, 1974)—but it may have nothing to do with moral socialization. Indeed, achievement socialization may at times serve as an obstacle to moral socialization (Burton, 1972; Pearlin, 1967). We are thus left with a tentative conclusion that may also serve as a working hypothesis for future research: There may be a division of labor in the home, in which mothers are the primary socializers in moral internalization and fathers are the primary socializers in a more egoistic achievement motivation.

---

[1]The following argument could be made, however, suggesting that there may be a biological basis for males being less moral than females, at least regarding the kind of interpersonal morality discussed here. First, there is evidence that empathy may provide a biologically based motive for an interpersonal morality (Hoffman, 1981). Second, there is suggestive evidence that males may be somewhat less empathic than females at all ages, even shortly after birth (Hoffman, 1975c).

CONCLUSIONS

The evidence adduced here suggests, contrary to Freud and others, that fathers are far less important than mothers as direct agents of moral socialization. Fathers do appear to serve as identification figures that help foster the acquisition of overt moral behavior by their sons as well as the use of moral standards in evaluating the actions of other people. Fathers generally do not appear to have such influence on their daughters. Even for sons, it is the mother's rather than the father's behavior that contributes to the tendency to use one's moral standards in evaluating one's own behavior. The fathers do appear to have an indirect role: they contribute to the credibility that mothers have with their children, and this may be an important factor in the mother's effectiveness.

The possibility that fathers do not as a rule make a direct contribution to moral internalization needs further investigation, for several reasons. First, it is important to know if the society's instrumental pressures have indeed had the effect of undermining the father's role in moral socialization. Something is wrong with our society if they have. And if the instrumental pressures do have this effect, has the effect been intensified by the countercultural movement which, to a large extent, was a *counterinstrumental* culture movement, as well as by revelations such as Watergate? Are fathers, because of their occupational role, sometimes tagged with a kind of guilt by association, with the result that no matter how moral they may act at home they are compromised as moral socializers? Finally, will the instrumental pressures of the occupational world have the same effect on mothers who go to work? If so, what impact will the increasing employment of mothers have on the moral status of this country? Will the level of moral internalization in girls, as well as boys, decline? And what will be the effect of all this on the future generation of mothers?

There is a clear need for systematic research on the content of the moral norms held by men in our society, the extent to which the norms are internalized, the possible antimoral pressures to which many men may be exposed, how they handle the resulting conflict, and how the conflict is reflected in their behavior as moral socializers of their children. Only then will a true assessment of the actual and potential roles of fathers in the child's moral development be possible.

REFERENCES

Aronfreed, J., & Reber, A. Internalized behavioral suppression and the timing of social punishment. *Journal of Personality and Social Psychology*, 1965, **1**, 3–16.

Baumhart, R. C. How ethical are businessmen? *Harvard Business Review*, 1961, **39**, 6–19, 156–176.

Berentson, J. *The American Lawyer,* May 1980.

Biller, H. B. *Paternal deprivation: Family, school, sexuality and society.* Lexington, Mass.: Heath, 1974.

Block, J. H., Block, J., & Harrington, D. M. The relationship of parental teaching strategies to ego resiliency in preschool children. Presented at Western Psychological Association, San Francisco, 1974.

Burton, R. V. Cheating related to maternal pressures for achievement. Unpublished manuscript, State University of New York at Buffalo, Department of Psychology, 1972.

Erikson, E. H. Reflections on the dissent of contemporary youth. *International Journal of Psychoanalysis,* 1970, **51**, 11–22.

Gross, A. E. Sex and helping: Intrinsic glow and extrinsic show. Paper presented at meetings of the American Psychological Association, Honolulu, September 1972.

Haan, N., Langer, J., & Kohlberg, L. Family patterns of moral reasoning. *Child Development,* 1976, **47**, 1204–1206.

Hetherington, E. M., Cox, M., & Cox, R. The aftermath of divorce. In J. H. Stevens, Jr., & M. Matthews (Eds.), *Mother–child, father–child relations.* Washington, D.C.: National Association for the Education of Young Children, 1978.

Hoffman, L. W. Changes in family roles, socialization, and sex differences. *American Psychologist,* 1977, **32**, 644–657.

Hoffman, M. L. Personality, family structure, and social class as antecedents of parental power assertion. *Child Development,* 1963, **34**, 869–884.

Hoffman, M. L. Parent discipline and child's moral development. *Journal of Personality and Social Psychology,* 1967, **5**, 45–57.

Hoffman, M. L. Moral development. In P. Mussen (Ed.), *Handbook of child psychology,* New York: Wiley, 1970.

Hoffman, M. L. Father absence and conscience development. *Developmental Psychology,* 1971, **4**, 400–406 (a).

Hoffman, M. L. Identification and conscience development. *Child Development,* 1971, **42**, 1071–1082 (b).

Hoffman, M. L. Moral internalization, parental power, and the nature of parent–child interaction. *Developmental Psychology,* 1975, **11**, 228–239 (a).

Hoffman, M. L. Altruistic behavior and the parent–child relationship. *Journal of Personality and Social Psychology,* 1975, **31**, 937–943 (b).

Hoffman, M. L. Sex differences in moral internalization. *Journal of Personality and Social Psychology,* 1975, **32**, 729–729 (c).

Hoffman, M. L. Developmental synthesis of affect and cognition and its implications for altruistic motivation. *Developmental Psychology,* 1975, **11**, 607–622 (d).

Hoffman, M. L. Moral internalization: Current theory and research. In L. Berkowitz (Ed.), *Advances in experimental social psychology*, Vol. 10. New York: Academic Press, 1977. (a).

Hoffman, M. L. Empathy, its development, and prosocial implications. In C. B. Keasey (Ed.), *Nebraska Symposium on Motivation*, 1977, **25**, 169–218 (b).

Hoffman, M. L. Sex differences in empathy and related behaviors. *Psychological Bulletin*, 1977, **84**, 712–722 (c).

Hoffman, M. L. Adolescent morality in developmental perspective. In J. Adelson (Ed.), *Handbook of adolescent psychology*. New York: Wiley, 1980.

Hoffman, M. L. Is altruism part of human nature? *Journal of Personality and Social Psychology*, 1981, **40**, 121–137.

Hoffman, M. L. Affective and cognitive processes in moral internalization: An information processing approach. In E. T. Higgins, D. Ruble, & W. Hartup (Eds.), *Social cognition and social behavior*. New York: Cambridge University Press, in press.

Johnson, C. D., & Gormly, J. Academic cheating: The contribution of sex, personality, and situational variables. *Developmental Psychology*, 1972, **6**, 320–325.

Kagan, J. The concept of identification. *Psychological Review*, 1958, **65**, 296–305.

Kohlberg, L. The cognitive-developmental approach. In D. A. Goslin (Ed.), *Handbook of socialization theory and research*. Chicago: Rand McNally, 1969.

Longabaugh, R. Mother behavior as a variable moderating the effects of father absence. *Ethos*, 1973, **1**, 456–465.

Lytton, H. The socialization of two-year-old boys: Ecological findings. *Journal of Child Psychology and Psychiatry*, 1976, **17**, 286–304.

Lytton, H. Disciplinary encounters between young boys and their mothers and fathers: Is there a contingency system? *Developmental Psychology*, 1979, **15**, 256–268.

Mischel, W. Sex differences, sex typing, and identification. In P. Mussen (Ed.), *Handbook of child psychology*. New York: Wiley, 1970.

Mowrer, O. H. *Learning theory and behavior*. New York: Wiley, 1960.

Parsons, T., & Bales, R. F. *Family, socialization and interaction process*. Glencoe, Ill.: Free Press, 1955.

Pearlin, L. I., Radke-Yarrow, M., & Scarr, H. A. Unintended effects of parental aspirations: The case of children's cheating. *American Journal of Sociology*, 1967, **73**, 73–83.

Santrock, J. W. Father absence, perceived maternal behavior and moral development in boys. *Child Development*, 1975, **46**, 753–757.

Shinn, M. Father absence and children's cognitive development. *Psychological Bulletin*, 1978, **85**, 295–324.

Stein, A. H. Imitation of resistance to temptation. *Child Development*, **38**, 157–169.

Walters, R. H., and Parke, R. D. Influence of response consequences to a social model on resistance to deviation. *Journal of Experimental Child Psychology,* 1964, **1,** 269–280.

Whiting, J. W. M. Social structure and child rearing: a theory of identification. Paper read at Tulane University as part of the Mona Brorsman Sheckman Lectures in Social Psychiatry, New Orleans, March 17–19, 1960.

Zussman, J. U. Relationship of demographic factors to parental discipline techniques. *Developmental Psychology,* 1978, **14,** 685–686.

CHAPTER 11

The Role of the Father
in Cognitive, Academic, and
Intellectual Development

NORMA RADIN

University of Michigan

In spite of the deficiencies in the literature, it is important to summarize what is known about the father's role in the child's intellectual functioning, so that some myths can be dispelled—for example, that father absence is invariably damaging to the children involved. In addition, the mass of data about maternal influence on the child's cognitive development tends to mask the influence that fathers exert, and the relative scarcity of discussions about fathers until very recently suggested that his role was unimportant. As the ensuing discussion suggests, this is indeed an invalid conclusion. Finally, an examination of the knowledge that is available may facilitate the generation of new hypotheses and highlight fruitful directions for future research.

OVERVIEW OF THE CHAPTER

This chapter is organized in the following manner. A discussion of the limitation of the literature is first presented, with the deficiencies common to research on mothers and fathers differentiated from the deficiencies unique to the studies of fathers. Emergent trends concerning the father's influence on the child's cognitive and academic growth are then delineated. The first such trend is the link between fathers and sons. Theoretical support for this association is presented followed by a summary of the literature demonstrating the relationship between the child's intellectual development and paternal factors (quantity and quality of contact, power, and self-confidence). The influence of paternal behavior on the boy's cognitive style concludes this section. The second trend is the differential impact fathers have on the cognitive growth of boys and girls. The third and fourth trends concern the nature of fathers' influence on their daughters' intellectual development—specifically, the effect of girls' autonomy and moderate distance from fathers, and fathers' influence on daughters' mathematical abilities. The next two trends discussed are the consequences of paternal participation in the child's problem-solving activities and the role of the mother as mediator of the father's impact on children's intellectual growth.

A discussion of the association between fathers' status characteristics and children's cognitive competence ensues, followed by a review of the literature on the impact of father absence. The latter topic includes coverage of the cumulative deficit hypothesis, sex differences in the impact of father absence, age-of-child differences, and racial, ethnic, economic, and family structural factors. Finally, an overall summary of the statements that can be made concerning the father's influence on the child's cognitive development is presented.

In offering a very brief overview of those conclusions before beginning the detailed discussion, it can be said that paternal nurturance fosters the cognitive growth of boys, and the more such contact, the greater the cognitive growth, except when the child is involved in tasks that require mastery efforts. Under such conditions, father participation tends to be detrimental. Insofar as girls are concerned, autonomy and moderate distance from fathers appear to be associated with the youngsters' cognitive proficiency under all conditions. For both boys and girls, authoritarian paternal behavior tends to be associated with reduced academic competence. Nondeath-related father absence appears to be most damaging to the intellectual functioning of boys when the absence occurs before the age of 5. For girls, father absence appears to be less damaging, but the development of mathematical abilities tends to be damaged when father absence occurs before the age of 9. Overall, fathers appear to influence their children's intellectual and academic growth through diverse channels, including their attitudes and behavior toward the youngsters, their ethnic and genetic heritage, their position in the family structure, and the nature of their relationships with their wives.

LIMITATIONS TO THE LITERATURE

Deficiencies Common to Research on Mothers and Fathers

The nature of cognitive functioning itself creates difficulties for anyone attempting to analyze the influence of any single variable or individual. Biller (1968) and Lynn (1974) in their books on fathers both stated that biological and environmental factors interact in their contribution to the child's intellectual growth; both recommended caution in analyzing the influence that fathers might exert. Lynn pointed out that even when there is a similarity in some particular aspect or style of thinking between father and child, it is difficult to determine how much of the similarity can be attributed to genetic heritage and how much to the social influence of the father. Many other researchers in child development, such as Bayley (1968), Zigler and Child (1969), Honzik (1963), Maccoby and Jacklin (1974), Munsinger and Douglass (1976), and Wilson (1977, 1978) have also discussed genetic influences on cognitive development. For example, Wilson (1977) concluded, after conducting a longitudinal study of monozygotic and dizygotic twins, that individual differences in intelligence will never be abolished because "the variation coded in the genotype is too deeply rooted" (p. 215). Data from a study conducted in France (Dumaret, Stewart, Tomklewicz, & Feingold, 1978), however, of working-class children adopted under 6 months of age led the investigators to state that there are no important genetic differences between social groups for factors relevant to school failure. The longitudinal study by Heber (1976) of black children in this country tends to support this conclusion. Perhaps the most useful comment on the complex nature–nurture question was made by Bane and Jencks (1977) who stated that genes may influence actual learning capacity, which may then affect opportunities and incentives to learn. The resulting inequality is thus caused by both genes and environment, and no one has yet devised a method for separating the two effects.

The preponderance of research on white middle-class families endemic to research on mothers contaminates the information available on fathers as well. Generalizations about the findings to other groups are therefore questionable. Investigations of fathers in Chicano, Puerto Rican, and Asian families are particularly scarce. Such data would be of great importance to those interested in cognitive development, since the academic performance of these youngsters differs considerably (Coleman, Campbell, Hobson, McPartland, Mood, Weinfeld, & York, 1966). Another difficulty prevalent in the study of maternal behavior and pervading research on father behavior is the question of the direction of influence in correlational investigations. All researchers in the field indicate it is possible that the father is responding to the behavior evinced by the child rather than the reverse. Osofsky and O'Connell (1972) and Frodi, Lamb, Leavitt, Donovan, Neff, and Sherry (1978) demonstrated experimentally that this phenomenon occurs. Bell (1968) reviewed many classic studies and demonstrated that other interpretations of the data were possible if one assumed that the child, rather than the parent, was the initiator of the interaction. Hoffman (1975) responded that in some instances it is reasonable to assume that parents initiate more interactions than children, but that in others it is not. The possibility also exists that the influence system is cyclical, as Clark-

Stewart (1978) suggested, with mothers influencing children who influence fathers who in turn influence mothers.

No attempt will be made in this review to interpret all of the findings in terms of the child's impact on the father as well as the father's impact on child. It will be assumed that both directions of influence exist. There is no question, as Harrington, Block, and Block (1978) indicated in interpreting their data, that the boy's inability to solve a problem may well arouse hostility and rejection in the young boy's father. One can never be certain that it is the father's hostility that is interfering with the boy's problem-solving capabilities. However, as this chapter's goal is to analyze possible influence fathers exert on their children's capabilities, the direction of influence emphasized is from adult to child.

Deficiencies Unique to Studies of Fathers

Perhaps the most severe limitation in the research literature available on the father's role in the intellective development of the child is the absence of long-term investigations of paternal behavior comparable to the Berkeley Growth Study or the Fels Research Institute investigation, in which repeated observations of maternal behavior and children's cognitive performance were made. Thus correlational data of father behavior with children's intellective ability through the years do not exist. A second limitation unique to father research is that many studies, particularly those published prior to 1974, purporting to focus on fathers, use data obtained entirely from mothers or from children, probably because housewives and students are more readily available. Mothers' views of fathers' behavior are of course important, as are the perceptions of the children. However, such information cannot replace direct observation of fathers or fathers' views directly expressed. Data obtained from different family members are not isomorphic and cannot be used interchangeably.

An additional constraint on father data is that many of the studies on paternal childrearing involve mothers as well as fathers interacting with their children. This method is rarely used in research on maternal behavior. It is difficult to know how the father would behave with his child if his wife were not present. Few studies have involved a father interacting spontaneously with his child alone, and again when his wife is present, so that a comparison of paternal behavior under the two conditions might be made. Lamb (1977a, 1976) studied attachment and affiliative behaviors of infants under 18 months with one and two parents present, but the focus of these investigations was on child behavior and the laboratory research design did not permit the fathers to interact freely with the children. There are some suggestions in the data that different correlational patterns may exist between father and child behaviors as fathers and children interact spontaneously in the presence and absence of mothers. These may be similar to the differences observed in maternal behavior in the presence and absence of fathers (Lytton, 1979; Clarke-Stewart, 1978; Lamb, 1979). The man who is fulfilling the husband and father role simultaneously may behave differently from the man who is only playing the father role. Fathers who "perform" in front of their wives may feel obligated to meet the women's demands in addition to, or instead of, meeting his own or his child's expectations. Thus there may be a tendency to play the stern disciplinarian or the loving parent when mother is watching, but not when she is absent. We do not know at this point if the mother's presence spurs the father on to his best behavior with the child the way that the father's presence appears to elicit positive behavior in mothers (Lytton, 1979). Perhaps "spouse manners" are the counterpart of family manners, at least insofar as interactions with young obstreperous children are concerned.

A complication that may be most unique to a study of fathers is the importance of the economic context in which the behavior occurs. Parsons and Bales' (1955) description of the father as playing the instrumental role in the family is still largely valid, although conditions are changing. It is still primarily the father who is the family's link with the world of work and whose status in the family is dependent to a great extent on his ability to fulfill that role. As Strodtbeck (1958) succinctly phrased it, "The father's occupational success is something else again . . . if he fails in his function of 'bringing home the bacon'—of adapting successfully outside—his power is reduced at home, too" (p. 189). Since paternal power has been shown by a number of investigators to mediate the child's modeling of the father, the employment status of the father may well affect his influence on his youngsters. There are suggestions that there may be racial, ethnic, and class differences in this area. Schulz (1969) indicated that many black fathers play an expressive role in the family that is not dependent on his employment status. We know too little about paternal behavior at present to understand how the child's cognitive development might be affected by extensive father unemployment, or underemployment, beyond the obvious financial deprivation on the family.

Another problem in understanding the role of fathers in the child's cognitive development is the abundance of research data assessing his influence by his absence. Herzog and Sudia (1970) presented strong evidence that little is known about the effect of father absence *per se*, because so many other variables confound the findings. Among those variables are the reactions of other family members to his absence, his relationship to the mother and child prior to his departure, the economic condition of the family, the child's age when the father leaves, the reason for his leaving, and the support system available. Other variables mediating the effects of divorce on children are custody disposition (Santrock & Warshak, 1979) and the birth order of the children of each sex (Sutton-Smith, Rosenberg, & Landy, 1968). Pederson (1976) went so far as to say that the research paradigm in which father-present and father-absent families are compared has outlived its usefulness. Perhaps that view is too extreme since some consistent data are emerging from recent well-controlled studies, but there is no question that there is a need to examine the father's influence when he is present, rather than focusing on an individual who is no longer there. Finally, much of the information about the father's influence on the cognitive competence of the child is contradictory, partially as a result of the different samples and methodologies employed. Sears (1965), Bing (1963), and Lytton (1973), among others, have underscored the fact that diverse results are obtained in the study of parent–child relations when different research strategies are used. Some trends do emerge, however, and appear to have substantial support. These are discussed first, and the more tenuous trends and findings follow.

EMERGENT TRENDS

Link Between Fathers and Sons

The most pronounced current theme concerning fathers and their children's intellectual growth is that the bond between fathers and sons is stronger than the bond between fathers and daughters. There are two probable reasons for this phenomenon. The first is the tendency for boys to identify with and model their fathers, particularly from about 4 to 9 years of age. The second is that fathers appear to identify with their sons so that they react in a different way to sons than to daughters; they become more invested in the young boy's activities, abilities, and behavior patterns.

Theoretical Support. Insofar as boys' identification with fathers is concerned, learning theorists such as Gewirtz and Stingle (1968) and Mischel (1970) assert that the boy will imitate his father because he is rewarded for doing so. Further, since an intermittent reinforcement schedule produces the most persistent behavior, a considerable amount of imitation can result from relatively little reinforcement. Since behaviors that are frequently rewarded acquire reinforcement value themselves, other learning theorists such as Baer and Sherman (1964) indicated that imitation itself can become rewarding. Bandura (1962), who stresses cognitive processes, stated that modeling can take place even without external reward, and described identification as virtually synonymous with imitation. Both involve matching the behavior, attitude, or emotional reactions exhibited by the models. Other child development theorists such as Sears

(1953), Kagan (1968), and Mussen and Rutherford (1963) discussed the relationship of reinforcement and imitation in other terms. They indicated that children will imitate models who are nurturant or rewarding. Such modeling is particularly strong with models who resembles themselves. According to Mowrer (1950), in developmental identification it is assumed that parental characteristics will be adopted to the extent that the parent is an important source of nurturance and reward, because by imitating the source of reinforcement, children can become their own reinforcers. Thus boys are likely to imitate fathers who are loving and warm even if they are not specifically rewarded for doing so.

Nelsen and Maccoby (1966) discussed another type of identification, identification with the aggressor, or defensive identification, in Mowrer's (1950) terminology. Mowrer hypothesized that defensive identification is a function of the threat qualities of the parent. Using other words but conveying the same idea, Nelsen and Maccoby (1966) suggested that boys identify with fathers they fear in order to relieve their anxiety. Others have focused on father power rather than fear of the father. Mussen and Distler (1960) and Hetherington and Frankie (1967) found that paternal power or dominance fostered the boy's identification with his father. Kohlberg and Zigler (1967) proposed that boys must develop the concept of constancy of identity before they can identify with their fathers. Once the child learns that his sex is invariant he will seek someone of the same sex as a model—his father—and ultimately identify with him. Finally, according to Maccoby and Jacklin (1974), sex identification and same-sex modeling is initiated by the child, not the adult; it is the result of self-socialization by the youngster and shows up in "rudimentary form" as early as 3 years of age.

There may be disagreement about the basis for identification among theorists and researchers, but there is little disagreement about the fact that young boys identify with, imitate, and/or model their fathers. As boys identify with their fathers, not only are attitudes, values, roles, gestures, and emotional reactions emulated, but problem-solving strategies, thinking processes, and vocabulary as well. This matching of the intellective behavior of the child's to that of the adult should foster the cognitive development of young boys.

Insofar as counteridentification (parent identification with the same-sex child) is concerned, Rothbart (1971), Maccoby and Jacklin (1974), Aberle and Naegele (1952), Sears (reported by Maccoby and Jacklin, 1974), and Gewirtz and Gewirtz (1968) found evidence of it. Counteridentification may also partially explain the observation that fathers are particularly upset when their retarded child is a boy (Farber, 1962) and react in extremes of total involvement or total withdrawal (Price-Bonham & Addison, 1978). Aberle and Naegele discussed parent identification with the same-sex child at some length:

Whereas the father's present situation represents to him his son's probable future situation (broadly speaking), the son's present behavior may represent to the father his own past . . . Perhaps difficulties now observed in the son were once successfully overcome by the father, sometimes after a struggle, and these may now be unconsciously reactivated. The identification may thus intensify the degree to which the father attempts to counteract the disturbing behaviors in his son, attempting at the same time to stifle the same tendencies in himself. (p. 374)

Such counteridentification may be related to the conclusions of Tauber (1979), Lynn (1974), Maccoby and Jacklin (1974), and Fagot (1978), among others, that greater emphasis is given by fathers than mothers to the appropriate sex role behaviors of their children, particularly their sons.

The paternal counteridentification construct may also help explain the consistent evidence that fathers attend to their young sons more than to young daughters. For example, Belsky (1979) who observed 40 middle-class families with 15-month-old children discovered that fathers preferentially vocalized to and interacted with their young sons. Weinraub and Frankel (1977) similarly observed 18-month-old boys and girls with their parents in a laboratory free-play situation and noted that each parent talked to and tended to play more with the same-sex infant. The authors speculated that the differentiated attentiveness could reflect identification with the child of the same sex. These findings are concordant with those of Lamb (Lamb, 1977b; Lamb & Lamb, 1976), who observed parents interacting with their infants on several occasions at home between the time the children were 7 and 24 months of age. According to Lamb, during the child's second year, fathers make themselves especially salient to their sons, becoming far more active in interactions with their sons than their daughters.

Other researchers have found that fathers display preferences for sons virtually from the moment of their birth. Parke and Sawin (1976) observed that fathers touched their firstborn male newborns and vocalized more to them than to their firstborn girls. As a result of these findings, the investigators concluded that there was clearly some basis to the claim that fathers prefer boys, especially firstborn boys. The same researchers noted that the preference continues for the next few months. When the infants reached 3 months of age Parke and Sawin (1980) found that fathers were more likely to diaper and feed sons than daughters.

Counteridentification is more likely to facilitate than hinder the young boy's cognitive growth although the opposite possibility exists. If the father's counteridentification results in his spending more time with the boy, encouraging his academic pursuits, and doing "daddish" things with the child such as interacting physically and actively with the youngster (Parke & Sawin, 1977;

Lytton, 1976; Clarke-Stewart, 1978; Pedersen, 1976), or engaging in stimulating and nonstereotyped play (Lamb & Lamb, 1976), it should facilitate cognitive growth. If, however, counteridentification leads to critical, domineering, paternal behavior, it could be damaging. Fortunately, the research literature suggests that this phenomenon is relatively rare.

By the time the son approaches adolescence a potential problem of a different nature arises. Rosen and D'Andrade (1959) suggested that boys and their fathers may see each other as competitors. Maccoby and Jacklin (1974) supported this view, stating that fathers may begin to treat older children the way they do adults of that sex and "there are simply discreet elements of flirtation with the opposite sex child and elements of rivalry with the same sex child" (p. 316). It is highly likely that such a rivalrous paternal stance will be detrimental to the boy's cognitive functioning, particularly if the hostility and power of the father are not restrained. In general, however, it can be said that young boys are particularly sensitive to their fathers' behaviors and respond more strongly to fathers than mothers; fathers in turn are particularly sensitive to, or empathetic with the behaviors of their young sons and react in a more differentiated way to sons than to daughters.

Investigations that found a relationship between paternal behavior, or presence, and the young boy's cognitive development are summarized below. They can all be interpreted to a considerable extent in terms of boys' identification with fathers and/or rivalry between fathers and sons. When counteridentification appears to be involved, this possibility is noted. Although some of the studies report data for older children, the researchers (e.g., Rosen & D'Andrade, 1967, and Dyk & Witkin, 1965) either implicitly or explicitly assume that the parental behavior assessed at one point in time had been taking place for some time previously. Thus the findings reflect an ongoing process whose consequences were evidenced at the time the study was conducted.

Quantity of Contact. Pedersen, Rubinstein, and Yarrow (1973, 1979) found that for black boys, 5 to 6 months of age, the amount of interaction between father and child was positively correlated with measures of the son's cognitive functioning (e.g., scores on the Mental and Psychomotor Developmental Indices from the Bayley Tests of Infant Development). The correlations with daughters' scores did not even approach significance. Since no differences could be found in the behaviors of the mothers, Pedersen et al. concluded that the link between father and son was direct and not mediated by the women. No hypothesis was offered, however, about the nature of the link except the negative one that the children were obviously too young to have been modeling anyone. One could interpret the results as evidence of counteridentification by fathers resulting in different behaviors by fathers of sons and fathers of daughters. The nature of the interaction between father and child was not investigated—merely the amount. Perhaps, just as qualitatively different paternal behavior with sons and daughters 4 years of age was found (Radin & Epstein, 1975a), paternal behavior with 6-month-old boys and girls also may be different, at least in black families.

A study of children several years older provided additional evidence of the association between the quantity of time fathers spend with sons and the youngsters' cognitive competence. Reis and Gold (1977) conducted a study of white middle-class boys, some with more available fathers and others with less available fathers based on paternal responses to a questionnaire. The boys were administered three problem-solving tasks, and for the total sample a significant correlation was found between one of those tasks and father availability. Further, within the high father available families, father availability was significantly correlated with the boys' scores on all three tests. The only paradoxical correlation emerging from the study was found within the low father available group; there was a significant negative relationship between the children's scores on one of the tasks and father availability during the week. The authors speculated that this finding may be related to father responses to poor child performance or to the poor quality of father behavior with sons for this subgroup. The implication of the Reis and Gold study is that, although in general the more father availability, the better the young boy's problem solving ability, for fathers who are highly involved with their sons the relationship is even stronger. Whether this is caused by such fathers understanding their sons more or to a selective factor in which fathers who are more child-sensitive choose to spend more time with their sons cannot be determined at this time.

Blanchard and Biller (1971) assessed the effect of different levels of father availability on the academic performance of third-grade boys from working-class and lower middle-class families and, controlling for age of child, IQ, socioeconomic status, and sibling constellation, learned that boys whose fathers interacted frequently with them (more than 2 hours per day) received higher grades in school than boys whose fathers infrequently (less than 6 hours per week) interacted with them. When four groups—early father-absent (beginning before age 5), late father-absent (beginning after age 5), low father-present (less than 6 hours per week), and high father-present (over 2 hours per day)—were compared, it was found that the rank order for school grades (controlling for the same variables) was: (1) high father-present boys who were doing superior work; (2) late father-absent and low father-present boys who were both functioning somewhat below grade level; and (3) early father-absent boys who were generally underachievers. The reason for absence or the mothers' reaction to the absence was not assessed in the study, but so many other variables were controlled that the research has major significance.

Another study of third- and fourth-grade children, only middle-class in this instance, provided similar data: The time fathers spent in a supervisory capacity with their youngsters was found to be positively associated with teacher ratings of the children's cognitive skills. It was noteworthy that the supervisory time spent by mothers was negatively associated with the same ratings (Ziegler, 1979).

Supporting Blanchard and Biller's findings that early father absence has a greater impact on boys' intellectual performance than later absence were the data collected by Carlsmith (1964). She investigated the College Board Aptitude scores of middle-class high school boys and found that those who were father-absent early in their childhood were more likely than boys who were father-present to have a feminine patterning of aptitude test scores—that is, a higher verbal score than mathematics score. The incidence of feminine patterning was negatively related to the child's age at the onset of the father's absence and was positively related to the length of his absence. Carlsmith attributed the findings to sex role identification. She hypothesized that the greater incidence of higher verbal than mathematics scores in boys who were father-absent early in life was because the boys' identified with their mothers rather than their fathers since the Vm (higher verbal than mathematics score) pattern of aptitude scores reflects an underlying "feminine conceptual approach." It was further assumed that the cognitive styles are maintained through childhood and adolescence despite the return of the father to the family. There is much in common between Carlsmith's view of the father's role in the cognitive development of the child and the view presented in this chapter. In both cases, it is suggested that a cognitive style can be modeled just as any other behavioral style can be emulated.

A more recent study of high school students and their parents tended to confirm the view that the quantity of paternal contact with sons was positively associated with measures of the boy's cognitive competence, at least in moderately affluent families. Gold and Andres (1978) explored the impact of maternal employment on adolescents 14 to 16 years of age and discovered that for middle-class boys, fathers' direct estimates of their interactions with their children correlated positively and significantly with self-reported grades. The correlation was not significant for middle-class girls or working-class males or females.

Quality of Contact. Nelsen and Maccoby (1966) replicated Carlsmith's work to test an alternate hypothesis explaining a feminine patterning of scores on father-absent males. They posed the tension-interference hypothesis that suggested that stress and tension interfere more with cognitive functioning basic to mathematical ability than with functioning involved in verbal ability. Thus stress caused by a number of factors could produce a Vm pattern in males. To test this theory, Nelsen and Maccoby examined the Scholastic Aptitude Test scores of college freshmen and related the patterning of verbal and mathematics scores to various experiences the students had reported having with their parents. One of the major findings was that there was support for the sex role identification theory of Carlsmith but only for males, not females. Supporting the sex role identification theory were the findings that males who were father-absent or whose fathers were frequently absent from home for extended periods had higher verbal than mathematics scores than males whose fathers were not frequently absent. In addition, males who reported having talked over their personal problems with their fathers and not having feared their fathers tended to obtain higher mathematics than verbal scores. Support for defensive identification was also found. Boys who reported being punished only by their fathers had higher mathematics scores in relation to their verbal scores than males who were not punished only by their fathers.

Multimer, Laughlin, and Powell (1966) found that boys 8 to 12 years old who read well preferred to be with their fathers; girls who read well preferred to be with their mothers. Shaw and White (1965), in an investigation of high school students with above average intelligence, obtained results that indicated that the boys who had a B average or better perceived themselves as more similar to their fathers than boys with a below-B average. Further, father and son self-ratings were correlated in the high-achieving group but not in the low-achieving group. Girls with high grades saw themselves as more like their mothers than their fathers. Similar results were obtained by Teahan (1963), who compared low- and high-achieving college freshmen. High-achieving males completed an attitude questionnaire the same way that their fathers' did; low-achieving males did not. High-achieving females' questionnaires resembled their mothers'; low-achieving girls' questionnaires did not. The author speculated that the disparity seen in attitudes of low-achieving girls and low-achieving boys and their mothers and fathers might be caused by a possible lack of identification with these parental figures. Also supportive of the relationship between developmental identification and cognitive competence of young boys were the findings of Andersland and Kimball. In the Andersland (1968) investigation, paternal rejection was related to underachievement in high school boys but not high school girls. In the Kimball (1952) study, very intelligent adolescent boys who had poor relations with their fathers had lower grades than the boys whose relationships with their fathers was considered average.

In my own observational research (Radin, 1972a, 1973; Jordan, Radin, & Epstein, 1975; Radin & Epstein, 1975a) with preschool children, paternal nurturance was found to be significantly related to cognitive competence in white boys, particularly middle-class youngsters. These findings were supported in a later study of 59 middle-class white families with varying degrees of paternal involvement (Radin, 1978, 1980). The father responses to a questionnaire that included six items about his nurturing behavior with his preschool son were correlated with the two child cognitive measures, the Peabody Picture Vocabulary Test, and the Raven's Coloured Progressive Matrices Test. It was found that the boys' score on the latter instrument correlated significantly with their fathers' estimate of how often he gave "a lot" of care and attention to his son. When the mother was asked the same questions in a separate interview, her estimates of how often her husband showed his love to the children, was concerned about the children's problems, and tried to help with these problems correlated significantly with the boy's mental age percentile on the Peabody Picture Vocabulary Test. None of the responses of the mothers or the fathers correlated significantly with girls' cognitive scores.

A significant link between paternal nurturance and the cognitive performance of sons also emerged in an observational study involving 8- and 9-year-old boys and their fathers engaged in cognitive tasks together (Ziegler, 1979). According to the researcher, the approval displayed by the fathers toward their children accounted for a significant proportion of the variance in the boys' task performance. In contrast, Baumrind's (1971) observational study of middle-class preschool children found no significant correlation between paternal nurturance and sons' cognitive competence. The difference in methodology employed in the three observational studies may help explain the divergent results. In the Baumrind investigation, both mother and father were present; in Radin's (1978, 1980) and Ziegler's (1979) studies, only the father and child were present with the interviewer. Perhaps fathers behave differently when their wives are present.

There is considerable evidence that paternal authoritarianism and hostility have detrimental effects on young men attending college and boys likely to become college students. Teahan (1963) found that fathers of low-achieving freshmen, male and female, were more punitive in their attitudes than fathers of high achievers. Cross and Allen (1969) discovered that high-achieving college men had fathers they viewed as accepting and child-centered; Heilbrun's (1973) data indicated that late adolescent males who experienced aversive paternal control—that is, much control in a context of low nurturance, had thinking deficits. Baumrind's (1971) study revealed that authoritarian attitudes expressed on a questionnaire by middle-class fathers were negatively associated with the cognitive competence of young boys, although observed authoritarian behaviors were not. Data from our study (Radin & Epstein, 1975a) indicated that observed paternal restrictiveness was negatively correlated with measures of cognitive ability in preschool middle- and lower-class boys.

Harrington, Block, and Block (1978), in a longitudinal study involving questionnaire data and observations during a teaching session found that 3-year-old middle-class boys whose fathers displayed impatience, authoritarian control, and lack of spontaneously expressed emotion obtained scores in a puzzle situation reflecting intolerance of ambiguity. The same finding did not apply to girls whose performance was affected by their mothers' behavior. Further, early intolerance of ambiguity in boys was related to less effective cognitive functioning when the youngsters were 7 years old. Prematurely imposing a solution on a problem before examining all of its aspects understandably should reduce the child's problem-solving competence. However, intolerance of ambiguity in young girls did not predict future intellectual functioning but rather stable peer relations. One conclusion that can be drawn from the Harrington et al. study is that relatively distant and authoritarian fathers who are impatient and critical with their preschool sons in a teaching session tend to hinder the youngsters' cognitive growth in the next few years, possibly by fostering anxiety in ambiguous situations. The investigators acknowledged that other interpretations are possible—for instance, the fathers might have been reacting to incompetent sons and therefore the influence was bidirectional.

Overall, the literature indicates that paternal punitiveness and hostility are associated with lack of cognitive ability in middle-class males. There is little evidence that fear of father facilitates their cognitive growth. The Nelsen and Maccoby (1966) study suggesting that defensive identification enhances mathematics skills contradicts this trend, but males who scored high in mathematics in this study did not fear their fathers. Thus some other factor, such as paternal dominance, may be involved rather than punitiveness. Perhaps middle-class boys who fear their fathers are also fearful about exploring the environment, and the child's cognitive growth is thereby hindered regardless of his identification with his father. Both modeling of an adult and freedom to explore may be needed for optimum intellectual development. Developmental identification may supply both of these essential factors by fostering imitation and also suggesting to the child that interaction with the environment (of which his father is part) is likely to be reinforcing. Defensive identification may only provide the first element.

Paternal Power. Several studies underscore the importance of paternal power in boys' cognitive performance, possibly because of the role that power plays in enhancing identification with the child's father. Bowerman and Elder (1964) found that 13- to 18-year-old, middle-class and lower-class boys who were high achievers had fathers who were the most powerful individual in the family and were democratic in their relationship with the children. Marjoribanks (1972), in an extensive study of 11-year-old boys in England, obtained similar results indicating that father dominance correlated significantly, although at a low level, with boys' verbal ability on a standard achievement test. In my own study of families varying in paternal involvement in childcare, paternal power in decision making concerning childrearing issues correlated significantly with the preschool boys' mental age on the Peabody Picture Vocabulary Test; the correlation was insignificant for girls (Radin, 1978). There is also evidence that low father power fosters cognitive competence in boys. Strodtbeck (1958) found that low father power vis-à-vis the son and wife was associated with high achievement. The one point of agreement between the work of Strodtbeck and Bowerman and Elder is that power assertion by the father over the son does not facilitate achievement or achievement striving. Rosen and D'Andrade's (1959) study of paternal influence on achievement in young boys supports this view. These researchers studied achievement motivation in lower- and middle-class white boys in grades four through six and concluded that for the development of a high motivation to achieve, the boy needs more autonomy from his father than from his mother. The father who gives the boy a relatively high degree of autonomy "provides him with the opportunity to compete on his own ground, to test his skill, and to gain a sense of confidence in his own competence" (p. 216). Although intellectual achievement and motivation to achieve are not the same, they are highly correlated when need achievement is assessed by projective techniques (Strodtbeck, 1959), and this was the procedure followed in the Rosen and D'Andrade study.

The different results regarding paternal power obtained by Bowerman and Elder, Marjoribanks, and Radin on one hand, and by Strodtbeck, and Rosen and D'Andrade on the other, may be reconciled when the methods used by the two groups are examined. The former investigators relied on questionnaire data about general paternal behavior; the latter group of researchers conducted observational studies in which fathers were watched as they interacted with their sons completing tasks. There is evidence that paternal interference, or even involvement, in the boy's mastery efforts may be detrimental to the youngster's cognitive growth. Paternal behavior in nonmastery situations may have different consequences for offspring. Perhaps a father who is perceived as competent and strong but who permits his son to master tasks and solve problems independently provides the most fertile background for the youngster's intellectual growth.

Paternal Self-Confidence. Grunebaum, Hurwitz, Prentice, and Sperry (1962) studied elementary school-aged boys of average IQ who were 2 years below grade level. The researchers discovered that the boys had fathers who felt inadequate and considered themselves failures. In support of these findings were those of Busse (1969), who found that flexibility in thinking (defined as considering alternative solutions to problems) of 11-year-old, lower-class black boys was related to the fathers' feelings of power toward his spouse, the world, and his offspring. Possibly a model who is ineffectual fosters ineffective problem solving in those who emulate him. An alternate possibility is that the powerless father is not as readily modeled as one who is perceived as powerful. Related to the Grunebaum and Busse findings were those of Honzik (1967). Describing some data obtained in the longitudinal Berkeley Guidance Study, Honzik reported that father satisfaction with his own occupation was significantly correlated with his son's IQ from ages 5 to 15 but not with his daughter's. The father who is pleased with his own job may present a more adequate and self-confident model for his son to emulate.

Cognitive Style. The literature on cognitive style tends to support the view that boys' approaches to problem solving are influenced by their relationships with their fathers. Various terms have been used to describe an approach that involves disembedding details of a problem from its context or ignoring irrelevant cues in the environment in solving certain types of problems. The cognitive style is sometimes called analytic as opposed to global, or field independent as opposed to field dependent or field sensitive. Dyk and Witkin (1965) in their research on young boys, reported that there was a significant correlation between an analytic approach and some components of intellectual competence such as spatial ability, and between an analytic approach and several nonverbal items on the Weschler Intelligence Scale for Children such as block design and object assembly. Corah (1965), in keeping with the findings of Dyk and Witkin, obtained significant associations between scores on tests of field independence and the verbal IQ of adult males, adult females, and young girls, but not young boys. Thus there appears to be an overlap between field independence and intellectual competence, and the findings pertaining to the latter are relevant to the former.

Several investigators have found that a positive association with fathers is linked to field independence in boys. Dyk and Witkin (1965), using 10-year-old, middle-class white boys as subjects, learned that field independent boys were more likely to perceive warm father–son relationships in their scores on the Thematic Apperception Test than field dependent boys. Seder's (1957) study of surburban families, as reported by Dyk and Witkin, revealed that fathers of field dependent boys, but not girls, spent time with their sons in relatively passive activities such as watching television. Seder also found that fathers of global boys used more physical punishment and verbal aggression than fathers of analytic boys, whose punishment tended to be more restrained. This relationship did not hold for girls. Analytic boys were punished more often by their fathers than their mothers, a finding resembling Nelsen and Maccoby's (1966) observation that college males with higher mathematics than verbal scores were punished by their fathers rather than their mothers. The similarity is not surprising in view of the relationship often found between an analytic approach, mathematical ability, and spatial ability (Maccoby & Jacklin, 1974; Bing, 1963; Carlsmith, 1964). Barclay and Cusumaro's (1967) and

Chapman's (1977) investigations indicated that father-absent adolescent boys were more field dependent than those whose fathers were present, a finding again resembling those of Nelsen and Maccoby and Carlsmith concerning the more limited mathematical ability of father-absent males in high school and college.

Lynn (1969) hypothesized that there was a curvilinear relationship between father availability and field independence. According to Lynn, when there is a moderate amount of father availability, the boy has an idea of masculine role but has to interact actively with his environment to develop his masculine role fully. Thus if the boy's father is constantly available, the boy will not develop an analytic, independent stance in interaction with his environment. Support for this hypothesis came from research on Eskimo boys who spend a good deal of time with their fathers. Berry (1966) and MacArthur (1967) found that Eskimo boys imitate their fathers more closely, but are not more field independent than girls. Sherman and Smith's (1967) study also gave support to Lynn's hypothesis when it was found that orphans receiving full-time care from male counselors were less field independent than males from normal families. Some additional indirect support for Lynn's proposition appeared in the data obtained by Corah (1965) who correlated scores of field dependence of middle-class fathers and their children. Little evidence was found of a relationship between fathers' and sons' scores, but there was a significant association between the scores of fathers and daughters. Thus it appears that the process by which fathers influence their sons' cognitive style may not be modeling. This suggests the possibility that the development of independence while interacting with the environment may be one of the antecedents of field independence.

Sex Differences

Our own work strongly supports the hypothesis that developmental identification fosters, or is associated with, cognitive competence in 4-year-old boys, but the picture is unclear concerning girls (Radin, 1972a, 1973, 1978; Radin & Epstein, 1975a, 1975b; Epstein & Radin, 1975). The data obtained have consistently shown paternal nurturance to be linked with intellectual ability in young boys and paternal restrictiveness to be linked with lack of such competence. There was no evidence of defensive identification or of a positive association between paternal punitiveness and intellectual ability. Rather, the conclusion was reached that paternal restrictiveness tended to hinder the boy's identification with his father and hence with the youngster's cognitive development. However, the link between father behavior and girls' cognitive competence was positive in one study and negligible in another. The factors that might account for this discrepancy are discussed below.

Two studies with white traditional families (that is, families in which mothers were the primary caregivers and fathers worked or attended school full-time) were conducted. The first, a pilot study for the second, involved only boys, with one-half of the sample middle-class and the other half lower-class families. The second study contained both boys and girls and three social classes, middle, working, and lower. The methodology used in both studies was the same. Fathers were interviewed at home in the presence only of their 4-year-old child. The child was asked to be in the room so that he or she could perform some tasks at the end of the interview. It was assumed that the child would make some demands on the father during the interview that he would have to handle or anticipate in some way. These paternal behaviors provided the raw data and were recorded on audiotape and subsequently coded, using 25 predetermined categories. Interviewer notations about nonverbal paternal behavior that took place were also coded. The categories were as behaviorally specific as possible (e.g., praised the child, asked the child a question). The child was administered intelligence tests within a few weeks, and the father behaviors were correlated with the child's test scores. In the pilot study the Stanford-Binet Intelligence Scale and the Peabody Picture Vocabulary Test were used; in the larger study the Stanford-Binet Intelligence Scale and some standardized Piagetian tasks were employed.

In both studies, paternal nurturance was positively and significantly associated with cognitive measures of boys. Paternal restrictiveness was negatively associated. In the pilot study, paternal behaviors were placed in these categories on an *a priori* basis. In the second study, separate factor analyses were performed on father behaviors with boys and father behaviors with girls. For boys, four factors emerged, two clearly nurturant and two essentially restrictive in quality. Although there were class differences (e.g., the restrictive variable was more important than the nurturant variable in the lower class) in general, nurturance was positively associated and restrictiveness negatively associated with cognitive competence.

For girls, the picture was sharply different. Six different factors emerged from the factor analysis, and only one of the six factors was associated with a child's cognitive score (this was in only one social class subgroup). In view of the large number of correlations performed, this may well have been caused by chance factors. Evidence also emerged of differential paternal behavior with sons and daughters. Although there had been a significant sex difference in the mean frequency of only two of the 25 behavior categories, the factor structure underlying father behavior with boys was completely different from the factor structure underlying father behavior with girls. For sons, as indicated above, there were two nurturant factors and two restrictive factors. For girls, however, three of the six factors were ambivalent in quality. For example, they contained contradictory behaviors such as meeting and ignoring explicit needs or requesting and ordering aversively. This mixed-message phenomenon did not occur in any of the boys' factors. The interpretation given to the finding was that the ambivalent message coming from the father to the daughter tended to alienate her and reduce the likelihood of the girl using him as a model for problem solving, intellectual striving, or vocabulary development. Thus his behaviors were unrelated to her cognitive scores. Even the three non-ambivalent factors that were either restrictive or nurturant in nature were unrelated to measures of the girls' intellective competence. It was suggested that 4-year-old girls were using their mothers as their primary model as a previous study (Radin, 1974) using the same methodology has indicated. Lynn and Cross' (1974) findings concerning the preference of 4-year-old girls for their mothers over their fathers tended to support this hypothesis.

A recent dissertation by Ziegler (1979) involving children 8 and 9 years of age tended to confirm the ambiguous and ambivalent nature of paternal behavior with daughters. In Ziegler's investigation, part of which involved observations of middle-class fathers interacting with their third- and fourth-grade youngsters, it was noted that girls sought their fathers' assistance more often than boys. According to the researcher, one might have then expected fathers to comply more often with their daughters than their sons, but the opposite proved to be true, leading Ziegler to conclude that ambiguity and mixed messages may indeed be characteristic of the father–daughter relationship. He hypothesized that "these paternal behaviors could serve to distance the girls emotionally by creating tension and frustration, and ultimately reduce the father's effectiveness as a model and teacher . . . such a relationship precludes the father's helping his daughter in the same way he can help his son at this age" (pp. 144–145). In spite of these findings, Ziegler's study also indicated that paternal support and encouragement as daughters completed cognitive tasks was associated with higher scores on these measures.

Adding to the accumulating evidence of a complex relationship between the father's behavior and the daughter's intellectual competence were the data emerging from the study referred to earlier of families of preschoolers with divergent patterns of childcare (Radin, 1978, 1980). When the subset of 27 girls was considered, a positive relationship was found between the fathers' global estimate of his involvement with his preschooler and the girls' mental age as measured by the Peabody Picture Vocabulary Test. However, no measures of paternal nurturance correlated with assessments of girls' mental ability. A significant interaction effect was found between sex of child and degree of father involvement on responses to a questionnaire (the Cognitive Home Environment Scale) concerning the cognitive stimulation present in the home (Radin & Sonquest, 1968; Radin & Epstein, 1975). Included in this questionnaire are items pertaining to the father's efforts to foster the child's intellective abilities by engaging in activities such as teaching the child to write and reading to the youngster. The questionnaire also contains items tapping the respondents' aspirations for the education and occupation of the child under consideration. Fathers who were primary caretakers (responsible for the children more than half the time they are awake) and had preschool daughters attained higher scores on the Cognitive Home Environment Scale than three other groups in the study: primary caregiving fathers of preschool boys, traditional fathers of boys (men who worked while their wives cared for the children on a full-time basis), and traditional fathers of preschool girls. The latter group of men had the lowest scores, in keeping with previous research in the area (Hoffman, 1977).

The results of this study were interpreted as indicating that nontraditional fathers who rejected society's sex role stereotypes for themselves and assumed the major responsibility for raising their youngsters while their wives worked or attended school also rejected sex role stereotypes for their young girls. These men may have put forth considerable effort to promote their daughter's intellectual growth, possibly to overcome the sexist socialization they would undoubtedly experience outside the home. The findings concerning greater home stimulation for girls are particularly significant, because several studies have suggested that such activities have long-term benefits for the children involved, whether fathers' activities (Radin, 1973) or mothers' (Elardo, Bradley, & Caldwell, 1975; Bradley & Caldwell, 1976; Radin, 1972b) are assessed.

These data concerning fathers and daughters appear to conflict with those obtained in the earlier observational study of traditional families in which father behavior was unrelated to girls' cognitive competence. The explanation of these contradictions may lie in the different aspects of paternal behavior measured. In the earlier study of traditional fathers, observed paternal behavior was audiotaped and coded into discrete categories; in the study of families with differing childcare arrangements, questionnaire data were used to assess the total amount of involvement the father had with the child and the content of his activities with the youngster. Thus different parental variables and different methodologies were involved.

It is also possible for fathers to spend much time with their daughters engaged in activities that foster the children's intellective growth and at the same time communicate ambivalent messages to them. The net effect may be that the girls' cognitive development is enhanced in spite of the mixed messages. Some support for this hypothesis is found in Ziegler's study in which fathers' behavior was described as ambivalent toward girls, and yet his encouragement was associated with daughters' problem-solving ability. Baumrind's (1979) theory that some abrasiveness in fathers fosters effectiveness in young girls is also supportive of this proposition, as are Bing's (1973) data indicating that fathers' reading to daughters, accompanied by paternal strictness, was linked with verbal achievement in the girls.

Thus it appears possible that paternal instructional activities with daughters, in the context of some strictness and warmth, may facilitate the girls' intellectual growth. Why this should be so is not apparent. Bing attributed it to the father's fostering femininity in the daughter; Baumrind speculated conversely that father abrasiveness may help girls overcome their female socialization and interact assertively instead of passively with the environment. It is clear that the issue is a perplexing one that will not be resolved until considerably more research is conducted.

Contributing to the complexity of this data are the findings suggesting that fathers respond to their daughters to some extent in the stereotypic ways that males behave with females. Aberle and Naegele's (1962) study of middle-class men found fathers expressing just such views. The men interviewed gave evidence that they thought of their sons as future occupants of middle-class occupational roles for which certain behaviors were of great importance. Their orientation toward their daughters, however, was as future occupants of different middle-class roles—wife and mother—for which their own standards were less exacting. In keeping with these orientations, the men voiced serious concerns about their sons' but not their daughters' success in school and attending a good college. Among the concerns voiced about girls but not boys was that they marry and not be too bossy.

More recently, Hoffman (1977) described a number of studies suggesting that fathers still aspire differentially for achievement and careers for their sons. For example, Block, Block, and Harrington (1974) observed parents in a teaching situation with their preschoolers and noted that fathers of boys were concerned with the child's achievement and emphasized the cognitive aspects of the teaching situation. With girls however, fathers were more attuned to the interpersonal aspects of the situation. Hoffman (1977) described another study by Block revealing the same sex bias. In describing their interactions with their sons, mothers and fathers were found to emphasize achievement to a greater extent than did parents who described their daughters.

Lynn (1974, 1976) also supported the hypothesis that fathers tend to respond to their daughters in a sex-stereotyped manner. He expanded on this concept by indicating that such stereotypic behavior may interfere with the cognitive development of daughters, because fathers may perceive intellectual growth and achievement as masculine rather than feminine qualities. A father who treats his daughter in a fashion that elicits a traditionally feminine reaction may thus retard her intellectual and academic development. However, if he sets up a relationship in which she can model his intellectual efforts and achievement motivation and be reinforced for doing so, he can heighten these attributes in his daughter. Perhaps this is the nature of the relationship between young girls and fathers who assume major childcare responsibilities.

Father–Daughter Trends

Moderate Distance and Autonomy. One salient difference in the research findings concerning boys and girls is that paternal warmth is seldom associated negatively with cognitive functioning in boys whereas there are indications that too much warmth may be detrimental to the development of intellective capacity in young girls. Honzik (1967), using the longitudinal data of the Berkeley Guidance Study, found that friendliness on the part of the father toward his daughter but not a close bond or expressions of affection were significantly and positively related with the girls' IQ at 7 to 9 years of age. However, a close bond between father and son was positively related with the IQ of boys.

The data of Crandall, Dewey, Katkovsky, and Preston (1964) did not fit the pattern exactly, but there is some evidence in their study that a moderate distance between father and daughter enhances the girl's intellectual competence. Crandall and her colleagues found that the academic achievement of girls but not boys in grades two through four was positively correlated with positive paternal reactions to her intellective efforts and negatively correlated with negative reactions. However, fathers who encouraged and instigated intellectual pursuits in girls had less proficient daughters. The investigators interpreted the latter finding as the result of paternal reactions to daughters of low ability. Other interpretations can be made, however, in view of the absence of a significant correlation between paternal instigative behavior and boys' intellective ability. It is possible that some distance and autonomy from fathers fosters girls' cognitive functioning. High father praise for daughters' intellectual efforts may also suggest a father who does not hold stereotypic views of girls as nonintellectual individuals. Thus these fathers may provide the enhancement Lynn (1974, 1976) suggested was possible by nonsexist fathers, provided the father does not become too involved in the girls' work.

Supporting the hypothesis that some degree of paternal distance and cognitive competence in girls are positively associated were the findings of Teahan (1963) who compared parental attitudes of high- and low-achieving college freshmen. It was found that the fathers of high-achieving girls expressed less dominating attitudes and less approval of ignoring the girls than the fathers of low-achieving female students. Thus an orientation that involves neither dominance nor ignoring appears to be associated with academic college women. The same pattern was not found for high-achieving college men. Similar results were obtained by Heilbrun, Harrel, and Gellard (1967), who also studied college women. These investigators found that the subjects did best on tasks requiring an analytic style of thinking when they viewed their fathers as having exerted little control over them and expressing little nurturance. More relevant to autonomy than moderate distance were the findings of another study by Heilbrun (1973). In this investigation it was found that female undergraduates did poorly on cognitive tasks under stress when they perceived their fathers as having exerted aversive control over them.

Investigating preschool children, Baumrind (1971) obtained results similar to those of Heilbrun who studied 18-year-old women. Baumrind discovered that observed paternal authoritarianism with preschool-age girls was negatively associated with the youngsters' cognitive performance. Our study with a similar age group found no significant correlations between these variables (Radin & Epstein, 1975a). The difference in results may be attributable to the different observational methodologies (i.e., regarding the mother's presence, discussed previously). Some support for this suggestion was found in the Harrington et al. (1978) study that used a procedure similar to ours; fathers and preschool-age girls were observed interacting alone without mothers present. Harrington's results, like ours, indicated that there was not a significant correlation between negative father behavior and girls' cognitive competence. Perhaps fathers are a bit more restrained when alone with their daughters. Further research is needed to clarify this issue.

Finally, the data from the study of families with different childcare arrangements lend support to the moderate distance hypothesis; father availability was positively associated with daughter's verbal intelligence, but assessments of his nurturance were not (Radin, 1978, 1980). Perhaps the father's presence stimulates cognitive growth of girls provided the relationship is not too loving.

Related to the autonomy issue are indications from both the Baumrind (1971) study of preschool children and our own (Jordan, Radin, & Epstein, 1975) that young girls but not young boys are hindered by paternal pressure to advance or grow. Baumrind found in her largely middle-class sample that early maturity demands and discouragement of infantile behavior by the child's father as assessed by questionnaire data were negatively correlated with the girl's IQ but not the boy's. Our investigation yielded similar results; early paternal demands for mastery and late independence granting, also assessed by questionnaire, were negatively associated with intellective scores of lower-class, 4-year-old girls. In contrast, for middle-class boys, late independence granting was positively associated with the boys' IQ scores on Piagetian tasks.

One study appears to contradict the hypothesis that some distance and autonomy from fathers fosters the cognitive growth of young girls. Cain (1971), using data supplied by the youngsters, found that high arithmetic achievement in Mexican-American children, 7 to 13 years of age, was associated with father love; low reading achievement was related to his casual attitude. Possibly father–child relationships within a Chicano culture are qualitatively different from those in Anglo families. As we mentioned previously, there is a dearth of data about paternal behavior in Mexican-American families. Perhaps love and control are not expressed the same way in these families; possibly values Chicano families hold concerning the extended family interact with father behavior to produce effects unique to that setting. We simply do not know.

Influence on Mathematics Skills. Several researchers have suggested that the relationship between fathers and daughters affects the girls' mathematical skills. The assumption is often made that relatively close contact with the father tends to foster her adoption of the fathers' masculine approach to thinking. Landy, Rosenberg, and Sutton-Smith (1968) studied the American College Entrance Examination scores of college sophomores and found that the Q or quantitative scores of women whose fathers were not present were significantly lower than Q scores of women whose fathers started working on the night shift after the girls were 10 years of age. There were no significant differences in the language scores of the two groups. Since there were no differences in the Q scores of the group with totally absent fathers and the group whose fathers started working on the night shift when the girls were under 10 years old, the authors concluded that the ages of 1 through 9 composed a critical period for the development of quantitative skills in girls, and that fathers who are available to girls influence this development.

Another study by the same investigators (Sutton-Smith, Rosenberg, & Landy, 1968) supported this conclusion. The ACE scores of college freshmen, with and without fathers, were compared in students from families of different size and sibling composition. The details of the interaction with these variables will be discussed in the section on father absence, but relevant to Q scores was the finding that there was a significant difference between father-present and father-absent groups in Q score only for females (except in one small subgroup) but in Q and L (language) scores for males. In addition, it was found that women whose fathers were absent starting when they were below 9 years of age obtained lower Q scores than women whose fathers' absence commenced after the age of 10. The age of onset of absence was not significant for men.

It is not clear why quantitative skills should be linked to father presence, especially for girls. A possible clue was offered by the authors (Rosenberg & Sutton-Smith, 1966), who postulated that independence as a personality trait mediates an interest in stimuli emanating from a variety of sources, particularly the world of objects. The authors added, "It is this interest in the object world that has often been said to underlie the superiority of boys in quantification and problem solving" (p. 27). When conditions foster the girls' emulation of brothers, described by Sutton-Smith et al. (1968) as already oriented toward independence by sex-typed reinforcement, the sisters' quantification scores are enhanced. Bing (1963) also linked independence and mathematical ability, and Lynn saw a connection between independence in the environment and field independence. One can extrapolate from the statement about brothers that any factor fostering female emulation of males—brothers, or fathers—may have a beneficial effect on quantification skills. Hence the possible link between father absence and low Q scores for women in college. The correlation obtained by Corah (1965) between field independence scores of fathers and daughters tends to support the view that women's analytic or mathematical ability may be based to some extent on modeling their fathers' thinking processes in this area.

Trends Common to Boys and Girls

Participation in Problem Solving. There are indications, although the data are not in complete agreement, that extensive father participation in the child's intellective efforts are not facilitative of the youngster's cognitive development. Boerger (1971) studied variables associated with pressure to achieve in fathers of boys in grades five and six. His data indicated that paternal participation was negatively and linearly related to achievement—that is, the fathers claiming the least participation in responding to a mailed questionnaire had the highest achieving sons, and as participation increased achievement decreased. A *post hoc* analysis of the data showed that the negative correlation was centered in arithmetic rather than in language arts or science. The results were interpreted as suggesting that although the fathers of high-achieving boys hold high aspirations for them, these fathers tend to be only indirectly involved in their sons' academic activities (e.g., providing opportunities and materials for achievement without actually directing specific tasks). Fathers of low-achieving boys appear to involve themselves directly in completion of school tasks.

Crandall et al. (1964) found that fathers' participation in boys' intellective activities were negatively associated with the boys' arithmetic achievement. The Crandall data also revealed that fathers who encouraged and instigated the intellectual pursuits of daughters had girls who were less proficient in school. Solomon, Houlihan, Busse, and Parelius (1971) conducted an observational study of black fifth-grade children and their parents in a problem-solving situation. The investigators found that a moderate amount of paternal involvement facilitated the girls' intellectual functioning, as assessed by school tests and grades. For girls, a moderate amount of paternal encouragement to engage in independent efforts free of hostility or efforts to dominate the girl was associated with high academic achievement. For boys, this curvilinear relationship did not exist. No father behavior in isolation from mother behavior during the puzzle-solving session was significantly associated with the boy's academic competence. In addition, the researchers found a negative relationship between paternal participation in the child's efforts to solve problems and the child's tendency to use efficient and constructive problem-solving techniques. Solomon and his colleagues reported studying the data carefully to determine if there was evidence, as Crandall had suggested, that parents were responding to poor academic performance in the child. They found only a slight tendency for fathers to participate more if they felt their child had low ability. The explanation offered by the Solomon group for the negative relationship between father participation and achievement behavior by the child was that the child may become more distracted when his or her father becomes involved in the problem-solving effort by the youngster.

Busse's (1969) study of black lower-class parents teaching tasks to their fifth-grade sons concluded that moderately active paternal participation while the boys were working on the tasks was associated with flexible thinking in the youngsters. Further, fathers who expressed preference in a questionnaire for a moderately active role with their children had sons higher in flexible thinking than fathers who preferred either a very active or ignoring role with their youngsters. There is also indirect evidence that father independence granting in a task situation is associated with intellectual growth in young black boys. Dill (1975) observed black fathers and sons aged 4 to 6 and 8 to 10 interacting at home in a middle-class and lower-class sample and noted that middle-class fathers had a tendency to remove themselves from the puzzle given the child, or serve as a consultant, whereas lower-class fathers became involved and acted as partners or supervisors. Dill described the middle-class men's behavior as seeming to foster independence in the boys. In view of the consistent finding that middle-class children obtain higher scores on cognitive measures than lower-class youngsters (Hess, 1970), it can be inferred that in black families, paternal fostering of autonomy in boys as they attempt to master problems may stimulate intellectual growth.

Our own research on traditional families also suggested that lack of paternal involvement when 4-year-old children were solving puzzles was related to cognitive competence in the youngsters (Radin & Epstein, 1975b). At the conclusion of the interview with the fathers, the children were given tasks to work on such as jigsaw puzzles, and fathers were told they could help if they wished. Whereas nurturant paternal behaviors during the interview were associated with intellective competence of the boys, paternal nurturance during the problem-solving segment was negatively correlated with IQ and other cognitive measures of the boys. For girls, the correlation was not significant, but there was a trend in this direction: When the total sample was grouped together, the correlation was negative and significant between a group of behaviors labeled nurturant and intellective measures of the children. A cluster of paternal behaviors labeled restrictive was not related to the cognitive measures. Regrouping the father behaviors into other categories produced the similar results. The behaviors were divided into "Father Responses to Requests for Help from the Child" and "Father-Initiated Behaviors." Each of these categories was negatively correlated with cognitive measures for the total sample and for boys. The total number of father interactions during the task-solving segment was also negatively associated with cognitive measures for the total sample and for boys. The only significant positive correlations with intellective scores were found with one father initiating behavior, "spontaneously announcing to the child that he won't help with the puzzles or showing no interest in the child's progress." This variable correlated positively with performance of Piagetian tasks for the total sample for boys.

It was possible to gain some clues about the direction of influence because the children were tested one year later on the same intellective measures. For girls, the cluster of nurturant paternal behaviors observed the previous year was now negatively related to measures of the girls' cognitive competence. Thus there was an indication that paternal efforts to be helpful were detrimental to girls' cognitive growth; it was not a case of fathers helping inept daughters. Similarly for boys and for the total sample, paternal restrictiveness, not correlated with concurrent measures of the youngsters' cognitive competence, were negatively correlated with the scores 1 year later. Again the direction of influence appeared to be from father to child; giving orders and making threats during the child's efforts to solve tasks hindered intellective development.

The contrast in correlations between paternal nurturance during the interview and boys' IQ and between paternal nurturance as the boy solved problems and his IQ was surprising. It appears evident that very similar behavior by fathers can have very different meaning in different contexts. As with the case of paternal power, paternal nurturance and helping may have generally beneficial effects, but not when the youngster is engaged in mastery efforts.

Mother as Mediator. All of the investigations reviewed and trends delineated have referred to a direct link between father and child. Another channel of influence may exist, however. Maternal behavior may mediate the relationship between father's behavior and the child's cognitive functioning. Mediation effects must be differentiated from second order effects, which have been defined as mother and father interactions with their children affected by the presence of the other spouse (Lytton, 1979). This phenomenon was described earlier in the discussion of the deficiencies of much of the earlier research on paternal influence.

A subtle illustration of the second order effect was offered by Clarke-Stewart (1978), who compared maternal behavior with her young child, 1 to 2½ years of age, in the presence and absence of her husband. According to Clarke-Stewart, mothers initiate less play with their children when fathers are around, virtually stepping back and permitting fathers to undertake as much of the childcare as they want. This phenomenon can be described in slightly different terms to make it comparable to the second order effect reported by Lytton (1979). In Clarke-Stewart's study, the father's presence reduced the play activity of the mother. In Lytton's study, the father's presence spurred the mother on to do what was expected of her but which she did not always carry out.

The concept of the mother as a mediator of father influence typically involves a longer time span than the second order effect. Pedersen (1976) graphically described the phenomenon as a psychological domino theory. The underlying principle is that an individual (in this case the father) does something to a second (the mother) and as a result, the second individual behaves differently to a third. Examples of such indirect father effects are plentiful in the literature. Pedersen (1976) found that when fathers are more supportive of mothers, the women were more effective in feeding the baby. Lamb et al. (1978) suggested that a husband's attitude toward a wife's employment influences her behavior with her infant and thereby influences the child's development. In the Gold and Reis (1978) study of preschool boys, a significant relationship was found between the quality of the mother–father relationship and the time spent by the mother with the child; the better the relationship, the more time spent with the child. Since one of the study's findings was that time spent with the boy by either parent enhanced his problem-solving ability, it can be said that the paternal influence here was both direct and indirect.

Support for the mother-as-mediator concept's applicability to older children was found in the Dyk and Witkin (1965) study of middle-class mothers of 10-year-old boys. According to the investigators, wives who felt their husband did not participate in childrearing fostered a global approach in their sons. Dyk and Witkin suggested that this indicated a father's behavior toward his wife may significantly affect her mothering. For example, he may add to her security by accepting her; he may add to her uncertainty by criticizing her.

In one of our studies, paternal expectations of daughters appeared to affect the mothers' behavior with the girls (Radin & Epstein, 1975a). Fathers' long-term and short-term academic expectations, as assessed by a questionnaire, were positively and significantly correlated with measures of the girls' cognitive functioning; his observable behaviors were not, however. It was hypothesized that these future expectations may have been communicated to his wife who consequently altered her own expectations and altered her own expectations and behavior with the young girl. Some support for this view was found in the data concerning another factor on the questionnaire: "mother stimulates child" (e.g., mother assists child with learning). This dimension was significantly related to the intellective competence of girls but not boys. Thus fathers' expectations concerning daughters may have influenced mothers' behaviors and thereby indirectly fostered the girls' cognitive development.

If paternal expectations for children can influence maternal behavior toward them, it is not unlikely that those expectations may continue to exert influence when the father is no longer in the home, especially if his departure did not engender hostile maternal feelings. Pedersen, Andersen, and Cain (1977) suggested that the influence of a family member may be so enduring in a psychological sense that the effects are manifest in situations that do not include the person. It is possible that the influence endures even beyond the time that the family member remains at home.

STATUS CHARACTERISTICS

In addition to what the father does, feels, or thinks, the socioeconomic rank the father holds appears to relate to his children's cognitive competence. For example, one longitudinal study found that the father's education alone predicted his child's attained educational level at 26 years as well as the combination of both mother's and father's education, and even the child's own IQ (McCall, 1977). Many significant correlations have been reported between the father's education or occupation and the child's intellective competence, but the reason for the relationship remains obscure. The material resources, such as books, that an affluent parent can provide may be important. Trips to museums, motivated peers, successful models in the neighborhood, and so forth may all be relevant, as Coleman et al. (1966) have shown. Certain parental linguist modes may facilitate mental growth (Hess et al., 1968) and these tend to be class linked. Finally, one is left with the question raised earlier about the role of constitutional and environmental factors in any significant correlation between father and child characteristics. In any case, since the correlations between children's cognitive scores and parent's education are generally higher for fathers than mothers (Honzig, 1963; McCall, 1977), it is not reasonable to dismiss the link between child scores and father status characteristics as mere artifacts of the association between mother and child variables.

Jencks, Smith, Acland, Bane, Cohen, Gintis, Heyns, and Michelson (1972) reported the following correlations between nonfarm males' cognitive ability at 11 years of age and father data: with father's education, $r = .300$; with father's occupation, $r = .300$. The correlations for the adult nonfarm males' cognitive ability and their fathers' characteristics were as follows: with father's education, $r = .305$; with father's occupation, $r = .314$. To obtain a numerical value for the father's occupation in the above calculation, the occupation was rated, using the Duncan scale where possible. The male's score at 11 was usually the sixth grade aptitude test score. The adult male's cognitive score was one of the military classification test scores. Majoribanks' (1972) study of 11-year-old English boys from the middle and lower classes yielded comparable results.

The correlation between total score on the SRA Primary Test of Mental Ability was .31 ($p < .01$) with father's education and .43($p < .01$) with father's occupation. Thus the Jencks, Honzik, and Marjoribanks studies all reported correlations between father's education and boy's IQ at 11 between .30 and .35; the figures are remarkably close.

Honzik's (1963) data were similar. Using a sample of individuals described as representative of the children born in Berkeley between January 1, 1928 and June 30, 1929, Honzik obtained the correlations shown in Table 1 between father's education and the child's IQ at different ages.

Table 1. Correlations Between Father's Education and Child's IQ[a]

Age of Child (years)	Correlations for Boys	Correlations for Girls
1¾	.01	.17
3	-.08	.32*
4	.10	.36*
5	.23	.34**
6	.17	.43**
7	.34**	.44**
8	.27**	.41**
9	.29**	.41**
10	.27**	.40**
12–13	.35**	.42**
14–15	.41**	.33**

[a]The data are from Honzik (1963).
*$p < .05$
**$p < .01$

The results did not differ much when Honzik employed an index of the father's social class, the Warner Index of Status Characteristics, based on father's occupation, the source of his income, house type, and dwelling area. The correlation between this measure and the girls' IQ reached significance at age 3 when the correlation was .27; the correlation reached significance at age 5 for boys when it was .37. In support of these findings were those of Reppucci (1971) who studied 48 27-month-old, middle-class children to explore the relationship between parents' education and measures of the children's cognitive competence. The correlations between the fathers' education and boys' performance on a number of cognitive tasks were not significant, but father education was significantly associated with the girls' performance on a number of tasks with the coefficients of correlation ranging between .49 and .72.

Kohn and Rosman (1973), Baumrind (1971), and our investigation (Radin & Epstein, 1975b) presented correlational data between father's education and intelligence scores of children at 4 to 6 years of age. Baumrind obtained a correlation of .25 for girls 4 years of age and .09 for boys. Neither figure was significant. Similar figures were obtained when a measure of the father's occupation was used in the correlation in place of his education. Kohn and Rosman combined father's education and occupation into one index, the Hollingshead Two-Factor Index of Social Position. A correlation of .24, which was significant, was obtained between the IQ of kindergarten boys and the Hollingshead Index. According to the authors, the correlation obtained in their study was lower than many reported in the literature (typically .40 between parent occupation and the child's intelligence) because their sample consisted of 5-year-old males, and the work of Honzik and others indicated that social class variables do not usually become predictive of boys' IQ until 5 or 6 years of age.

Our study also employed the Hollingshead Two-Factor Index of Social Position and found the correlation with boys' IQ at the end of the kindergarten year to be .12 for boys (not significant) and .34 ($p < .01$) for girls. The correlation between father's education and IQ were similar: .08 for boys and .31 for girls. Thus there is some consistency in correlational pattern across studies, although not as much as there was for 11-year-old children. This is not surprising since the IQ has stabilized by 11 years, whereas at the ages of 4 to 6, it is just beginning to stabilize (Honzik, 1963). Considering the data from the Baumrind, Kohn and Rosman, Honzik, and Radin studies, the range of correlations for boys aged 4 to 6 was .09 to .24; for girls the range extended from .25 to .36. The correlations were clearly higher for girls; there was not even an overlap. Further, in the studies that included both boys and girls, the correlations were consistently higher for girls. The reason for the earlier association of girls' cognitive scores and fathers' education or occupation is not entirely clear. Honzig (1963) attributed the differential pattern to sex differences in the rate of physical growth. Just as girls achieve their full height at an earlier age, so too does their central nervous system, and consequently their mental growth, develop more rapidly. Whether this hypothesis is true remains to be determined.

None of the above studies reported correlations of over .50 between father characteristics and child's cognitive competence. Thus one can say that, at most, under 25 percent of the variation in a child's cognitive score is attributable to the social class status of the child's father. It is of interest that both the Baumrind and Radin studies obtained higher correlations between observed paternal behavior and the child's IQ than between the father's education and the youngster's IQ.

FATHER ABSENCE

Much of the evidence concerning the father's role in the child's intellective functioning is contradictory, although some trends are emerging. A recent review of the relevant literature concluded that growing up in a fatherless home is likely to have a damaging effect on the child's cognitive development (Shinn, 1978) although there are exceptions to this conclusion. The issue of the effects of father absence is particularly important in the light of the current estimates that one out of every four children under 18 years of age in the United States will be living with one parent by 1990, virtually all living with mothers (Glick, 1979). In 1960, the figure was less than one out of 10; in 1978 it was almost one out of five. Perhaps the very prevalence of single-parent families in the 1980s and 1990s will make the research of the past two decades on father absence inapplicable, because as the number of single-parent families raising children sharply increases, particularly in middle-class families (Bronfenbrenner, 1975), the attitudes of society and the mass media are also likely to change, and more support groups and extended family networks may emerge. What was once considered a ''broken family'' may become accepted as a functional, alternative family structure. There is evidence that some sociologists already conceptualize the single black parent raising a child in this manner (Billingsley, 1968). In spite of the possibly outdated nature of the past findings concerning the effects of father absence on children's cognitive growth, it is important to know what has been discovered if for no other reason than to compare these conclusions with those that may be reached in the coming decades in a changed societal context.

Cumulative Damage

Among those who reported a negative impact are Deutsch (1960) and Deutsch and Brown (1964) who studied the school performance of black, primarily lower-class children. Deutsch found that 10- to 13-year-old children without fathers scored lower on academic tests than their classmates with fathers. Deutsch and Brown found no significant difference in achievement of father-present and and father-absent youngsters in the first grade, but by the fifth grade a significant difference appeared. The researchers attributed these results to a cumulative damaging effect of father absence. Generally in support of this view were the findings of Sciara (1975) who collected fourth grade reading and arithmetic test scores of over 1,000 black children from low-income metropolitan areas. When the total sample was considered, Sciara found significant differences in favor of the father-present children in both reading and arithmetic, although the differences were small (i.e., 0.3 of a school year in each subject). When each sex was considered alone, there was no difference in arithmetic or reading scores between father-present and father-absent boys, and a small significant difference (0.4 of a school year) in arithmetic in favor of girls with fathers present. The most significant finding of the study was the relatively large difference between father-present and father-absent children with IQ's over 100; the difference in scores here was approximately one full school year in both mathematics and reading. For those with IQ's under 100 the differences were 0.1 of a school year in both areas. Further support for the cumulative deficit theory was provided by Hess and his colleagues (Hess, Shipman, Brophy, Bear, & Adelberger, 1969; Hess, Shipman, Brophy, & Bear, 1968), who failed to find cognitive deficits associated with father absence in lower-income black kindergarten and first-grade children but did find such deficits in later grades. However, Santrock and Wohlford (1970) compared lower-class white boys in fifth grade who were father-present and father-absent and discovered that the lowest scores were obtained by boys whose fathers' absence began when the youngsters were 6 to 9 years of age. This suggested that recency of departure was more critical than the total number of years of absence. But in support of the cumulative deficit hypothesis, the researchers found that the next worst scores were obtained by boys whose fathers' absence commenced when the youngsters were under 2 years of age; the next lowest marks appeared among boys who became father-absent when they were 3 to 5 years old.

Sex Differences

Shelton's (1968) findings resembled those of Deutsch and Brown (1964). He compared junior high school students from Iowa who were father-absent and father-present and found the former group was significantly lower in academic grade point average, controlling for IQ. In addition, there was evidence that the family dissolution had a greater impact on boys than on girls. The boys who were father-absent obtained significantly lower grades than the father-absent girls, although there were no differences in the grades of father-present boys and girls. Further, although father-absent boys scored significantly below father-present boys, there was no difference in the grades of father-present and father-absent girls. In accord with these data are the findings of the Pedersen, Rubenstein, and Yarrow study (1973, 1979) indicating that black male infants raised without fathers were less cognitively competent than infants raised in two-parent families, even when the average number of persons in the household was the same in the two groups. Pedersen et al. did not find father absence affecting the development of girls.

The data obtained by Lessing, Zagorin, and Nelson (1970) gave additional support to the hypothesis that there are sex differences in the impact of father absence. These investigators found that the father-absent youngsters, all of whom were between 9 and 15 years of age and had been father-absent for at least 2 years, obtained lower Performance IQ scores on the Weschler Intelligence Scale than their father-present counterparts, regardless of sex or social class. However, boys but not girls who were father-absent obtained lower scores than their father-present peers on the arithmetic subtest. All of the children had been referred for diagnosis to a research institute and were considered a clinic sample by the authors. This factor may account for the difference in findings regarding father-absent girls between the Shelton study and that of Lessing et al.; the impact appeared to be much greater in the latter investigation.

In an extensive study, Santrock (1972) explored the differential impact on lower-class white children of father absence through death versus father absence because of divorce, desertion, or separation. The effect of the child's sex and age at the onset of the absence was also investigated by examining the children's third and sixth grade scores on standard achievement tests. The major conclusions were that the sex of the child, the age at the onset of absence, and the reason for absence were all significant variables mediating the impact of father absence on the child's academic and intellective performance. In general, boys were found to be more damaged by father absence than girls were. However, both boys and girls who were father-absent for any reason scored lower on third grade achievement tests than their father-present peers. For both boys and girls, greater impairment was found when the father's absence was because of divorce, desertion, or separation than it was because of death.

When not death-related, father absence occurring before the age of 5 was more damaging than an absence for the same reason occurring between 6 and 11 for children of either sex. The ages of 0 to 2 were particularly vulnerable ones for both boys and girls when the father left home because of divorce, desertion, or separation. When the father's absence was because of death, however, the most vulnerable age for boys was 6 to 9. There was no evidence of cognitive impairment in the boys whose fathers died before the boys were 2; there was even a trend for such boys to be superior in IQ to their father-present peers. An additional difference between boys and girls was their reaction to the presence of a stepfather in the home. If a stepfather entered a family in which the father's absence was because of divorce, desertion, or separation before the child was 5, the academic scores of boys improved; those of girls did not. Thus the study tended to support the proposition that modeling of the same sex parent influences the cognitive functioning of young boys.

Investigating an older group of students, Chapman (1977) arrived at similar conclusions. In a tightly controlled study with 16 white male and 16 white female college students in each of three family structures: intact, father-absent, and stepfather-present, Chapman's data indicated that the presence of a stepfather was associated with the attenuation of the damaging effect on SAT scores in father-absent males, and the younger the boy was when his mother remarried the higher his SAT scores. However, Chapman found no consistent father absence effects on the cognitive performance of females and hence no consistent stepfather effect. Further, contrary to the findings of Carlsmith (1964) discussed earlier, Chapman found that father absence was more strongly associated with lower verbal scores than lower mathematics scores for the males in her sample.

Age of Onset of Absence

In addition to the Santrock investigation, several other studies focused on the child's age at onset of the father's absence. Maxwell's (1961) investigation of British children 8 to 13 years of age and under treatment in a psychological clinic revealed that those who were father-absent starting when the youngsters were over 5 years of age were below average on the Weschler Intelligence Scale. Those whose fathers were absent commencing when the children were below 5 were not below average. Although both boys and girls were included in the study, no breakdown was given by sex of child. In the area of mathematics, Sutton-Smith and his colleagues (1968) found the ages of 1 through 9 to be the vulnerable period for girls. The total number of years the father was absent was not important. Shelton (1968) found no difference in achievement among three subgroups of children in junior high school without fathers who were identified according to the time of the dissolution of the home. As indicated above, Santrock found that both the sex of the child and the reason for the father's absence influenced the most vulnerable age of onset of absence. Thus there appears to be little consensus about a single critical age when the death or departure of the father is most damaging.

Impact on Young Children

Kohn and Rosman (1973) reported no significant differences in Stanford-Binet IQ of father-present and father-absent kindergarten boys from three social classes. Both white and black youngsters were included in their sample. Many other cognitive measures were used as well but for "very few" were significant correlations obtained with father absence. The authors stated that these results supported their previous findings that family intactness was not very relevant for cognitive functioning at kindergarten age. This conclusion would be in accordance with findings of Deutsch and Brown (1964) and Hess et al. (1968) in their studies of young black children. Coleman et al. (1966) similarly found no difference in ability test scores of father-present and father-absent kindergarten children in a sample that included black and white youngsters. According to Hetherington, Cox, and Cox (1978a) cognitive differences in children from one- and two-parent homes are rarely found in the preschool years. The reason may be that no cumulative deficit has occurred yet, as Deutsch (1960) suggested, or that the types of cognitive skills measured in very young children are more impervious to father absence, as Shinn (1978) postulated.

Race and Ethnicity

The importance of ethnicity in father absence was demonstrated in Coleman's study when the sixth, ninth, and twelfth grade achievement test scores were examined. There were no differences in school achievement between black or white students from structurally intact homes and their peers from nonintact homes. However, there were significant differences for other minority groups, particularly Oriental-Americans, Mexican-Americans, and, to a lesser extent, Puerto Ricans. Although Coleman and his colleagues did not comment on the fact, it appeared that families from cultures in which fathers tend to be very powerful are most adversely affected by their absence. The authors noted, however, that "contrary to much that has been written, the structural integrity of the home (principally the father's presence or absence) shows very little relation to achievement for Negroes. It does, however, show a strong relation to achievement for other minority groups" (p. 302).

Other researchers similarly failed to find differences in cognitive performance between father-present and father-absent black youngsters. Wasserman (1968) found father-absent, lower-class black boys, 10 to 16 years of age, no worse in academic work than their father-present peers, although approximately 60 percent of both groups repeated a grade. Cortes and Fleming (1968) found no difference in achievement between lower-class black boys, 9 to 11 years of age, who were with or without fathers or father substitutes. Both groups were below norms on standard achievement tests, particularly in the area of arithmetic. Further, in Shinn's (1978) review of recent literature on father absence, she found that 43 percent, or six out of 14 studies involving black families, evidenced detrimental effects of father absence, whereas the figure was 57 percent, or 12 out of 21 studies for investigations conducted with whites. Perhaps the lower-class black child is already so overwhelmed by adversity that the additional handicap of fatherlessness does not have a critical impact. It may be that the children who suffer the most are those whose intellectual potential has at least a moderate chance of being fulfilled. Sciara's (1975) finding that there were far more damaging effects of father absence on low-income black children with IQs above 100 than on children with IQs under 100 would tend to support this view. It was the more advantaged children in this population—that is, those with IQs over 100, whose growth was curtailed when a father was no longer in the home.

Affluence and Giftedness

Hilgard, Neuman, and Fisk (1960) investigated a representative sample of people 19 to 49 years of age from a university town who had lost their fathers in childhood. The findings indicated that the men were highly successful academically and occupationally. Albert (1969), as reported by Biller (1971), analyzed the family background of geniuses and discovered a high rate of father loss during childhood. He attributed this phenomenon to the possibility that father-absent gifted children were freer to explore their environment and develop a more creative type of behavior. Biller (1971) offered an alternate explanation. He posed the possibility that an intense relationship with an intellectually-oriented mother may have facilitated the development of the gifted, father-absent children. In support of this view, Biller cited the findings of Levy (1943) that middle-class, maternally overprotected boys did superior work in school, especially in subjects requiring verbal skill; their mathematics performance was not at the same level. This finding is consistent with Carlsmith's (1964) conclusion that fathers play an important role in the development of mathematical ability in boys.

Lessing et al. (1970) found that working-class children with no father earned significantly lower Verbal and Full Scale IQs on the Weschler Intelligence Scale than their father-present peers, but middle-class, father-absent children showed significantly higher mean Verbal IQs than father-present children from the same background. According to the authors, "The pervasive cognitive deficit found among working-class, father-absent children is most plausibly interpreted as a massive stress reaction to the loss of many resources provided by the father, in the absence of any compensatory gains" (p. 192). This suggests that middle-class families are able to continue providing material resources to their youngsters even after the departure or death of the father, and the children are thereby able to withstand the loss more effectively. Lessing et al., however, did not indicate what the compensatory gain experienced by middle-class, father-absent children could be. Perhaps it is closeness to an intellectually oriented mother that Biller discussed, but another possible source of strength to the child in a father-absent home may exist, that of added responsibility and autonomy. This conclusion was reached by a researcher who intervieweed over 200 single parents from a wide range of educational backgrounds and approximately 40 children, ranging in age from 6 years to adulthood and living with single parents (Weiss, 1979). Weiss proposed that women without husbands who work full-time are likely to forgo a power hierarchy present in two-parent families and share managerial responsibilities with their children. As a consequence, there may be a fostering of early maturity in the youngsters. "For many children, both younger and older, the new demands on them for autonomy and responsibility may lead to growth . . . independence and a sense of competence" (p. 110).

Conversely, in a longitudinal study of divorced families with preschoolers, Hetherington, Cox, and Cox (1978a, 1979b) found that 2 years after the divorce the mother was making fewer demands for mature, independent behavior in the children. This led to short attention spans and distractability in the young children that resulted in a drop in scores on cognitive tasks requiring sustained attention. The discrepancy in the Weiss and Hetherington findings highlights the fact that the age of the child and possibly the number of years spent in a single-parent family mediate the effects of father absence on the child's development. It is clearly dangerous to generalize the conclusions concerning the father absence beyond the characteristics of the sample studied.

Family Structure and Composition

The importance of the family structure and composition on the impact of father absence was made salient by the research of Sutton-Smith, Rosenberg, and Landy (1968). They compared the American College Entrance Examination scores of father-present and father-absent, middle-class college sophomores from one-child, two-child, and three-child families. Also examined were the effects of birth order and sex of siblings. The findings indicated that for the majority of the sample, quantitative, language, and total scores were lower for father-absent than for father-present students, regardless of the student's age at the onset of the father absence or the length of time the father was away. However, the effects of father absence were more pervasive for males than for females and were strongest in three-child families, moderate in two-child families, and minimal in one-child families.

Blanchard and Biller (1971) found third grade boys who became father-absent when they were over 5 years old performed better than their peers whose father absence commenced when they were under 5. The grades of boys with little father interaction resembled those of the latter boys. High school boys who were father-absent in their early childhood were shown by Carlsmith (1964) to have higher verbal than mathematics scores. The incidence of this feminine pattern was correlated with the length of father absence and the age of onset of absence. Male college freshmen in the Nelsen and Maccoby (1966) investigation who were father-absent were significantly higher in verbal and mathematics scores than their father-present peers. Landy, Rosenberg, and Sutton-Smith (1969) found that college women who were father-absent as a result of their fathers working the night shift obtained lower quantitative scores, but not lower language scores, when the absence occurred before they were 9 years old. Finally, Chapman (1977) and Barclay and Cusumano (1967) reported that father-absent boys were less field independent than their father-present counterparts.

Trends Regarding Father Absence

Several trends emerge from the array of contradictory and nonoverlapping evidence concerning father absence. It appears that father-present/father-absent is not a dichotomous variable and should not be treated in that fashion. More relevant is the amount of father involvement with the child. In general, boys appear to be more damaged than girls by father absence. For both sexes, quantitative scores appear to be more sensitive to paternal involvement than verbal scores, particularly for college-bound high school students, where such separate scores are readily available. Other skills related to mathematics also appear to be responsive to father involvement. Although the evidence is not uniform, the preponderance of data suggest that father absence is most damaging when the child is under 5 years old. However, the effect of the damage on cognitive performance does not become evident until the youngster is at least 8 years old. For boys, the presence of a stepfather appears to attentuate the damaging effect of a missing father, and a recent death appears to be more debilitating than a recent divorce or separation. There is some evidence that father absence has the most debilitating effects in ethnic groups that tend to be patriarchal.

It is clear that the effect of diminished paternal involvement with children must be examined in the context of the entire family. When the circumstances are quite positive (e.g., university-based families or middle-class families with one child,) father absence appears to have relatively little detrimental effect on the intellectual functioning of the child and may even stimulate the child's cognitive growth in some instances, particularly in the area of verbal ability. When the circumstances are extremely impoverished (e.g., lower-class black families,) the additional damage wrought by father absence may be fairly limited since there are already numerous factors hindering the actualization of the child's mental ability. Father absence may have the most impact when conditions are intermediate, in working-class families or lower-class families with very bright children. Here the possibility of full cognitive development exists but it is problematic. The subtlety of the findings regarding family structure and composition opens a Pandora's box of questions concerning the possible interaction effects of father absence with social class, ethnicity, age of child, and cause of absence in families of any given structure and composition. The number of permutations and combinations to be studied is overwhelming. Perhaps some explanatory principles will soon emerge to create order out of the mass of data that has been collected about single-parent families.

SUMMARY

In spite of the problematic nature of the data available on the father's role in the child's cognitive development, several trends, varying in strength, can be detected. Paternal nurturance appears to be more closely associated with the cognitive competence of boys than girls. A close relationship between father and son seems to foster an analytic cognitive style in the child. There are indications that powerful fathers foster their sons' cognitive development provided the power is not used to intimidate the boys while they are engaged in mastery efforts. Insofar as girls are concerned, the father's influence is more complex and includes contradictory elements. For example, some degree of autonomy and distance from fathers appears to be associated with girls' cognitive proficiency, although specific father interest in their academic progress appears to stimulate their intellective growth. For both males and females, authoritarian paternal behavior tends to be associated with reduced academic competence, as does intense paternal involvement in problem-solving activities of the child. There are indications that fathers can influence their children indirectly through the impact the men have on their wives. This can be on a relatively long-term basis as well as immediately by the impact of his presence during mother–child interactions.

Many variables appear to mediate the effect of father absence on the child's intellectual performance, including the reason for his absence, the child's age at the onset of absence, the sex of the child, family composition and structure, ethnicity, and the socioeconomic status of the family. Father absence prior to age 5 appears to be the most damaging to the intellective functioning of young boys, except in the case of death where recency is the most important variable. Father absence in children's early years appears to result in a cognitive profile in college men more typical of females than males—that is, a higher verbal than mathematics score. Father absence prior to age 9 tends to hinder the development of girls' mathematical skills.

Less than 25 percent of the variance in the child's IQ is accounted for by fathers' education, leaving 75 percent to be accounted for by other variables. The relationship between the child's IQ and father's education becomes manifest at an earlier age for girls (about 3) than for boys (about 6). Whether the link between the father's education and the child's intellective competence is because of genetic heritage, environment, or both in varying degrees, is unknown at this time.

It is clear that much additional research is needed to clarify the father's role in the child's cognitive growth. Among the most pressing needs are longitudinal studies with repeated observations of the father's behavior and the child's intellective performance and investigations of paternal childrearing practices and their correlates in black, Hispanic, and Asian families. Observational studies of father behavior in the presence and absence of his wife and other family members are also needed to determine some of the ecological influences on father–child interactions. Perhaps most provocative at the moment are questions concerning how much of paternal behavior is constitutionally determined, how much is caused by early socialization, and how much is attributable to current circumstances. A comparison of the behaviors of fathers who were primary caretakers of infants and those who were secondary caretakers found that some behaviors, such as more playfulness, were common to both groups of men compared to their wives (Field, 1978). There were also differences between the two groups of men, however. For example, there was more "infanticized" imitative behaviors by both male and female primary caretakers than by secondary fathers. As in the case of our study of primary caretaking fathers, the elusive question of selectivity remains: Are the men who choose to care for children inherently different from their traditional peers, or did circumstances shape their behaviors? Only a longitudinal investigation will provide the answer.

One is left with the overall conclusion that in spite of the limitations in the state of our knowledge, a father influences his children's mental development through many and diverse channels: through his genetic background, through his manifest behavior with his offspring, through the attitudes he holds about himself and his children, through the behavior he models, through his position in the family system, through the material resources he is able to supply for his children, through the influence he exerts on his wife's behavior, through his ethnic heritage, and through the vision he holds for his children. Finally, when he dies or separates from the family, the memories he leaves with his wife and children continue to exert an influence perhaps equal to the impressions he made on the youngsters when he was physically present.

REFERENCES

Aberle, D. F., & Naegele, K. D. Middle-class fathers' occupational role and attitudes toward children. *American Journal of Orthopsychiatry*, 1952, **22**, 366–378.

Albert, R. S. Early cognitive development among the gifted. Paper presented at the meeting of the Western Psychological Association, Vancouver, British Columbia, June 1969.

Andersland, P. B. Parental rejection and adolescent academic achievement. *Dissertation Abstracts*, 1968, **28**, (11-B), 4751.

Baer, D. M., & Sherman, J. A. Reinforcement control of generalized imitation in young children. *Journal of Experimental Child Psychology*, 1964, **1**, 37–49.

Bandura, A. Social learning through imitation. In M. R. Jones (Ed.), *Nebraska symposium on motivation*. Lincoln: University of Nebraska Press, 1962.

Bane, M. J., & Jencks, C. Five myths about your I.Q. In E. M. Hetherington and R. D. Parke (Eds.), *Contemporary readings in child psychology*. New York: Mc-Graw-Hill, 1977.

Barclay, A. G., & Cusumano, D. Father absence, cross-sex identity, and field-dependent behavior in male adolescents. *Child Development*, 1967, **38**, 243–250.

Baumrind, D. Current patterns of parental authority. *Developmental Psychology Monographs*, 1971, **4**, 1–103.

Baumrind, D. Current issues in socialization. Paper presented at the Society for Research in Child Development, San Francisco, March 14, 1979.

Bayley, N. Behavior correlates of mental growth: Birth to thirty-six years. *American Psychologist,* 1968, **23,** 1–17.

Bell, R. Q. A reinterpretation of the direction of effects in studies of socialization. *Psychological Review,* 1968, **75,** 81–95.

Belsky, J. Mother-father-infant interaction: A naturalistic observational study. *Developmental Psychology,* 1979, **15,** 601–607.

Berry, J. W. Temne and Eskimo perceptual skills. *International Journal of Psychology,* 1966, **1,** 207-229.

Biller, H. B. *Father, child, and sex role.* Lexington, Mass.: Heath, 1971.

Biller, H. B. *Paternal deprivation: Family, school, sexuality, and society.* Lexington, Mass.: Heath, 1974.

Billingsley, A. *Black families in white America.* Englewood Cliffs, N.J.: Prentice-Hall, 1968.

Bing, E. The effect of childrearing practices on development of differential cognitive abilities. *Child Development,* 1963, **34,** 631–648.

Blanchard, R. W., & Biller, H. B. Father availability and academic performance among third-grade boys. *Developmental Psychology,* 1971, **4,** 301–315.

Block, J. H., Block, J. & Harrington, D. M. The relationship of parental teaching strategies to ego-resiliency in pre-school children. Paper presented at the meeting of Western Psychological Association, San Francisco, 1974.

Boerger, P. H. The relationship of boys' intellectual achievement behavior to parental involvement, aspirations, and accuracy of IQ estimate. *Dissertation Abstracts International,* 1971, **31,** 5191.

Bowerman, C. E., & Elder, G. H., Jr. Variations in adolescent perception of family power structure. *American Sociological Review,* 1964, **29,** 551–567.

Bradley, R. H., & Caldwell, B. M. The relation of infants' home environment to mental test performance at fifty-four months: A follow-up study. *Child Development,* 1976, **47,** 1172–1174.

Bronfenbrenner, U. The challenge of social change to public policy and developmental research. Paper presented at the biennial meeting at the Society for Research in Child Development, Denver, April 12, 1975.

Busse, T. V. Child-rearing antecedents of flexible thinking. *Developmental Psychology,* 1969, **1,** 585–591.

Cain, M. A. A study of relationship between selected factors and the school achievement of Mexican migrant children. *Dissertation Abstracts International,* 1971, **31,** (8-A), 3947.

Carlsmith, L. Effect of early father absence on scholastic aptitude. *Harvard Educational Review,* 1964, **34,** 3–21.

Chapman, M. Father absence, stepfather and the cognitive performance of college students. *Child Development,* 1977, **48,** 1155–1158.

Clarke-Stewart, K. A. Interaction between mothers and their young children: Characteristics and consequences. *Monographs of the Society for Research in Child Development,* 1973, **38,** Serial No. 153.

Clarke-Stewart, K. A. And daddy makes three: The father's impact on mother and young child. *Child Development,* 1978, **49,** 466-478.

Coleman, J. S., Campbell, E. Q., Hobson, C. J., McPartland, J., Mood, A. M., Weinfeld, F. D., & York, R. L. *Equality of educational opportunity.* Washington, D.C.: U.S. Department of Health, Education and Welfare, Office of Education, 1966.

Corah, N. L. Differentation in children and their parents. *Journal of Personality,* 1965, **33,** 300-308.

Cortes, C. F., & Fleming, R. The effects of father absence on the adjustment of culturally disadvantaged boys. *Journal of Special Education,* 1968, **2,** 413-420.

Crandall, V., Dewey, R., Katkovsky, W., & Preston, A. Parents' attitudes and behaviors and grade-school children's academic achievements. *Journal of Genetic Psychology,* 1964, **104,** 53-66.

Cross, H. J., & Allen, J. Relationship between memories of parental behavior and academic achievement motivation. *Proceedings of the 77th Annual Convention, American Psychological Association,* 1969, 285-286.

Deutsch, M. Minority group and class status as related to social and personality factors in scholastic achievement. *Monographs of Sociology and Applied Anthropology,* 1960, **2,** 1-32.

Deutsch, M., & Brown, R. Social influences in Negro-white intelligence differences. *Journal of Social Issues,* 1964, **20,** 24-35.

Dill, J. R. Indices of socialization: Black father-son interactions (a preliminary report). Paper presented at the Society for Research in Child Development Bienniel Conference, Denver, April 11, 1975.

Dyk, R. B., & Witkin, H. A. Family experiences related to the development of differentiation in children. *Child Development,* 1965, **36,** 21-55.

Elardo, R., Bradley, R., & Caldwell, B. M. The relation of infants' home environments to mental test performance from six to thirty-six months: A longitudinal analysis. *Child Development;* 1975, **46,** 71-76.

Epstein, A. S., & Radin, N. Motivational components related to father behavior and cognitive functioning in preschoolers. *Child Development,* 1975, **46,** 831-839.

Farber, B. Effects of a severely mentally retarded child on the family. In E. P. Trapp & P. Himelstein (Eds.), *Readings on the exceptional child.* New York: Appleton-Century-Crofts, 1962, pp. 227-246.

Fagot, B. I. Sex differences in toddlers' behavior and parental reaction. *Developmental Psychology,* 1974, **10,** 554-558.

Field, T. Interaction behaviors of primary versus secondary caretaker fathers. *Developmental Psychology,* 1978, **14,** 183-184.

Frodi, A. M., Lamb, M. E., Leavitt, L. A., Donovan, W. L., Neff, C., & Sherry, D. Fathers' and mothers' responses to the faces and cries of normal and premature infants. *Developmental Psychology*, 1978, **14**, 490–498.

Gewirtz, H. B., & J. L. Gewirtz. Visiting and caretaking patterns for kibbutz infants: Age and sex trends. *American Journal of Orthopsychiatry*, 1968, **38**, 427–443.

Gewirtz, J. L., & Stingle, K. G. Learning of generalized imitation as the basis for identification. *Psychological Review*, 1968, **75**, 374–397.

Glick, P. C. Children of divorced parents in demographic perspective. *Journal of Social Issues*, 1979, **35**, 170–182.

Gold, D., & Andres, D. Comparisons of adolescent children with employed and nonemployed mothers. *Merrill-Palmer Quarterly*, 1978, **24**, 243–254.

Grunebaum, M. G., Hurwitz, I., Prentice, N. M., & Sperry, B. M. Fathers of sons with primary neurotic learning inhibition. *American Journal of Orthopsychiatry*, 1962, **32**, 462–473.

Harrington, D. M., Block, J. H., & Block, J. Intolerance of ambiguity in preschool children: Psychometric considerations, behavioral manifestations, and parental correlates. *Developmental Psychology*, 1978, **14**, 242–256.

Heber, F. R. Sociocultural mental retardation—A longitudinal study. Paper presented at the Vermont Conference on the Primary Prevention of Psychopathology, Burlington, June 1976.

Heilbrun, A. B., Jr. *Aversive maternal control*. New York: Wiley, 1973.

Heilbrun, A. B., Jr., Harrell, S. N., & Gillard, B. J. Perceived childrearing attitudes of fathers and cognitive control in daughters. *Journal of Genetic Psychology*, 1967, **111**, 29–40.

Herzog, E., & Sudia, C. *Boys in fatherless families*. Washington, D.C.: U.S. Department of Health, Education and Welfare, 1970.

Hess, R. D. Social class and ethnic influences upon socialization. In P. H. Mussen (Ed.), *Carmichael's manual of child psychology*, 3rd ed., Vol. 2. New York: Wiley, 1970.

Hess, R. D., Shipman, V. C., Brophy, J. E., & Bear, R. M. *The cognitive environment of urban preschool children*. Chicago: University of Chicago, 1968 (ERIC Document Reproduction Service No. ED039264).

Hess, R. D., Shipman, V. C., Brophy, J. E., Bear, R. M., & Adelberger, A. B. *The cognitive environments of urban preschool children: Follow-up phase*. Chicago: Graduate School of Education, University of Chicago, 1969 (ERIC Document Reproduction Service No. 039270).

Hetherington, E. M., Cox, M., & Cox, R. Family interaction and the social, emotional, and cognitive development of children following divorce. Johnson and Johnson Conference on the Family, Washington, D.C., May 1978(a).

Hetherington, E. M., Cox, M., & Cox, R. The aftermath of divorce. In J. H. Stevens, Jr., & M. Matthew (Eds.), *Mother-child, father-child relationships*. Washington, D.C.: National Association for the Education of Young Children, 1978(b).

Hetherington, E. M., & Frankie, G. Effects of parental dominance, warmth, and conflict on imitation in children. *Journal of Personality and Social Psychology*, 1967, **6**, 119–125.

Hilgard, J. R., Neuman, M. F., & Fisk, F. Strength of adult ego following bereavement. *American Journal of Orthopsychiatry*, 1960, **30**, 788–798.

Hoffman, L. W. Changes in family roles, socialization, and sex differences. *American Psychologist*, 1977, **32**, 644–657.

Hoffman, M. Moral internalization, parental power, and the nature of parent-child interaction. *Developmental Psychology*, 1975, **11**, 228–239.

Honzik, M. P. A sex difference in the age of onset of the parent-child resemblance in intelligence. *Journal of Educational Psychology*, 1963, **54**, 231–237.

Honzik, M. P. Environmental correlates of mental growth: Prediction from the family setting at 21 months. *Child Development*, 1967, **38**, 337–364.

Jencks, C., Smith, M., Acland, H., Bane, M. J., Cohen, D., Gintis, D., Heyns, B., & Michelson, S. *Inequality*. New York: Basic Books, 1972.

Jordan, B., Radin, N., & Epstein, A. S. Paternal behavior and intellectual functioning in preschool boys and girls. *Developmental Psychology*, 1975, **11**, 407–408.

Kagan, J. The concept of identification. *Psychological Review*, 1958, **65**, 296–305.

Kimball, B. The sentence completion technique in a study of scholastic underachievement. *Journal of Consulting Psychology*, 1952, **16**, 353–358.

Kohlberg, L., & Zigler, E. The impact of cognitive maturity on the development of sex-role attitudes in the years 4 to 8. *Genetic Psychology Monographs*, 1967, **75**, 89–165.

Kohn, M. & Rosman, B.L. Cognitive functioning in five-year-old boys as related to social–emotional and background–demographic variables. *Developmental Psychology*, 1973, **8**, 277–294.

Lamb, M. E. Twelve-month-olds and their parents: Interaction in a laboratory playroom. *Developmental Psychology*, 1976, **12**, 237–244.

Lamb, M. E. Father–infant and mother– infant interaction in the first year of life. *Child Development*, 1977, **48**, 167–181 (a).

Lamb, M. E. Developmpent and function of parent–infant relationships in the first two years of life. Paper presented at the biennial meeting of the Society for Research in Child Development, New Orleans, March 1977 (b).

Lamb, M. E. The effects of the social context on dyadic social interaction. In M. E. Lamb, S. J. Suomi, & G. R. Stephenson (Eds.), *Social interaction analysis: Methodological issues*. Madison: University of Wisconsin Press, 1979.

Lamb, M. E., Frodi, A. M., Chase-Lansdale, L., & Owen, M. T. The fathers' role in non-traditional family contexts: Direct and indirect effects. Paper presented at the American Psychological Association Convention, Toronto, September 1978.

Lamb, M. E. & Lamb, J. E. The nature and importance of the father–infant relationship. *The Family Coordinator*, 1976, **25**, 379–385.

Lambert, L., & Hart, S. Who needs a father? *New Society*, 1976, **37**, 80.

Landy, F., Rosenberg, B. G., & Sutton-Smith, B. The effect of limited father absence on cognitive development. *Child Development,* 1969, **40,** 941–944.

Lessing, E. E., Zagorin, S. W. & Nelson, D., WISC subtest IQ score correlates of father absence. *Journal of Genetic Psychology,* 1970, **117,** 181–195.

Levy, D. M. *Maternal overprotection.* New York: Columbia University Press, 1943.

Lynn, D. B. *Parental and sex-role identification.* Berkeley: McCutchan, 1969.

Lynn, D. B. *The father: His role in child development.* Monterey, Calif.: Brooks/Cole, 1974.

Lynn, D. B. Fathers and sex-role development. *The Family Coordinator,* 1976, **25,** 403–409.

Lynn, D. B. & Cross, A. D. Parent preference of preschool children. *Journal of Marriage and the Family,* 1974, **36,** 555–559.

Lytton, H. Three approaches to the study of parent–child interaction: Ethological, interview, experimental. *Journal of Child Psychology and Psychiatry,* 1973, **14,** 1–17.

Lytton, H. The socialization of two-year-old boys: Ecological findings. *Journal of Child Psychology and Psychiatry,* 1976, **17,** 287–304.

Lytton, H. Disciplinary encounters between young boys and their mothers and fathers: Is there a contingency system? *Developmental Psychology,* 1979, **15,** 256–268.

MacArthur, R. Sex differences in field dependence for the Eskimo: Replication of Berry's findings. *International Journal of Psychology,* 1967, **2,** 139–140.

Maccoby, E. E., & Jacklin, C. N. *The psychology of sex differences.* Stanford: Stanford University Press, 1974.

Marjoribanks, K. Environment, social class, and mental abilities. *Journal of Educational Psychology,* 1972, **63,** 103–107.

Maxwell, A. E. Discrepancies between the pattern of abilities for normal and neurotic children. *Journal of Mental Science,* 1961, **107,** 300–307.

McCall, R. B. Childhood IQ's as predictors of adult educational and occupational status. *Science,* 1977, **197,** 482–483.

Mischel, W. Sex-typing and socialization. In P.H. Mussen (Ed.), *Carmichael's manual of child psychology,* 3rd ed., Vol. 2. New York: Wiley, 1970.

Mowrer, O. H. *Learning theory and personality dynamics.* New York: Ronald Press, 1950.

Multimer, D., Loughlin, L., & Powell, M. Some differences in the family relationships of achieving and underachieving readers. *Journal of Genetic Psychology,* 1966, **109,** 67–74.

Munsinger, H., & Douglass, A. The syntactic abilities of identical twins, fraternal twins and their siblings. *Child Development,* 1976, **47** 40–50.

Mussen, P., & Distler, L. Child rearing antecedents of masculine identification in kindergarten boys. *Child Development,* 1960, **31,** 89–100.

Mussen, P., & Rutherford, E. Parent–child relations and parental personality in relation to young children's sex-role preferences. *Child Development,* 1963, **34,** 589–607.

Nelsen, E. A., & Maccoby, E. E. The relationship between social development and differential abilities on the scholastic aptitude test. *Merrill-Palmer Quarterly,* 1966, **12,** 269–289.

Osofsky, J. D., & O'Connell, E. J. Parent–child interaction: Daughters' effects upon mothers' and fathers' behaviors. *Developmental Psychology,* 1972, **7,** 157–168.

Parke, R. D., & Sawin, D. B. Infant characteristics and behavior as elicitors of maternal and paternal responsibility in the newborn period. Paper presented at the Society for Research in Child Development, Denver, April 1975.

Parke, R. D., & Sawin, D. B. The father's role in infancy: A reevaluation. *The Family Coordinator,* 1976, **25,** 365–371.

Parke, R. D., & Sawin, D. B. Fathering: It's a major role. *Psychology Today,* 1977, **11,** 109–112.

Parke, R. D., & Sawin, D. B. The family in early infancy: Social- interactional and attitudinal analyses. In F. A. Pedersen (Ed.), *The father–infant relationship: Observational studies in a family context.* New York: Praeger, 1980.

Parsons, T., & Bales, R. F. *Family socialization and interaction process.* New York: Free Press, 1955.

Pedersen, F. A. Does research on children reared in father-absent families yield information on father influences. *The Family Coordinator,* 1976, **25,** 459–464.

Pedersen, F. A., Anderson, B. J., & Cain, R. L. An approach to understanding linkages between the parent–infant and spouse relationships. Paper presented at the biennial meeting of the Society for Research in Child Development, New Orleans, March 1977.

Pedersen, F. A., Rubenstein, J., & Yarrow, L. J. Father absence in infancy. Paper presented at the meeting of the Society for Research in Child Development, Philadelphia, March 1973.

Pedersen, F. A., Rubenstein, O. L., & Yarrow, L. J. Infant development in father-absent families. *Journal of Genetic Psychology,* 1979, **135,** 51–61.

Price-Bonham, S., & Addison, S. Families and mentally retarded children: Emphasis on the father. *The Family Coordinator,* 1978, **27,** 221–230.

Radin, N. Father–child interaction and the intellectual functioning of four-year-old boys. *Developmental Psychology,* 1972, **6,** 353–361 (a).

Radin, N. Three degrees of maternal involvement in a preschool program: Impact on mothers and children. *Child Development,* 1972, **43,** 1355–1364 (b).

Radin, N. Observed paternal behaviors as antecedents of intellectual functioning in young boys. *Developmental Psychology,* 1973, **8,** 369–376.

Radin, N. Observed maternal behavior with four-year-old boys and girls in lower-class families. *Child Development,* 1974, **45,** 1126–1131.

Radin, N. Childrearing fathers in intact families with preschoolers. Paper presented at the Annual Meeting of the American Psychological Association, Toronto, September 1978.

Radin, N. Childrearing fathers in intact families: An exploration of some antecedents and consequences. Paper presented at a study group on The Role of the Father on Child Development, Social Policy, and the Law, sponsored by the Society for Research on Child Development and the University of Haifa, Haifa, Israel, July 14, 1980.

Radin, N., & Epstein, A. S. Observed paternal behavior and the intellectual functioning of preschool boys and girls. Paper presented at the meeting of the Society for Research in Child Development, Denver, Colorado, April 1975 (a).

Radin, N., & Epstein, A. S. *Observed paternal behavior with preschool children: Final report.* Ann Arbor: The University of Michigan, School of Social Work, 1975 (ERIC Document Reproduction Service No. ED 174 656) (b).

Radin, N., & Sonquist, H. *The Gale preschool program: Final report.* Ypsilanti, Mich.: Ypsilanti Public Schools, 1968.

Reis, M., & Gold, D. Relation of paternal availability to problem-solving and sex-role orientation in young boys. *Psychological Report,* 1977, **40,** 823–829.

Reppucci, N. D. Parental education, sex differences and performance on cognitive tasks among two year-old children. *Developmental Psychology,* 1971, **4,** 248–253.

Rosen, B., & D'Andrade. R. D. The psychosocial origins of achievement motivation. *Sociometry,* 1959, **22,** 185–218.

Rosenberg, B. G., & Sutton-Smith, B. Sibling association, family size, and cognitive abilities. *Journal of Genetic Psychology,* 1966, **107,** 271–279.

Rothbart, M. D. Birth order and mother–child interaction in an achievement situation. *Journal of Personality and Social Psychology,* 1971, **17,** 113–120.

Santrock, J. W. The relation of type and onset of father absence to cognitive development. *Child Development,* 1972, **43,** 455–469.

Santrock, J. W., & Warshak, R. A. Father custody and social development in boys and girls. *Journal of Social Issues,* 1979, **35,** 112–125.

Santrock, J. W., & Wohlford P. Effects of father absence: Influence of the reason for the onset of the absence. *Proceedings of the 78th Annual Convention of the American Psychological Association,* 1970, **5,** 265–266.

Schiff, M., Duyme, M., Dumaret, A., Stewart, J., Tomkiewicz, S., & Feingold, J. The intellectual status of working-class children adapted early into upper-class families. *Science,* 1978, **200,** 1503–1504.

Schulz, D. *Coming up black.* Englewood Cliffs, N.J.: Prentice-Hall, 1969.

Sciara, F. J. Effects of father absence on the educational assessment of urban black children. *Child Study Journal,* 1975, **5,** 45–55.

Shinn, M. Father absence and children's cognitive development. *Psychological Bulletin,* 1978, **85,** 295–324.

Sears, P. S. Childrearing factors related to the playing of sex-typed roles. *American Psychologist,* 1953, **8,** 431 (Abstract).

Sears, R. R. Comparison of interviews with questionnaires for measuring mothers' attitudes toward sex and aggression. *Journal of Personality and Social Psychology*, 1965, **2**, 37–44.

Sears, R. R. Relation of early socialization experiences to self-concepts and gender role in middle childhood. *Child Development*, 1970, **41**, 267–289.

Seder, J. A. The origin of differences in extent of independence in children: Developmental factors in perceptual field dependence. Unpublished bachelor's thesis, Radcliff College, 1957.

Shaw, M. C., & White, D. L. The relationship between child–parent identification and academic underachievement. *Journal of Clinical Psychology*, 1965, **21**, 10–13.

Shelton, L. A. A comparative study of educational achievement in one-parent families and in two-parent families. *Dissertation Abstracts*, 1969, **29** (8-A), 2535–2536.

Sherman, R. C. & Smith, F. Sex differences in cue-dependency as a function of socialization environment. *Perceptual and Motor Skills*, 1967, **24**, 599–602.

Solomon, F., Houlihan, D. A., Busse, T. C., & Parelius, R. J. Parent behavior and child academic achievement, achievement striving, and related personality characteristics. *Genetic Psychology Monographs*, 1971, **83** 173–273.

Strodtbeck, F. L. Family interaction, values, and achievement. In D. C. McClelland, A. L. Baldwin, U. Bronfenbrenner, & F. L. Strodtbeck (Eds.), *Talent and society*. Princeton: Von Nostrand, 1958.

Sutton-Smith, B., Rosenberg, B. G., & Landy., F. Father-absence effects in families of different sibling compositions. *Child Development*, 1968, **39**, 1213–1221.

Tauber, M. A. Sex differences in parent–child interactions styles during a free-play session. *Child Development*, 1979, **50**, 981–988.

Teahan, J. E. Parental attitudes and college success. *Journal of Educational Psychology*, 1963, **54**, 104–109.

Wasserman, H. L. Father-absent and father-present lower-class Negro families: A comparative study of family functioning. *Dissertation Abstracts*, 1969, **29**, (12-A), 4569–4570.

Weinraub, M., & Frankel, J. Sex differences in parent–infant interaction during free-play, departure and separation. *Child Development*, 1977, **48**, 1240–1249.

Weiss, R. S. Growing up a little faster: The experience of growing up in a single-parent household. *Journal of Social Issues*, 1979, **35**, 97–111.

Wilson, R. S. Twins and siblings: Concordance for school-age mental development. *Child Development*, 1977, 211–216.

Wilson, R. S. Synchronies in mental development: An epigenetic perspective. *Science*, 1978, **202**, 939–948.

Ziegler, M. E. The father's influence on his school-age child's academic performance and cognitive development. Doctoral dissertation, University of Michigan, 1979.

Zigler, E., & Child, I. L. Socialization. In G. Lindzey, & E. Aronsen (Eds.), *The handbook of social psychology*, 2nd ed., Vol 3. Reading, Mass.: Addison-Wesley, 1969.

CHAPTER 12

The Father's Role in Infancy: Determinants of Involvement in Caregiving and Play

ROSS D. PARKE

University of Illinois at Urbana-Champaign

BARBARA R. TINSLEY

University of Illinois at Urbana-Champaign

There has recently been a proliferation of research documenting the father's role in infancy. Fathers have increased opportunities to participate in the care, feeding, and stimulation of their infants from the earliest days of life. The aim of this chapter is to present an overview of this recent research and to discuss the factors that affect both the quality and quantity of father–infant interaction. Our thesis is that fathers are capable participants in early care and stimulation, but more needs to be known about the determinants of the variability in participation of fathers across families. First, we outline studies suggesting that fathers are capable and interested interactive partners in both caregiving and noncaregiving contexts. Second, stylistic differences in mother and father play patterns are reviewed. Third, factors that modify the level of father involvement in caregiving and both the quantity and quality of play are discussed. Finally, the need for further cultural support systems for fathers is emphasized.

Preparation of this chapter was supported by NICHD Grant HEW PHS HD 05951, NICHD Training Grant HDO 7205-01, and a grant from the National Foundation March of Dimes. Thanks to Eileen Posluszny and Mary Johnson for their preparation of the manuscript.

PATTERNS OF FATHER–INFANT INTERACTION: NEWBORN PERIOD AND EARLY INFANCY

In one of the earliest studies to examine this issue, Greenberg and Morris (1974) used fathers' verbal reports to assess their level of involvement with their newborn infants. These investigators questioned two groups of fathers: (1) a group whose first contact with the newborn occurred at birth (in the delivery room), and (2) a group whose first contact with the infant occurred after the birth when it was shown to them by nursing personnel. Both groups of fathers showed evidence of strong paternal feelings and of involvement with their newborn infants, and 97 percent of the fathers rated their paternal feelings from average to very high. The majority were generally "very glad" immediately after the delivery, and almost all the fathers were pleased about the sex of their infant. There was some indication that fathers who were present at the delivery felt more comfortable holding their babies. Based on these findings and additional interview data, Greenberg and Morris (1974) suggest that "fathers begin developing a bond to their newborn by the first three days after birth and often earlier. Furthermore, there are certain characteristics of this bond which we call 'engrossment' . . . a feeling of preoccupation, absorption and interest in their newborn" (p. 526).

Although they are suggestive of fathers' very early involvement with their infants, these verbal reports can be supplemented by direct behavioral observations to demonstrate that positive feelings about and interest in newborns are reflected in actual paternal behavior. A series of observational studies by Parke and his associates have been conducted to describe—in behavioral terms—the nature of fathers' interaction with newborn infants. In the first study, Parke, O'Leary, and West (1972) observed the behavior of fathers in the family triad of mother, father, and infant. Observation sessions lasted 10 minutes and occurred during the first 3 days following delivery. A time-sampling procedure was used in which 40 intervals of 15-second duration were scored for the following behaviors for each parent: hold infant, change position, look at infant, smile, vocalize, touch, rock, kiss infant, explore infant, imitate infant, feed infant, and give infant to other parent.

Results of this study indicated that fathers were just as involved with their infants as mothers were and that mothers and fathers did not differ in the frequency of the majority of these behaviors. Moreover, fathers tended to hold the infant more than mothers and rock the infant in their arms more than mothers. Fathers, when participation was voluntary, were just as involved as the mothers in interaction with their newborn infants.

A variety of questions could be raised about this study. First, since the mother and father were observed together, it is possible that the high degree of father–infant interaction observed was because of the supporting presence of the mother. Second, the sample of fathers was unique in ways that may have contributed to their high degree of interaction with their infants. Over half of the fathers had attended Lamaze childbirth classes, and, with one exception, all fathers were present during the delivery of the child. Both of these factors could account for the fathers' high degree of involvement with their infants (Entwisle & Doering, 1980). Finally, the substantial early involvement of these fathers might be explained by their high educational level and middle-class status; paternal involvement might be less in lower-class samples because of a typically more rigid definition of parental roles among lower-class parents.

To overcome these limitations, a group of lower-class fathers who neither participated in childbirth classes nor were present during delivery were observed in two contexts: (1) alone with their infant and (2) in the presence of the mother (Parke & O'Leary, 1976). This study permitted a much more stringent test of father–infant involvement and allowed broader generalization of the previous findings. As in the earlier study, fathers were found to be very interested and active participants in early interaction. In fact, in the family triad, the father was more likely to hold and visually attend to the infant than the mother was. Nor was the mother's presence necessary for the father's active involvement. The father was an equally active interactor in both settings— alone and with his wife. Fathers in this series of studies (Parke et al., 1972; Parke & O'Leary, 1976; Parke & Sawin, 1975) were just as nurturant as mothers. For example, in the first study, they touched, looked at, vocalized to, and kissed their newborn offspring just as often as mothers did. In the second study an even more striking picture emerged—the father exhibited more nurturant behavior in the triadic context than the mother and an equal amount when alone with the baby. There was only a single nurturant behavior—smiling—in which the mother surpassed the father in both studies.

These patterns of nurturant activity on the part of fathers are not restricted to samples of American fathers. In a recent cross-cultural study, Parke, Grossman, and Tinsley (1981) compared the behaviors of American and German mothers and fathers when they were together with their newborn infants during the regular feeding periods in the postpartum hospital stay. Each triad of mother, father, and newborn infant was observed for 30 minutes. A slightly modified version of the observational system used in our earlier studies (Parke & O'Leary, 1976) was employed. Specifically, a 15-second time sampling method was used in which the observer watched the triad for the first 15 seconds of each 30-second period, and in the next 15-second interval the observer recorded the behaviors that occurred during the previous 15-second period. Each family triad was observed for 30 minutes (60 15-second observation intervals). A similar set of parental behaviors derived from our earlier studies was used. In contrast to our earlier observations in which an unstructured situation was utilized, all observations were made during the regular feeding period. The majority of babies were breast-fed (15 out of 18 in the American sample and 14 out of 19 in the German sample), and therefore mothers held the infants for longer periods than fathers during the observations. However, fathers held their infants sufficiently often to permit a comparison of the *quality* of mother and father behavior while holding was held constant. Proportions for each parent behavior while the infant was being held by either mother or father were calculated. When the father was holding the infant, he was significantly more likely than mother to rock, vocalize, and imitate; touching, exploration, looking, and smiling were similar for both mother and father while the father was holding the infant. A similar pattern was evident when the mother was holding; she engaged in more rocking, touching, vocalizing, and smiling than the father, and exploration and imitation were similar for both the mother and father while the mother was holding the infant.

In sum, the amount of stimulatory and affectional behavior depends on the opportunity to hold the infant. Once the father has this opportunity, he equals or exceeds the mother in his display of stimulatory and affectional behavior. This type of analysis suggests that parents—regardless of sex—interact in relatively similar ways when they are holding their infants. Moreover, it underlines the importance of contextual variables in modifying the nature of mother–father interaction patterns and suggests the importance of controlling the opportunity to hold the infant in naturalistic studies of early parent–infant interaction. Finally, there was a marked degree of similarity in the interaction patterns of the German and American parents. In terms of stimulatory patterns, American parents are more physical than German parents; American mothers and fathers actually explore and rock their infants more than German parents. The effect was particularly true for mothers; American and German fathers rocked approximately the same amount. In contrast, German parents used more auditory–visual modes of interaction than American parents. They looked at and imitated their infants more than American mothers and fathers. However, these differences are relatively minor in relation to the total array of similarities in parent behaviors across the two cultures.

To summarize briefly, our studies with both American and German families suggest that fathers as well as mothers are interested, nurturant, and stimulating interactive partners in the newborn period.

Parental Speech to Newborn and Young Infants

A closer examination of one aspect of parental interactional behavior—parental speech to infants during the first three months of life—was undertaken by Phillips and Parke (1981). Parental speech is of interest since prior researchers have found that mothers adjust their speech when addressing infants and children. They speak in shorter phrases, use a higher pitch, and repeat the content of their speech more often than when speaking to adults. According to Phillips and Parke, fathers as well as mothers show a variety of shifts in speech when talking to young infants. In 5-minute toy-play interaction periods and 10-minute feeding sessions, parents of either sex spoke in shorter phrases when talking to infants than when speaking to each other. The mean length of utterance (MLU) for fathers and mothers was 3.29 and 3.84, respectively, when talking to their newborn or 3-month-old infants. In contrast, these same parents showed an average MLU of 10.78 when addressing each other. This latter value is similar to earlier research, which found a value of 8.43 MLU for adult-to-adult speech (Sachs, 1977). Although fathers and mothers repeated approximately 12 percent of the time when verbally interacting with their infants, this percentage dropped to zero for speech directed at the other parent. Similar adjustments in father speech to 5-month-old infants have been noted by Pedersen et al. (1980).

Both fathers and mothers were sensitive to contextual cues as well. During feeding, the rate of speech of both parents was slower and the pauses longer than during play. Parents repeated phrases more during play than during feeding and used a conversational style of speech (e.g., questions, attention-getting tactics) more during play than feeding sessions. These contextual differences support our interpretation of the significance of these parental speech adjustments—that "baby talk" serves the function of eliciting and maintaining infant attention. When the infant's attention is focused more closely on the parents' faces, the infant's learning of the characteristics of the parents' voices and faces may be facilitated. Thus modifications in parental speech may serve the process of discriminating among caregivers and in turn may promote closer parent–infant relationships. Although this explanation is not inconsistent with or exclusive of earlier psycholinguistic arguments that mothers may facilitate language development, the limited data in support of this linguistic function suggests that other hypotheses, such as those of social learning, merit serious consideration.

FATHER–INFANT INTERACTION IN DYADIC AND TRIADIC SETTINGS

Fathers interact with their young infants both alone and in the presence of others. To assess whether the father's behavior is modified in the presence of others—specifically, the mother—Parke and O'Leary (1976) compared parental behavior alone with the infant and in a triadic situation with the other parent present. Two sets of results are noteworthy. First, the presence of a second adult has the effect of reducing the overall rate of occurrence for most categories of behavior. When a second adult is present, rates of vocalization, touching, holding, rocking, imitating, and feeding are reduced. This finding of a reduction in the overall quantity of the majority of behaviors exhibited by parents in a triadic rather than a dyadic context is consistent with a number of other studies in both the laboratory (Lamb, 1976, 1977, 1978, 1979) and at home (Belsky, 1979; Clarke-Stewart, 1978; Pedersen, Anderson, & Cain, 1980) with infants of varying ages.

In contrast to a number of other investigators, Parke and O'Leary (1976) have found that certain behaviors *increase* rather than *decrease* from dyadic to triadic situations. Both fathers and mothers smiled more at their infants and mothers exhibited more exploratory behavior (counting toes, checking fontanels) in the presence of their spouses than when they were alone with the infant. However, the increase in exploratory behavior was significant only for mothers. The context of the family triad, in this case, appeared to elicit greater affective and exploratory behavior on the part of both parents, especially mothers. Our hypothesis is that parents verbally stimulate each other by focusing the partner's attention on aspects of the baby's behavior or by commenting on the infant's appearance, which in turn elicits either positive action directed toward the baby or exploration or checking on an aspect of behavior noted by the spouse. In addition to the obvious difference that our studies involved newborn infants in a hospital context whereas others involved older infants in laboratory or home settings, there may be other reasons for the discrepancy between our results and the findings of other investigators. Some behaviors such as smiling may be socially mediated, or may depend on a responsive social partner for their display. In the case of newborn infants who show no social smiling, the presence of a responsive spouse may be a necessary eliciting and maintaining condition for smiling. Moreover, it is assumed that smiling, elicited by a spouse, may in turn be directed to the infant. Greater attention should be given to the specification of conditions that are likely to increase as well as decrease parental behavior in the presence of a spouse. By focusing on the interactions between husband and wife (Pedersen et al., 1977) as well as on parent–infant interaction, these conditions may become evident.

FATHER–MOTHER DIFFERENCES IN CARETAKING ACTIVITIES

Father as a Direct Participant in Feeding

Although there were few differences in the nurturance and stimulatory activities of parents of young infants, fathers do play a less active role in caretaking activities than mothers. In the second Parke and O'Leary (1976) study in which all infants were bottle-fed, fathers fed significantly less than mothers when they were alone with the baby. Additional support for this mother–father difference comes from another study (Parke & Sawin, 1975) of father–newborn interaction, which involved a detailed examination of early parent–infant interaction in a feeding context. Comparisons of the frequencies and durations of specific caretaking activities of mothers and fathers while alone with their infants in a feeding context indicate that mothers spend more time engaged in feeding the infant and in related caretaking activities, such as wiping the baby's face, than do fathers. These findings suggest that although both parents are actively involved with very young infants, parental role allocation begins in the earliest days of life.

Many of the features that are evidenced in father–infant interactions in the newborn period characterize the interaction patterns both in later infancy and in home settings. Differences between mother and father in terms of caretaking are evidenced in home observations. In studies conducted in both the United States (Kotelchuck, 1976; Rendina & Dickerscheid, 1976) and Great Britain (Richards, Antonis, & Dunn, 1977), it was found that fathers spend less time than mothers in feeding and caretaking. For a more detailed review of these time distribution studies of mother and father caregiving, see Parke, 1978.

These findings are consistent with the more general proposition that pregnancy and birth of a first child, in particular, are occasions for a shift toward a more traditional division of roles (Arbeit, 1975; Cowan et al., 1978; Shereshefsky & Yarrow, 1973). Other studies confirm these general trends. Hoffman (1978) found that husbands help less with housework after the arrival of a first child than they did before. Cowan and her co-workers (1978) studied couples before and up to 6 months after the birth of a first child. They reported that the shift was most marked in the household tasks, next in the family decision-making roles, and least in the babycare items. Of particular interest is the fact that these patterns held regardless of whether their initial role division was traditional or egalitarian. "Despite the current rhetoric and ideology concerning equality of roles for men and women, it seems that couples tend to adopt traditionally defined roles during times of stressful transition such as around the birth of a first child" (Cowan et al., 1978, p. 20).

The lower level of father involvement in feeding does not imply that fathers are less competent than mothers to care for the newborn infant. Competence can be measured in a variety of ways; one approach is to measure the parent's sensitivity to infant cues in the feeding context. Success in caretaking, to a large degree, depends on the parent's ability to correctly "read" or interpret the infant's behavior so that his or her own behavior can be regulated to respond appropriately. In the feeding context, the parent attempts to facilitate the food intake of the infant. The infant, in turn, by a variety of behaviors such as sucking or coughing, provides the caretaker with feedback concerning the effectiveness or ineffectiveness of his or her current behavior in maintaining the food intake process. In this context, one approach to the competence issue involves an examination of the degree to which the caretaker modifies his or her behavior in response to infant cues. Parke and Sawin (1975) found that the father's sensitivity to an auditory distress signal in the feeding context—sneeze, spit up, cough—was just as marked as the mother's was to this infant cue. Using a conditional probability analysis, they demonstrated that fathers, like mothers, adjusted their behavior by ceasing their feeding activity momentarily, looking more closely to check on the infant, and vocalizing to their infant. The only difference found concerned the greater cautiousness of the fathers, who were more likely than mothers to inhibit their touching in the presence of infant distress signals. The implication of this analysis is clear: in spite of the fact that they may spend less time overall in caretaking activities, fathers are as sensitive as mothers to infant cues and as responsive to them in the feeding context.

Moreover, the amount of milk consumed by infants with their mothers and fathers in this study was very similar (1.3 versus 1.2 ounces, respectively), suggesting that fathers and mothers are not only comparable in their sensitivity but are equally successful in feeding the infant based on the amount of milk consumed. Fathers may not necessarily be as frequent contributors to infant feeding, but when called on have the competence to execute these tasks effectively.

Fathers are just as responsive as mothers to other infant cues such as vocalizations and mouth movements. Both mothers and fathers in this study increased their rate of positive vocalizations following an infant's vocal sound. Both fathers and mothers also touched and looked more closely at the infant after the infant had vocalized. However, mothers and fathers differed in the other behaviors that they showed in response to this type of infant elicitation: upon infant vocalization, fathers were more likely than mothers to increase their vocalization rate. Mothers, however, were more likely than fathers to react to infant vocalization with touching. The fathers were possibly more cautious than mothers in their use of tactile stimulation during feeding because of their concern about disrupting infant feeding behavior. A further demonstration of the modifying impact of the infant's behavior on caregiving by fathers as well as mothers comes from an examination of the impact of infant mouth movements: parents of both sexes increase their vocalizing, touching, and stimulation of feeding activity in response to mouth movements. These data indicate that fathers and mothers both react to the newborn infant's cues in a contingent and functional manner even though they differ in their specific response patterns. The interaction patterns in the newborn period are reciprocal; although our focus in the Parke and Sawin (1975) study was on the role of infant cues as elicitors of parent behavior, in a later study (Parke & Sawin, 1980) it was shown that parent vocalizations can modify newborn infant behavior such as infant vocalizations. Interaction between fathers and infants—even in the newborn period—is clearly bidirectional in quality; both parents and infants mutually regulate each other's behavior in the course of interaction.

Fathers do have the capability to execute caregiving activities competently even though they directly contribute less to this type of activity than mothers. In a later section, some of the conditions that may modify the amount of father participation in routine caregiving are explored.

Father as an Indirect Influence on Feeding

Although research on the father's influence in infancy has centered primarily on the direct impact of the father's behavior (e.g., as a feeding or stimulatory agent), his influence in some cases may be indirectly mediated through the mother or other members of the family as well (see Lewis & Feiring, 1981; Parke, Power, & Gottman, 1979, for detailed discussion of this issue). Even when they are not directly participating in feeding, fathers can indirectly affect this activity by modifying the behavior of the feeding agent. The father's indirect role in feeding is illustrated by Pedersen's (1975) investigation of the influence of the husband–wife relationship on mother–infant interaction in a feeding context. Ratings were made of the quality of the mother–infant relationship in connection with two time-sampling home observations when the infants were 4 weeks old. Of particular interest was "feeding competence," which refers to the appropriateness of the mother in managing feeding. "Mothers rated high are able to pace the feeding well, intersperse feeding and burping without disrupting the baby and seem sensitive to the baby's needs for either stimulation of feeding or brief rest periods during the course of feedings" (Pedersen, 1975, p. 4). In addition, the husband–wife relationship was assessed through an interview.

Pedersen (1975, p. 6) summarized his results as follows:

The husband–wife relationship was linked to the mother–infant unit. When the father was more supportive of the mother, that is, evaluated her maternal skills more positively, she was more effective in feeding the baby. Then again, maybe competent mothers elicit more positive evaluations from their husbands. The reverse holds for marital discord. High tension and conflict in the marriage was associated with more inept feeding on the part of the mother.

In short, even if fathers do not feed the infant directly, they may still influence the process by their relationship with their wives.

When the mother breast-feeds the infant, the father can be involved in a number of ways. In addition to being supportive to the mother in her efforts to breast-feed, he can also participate in feeding by providing supplemental bottle-feeding and sharing in nonfeeding-related aspects of caretaking such as bathing and diapering. Although recent evidence by Entwisle and Doering (1980) suggests that supplemental bottle-feedings by the father may be associated with the early cessation of breast-feeding, their results must be interpreted carefully. These researchers found that the husbands of women who stopped breast-feeding by 6 months were bottle-feeding about once a day; husbands of those mothers who continued to breast-feed were bottle-feeding only once in 4 days. As the researchers note, "Frequent bottle-feeding at this early stage could interfere with breast-feeding because establishing a good milk supply depends on frequent stimulation. Women who give supplementary formula because they 'don't have enough milk' are exacerbating their problem rather than curing it, and fathers who feed babies formula may contribute to early cessation of breast-feeding" (Entwisle & Doering, 1980). Thus the father who feeds his infant supplemental bottles of formula may be causing problems, but the father who gives supplemental bottles of breast milk may be providing constructive support for the mother as well as enhancing his own relationship with the infant.

The importance of these findings is clear: to fully appreciate the father's role in early caregiving, both direct and indirect ways in which he contributes must be considered. These studies underline the necessity of viewing fathers in a family context and suggest the importance of assessing the total set of relationships among the members of the family.

FATHER–MOTHER DIFFERENCES IN PLAY

Fathers participate less than mothers in caregiving but spend a greater percentage of the time available for interaction in play activities than mothers do. Kotelchuck (1976) found that fathers spent a greater percentage of their time with their infants in play (37.5 percent) than mothers did (25.8 percent), although in absolute terms mothers spent more time than fathers in play with their children.

Nor are these differences in mother and father participation in play restricted to U.S. families. Similar findings have been reported from a longitudinal investigation of parent–infant interaction in England (Richards et al., 1977). These investigators interviewed mothers concerning fathers' participation in a wide range of activities when the infant was 30 and 60 weeks old. At both ages, playing with their infants was the most common activity of these fathers, and over 90 percent of the fathers played regularly with their infants.

Further evidence comes from Lamb (1977a), who observed interactions among mother, father, and infant in their homes at 7 to 8 months and again at

12 to 13 months. Based on 4 to 8 hours of home observation, Lamb reported marked differences in the reasons that fathers and mothers pick up infants: fathers were more likely to hold the babies simply to play with them, whereas mothers were far more likely to hold them for caretaking purposes.

It is not merely the quantity of time *per se* that discriminates between mother and father involvement in infancy; it is the quality of play activity as well. Differences in the style of mother–father play have been examined in a recent series of studies by Yogman and his colleagues (Yogman, Dixon, & Tronick, 1977; Yogman, 1981). They compared mothers, fathers, and strangers in their interactions with infants in a face-to-face play context. Each of six infants was studied in 2 minutes of interaction with his or her mother, father, and a stranger when they were from 2 weeks to 6 months of age in a laboratory arrangement in which the adult faces the infant and is instructed to play without using toys and without removing the infant from an infant seat. With the use of videotaped records a variety of microbehavioral analyses of the adult–infant interaction patterns were scored. Adults differed in their play with infants as indicated by differences in vocalization and touching patterns. Mothers vocalized in soft, repetitive, imitative burst-pause talking (47 percent) more than fathers (20 percent), who did so significantly more often than strangers (12 percent). Fathers, however, touched their infants with rhythmic tapping patterns (44 percent) more often than either mothers (28 percent) or strangers (29 percent) did.

Differences are revealed not only in discrete behaviors but also in the patterns of behavior. As Yogman et al. (1977) comment, "These adult behaviors were often part of an interactive 'game' in the sense defined by Stern (1974): 'a series of episodes of mutual attention in which the adult uses a repeating set of behaviors with only minor variations during each episode of mutual attention' " (Yogman et al., 1977, p. 8). Moreover, Yogman (1981) reported that these "games" were more likely to occur during sessions with fathers than with mothers. Mothers and infants played games during 75 percent of the face-to-face interaction sessions, whereas fathers played games during 87 percent of the sessions. The types of games that mothers and fathers played differed as well. Visual games in which the parent displays distal motor movements that may be observed by the infant and appear to be attempts to maintain the visual attention of the infant" (Yogman, 1981, p. 30) were the most common type mother's game (31 percent of all games played). For fathers, this type of game represented only 19 percent of the games played. The most common type of father–infant games were tactile and limb-movement games. Limb-movement games, which were associated with increases in infant arousal, represented 70 percent of all father–infant games and only 4 percent of mother–infant games. In contrast to this type of physically arousing game used by fathers, mothers played physically by utilizing more conventional motor games such as pat-a-cake, peek-a-boo, or waving. "The visual games more often played by mothers represent a more distal attention-maintaining form of interactive play than the more proximal, idiosyncratic limb movement games played more often by fathers" (Yogman, 1981, p. 39).

Stylistic differences in mothers' and fathers' play are not restricted to very young infants. In a recent series of studies by Power and Parke (1981), mothers and fathers were videotaped while playing with their firstborn, 8-month-old infants in a laboratory playroom. Fathers played more bouncing and lifting games than mothers. In contrast, mothers played more watching games in which a toy is presented and made salient by moving or shaking it. The mother–father difference in lifting games was qualified by the sex of the infant; the game was played primarily by fathers of boys.[1] In addition to examining the amount of time that mothers and fathers devoted to different types of play, Power and Parke examined the sequencing of various types of play for mothers and fathers. Two further ways in which mothers and fathers differ in interaction style are illustrated by this type of analysis. Fathers were more likely than mothers to engage in extended physical, no-toy play interaction; even if they were engaged in toy-mediated play, they were generally less successful than mothers in maintaining play of this type successfully. When fathers failed to elicit their infants' attention in toy play, they often shifted to physical no-toy play. In contrast, mothers were better able to maintain infant attention during toy play, and a loss in infant attention led to continued toy play as opposed to a shift to the physical mode in the case of fathers. In short, there is a general tendency for parents to rely on familiar and predominant modes of play, particularly when infant interest lessens. For mothers this involves prolonging toy play; for fathers it involves shifting to physical play.

Recent observations of father– and mother–infant interaction in unstructured home contexts with older infants indicates mother–father differences in style of play. Lamb (1977a), in an observational study of infants at 7 and 8 months and again at 12 and 13 months in their homes, found that fathers engage in more physical (i.e., rough-and-tumble type) and unusual play activities than mothers. Mothers, in contrast, engaged in more conventional play activities (e.g., peek-a-boo, pat-a-cake), stimulus toy play (where a toy was jiggled or operated to stimulate the child directly), and reading than fathers. Power and Parke (1981) also found that fathers engaged in more physical play than mothers in home observations of 7½- and 10½-month-old infants. Similar differences in the style of play patterns were found by Clarke-Stewart (1980) in a study of 15- to 30-month-old infants and their parents: "Fathers' play was

---

[1] In many studies of father–infant interaction, fathers have been found to treat boys and girls differently. A detailed discussion of these findings is beyond the scope of this chapter. For reviews of this issue, see Clarke-Stewart (1980), Lamb (Chapter 13), Parke (1979), and Pedersen (1980).

relatively more likely to be physical and arousing rather than intellectual, didactic or mediated by objects—as in the case of mothers'' (Clarke-Stewart, 1977, p. 37).

In all studies reviewed, a reasonably consistent pattern emerges: fathers are tactile and physical, whereas mothers tend to be verbal. It is clear that infants do not experience simply more stimulation from their fathers; they experience a qualitatively different stimulatory pattern.

The father's role as playmate shows developmental changes; in the Clarke-Stewart study, at 15 months the child's primary playmate was the mother, by 20 months both the mother and father shared this role, and by 30 months the father played more than the mothers. The mother's role as caretaker was also diminishing over this same period, and by 30 months there was little difference in caretaking between mothers and fathers. Of particular interest is the pattern of relationships between playful behaviors and other behavior patterns. For mothers, positive emotion and physical stimulation were highly correlated with other measures of stimulation and responsiveness. For fathers, expressions of negative emotion, including scolding, criticizing, and speaking sharply were related to father's physical playfulness.

Not only do fathers and mothers differ in their play patterns, but infants react differently to mother and father play. Lamb (1976b), in his study of 8- to 13-month-old infants, found that the infants' response to play with their fathers was significantly more positive than their response to play with their mothers.

Consistent with Lamb's observations is Clarke-Stewart's (1977) finding that 20-month-old children were significantly more responsive to playful social interaction initiated by the father than to play initiated by the mother. At 2½ years of age, children were more cooperative, close, involved, excited, and interested in play with their fathers. Over two-thirds of the children chose to play with their fathers first in a choice situation and displayed a stronger preference for him as a playmate. Just as the structured/unstructured distinction is important in the "attachment" studies, a similar distinction is useful in the play sphere. Although there were clear mother–father differences in the play-probe sessions, fewer differences in infant initiations occurred in unstructured home observations (Clarke-Stewart, 1977).

Just as fathers and mothers behave differentially toward male and female infants, opposite sexed infants react differently to their mothers and fathers. In the Lamb studies (1977a, b) boys were in proximity to, approached, and fussed to their fathers more than girls; female infants, however, were in proximity to and fussed to their mothers more than the boys, although they approached their mothers about as often as boys did. Spelke et al. (1973) observed that 1-year-old infants vocalized more to the same- than to the opposite-sexed parent, while Ban and Lewis (1974) found that 1-year-old boys looked more at their fathers than at their mothers. Finally, Lynn and Cross

(1974) found that 2-year-old boys prefer to play with their fathers than with their mothers; girls, however, show a shift between 2 and 4 years of age to preferring mother as a play partner.

In general, this pattern of findings suggests that father involvement in infancy is quantitatively less than mother involvement, but the types of roles that mothers and fathers play clearly differ as well. Less quantity of interaction, does not imply that fathers do not have an important impact on infant development. Just as earlier research (e.g., Hoffman & Nye, 1974; Schaffer & Emerson, 1964) has indicated that quality rather than quantity of mother–infant interaction was the important predictor of infant cognitive and social development, it is likely that a similar assumption will hold for fathers as well.

FACTORS ALTERING TRADITIONAL FATHER–MOTHER DIFFERENCES IN CAREGIVING AND PLAY

Although the general picture emerging from our review of mother as caregiver and father as playmate is still prevelant, there is a high degree of variability across families in the extent to which this traditional division of behaviors applies. In this section, recent research is reviewed that illustrates some of the parameters modifying this general set of findings. Changes in sex role definitions, the work status of women, the type of childbirth and timing of the birth are all modifying both mothers' and fathers' levels of participation in caregiving as well as the amounts of play exhibited by mothers and fathers. It is recognized that caregiving responsibilities of fathers and mothers will obviously be markedly different in families that have explicitly reorganized and redefined role divisions. Recent studies in Australia (Russell, 1980), the United States (Levine, 1976; Radin, 1980), Norway (Groseth, 1975), and Sweden (Lamb, Frodi, Hwang, & Frodi, in press a; Lamb, Frodi, Hwang, Frodi, & Steinberg, in press b) illustrate the nonuniversality of traditional role divisions within families. Although detailed discussion of the full range of this recent work is beyond the scope of this chapter, selected findings are presented to illustrate how family organization can influence caregiving and play patterns. In addition, a variety of other factors, including the medical status of the infant, type of birth, and working arrangements of parents that alter the general patterns of caregiving and play are noted.

First, an individual's definitions of masculinity and femininity may affect the degree to which fathers participate in caregiving. Russell's (1978) recent finding that androgynous men in Australia participate more in caregiving than traditionally masculine men do illustrates the impact of self-defined sex-related attributes on the distribution of caregiving responsibilities. Entwisle and Doering (1980) found that men who adhered to rigid stereotypes (e.g., nurturing an infant is unmasculine) showed less interest in their new babies. However, recent studies in the United States (Radin, 1980) and Sweden (Lamb et al., in press a) have failed to confirm this relationship between caregiving levels of fathers and androgyny.

Second, recent research suggests that certain medical practices such as cesarean childbirth can alter the fathers' level of participation in routine caretaking activities. In a recent study, Pedersen, Zaslow, Cain, and Anderson (1980) found that fathers of cesarean-delivered infants engaged in significantly more caregiving at 5 months than fathers in a comparison group whose infants were vaginally delivered. Whereas the fathers of the cesarean-delivered infants were more likely to share caregiving responsibilities in several different areas on an equal basis with the mother, fathers in the comparison sample tended only to "help out"—the mothers still met the major proportion of caregiving needs. Other investigators have found similar patterns. In an interview study of 84 couples through pregnancy, birth, and their child's infancy, Grossman, Winickoff, and Eichler (1980) found that in families in which the infant was cesarean-delivered, fathers seemed more involved with their infants at 2 months of age than fathers of vaginally delivered infants did. Vietze, Mac-Turk, McCarthy, Klein, and Yarrow (1980) also report that cesarean delivery results in more active paternal caretaking. Seventy-five families with a first child were observed through the first year of the child's life. Fathers of cesarean-delivered, 6-month-old infants demonstrated more soothing behavior toward their infants than fathers of vaginally delivered infants of the same age, although this was not observed at 12 months. The most probable explanation for these findings is that mothers, as a result of the surgery, are unable to assume a fully active role in caregiving during the early postpartum weeks. Fathers, as a result of their increased involvement in early care, continue this caregiving activity even after the time that the mothers are able to resume a more active role. Support for this analysis comes from a recent study by Doering and Entwisle (1980), who found that women who underwent cesarean delivery were less positive about caring for their baby than mothers who were vaginally delivered.

The Pedersen et al. study, as well as other studies of the effects of cesarean birth on paternal involvement, underlines the importance of the early postpartum period for establishing role definitions. However, this should not imply that these early established patterns are not modifiable, as evidence by Vietze et al. (1980), who suggest that by the end of the first year these differences in father participation between the two types of deliveries have disappeared. The research, however, does alert us to another type of second-order effect: the mother's behavior and needs—as a result of the cesarean birth—may influence the father–infant interaction (Pedersen et al., 1980).

The birth of a premature infant may also modify the father's role in a similar fashion by creating a situation in which it is more important than usual for the father to provide nurturance for the mother as well as increasing the need for paternal involvement in caretaking. In an interview study of over 100 families with premature infants, Herzog (1979) found that the most important function of fathers of premature infants was to provide support for the mother to facilitate her caretaking role and her positive feelings toward the infant. Further support for this position comes from a study of parental visiting patterns in an English high-risk nursery (Hawthorne, Richards, & Callon, 1978). These investigators found that mothers of premature infants were helped by fathers who became highly involved in the caretaking of the infant. Similar evidence comes from a recent Canadian study by Marton and Minde (1980) who reported that fathers of preterm infants are highly involved with their infants as indexed by visitation patterns to the perinatal unit. Finally, in a U.S. sample, Yogman (1980) found that fathers of premature infants exhibit higher levels of caretaking involvement (e.g., bathing, diapering) than fathers of full-term infants. These patterns of heightened father involvement may, in part, be in response to the difficulties associated with the care of the preterm infant.

A number of investigators have suggested that premature infants place greater interactional demands on their parents than full-term infants because of their limited alertness and responsivity (Goldberg, 1979, Field, 1979). Brown and Bakeman (1979) report that parents find preterm infants less enjoyable and less satisfying to feed. Moreover, because of their low weight, these infants often are fed more often than full-term infants. In a series of observational studies comparing parent–infant interaction with full-term and preterm infants, Goldberg (1979) finds that in the newborn period, mothers of preterm infants are less actively involved with their babies than mothers of full-term infants. Preterm infants were held farther from the mother's body, touched less, talked to less, and placed in a face-to-face position less often than full-term infants. Other studies of mother–premature infant interaction have found that in the feeding context, mothers are more likely to stimulate their infants' feeding in a less contingent manner than mothers of full-term infants (Brown & Bakeman, 1979; Goldberg, 1979). This has been hypothesized to be a reaction to the premature infant's lower responsivity and alertness. Thus prematurity may elicit greater father involvement in caretaking at least partially because of the father's desire to relieve the mother of full responsibility for the extra time and skill required in caring for these infants.

Play patterns as well as levels of involvement in caregiving may be different for fathers of preterm infants than fathers of full-term infants. In a comparative observational investigation of the interaction patterns of fathers with premature and full-term infants in the high-risk nursery and at home shortly after the infants' discharge, styles of father–infant play with these infants differed

(Parke, Thomas, Neff, Szczypka, Tinsley, & Zarling, 1981). Fathers exhibited their characteristic higher rate of physical play (bounce-stretch) than mothers— but only when the infant was full-term. When the infant was born prematurely, there was no mother–father difference in play style. Although there were no differences at the hospital period, differences between mothers and fathers of full or preterm infants were evident at 3 weeks. Possibly fathers assume that the premature infant is fragile and unable to withstand robust physical stimulation, which leads to an inhibition of fathers' usual play style. Follow-up observations are currently underway to determine the stability of this pattern at later developmental points in the first year of infancy. In sum, play as well as caregiving can be altered by the medical status of the infant.

    Another factor that may alter both the quality and quantity of father–infant play is the nature of work arrangements for fathers and mothers. Dual wage earner families in which both mother and father work are becoming increasingly common. A recent study by Pedersen, Cain, Zaslow and Anderson (1980) assessed the impact of this type of alternative family role organization on mother–infant and father–infant interaction patterns. These investigators observed single and dual wage earner families for a 1-hour period in the evening with their 5-month-old infants. Fathers in single wage earner families tended to play with their infants more than mothers did. However, in the two wage earner families, the mothers' rate of social play was higher than the fathers' rate of play. In fact, the fathers in these dual wage earner families played at a lower rate than even the mothers in the single wage earner families. Since the observations took place in the evenings after both parents returned from their jobs, Pedersen et al. suggested that the mother used increased play as a way of reestablishing contact with her infant after being away from home for the day. "It is possible that the working mother's special need to interact with the infant inhibited or crowded out the father in his specialty" (Pedersen, Cain, Zaslow, & Anderson, 1980, p. 10). It is still unclear whether these patterns of increased mother play continue after the mother–infant relationship is more firmly established than it is at 5 months. Is this pattern of increased play evident in dual wage earner families in which the mother begins work when the infant is older? Comparison of families in which the age of the infant differs when the mother returns to work would help to clarify these issues.

    The style of interaction that the mothers in these working-mother families exhibited was similar to the predominant style of mother play characterized by verbal behavior. Mothers in these families increased the amount of their play with their infants but remained within their stylistic mode. There was no evidence of a shift to a more typically "masculine" style of physical play.

    In an even more stringent test of the modifiability of play styles as a function of family organization, Field (1978) compared fathers who act as primary caregivers with fathers who are secondary caregivers in contrast to the Pedersen et al. families in which both parents were employed outside the home. Mothers and fathers reversed roles in Field's families. Field found that primary-caregiver fathers retained the physical component in their interaction styles just as secondary fathers did. However, in other subtle ways the play styles of primary caregiving fathers were similar to the play styles of mothers. Primary caretakers—both mothers and fathers—exhibited less laughing and more smiling, imitative grimaces, and high-pitched vocalizations than secondary-caretaker fathers did. However, fathers—both primary-caregiving and secondary-caregiving—engaged in less holding of the infants' limbs and in more game-playing and poking than mothers. Together with the Pedersen et al. (1980) study, these data suggest that both mothers and fathers may exhibit distinctive play styles, even when family role arrangements modify the quantity of their interaction. Further research is necessary to assess more completely the modifiability of these interactive styles as a result of differing family arrangements. A complete comparative study of families in which there is a full reversal of primary and secondary caregiving roles with traditional families in which the father is the secondary caregiver would clarify the extent to which interactional behavior is dependent on the differential distribution of caregiving tasks. Just as investigators are examining the impact of self-defined concepts of masculinity, femininity, and androgyny on caregiving patterns it would clearly be worthwhile to evaluate the relationship between sex role attitudes and play styles. Perhaps androgynous individuals—male or female—would exhibit less stereotypically masculine or feminine play styles. Such research is currently being performed by Lamb and his co-workers (in press, a, in press, b).

CULTURAL SUPPORT SYSTEMS FOR FATHERS

In the light of the social and economic changes that are promoting increased father involvement in the caregiving of infants, it is important to provide cultural supports for fathering activities (see Parke and Tinsley, in press). First, there needs to be an increase in opportunities for learning fathering skills. These supports can assume a variety of forms such as the provision of both pre- and postpartum training classes for fathers to both learn and practice caretaking skills and to learn about normal infant development (Biller & Meredith, 1974). Parenthood training, however, need not wait until pregnancy or childbirth. As many have advocated—as early as a 1925 PTA report (cited by Schlossman, 1976) and more recently (Hawkins, 1971; Sawin & Parke, 1976)—parenthood training, including information about infant development, infant care, and the economic realities of childrearing should be provided in high school or even at an earlier age in light of the increasing number of teenage pregnancies. As noted elsewhere (Parke, 1981a; Parke & Collmer, 1975), such training may also aid in the prevention of child abuse.

Second, there must be more opportunities to practice and implement these skills. To provide the opportunity to share in the early caretaking of the infant, paternity leaves should be given wider support. These leaves could be usefully extended to the pregnancy period to permit the father to attend classes and to share in obstetrician visits with the mother. Other shifts in societal arrangements such as shorter work weeks, flexible working hours, and split jobs whereby a male and female share the same position are all changes that can increase the potential participation of males in fathering (see Parke, 1981b).

Another positive change involves modification of maternity ward visiting arrangements to permit fathers to have more extended contact with the newborn infants. To date, father–infant interaction in the newborn period is largely under institutional control, and as a result it is frequently hospital policy rather than father interest that determines the degree of father–newborn involvement. Although some countries, such as Russia, are still highly restrictive of father–infant visitation, other countries such as Denmark and Sweden encourage father involvement in labor and delivery and support frequent visitation during the immediate postpartum period (Klaus & Kennell, 1976). In the United States, there is an increasing trend toward greater father participation. For example, in New York City, 60 percent of the hospitals permit father–infant visitation (*New York Times,* December 5, 1975). As Klaus and Kennell (1976) have documented, opportunities for early contact in the postpartum period with the infant may alter mother–infant interaction patterns. Some preliminary evidence from Sweden (Lind, 1974) suggests that a parallel effect may hold for fathers as well. Fathers who were provided the opportunity to learn and practice basic caretaking skills during the postpartum hospital period were more involved at home in the care of the 3-month-old infant and in household tasks.

The effectiveness of supportive intervention for fathers has been demonstrated by a recent hospital-based study (Parke, Hymel, Power, & Tinsley, 1980). During the mother's postpartum hospitalization, one group of 16 fathers was shown a short videotape designed to increase father–infant interaction and caretaking involvement. In the videotape, three different fathers were shown playing with, feeding, and diapering their babies. In addition, a narrator emphasized the wide range of newborn cognitive and social capacities as well as the active role that fathers can assume in early care and stimulation of infants. The videotape was designed to serve four purposes: (1) modification of father's sex role attitudes concerning the appropriateness of infant caretaking for adult males; (2) provision of specific demonstrations of feeding and diapering; (3) provision of information concerning newborn infants' perceptual and cognitive capabilities; and (4) demonstration of a number of ways in which fathers can interact with babies, emphasizing contingent responses to infant cues.

To assess the impact of the intervention, attitudinal and observational measures of father–infant interaction were secured in the hospital in the early postpartum period and in the home at 3 weeks and 3 months for both the group of fathers who viewed the tape and a group of 16 fathers who did not. At 3 months, the typical level of father participation in routine caretaking activities in the home was also assessed. Results showed that fathers who viewed the tape in the hospital increased their knowledge about infant perceptual abilities and believed more strongly than fathers who did not see the videotape that infants need stimulation. In addition, for fathers of boys, viewing the tape modified their sex role attitudes concerning the appropriateness of their participation in caretaking activities. Based on diary reports of caretaking activities in the home, fathers who saw the tape were more likely to diaper and feed their 3-month-old sons than fathers in the no-tape control group. The observational data revealed that the videotape modified father behavior in a variety of ways. It was effective in increasing the amount of caretaking behavior exhibited during feeding, both in the hospital and at 3 months. The tape significantly increased the stimulatory behavior of fathers of firstborn boys during the hospital period but not at later time periods. Examination of father–infant behavior sequences showed that as the fathers decreased their total amount of stimulation over the three time points, there was a concurrent increase in the probability of these behaviors being contingent on infant cues. Thus as the infant's behavioral repertoire expanded over the first 3 months, fathers who viewed the videotape changed from a highly stimulating interaction style to one that was highly contingent on infant behavior.

A similar pattern emerged for affection behaviors. There were no effects of the tape in the hospital or at 3 weeks, but at 3 months fathers who viewed the tape displayed more affection than control fathers during feeding, but control fathers were more affectionate than the others during play. Once again, examination of sequences revealed that this decrease in overall frequency was coupled with an increase in responsiveness. In spite of the lower amount of affection that fathers who viewed the tape displayed during play, the manner with which affection was displayed was more closely linked to infant signals in these fathers than in control fathers.

In summary, the videotape intervention significantly modified selected aspects of fathers' behavior and attitudes both in the hospital and through the first 3 months of their infants' lives. Of particular interest was the finding that the level of father participation in feeding and diapering increased as a result of this very limited intervention even after a 3-month period—at least in the case of boys. The heightened impact of the tape for fathers of boys merits comment. The most plausible explanation for this finding is a predispositional one. Since fathers are already differentially predisposed to interact more with male infants than female infants, the tape served to strengthen these already existing tendencies. There is a substantial body of literature in support of the claim that fathers both expect to and do show higher involvement with male than female infants (Lamb, Chapter 13; Parke, 1979; Pedersen, 1980). Previous social influence literature suggests that it is easier to produce further change in a direction that is already favored than in a nonfavored direction (McGuire, 1968).

In a recent study, Dickie and Carnahan (1979) provided training to mothers and fathers of 4- to 12-month-old infants in order to increase the parents' competence. Utilizing Goldberg's notion of competence as parental ability to assess, predict, elicit, and provide contingent response experiences for their infants, these investigators provided eight 2-hour weekly sessions. Training emphasized individual infant variation, knowledge of the infant's temperament and cues, provision of contingent experiences, and awareness of the infant's effect on the parents. Fathers who had participated in the training sessions, in contrast to fathers who had not participated, increased their interactions with their infants; they talked, touched, held, attended more, and gave more contingent responses to infant smiles and vocalizations. The infants of the trained fathers sought interaction more than infants of fathers in the control group. However, mothers in the trained group decreased their interactions. In view of the fact that training did increase competence, it is possible that the wives of the trained fathers encouraged their competent husbands to assume a greater share of the infant care and interactional responsibilities. This finding underlines the reciprocal nature of the mother–father relationship and provides further support for viewing the family as a social system in which the activities of one member have an impact on the behavior of other family members. Finally, these data are consistent with nonhuman primate findings that father–infant involvement varies inversely with the degree of maternal restrictiveness (see Redican, 1976; Redican & Taub, chapter 6, Parke & Suomi, 1981, for reviews).

As a number of recent studies suggest, efforts to modify father–infant interaction need not be restricted to young infants. Zelazo, Kotelchuck, Barber, and David (1977) selected 20 very low-interacting fathers and their 12-month-old first-born sons for an intervention study. These fathers did little caretaking or playing and were present only occasionally when their child was awake. Twelve fathers received an intervention involving playing with their infants for 30 minutes each day for 4 weeks in their homes. To facilitate the play interaction, a schedule of games and toys was provided for the father. Using a social learning strategy (Bandura, 1977), the experimenters both demonstrated the games, toys, and styles of interaction and coached the fathers in these activities prior to the intervention period. A control group of eight low-interacting fathers received no intervention. To assess the impact of the intervention on the infant's behavior, a laboratory-based parent–infant interaction session was held before and after the training period. This consisted of a 20-minute free-play period, with both parents in the room reading, followed by a series of maternal and paternal departures. In comparison to the control group, infants in the experimental group increased their interaction with their fathers in the free-play session; these infant boys looked more at their fathers and initiated more interaction with them. Separation protest was not affected by the experimental intervention. This was surprising in view of earlier reports that as father involvement increased, separation upset in the presence of a stranger lessened (Kotelchuck, 1972; Spelke et al., 1973). Although it was a pioneering study, there were several limitations. The fathers were instructed to initiate interactions in the laboratory sessions, so it is unclear whether there were increases in father behaviors directed to their infants. It is also unfortunate that these investigators did not monitor the amount of interaction between fathers and infants in their homes as a follow-up to their intervention program. In spite of these limitations, the investigation further underlines the modifiability of the father–infant relationship. It also serves as a corrective reminder of the fact that modification of early social interaction patterns are not necessarily limited to a particular "critical" period. As both Zelazo and his colleagues and earlier intervention studies (Rheingold, 1956; Skeels, 1966) have demonstrated, infant responsiveness can be modified at a variety of age levels. A similar caution applies to the development of parental responsiveness to infants. Although the early contact studies (Klaus & Kennell, 1976) suggest the importance of the immediate postpartum period for the facilitation of parental responsiveness to their infants, it should be recalled that adoption studies indicate that parents can learn to develop satisfactory relationships with infants and children who are adopted at older ages. The capacity of both parents and infants for continual adaptation to shifting social circumstances probably overrides the paramount importance of any single time period for the formation of social relationships (Cairns, 1977).

Considerable care must be taken in the implementation of these support systems; the important issue of parent's rights needs to be considered. It is not the aim to inflict these supports (with their implicit scenario of the liberated family versus more traditional family organization) on all families. The goal should be to provide as much support as the couple's ideology and role definition dictates is necessary for the successful fulfillment of these functions. Too often "more" is equated with "improvement;" however, in many families, increased father participation may cause conflict and disruption as a result of the threat to well-established and satisfying role definitions. Intervention, therefore, should be geared to the needs of individual families, and the dynamics and ideology of the couple should be given primary recognition.

CONCLUSION

In this chapter we have argued that fathers and mothers play distinctive but complementary roles in infancy. By utilizing a competence–performance distinction, it is clear that mothers and fathers are both competent caregivers even though in traditional families fathers play a less direct role in caregiving. Fathers, however, influence the caregiving activities of the mother in a variety of indirect ways. Play patterns of mothers and fathers were examined and differences in quantity and quality of play were noted. Each parent has a distinctive play style, fathers being more robust and physical and mothers more verbal.

Evidence was presented that illustrated the modifiability of these traditional distinctions between mother and father patterns of play. In addition to shifts in sex role ideologies and work patterns that are producing alternative family organizations, medical practices associated with childbirth and the child's birth status are among the factors shown to undermine stereotyped conceptions of the mother as caregiver and the father as playmate. Recognition of a wider range and modifiability of mother and father roles in infancy clearly is necessary. It is important to continuously monitor variations in father–infant and mother–infant interaction patterns attributable, at least in part, to secular and societal change. Eventually we may be able to isolate the principles that govern the process of change in social interaction patterns as well as describe the nature of these secular changes.

We have argued that more attention needs to be given to social support systems for fathers to facilitate their execution of parenting activities. Finally, a multilevel analytic approach to understanding fathers that recognizes the embeddedness of fathers and families within a network of social systems, including neighborhoods and communities, is advocated (Brim, 1975; Bronfenbrenner, 1979; Parke & Thomas 1981; Parke & Tinsley, in press). Eventually, the complexity of our models may match the complexity of father–infant relationships.

REFERENCES

Arbeit, S. A. A study of women during their first pregnancy. Unpublished doctoral dissertation, Yale University, 1975.

Ban, P., & Lewis, M. Mothers and fathers, girls and boys: Attachment behavior in the one-year-old. *Merrill-Palmer Quarterly,* 1974, **20,** 195–204.

Bandura, A. *Social learning theory*. Englewood Cliffs, N.J.: Prentice-Hall, 1977.

Belsky, J. Mother-father-infant interaction: A naturalistic observational study. *Developmental Psychology*, 1979, **15**, 601–607.

Biller, H. B., & Meredith, D. L. *Father power*. New York: McKay, 1974.

Brim, O. G. Macro-structural influences on child development and the need for childhood social indicators. *American Journal of Orthopsychiatry*, 1975, **45**, 516–524.

Bronfenbrenner, U. *The ecology of human development: Experiments by nature and design*. Cambridge, Mass.: Harvard University Press, 1979.

Brown, J. V., & Bakeman, R. Relationships of human mothers with their infants during the first year of life: Effects of prematurity. In R. W. Bell & W. P. Smotherman (Eds.), *Maternal influences and early behavior*. Holliswood, N.Y.: Spectrum, 1980.

Cairns, R. B. Beyond social attachment: The dynamics of interactional development. In T. A. Alloway, P. Pliner, & L. Krames (Eds.), *Attachment behavior*. New York: Plenum, 1977.

Clarke-Stewart, K. A. The father's impact on mother and child. Paper presented at the biennial meeting of the Society for Research in Child Development, New Orleans, March 1977.

Clarke-Stewart, K. A. And daddy makes three: The father's impact on mother and young child. *Child Development*, 1978, **49**, 466–478.

Clarke-Stewart, K. A. The father's contribution to children's cognitive and social development in early childhood. In F. A. Pedersen (Ed.), *The father–infant relationship: Observational studies in the family setting*. New York: Praeger, 1980.

Cowan, C. P. Cowan, P. A., Coie, L., & Coie, J. D. Becoming a family: The impact of a first child's birth on the couple's relationship. In W. B. Miller & L. F. Newman (Eds.), *The first child and family formation*. Chapel Hill, N.C.: Carolina Population Center, 1978.

Dickie, J., & Carnahan, S. Training in social competence: The effect on mothers, fathers and infants. Paper presented at the biennial meeting of the Society for Research in Child Development, San Francisco, 1979.

Entwisle, D. R., & Doering, S. G. *The first birth*. Baltimore: John Hopkins University Press, 1980.

Field, T. M. Interaction behaviors of primary versus secondary caretaker fathers. *Developmental Psychology*, 1978, **14**, 183–185.

Field, T. M. Interaction patterns of preterm and full term infants. In T. M. Field (Ed.), *Infants born at risk: Behavior and development*. New York: S. P. Medical and Scientific Books, 1979.

Goldberg, S. Premature birth: Consequences for the parent–infant relationship. *American Scientist*, 1979, **67**, 214–220.

Greenberg, M., & Morris, N. Engrossment: The newborn's impact upon the father. *American Journal of Orthopsychiatry*, 1974, **44**, 520–531.

Gronseth, E. Work-sharing adaptations of pioneering families with husband and wife in part time employment. *Acta Sociologia,* 1975, **18,** 202–221.

Grossman, F. K., Eichler, L. S., Winickoff, S. A., et al. *Pregnancy, birth, and parenthood.* San Francisco: Jossey-Bass, 1980.

Hawkins, R. P. Universal parenthood training: A proposal for preventative mental health. *Educational Technology,* 1971, **11,** 28–35.

Hawthorne, J. T., Richards, M. P. M., & Callon, M. A study of parental visiting of babies in a special care unit. In F. S. W. Brimblecombe, M. P. M. Richards, & N. R. C. Robertson (Eds.), *Early separation and special care nurseries: clinics in developmental medicine.* London: SIMP/Heinemann Medical Books, 1978.

Herzog, J. M. Disturbances in parenting high-risk infants: Clinical impressions and hypotheses. In T. M. Field (Ed.), *Infants born at risk: Behavior and development.* New York: S. P. Medical and Scientific Books, 1979.

Hoffman, L. W. Effects of the first child on the women's role. In W. B. Miller & L. F. Newman (Eds.), *The first child and family formation.* Chapel Hill, N.C.: Carolina Population Center, 1978.

Hoffman, L. W., & Nye, F. I. *Working mothers.* San Francisco: Jossey-Bass, 1974.

Klaus, M. H., & Kennell, J. H. *Parent–infant bonding.* St. Louis: Mosby, 1976.

Kotelchuck, M. The infant's relationship to the father: Experimental evidence. In M. E. Lamb (Ed.), *The role of the father in child development.* New York: Wiley, 1976.

Kotelchuck, M. The nature of the child's tie to his father. Unpublished doctoral dissertation, Harvard University, 1972.

Lamb, M. E. Twelve-month-olds and their parents: Interactions in a laboratory playroom. *Developmental Psychology,* 1976, **12,** 237–244.

Lamb, M. E. Father–infant and mother–infant interaction in the first year of life. *Child Development,* 1977, **48,** 167–181 (a).

Lamb, M. E. The development of mother–infant and father–infant attachments in the second year of life. *Developmental Psychology,* 1977, **13,** 637–648 (b).

Lamb, M. E. Infant social cognition and "second-order" effects. *Infant Behavior and Development,* 1978, **1,** 1–10.

Lamb, M. E. The effects of the social context on dyadic social interaction. In M. E. Lamb, S. J. Suomi, & G. R. Stephenson (Eds.), *Social interaction analysis: Methodological issues.* Madison: University of Wisconsin Press, 1979.

Lamb, M. E., Frodi, A. M., Hwang, C. P., & Frodi, M. Varying degress of paternal involvement in infant care: Attitudinal and behavioral correlates. In M. E. Lamb (Ed.), *Nontraditional families: Parenting and child development.* Hillsdale, N.J.: Lawrence Erlbaum Associates, in press (a).

Lamb, M. E., Frodi, A. M., Hwang, C., P., Frodi, M., & Steinberg, J. Effects of gender and caretaking roles on parent–infant interaction. In R. N. Emde & R. J. Harmon (Eds.), *Attachment and affiliative systems.* New York: Plenum, in press (b).

Levine, J. A. *Who will raise the children: New options for fathers (and mothers)*. New York: Lippincott, 1976.

Lewis, M., & Feiring, C. Direct and indirect interactions in social relationships. In L. Lipsitt (Ed.), *Advances in infancy research*, Vol. 1. Norwood, N.J.: Ablex Publishing Corp., 1981.

Lind, R. Observations after delivery of communications between mother–infant–father. Paper presented at the International Congress of Pediatrics, Buenos Aires, October 1974.

Lynn, D. B., & Cross, A. R. Parent preference of preschool children. *Journal of Marriage and the Family*, 1974, **36**, 555–559.

Marton P. L., & Minde, K. Paternal and maternal behavior with premature infants. Paper presented to the American Orthopsychiatric Association, Toronto, April 1980.

McGuire, W. J. The nature of attitudes and attitude change. In G. Lindzey & E. Aronson (Eds.), *Handbook of social psychology*, Vol. 3. Reading, Mass.: Addison-Wesley, 1968.

Parke, R. D. Perspectives on father–infant interaction. In J. Osofsky (Ed.), *Handbook of infancy*. New York: Wiley, 1979.

Parke, R. D. Theoretical models of child abuse: Their implications for prediction, prevention and modification. In R. Starr (Ed.), *Prediction of Abuse*. New York: Ballinger, in press (a).

Parke, R. D. *Fathers*. Cambridge: Harvard University Press, 1981 (b).

Parke, R. D., & Collmer, C. W. Child abuse: An interdisciplinary analysis. In E. M. Hetherington (Ed.), *Review of child development research*, Vol. 5. Chicago: University of Chicago Press, 1975.

Parke, R. D., Grossman, K., & Tinsley, B. R. Father–mother–infant interaction in the newborn period: A German–American comparison. In T. Field (Ed.), *Culture and early interactions*. Hillsdale, N.J.: Lawrence Erlbaum Associates, 1981.

Parke, R. D., Hymel, S., Power, T. G., & Tinsley, B. R. Fathers and risk: A hospital based model of intervention. In D. B. Sawin, R. C. Hawkins, L. O. Walker, & J. H. Penticuff (Eds.), *Psychosocial risks in infant–environment transactions*, New York: Bruner/Masel, 1980.

Parke, R. D., & O'Leary, S. E. Father–mother–infant interaction in the newborn period: Some findings, some observations and some unresolved issues. In K. Riegel & J. Meacham (Eds.), *The developing individual in a changing world*, (Vol. 2). *Social and environmental issues*. The Hague: Mouton, 1976.

Parke, R. D., O'Leary, S. E., & West, S. Mother–father–newborn interaction: effects of maternal medication, labor and sex of infant. *Proceedings of the American Psychological Association*, 1972, 85–86.

Parke, R. D., Power, T. G., & Gottman, J. Conceptualizing and quantifying influence patterns in the family triad. In M. E. Lamb, S. J. Suomi, & G. R. Stephenson (Eds.), *Social interaction analysis: Methodological issues*. Madison: University of Wisconsin Press, 1979.

Parke, R. D., & Sawin, D. B. Infant characteristics and behavior as elicitors of maternal and paternal responsibility in the newborn period. Paper presented at the biennial meeting of the Society for Research in Child Development, Denver, April 1975.

Parke, R. D., & Sawin, D. B. The family in early infancy: Social interactional and attitudinal analyses. In F. A. Pedersen (Ed.), *The father–infant relationship: Observational studies in the family setting.* New York: Praeger, 1980.

Parke, R. D. & Suomi, S. J. Adult male–infant relationships: Human and nonhuman primate evidence. In K. Immelman, G. Barlow, M. Main, & L. Petrinovitch (Eds.), *Behavioral development: The Bielefeld Interdisciplinary project.* New York: Cambridge University Press, 1981.

Parke, R. D., & Thomas, N. G. The family in context: A multi-level interactional analysis of child abuse. In R. W. Henderson (Ed.), *Parent-child interaction: Theory, research and prospect.* New York: Academic Press, 1981.

Parke, R.D., Thomas, N. G., Neff, C., Szcyzypka, D., Tinsley, B. R., & Zarling, C. Parent–infant interaction with full term and premature infants: In the hospital and at home. Unpublished manuscript.

Parke, R. D. & Tinsley, B. R. The early environment of the high-risk infant: Expanding the social context. In D. Bricker (Ed.), *Application of research findings to intervention with at-risk and handicapped infants.* Baltimore: University Park Press, in press.

Pedersen, F. A. Mother, father, and infant as an interactive system. Paper presented to the American Psychological Association, Chicago, September 1975.

Pedersen, F. A., Anderson, B. J., & Cain, R. L. An approach to understanding linkages between the parent–infant and spouse relationships. Paper presented at the Society for Research in Child Development, New Orleans, March 1977.

Pedersen, F. A., Anderson, B. J. & Cain, R. L. Parent–infant and husband–wife interactions observed at age five months. In F. A. Pedersen (Ed.), *The father–infant relationship: Observational studies in the family setting.* New York: Praeger, 1980.

Pedersen, F. A., Cain, R., Zaslow, M., & Anderson, B. Variation in infant experience associated with alternative family role organization. Paper presented at the International Conference on Infant Studies, New Haven, April 1980.

Pedersen, F. A., Zaslow, M. J., Cain, R. L., & Anderson, B. J. Cesarean birth: The importance of a family perspective. Paper presented at the International Conference on Infant Studies, New Haven, April 1980.

Phillips, D., & Parke, R. D. Father and mother speech to prelinguistic infants. Unpublished manuscript, University of Illinois, 1981.

Power, T. G., & Parke, R. D. Play as a context for early learning: Lab and home analyses. In L. M. Laosa & I. E. Sigel (Eds.), *The family as a learning environment,* New York: Plenum, in press.

Radin, N. Childbearing fathers in intact families: An exploration of some antecedents and consequences. Paper presented at a study group on ''The Role of the Father in

Child Development, Social Policy, and the Law,'' University of Haifa, Haifa, Israel, July 15–17, 1980.

Redican, W.K. Adult male–infant interactions in nonhuman primates. In M. E. Lamb (Ed.), *The role of the father in child development*. New York: Wiley, 1976.

Rendina, I., & Dickerscheid, J. D. Father involvement with first-born infants. *Family Coordinator*, 1976, **25**, 373–379.

Rheingold, H. The modification of social responsiveness in institutional babies. *Monographs of the Society for Research in Child Development*, 1956, **21**, No. 63.

Richards, M. P. M., Dunn, J. F. & Antonis, B., Caretaking in the first year of life: The role of fathers' and mothers' social isolation. *Child: Care, Health and Development*, 1977, **3**, 23–26.

Russell, G. The father role and its relation to masculinity, femininity and androgyny. *Child Development*, 1978, **49**, 1174–1181.

Russell, G. Fathers as caregivers: Possible antecedents and consequences. Papers presented to a study group on "The Role of the Father in Child Development, Social Policy and the Law," University of Haifa, Haifa, Israel, July 15–17, 1980.

Sachs, J. The adaptive significance of linguistic input to prelinguistic infants. In C. E. Snow & C. A. Ferguson (Eds.), *Talking to children*. Cambridge, Mass.: Cambridge University Press, 1977.

Sawin, D. B., & Parke, R. D. Adolescent fathers: Some implications from recent research on parental roles. *Educational Horizons*, 1976, **55**, 38–43.

Schaffer, H. R., & Emerson, P. E. The development of social attachments in infancy. *Monographs of the Society for Research in Child Development*, 1964, **29**, Serial No. 94.

Schlossman, S. L. Before home starts: Notes toward a history of parent education in America, 1897–1929. *Harvard Educational Review*, 1976, **46**, 436–467.

Shereshefsky, P. M., & Yarrow, L. J. *Psychological aspects of a first pregnancy and early postnatal adaptation*. New York: Raven Press, 1973.

Skeels, H. Adult studies of children with contrasting early life experiences. *Monographs of the Society for Research in Child Development*, 1966, **31**, No. 105.

Spelke, E., Zelazo, P., Kagan, J., & Kotelchuck, M. Father interaction and separation protest. *Developmental Psychology*, 1973, **9**, 83–90.

Stern, D. N. Mother and infant at play: The dyadic interaction involving facial, vocal, and gaze behaviors. In M. Lewis & L. A. Rosenblum (Eds.), *The effect of the infant on its caregiver*. New York: Wiley, 1974.

Vietze, P. M., MacTurk, R. H., McCarthy, M. E., Klein, R. P., & Yarrow, L. J. Impact of mode of delivery on father– and mother–infant interaction at 6 and 12 months. Paper presented at the Second International Conference on Infant Studies, New Haven, 1980.

Yogman, M. W. Development of the father–infant relationship. In H. Fitzgerald, B. Lester, & M. W. Yogman (Eds.), *Theory and Research in Behavioral Pediatrics,* Vol. 1. New York: Plenum, 1981.

Yogman, M. W., Dixon S., & Tronick, E. The goals and structure of face-to-face interaction between infants and fathers. Paper presented at the biennial meeting of the Society for Research in Child Development, New Orleans, 1977.

Zelazo, P. R., Kotelchuck, M., Barber, L., & David, J. Fathers and sons: An experimental facilitation of attachment behaviors. Paper presented at the biennial meeting of the Society for Research in Child Development, New Orleans, March 1977.

CHAPTER 13

The Development of Father–Infant Relationships

MICHAEL E. LAMB

University of Utah

Since 1970 there has been considerable research on the development of father–infant relationships. This represents a remarkable shift, since in earlier years students of infant social development barely acknowledged the father's existence, much less considered that fathers might play a formatively significant role in the socialization of infants and young children. Although many researchers and theorists still disregard paternal contributions to socioemotional development, it is widely recognized today that most infants develop in the context of a complex social system—the family. Unfortunately, the amount of research conducted thus far is too limited to permit many firm conclusions, and we currently lack the statistical and conceptual sophistication necessary to understand the complex and multidirectional paths of influence operating within families. This obviously limits our comprehension of the father–infant relationship.

Another limitation should also be acknowledged. With a few recent exceptions, almost all the research has been concerned with the behavior and impact of "traditional" fathers—that is, fathers whose primary role, breadwinning, limits the amount of contact they have with their infants. It is readily apparent, however, that increasing numbers of infants are not cared for exclusively by their mothers, and that as the number of working mothers increases, the possibility (and, for many, the desirability and necessity) for paternal involvement also increases. There is no reason to assume that "nontraditional" fathers influence their children in the same way that traditional fathers do, and this restricts the generalizability of the research that has been conducted.

It is not difficult to determine why developmental psychologists ignored the father–child relationship for so long. In their assumption of maternal prominence they simply reflected common cultural presumptions that were reinforced by evaluations of paternal involvement in nonhuman species. Experimental analyses showed that the female hormones—estrogen, prolactin, and progesterone—were crucial in rodents (see reviews by Lamb, 1975b; Rosenblatt, 1970). Among nonhuman primates, males appeared to have minimal involvement in infant care (e.g., Chamove, Harlow, & Mitchell, 1967; DeVore, 1963), mirroring the reports by anthropologists that human women everywhere assumed primary responsibility for childcare. Only later did it become apparent that the rodent model was a poor one to apply to humans (e.g., Lamb & Goldberg, 1982) and that there was vast variability among primate species. The greatest paternal involvement occurs when mothers are not protectively restrictive and adults form enduring monogamous bonds—characteristics that lead to predictions of relatively high paternal involvement among humans (see Parke & Suomi, 1980; Redican, 1976 and Chapter 6 for reviews).

When research on human father–infant relationships first began, researchers sought to determine whether (and when) most infants formed relationships to their fathers. Having shown that most infants indeed became attached to their fathers, investigators then attempted to define the similarities and differences between mother– and father–infant relationships. At about the same time, two other issues became popular: the analysis of paternal behavior in the early (preattachment) months of life and the interest in the formative significance of father–infant relationships. It is clear that the concerns of researchers have become broader and more inclusive over the years. Furthermore, the discovery of father–infant relationships has brought with it the realization that infants are raised within complex social systems in which each person or relationship probably affects all other persons and relationships. As a result, there is increasing interest in the influence of the mother–father relationship on the infant (and vice versa) and in the potential for indirect as well as direct influences on infant development.

In this review I address each of these issues, although I do not take them up in the order in which they achieved prominence. Instead, I start with a brief review of the research on paternal responses to very young infants—a topic discussed more thoroughly by Parke and Tinsley in Chapter 12. I then consider the development of father–infant attachments, evaluating the proposition that there is a preference hierarchy among attachment figures in which mothers typically are preferred over fathers. In the third section, I describe research on the differences and similarities between maternal and paternal behavior. The characteristics of paternal behavior are again of concern in section four, in which paternal influences on the course of social and personality development are considered. Patterns of indirect effects are reviewed in the final substantive section.

PATERNAL SENSITIVITY

Sensitivity, or responsiveness to infant signals, is a topic that has been of interest to developmental psychologists for many decades. Unfortunately, the relevant research is of variable quality, and the concept itself has been operationalized in many different ways. Perhaps the most useful formulation is that of the ethological attachment theorists (Ainsworth, 1973; Bowlby, 1969; Lamb, 1978c, 1981; Lamb & Easterbrooks, 1981) who propose that human infants are biologically predisposed to emit signals (e.g., cries, smiles) to which adults are biologically predisposed to respond. When adults consistently respond promptly and appropriately to infant signals, the infants come to perceive the adults concerned as predictable and reliable. This perception assures the formation of secure infant–parent attachments (Ainsworth, Bell, & Stayton, 1974; Lamb, 1981). In contrast, when adults do not respond sensitively, insecure attachments result, and when they respond rarely, no attachments at all may develop. Thus it is crucial to determine whether fathers are appropriately responsive to their infants; when they are not, the likelihood of father–infant relationships forming would be minimal.

There is another (related) reason that research on paternal sensitivity is important. Several theorists (e.g., Klaus, Trause, & Kennell, 1975) have speculated that the biological predisposition to respond to infant signals is stronger in females than it is in males. If true, this would imply that biology limits the potential for males to have significant and direct influences on infant development. Unfortunately, the speculation is based largely on evidence concerning hormonal influences on parental behavior in rodents, and this animal model may be very inappropriate (Lamb & Goldberg, 1982). Nevertheless, the implications are such that the speculation merits serious consideration.

In an early interview study, Greenberg and Morris (1974) reported that most fathers were elated by the birth of their infants and experienced strongly positive emotions that Greenberg and Morris termed ''engrossment.'' In the first two of the studies undertaken by Parke and his colleagues (Parke & O'Leary, 1976; Parke, O'Leary, & West, 1972; Chapter 12), mothers and fathers were observed in a maternity ward interacting with their newborn infants. Contrary to popular misconceptions, the fathers were neither inept nor uninterested in interaction with the newborns. Indeed, all but a couple of measures showed that the fathers and mothers were equivalently involved in interaction. Observing each parent alone with the infant as well as with the spouse present, Parke and his colleagues found that fathers were somewhat more interactive when their wives were present than when the fathers and infants were alone together. This effect is difficult to explain, particularly because many other studies (involving parents and children ranging in age from 4 months to school age) show that parents are typically *less* interactive in triadic than in dyadic contexts (see Lamb, 1979, for a review).

In his subsequent research, Parke has considered not only the affectionate manner in which fathers behave but also their behavioral responsiveness or sensitivity—that is, their propensity to attend to their infants' cues and emit appropriate responses. Phillips and Parke (1979), like Gleason (1975), Golinkoff and Ames (1979), Kauffman (1977), and Blount and Padgug (1976), found that fathers, like mothers, adjusted their speech patterns when interacting with infants—they spoke more slowly, used shorter phrases, and repeated themselves more often when talking to infants than to adults. When observed feeding their infants, both fathers and mothers responded to infant cues either with social bids or by adjusting the pace of the feeding (Parke & Sawin, 1977). Although the fathers were capable of behaving sensitively, they tended to yield responsibility for childtending chores to their wives when not asked to demonstrate their competence for the investigators.

Alternative ways of studying parental responsiveness to infant signals have been pursued by Feldman and Nash and by Frodi and Lamb. Both of these research teams have observed parents with unfamiliar infants rather than with their own. Feldman and Nash (1977, 1978; Nash & Feldman, 1981; Feldman, Nash, & Cutrona, 1977) observed parents individually while they sat in a waiting room containing an infant and its mother. The subjects were observed interacting with the baby by concealed observers. These studies by Feldman and Nash showed that sex differences in "baby responsiveness" waxed and waned depending on the subject's age and social status. Thus females were more responsive than males in early adolescence and in early parenthood, whereas there were no sex differences among 8-year-olds, childless couples, and unmarried college students. Feldman and Nash concluded that sex differences in responsiveness to infants are experientially rather than biologically determined: they are evident when individuals are under increased social pressure to respond in a conventionally sex-typed fashion. The data indicated that in response to presumed social pressures, mothers were more responsive than fathers.

In contrast, the studies conducted by Frodi and Lamb revealed no sex differences in responsiveness to infants. In their first two studies (Frodi, Lamb, Leavitt, & Donovan, 1978; Frodi, Lamb, Leavitt, Donovan, Neff, & Sherry, 1978), the psychophysiological responses (heart rate, blood pressure, skin conductance) of mothers and fathers were monitored while the parents observed quiescent, smiling, or crying infants on a television monitor. Crying and smiling infants elicited characteristic and distinct physiological response patterns in both mothers and fathers. In a later study (Frodi & Lamb, 1978), we found no sex differences in physiological responses among either 8- or 14-year-olds, whereas 14-year-old females were more behaviorally responsive than males in a waiting room situation similar to Feldman's. Like Feldman and Nash, we concluded that there were no biologically based sex differences in responsiveness to infants and that behavioral dimorphisms emerged in response to societal pressures and expectations.

This conclusion appears to be consistent with all the relevant data currently available. Nevertheless, the fact that men *can* be as responsive as women does not mean that mothers and fathers typically *are* equivalently responsive. Fathers are not always highly responsive, and their responsiveness probably varies depending on the degree to which they assume responsibility for infant care, since caretaking experience appears to facilitate parental responsiveness (Zelazo, Kotelchuck, Barber, & David, 1977). Nevertheless, most fathers are sufficiently responsive to their infants that attachments should form provided only that a sufficient amount of father–infant interaction takes place.

The Extent of Father–Infant Interaction

Several researchers have attempted to determine how much time the "average" father spends with his infant. As one might expect, the estimates vary widely even when one considers only traditional family structures in which mothers assume primary and full-time responsibility for childcare, and fathers are concerned primarily with breadwinning. One early study found that, according to maternal reports, fathers of 8- to 9½-month-old infants were home between 5 and 47 hours per week at times when the infants were awake (Pedersen & Robson, 1969). The average was 26 hours. The fathers reportedly spent between 45 minutes and 26 hours each week actually interacting with their babies. From interviews with the parents of 6- to 21-month-olds, meanwhile, Kotelchuck (1975) determined that mothers spent an average of 9 waking hours per day with their children, whereas fathers spent 3.2 hours. The parents interviewed by Golinkoff and Ames (1979) reported figures of 8.33 and 3.16 hours. In contrast, fathers interviewed by Lewis and Weinraub (1974) reported much less interaction than this: the average was 15 to 20 minutes per day. The variability among these estimates presumably is attributable to socioeconomic and subcultural differences in the populations studied. It may also differ depending on the amount of encouragement and support fathers receive: Lind (1974), for example, found that Swedish fathers who were taught how to care for their newborns and were encouraged to do so were more involved with their infants 3 months later. When babies are hospitalized because of their premature birth status, fathers visit as frequently as mothers (Marton & Minde, 1980), indicating that there is a desire for interaction. Finally, it is important to distinguish between time spent in the same house and time spent in actual and intensive interaction: The mothers and children studied by Clarke-Stewart (1973) spent 90 percent of the observational sessions in the same room, but only 10 to 15 percent of the time was spent in interaction with one another. Most investigators would agree that traditional fathers spend relatively little time each day interacting with their infants, regardless of their class status. Unfortunately, although most theorists believe that at least a minimum amount of regular interaction is necessary if attachments are to form, no one has yet determined the minimum necessary amount. It is unlikely that such an estimate will ever be possible given the fact that the quality of interaction appears to be more important than its quantity (e.g., Schaffer & Emerson, 1964; see also Chapter 1). Furthermore, Schaffer's research on hospitalized infants suggested that the amount and quality of social interaction in general may facilitate the later formation of bonds to people other than the sources of stimulation (Schaffer, 1963). It is conceivable, therefore, that the quality of mother–infant interaction may facilitate the formation of father–infant attachments and affect the amount of interaction necessary for the attachment to form. We can simply say, on the basis of the evidence reviewed in the next section, that most infants must have enough "quality" interaction with their fathers since most infants do become attached to their fathers.

THE DEVELOPMENT OF FATHER–INFANT ATTACHMENTS

It took a major shift in predominant theoretical orientation to encourage the study of father–infant attachments. Prior to the late 1950s, it was presumed that infants formed attachments only to those involved in their basic physical care, but Harlow's (1958) provocative findings and the general fall from favor of secondary drive theories (e.g., Hinde, 1960; White, 1959) produced a shift from an emphasis on caretaking to a focus on the quantity and quality of social stimulation (Berlyne, 1969; Rheingold, 1956; Welker, 1971). This emphasis has remained prominent, and in the course of attempts to specify what constitutes high-quality interaction, many theorists have converged on the notion of parental sensitivity that I introduced in an earlier section (see Lamb & Easterbrooks, 1981, for a review). Not all theorists would share my views on the nature and significance of parental sensitivity, but most would agree that the sheer quantity of interaction is less significant than its quality.

The first attempt to determine empirically whether and when infants formed attachments to their fathers was made by Schaffer and Emerson in 1964, although unfortunately these researchers relied solely on maternal reports for their evidence. Mothers reported that their infants began to protest separations from them at 7 to 9 months of age; many also reported that their infants began to protest separations from their fathers at about the same time. By 18 months of age, 71 percent of the subjects appeared to be attached to (i.e., they protested separation from) both parents. According to Schaffer and Emerson (1964), the babies formed attachments to those with whom they interacted regularly; involvement in caretaking seemed insignificant.

The next published study (Pedersen & Robson, 1969) also relied on maternal reports, although here the focus was on responses to reunion following separation rather than on protest concerning the onset of separation. The majority of the mothers (75 percent) reported that their infants responded positively and enthusiastically when their fathers' returned from work, and this led Pedersen and Robson to conclude that these infants were attached to their fathers. Among the boys, intensity of greeting behavior was correlated with the frequency of paternal caretaking, paternal patience with infant fussing, and the intensity of father–infant play. Among daughters, however, intensity of greeting behavior was correlated only with reported paternal "apprehension over well-being."

Observational studies of father–infant attachment began in the 1970s—a decade marked by a sharp shift from interviews to observations as the most popular sources of data. For his doctoral dissertation, Kotelchuck (1972) developed an experimental procedure that permitted him to observe the reactions of 6-, 9-, 12-, 15-, 18-, and 21-month-old infants to brief separations from mothers, fathers, and strangers. Although no usable data were obtained from the 6- and 9-month-olds (perhaps because the sequence of 13 3-minute episodes was too confusing or exhausting for them), it seemed that the older infants were attached to both of their parents. They predictably protested when left alone by either parent, explored little while the parents were absent, and greeted them positively when they returned. Few infants protested separation from either parent when the other parent remained with them. A majority (55 percent) of the infants were more concerned about separation from, and thus seemed to prefer, their mothers, but 25 percent preferred their fathers and 20 percent showed no preference for either parent.

Kotelchuck and his colleagues proceeded to conduct a series of investigations using the same experimental procedure (Spelke, Zelazo, Kagan, & Kotelchuck, 1973; Ross, Kagan, Zelazo, & Kotelchuck, 1975; Lester, Kotelchuck, Spelke, Sellers, & Klein, 1974; Zelazo et al., 1977). The results of these studies confirmed the conclusions drawn in the initial study. In addition, Spelke et al. (1973) replicated Kotelchuck's (1972) finding that there is a relationship between amount of separation protest following separation from fathers and the degree of paternal involvement in caretaking. Somewhat unexpectedly, however, infants protested *least* when they had highly involved fathers. Heightened paternal involvement also delayed the onset of separation protest. American infants with highly interactive fathers strongly protested separation from both parents at 15 and 18 months of age (Kotelchuck, 1972), whereas those with less interactive fathers protested at 12 months of age (Spelke et al., 1973). Guatemalan infants, who rarely interacted with their fathers, protested separation at 9 months (Lester et al., 1974). In general, the data collected by Kotelchuck and his colleagues indicated that babies who experienced a great deal of interaction with their fathers started to protest separation later than those whose fathers were uninvolved, and the phase during which protest occurred was briefer when involvement was greater. It is still not at all clear what these data mean. The consistently counterintuitive nature of the correlations between measures of protest and measures of involvement suggests that intensity of separation protest may not be a good measure of intensity of attachment. This interpretation is strengthened by the fact that measures of separation protest may fail to reveal differences that are evident on more sensitive measures (e.g., Cohen & Campos, 1974; Stayton, Ainsworth, & Main, 1973).

The other dependent measures recorded in Kotelchuck's studies yielded more interpretable findings, however. Low paternal involvement in caretaking was associated with reduced interaction and proximity seeking in the laboratory (Kotelchuck, 1972; Spelke et al., 1973), and an intervention study (Zelazo et al., 1977) showed that when paternal involvement at home increased, there was a concomitant increase in the amount of father–infant interaction in the laboratory. Measures of separation protest were unaffected.

Like Kotelchuck and his colleagues, Cohen and Campos (1974) observed infants' responses to brief separations from each of their parents, but they also recorded the infants' propensity to seek comfort from the people (mother, father, or stranger) remaining with them. Distress did not discriminate between mothers and fathers, but on measures such as frequency of approach, speed of approach, time in proximity, and use of the parent as a "secure base" from which to interact with a stranger, 10-, 13-, and 16-month-old infants showed preferences for their mothers over their fathers, as well as clear preferences for fathers over strangers. This finding contrasts with that of Feldman and Ingham (1975), and Willemsen, Flaherty, Heaton, and Ritchey (1974), who used the Strange Situation procedure (Ainsworth & Wittig, 1969) but not Ainsworth's scoring procedure. Both of the latter studies revealed no preferences for either parent over the other. In a study of 2-year-olds, Lamb (1976c) found no preferences for either parent on measures of separation protest or greeting behavior.

Instead of a separation–reunion paradigm, Lewis and his colleagues observed 1- and 2-year-old infants in 15-minute free-play sessions—once with each parent. One-year-olds touched, stayed near, and vocalized to their mothers more than their fathers, whereas no comparable preferences were evident among 2-year-olds (Ban & Lewis, 1974; Lewis & Ban, 1971; Lewis, Weinraub, & Ban, 1972).

By the mid-1970s, therefore, there was substantial evidence that children developed attachments to their fathers in infancy. However, it was unclear how early in their lives infants formed these attachments, since there were no data available concerning the period between 6 and 9 months of age during which infants form attachments to their mothers (Bowlby, 1969). There was also controversy concerning the existence of preferences for mothers over fathers—some studies reported such preferences and others did not—and there were no data available concerning father–infant interaction in the unstructured home environment rather than in the laboratory.

It was in this context that I initiated a naturalistic longitudinal study of mother– and father–infant attachment in 1974. Lengthy home observations revealed that 7-, 8-, 12-, and 13-month-old infants showed no preference for either parent over the other on attachment behavior measures (measures of their propensity to stay near, approach, touch, cry to, and ask to be held by specific adults), although these measures all showed preferences for parents over a relatively unfamiliar adult visitor (Lamb, 1976b, 1977c). Measures of separation protest and greeting behavior also showed no infant preferences for either parent (Lamb, 1976b). During the second year of life, however, the situation changed. Boys began to show significant preferences for their fathers on the attachment behavior measures, whereas girls as a group showed no significant or consistent preference for either parent (Lamb, 1977a). By the end of the second year, all but one of the nine boys showed consistent preferences for their fathers on at least four of the five attachment behavior measures (Lamb, 1977b).

The results of this longitudinal study indicated that most infants formed attachments to both their parents at about the same time, and that by the second year of life boys preferred to interact with their fathers. On superficial examination, these findings appear to be at odds with Bowlby's (1969) claim that there is a hierarchy among attachment figures, with the primary caretaker usually becoming the preferred attachment figure. My data, however, were not really appropriate for testing this hypothesis. According to attachment theory, preferences among attachment figures may not be evident in stress-free situations in which infants do not need comfort from or protection by attachment figures. Under stress, however, infants should inhibit affiliation with nonattachment figures and focus their attachment behavior more narrowly on primary attachment figures.

In fact, the participants in my longitudinal study were also observed in more stressful laboratory contexts at 8, 12, and 18 months (Lamb, 1976a, 1976d, 1976f). The results of the 12- and 18-month observations were clear-cut and consistent with Bowlby's hypothesis. In stress-free episodes, infants behaved much as they did at home; the attachment behavior measures showed no significant preferences for either parent, although there was more affiliative interaction with fathers. When distressed, the display of attachment behaviors increased, and the infants organized their behavior similarly around whichever parent was present. When both parents were present, distressed infants turned to their mothers preferentially (Lamb, 1976a, 1976f). At 8 months of age the infants showed no preferences (Lamb, 1976d), nor did a sample of 24-month-olds (Lamb, 1976c). Evidently, the hierarchy among attachment figures is marked only during a relatively brief period. Notice also that the boys showed strong preferences for their fathers at home during the period that they turned to their mothers preferentially when distressed. This indicates that mothers were still deemed more reliable sources of comfort and security, even though fathers had become more desirable partners for playful interaction.

The fact that stress affects the display of preferences may help explain some of the inconsistency evident in the results of the studies reviewed earlier. Primary caretaking mothers become primary attachment figures for most infants, but preferences for them may not be apparent unless the infants are distressed. Studies in which infants either are not distressed or cannot choose between the parents when distressed are less likely to uncover reliable preferences than studies in which distressed infants can choose between two potential sources of comfort and security.

The results of studies on the development of attachment and parental preferences also underscore important methodological concerns having to do with the assessment of social relationships. Following Bowlby (1969), I have suggested a distinction between *affiliative behaviors* (such as smiling and vocalizing) and *attachment behaviors* (such as crying or asking to be held). Affiliative behaviors are employed in friendly interaction with individuals whether or not the infant is attached to them, whereas attachment behaviors, which are more directly useful in promoting proximity/contact, should be focused fairly narrowly on attachment figures. It is only by examining the occurrence of attachment behaviors that we can determine whether an infant is attached to a person[1] and whether there exists a hierarchy of preference among multiple attachment figures. The attachment behavior measures show that infants are attached to both parents (e.g., Lamb, 1977c) and that they prefer their mothers when distressed (Lamb, 1976a, 1976f), whereas affiliative behavior measures tend to show "preferences" for fathers throughout the first 2 years of life (Clarke-Stewart, 1978; Lamb, 1977a, 1977c). These preferences on the affiliative behavior measures seem attributable to the relative novelty of fathers (who are away much of the day), and to the fact that fathers themselves elicit more

---

[1] Even when relying solely on attachment behavior measures, it is necessary to be cautious, since it is known that distressed infants will seek comfort from nonattachment figures when no attachment figure is present (see, for example, Bowlby, 1969). Ideally, therefore, one would want to demonstrate clear preferences for a putative attachment figure over friendly but unfamiliar comparison persons (Cohen, 1974).

affiliative interaction than mothers do (Clarke-Stewart, 1978; Lamb, 1977a, 1977c).

Finally, it is interesting that infants learn to use labels ("papa," "dada," etc.) for their fathers earlier than they label their mothers (Brooks-Gun & Lewis, 1979). Perhaps frequent paternal absences make it necessary to refer to them more often. It would be revealing to determine what happens when parental roles are reversed.

CHARACTERISTICS OF MOTHER– AND FATHER–INFANT INTERACTION

Evidence that most infants form attachments to their fathers as well as to their mothers is not sufficient to demonstrate that fathers play a formatively significant role in infant development. It could be argued, for example, that fathers are essentially redundant—that they are occasional mother substitutes but have little independent impact on infant development. This possibility has stimulated research designed to determine whether mothers and fathers represent different types of experiences for their infants. The data consistently show that they do.

Even in the first trimester, fathers and mothers appear to engage in different types of interactions with their infants. When videotaped in face-to-face interaction with their 2- to 25-week-old infants, for example, fathers tended to provide staccato bursts of both physical and social stimulation, whereas mothers tended to be more rhythmic and containing (Yogman, Dixon, Tronick, Als, Adamson, Lester, & Brazelton, 1977). Mothers addressed their babies with soft, repetitive, imitative sounds, whereas fathers touched their infants with rhythmic pats (Yogman et al., 1977). During visits to hospitalized premature infants, mothers were responsive to social cues, fathers to gross motor cues (Marton & Minde, 1980).

Older infants are often unwilling to sit in infant seats to engage in face-to-face interaction, and thus most of the data concerning the characteristics of parent–infant interaction have been gathered in the course of naturalistic home observations. In my longitudinal study, I found that fathers tended to engage in more physically stimulating and unpredictable or "idiosyncratic" play than mothers did (Lamb, 1976b, 1977c). Since these types of play elicited more positive responses from the infants, the average response to play bids by fathers was more positive than the average response to maternal bids. Power and Parke (1979) and Clarke-Stewart (1978) later confirmed that mothers and fathers engaged in different types of play. Belsky (1979), by contrast, did not find any differences of this kind. Since he used different observational codes and studied older infants, however, direct comparison of the findings is not possible.

When I examined the reasons that mothers and fathers picked up and held their 7- to 13-month-old infants, I found that mothers were more likely to hold infants in the course of caretaking, whereas fathers were more likely to do so in playing with the babies or in response to the infants' requests to be held (Lamb, 1976c, 1977c). These findings were replicated by Belsky (1979). It is not surprising that infants responded more positively to being held by their fathers than by their mothers (Lamb, 1976a, 1977c).

Data gathered by interview confirm that fathers are identified with playful interactions whereas mothers are associated with caretaking. According to Kotelchuck's (1975) informants, mothers spent an average of 1.45 hours per day feeding their 6- to 21-month-olds, whereas fathers averaged 15 minutes. Mothers spent 55 minutes per day cleaning their infants and 2.3 hours playing with them, whereas the comparable figures for fathers were 9 minutes and 1.2 hours. Mothers thus spent a greater proportion of their total interaction caretaking, and fathers spent a greater proportion of their interaction time in playful social interaction. Relative to the total amount of interaction, Clarke-Stewart's (1978) data also suggested that fathers were consistently notable for their involvement in play, and that their relative involvement in caretaking increased over time. Although Rendina and Dickerscheid (1976) did not record maternal behavior (making a comparison of maternal and paternal behavior impossible), it is clear that fathers spent most of their time in playful interaction; on average, only 3.8 percent of the time was spent in caretaking. A study of English families reported similar findings. From maternal interviews, Richards, Dunn, and Antonis (1975) found that at both 30 and 60 weeks, the most common father–infant activity in 90 percent of the families was play. Routine involvement in caretaking was rare: only 35 percent regularly fed their infants at 30 weeks and 46 percent at 60 weeks. Diaper-changing and bathing were the least common paternal activities. However, Marton and Minde (1980) found that the fathers of preterm infants were more involved in caretaking than the fathers of full term infants.

Further evidence that fathers are especially notable for their involvement in play comes from a small (n=14) but intensive longitudinal study of 15- to 30-month-olds undertaken by Clarke-Stewart (1978, 1980). In this study, it was found that fathers gave more verbal directions and positive reinforcements than mothers did. Fathers were rated higher than mothers on ability to engage children in play. For their part, babies showed more enjoyment and involvement when playing with fathers than with mothers. No differences were found in parental responsiveness. When the parents were asked (as part of a laboratory task) to choose an activity in which to engage their infants, mothers tended to choose intellectual activities, whereas fathers selected playful social-physical activities. Given the playfulness of much father–infant interaction, it is little wonder that young children come to prefer play with their fathers when they have the choice (Clarke-Stewart, 1978; Lamb, 1976c, 1977c; Lynn & Cross, 1974).

Diaries kept by the mothers of Clarke-Stewart's (1978) subjects also suggested important age changes not explored in the other studies. At 15 months, mothers and infants engaged in more play than fathers and infants; at 20 months, mothers and fathers spent equivalent amounts of time in play, and by 30 months, fathers were spending more time than mothers in play. There was also a change with age in relative responsibility for caretaking. At 15 months, mothers spent far more time than fathers in caretaking, but by 30 months, both parents devoted equivalent amounts of time to this.

Finally, the results of a recent study by Pedersen, Cain, and Zaslow (1982) suggested that the patterns of involvement may differ when both parents work full-time during the day. When observed with their infants, working mothers stimulated their infants more than nonworking mothers did, and they were far more active than their husbands were. In accordance with the findings just reviewed, fathers with nonworking wives played with their infants more than the mothers did, but this pattern was reversed in the families with working mothers. Maternal responsibility for caretaking did not differ depending on the mothers' working status. This contradicts Hoffman's (1977) conclusion that paternal involvement increases when mothers work outside the home.

There is no solid evidence yet available concerning the origins of the paternal and maternal play styles. Brazelton and his colleagues (1979) have argued that they reflect biologically determined differences, and that because even very young infants innately "expect" fathers and mothers to behave differently, they behave in ways that elicit "appropriate" paternal behavior from fathers who assume a primary caretaking role. This would be consistent with the fact that playfulness is also characteristic of father–child relationships in monkeys (Zucker, Mitchell, & Maple, 1978), but it seems implausible, since it attributes to young infants greater cognitive and perceptual skills than they are known to possess (see Lamb & Sherrod, 1981, for reviews of the relevant literature). It seems more likely that maternal and paternal styles are consequences of the socially prescribed roles assumed by mothers and fathers in traditional families. Unfortunately, there has been only one published study in which the behavior of primary and secondary caretaking fathers was compared (Field, 1978). According to Field, the primary caretaking fathers behaved more like mothers than the secondary caretaking fathers did, although there were still differences between primary caretaking mothers and fathers. Particularly noteworthy was the fact that playful and noncontaining interactions were more common among fathers regardless of their caretaking responsibilities.

Together with Frodi, Hwang, and Frodi, I am currently undertaking a longitudinal study of primary and secondary caretaking fathers that should help us determine the extent to which biological gender and social role determine the distinctive styles of mothers and fathers. Naturalistic observation of the interactions between 3- and 8-month-olds and their parents have shown that sex of parent is a more powerful determinant of parental behavior than is family type (Lamb, Frodi, Hwang, & Frodi, in press). Later observations will focus on play and caretaking involvement with older infants.

Whatever the findings of this longitudinal study, it is clear that mothers and fathers generally do represent different types of experiences for their infants. This fact increases the likelihood that both parents may have independent and significant (as well as interrelated) influences on infant development.

PATERNAL INFLUENCES ON INFANT DEVELOPMENT

Beacuse researchers have focused on two questions—"Do infants form attachments to their fathers?" and "Do mother- and father-infant relationships differ in any way?"—relatively few attempts have been made to determine *how* fathers contribute to infant development. There has been a great deal of speculation, however, about the possibility that fathers contribute to the development of sex role and gender identity, especially in boys (see, for example, Lamb & Lamb, 1976; Lamb & Stevenson, 1978; Parke, 1979). This interest probably stems from the common assumption that fathers affect this aspect of development in their older children (see Chapters 1, 9, and 14).

Although both men and women have a preference for sons, this preference is especially marked among men (e.g., Arnold, Buripakdi, Ching, Fawcett, Iritani, Lee, & Wu, 1975; Hoffman, 1977). It is perhaps not surprising, therefore, that fathers tend to interact preferentially with sons from shortly after delivery. Thus Parke and O'Leary (1975) found that fathers vocalized to, touched, and responded to their first-born sons more frequently than their first-born daughters. In a later study of 3-week-olds and 3-month-olds, Parke and Sawin (1975) found that fathers looked at sons more than at daughters and provided them with more visual and tactile stimulation than daughters. Mothers, in contrast, stimulated girls more than boys. Weinraub and Frankel (1977) reported analogous cross-sex preferences with much older infants. Parke and Sawin (1980) found that fathers were more likely to diaper and feed 3-month-old sons than 3-month-old daughters. Rendina and Dickerscheid (1976) confirmed that the fathers of 6- and 13-month-olds watched boys more than girls. In Israeli kibbutzim, fathers spent more time visiting their 4-month-old sons that their 4-month-old daughters (Gewirtz & Gewirtz, 1968).

During the second year of life, sex-differentiated treatment appears to intensify: some studies that report no sex-differentiated treatment in the first year find substantial differentiation thereafter (e.g., Lamb, 1977b). Fathers verbalize to their sons more than to their daughters during the second year (Lamb, 1977a, 1977b), and they report spending more time (about 30 minutes more per day) playing with first-born sons than with first-born daughters (Kotelchuck, 1976). Even among the nomadic !Kung Bushmen, fathers spend more time with sons than with daughters (West & Konner, 1976). Among the parents of infants (Lamb, 1977b), as among the parents of older children (Lamb, 1976e), fathers appear to differentiate between boys and girls more than mothers do. For example, a small interview study (Fagot, 1974) found that the parents of boys believed that there was a special paternal role (as play partner and role model), whereas the parents of girls did not think that mothers and fathers had different roles.

From early in their sons' lives, in fact, fathers make themselves especially salient to male offspring. Although I found that mothers and fathers treated boys and girls similarly in the first phase of my longitudinal study (Lamb, 1977c), there was a dramatic change early in the second year (Lamb, 1977a, 1977b). Fathers began to direct more social behavior to sons than to daughters, and this appeared to encourage sex differences in the infants' behavior. As noted earlier, boys focused their attachment behaviors on fathers during the second year, whereas girls continued to show no consistent preference for either parent. Thus the fathers behaved in a manner that encouraged preferential relationships with sons; this behavior may contribute to the development of gender identity and sex role orientation (Lamb, 1977b).

Furthermore, fathers and mothers tend to behave in a sex-differentiated fashion, which should facilitate the fathers' influence on the development of gender identity. Unfortunately, there is no substantive support for this speculation, but circumstantial support comes from two sources. First, there is Money's claim that gender identity must be established in the first 2 to 3 years of life if it is to be established securely (Money & Ehrhardt, 1972). Second, there is the evidence that father absence is most likely to affect the development of masculinity in boys when the absence occurs early in the children's lives (Lamb, 1976e and Chapter 1; Biller, 1971, 1974, and Chapter 14; Hetherington & Deur, 1971). Nevertheless, the tenuousness of these data underscores the need for further research in this area. In addition, we do not know whether and how fathers affect the development of femininity in young daughters (Lamb, Owen, & Chase-Lansdale, 1979).

Instead of paternal influences on sex role development, several recent studies have explored paternal influences on cognitive and motivational development. This focus is attributable partly to evidence concerning the impact of mother–infant interaction on cognitive development (see Stevenson & Lamb,

1981, for a review) and partly to evidence that male infants raised without fathers are less cognitively competent than infants raised in two-parent families (Pedersen, Rubenstein, & Yarrow, 1979). Since Pedersen et al. found no differences between the behavior of the single and married mothers, they concluded "that it is the father's direct interaction with his son that significantly influences development in areas such as social responsiveness, the development of secondary circular behavior, and preferences for novel stimulation" (p. 59). Father absence did not affect the development of girls. It was not simply that the fatherless infants lacked sources of stimulation, since the average number of household members was the same in father-absent and father-present families: "With the number of people who are potential sources of stimulation comparable, it appears that the father has an impact that is qualitatively different from other adults" (p. 58). This conclusion appears consistent with Wachs, Uzgiris, and Hunt's (1971) finding that increased paternal involvement is associated with better performance on the Uzgiris-Hunt scales.

In her observational study of 15- to 30-month-olds, Clarke-Stewart (1978) found that intellectual competence was correlated with measures of maternal stimulation (both material and verbal), intellectual acceleration, and expressiveness, as well as with measures of the fathers' engagement in play, their positive ratings of the children, the amount they interacted, and the fathers' aspirations for the infants' independence. However, examination of the correlational patterns over time indicated that the mothers affected the children's development and that this, in turn, influenced the fathers' behavior. In other words, paternal behavior appeared to be a consequence of, not a determinant of, individual differences in child behavior. These findings illustrate a notion we pursue in the next section—that children develop within family systems, in which all parties affect and are affected by one another. Influences do not always run directly *from* parents *to* children. On the other hand, Clarke-Stewart's sample was very small (especially for the types of analyses conducted) and so her findings must be treated cautiously until replicated.

Some of the speculations concerning paternal influences focus less on the specific differences between maternal and paternal styles than on the fact that they differ in many ways. In the early months, for example, it may be easier for infants to learn to recognize the distinctive features of one parent when they are exposed relatively frequently to a distinctly different person. Furthermore, because mothers and fathers represent different types of interaction, infants are likely to develop different expectations of them (Lamb, 1981), which should in turn increase their awareness of different social styles and perhaps facilitate a perceptual sensitivity to such subtle differences. This would contribute to the development of social competence. Pedersen et al. (1979) found that the degree of paternal involvement (as reported by mothers) was positively correlated with the social responsiveness of 5-month-olds. From a very different perspective, psychoanalysts who follow Margaret Mahler (1968; Mahler & Gosliner, 1955) argue that fathers serve to extract infants from symbiotic relationships with their mothers (Abelin, 1975, 1980, in preparation).

Finally, we should consider the formative significance of parental sensitivity once again. There is impressive evidence that maternal sensitivity determines the security of the mother–infant attachment (Ainsworth, Blehar, Waters, & Wall, 1978) and that the security of this relationship determines how the child will later behave in problem-solving situations and in the peer group (Lieberman, 1977; Easterbrooks & Lamb, 1979; Matas, Arend, & Sroufe, 1978; Waters, Wippman, & Sroufe, 1979; Arend, Gove, & Sroufe, 1979) as well as other aspects of personality (Arend et al., 1979). As yet, no published studies have examined the effects of paternal sensitivity on the security of father–infant attachments. However, two studies have shown that many infants have secure relationships with one parent and insecure relationships with the other, suggesting that the security of each attachment is independently determined—presumably by the sensitivity of the parent concerned (Lamb, 1978b; Main & Weston, in press). Main and Weston found that the security of both mother–infant and father–infant attachments affected infants' responses to an unfamiliar person (dressed as a clown). Unfortunately, it was not possible to determine which relationship had the greater impact since the clown session took place at the same time as the assessment of the mother–infant attachment—6 months before assessment of the father–infant attachment. It seems plausible, however, that the relationship with the primary caretaker is more influential and that the child who has at least one secure attachment relationship is better off than a child who has no secure attachment. It is clearly inadequate to assess the behavior of only one parent or the nature of only one parent–child relationship if we wish to understand how parent–child relationships affect child development. Neither parent–child relationship exists in a vacuum, and its effects cannot be understood without considering other important sources of influence.

DIRECT AND INDIRECT EFFECTS

Since several other chapters in this book (Lewis, Feiring, & Weinraub, Chapter 7; Parke & Tinsley, Chapter 12; Pedersen, Chapter 8) deal with this topic in greater detail, my discussion is abbreviated despite the manifest importance of the issues involved. Since students of infancy have come to recognize that there are multiple influences (e.g., maternal, paternal, sibling, biological) on infant development, they have come to appreciate that many influences are indirectly mediated through complex paths and networks (Belsky, 1981; Lewis

& Weinraub, 1976). According to Lewis and Weinraub (1976 and Chapter 7) *most* paternal influences on infant development are indirectly mediated through the fathers' impact on their wives. Although this suggestion remains unsubstantiated, several studies confirm that indirect influences are indeed significant. Pedersen, Anderson, and Cain (1977), for example, showed that the affective quality of parent–infant interaction could be predicted from observational measures of mutual criticism in the spousal relationship. There were, however, no significant relationships between measures of positive affect in the spousal and parent–child relationships. In contrast, Price (1977) reported that the ability of mothers to enjoy and be affectionate with their infants was associated with the quality of the marital relationship, and Minde, Marton, Manning, and Hines (1979) reported that the quality of the marital relationship predicted the frequency of maternal visits to hospitalized premature infants. The suggestion of Pedersen et al. that marital conflict produces unsatisfactory parent–child relations is consistent with evidence (reviewed by Rutter, 1972, 1979) indicating that marital conflict has a more harmful impact on socioemotional development than does parent–child separation or father absence. Bronson (1966), for example, reported that poor marital adjustment and spousal hostility or indifference predicted reactive explosive patterns of emotional expression in children's elementary school years.

The only experimental investigations of indirect effects have examined the impact of one parent's presence on the interaction between the other parent and the infant. In general, the presence of the other parent leads to a reduction in interaction between parent and child—whether the interaction takes place at home (Belsky, 1979; Clarke-Stewart, 1978; Pedersen, Anderson, & Cain, 1980) or in structured laboratory settings (Lamb, 1976a, 1976f, 1977a, 1978a, 1979). A similar effect has been noted in naturalistic studies of family behavior in public places (Rosenblatt, 1974; Cleaves & Rosenblatt, 1977) as well as in studies of maternal and paternal speech (Golinkoff & Ames, 1979). Lewis and Kreitzberg (1979) reported that the fathers and mothers of first-borns vocalized to their infants more than the parents of later-borns did—perhaps because, as the authors report, other siblings were often present during the observations. As Parke & Tinsley note in Chapter 12, however, the effects observed within the mother–father–neonate triad are somewhat different.

Unfortunately, although these studies have yielded a tool for investigating some aspects of infant social cognition (Lamb, 1979) and have methodological implications for research of parent–child relationships, they tell us little about indirect influences on infant development. Lytton's (1979) recent study may be an exception. Lytton found that paternal presence increased the likelihood that mothers would respond positively to toddlers' compliance, reduced the number of maternal efforts to exert control, and increased the mothers' effectiveness as disciplinarians.

As Parke, Power, and Gottman (1979) point out, there are many ways in which indirect effects may be mediated, and this makes it difficult to explore the patterns of influence within the family. It is not sufficient to compute correlations between characteristics of the individual family members and of the relationships among them. Instead, researchers need to develop clear theoretical frameworks from which to derive precise hypotheses that are then subjected to empirical scrutiny. Belsky (1981), Parke et al. (1979), and Lewis, Feiring, and Weinraub (Chapter 7) have begun to develop such frameworks and hypotheses.

One way in which fathers may indirectly affect their children's development, despite limited opportunities for interaction, was described by Bowlby (1951) in an early discussion of the significance of mother–infant attachment. Bowlby (p. 13) wrote in his introduction:

Fathers . . . provide for their wives to enable them to devote themselves unrestrictedly to the care of the infant and toddler [and] by providing love and companionship, they support her emotionally and help her maintain that harmonious contented mood in the aura of which the infant thrives. In what follows, therefore, while continual reference will be made to the mother–child relation, little will be said of the father–child relation; his value as the economic and emotional support of the mother will be assumed.

The importance of paternal support has been noted by several others, although we have available only correlational data concerning its import. Hennenborn and Logan (1975) and Anderson and Standley (1976) reported that women whose husbands were supportive during labor were themselves less distressed, and Feiring (1976) found that women who reported supportive relationships with "secondary parents" (spouses, lovers, or grandparents) were more sensitively responsive to their infants. Lamb (Lamb, Chase-Lansdale, & Owen, 1979; Lamb, Owen, & Chase-Lansdale, 1980) suggested that paternal and familial support may be an especially significant determinant of maternal sensitivity today, when many young mothers feel the conflicting attractions of parenthood and career aspirations.

According to Pedersen (1975), mothers whose husbands evaluated their maternal skills positively were more effective in feeding 4-month-old infants, although the direction of effects is especially difficult to determine in this case. In a recent study, Belsky (1980) found significant correlations between the frequency of the parents' comments about the baby and the amount of father–infant interaction as well as between the frequency of comments *not* about the baby and the frequency of ignoring. Perhaps the most complicated and intriguing set of relationships was reported by Clarke-Stewart (1978), who found that maternal behavior appeared to facilitate the children's cognitive development and that this in turn provoked the fathers to become more involved.

An increasing awareness of the interface between spousal and parent–child relationships has accompanied recognition of the fact that both parents, the infant, and the marriage all develop and change with time. The changes within any individual or relationship may affect all other persons and relationships. Instead of the unidirectional pattern of influences (from parent to infant) once assumed, there exists a complex network of influences and interrelations. Few researchers have attempted to assess parenting, infant development, and marital quality simultaneously, although Parke, Pedersen, Belsky, and Lamb are all working in this area today. As we proceed, however, we become increasingly aware of the methodological and conceptual revisions this research demands. As Parke (1979) noted, for example, it is imperative to collect multiple types of data representing multiple levels of analysis. It is only by interviewing parents that we learn about their attitudes and perceptions, and this information may help us explain *why* parents behave as they do. Ideally, observational and interview data should be used to supplement and complement one another. They should not be viewed as alternatives. Exemplary studies involving multiple types of data are discussed by Parke and Tinsley in Chapter 12 and Pedersen in Chapter 8.

CONCLUSION

Fathers clearly can no longer be deemed "forgotten contributors to child development" (Lamb, 1975a), because the relationships between fathers and infants are now being studied widely and thoroughly. Of course, many important questions remain unanswered, but at least some issues have been resolved. First, there is substantial evidence that infants form attachments to both mothers and fathers at about the same point during the first year of life. Second, there appears to exist a hierarchy among attachment figures such that most infants prefer their mothers over their fathers. These preferences probably developed because the mothers were primary caretakers; the preference patterns may well disappear or be reversed when fathers share caretaking responsibilities or become primary caretakers, but the necessary research has not yet been done.

Third, the traditional parental roles affect styles of interaction as well as infant preferences. Several observational studies have now shown that fathers are associated with playful—often vigorously stimulating—social interaction, whereas mothers are associated with caretaking. These social styles obviously reflect traditionally sex-stereotyped roles, and it has been suggested that they play an important role in the early development of gender role and gender identity. We do not yet know whether the maternal and paternal styles are purely products of social influences or whether there are biological determinants as well.

We do know, however, that both mothers and fathers are capable of behaving sensitively and responsively in interaction with their infants. With the exception of lactation, there is no evidence that women are biologically predisposed to be better parents than men are. Social conventions, not biological imperatives, underlie the traditional division of parental responsibilities.

In the immediate future, the most conceptually important advances will involve attempts to determine how patterns of interaction within the family system affect the course of infant development. It is clear that the way either parent interacts with the infant is determined jointly by his or her personality, relationship with the spouse, and the infant's unique characteristics, but we do not know just how these diverse influences supplement one another. Therefore, it will be difficult to unravel the network of direct and indirect influences within the family, although it is ultimately more useful to attempt this than to try to identify the independent contributions of mothers and fathers to infant development.

REFERENCES

Abelin, E. L. The role of the father in the separation-individuation process. In J. B. McDevitt & C. F. Settlage (Eds.), *Separation-Individuation*. New York: International Universities Press, 1971.

Abelin, E. L. Some further observations and comments on the earliest role of the father. *International Journal of Psychoanalysis,* 1975, **56,** 293–302.

Abelin, E. L. Triangulation, the role of the father, and the origins of core gender identity during the rapprochement subphase. In R. Lax, A. Burland, & S. Bach (Eds.), *Rapprochement.* New York: Jason Aronson, 1980.

Abelin, E. L. *Self image, gender identity and early triangulations.* Manuscript in preparation.

Ainsworth, M. D. S. The development of infant–mother attachment. In B. M. Caldwell & H. N. Ricciuti (Eds.), *Review of child development research,* Vol. 3. Chicago: University of Chicago Press, 1973.

Ainsworth, M. D. S., Bell, S. M., & Stayton, D. J. Infant–mother attachment and social development: Socialisation as a product of reciprocal responsiveness to signals. In M. P. M. Richards (Ed.), *The integration of a child into a social world.* Cambridge, England: Cambridge University Press, 1974.

Ainsworth, M. D. S., Blehar, M. C., Waters, E., & Wall, S. *Patterns of attachment.* Hillsdale, N.J.: Lawrence Erlbaum Associates, 1978.

Ainsworth, M. D. S., & Wittig, B. A. Attachment and exploratory behavior of one-year-olds in a strange situation. In B. M. Foss (Ed.), *Determinants of infant behavior*, Vol. 4. London: Methuen, 1969.

Anderson, B. J., & Standley, K. A methodology for observation of the childbirth environment. Paper presented to the American Psychological Association, Washington, D.C., September 1976.

Arnold, R., Bulatas, R., Buripakdi, C., Ching, B. J., Fawcett, J. T., Iritani, T., Lee, S. J., & Wu, T. S. *The value of children: Introduction and comparative analysis.* Honolulu: East West Population Institute, 1975.

Ban, P., & Lewis, M. Mothers and fathers, girls and boys: Attachment behavior in the one-year-old. *Merrill-Palmer Quarterly,* 1974, **20,** 195–204.

Belsky, J. Mother–father–infant interaction: A naturalistic observational study. *Developmental Psychology,* 1979, **15,** 601–607.

Belsky, J. A family analysis of parental influence on infant exploratory competence. In F. A. Pedersen (Ed.), *The father–infant relationship: Observational studies in a family setting.* New York: Praeger, 1980.

Belsky, J. Early human experience: A family perspective. *Developmental Psychology,* 1981, **17,** 3–19.

Berlyne, D. E. Laughter, humor, and play. In G. L. Lindzey, & E. Aronson (Eds.), *Handbook of social psychology.* Reading, Mass: Addison–Wesley, 1969.

Biller, H. B. *Father, child, and sex role.* Lexington, Mass: Heath, 1971.

Biller, H. B. *Paternal deprivation: Family, school, sexuality and society.* Lexington, Mass: Heath, 1974.

Blount, G. B., & Padgug, E. J. Mother and father speech: Distribution of parental speech features in English and Spanish. *Papers and Reports on Child Language Development,* 1976, **12,** 47–59.

Bowlby, J. *Maternal care and mental health.* Geneva: WHO, 1951.

Bowlby, J. *Attachment and loss,* Vol. 1. *Attachment.* New York: Basic Books, 1969.

Brazelton, T. B., Yogman, M. W., Als, H., & Tronick, E. The infant as a focus for family reciprocity. In M. Lewis, & L. A. Rosenblum (Eds.), *The child and its family.* New York: Plenum, 1979.

Bronson, W. C. Early antecedents of emotional expressiveness and reactivity control. *Child Development,* 1966, **37,** 793–810.

Brooks–Gun, J., & Lewis, M. "Why Mama and Papa?" The development of social labels. *Child Development,* 1979, **50,** 1203–1206.

Chamove, A., Harlow, H. F., & Mtichell, G. D. Sex differences in the infant-directed behavior of preadolescent rhesus monkeys. *Child Development,* 1967, **38,** 329–335.

Clarke–Stewart, K. A. Interactions between mothers and their young children: Characteristics and consequences. *Monographs of the Society for Research in Child Development,* 1973, **38,** Serial No. 153.

Clarke–Stewart, K. A. And daddy makes three: The father's impact on mother and young child. *Child Development*, 1978, **49**, 466–478.

Clarke–Stewart, K. A. The father's contribution to children's cognitive and social development in early childhood. In F. A. Pedersen (Ed.), *The father–infant relationship: Observational studies in a family setting*. New York: Praeger, 1980.

Cleaves, W., & Rosenblatt, P. Intimacy between adults and children in public places. Paper presented to the Society for Research in Child Development, New Orleans, March 1977.

Cohen, L. J. The operational definition of human attachment. *Psychological Bulletin*, 1974, **81**, 207–217.

Cohen, L. J., & Campos, J. J. Father, mother, and stranger as elicitors of attachment behaviors in infancy. *Developmental Psychology*, 1974, **10**, 146–154.

DeVore, I. Mother–infant relations in free-ranging baboons. In H. L. Rheingold (Ed.), *Maternal behavior in mammals*. New York: Wiley, 1963.

Easterbrooks, M. A., & Lamb, M. E. The relationship between quality of infant–mother attachment and infant competence in initial encounters with peers. *Child Development*, 1979, **50**, 380–387.

Fagot, B. I. Sex differences in toddler's behavior and parental reaction. *Developmental Psychology*, 1974, **10**, 554–558.

Feiring, C. The preliminary development of a social systems model of early infant–mother attachment. Paper presented to the Eastern Psychological Association, New York, March 1976.

Feldman, S. S., & Ingham, M. E. Attachment behavior: A validation study in two age groups. *Child Development*, 1975, **46**, 319–330.

Feldman, S. S., & Nash, S. C. The effect of family formation on sex stereotypic behavior: A study of responsiveness to babies. In W. Miller, & L. Newman (Eds.), *The first child and family formation*. Chapel Hill: University of North Carolina Press, 1977.

Feldman, S. S., & Nash, S. C. Interest in babies during young adulthood. *Child Development*, 1978, **49**, 617–622.

Feldman, S. S., Nash, S. C., & Cutrona, C. The influence of age and sex on responsiveness to babies. *Developmental Psychology*, 1977, **13**, 675–676.

Field, T. Interaction behaviors of primary versus secondary caretaker fathers. *Developmental Psychology*, 1978, **14**, 183–184.

Frodi, A. M., & Lamb, M. E. Sex differences in responsiveness to infants: A developmental study of psychophysiological and behavioral responses. *Child Development*, 1978, **49**, 1182–1188.

Frodi, A. M., Lamb, M. E., Leavitt, L. A., & Donovan, W. L. Fathers' and mothers' responses to infant smiles and cries. *Infant Behavior and Development*, 1978, **1**, 187–198.

Frodi, A. M., Lamb, M. E., Leavitt, L. A., Donovan, W. L., Neff, C., & Sherry, D. Fathers' and mothers' responses to the faces and cries of normal and premature infants. *Developmental Psychology*, 1978, **14**, 490–498.

Gewirtz, H. B., & Gewirtz, J. L. Visiting and caretaking patterns for Kibbutz infants: Age and sex trends. *American Journal of Orthopsychiatry*, 1968, **38**, 427–443.

Gleason, J. B. Fathers and other strangers: Men's speech to young children. In D. P. Dato (Ed.), *Language and linguistics*. Washington D.C.: Georgetown University Press, 1975.

Golinkoff, R. M., & Ames, G. J. A comparison of fathers' and mothers' speech with their young children. *Child Development*, 1979, **50**, 28–32.

Gove, F., Arend, R., & Sroufe, L. A. Continuity of individual adaptation from infancy to kindergarten. Paper presented to the Society for Research in Child Development, San Francisco, March 1979.

Greenberg, M., & Morris, N. Engrossment: The newborn's impact upon the father. *American Journal of Orthopsychiatry*, 1974, **44**, 520–531.

Harlow, H. F. The nature of love. *American Psychologist*, 1958, **13**, 673–685.

Henneborg, W. J., & Cogan, R. The effect of husband participation in reported pain and the probability of medication during labor and birth. *Journal of Psychosomatic Research*, 1975, **19**, 215–222.

Hetherington, E. M., & Deur, J. L. The effect of father absence on child development. *Young Children*, 1971, **26**, 233–248.

Hinde, R. A. Energy models of motivation. *Symposium for the Society of Experimental Biology*, 1960, **14**, 119–213.

Hoffman, L. W. Changes in family roles, socialization and sex differences. *American Psychologist*, 1977, **32**, 644–658.

Kauffman, A. L. Mothers' and fathers' verbal interactions with children learning language. Paper presented to the Eastern Psychological Association, Boston, April 1977.

Klaus, M. H., Trause, M. A., & Kennell, J. H. Human maternal behavior following delivery: Is it species specific? Unpublished manuscript, Case Western Reserve University, 1975.

Kotelchuck, M. *The nature of the child's tie to his father*. Unpublished doctoral dissertation, Harvard University, 1972.

Kotelchuck, M. Father caretaking characteristics and their influence on infant father interaction. Paper presented to the American Psychological Association, Chicago, September 1975.

Kotelchuck, M. The infant's relationship to the father: Experimental evidence. In M. E. Lamb (Ed.), *The role of the father in child development*. New York: Wiley, 1976.

Kotelchuck, M., Zelazo, P. R., Kagan, J., & Spelke, E. Infant reactions to parental separations when left with familiar and unfamiliar adults. *Journal of Genetic Psychology*, 1975, **126**, 255–262.

Lamb, M. E. Fathers: Forgotten contributors to child development. *Human Development*, 1975, **18**, 245–266(a).

Lamb, M. E. Physiological mechanisms in the control of maternal behavior in rats: A review. *Psychological Bulletin*, 1975, **82**, 104–119(b).

Lamb, M. E. Effects of stress and cohort on mother– and father–infant interaction. *Developmental Psychology*, 1976, **12**, 435–443(a).

Lamb, M. E. Interaction between eight-month-old children and their fathers and mothers. In M. E. Lamb (Ed.), *The role of the father in child development*. New York: Wiley, 1976(b).

Lamb, M. E. Interactions between two-year-olds and their mothers and fathers. *Psychological Reports*, 1976, **38**, 447–450(c).

Lamb, M. E. Parent–infant interaction in eight-month-olds. *Child Psychiatry and Human Development*, 1976, **7**, 56–63(d).

Lamb, M. E. The role of the father: An overview. In M. E. Lamb (Ed.), *The role of the father in child development*. New York: Wiley, 1976(e).

Lamb, M. E. Twelve-month-olds and their parents: Interaction in a laboratory play-room. *Developmental Psychology*, 1976, **12**, 237–244(f).

Lamb, M. E. The development of mother–infant and father–infant attachments in the second year of life. *Developmental Psychology*, 1977, **13**, 637–648(a).

Lamb, M. E. The development of parental preferences in the first two years of life. *Sex Roles*, 1977, **3**, 495–497(b).

Lamb, M. E. Father–infant and mother–infant interaction in the first year of life. *Child Development*, 1977, **48**, 167–181(c).

Lamb, M. E. Infant social cognition and ''second-order'' effects. *Infant Behavior and Development*, 1978, **1**, 1–10(a).

Lamb, M. E. Qualitative aspects of mother– and father–infant attachments. *Infant Behavior and Development*, 1978, **1**, 265–275(b).

Lamb, M. E. Social interaction in infancy and the development of personality. In M. E. Lamb (Ed.), *Social and personality development*. New York: Holt, Rinehart, & Winston, 1978(c).

Lamb, M. E. The effects of the social context on dyadic social interaction. In M. E. Lamb, S. J. Suomi, & G. R. Stephenson (Eds.), *Social interaction analysis: Methodological issues*. Madison: University of Wisconsin Press, 1979.

Lamb, M. E. Separation and reunion behaviors as criteria of attachment to mothers and fathers. *Early Human Development*, 1979, **3/4**, 329–339.

Lamb, M. E. The development of social expectations in the first year of life. In M. E. Lamb & L. R. Sherrod (Eds.), *Infant social cognition: Empirical and theoretical considerations*. Hillsdale N.J.: Lawrence Erlbaum Associates, 1981.

Lamb, M. E., Chase-Lansdale, L., & Owen, M. T. The changing American family and its implications for infant social development: The sample case of maternal employment. In M. Lewis, & L. A. Rosenblum (Eds.), *The child and its family*. New York: Plenum, 1979.

Lamb, M. E., & Easterbrooks, M. A. Individual differences in parental sensitivity: Origins, components and consequences. In M. E. Lamb, & L. R. Sherrod (Eds.), *Infant social cognition: Empirical and theoretical considerations*. Hillsdale N.J.: Lawrence Erlbaum Associates, 1981.

Lamb, M. E., Frodi, A. M., Hwang, C-P, & Frodi, M. Varying degrees of paternal involvement in infant care: Attitudinal and behavioral correlates. In M. E. Lamb (Ed.), *Nontraditional families: Parenting and child development*. Hillsdale N.J.: Lawrence Erlbaum Associates, in press.

Lamb, M. E., & Goldberg, W. A. The father–child relationship: A synthesis of biological, evolutionary and social perspectives. In L. W. Hoffman & R. Gandelman (Eds.), *Perspectives on parental behavior*. Hillsdale N.J.: Lawrence Erlbaum Associates, 1982.

Lamb, M. E., & Lamb, J. E. The nature and importance of the father–infant relationship. *Family Coordinator*, 1976, **25**, 379–385.

Lamb, M. E., & Sherrod, L. R. (Eds.) *Infant social cognition: Empirical and theoretical considerations*. Hillsdale N.J.: Lawrence Erlbaum Associates, 1981.

Lamb, M. E., & Stevenson, M. B. Father–infant relationships: Their nature and importance. *Youth and Society*, 1978, **9**, 277–298.

Lamb, M. E., Owen, M. T., & Chase-Lansdale, L. The father–daughter relationship: Past, present and future. In C. B. Kopp & M. Kirkpatrick (Eds.), *Becoming female: Perspectives on development*. New York: Plenum, 1979.

Lamb, M. E., Owen, M. T., & Chase-Lansdale, L. The working mother in the intact family: A process model. In R. R. Abidin (Ed.), *Handbook of parent education*. Springfield, Ill.: Thomas, 1980.

Lester, B. M., Kotelchuck, M., Spelke, E., Sellers, M. J., & Klein, R. E. Separation protest in Guatemalan infants: Cross-cultural and cognitive findings. *Developmental Psychology*, 1974, **10**, 79–85.

Lewis, M., & Ban, P. Stability of attachment behavior: A transformational analysis. Paper presented to the Society for Research in Child Development, Minneapolis, April 1971.

Lewis, M., & Kreitzberg, V. S. Effects of birth order and spacing on mother–infant interactions. *Developmental Psychology*, 1979, **15**, 617–625.

Lewis, M., & Weinraub, M. Sex of parent × sex of child: Socioemotional development. In R. Richart, R. Friedman, & R. Vande Wiele (Eds.), *Sex differences in behavior*. New York: Wiley, 1974.

Lewis, M., & Weinraub, M. The father's role in the infant's social network. In M. E. Lamb (Ed.),*The role of the father in child development*. New York: Wiley, 1976.

Lewis, M., Weinraub, M., & Ban, P. Mothers and fathers, girls and boys: Attachment behavior in the first two years of life. Educational Testing Service Research Bulletin, Princeton, N.J., 1972.

Lieberman, A. F. Preschoolers' competence with a peer: Relations with attachment and peer experience. *Child Development*, 1977, **48**, 1277–1287.

Lind, R. Observations after delivery of communications between mother–infant–father. Paper presented to the International Congress of Pediatrics, Buenos Aires, October 1974.

Lynn, D. B., & Cross, A. R. Parent preference of preschool children. *Journal of Marriage and the Family*, 1974, **36**, 555–559.

Lytton, H. Disciplinary encounters between young boys and their mothers and fathers: Is there a contingency system? *Developmental Psychology*, 1979, **15**, 256–268.

Mahler, M. *On human symbiosis and the vicissitudes of individuation.* New York: International Universities Press, 1968.

Mahler, M., & Gosliner, B. J. On symbiotic child psychosis: Genetic, dynamic, and restitutive aspects. *The Psychoanalytic Study of the Child*, 1955, **10**, 195–212.

Main, M., & Weston, M. The independence of infant–mother and infant–father attachment relationships: Security of attachment characterizes relationships, not infants. *Child Development*, 1981, **52**, in press.

Marton, P. L., & Minde, K. Paternal and maternal behavior with premature infants. Paper presented to the American Orthopsychiatric Association, Toronto, April 1980.

Matas, L., Arend, R., & Sroufe, L. A. Continuity of adaptation in the second year of life. *Child Development*, 1978, **49**, 547–556.

Minde, K., Marton, P., Manning, D., & Hines, B. Some determinants of mother–infant interaction in the premature nursery. *Journal of the Academy of Child Psychiatry*, 1979, in press.

Money, J., & Ehrhardt, H. A. *Man and woman, boy and girl.* Baltimore: Johns Hopkins University Press, 1972.

Nash, S. C., & Feldman, S. S. Sex role and sex-related attributions: Constancy and change across the family life cycle. In M. E. Lamb & A. L. Brown (Eds.), *Advances in developmental psychology*, Vol. 1. Hillsdale, N. J.: Lawrence Erlbaum Associates, 1981.

Parke, R. D. Parent–infant interaction: Progress, paradigms and problems. In G. P. Sackett (Ed.), *Observing behavior.* Baltimore: University Park Press, 1978.

Parke, R. D. Perspectives on father–infant interaction. In J. D. Osofsky (Ed.), *Handbook of infant development.* New York: Wiley, 1979.

Parke, R. D., & O'Leary, S. E. Father–mother–infant interaction in the newborn period: Some findings, some observations and some unresolved issues. In K. Riegel, & J. Meacham (Eds.), *The developing individual in a changing world*, Vol. 2. *Social and environmental issues.* The Hague: Mouton, 1976.

Parke, R. D., O'Leary, S. E., & West, S. Mother–father–newborn interaction: Effects of maternal medication, labor and sex of infant. *Proceedings of the American Psychological Association*, 1972, 85–86.

Parke, R. D., Power, T. G., & Gottman, J. Conceptualizing and quantifying influence patterns in the family triad. In M. E. Lamb, S. J. Suomi, & G. R. Stephenson (Eds.), *Social interaction analysis: Methodological issues.* Madison: University of Wisconsin Press, 1979.

Parke, R. D., & Sawin, D. B. Infant characteristics and behavior as elicitors of maternal and paternal responsivity in the newborn period. Paper presented to the Society for Research in Child Development, Denver, April 1975.

Parke, R. D., & Sawin, D. B. The family in early infancy: Social interactional and attitudinal analyses. In F. A. Pedersen (Ed.), *The father–infant relationship: Observational studies in a family setting.* New York: Praeger, 1980.

Parke, R. D., & Suomi, S. J. Adult male–infant relationships: Human and nonhuman primate evidence. In K. Immelman, G. Barlow, M. Main, & L. Petrinovich (Eds.), *Early development in animals and man.* Cambridge, England: Cambridge University Press, 1980.

Pedersen, F. A. Mother, father, and infant as an interactive system. Paper presented to the American Psychological Association, Chicago, September 1975.

Pedersen, F. A., Anderson, B., & Cain, R. An approach to understanding linkages between the parent–infant and spouse relationships. Paper presented to the Society for Research in Child Development, New Orleans, March 1977.

Pedersen, F. A., Anderson, B., & Cain, R. Parent–infant and husband–wife interactions observed at age 5 months. In F. A. Pedersen (Ed.), *The father–infant relationship: Observational studies in a family setting.* New York: Praeger, 1980.

Pedersen, F. A., Cain, R., & Zaslow, M. Variation in infant experience associated with alternative family roles. In L. Laosa & I. Sigel (Eds.), *The family as a learning environment.* New York: Plenum, 1982.

Pedersen, F. A., & Robson, K. Father participation in infancy. *American Journal of Orthopsychiatry,* 1969, **39,** 466–472.

Pedersen, F. A., Rubinstein, J. L., & Yarrow, L. J. Infant development in father–absent families. *Journal of Genetic Psychology,* 1979, **135,** 51–61.

Phillips, P., & Parke, R. D. Father and mother speech to prelinguistic infants. Unpublished manuscript, University of Illinois, 1979.

Power, T. G., & Parke, R. D. Toward a taxonomy of father–infant and mother–infant play patterns. Paper presented to the Society for Research in Child Development, San Francisco, March 1979.

Price, G. Factors influencing reciprocity in early mother–infant interaction. Paper presented to the Society for Research in Child Development, New Orleans, March 1977.

Redican, W. K. Adult male–infant interactions in nonhuman primates. In M. E. Lamb (Ed.), *The role of the father in child development.* New York: Wiley, 1976.

Rendina, I., & Dickerscheid, J. D. Father involvement with first-born infants. *Family Coordinator,* 1976, **25,** 373–379.

Rheingold, H. L. The modification of social responsiveness in institutional babies. *Monographs of the Society for Research in Child Development,* 1956, **21,** Whole No. 63.

Richards, M. P. M., Dunn, J. F., & Antonis, B. Caretaking in the first year of life: The role of fathers' and mothers' social isolation. Unpublished manuscript, Cambridge University, 1975.

Rosenblatt, J. S. The development of maternal responsiveness in the rat. *American Journal of Orthopsychiatry*, 1970, **39**, 36–56.

Rosenblatt, P. C. Behavior in public places: Comparison of couples accompanied and unaccompanied by children. *Journal of Marriage and the Family*, 1974, **36**, 750–755.

Ross, G., Kagan, J., Zelazo, P., & Kotelchuck, M. Separation protest in infants in home and laboratory. *Developmental Psychology*, 1975, **11**, 256–257.

Rutter, M. *Maternal deprivation reassessed.* Harmondsworth, England: Penguin, 1972.

Rutter, M. Maternal deprivation, 1972–1978: New findings, new concepts, new approaches. *Child Development*, 1979, **50**, 283–305.

Schaffer, H. R. Some issues for research in the study of attachment behaviour. In B. M. Foss (Ed.), *Determinants of infant behaviour*, Vol. 2. London: Methuen, 1963.

Schaffer, H. R., & Emerson, P. E. The development of social attachments in infancy. *Monographs of the Society for Research in Child Development*, 1964, **29**, Whole No. 94.

Spelke, E., Zelazo, P., Kagan, J., & Kotelchuck, M. Father interaction and separation protest. *Developmental Psychology*, 1973, **9**, 83–90.

Stayton, D. J., Ainsworth, M. D. S., & Main, M. B. Development of separation behavior in the first year of life: Protest, following, and greeting. *Developmental Psychology*, 1973, **9**, 213–225.

Wachs, T., Uzgiris, I., & Hunt, J. Cognitive development in infants of different age levels and from different environmental backgrounds. *Merrill–Palmer Quarterly*, 1971, **17**, 283–317.

Waters, E., Wippman, J., & Sroufe, L. A. Attachment, positive affect and competence in the peer group: Two studies in construct validation. *Child Development*, 1979, **50**, 821–829.

Weinraub, M., & Frankel, J. Sex differences in parent–infant interaction during free play, departure, and separation. *Child Development*, 1977, **48**, 1240–1249.

Welker, W. I. Ontogeny of play and exploratory behaviors: A definition of problems and a search for new conceptual relations. In H. Moltz (Ed.), *The ontogeny of vertebrate behavior*. New York: Academic, 1971.

West, M. M., & Konner, M. J. The role of the father: An anthropological perspective. In M. E. Lamb (Ed.), *The role of the father in child development*. New York: Wiley, 1976.

White, R. W. Motivation reconsidered: The concept of competence. *Psychological Review*, 1959, **66**, 297–333.

Willemsen, E., Flaherty, D., Heaton, C., & Ritchey, G. Attachment behavior of one-year-olds as a function of mother vs father, sex of child, session, and toys. *Genetic Psychology Monographs*, 1974, **90**, 305–324.

Yogman, M. J., Dixon, S., Tronick, E., Als, H., & Brazelton, T. B. The goals and structure of face-to-face interaction between infants and their fathers. Paper presented to the Society for Research in Child Development, New Orleans, March 1977.

Zelazo, P. R., Kotelchuck, M., Barber, L., & David, J. Fathers and sons: An experimental facilitation of attachment behaviors. Paper presented to the Society for Research in Child Development, New Orleans, March 1977.

Zucker, E. L., Mitchell, G. D., & Maple, T. Adult male-offspring play interactions within a captive group of orangutans *(Pongo pygmaeus)*. *Primates,* 1978, **19,** 379–384.

CHAPTER 14

Father Absence, Divorce, and Personality Development

HENRY B. BILLER

University of Rhode Island

Much of the current interest in the father's role has been intensified by the growing awareness of the prevalence of fatherless families and the social, economic, and psychological problems that such families often encounter. The fatherless family is a source of increasing concern in many industrialized countries. More than 20 percent of the children in the United States, a total in excess of 10 million, live in fatherless families. Father-absent families are especially common among lower-class black families, surpassing 50 percent in some areas (Biller, 1974c; Moynihan, 1965). Although there are many different contexts in which father absence occurs, divorce is frequently the cause. Because of the currently high divorce rate, it is estimated that 40 to 50 percent of children born in the last decade will spend at least a significant portion of their childhoods in single-parent families. At the present time, only about 10 percent of children living in single-parent homes live with their fathers, although this percentage is increasing (Glick & Norton, 1978; Hetherington, 1979).

Father absence, or at least decreased father availability, is a typical concomitant of divorce. There has been a great deal of controversy about the consequences of both divorce and father absence on child development. On one extreme are those who attribute all undesirable effects in fatherless homes simply to father absence; on the other extreme are those who believe that adequate financial and emotional support of single mothers will alleviate any of the so-called detrimental effects of father absence and divorce on children. Research reviewed in this chapter makes it clear that an understanding of the influence of father absence and divorce on development demands the consideration of many different and complex factors.

There is a surprisingly vast literature on the alleged effects of father absence. This chapter is an effort to give the reader an overview of an often seemingly disparate and fragmented literature. It is not a completely exhaustive review, but it does highlight the most methodologically sound and/or provocative research endeavors.

The first major section contains a summary of studies dealing with father absence and masculine development. The relevance of developmental stages, different aspects of sex role development, and surrogate models are also discussed in this section. The second major section focuses on father absence and feminine development, with a particular emphasis on social factors and heterosexual functioning. The third major section analyzes data relating to father absence and cognitive functioning. There is a consideration of issues relating to academic success and various facets of intellectual ability. The fourth major section reviews research that pertains to father absence and personal and social adjustment. Topics in this section include anxiety, self-control, moral development, delinquency, and psychopathology. The fifth major section integrates data pertaining to influences of individual differences in mothering on the father-absent child's development. There is a discussion of matrifocal families, maternal overprotection, sociocultural context, and patterns of effective mothering. The final section presents a brief summary of some therapy and prevention techniques that are relevant in confronting problems associated with father absence.

METHODOLOGICAL ISSUES

It is important to emphasize that father absence *per se* does not necessarily lead to developmental deficits and/or render the father-absent child inferior in psychological functioning relative to the father-present child. Fatherless children are far from a homogeneous group. An almost infinite variety of patterns of father absence can be specified. Many factors need to be considered in evaluating the father-absent situation: length of separation from the father; type of separation, (constant, intermittent, temporary, etc.); cause of separation (divorce, death of father, etc.); the child's age, sex, and constitutional characteristics; the mother's reaction to husband absence; the quality of mother–child interactions; the family's socioeconomic status; and the availability of surrogate models. Father-absent children may not be paternally deprived if they have adequate father surrogates, or they may be less paternally deprived than are many father-present children.

The child who has an involved and competent mother *and* father is more likely to have generally adequate psychological functioning and is less likely to suffer from developmental deficits and psychopathology than the child who is reared in a one-parent family is. However, this generalization is not the same as assuming that all father-absent children are going to have more difficulties in their development than are all father-present children. For example, there is evidence that children with competent mothers are less likely to have certain types of developmental deficits than children who have a dominating mother and a passive ineffectual father are. The father-absent child may develop a more flexible image of adult men and may seek out some type of father surrogate, whereas the child with a passive, ineffectual, and/or rejecting father may have a very negative image of adult males and avoid interacting with them, (Biller, 1971a, 1974c).

In addition to the obvious theoretical and practical relevance of studying the effects of father absence, a possible methodological justification is that father absence is a naturalistic manipulation. It can be argued that father absence is an antecedent rather than a consequence of certain behaviors in children. (Of course, in some instances a child's handicaps or "abnormalities" may actually be a factor in divorce and subsequent father absence.) A general problem with studies comparing father-absent and father-present children is that investigators have usually treated both father-absent and father-present children as if they represent homogeneous groups. There has been a lack of concern for the meaning of father absence and father presence. For example, there have been few attempts to ensure that a group of consistently father-absent boys is compared with a group of boys who have a high level and quality of father availability (Biller, 1971a; 1974c).

Most researchers have treated father absence in an overly simplistic fashion. In many studies there have been no specifications of such variables as type, length, and age of onset of father absence. Potentially important variables such as the child's sex, IQ, constitutional characteristics, birth order, relationship with the mother, and sociocultural background, as well as the availability of father surrogates, are not taken into account, either in subject matching or data analysis. When careful matching procedures are followed, more clear-cut findings seem to emerge (e.g., Biller, 1968b, 1971a; Blanchard & Biller, 1971; Hetherington, 1966, 1972; Hetherington, Cox & Cox, 1978).

Even though children living with their mothers subsequent to a divorce technically may be considered father-absent, there is tremendous variability in the amount of contact they have with their fathers (Biller & Meredith, 1974; Keshet & Rosenthal, 1978). In some families children whose parents are divorced may never again see their fathers, whereas in other families they may have contact with them on a daily basis and may even spend more time with them than they did prior to the divorce. Many children whose fathers do not live with them spend more time with their fathers than do children in so-called father-present families. Recent research has clearly supported the advantages for children of a high level of father–child interaction, even when the parents are divorced (Abarbanel, 1979; Biller & Meredith, 1974; Grief, 1979; Hether-ington, Cox, & Cox, 1978; Wallerstein & Kelly, 1980a).

I have dealt with many of the methodological issues considered in this section in some of my earlier publications (e.g., Biller, 1970, 1971a, 1974c, 1976b, 1978). There have also been some other analyses of methodological issues relating to divorce and father absence that are particularly worthy of the reader's consideration (e.g., Hetherington, 1979; Lamb, 1976, 1979; Pedersen, 1976; Shinn, 1978).

MASCULINE DEVELOPMENT

Many researchers have speculated that the primary effects of father absence are manifested in terms of deficits and/or abnormalities in the boy's sex role development. In this section, research findings concerning the relationship between father absence and the boy's sex role development are discussed. (In Chapter 9 I have summarized data relating to the quality of fathering and sex role development.) A comparison of the sex role development of father-absent and father-present boys suggests some of the ways that paternal deprivation can influence personality development.

Sears and Sears conducted a pioneering investigation of the effects of father absence on 3- to 5-year-old boys whose fathers were in military service during World War II. Each child was given an opportunity to play with a standardized set of doll play equipment and the investigators recorded his behavior. Compared to the father-present boys, the father-absent boys were less aggressive, and they also had less sex role differentation in their doll play activity. For example, their play contained less emphasis on the maleness of the father and boy dolls (Sears, 1951; Sears, Pintler, & Sears, 1946).

Bach (1946) used a similar procedure to study the effects of father absence on 6- to 10-year-old children. As in the Sears study, father-absent boys were less aggressive than father-present boys in doll play. Bach observed that "the father-separated children produced an idealistic and feminine fantasy picture of the father when compared to the control children who elaborated the father's aggressive tendencies" (p. 79).

In Santrock's (1970a) study of 4- and 5-year-old disadvantaged black children, father-absent boys exhibited less masculine and more dependent behavior in standardized doll play situations than did father-present boys, although the two groups of boys did not differ in amount of aggressive behavior. In addition, maternal interviews suggested that the father-absent boys were less aggressive as well as less masculine and more dependent in their interpersonal relations.

In a very thorough investigation, Stolz et al. (1954) gathered data concerning 4- to 8-year-old children, who for approximately the first 2 years of their lives had been separated from their fathers. Interview results revealed that the previously father-separated boys were generally perceived by their fathers as being "sissies." Careful observation of these boys supported this view. The previously father-separated boys were less assertively aggressive and independent in their peer relations than boys who had not been separated from their fathers. They were more often observed to be very submissive or to react with immature hostility. The boys who had been father-absent were actually more aggressive in doll play than boys who had not been separated from their fathers. However, the facts that the fathers were present in the home at the time of this study and that the father–child relationships were stressful make it difficult to speculate about what influence father absence *per se* had on the children's personality development (Biller, 1978).

There is additional evidence that the effects of early father absence on boys persist even after their fathers return. Carlsmith (1964) studied middle-class and upper middle-class high school males who had experienced early father absence because of their father's military service during World War II. Father absence before the age of 5 was related to the patterning of College Board Aptitude Scores. Compared to the usual male pattern of math score higher than verbal score, the pattern of the father-absent subjects was more frequently the same as the female pattern: verbal score higher than math score. Moreover, "the relative superiority of verbal to math aptitudes increases steadily the longer the father is absent and the younger the child when the father left" (p. 10). Other researchers have also found that early father absence is related to a feminine patterning of aptitude test scores (e.g., Altus, 1958; Nelsen & Maccoby, 1966.)

Leichty (1956) compared the projective test responses of male college students who were father absent between the ages of 3 and 5 to those of a matched group of students who had not been father absent. In responses to Blacky Pictures, fewer of the father-absent students said "Blacky" would like to pattern himself after his father, more often choosing "Mother" or "Tippy," a sibling. Such a response can be conceived of as a projective indication of underlying sex role orientation, the father-absent males being less masculine. However, it is not clear from the data Leichty presented how many of the father-absent group chose Tippy. This response might also indicate a masculine sex role orientation if Tippy was depicted by the respondent as being a male sibling.

Paternal occupation can be related to frequent father absence. In a very extensive investigation, Tiller (1958) and Lynn and Sawrey (1959) studied Norwegian children aged 8 to 9½ whose fathers were sailors, absent at least 9 months a year. They compared these father-separated children with a matched group of children whose fathers had jobs that did not require them to be separated from their families. The boys' responses to projective tests and interviews with their mothers indicated that father separation was associated with compensatory masculinity (the boys at times behaving in an exaggerated masculine manner, at other times behaving in a highly feminine manner). The father-separated boys appeared to be much less secure in their masculinity than did the control group boys. Consistent with the findings of Bach (1946) and Sears (1951), the father-separated boys were less aggressive in doll play than the control group.

Rogers and Long's (1968) data also suggest that boys whose fathers are away for long periods of time have difficulties in their masculine development. These investigators studied children from two communities in the Out Island Bahamas. In one community, Crossing Rocks, there was a high level of paternal deprivation because men were involved in lengthy fishing trips, being away for weeks at a time for a total of at least 6 months a year. In the other community, Murphy Town, men were primarily wage laborers, sometimes unemployed but generally not away from home for any lengthy period. A preference-for-shapes procedure was administered to 6- to 15-year-old children, and, among the boys, a much lower percentage (25 versus 61 percent) of those from the paternally-deprived community made masculine responses (chose the angular shape rather than the curved shape). The majority (80 percent) of the adult males in the paternally deprived community who were tested made masculine responses on the preference-for-shapes procedure. Rogers and Long speculated that there was often a shift from a feminine to a masculine sex role identification as a result of informal initiation rites during the adolescent male's first year of going on fishing trips.

Several investigators have attempted to assess differences between father-absent and father-present boys in terms of their human figure drawings. Phelan (1964) assumed that boys who drew a female when asked to draw a person had failed to make a shift from an initial identification with the mother to an identification with the father. In her study, there was a higher rate of father absence among elementary school-age boys who drew a female first than among those who drew a male first. An additional analysis of some of Biller's (1968a) data with kindergarten-age children revealed that father-absent, as compared to father-present, boys were less likely to draw a male first or to clearly differentiate their male and female drawings, particularly if they became father absent before the age of 4.

Burton (1972) asked 8- to 15-year-old Caribbean children to draw human figures. His evidence suggested that father absence during the first 2 years of life was associated with relatively unmasculine self-concepts for boys. Compared to father-present boys, boys who had been father absent during their first 2 years of life (and did not subsequently have a permanent father figure) less frequently drew a male first and drew males shorter. (The father-absent boys generally drew males shorter than they drew females.)

However, clear-cut correlations between father absence and figure drawings have not been consistent with older children. A problem in many of the studies concerned with figure drawings is that there is no presentation of specific information regarding length and age of onset of father absence (e.g., Donini, 1967; Lawton & Sechrest, 1962).

Difficulty in forming lasting heterosexual relationships often appears to be linked to father absence during childhood. Andrews and Christensen's (1951) data suggested that college students whose parents had been divorced were likely to have frequent but unstable courtship relationships. Winch (1949, 1950) found that father absence among college males was negatively related to degree of courtship behavior (defined as closeness to marriage). He also reported that a high level of emotional attachment to the mother was negatively related to the degree of courtship behavior. In their interview study, Hilgard, Neuman, and Fisk (1960) detected that many men whose fathers died when they were children continued to be very dependent on their mothers if their mothers did not remarry. For example, only one of the 10 men whose mothers did not remarry seemed to manifest a fair degree of independence in his marital relationship.

Jacobson and Ryder (1969) conducted an exploratory interview study with young married men who suffered the death of a parent prior to marriage. Death of the husband's father prior to the age of 12 was associated with a high rate of marriage difficulty. Husbands who were father absent early in life were described as immature and as lacking interpersonal competence. Participation in feminine types of domestic activities and low sexual activity were commonly reported for this group. In general, their marriages were relatively devoid of closeness and intimacy. However, when the husbands had lost their fathers after the age of 12, they were more likely to be involved in positive marriage relationships.

Other researchers have reported evidence that individuals who have experienced father absence because of a broken home situation in childhood are more likely to have their own marriages end in divorce or separation (Landis, 1965; Rohrer & Edmonson, 1960). In many of these situations there is probably a strong modeling effect; children see parents attempting to solve their marital conflicts by ending a marriage and are more likely to behave in a similar fashion themselves. Research by Pettigrew (1964) with lower-class blacks is consistent with the supposition that father-absent males frequently have difficulty in their heterosexual relationships. Compared to father-present males, father-absent males were "more likely to be single or divorced—another manifestation of their disturbed sexual identification" (p. 420).

Because of frequent paternal deprivation and maternal disparagement of maleness, lower-class black males often suffer in terms of their sex role orientations, even though they may be quite masculine in other facets of their behavior. In two studies, both father availability and sociocultural background were significantly related to what could be considered measures of sex role orientation (Barclay & Cusumano, 1967; Biller, 1968b). Studying lower-class black and white boys, I did not find any clear-cut differences in sex role preference or adoption. However, in terms of projective sex role orientation responses, black father-absent boys were the least masculine; there was no significant difference between white father-absent and black father-present boys; and white father-present boys were the most masculine (Biller, 1968b).

A great deal of the heterosexual difficulty that many paternally deprived, lower-class males experience is associated with their compulsive rejection of anything that they perceive as related to femininity. Proving that they are not homosexual and/or effeminate is a major preoccupation of many lower-class males. They frequently engage in a Don Juan pattern of behavior, making one conquest after another, and a stable emotional relationship with a female may not be formed even during marriage. The fear of again being dominated by a female, as they were as children, contributes to their need to exhibit their masculinity continually by new conquests. The perception of child rearing as an exclusively feminine endeavor also interferes with their interaction with their own children and helps perpetuate the depressing cycle of paternal deprivation in lower-class families. Although such a pattern of behavior seems particularly prevalent among lower-class black males, it is by no means exclusive to this group.

Developmental Stages

The quality of the early father–child attachment is an important factor in the child's sex role and personality development. The degree and quality of the father's involvement, even in the first year of life, has much influence on the child's behavior (Biller, 1974c; Lamb, 1976). Research by Money and his co-workers has also pointed to the first 2 to 3 years of life as being of crucial importance in the formation of an individual's sex role orientation (Money & Ehrhardt, 1972). On the basis of their clinical observations of individuals with physical–sexual incongruencies, these investigators have concluded that self-conceptions relating to sex role appear particularly difficult to change after the second and third years of life. The possibility of critical periods in sex role development is suggested and early father absence seems to interfere particularly with the development of a secure sex role orientation.

Father absence before the age of 4 or 5 appears to have a retarding effect on masculine development. Hetherington (1966) reported that 9- to 12-year-old father-absent boys manifested less masculine projective sex role behavior and were rated as more dependent on their peers, less aggressive, and as engaging in fewer physical contact games by male recreation directors than were father-present boys. However, there were no consistent differences on sex role measures when the father-present boys were compared with boys who had become father absent after the age of 4.

I found that father-absent 5-year-old boys had less masculine sex role orientations (fantasy game measure) and sex role preferences (game choice) than did father-present boys (Biller, 1969b). Moreover, the boys who became father absent before the age of 4 had significantly less masculine sex role orientations than those who became father absent in their fifth year. In an investigation Bahm and I conducted with junior high school boys, those who became father-absent before the age of 5 scored less masculine on an adjective checklist measure of masculinity of self-concept than did those who were father-present (Biller & Bahm, 1971). Research by Burton (1972) with Caribbean children also indicates the disruptive effect of early father absence on a masculine self-concept.

In a study that included a longitudinal format and an impressive array of sex role measures, Hetherington, Cox, and Cox (1978) found relatively clear-cut differences in sex role functioning between 5- to 6-year-old boys from intact families and those who were father absent for 2 years because of divorce. The father-absent boys had lower masculine sex role preference scores but higher feminine sex role preference scores than the father-present boys did. On the Draw-A-Person Test, the father-absent boys more often drew a female first and also demonstrated less differentiation between their drawings of males and females than the father-present boys did. In addition, father-absent boys spent more time playing with females and younger peers and in activities generally regarded as feminine.

Almost half (17 out of 38) of the extremely feminine boys in Green's (1974) investigation experienced at least 3 consecutive months of father absence prior to the age of 4. The separations were temporary in only three of the cases and most, if not all, of the other 21 feminine boys who were not father absent appeared to suffer from some other form of paternal deprivation during their first few years of life. However, Green's research reveals that many factors in addition to early paternal deprivation are involved in the development of extremely feminine behavior patterns among boys.

From their cross-cultural perspective, Burton and Whiting (1961) discussed the possible differential impact of father absence at different stages of the sex role development process. Burton and Whiting pointed out that many societies have a "discontinuous identification process." The father is virtually excluded from contact with his young children. A discontinuity in identification supposedly is produced when the boy is pushed into masculine behavior sometime in preadolescence or adolescence, particularly through his experiences during initiation rites. In contrast to earlier female domination, the boy is suddenly under the direct control of adult males, and feminine behavior is negatively reinforced. It is assumed that the boy has to learn to repress his earlier feminine identification. Whiting, Kluckhohn, and Anthony (1958) discovered that societies with exclusive mother–son sleeping arrangements and long postpartum sex taboos were likely to have elaborate male initiation rites; Burton and Whiting hypothesized "that the initiation rites serve psychologically to brainwash the primary feminine identity and establish firmly the secondary male identity" (p. 90).

In support of their "sex-role identification conflict hypothesis" Burton and Whiting (1961) reported some rather dramatic cross-cultural evidence. In societies in which the infant sleeps and interacts almost exclusively with females during the first few years of his life, a custom called the couvade was likely to occur. This custom stipulates that the husband retire to his bed on the birth of his offspring and act as though he had just gone through childbirth. This custom can be interpreted as symbolic of an underlying feminine identification.

The effects of early father absence are not restricted to sex role functioning, and many other personality characteristics can be influenced. A study of lower-class fifth-grade boys by Santrock (1970b) revealed that boys who became father absent before the age of 2 were more handicapped in terms of several dimensions of personality development than boys who became father absent at a later age were. For example, boys who became father absent before age 2 were found to be less trusting, less industrious, and to have more feelings of inferiority than boys who became father absent between the ages of 3 and 5. Other evidence is consistent with the supposition that early father absence is associated with a heightened susceptibility to a variety of psychological problems (Biller 1971a, 1974c). Research by Wallerstein and Kelly (1974, 1975, 1976, 1980a,b) has clearly shown that the developmental stage is a crucial factor in determining the type of reaction that children have to divorce and separation from the father. Studies relating to the effects of the timing of father absence on various dimensions of personality development are reviewed in later sections of this chapter.

Different Aspects of Sex Role Development

As the findings relating to developmental stages have suggested, father absence may not affect different aspects of sex roles in the same way. It is common for young father-absent children to intensely seek the attention of older males. Because of deprivation effects, father-absent children often have a strong motivation to imitate and please potential father figures. Father-absent boys may strive to act masculine in some facets of their behavior while continuing to behave in an unmasculine or feminine manner in others. For example, a paternally deprived boy may interact only with females who encourage passivity and dependency in the first 4 or 5 years of his life, whereas later there is much peer pressure and societal pressure for him to behave in a masculine manner. Demands for masculine behavior may not become apparent to the boy until he reaches school age or even adolescence, but in any case under such conditions his sex role preference and/or adoption may differ from his basic sex role orientation (Biller & Borstelmann, 1967).

Barclay and Cusumano (1967) did not find any differences between father-present and father-absent adolescent males on a measure of sex role preference (Gough Femininity Scale). However, the father-absent males were more field dependent in terms of Witkin's rod and frame test. Barclay and Cusumano conceptualized the field dependence–field independence dimension as reflecting underlying sex role orientation. In a study with lower-class, 6-year-old children, I found that father-absent boys were significantly less masculine than father-present boys on a measure of projective sex role behavior used to assess sex role orientation (Biller, 1968b). However, the two groups were not consistently different in terms of their direct sex role preferences (the toys and games that they said they liked) or teachers' ratings of sex role adoption. My results from a study with 5-year-old boys also suggested that sex role orientation is more affected by father absence than are sex role preference or sex role adoption (Biller, 1969b). Even though the father-absent boys had significantly less masculine game preferences than the father-present boys, differences between the groups were most clear-cut in terms of responses to the sex role orientation procedure. No consistent differences were apparent with respect to the sex role adoption measure.

An examination of data from several other studies suggests the hypothesis that, particularly by adolescence, there is relatively little difference among lower-class father-present and father-absent boys in many facets of sex role awareness, preference, and adoption (e.g., Barclay & Cusumano, 1967; D'Andrade, 1973; Greenstein, 1966; Mitchell & Wilson, 1967; McCord, McCord, & Thurber, 1962; Santrock, 1977; Tiller, 1961).

Surrogate Models

Paternal absence or paternal inadequacy does not rule out the presence of other male models. A brother, uncle, grandfather, or male boarder may provide the boy with much competent adult male contact. Important roles can be played by peers, neighbors, and teachers. Male teachers seem to have much potential for influencing father-absent boys (Biller, 1974a,b,c; Lee & Wolinsky, 1973).

The child may even learn some masculine behaviors by patterning himself after a movie or television star, an athlete, or a fictional hero. Freud and Burlingham (1944) described how a fatherless 2-year-old boy developed a fantasy role model. Bob's mother had told him about a 9-year-old boy to whom he referred as "Big Bobby," and thereafter Bob actively used Big Bobby as a masculine model, attempting physical feats that he thought Big Bobby could perform. Bob perceived Big Bobby as physically superior to everyone else.

Some investigators have found that masculinity is related to the general amount of contact boys have with adult males. Nash (1965) studied a group of Scottish orphans who went to live in cottages run by married couples, the husbands thus offering them a masculine model. Even though they were less masculine (on a variety of sex role measures) than boys who were raised in a typical family setting, they were more masculine than a group of orphans brought up entirely by women.

There are also data suggesting that stepfathers can have a facilitating effect on the father-absent child's development, particularly if the stepfather–child relationship begins before the child is 4 or 5 years old. Research relating to cognitive functioning has indicated that previously father–absent children who gain a stepfather in early childhood are not usually handicapped in their cognitive functioning, whereas children who remain without a father substitute are likely to suffer in at least some facets of their cognitive functioning, often in areas that are considered to be masculine-related skills (Lessing, Zagorin, & Nelson, 1970; Santrock, 1972). Some investigators have found evidence suggesting that the presence of a stepfather can negatively affect the child's psychological functioning (e.g., Benson, 1968; Langner & Michael, 1963). However, Anderson (1968) reported evidence that the early presence of a stepfather can lessen the chance of the father-absent boy becoming delinquent. It is, of course, the quality of the stepfather–child relationship and not the presence of a stepfather *per se* that affects the child's personality development. The child's age at the time the mother remarries seems to be a critical variable. For example, the young child who feels paternally deprived may find it much easier to accept a stepfather than the adolescent who may have established a strong sense of independence. The stepfather may react more favorably to a young affectionate child than to an older child who refuses to accept his authority. The quality of the mother–child relationship and the mother's attitude toward the stepfather are also very important factors (Biller & Meredith, 1974).

Siblings. Older brothers can be very important masculine models for children. For example, paternal deprivation may have a very different effect on a 5-year-old boy who is an only child than on a 5-year-old boy who has two older brothers who themselves were not paternally deprived in early childhood. Obviously, many other variables have to be considered, including the frequency and quality of interactions among siblings. A problem with many of the sibling studies is that they consider only the presence or absence of a particular type of sibling. This is somewhat analogous to studies that take into account only whether a child is a father present or father absent (Biller, 1974c).

In two-child father-absent families there is some evidence that boys with brothers suffer less of a deficit in academic aptitudes than boys with sisters do (Sutton-Smith, Rosenberg, & Landy, 1968). In Santrock's (1970) study, father-absent boys with only older male siblings scored more masculine (on a maternal interview measure of sex role behavior) than father-absent boys with only female siblings. In an extension of Santrock's investigation, Wohlford et al. (1971) found that father-absent children with older brothers were less dependent than those with older sisters in terms of both doll play and maternal interview measures. However, the presence or absence of older female siblings was not related to the sex role measures and did not affect the older brother's influence.

Although the presence of male siblings may lessen the effects of father absence, data from one of my investigations were consistent with the conclusion that the presence of a father is generally a much more important factor in masculine development than the presence of an older brother is (Biller, 1968a).

Peers. The masculine role models provided by the peer group can be particularly influential for the paternally deprived boy. In a subculture in which instrumental aggression and physical prowess are very important means of achieving peer acceptance, many father-absent boys are likely to emulate their masculine peers. Peer models seem especially important in lower-class neighborhoods. Miller (1958) emphasized the centrality of such traits as toughness and independence in the value system of lower-class adolescents. Lower-class boys honor aggressiveness more than middle-class boys do, and one of the types of boy that they most admire is the aggressive, belligerent youngster who earns their respect because of his toughness and strength (Pope, 1953).

The boy who is physically well-equipped may find it relatively easy to gain acceptance from his peers. Many paternally-deprived boys behave in a generally effective and masculine manner. For example, an additional case study analysis of some of the 5-year-old-boys in my studies has indicated that father-absent boys who are relatively mesomorphic are less likely to be retarded in their sex role development than are father-absent boys with unmasculine physiques (Biller, 1968a, 1969b). A boy's physique has important stimulus value in terms of the expectations and reinforcements it elicits from others, and it may, along with correlated constitutional factors, predispose him toward success or failure in particular types of activity. The influence of the child's anatomical, temperamental, and cognitive predispositions on parental and peer behavior must be taken into account (Biller, 1974c).

FEMININE DEVELOPMENT

Some data suggest that females are less affected by father absence than males are (e.g., Bach, 1946: Lessing, Zagorin, & Nelson, 1970; Hetherington, Cox, & Cox, 1978; Lynn & Sawrey, 1959; Santrock, 1972; Winch, 1950). However, there is other research that supports the conclusion that girls are at least as much influenced in their social and heterosexual development by father absence as boys are (e.g., Biller 1971a; Biller & Weiss, 1970; Hetherington, 1972; Wallerstein & Kelly, 1976, 1980a). The extent and direction of the differential impact of father absence on males and females probably vary with respect to which dimensions of personality are considered.

Father absence can interfere with the girl's feminine development and her overall heterosexual adjustment. In Seward's (1945) study, women who rejected the feminine role of wife and mother were more likely to come from broken homes than were women who accepted these roles. White (1959) reported similar results. Landy, Rosenberg, and Sutton-Smith's (1967) results suggest that among college females, father absence during adolesence is sometimes associated with a rejection of feminine interests. Although she studied father-present females, Fish's (1969) data also seem relevant. College females who reported that their father spent little time with them during their childhoods had less feminine self-concepts than those who reported moderate or high father availability. It is also interesting to note anthropological evidence suggesting that low father availability is associated with sex role conflicts for girls as well as boys (Brown, 1963; Stephens, 1962).

In Jacobson and Ryder's (1969) interview study, many women who had been father absent early in life complained of difficulties in achieving satisfactory sexual relationships with their husbands. Lack of opportunity to observe meaningful male–female relationships in childhood can make it much more difficult for the father-absent female to develop the interpersonal skills necessary for adequate heterosexual adjustment. Case studies of father-absent girls are often filled with details of problems concerning interactions with males, particularly in sexual relationships (e.g., Leonard, 1966; Neubauer, 1960).

However, other findings suggest that father-absent girls are not inhibited in terms of their development of sex-typed interests or perceptions of the incentive value of the feminine role (Hetherington, 1972; Hetherington, Cox, & Cox, 1978; Lynn & Sawrey, 1969; Santrock, 1970). In fact, in a study with disadvantaged black children, Santrock (1970) found a tendency for father-absent girls to be more feminine than father-present girls on a doll play sex role measure. A very high level of femininity may be associated with a rigid sex role development that devalues males and masculine activities. In any case, father absence seems to have more effect on the girl's ability to function in interpersonal and heterosexual relationships than it does on her sex role preference. (In Chapter 9 I have summarized data relating to the quality of fathering and the daughter's sexual development.)

The father-absent girl often has difficulty in dealing with her aggressive impulses. In their study of doll play behavior, Sears et al. (1946) found "no indication that the girls are more frustrated when the father is present; on the contrary, his absence is associated with greater aggression, especially self-aggression." (p. 240). These investigators speculated that a high degree of aggressive doll play behavior may be a function of the father-absent girl's conflict with her mother. In a clinical study, Heckel (1963) observed frequent school maladjustment, excessive sexual interest, and social acting-out behavior in five fatherless preadolescent girls. Other investigators have also found a high incidence of delinquent behavior among lower-class father-absent girls (Monahan, 1957; Toby, 1957). Such acting-out behavior may be a manifestation of frustration associated with the girl's unsuccessful attempts to find a meaningful relationship with an adult male. Father absence appears to increase the probability that a girl will experience difficulties in interpersonal adjustment.

The devaluation of maleness and masculinity, so prevalent in paternally deprived, matrifocal families, adversely affects many girls as well as boys. Children in lower-class families often do not have opportunities to interact with adequate adult males. Even in intact lower-class families, father–daughter relationships are generally not very adequate. The father may be very punitive and express little affection toward his daughter (Elder & Bowerman, 1963). Many investigators have observed that lower-class black girls in families in which the father is absent or ineffectual quickly develop derogatory attitudes toward males (e.g., Pettigrew, 1964; Rohrer & Edmonson, 1960).

The downgrading of males in terms of their seeming social and economic irresponsibility is common among lower-class black families. Negative attitudes toward males are transmitted by mothers, grandmothers, and other significant females and, unfortunately, are often strengthened by the child's observation or involvement in destructive male–female relationships. Paternal deprivation, in the rubric of the devaluation of the male role, is a major factor in the lower-class females' frequent difficulties in interacting with their male relatives, boyfriends, husbands, and children. Maternally based households seem to become family heirlooms—passed from generation to generation (Mueller & Pope, 1977; Rohrer & Edmonson, 1960).

Male–Female Interactions

The most comprehensive and well-controlled study concerning father absence and the girl's development was conducted by Hetherington (1972). Her subjects were white, adolescent, lower middle-class girls (aged 13 to 17) who regularly attended a community recreation center. Hetherington was particularly interested in the possible differential effects of father absence due to divorce or death. She compared three groups of girls: girls whose fathers were absent because of divorce and who had no contact with their fathers since the divorce; girls who fathers were absent because of death; and girls with both parents living at home. She was careful to control for sibling variables (all the girls were first-borns without brothers and none of the father-absent children had any adult males living in their homes following separation from the father).

The most striking finding was that both groups of father-absent girls had great difficulty in interacting comfortably with men and male peers. Hetherington discovered that the difficulties were manifested differently for the daughters of divorcees than for the daughters of widows. The daughters of divorcees tended to be aggressive and forward with males whereas the daughters of widows tended to be extremely shy and timid in interacting with males. In contrast, all three groups of girls generally appeared to have appropriate interactions with their mothers and with female adults and peers. One of the exceptions was that the father-absent girls seemed more dependent on women, which is consistent with Lynn and Sawrey's (1959) findings of increased mother dependency among father-separated girls.

Observations at the recreation center revealed that, compared with the other girls, daughters of divorcees sought more attention from men and tried to be near and have physical contacts with male peers. The daughters of widows, however, avoided male areas and much preferred to be with females. Compared with other girls, the daughters of widows reported less heterosexual activity; the daughters of divorcees reported more heterosexual activity.

The daughters of widows sat as far away from male interviewers as possible, whereas the daughters of divorcees tended to sit as close as possible. (The girls from intact families generally sat at an intermediate distance.) Daughters of widows also showed avoidance behavior in their postures during interactions with male interviewers; they often sat stiffly upright, leaned backward, kept their legs together, and showed little eye contact. In contrast, the daughters of divorcees tended to sprawl in their chairs, have an open leg posture, lean slightly forward, and exhibit eye contact and smiling. Nelsen and Vangen (1971) also found that among lower-class eighth-grade black girls, those who were father absent because of divorce or separation were more precocious in their dating behavior and in their knowledge of sex than father-present girls were. Nelsen and Vangen emphasized that when the father is in the home he is an important limit setter for the girl's sexual behavior and that when he is absent there is a great decrease in parental control.

However, the presence of the father during preadolescence or early adolescence does not appear to be the key factor in preventing the girl's sexual difficulties. As with data concerning boys' development, Hetherington generally found that girls had the most difficulties in their heterosexual interactions when their father absence began before they were 5. Early father separation was usually more associated with inappropriate behavior in the girls' interactions with males than father absence after the children were 5 was, although differences were not significant for every measure. Early father absence was also associated with more maternal overprotection. There is other evidence indicating that early father absence is more associated with maternal overprotection than is father absence beginning later in the child's life (e.g., Biller and Bahm, 1971). A more recent study has not replicated Hetherington's (1972) findings, but the subjects were college students and different in sociocultural background from those in her research (Hainline & Feig, 1978).

There were additional findings in Hetherington's study that indicated the importance of taking into account the context of and reason for father absence. Daughters of widows recalled more positive relationships with their fathers and described them as warmer and more competent than did daughters of divorcees. The divorced mothers also painted very negative pictures of their marriages and former husbands. Daughters of divorcees were low in self-esteem, but daughters of widows did not differ significantly in their self-images from daughters of father-present homes. Nevertheless, both groups of father-absent girls had fewer feelings of control over their lives and more anxiety than father-present girls did.

Hetherington has found evidence that suggests the continuing influence of father absence on adult female development (Hetherington & Parke, 1979). She has followed the development of daughters of divorcees, daughters of widows, and daughters from intact families for several years. The daughters of divorcees seem to have especially troubled heterosexual relationships. They were likely to marry at an earlier age than the other groups, but were also likely to be pregnant at the time of marriage. Some of these women have already been separated or divorced from their husbands. A variety of data from interview, observational, and test measures indicated that the daughters of divorcees married less adequate men than the women from the other groups did. The husbands of the daughters of divorcees appeared to have a lower level of educational and vocational accomplishments and had been involved more often in difficulties with the law. These men also had more negative feelings toward their wives and infants and had more difficulty in controlling their impulses and behaving in an emotionally mature manner than the husbands of the women in other groups.

In contrast, there were findings that revealed that daughters of widows tended to marry vocationally successful and ambitious men who were overly controlled and inhibited in their social interactions. In general, the results of Hetherington's follow-up study suggested that women from intact families tended to make the most realistic marital choices. These women also reported more orgasmic satisfaction in sexual relationships with their husbands than the two groups of women who grew up in father-absent homes did (Hetherington & Parke, 1979).

COGNITIVE FUNCTIONING

Much of the evidence supporting the father's importance in cognitive development has come indirectly from studies in which father-absent and father-present children have been compared. The first investigator to present data suggesting an intellectual disadvantage among father-absent children was Sutherland (1930). In a rather ambitious study involving Scottish children, he discovered that those who were father-absent scored significantly lower than those who were father present did. Unfortunately, specific analyses concerning such variables as length of father absence, sex of child, and socioeconomic status are not included in his report. A number of more recent and better controlled studies are also generally consistent with the supposition that father-absent children, at least from lower-class backgrounds, are less likely to function well on intelligence and aptitude tests tha father-present children are (e.g., Blanchard & Biller; 1971; Deutsch & Brown, 1964; Lessing, Zagorin, & Nelson, 1970; Santrock, 1972).

Maxwell (1961) reported some evidence indicating that father absence after the age of 5 negatively influences children's functioning on certain cognitive tasks. He analyzed the Wechsler Intelligence Test scores of a large group of 8- to 13-year-old children who had been referred to a British psychiatric clinic. He found that children whose fathers had been absent since the children were 5 performed below the norms for their age on a number of subtests. Children who had become father absent after the age of 5 had lower scores on tasks tapping social knowledge, perception of details, and verbal skills. Father absence since the age of 5 was the only family background variable consistently related to subtest scores; it seems surprising that there were no findings related to father absence before the age of 5.

Sutton-Smith, Rosenberg, and Landy (1968) explored the relationship between father absence and college sophomores' aptitude test scores (American College Entrance Examination). These investigators defined father absence as an absence of the father from the home for at least 2 consecutive years. Compared to father-present students, those who were father absent performed at a lower level in terms of verbal, language, and total aptitude test scores. Although father absence appeared to affect both males and females, it seemed to have more influence on males. Some interesting variations in the effects of father absence as a function of sex of subject and sex of sibling are also reported; for example, in two-child father-absent families, boys with brothers appeared to be less deficient in academic aptitude than boys with sisters did. In contrast, the father-present girl who was an only child seemed to be at a particular advantage in terms of her aptitude test scores.

In a related investigation, Landy, Rosenberg, and Sutton-Smith (1969) found that father absence had a particularly disruptive effect on the quantitative aptitudes of college females. Total father absence before the age of 10 was highly associated with a deficit in quantitative aptitude. Their findings also suggested that father absence when children are between the ages of 3 and 7 may have an especially negative effect on academic aptitude.

Lessing, Zagorin, and Nelson (1970) conducted one of the most extensive investigations of father absence and cognitive functioning. They studied a group of nearly 500 children (ages 9 to 15) who had been seen at a child guidance clinic, and they explored the relationship between father absence and functioning on the Wechsler Intelligence Test for Children. They defined father absence as separation from the father for 2 or more years, not necessarily for a consecutive period of time.

Father absence for both boys and girls was associated with relatively low ability in perceptual–motor and manipulative–spatial tasks (Block Design and Object Assembly). Father-absent boys also scored lower than father-present boys on the arithmetic subtest. In terms of our society's standards, such tasks are often considered to require typically male aptitudes. In a study with black elementary school boys, Cortés and Fleming (1968) also reported an association between father absence and poor mathematical functioning.

The results of the Lessing, Zagorin, and Nelson investigation suggest some rather complex interactions between father absence and social class. Among working-class children, those who were father absent performed at a generally lower level than those who were father-present. They were less able in their verbal functioning as well as on perceptual–motor and manipulative–spatial tasks. In comparison, middle-class children did not appear to be as handicapped by father absence. They earned lower performance scores (particularly in Block Design and Object Assembly), but they actually scored higher in verbal intelligence than father-present children did.

Lessing, Zagorin, and Nelson also found that previously father-absent children who had father surrogates in their homes (e.g., a stepfather) did not have intelligence test scores that were significantly different from father-present children. (In general, children with no father figure in the home accounted for most of the differences between father-absent and father-present children.)

These findings can be interpreted in terms of a stepfather presenting a masculine model and/or increasing stability in the home. The Lessing, Zagorin, and Nelson study is very impressive. In many ways, it is a vast improvement over earlier research in which there was an attempt to link father absence and intellectual deficits. For example, there is more detail in the analysis of sex differences, social class, and specific areas of intellectual functioning. In general, the investigators show awareness of potential variables that may interact with father absence. Nevertheless, a number of serious questions can be raised in regard to the methodology of the research. The investigation can be criticized because it is based solely on findings from a clinic population. Of even more direct relevance, the study has a weakness similar to almost all of its predecessors in that the variables of father absence and father presence are not defined clearly enough. Two years of not necessarily consecutive separation from the father was used as the criterion for father absence. An obvious question is whether age at onset of father absence is related to intellectual functioning. There is also no consideration of the amount of availability of father-present fathers or the quality of father–child interactions within the intact home. Similar inadequacies may account for the lack of clear-cut findings concerning father absence and academic functioning in some studies (Biller, 1974c; Herzog & Sudia, 1973).

Early Paternal Deprivation

Blanchard & Biller (1971) attempted to specify different levels of father availability and to ascertain their relationship to the academic functioning of third-grade boys. We examined both the timing of father absence and the degree of father–son interaction in the father-present home. The boys were of average intelligence and were from working-class and lower middle-class backgrounds. Four groups of boys were studied: early father absent (beginning before age 3), late father absent (beginning after age 5), low father present (less than 6 hours per week), and high father present (more than 2 hours per day). To control for variables (other than father availability) that might affect academic performance, there was individual subject matching so that each boy in the early father-absent group was matched with a boy from each of the other three groups in terms of essentially identical characteristics of age, IQ, socioeconomic status, and presence or absence of male siblings.

Academic performance was assessed by means of Stanford Achievement Test scores and classroom grades. (The teachers did not have the children's achievement test scores available to them until after final classroom grades had been assigned.) The high father-present group was very superior to the other three groups. With respect to both grades and achievement test scores, the early father-absent boys were generally underachievers, the late father-absent boys and low father-present boys usually functioned somewhat below grade level, and the high father-present group performed above grade level.

The early father-absent boys were consistently handicapped in their academic performance. They scored significantly lower on every achievement test index as well as in their grades. The early father-absent group functioned below grade level in both language and mathematical skills. When compared to the high father-present group, the early father-absent group appeared to be very inferior in skills relating to reading comprehension.

Santrock (1972) presented additional evidence indicating that early father absence can have a very significant debilitating effect on cognitive functioning. Among lower-class junior-high and high-school children, those who became father absent before the age of 5, and particularly before the age of 2, generally scored significantly lower on measures of IQ (Otis Quick Test) and achievement (Stanford Achievement Test) that had been administered when they were in the third and sixth grades than did those from intact homes. The most detrimental effects occurred when father absence was due to divorce, desertion, or separation, rather than death. The findings of this study also provided support for the positive remedial effects of a stepfather for boys, especially when the stepfather joined the family before the child was 5 years old.

Hetherington, Cox, and Cox (1978) also reported data indicating that early father absence can impede cognitive development. They found differences between the cognitive functioning of young boys (5- and 6-year-olds) who had been father absent for 2 years because of divorce and boys from intact families. Boys from intact families scored significantly higher on the Block Design, Mazes, and Arithmetic subtests of the WIPSI and achieved higher Performance Scale Intelligence scores and marginally higher ($p < .07$) Full-Scale Intelligence scores. Other data from this study clearly suggest that the decreasing availability of the divorced fathers for their sons during the 2 years following the divorce was a major factor in these boys performing at a lower level than boys from intact families. In contrast, no clear-cut differences in cognitive functioning were found between father-absent girls and girls from intact homes.

Carlsmith (1964) made an interesting discovery concerning the relationship between father absence and intellectual abilities. She examined the College Board Aptitude Test scores of middle-class and upper middle-class high school males who had experienced early father absence because of their father's military service during World War II. Boys who were father absent in early childhood were more likely to have a feminine patterning of aptitude test scores. Compared to the typical male pattern of higher math than verbal scores, males who had experienced early separation from their fathers more frequently had a higher verbal score than math score. She found that the earlier the onset of father absence, the more likely the male was to have a higher verbal than math score. The effect was strongest for students whose fathers were absent at birth and/or were away for over 30 months. Higher verbal than math functioning is the usual pattern among females, and Carlsmith speculated that it reflects a feminine global style of cognitive functioning. Results from other studies have also indicated a relationship between father absence and a feminine patterning of aptitude test scores among males (e.g., Altus, 1958; Nelsen & Maccoby, 1966).

A study with adolescent boys by Barclay and Cusumano (1967) supports the hypothesis that difficulties in analytical functioning are often related to father absence. Using Witkin's rod and frame procedure, Barclay and Cusumano found that father-absent males were more field dependent than those who were father present. Wohlford and Liberman (1970) reported that father separation (after the age of 6) was related to field dependency among elementary school children from an urban section of Miami. Their procedure involved an embedded figures test. Field dependent individuals have difficulties in ignoring irrelevant environmental cues in the analysis of certain types of problems.

Louden (1973), in a very extensive study with college students, presented evidence indicating that both males and females who had been father absent during childhood were more field dependent than were those who were father present. Father absence was defined as the continuous absence of the father or father surrogate for at least 3 years during one of three age periods (0 to 5 years, 6 to 12 years, or 13 to 18 years). Field dependence–independence was measured by a group-administered embedded figures procedure. Father absence during each age period was associated with greater field dependence than was father presence, but, as in Wohlford and Liberman's research, father absence during the 6- to 12-year age period seemed to be most linked with field dependent behavior. Louden argued that this period is especially important for the development of an ability to adapt to changing environments. Such data suggest that the father may serve different functions at different stages of the child's development.

Sociocultural Variables

Paternal deprivation is often a major factor contributing to a disadvantaged environment (Bronfenbrenner, 1967). Father absence appears to hamper lower-class children particularly. Some investigators have reported that among lower-class black children, those who are father absent score considerably lower on intelligence and achievement tests than those who are father present do (e.g., Cortés & Fleming, 1968; Deutsch, 1960; Deutsch & Brown, 1964).

Radin (1976) emphasized that several studies did not reveal any cognitive deficits associated with father absence for black children. Shinn (1978) also noted that there appeared to be more consistency in the effects of father absence on white children than on black children. Shinn did point out, however, that almost half of the methodologically adequate studies involving black children did produce results suggesting detrimental effects of father absence on cognitive functioning. For example, Pedersen, Rubenstein, and Yarrow (1979) reported that among the black infants they studied, those who were father present generally scored higher on a variety of cognitive development measures than did those who were father absent.

Radin (1976) cited Coleman et al.'s (1966) data indicating that father absence may be more detrimental in societies in which the father generally has a strong role. The implication is that children are more likely to miss out on a particularly important source of cognitive stimulation. For example, Coleman et al. (1966) found that Oriental-American and Mexican-American children were negatively influenced by father absence although lower-class black children were not. Note that other investigators have reported that father absence may not have such detrimental effects in societies in which the mother is expected to have a particularly influential role in family and economic functioning (Ancona, Cesa-Bianchi, & Bocquet, 1964; Hunt & Hunt, 1975, 1977).

Socioeconomic and sociocultural variables have to be considered more carefully if there is to be a greater understanding of the effects of paternal deprivation on cognitive development. A problem in some research is the absence of specific comparisons among individuals from different social backgrounds. In particular, culturally disadvantaged groups and members of stable blue-collar occupations (e.g., truck drivers, skilled factory workers) are often considered lower class. Such generalized groupings seem to obscure possible relationships (Biller, 1971a). For example, the incidence of continual father absence is much higher among culturally disadvantaged families than among working-class families.

The classification becomes very difficult to untangle, because a family that has been working class may be redefined as disadvantaged or lower-class if it becomes father-absent. Herzog and Sudia (1973) pointed out that there have been inadequate controls for income levels in research with disadvantaged children. They emphasized that differences in income level between father-absent and father-present families may be more closely related to intellectual disadvantages than is father absence *per se*.

In any case, paternal deprivation seems to be associated with much more serious consequences among lower-class children than among middle-class children (Biller, 1971a). Some research already discussed in this section has suggested that among father-absent children, those who are from working-class backgrounds are consistently more handicapped in their cognitive functioning than are those from middle-class backgrounds. (Lessing, Zagorin, & Nelson,

1970). A general depression in academic achievement associated with father absence has usually been found with working-class or lower-class children (Blanchard & Biller, 1971; Santrock, 1972).

Middle-class father-absent children often do well in situations requiring verbal skills. Carlsmith's (1964) middle- and upper middle-class, father-absent group apparently was equal or superior to her father-present group in verbal aptitude, although inferior in mathematical aptitude. Lessing, Zagorin and Nelson (1970) found that middle-class father-absent children had higher verbal scores, but lower performance (e.g., perceptual–manipulative) scores than did father-present children. Dyl and Biller (1973) found that, although lower-class father-absent boys were particularly handicapped in their reading skills, middle-class father-absent boys functioned adequately in reading. Because academic achievement, particularly in elementary school, is so heavily dependent on verbal and reading ability, father-absent middle-class children do not seem to be very handicapped. There is also evidence that the loss of a father may be a stimulus for unusual achievement in certain individuals. In some cases, a child's abilities may be strengthened in the attempt to cope with the loss of a parent (Biller, 1974c).

Eisenstadt (1978) presented some provocative data suggesting that the death of a parent, particularly a father, when one is a child could be a stimulating factor in occupational eminence (and genius) as well as in serious psychopathology. He compared the family histories of individuals who were eminent in their professions with demographic data from various populations and consistently found that a greater proportion of those with unusual accomplishment had experienced the death of their fathers during childhood. He also cited some other research that supported the notion that the death of a father may, in some cases, spur an individual on to great creative accomplishment (e.g., Albert, 1971) even though the majority of studies he reviewed focused on the link between parent loss and psychopathology.

In general, Eisenstadt put forth the argument that the bereavement process can be worked through in a very constructive manner by some children so that they become particularly motivated and energized toward creative accomplishment. I would emphasize that such factors as the quality of mothering that the child receives and the child's own constitutional predispositions are particularly important in determining whether the bereavement process can lead an individual toward eminence and genius (Biller, 1974c).

Maternal Influence

The middle-class mother seems to influence her father-absent son's intellectual development strongly. In an interview study in a university town, Hilgard,

Neuman, and Fisk (1960) found that men who lost their fathers during childhood tended to be highly successful in their academic pursuits despite, or maybe because of, a conspicuous overdependence on their mothers. Clinical findings presented by Gregory (1965) also suggest that many upper middleclass father-absent students do well in college. Evidence reviewed by Nelsen and Maccoby (1966) reveals that high verbal ability in boys is often associated with a close and restrictive mother–son relationship. Levy (1943) reported that middle-class maternally overprotected boys did superior work in school, particularly in subjects requiring verbal facility. However, their performance in mathematics was not at such a high level, which seems consistent with Carlsmith's (1964) results.

Middle-class mothers are much more likely to place strong emphasis on academic success than lower-class mothers are (Kohn, 1959). Some findings suggest that among lower-class mothers, those without husbands are preoccupied with day-to-day activities and less frequently think of future goals for themselves or for their children (Hecksher, 1967; Parker & Kliener, 1956). Compared to the middle-class mother, the lower-class mother usually puts much less emphasis on long-term academic goals and is also generally a much less adequate model for coping with the demands of the middle-class school.

In homes in which the father is absent or relatively unavailable, the mother assumes a more primary role in terms of dispensing reinforcements and emphasizing certain values. A father-absent child who is strongly identified with an intellectually oriented mother may be at an advantage in many facets of school adjustment. He or she may find the transition from home to the typically feminine-oriented classroom quite comfortable. Such father-absent children might be expected to do particularly well at tasks in which verbal skills and conformity are rewarded.

Although they may stimulate the paternally deprived child's acquisition of verbal skills and adaptation to the typical school environment, middle-class, overprotecting mothers often inhibit the development of an active, problem-solving attitude toward the environment. A mother who is excessively overprotective and dominating may interfere with the development of the child's assertiveness and independence (Biller, 1971b). The psychological adjustment of the mother is a crucial factor; a mother who is emotionally disturbed and/or interpersonally handicapped can have a very negative effect on the father-absent child's self-concept and ability to relate to others. However, mothers who are self-accepting, have high ego strength, and are interpersonally mature can do much to facilitate positive personality development among their paternally deprived children (Biller, 1971a, 1971b).

Variations in fathering can influence the child's cognitive development, but it must be emphasized that father absence is only one of many factors that have an impact on the child's intellectual functioning. Sociocultural, maternal, and peer group values are especially important. For example, among male lower-class children, paternal deprivation usually intensifies lack of exposure to experiences linking intellectual activities with masculine interests. Many boys, in their desperate attempts to view themselves as totally masculine, become excessively dependent on their peer group and perceive intellectual tasks as "feminine." The school setting, which presents women as authority figures and makes strong demands for obedience and conformity, is particularly antithetical to such boys' fervent desires to feel masculine (Biller, 1974b).

Shinn (1978) conducted a very careful analysis of research concerning father absence and cognitive functioning. She focused her discussion on 28 studies that met some minimal methodological criteria; data were collected from nonclinical populations, there was some sort of "father-present" control group, and there was some effort to control for socioeconomic status. The majority of these studies indicated that father absence was associated with detrimental effects in cognitive functioning. Her survey suggested that father absence because of divorce may be particularly detrimental, and there was some evidence that early, long-term, and complete father absence was especially likely to be negatively associated with intellectual competence. However, she also found some data indicating that there are negative effects from later, short-term, and partial father absence. More clear-cut results were reported from studies involving lower-class males, although Shinn emphasized that there is much evidence that females' cognitive functioning generally also appears to be affected by father absence.

There have been several interpretations of the process by which father absence may influence the child's cognitive functioning (as well as other facets of personality development; Biller, 1974c). In her review, Shinn (1978) tried to systematically differentiate between the relevance of various hypotheses concerning underlying factors that may be responsible for an association between father absence and cognitive functioning. Some families may be predisposed to father absence through divorce because of the parent's family backgrounds, and the child's development may be negatively affected even before the divorce takes place. For example, high levels of father–mother conflict, financial stress, and paternal deprivation seem to be characteristic for some children in the years preceding the divorce.

The father's absence may be linked to a variety of factors more directly associated with deficits in the child's cognitive functioning. Shinn (1978) concluded that data linking disruption of sex role identification with impaired cognitive functioning are relatively meager, but Biller's (1974c) review has indicated that sex role functioning may interact with the cognitive development of the paternally deprived child in a variety of complex ways. There is much evidence suggesting that the family instability and financial difficulty often associated with father absence may be major factors interfering with the child's cognitive functioning. Shinn (1978) agreed, however, that the major influence of father absence appears to be lessened parental interaction and attention, which in turn often seems to result in a decrease in the child's level of cognitive stimulation and the opportunity to model more mature types of information processing and problem solving.

PERSONAL AND SOCIAL ADJUSTMENT

Although it did not focus on father-absent children, a study by Reuter and Biller (1973) appears to have some interesting implications concerning father absence and availability. We investigated the relationship between various combinations of perceived paternal nurturance-availability and college males' personality adjustment. A family background questionnaire was designed to assess perceptions of father–child relationships and the amount of time the father spent at home when the subjects were children. The personal adjustment scale of Gough and Heilbrun's Adjective Check List and the socialization scale of the California Psychological Inventory were employed as measures of personality adjustment. High paternal nurturance combined with at least moderate paternal availability, and high paternal availability combined with at least moderate paternal nurturance were related to high scores on the personality adjustment measures. A male who has adequate opportunities to observe a nurturant father can imitate his behavior and develop positive personality characteristics. The father who is both relatively nurturant and relatively available may have a more adequate personality adjustment than other types of father.

In contrast, high paternal nurturance combined with low paternal availability and high paternal availability combined with low paternal nurturance were associated with relatively poor scores on the personality adjustment measures. Males who reported that their fathers had been home much of the time but gave them little attention seemed to be especially handicapped in their psychological functioning. The nonnurturant father is an inadequate model, and his consistent presence appears to be a detriment to the child's personality functioning. To put it another way, the child with a nonnurturant father may be better off if the father is not very available. This is consistent with evidence that suggests that father-absent children often have better personality adjustments than children with passive ineffectual fathers (Biller 1971a, 1974c).

The child with a highly nurturant but seldom home father may feel quite frustrated that the father is not home more often and/or may find it difficult to imitate such an elusive figure. Children whose parents are divorced often fit this pattern; they see their fathers infrequently and/or unpredictably, but their fathers may be extremely nurturant during such interactions.

Anxiety

Inadequate fathering is sometimes associated with a high level of anxiety in children. The paternally deprived child's insecurity in interpersonal relationships can contribute to feelings of anxiety and low self-esteem. In addition, the paternally deprived child may experience much anxiety because of an overly intense relationship with the mother. The father-absent child, in particular, is likely to encounter economic insecurity and, depending on the reason for paternal absence, may be concerned with the father's well-being. Feelings of being different from other children may also increase anxiety and feelings of inadequacy. A principal role of the father is to help the family deal with environmental problems, and the paternally deprived child may encounter many seemingly insoluble crises. Children with adequate and available fathers are exposed to a model who can realistically and creatively deal with some of the problems that a mother may not have the experience or time to solve (Biller, 1971a).

Stolz et al. (1954) reported that 4- to 8-year-old children, father absent the first few years of life while their fathers were away in military service, were more anxious than children whose fathers had been consistently present. Previously father-separated children were observed to be more anxious with peers and adults, in story completion sessions when the situation involved the father and in terms of maternal reports of seriousness and number of fears. It is important to note that the fathers were not absent at the time of the study and were having stressful relationships with their children. In a study of nursery school children, Koch (1961) found that father-absent children (eight boys and three girls) exhibited more anxiety on a projective test than did a matched group from intact families. The father-absent children more often selected unhappy faces for the central child depicted in various situations.

McCord, McCord, and Thurber (1962) analyzed social worker's observations of 10- to 15-year-old lower-class boys. They concluded that father-absent boys manifested more anxiety about sex than a matched group of father-present boys, although the difference concerning the amount of general fearfulness was insignificant. In a retrospective study, Stephens (1961) asked social workers about their experiences with father-absent boys. Father-absent boys were described as being more effemininate and anxious about sex than were father-present boys. Leichty (1960) did not find any evidence that father absence during early childhood was associated with castration anxiety in college males, although some of her findings did suggest that father absence was related to anxiety concerning mother–father sexual interaction. There is at least some initial increase in anxiety level for all children whose parents divorce, although many are able to cope very well because of their developmental stage or other factors (Hetherington, Cox, & Cox, 1978; Wallerstein & Kelly, 1980a, b).

Self Control and Moral Development

Mischel (1961c) conducted a series of studies concerning the antecedents and correlates of impulse control in Caribbean children. In an earlier phase of his research, Mischel (1958) reported that 7- to 9-year-old black West Indian children chose immediate gratification significantly more frequently than white West Indian children. The difference among the black and white children appeared to be related to the greater incidence of father absence among the black children. Studying 8- and 9-year-olds, Mischel (1961) found that father-absent children showed a stronger preference for immediate gratification than did father-present children. Father-absent children, for instance, more often chose a small candy bar for immediate consumption rather than waiting a week for a large candy bar.

Santrock and Wohlford (1970) studied delay of gratification among fifth-grade boys. They found that boys who were father absent because of divorce, as compared to those who were father absent because of death, had more difficulty in delaying gratification. Boys who were father absent because of divorce more often chose an immediately available small candy bar than waiting until the next day for a much larger one. Boys who became father separated before the age of 2 or between the ages of 6 and 9 were more likely to choose the immediate reward than those who were separated from their fathers between the ages of 3 and 5.

There is also some evidence that individuals who have been father absent during childhood are likely to have difficulties making long term commitments. Studying Peace Corps volunteers, Suedfeld (1967) discovered that those who were father absent during childhood were much more likely not to complete their scheduled overseas tours than were those who had not been father absent. Premature terminations were associated with problems of adjustment and conduct and included some psychiatrically based decisions. Other research suggests that there is sometimes a relationship between father absence in childhood and unemployment in adulthood (Gay & Tonge, 1967; Hall & Tonge 1963).

Hoffman (1971a) analyzed data concerning the conscience development of seventh-grade children. Father-absent boys consistently scored lower than father-present boys on a variety of moral indexes. They scored lower on measures of internal moral judgment, guilt following transgressions, acceptance of blame, moral values, and rule conformity. In addition, they were rated as higher in aggression by their teachers, which may also reflect difficulties in self-control. Although the influence was less clear-cut, weak father identification among father-present boys was also related to less adequate conscience development. Father identification was determined by responses to questions involving the person the boy felt most similar to, most admired, and most wanted to resemble when he grew up. Boys with strong father identification scored higher on the measures of internal moral judgment, moral values, and conformity to rules than did boys with low father identifications (Hoffman, 1971a,b).

Whiting (1959) hypothesized that paternal deprivation is negatively related to the strength of the child's conscience development. Doing a cross-cultural analysis, he assumed that self-blame for illness is an indication of strong conscience development. In societies in which fathers have little interaction with their younger children, there is more of a tendency to blame others and/or supernatural beings for one's illness. Blaming one's self for illness was stronger in nuclear households and least in polygynous mother–child households: Such evidence is also consistent with the view that paternal deprivation can inhibit the development of trust in others. Some data also suggest that father loss due to death may be associated with the development of a fatalistic attitude and an external locus of control, at least among males (Duke & Lancaster, 1976; Parish & Copeland, 1980).

A number of clinicians, including Aichorn (1935) and Lederer (1964), have speculated about inadequacies in the self-control and conscience development of the father-absent child. In his experience as a psychotherapist, Meerloo (1956) found that a lack of accurate time perception, which is often associated with difficulties in self-control, is common among father-absent individuals. In a study of elementary school children in a Cuban section of Miami, Wohlford and Leiberman (1970) reported that father-absent children had less well developed future time perspective than did father-present children.

Meerlo (1956) assumed that the father represents social order and that his adherence to time schedules gives the child an important lesson in social functioning. The paternally deprived child may find it very difficult to follow the rules of society. Antisocial acts are often impulsive as well as aggressive, and there is evidence that inability to delay gratification is associated with inaccurate time perception, lack of social responsibility, low achievement motivation, and juvenile delinquency (e.g., Mischel, 1961a, 1961b).

The father-absent child often lacks a model from whom to learn to delay gratification and to control his aggressive and destructive impulses. A child who has experienced paternal deprivation may have particular difficulty in respecting and communicating with adult males in positions of authority. Douvan and Adelson (1966) observed much rebelliousness against adult authority figures and particularly a rejection of men among adolescent father-absent boys. (It is interesting to contrast such a reaction to the continual seeking of male adults among many young father-absent children; perhaps there has been a disillusionment process.)

Delinquency

Juvenile delinquency can have many different etiologies, but paternal deprivation frequently is a contributing factor. Many researchers have noted that father absence is more common among delinquent children than among nondelinquent children. Studying adolescents, Glueck and Glueck (1950) reported that more than two-fifths of the delinquent boys were father absent as compared with less than one-fourth of a matched nondelinquent group. McCord, McCord, and Thurber (1963) found that the lower-class father-absent boys in their study committed more felonies than the father-present group, although the rates of gang delinquency were not different. Gregory (1965a) listed a large number of investigations linking father absence with delinquent behavior and also detected a strong association between these variables in his study of high school students.

Early father absence has a particularly strong association with delinquency among males. Siegman (1966) analyzed medical students' responses to an anonymous questionnaire concerning their childhood experiences. He compared the responses of students who had been without a father for at least 1 year during their first few years of life with those of students who had been continuously father present. The father-absent group admitted to a greater degree of antisocial behavior during childhood. Anderson (1968) found that a history of early father absence was much more frequent among boys committed to a training school. He also discovered that father-absent nondelinquents had a much higher rate of father substitution (stepfather, father surrogate, etc.) between the ages of 4 and 7 than did father-absent delinquents. Kelly and Baer (1969) studied the recidivism rate among male delinquents. Compared to a 12 percent rate among father-present males, they found a 39 percent recidivism rate among males who had become father absent before the age of 6. However, boys who became father absent after the age of 6 had only a 10 percent recidivism rate.

Miller (1958) argued that most lower-class boys suffer from paternal deprivation and that their antisocial behavior is often an attempt to prove that they are masculine. Bacon, Child, and Barry (1953), in a cross-cultural study, found that father availability was negatively related to the amount of theft and personal crime. The degree of father availability was defined in terms of family structure. Societies with a predominantly monogamous nuclear family structure tended to be rated low in the amount of theft and personal crime, whereas societies with a polygamous mother–child family structure tended to be rated high in both theft and personal crime. Following Miller's hypothesis, Bacon, Child, and Barry suggested that such antisocial behavior was a reaction against a female-based household and an attempted assertion of masculinity. A large number of psychiatric referrals with the complaint of aggressive acting out are made by mothers of preadolescent and adolescent father-absent boys, and clinical data suggest that sex role conflicts are frequent in such boys (Biller, 1974c).

Herzog and Sudia (1973) carefully analyzed the methodological defects of studies linking father absence and delinquency. They pointed out that socio-economic and sociocultural factors are often not taken into account in comparisons of father-absent and father-present children. Furthermore, Herzog and Sudia emphasized that law enforcement officials and other community agents may react differently when a father-absent child, rather than a father-present child, behaves in an antisocial manner, especially when the child comes from an economically disadvantaged family. For example, they may expect father-absent children to commit increasingly serious offenses and may deal with them more severely. It is also relevant to note that Santrock and Tracy's (1978) data clearly indicate that teachers are likely to stereotype boys from father-absent and divorced families. Such treatment may negatively influence the father-absent child's self-concept and strengthen the probability that he or she will become involved in antisocial acts.

The difficulty that boys from father-absent homes often have in relating to male authority figures can also contribute to the reactions of law enforcement officials. The father-absent boy's "lack of respect" can lead to negative interactions with male authority figures. In fact, some data suggest that father-absent boys are more prone to commit offenses against authority than against property (Herzog & Sudia, 1973; Nye, 1958).

Herzog and Sudia (1973) also cited much evidence indicating that lack of general family cohesiveness and supervision, rather than father absence *per se*, is the most significant factor associated with juvenile delinquency. Many familial and nonfamilial factors have to be considered, and in only some cases is father absence directly linked to delinquent behavior. For example, children in father-absent families who have a positive relationship with highly competent mothers seem to be less likely to become delinquent than children in father-present families who have inadequate fathers (Biller, 1974c).

Psychopathology

Garbower (1959), studying children from Navy families, found that those who were seen for psychiatric problems had more frequent and lengthy periods of father absence than a nondisturbed comparison group did. The fathers of the disturbed children also seemed less sensitive to the effects of their being away from their families. In studying military families, Pedersen (1966) found a similar amount of father absence among 11- to 15-year-old boys, irrespective of whether they were referred for psychiatric help. However, he did find that the degree of their psychopathology was highly associated with the amount of father absence they had experienced.

Trunnell (1968) studied children seen at an outpatient clinic and found that severity of psychopathology varied with the length of father absence and the age of onset of the father's absence. The longer the absence and the younger the child at the onset, the more serious the psychopathology. Oltman and Friedman (1967) found particularly high rates of childhood father absence among adults who had chronically disturbed personalities and inadequate moral development. In addition, they found above average rates of father-absence among neurotics and drug addicts. Rosenberg (1969) also reported extremely high rates of frequent childhood father absence among young alcoholics and drug addicts. Maternal dominance combined with father absence or inadequacy is common in the histories of drug addicts (Chein et al., 1964; Wood & Duffy, 1966).

Rubenstein (1980) described data that are relevant to the consideration of the long-term effects of father absence because of divorce. She focused on the adjustment of adults who experienced parental divorce when they were children. Her survey research in collaboration with Phillip Shaver suggested that feelings of loneliness and low self-esteem were more common among adults who had grown up in one-parent families than among those whose families had remained intact. The earlier the divorce in individuals' lives, the more likely they were to have low self-esteem and experience profound loneliness as adults. Worry, despair, feelings of worthlessness, fearfulness, and general "separation anxiety" seemed especially common among those who grew up in families where the parents had divorced.

I have also reviewed data from other studies suggesting a possible link between father absence in childhood and depression and suicidal behavior in adulthood (Biller, 1974c). In a recent article, Crook and Eliot (1980) concluded that all the investigations indicating a connection between parental death during childhood (including orphanhood) and adult depression have been frought with methodological inadequacies. Although Crook and Eliot were not focusing on the effects of father loss, their criticisms are similar to those that have been directed towards studies concerning the influence of father absence on the development of depression (Biller, 1974c).

Brill and Liston (1966) reported that the childhood loss of the father through death was not unusually high among mental patients. However, the frequency of the loss of the father because of divorce or separation was much higher for individuals suffering from neurosis, psychosis, or personality disorders than for a number of different comparison groups. Consistent with Brill and Liston's data, father absence through divorce, separation, or desertion has also been found to be more highly associated with delinquency (Goode, 1961), maladjustment (Baggett, 1967), low self-esteem and sexual acting out (Hetherington, 1972), and cognitive deficits (Santrock, 1972). In a study concerning children who were referred for school adjustment problems, Felner, Stolberg and Cowen (1975) found that those whose parents were divorced were likely to display acting-out behavior whereas those from homes where the father had dies were likely to display moody withdrawal. Other researchers who have reported that rates of childhood father absence are higher among patients classified as neurotic or schizophrenic than among the general population have not considered the reason for father absence systematically (e.g., DaSilva, 1963; Madow & Hardy, 1947; Oltman, McGarry & Friedman, 1952; Wahl, 1954; 1956).

Gregory (1958, 1965b) critically evaluated many of the relevant studies and emphasized some of the methodological pitfalls in comparisons involving the relative incidence of mental illness among father-present and father-absent individuals. A major shortcoming of most of the studies is a lack of consideration of the possible effects of socioeconomic status. Cobliner (1963) reported some provocative findings suggesting that father absence is more likely to be related to serious psychological disturbance in lower-class than middle-class individuals. Middle-class families, particularly with respect to the mother–child relationship, may have more psychological as well as economic resources with which to cope with paternal deprivation (Biller, 1971a, 1974c).

There are some data suggesting that boys from father-absent homes are, in many cases, less retarded in their personality development than are boys from intact maternally dominated homes (Biller, 1968a; Reuter & Biller, 1973). In Nye's (1957) study, children from broken homes were found to have better family adjustments and lower rates of antisocial behavior and psychosomatic illness than children from unhappy unbroken homes were. Other research has also suggested that a child may function more adequately in a father-absent home than one in which there is an inappropriate husband-wife relationship (e.g., Benson, 1958; Hetherington, Cox, & Cox, 1978; Landis, 1962).

Father-absent children may be more influenced by factors outside the home than are children from intact but unhappy and/or maternally dominated homes. Some children may be particularly affected by attention from an adult male because of their intense feelings of paternal deprivation. Children with inadequate fathers often become resigned to their situation. For example, the father-present but maternally dominated child is likely to develop a view of men as ineffectual, especially if the father is continually being controlled by the mother. In contrast, the father-absent child may develop a much more flexible view of adult male behavior.

The research described in this chapter indicates that inadequate fathering and/or father absence predisposes children toward certain developmental deficits. However, there are many paternally deprived children who are generally well adjusted. Such children should be more carefully studied to determine why they differ from less well adjusted, paternally deprived children. Investigators should include consideration of both the type of child maladjustment and the type of family inadequacy.

Extremely severe psychopathology such as autism or childhood schizophrenia does not develop simply as a function of disturbed parent–child relationships. The child's genetic and/or constitutional predispositions play an important part in determining the severity of the psychopathology as well as the quality of parent–child interactions. Most children are handicapped if they have experienced paternal deprivation and are likely to have much difficulty in their emotional and interpersonal development. But in the great majority of cases, insufficient or inappropriate fathering (and/or mothering) *per se* does not account for children who are unable to develop basic communication skills or to form interpersonal attachments. For example, the child's neurological malfunctioning or extreme, temperamentally related hypersensitivity or hyposensitivity can make it very difficult for the parent to respond in a positive manner. In some cases, constitutionally atypical children contribute to the development of psychopathology in their parents (Biller 1971a, 1974c).

Longitudinal Perspective

The most important studies dealing with the effects of divorce on children's personal and social adjustment have been done by Hetherington, Cox, and Cox (1978) and Wallerstein and Kelly (1980a). These studies highlight the importance of the developmental and family-social system context, in evaluating the influence of divorce and father absence on children. The developmental stage of the child *and* the length of time that has elapsed since the initial family breakup must be considered in attempting to understand how boys and girls cope with the divorce process.

Hetherington and her co-workers have carried out a very interesting, exhaustive, and methodologically complex longitudinal research project on the effects of divorce on young children (Hetherington, Cox, & Cox, 1978). Because this study is so provocative and also much better controlled than other research endeavors relating to father absence, it is deserving of special consideration. These investigators presented data on the effects of divorce on families with preschool-age children. They analyzed a vast array of findings garnered from several types of procedure, including measures of social interaction at home and at school and observer, teacher, and peer ratings. Their longitudinal analyses included assessments of individual and family functioning at various periods of time during the first 2 years after the divorce.

They presented evidence clearly indicating that both father absence because of divorce and high family conflict in intact families are associated with difficulties in the personal and social adjustment of young children. On a variety of social interaction measures, children in father-absent homes and those from homes with a high degree of father–mother conflict were generally less mature and independent in their social interactions than children from families in which there was low or moderate father–mother conflict were. The relative standing of the father-absent children compared to children in high-conflict families changed during the aftermath of divorce. At 1 year after the divorce, the father-absent children generally were experiencing more interpersonal conflict at school and at home than were children from high-conflict, intact families. Two years after the divorce, however, the father-absent children seemed to be faring better than the children from high-conflict families. The girls seemed to be less affected than the boys by both marital discord and father-absence.

Data from the Hetherington, Cox, and Cox (1978) study revealed that father absence, or the decreased availability of the father because of divorce, is associated with a lower level of cognitive and sex role functioning in boys 2 years after the divorce. Girls at the same age did not appear to be similarly affected. However, individual differences in the quality of mother–child interactions in the father-absent home had a strong association for both the boys' and girls' cognitive functioning and personal and social adjustment 2 years after the divorce.

Wallerstein and Kelly (1974, 1976, 1980a, 1980b) have reported much interesting longitudinal data from their long-term project studying the effects of divorce on children. Their findings are based on extensive interviews with family members and the children's teachers at three intervals: just after the separation, 1 year later, and again after 5 years. The parents in the 60 families who were involved in the study had initially participated in a 6-week counseling program aimed at helping them cope with divorce-related issues. The families from Marin County, California, were generally white, middle-class, and well-educated. At the 5-year follow-up study the investigators were still able to locate and interview 58 of the 60 families and 101 of the 131 children, who at that point ranged in age from 7 to 23. Immediately after the divorce, almost all the children experienced some degree of father absence in the sense that they no longer lived with their fathers. Over 90 percent lived with their mothers at the start of the study; at the 5-year follow-up study 77 percent still remained with their mothers, 11 percent (many of the older adolescents) were now living in separate residences, 8 percent lived with their fathers, and 3 percent spent a significant period of time shuffling back and forth (often in reaction to some stress) between their parents' homes.

The wealth of findings from the Wallerstein and Kelly research is very provocative, but unfortunately there was no intact family comparison group used in this study. Such a comparison group could give a much clearer frame of reference for the relative severity of difficulties associated with divorce. Questions also could be raised about the representativeness of the families in this study (e.g., They were predominantly middle-class and were involved in a 6-week counseling program). Nevertheless, since the Wallerstein and Kelly study appears to the most extensive in terms of the number and variety of children at different ages and the span of years covered, the findings should be important in stimulating more focused and controlled research efforts.

To assess the effects of divorce on children at different developmental levels, Wallerstein and Kelly (1974, 1975, 1976) divided the children into several different groups on the basis of their age at the time of the initial separation. They divided the children into six different age groups: 2- to 3-year-olds; 3- to 4-year-olds; 5- to 6-year-olds; 7- to 8-year-olds; 9- to 10-year-olds, and 13- to 18-year-olds. The 2- to 3-year-olds were particularly prone to regress and express bewilderment, anger, clinging, and indescriminate neediness toward adults in reaction to parental divorce. Regression seemed to be brief if children received an adequate and consistent emotional involvement from adult family members. However, those children who experienced continuously intense parental conflict and had mothers who were devastated by the divorce appeared very depressed and developmentally delayed a year after the divorce (Wallerstein & Kelly, 1975).

Among the 3- and 4-year-olds, a poor self-image and loss of self-esteem was a frequent concomitant of parental divorce. A feeling of responsibility for the parents' divorce was common among many of the children. More of the 5- and 6-year-olds, in contrast to the younger children, seemed to be able to weather the divorce without manifesting clear-cut developmental setbacks. Such data are, of course, consistent with other findings indicating that children are particularly vulnerable to father absence beginning before the age of 5 (Biller, 1971a, 1974c).

Children who were 7 to 8 years old seemed intensely sad in response to parental divorce (Kelly & Wallerstein, 1976). They were more likely than the 9- and 10-year-olds to show regressive behaviors but were more directly communicative about the reason for their feelings than the younger children were. The 7- and 8-year-olds appeared to be frightened about the consequences of the divorce, and they all seemed to want their parents back together again desperately, even those were exposed to particularly intense and abusive parental conflict. Frequent expressions of sadness about not being with their fathers was especially prevalent for most of the 7- and 8-year-olds. A year after the divorce, the modal response seemed to be more a placid resignation than an energetic striving to make the family intact again.

As might be expected from the more mature cognitive development of 9- and 10-year-olds, they often seemed able to deal with divorce in a more controlled and realistic fashion (Wallerstein & Kelly, 1976). They were more likely to use a variety of defensive and coping patterns so that their everyday lives did not seem as disrupted as those of the younger children did. However, loneliness, physical symptoms, feelings of shame, and especially an intense conscious anger toward the parents was common among the 9- and 10-year-olds. About half the 9- and 10-year-olds appeared to cope adequately a year after the divorce, even though they were still dealing with some feelings of sadness and bitterness. In contrast, the rest of the children in this age group were severely handicapped by feelings of low self-esteem and depression, which often interfered with their peer relationships and academic functioning. Approximately one-fourth of the children were clearly more psychologically disabled 1 year after the divorce.

For adolescents, the divorce was characterized by much pain, anger, sadness, and often conflicts concerning their parents' sexual behavior (Wallerstein & Kelly, 1974). Those adolescents who were relatively mature at the time of the divorce and were able to maintain some distance from their parents' conflicts (not take sides) seemed to be doing better by the end of the first year after the divorce, having developed a strikingly realistic perception of their parents. In contrast, those adolescents who had emotional and social problems before the divorce tended to manifest even more serious difficulties after it.

At the 5-year follow-up study, many different patterns of adaptation were evident from Wallerstein and Kelly's data (1980a, 1980b). In general, about one-third (34 percent) of the children appeared to be doing especially well personally, socially, and educationally. They had very positive self-concepts and showed generally high levels of competence, including coping well with experiences related to the divorce. A slightly greater proportion (37 percent) expressed severe adjustment problems, including personal and social difficulties, many having particularly strong feelings of loneliness, alienation, and depression. They were extremely dissatisfied with their lives, although even among this group about half were able to do adequately in some areas, such as school. The remaining children (29 percent) made what could be termed mixed adjustments, showing typical ups and downs in coping with their life situations. These children appeared to be making an "average" adaptation to school and social demands, but there was some evidence that feelings about the divorce sometimes had negative effects on their self-esteem and overall competence.

Although they noted that other factors seemed to be operating for some children who made successful adjustments to the divorce, Wallerstein and Kelly

(1980a, 1980b) emphasized that in the majority of cases the most important variable was the positive involvement of both the father and the mother. At the 5-year postdivorce assessment, almost a third (30 percent) of the children had an emotionally meaningful *and* warm relationship with their fathers. This type of positive relationship with the father was strongly associated with a healthy adjustment for both boys and girls. The investigators point out the importance of frequent but flexible father–child visiting patterns. Again, such findings suggest that even when divorce results in the child not living with the father, it does not mean that he or she has to be father-absent in a general way. It is clear that many of the children who resided with their mothers still enjoyed much better relationships with their fathers than many children from intact families do.

Wallerstein and Kelly underscore the importance of the child's relationships with both parents, the support that the mother gives to the father's visitation (or that the father gives to the mother's visitation), and the ability of the divorced parents to develop ways to cooperate in terms of dealing with the needs of their children, even though they are no longer married. Only in instances where a father was seriously disturbed or abusive did it seem that the child was better off having no contact with him. Although there was often much initial conflict, a relationship with an interested stepfather appeared generally to have positive benefits for most of the children. Those over the age of 8 often had particular difficulties in accepting a stepfather, but at least most of the younger children seemed to be able to enlarge their view of their family constructively to allow for positive feelings toward both their fathers and stepfathers (Wallerstein & Kelly, 1980a, 1980b).

THE MOTHER–CHILD RELATIONSHIP

There are many factors that can affect the way in which the child is influenced by divorce and father absence. The quality of mothering a child receives is crucial and can become even more important when the child is paternally deprived. In this section, I emphasize the way in which variations in mothering may be related to individual differences in the father-absent deprived child's behavior. The major topics considered include the influence of the mother's evaluation of the absent father, matrifocal families, and dimensions of effective mothering.

Maternal attitudes are of critical significance when a boy's father is absent. In his study of children separated from their fathers during wartime, Bach (1946) described "curiously ambivalent aggressive affectionate father fantasies in some cases where maternal father-typing tended to be depreciative" (p. 75).

Wylie and Delgado (1959) analyzed the family backgrounds of aggressive fatherless boys referred to a child guidance clinic. With few exceptions, the mothers described their ex-husbands and sons in highly similar and negative terms, emphasizing the dangerously aggressive quality of their behavior. Koph (1970) found that poor school adjustment among father-absent boys was associated with their mothers' negative attitude toward their absent husbands. Clinical cases dramatically illustrate how the mother's consistently derogatory comments about the absent father can contribute to the development of a poor self-concept and maladaptive behavior in the child (Neubauer, 1960). As might be expected, maternal attitudes concerning the absent father influence the child's reaction if the father returns home (Biller, 1978; Stolz et al., 1954).

The mother's evaluation of the absent father is often related to the reason for his being absent. Feelings of resentment and loneliness can be associated with many different reasons for husband absence, but it is usually easier for a mother to talk positively about a husband who has died than one who has divorced or deserted her (Benson, 1968; Hetherington, 1972). Discussing the absent father with her children may be very frustrating for the mother, and when the father is absent because of divorce or desertion, such discussion may be even more painful. It is very difficult to maintain a positive image of the father in the face of the conflict and competition concerning children that often takes place before, during, and after a divorce. Sociocultural factors can also influence the family's reaction to father absence. For example, divorce seems to be less acceptable and more disruptive for Catholic and Jewish families than for Protestant families (Rosenberg, 1965).

Loss of the father through death may lead to more acute behaviorial reactions in children than loss of the father because of other factors, but father absence may have general effects on personality irrespective of the reason (Biller, 1971b). If the reason for father absence has an impact on the child's personality development, much of the effect is mediated through the mother–child relationship.[1]

The father–child relationship prior to father absence and the child's age at the onset of the absence are also very important factors in determining the extent of the influence of maternal attitudes toward the absent father. For example, the father-absent boy who has had a positive relationship with his father up until 10 years of age is less likely to be influenced by negative maternal views concerning the father than the boy who was paternally deprived even before his father's absence. Unfortunately, there have not been systematic investigations of how the reasons for father absence at different developmental periods influences the mother–child relationship.

---

[1] Researchers should also examine why certain women remain unmarried or without consistent male companionship. Long-term father or father surrogate absence, as well as onset of father absence is, in some cases, much a function of the mother's attitudes toward men.

Matrifocal Families

Negative evaluation of the father often occurs in matrifocal families, (The female-centered family is sometimes referred to as "matriarchal" but the term matrifocal seems a more accurate label.) This type of family is very common in lower socioeconomic neighborhoods and appears to be particularly prevalent among lower-class blacks (Pettigrew, 1964). There are many black families of lower socioeconomic status in which the father is a respected and integral member, but there seem to be even more in which he is absent or a relatively peripheral member (Dai, 1953; Frazier, 1939).

Sociocultural factors lessen the probability of long-term marriage relationships among lower-class blacks (Pettigrew, 1964). The instability of marriage relationships among lower-class blacks may be related to the fact that individuals with certain personality patterns are predisposed to become divorced and/or to seek out very tangential marriage relationships (Grønseth, 1957; Loeb, 1966). Because of their inability to tolerate close relationships with men, some women marry men whose personality functioning and/or occupational commitments do not allow them to get very involved in family life. The wife's negative attitudes concerning men can be a central factor in the husband's decision to desert her and his children.

The mother who has a positive attitude concerning masculinity can facilitate her father-absent child's personality development. For instance, by praising the absent father's competence she may be able to help her son learn to value his own maleness. However, maternal deprecation of the father's masculinity can lead the young boy to avoid acting masculine, at least until the time he comes into contact with his peer culture.

Maternal attitudes concerning masculinity and men form a significant part of the mother–son relationship, and a mother is apt to view her husband and her son in a similar manner. Nevertheless, maternal reactions are not independent from individual differences in children. The degree to which a mother perceives her son or daughter as similar to the father is often related to the child's behavorial and physical characteristics. For example, if a boy very much resembles his father facially and physically it is more likely that the mother will expect her son's behavior to approximate his father's than if there were little father–son resemblance.

Overprotection

Maternal overprotection is a frequent concomitant of paternal deprivation. In families in which maternal overprotection exists, the father generally plays a very submissive and ineffectual role (Levy, 1943). When fathers are actively involved with their families, they are usually very critical of having their children overprotected, and they also serve as models for independent behavior. If the father is absent, the probability of a pattern of maternal overprotection is often increased. The child's age at the onset of father absence is an important variable. The boy who becomes father absent during infancy or during his preschool years is more likely to be overprotected by his mother, but if father absence begins when the boy is older, he may be expected to take over many of the responsibilities that his father had previously assumed.

Stendler (1952) described two critical periods in the development of overdependency: (1) at around 9 months, when the child first begins to test if the mother will meet his or her dependency needs; and (2) from 2 to 3 years of age, when the child must give up the perceived control of the mother and learn to act independently in culturally approved ways. Paternal deprivation during these periods can make the child particularly prone to overdependency. Studying first-grade children, Stendler (1954) found that many children who were rated overdependent by their teachers came from families with high rates of father absence. Among the 20 overdependent children, 13 lacked the consistent presence of the father in the home during the first 3 years of life, compared to only six of 20 in the control group. Moreover, the six relatively father absent children in the control group generally had been without their fathers for a much shorter time than the overdependent children. The actively involved father discourages the mother's overprotecting tendencies and encourages independent activity, especially in the boy. Unfortunately, Stendler did not give separate data analyses for boys and girls.

Retrospective maternal reports compiled by Stolz et al. (1954) suggested that mothers whose husbands were away in military service tended to restrict their infants' locomotor activities to a greater extent than mothers whose husbands were present did. However, these findings might also be more meaningful if the researchers had presented separate analyses in terms of the sex of the child. Similar results were reported by Tiller (1958) in his study with mothers of 8- and 9-year-old Norwegian children. Compared to the control group mothers, those whose husbands were seldom home (sailor officers) were more overprotective, as judged by maternal interview data and by the children's responses to a structured doll play test.

The Stolz et al. (1954) and Tiller (1958) investigations suggest that paternally deprived and maternally overprotected boys are particularly likely to suffer in terms of their masculine development. In a study of 5-year-old children, Biller (1974) found that mothers of father-absent boys were less encouraging of independent and aggressive behavior than mothers of father-present boys were. Many of the informal responses of the husband-absent mothers indicated that they were particularly afraid that their children would be physically injured.

An intense relationship with the mother and little opportunity to observe appropriate male–female interactions is more common when the child is father-absent. A close-binding mother–son relationship in the context of paternal deprivation is a frequent factor contributing to difficulties in heterosexual relationships and in the etiology of homosexuality (Biller, 1974c).

Sociocultural Context

In assessing variables that influence the behavior of the husband-absent mother, economic and social difficulties cannot be overlooked (e.g., Glasser & Navarre, 1965). In a provocative article, Kriesberg (1967, p. 288) described the plight of the mother whose husband is absent:

His absence is likely to mean that his former wife is poor, lives in poor neighborhoods, and lacks social, emotional, and physical assistance in childrearing. Furthermore, how husbandless mothers accommodate themselves to these circumstances can have important consequences for their children.

The degree to which the husbandless mother has social and economic resources available to her can influence the child's interpersonal and educational opportunities. Kellam, Ensminger, and Turner's (1978) research indicates that a major difficulty in the economically disadvantaged father-absent home is that the mother is flooded with responsibilities but often has no other adult to help her. Mother-alone families were much more likely to be related to children's social and personal maladjustment among poor black children than father-present families were. Families in which there was both a mother and grandmother, however, were associated with less developmental risk for children than families where the mother had all the childraising responsibility.

Paternal absence or inadequacy adds to the generally debilitating effects already experienced by the economically disadvantaged segment of our society. Paternal absence or inadequacy is often associated with a lack of material resources. Economic deprivation can make it much more difficult for father-absent children to avail themselves of experiences that might positively affect their development. Consistent economic deprivation makes it easy to develop a defeatist attitude about one's potential impact on the environment. As Herzog and Sudia (1973) cogently pointed out, many researchers uncritically assume that a child's personality difficulties simply are caused by father absence and do not consider the impact of economic deprivation.

The mother's attitudes are related to her social and economic opportunities and are readily transmitted to the child. Maternal views concerning the worth of education are linked to sociocultural backgrounds. As a function of differing maternal values and reinforcement patterns, middle-class father-absent children are generally less handicapped in intellectual pursuits than are lower-class father-absent children. Middle-class father-absent boys appear to receive more maternal encouragement for school achievement than lower-class father-absent boys do (Biller, 1974a, 1974b).

Effective Mothering

The mother–child relationship can stimulate or hinder adequate personality development. When children are paternally deprived, their relationships with their mothers are particularly influential. McCord, McCord, and Thurber (1962) analyzed social workers' observations to 10- to 15-year-old lower-class boys. The presence of a rejecting and/or disturbed mother was related to various problems (sexual anxiety, regressive behavior, and criminal acts) in father-absent boys; but father-absent boys who had seemingly well-adjusted mothers were much less likely to have such problems.

Pedersen (1966) compared a group of emotionally disturbed boys with a group of nondisturbed boys. The boys were all from military families and ranged in age from 11 to 15. Relatively long periods of father absence were common for both the emotionally disturbed and nondisturbed children. However, it was only in the disturbed group that the degree of father absence was related to level of emotional disturbance (measured by the Rogers Test of Personality Adjustment). Pedersen also found that the mothers of the emotionally disturbed children were themselves more disturbed (in terms of MMPI responses) than the mothers of the nondisturbed children. An implication of these findings is that psychologically healthy mothers may be able to counteract some of the effects of paternal deprivation.

Using a retrospective interview technique, Hilgard, Neuman, and Fisk (1960) studied adults whose fathers had died when they were children. These investigators concluded that the mother's ego strength was an important determinant of her child's adjustment as an adult. Mothers who could utilize their own and outside resources and assume some of the dual functions of mother and father with little conflict appeared to be able to deal constructively with the problems of raising a fatherless family. Such women were described as relatively feminine while their husbands were alive but as secure enough in their basic sex role identifications to perform some of the traditional functions of the father after he had died. It is important to emphasize that the mother's ego strength rather than her warmth or tenderness seemed to be essential variable in her child's adjustment. When children are paternally deprived, excessive maternal warmth and affection may be particularly detrimental to their personality development. A close-binding, overprotective relationship can severely hamper their opportunities for interpersonal growth.

When a mother is generally competent in interpersonal and environmental interactions, she may be an important model for her child. However, children's personality development seems to be facilitated only if the parent allows them sufficient freedom and responsibility to imitate effective parental behaviors (Biller, 1969a, 1971a). Maternal encouragement of masculine behavior seems particularly important for the father-absent boy. In a study of kindergarten boys, Biller (1969b) assessed maternal encouragement of masculine behavior with a multiple choice questionnaire. The measure of maternal encouragement of masculine behavior was significantly related to the father-absent boys' masculinity as assessed by a game preference measure and a multidimensional rating scale filled out by teachers. Father-absent boys whose mothers accepted and reinforced assertive, aggressive, and independent behavior were more masculine than father-absent boys whose mothers discouraged such behavior. The degree of maternal encouragement for masculine behavior was not significantly related to the father-present boys' masculine development.

The father–son relationship appears to be more critical than the mother–son relationship when the father is present, and it can be predicted that maternal encouragement and expectations concerning sex role behavior are less important when the father is present than when he is absent. For instance, a warm relationship with a masculine and salient father can outweigh the effects of a mildly overprotective mother. However, maternal behavior is an especially significant variable in facilitating or inhibiting masculine development in the young, father-absent boy. The mother can, by reinforcing specific responses and expecting masculine behavior, increase the father-absent boy's perception of the incentive value of the masculine role. Such maternal behavior can promote a positive view of males as salient and powerful and thus motivate the boy to imitate their behavior.

Father absence generally has more of a retarding impact on the boy's sex role orientation than it does on his sex role preference or his sex role adoption. Sex role preference and adoption seem more easily influenced by maternal behavior. However, if a father-absent boy receives both consistent maternal and peer group reinforcement, he is likely to view himself and his masculinity positively and develop a masculine sex role orientation at least by his middle school years.

Father absence before the child is 5 years old has more effect on the boy's masculine development than father absence after that age, and the mother–child relationship is particularly crucial when a boy becomes father-absent early in life. Biller and Bahm (1971) found that the degree of perceived maternal encouragement for masculine behavior was highly related to the masculinity of junior high school boys who had been father-absent since before the age of 5. (Encouragement for aggressive behavior was assessed by the subjects' responses to a Q-sort procedure and by their masculinity by their self-descriptions on an adjective checklist.) Among the boys who became father absent before the age of 5, those who perceived their mothers as encouraging their assertive and aggressive behavior had much more masculine self-concepts than those who perceived their mothers as discouraging such behavior. Although the researchers have not systematically analyzed how such variables as the age of onset of father absence may interact with the quality of maternal behavior, other data also suggest that effective mothering can insulate the father–absent child from emotional and interpersonal adjustment problems (Biller, 1974c; Longabaugh, 1973; Kagel, White & Coyne, 1978; Santrock & Warshak, 1979).

Boss's (1977) work underscores the crucial role of the mother in the father-absent family. She cogently stressed the dysfunctioning of a family that focuses on the psychological presence of a father who is actually physically absent. The absent father can be treated as if he just left the home temporarily when in reality he is not coming back. Boss (and others who have studied families of fathers who are missing-in-action) was impressed by the tenacious rigidity of some of the families in supporting the notion of pervasive father presence, even though several years had passed since there had been any indication that the father was still alive.

It is very important for the family to resolve the ambiguity of the situation by redistributing various role functions and realistically acknowledging that the father is not coming back. Boss found that the emotional health of the family was highly related to the wife's ability to accept the reality that her husband was no longer an active part of the family, except in the sense that the family was still receiving a military allotment. The mother's ability to go on with her own life, strive for personal growth, have close relations with others, seek further education, and develop plans to remarry all were strongly related to her children's emotional adjustment. Of course, such data should not be seen as inconsistent with the mother supporting positive memories about the father. Letters, photographs, home movies, possessions and accomplishments relating to the father, as well as the mother's descriptions, can play a very constructive role in helping children develop a concrete and positive image of a father they may have never even known (Biller, 1974c; 1978). A major implication from Boss's work is that the mother should not encourage unrealistic expectations concerning the continuing and future role of a father who is not going to return.

Hetherington, Cox, and Cox's (1978) research revealed a wealth of data highlighting the importance of individual differences in the mother–child relationship in a father-absent home. In their study assessing the impact of divorce on young children, they found that a positive relationship with the mother was likely to be associated with a healthy social and emotional adjustment in the child. Even in the case where there were conflictual mother–father relations, a good mother–child relationship seemed capable of serving as a buffer for the child in the father-absent home. The quality of the mother–child relationship in the father-absent home had much impact on the cognitive, sex role, and social functioning of the young children. Mothers who were authoritative and helped present a structured and orderly environment seemed to facilitate the father-absent child's cognitive functioning and ability to develop self-control. Mothers who reinforced sex typed behavior, encouraged independent and exploratory behavior, were low in anxiety, and had a positive view of the child's father seemed particularly likely to facilitate the father-absent boy's masculine development. In contrast, a combination of maternal fearfulness and inhibition, maternal discouragement of independence, and maternal disapproval of the father were found to be associated with anxious dependency and a feminine pattern of behavior in some of the father-absent boys.

RESEARCH IMPLICATIONS

It is useful to note some of the major research avenues that are worthy of further exploration in the attempt to understand the complex impact of father absence and divorce on child development. I emphasize that we should take a developmental, longitudinal and multivariable perspective to gain more of a grasp on the influence of father absence and divorce. Carefully selected comparison groups obviously are needed, and any such approach should take process variables into account and consider possible advantages as well as deficits that the father-absent child may encounter. Researchers need to consider the potential interactions of biological-constitutional, family, and sociocultural variables.

A longitudinal developmental approach may help give more attention to both genetic and prenatal environmental factors. Further scientific advances could lead to a clearer indication of the father's genetic contribution even if he no longer plays a direct behavorial role in the child's life. For instance, how are positive and negative temperamental patterns in the child influenced by the father's genetic contribution? There is some evidence that father absence may be at least indirectly associated with maternal stress factors during the prenatal period, and this may have negative effects on fetal development. For example, among poor expectant mothers, those without husbands seem particularly unlikely to receive adequate prenatal care. Among couples, even when unwed, the expectant father can give the expectant mother an emotional source of support and in a practical way may be a factor in her going to a physician (Biller & Salter, 1981). Some research evidence has indicated that the expectant father's death during the prenatal period is associated with a higher probability of behavior disorders in the child (Huttunen & Niskanen, 1978). It is possible that in some cases a highly negative maternal stress reaction may damage the fetus, and the mother who lacks the father's support during the birth process is less likely to adequately nurture the newborn infant. Certainly these explanations are speculative, but they could provoke some exciting research projects.

It is important to consider the child's characteristics if we are to understand the impact of father absence. We need more research that will assess carefully how sex and temperament differences, as well as the level of intellectual and social functioning can influence children's adaptation to father absence. Some of my research, for example, suggests that young children who are highly physically and intellectually competent at the onset of father absence are not as handicapped as children who are average or below average in their developmental level (Biller, 1974c). We need more data on so-called invulnerable children. The child's temperament and behavior certainly can have a large impact on the quality of the mother–child relationship and other adult–child relationships. Researchers need to be aware of various family structure and social system variables, including the sibling composition of the family and availability of surrogate models. The child's characteristics and the parents' difficulty in dealing with them may actually be a factor contributing to the father's unavailability and/or parental divorce.

The reason for the father's absence is another important variable. Divorce seems to have very different consequences for the child than the death of the father or the father's absence because of employment do. The mother's reaction to her husband's absence can be very influential. There needs to be more research focusing on how the reasons and the perceptions of the reasons for divorce may relate to the child's adaptation. For example, how much difference does it make if the same-sex, noncustodial parent is perceived by the child as the parent who initiated the divorce? Of course, such variables need to be considered in a social-systems context.

Researchers comparing father-absent families with intact families can more carefully analyze individual differences in family functioning among all types (and subtypes) of family patterns. For example, although studying the father-absent family may be of heuristic value in suggesting certain functions of fathers that may not be fulfilled, such research is no substitute for direct analysis of the father's complex role in the intact family. We can profit from much more research on the family dynamics process in both father-present and father-absent homes, with particular emphasis on parent–child–sibling interactions. Other sources of interpersonal influence, including extended family and peers, should also be considered.

An approach that takes into account the developmental stages of various family members as well as the quality of family functioning could be very revealing in understanding the impact of the divorce process on the child. For example, the reaction of different individuals in the family at various times, pre- and postdivorce, may greatly influence the child's short and/or long-term adaptation. A longitudinal perspective will help differentiate what may be short-term setbacks or spurts in development from what may be long-term deficits or gains in later functioning. Certainly a more limited cross-sectional approach can still at least consider the impact of divorce and father absence for children at specific developmental periods.

It is very clear from data reviewed in this chapter that divorce does not necessarily mean that a child will be father absent. Many fathers are able to visit and be involved with their children, and still others have shared, joint, or full custody of their children. An analysis of different types of custody patterns can help us to learn more about how the father's availability and quality of functioning (along with the interaction of other factors) influences the child whose parents are divorced.

Future research also should lead to a much clearer delineation of the kinds of maternal behaviors and the dimensions of the mother–child relationship that are relevant to the father-absent child's personality development. In an earlier section of this chapter some research concerning the effects of father absence on the girl's personality development is reviewed, and it is important for investigators studying the impact of father absence to systematically examine the possible differential effects of the mother–child relationship as a function of the sex of a child. Data from such studies can be useful for programs designed to maximize the interpersonal and intellectual potential of father-absent children and to help mothers in father-absent families become more effective parents.

THERAPY AND PREVENTION

Since paternally deprived individuals are overrepresented among individuals with psychological problems, it is not surprising that they are found in abundance in the case reports of psychotherapists. Despite the lack of controlled research, there are many illuminating descriptions of how psychotherapists have attempted to help father-absent or inadequately fathered children. (e.g., Forrest, 1966, 1967; Green, 1974; Meerloo, 1956; Neubauer, 1960; Wylie & Delgado, 1959).

Glueck and Glueck (1950) reported that many delinquent boys who form a close relationship with a father surrogate resolve their antisocial tendencies. Trenaman (1952) found that young men who had been chronically delinquent while serving in the British army improved as a function of their relationships with father surrogates. A father-absent boy may be particularly responsive to a male therapist or role model because of his motivation for male companionship. Rexford (1964), in describing the treatment of young antisocial children, noted that therapists are more likely to be successful with father-absent boys than with boys who have strongly identified with an emotionally disturbed, criminal, or generally inadequate father.

There are many organizations, including Big Brothers, Y.M.C.A., Boy Scouts, athletic teams, camps, churches, and settlement houses. that provide paternally deprived children with meaningful father surrogates. Additional professional consultation and more community support (especially more father surrogates), would allow these organizations to be of even greater benefit to many more children (Biller, 1974c; Brody, 1978; Jenkins, 1979).

Available research indicates that even in the first few years of life, the child's personality development can be very much influenced by the degree and type of involvement of a father or father surrogate. Group settings such as daycare centers can be used as vehicles to provide father surrogates for many children. The facilities of such organizations as Big Brothers and the Y.M.C.A. could also be utilized to help younger children.

Educational Implications

Our educational system could do much to mitigate the effects of paternal deprivation if more male teachers were available, particularly in nursery school, kindergarten, and the early elementary school grades. Competent and interpersonally able male teachers could facilitate the cognitive development of many children as well as contribute to their general social functioning (Biller, 1974a, 1974b; Sexton, 1969).

There is much need for greater incentives to encourage more males to become teachers of young children. There has to be more freedom and autonomy to innovate, as well as greater financial rewards. We must make both men and women aware of the impact that males can have in child development and the importance of male influence in the early years of the child's development.

Fathers and father surrogates can be made more knowledgeable about the significance of the father in child development through education and the mass media (Biller & Meredith, 1972, 1974). Such exposure, along with other programs, can lessen the number of families that become father absent. Explicit advantages such as financial and other support for fathers remaining with their families in contrast to the current rewarding of father absence by many welfare departments might do much to keep some families intact and reconstitute other families.

Preventive programs can focus on families that seem to have a high risk of becoming father absent. Systematic techniques can be developed to determine the potential consequences of father absence for a family that is considering separation or divorce. There are many families in which both the parents and the children would be able to function better subsequent to divorce. When the divorce process is taking place, more consideration should be given to whether all or some of the children might benefit from remaining with their fathers (Biller & Meredith, 1974). Data collected by Santrock and Warshack (1979) suggest that it may be advantageous for children whose parents divorce to live with the same-sex parent. It is usually easier to find mother surrogates (e.g., grandmothers, housekeepers) than father surrogates. It is also relevant to consider potential paternal effectiveness in placing children with adoptive or foster parents. There is much evidence that fathers can be just as effective parents as mothers can whether in a typical nuclear family or as single parents (Biller & Meredith, 1974; Walters, 1976).

Much more needs to be done to support continued father–child interactions in families in which the parents are divorced or in the process of becoming divorced (Biller & Meredith, 1974). Recent research has clearly indicated the benefits of frequent father–child contact when parents are divorced (Abarbanel, 1979; Keshet & Rosenthal, 1978; Wallerstein & Kelly, 1980). Furthermore, there is increasing evidence concerning the advantages for children (and parents) when a joint custody and/or shared parenting arrangement is put into effect (Abarbanel, 1979; Biller & Meredith, 1974; Greif, 1979; Hetherington, Cox, & Cox, 1978; Roman & Haddad, 1978; Rosenthal & Keshet, 1981; Wallerstein & Kelly, 1980a, 1980b).

Much of the recent research on the impact of divorce on various family members has emphasized that parents' difficulties in coping with their own needs may interfere with their adequacy in dealing with their children's distress (Hetherington, Cox, & Cox, 1978; Wallerstein & Kelly, 1980a, b). Parents in the one-parent family must not be neglected. For example, the mother's reaction to husband absence may greatly influence the extent to which father absence or lack of father availability affects her children. She is often in need of psychological as well as social and economic support. Mental health professionals have outlined many useful techniques for helping mothers and children in fatherless families (e.g., Baker et al., 1968; Despert, 1953; Hill, 1949; Jenkins, 1979; Jones, 1963; Klein, 1973; Lerner, 1954; McDermott, 1968; Weiss, 1975; Wylie & Delgado, 1959).

In a pilot project, one of the central goals of a welfare mothers' group was to help husbandless mothers deal constructively with their social and familial problems (Biller & Smith, 1972). Pollak (1970) discussed the frequent interpersonal and sexual problems of parents without partners and gave some excellent suggestions for helping such parents cope with their concerns. Educational and therapeutic groups such as Parents Without Partners can be very meaningful for the wifeless father as well as the husbandless mother (e.g., Egelson & Frank, 1961; Freudenthal, 1959; Jenkins, 1979; Schlesinger, 1966; Wallerstein & Kelly, 1977; Weiss, 1975).

A significant part of community mental health efforts, both in terms of prevention and treatment, should be to support fathers in being effective parents and to locate father surrogates for paternally deprived children. Far-reaching community, state, and government programs are needed. A vast number of children do not have consistent and meaningful contact with adult males. This very serious situation must be remedied if all our children are to take full advantage of their growing social and educational opportunities.

REFERENCES

Abarbanel, A. Shared parenting after separation and divorce; A study of joint custody. *American Journal of Orthopsychiatry,* 1979, **49,** 320–329.

Aichorn, A. *Wayward youth,* New York: Viking, 1935.

Albert, R. Cognitive development and parent loss among the gifted, the exceptionally gifted, and the creative. *Psychological Reports,* 1971, **29,** 19–26.

Altus, W. D. The broken home and factors of adjustment. *Psychological Reports,* 1958, **4,** 477.

Ancona, L., Cesa-Bianchi, M., & Bocquet, C. Identification with the father in the absence of the paternal model: Research applied to children of Navy officers. *Archivo di Psicologia Neurologia e Psichiatria,* 1964, **24,** 339–361.

Anderson, R. E. Where's Dad? Paternal deprivation and delinquency. *Archives of General Psychiatry,* 1968, **18,** 641–649.

Andrews, R. O. & Christensen, H. T. Relationship of absence of a parent to courtship status: A repeat study. *American Sociological Review,* 1951, **16,** 541–544.

Bach, G. R. Father-fantasies and father typing in father-separated children. *Child Development,* 1946, **17,** 63–80.

Bacon, M. K., Child, I. L., & Barry, H. A cross-cultural study of correlates of crime. *Journal of Abnormal and Social Psychology,* 1963, **66,** 291–300.

Baggett, A. T. The effect of early loss of father upon the personality of boys and girls in late adolescence. *Dissertation Abstracts,* 1967, **28** (1-B), 356–357.

Baker, S. L., Cove, L. A., Fagen, S. A., Fischer, E. G., & Janda, E. J. Impact of father-absence: III. Problems of family reintegration following prolonged father-absence. Paper presented at the meeting of the American Orthopsychiatric Association, Washington, D.C., March 1968.

Barclay, A. G., & Cusumano, D. Father-absence, cross-sex identity, and field-dependent behavior in male adolescents. *Child Development,* 1967, **38,** 243–250.

Baxter, J. C., Horton, D. L., & Wiley, R. E. Father identification as a function of the mother–father relationship. *Journal of Individual Psychology* 1964, **20,** 167–171.

Beck, A. T., Sehti, B. B., & Tuthill, R. W. Childhood bereavement and adult depression. *Archives of General Psychiatry,* 1963, **9,** 295–302.

Beller, E. K. Maternal behaviors in lower-class Negro mothers. Paper presented at the meeting of the Eastern Psychological Association, Boston, April 1967.

Benson, L. *Fatherhood: A sociological perspective.* New York: Random House, 1968.

Biller, H. B. A multiaspect investigation of masculine development in kindergarten-age boys. *Genetic Psychology Monographs*, 1968, **76,** 89–139 (a).

Biller, H. B. A note on father-absence and masculine development in young lower-class Negro and white boys. *Child Development*, 1968, **39,** 1003–1006 (b).

Biller, H. B. Father-absence, maternal encouragement, and sex-role development in kindergarten-age boys. *Child Development*, 1969, **40,** 539–546.

Biller, H. B. Father-absence and the personality development of the male child. *Developmental Psychology*, 1970, **2,** 181–201.

Biller, H. B. *Father, child, and sex role*, Lexington, Mass.: Heath 1971(a).

Biller, H. B. The mother–child relationship and the father-absent boy's personality development. *Merrill-Palmer Quarterly*, 1971, **17,** 227–241 (b).

Biller, H. B. Paternal and sex-role factors in cognitive and academic functioning. In. J. K. Cole & R. Dienstbier (Eds.), *Nebraska symposium on motivation, 1973*, Lincoln: University of Nebraska Press, 1974 (a).

Biller, H. B. Paternal deprivation, cognitive functioning and the feminized classroom. In A. Davids (Ed.), *Child personality and psychopathology: Current topics.* New York: Wiley, 1974 (b).

Biller, H. B. *Paternal Deprivation.* Lexington, Mass.: Heath, 1974 (c).

Biller, H. B. The effects of intermittent but prolonged absence of the father. *Medical Aspects of Human Sexuality*, 1975, **9,** 179.

Biller, H. B. The father-child relationship: Some crucial issues. In V. C. Vaughn & T. B. Brazelton, (Eds.), *The family—Can it be saved?* Chicago: Year Book Medical Publishers, 1976 (a).

Biller, H. B. The father and personality development: Paternal deprivation and sex-role development. In M. E. Lamb (Ed.), *The role of the father in child development.* New York: Wiley, 1976 (b).

Biller, H. B. Sex-role learning: Some comments and complexities from a multidimensional perspective. In S. Cohen & T. J. Comiskey (Eds), *Child development: A study of growth processes.* Ithaca, Ill.: Peacock, 1977.

Biller, H. B. Father absence and military families. In E. J. Hunter (Ed.), *A report on the military family research conference.* San Diego: Family Studies Branch, Naval Health Research Center, 1978.

Biller, H. B., & Bahm, R. M. Father-absence, perceived maternal behavior and masculinity of self-concept among junior high school boys. *Developmental Psychology*, 1971, **4,** 178–181.

Biller, H. B., & Borstelmann, L. J. Masculine development: An integrative review. *Merrill-Palmer Quarterly*, 1967, **13,** 253–294.

Biller, H. B., & Meredith, D. L. The invisible American father. *Sexual Behavior*, 1972, **2**(7), 16–22.

Biller, H. B., & Meredith, D. L. *Father power.* New York: David McKay, 1974.

Biller, H. B., & Salter, M. The adolescent unwed father. In C. J. Poole (Ed.), *Children bearing children: Adolescent pregnancy and parenthood.* North Scituate, Mass.: Duxbury Press, 1981.

Biller, H. B., & Smith, A. E. An AFDC mothers group: An exploratory effort in community mental health. *Family Coordinator,* 1972, **21**, 287–290.

Biller, H. B., & Weiss, S. The father-daughter relationship and the personality development of the female. *Journal of Genetic Psychology,* 1970, **114**, 79–93.

Blanchard, R. W., & Biller, H. B. Father availability and academic performance among third grade boys. *Developmental Psychology,* 1971, **4**, 301–305.

Boss, P. A clarification of the concept of psychological father presence in families experiencing ambiguity of boundary. *Journal of Marriage and the Family,* 1977, **39**, 141–151.

Brill N. Q., & Liston, E. H. Parental loss in adults with emotional disorders. *Archives of General Psychiatry,* 1966, **14**, 307–314.

Brody, S. Daddy's gone to Colorado: Male staffed child care for father absent boys. *Counseling Psychologist,* 1978, **7**, 33–36.

Bronfrenbrenner, U. The psychological costs of quality in education. *Child Development,* 1967, **38**, 909–925.

Brown, F. Depression and childhood bereavement. *Journal of Mental Science,* 1961, **107**, 754–777.

Brown, J. K. A cross-cultural study of female initiation rites. *American Anthropologist,* 1963, **65**, 837–853.

Burton, R. V. Cross-sex identity in Barbados. *Developmental Psychology,* 1972, **6**, 365–374.

Burton, R. V., & Whiting, J. W. M. The absent father and cross-sex identity. *Merrill-Palmer Quarterly,* 1961, **7**, 85–95.

Carlsmith, L. Effect of early father-absence on scholastic aptitude. *Harvard Educational Review,* 1964, **34**, 3–21.

Chein, I., Gerrard, D. L., Lee, B. S., & Rosenfeld, E. *The road to H.* New York: Basic Books, 1964.

Cobliner, W. G. Social factors in mental disorders: A contribution to the etiology of mental illness. *Genetic Psychology Monographs,* 1963, **67**, 151–215.

Coleman, J. S., et al. *Equality of educational opportunity.* Washington, D.C.: National Center for Educational Statistics, Office of Education, 1966.

Cortés, C. F., & Fleming, E. The effects of father absence on the adjustment of culturally disadvantaged boys. *Journal of Special Education,* 1968, **2**, 413–420.

Crook, T. & Eliot, J. Parental death during childhood and adult depression: A critical review of the literature. *Psychological Bulletin,* 1980, **87**, 252–259.

Crumley, F. E., & Blumenthal, D. S. Children's reactions to temporary loss of the father. *American Journal of Psychiatry,* 1973, **130**, 778–782.

Dai, B. Some problems of personality development among Negro children. In L. Kluckhohn, H. A. Murray, & D. M. Schneider (Eds.), *Personality in nature, society and culture.* New York: Knopf, 1953.

D'Andrade, R. G. Father absence, identification and identity. *Ethos*, 1973, **1**, 440–445.

DaSilva, G. The role of the father with chronic schizophrenic patients. *Journal of the Canadian Psychiatric Association,* 1963, **8**, 190–203.

Dennehey, C. Childhood bereavement and psychiatric illness. *British Journal of Psychiatry,* 1966, **112**, 1049–1069.

Despert, I. J. The fatherless family. *Child Study,* 1957, **34**, 22–28.

Deutsch, M. & Brown, B. Social influences in negro-white intelligence differences. *Journal of Social Issues*, 1964, **20**, 24–35.

Donini, G. P. An evaluation of sex-role identification among father-absent and father-present boys. *Psychology,* 1967, **4**, 13–16.

Douvan, E., & Adelson, J. *The adolescent experience.* New York: Wiley, 1966.

Drake, O. T., & McDougall, D. Effects of the absence of a father and other male models on the development of boys' sex roles. *Developmental Psychology,* 1977, **13**, 537–538.

Duke, M. & Lancaster, W. A. note on locus of control as a function of father absence. *Journal of Genetic Psychology*, 1976, **129**, 335–336.

Dyl, A. S., & Biller, H. B. Paternal absence, social class and readings achievement. Unpublished study, University of Rhode Island, 1973.

Egelson, J., & Frank, J. F. *Parents without partners.* New York: Dutton, 1961.

Eisenstadt, J. M., Parental loss and genius. *American Psychologist,* 1978, **33**, 211–223.

Elder, G. H., Jr., & Bowerman, C. C. Family structure and child-rearing patterns: The effect of family size and sex composition. *American Sociological Review,* 1963, **28**, 891–905.

Felner, R., Stolberg, A., & Cowen, E. Crisis events and school mental health referral patterns of young children. *Journal of Consulting and Clinical Psychology*, 1975, **43**, 305–310.

Fish, K. D. Paternal availability, family role-structure, maternal employment and personality development in late adolescent females. Unpublished doctoral dissertation, University of Massachusetts, 1969.

Forrest, T. Paternal roots of female character development. *Contemporary Psychoanalyst,* 1966, **3**, 21–28.

Forrest, T. The paternal roots of male character development. *The Psychoanalytic Review,* 1967, **54**, 81–99.

Frazier, E. F. *The Negro family in the United States.* Chicago: University of Chicago Press, 1939.

Freud, A., & Burlingham, D. T. *Infants without families.* New York: International Universities Press, 1944.

Freudenthal, K. Problems of the one-parent family. *Social Work,* 1959, **4,** 44–48.

Garbower, G. *Behavior problems of children in Navy officers' families: As related to social conditions of Navy family life.* Washington, D.C.: Catholic University Press, 1959.

Gay, M. J., & Tonge, W. L. The late effects of loss of parents in childhood. *British Journal of Psychiatry,* 1967, **113,** 753–759.

Glasser, P., & Navarre, E. Structural problems of the one-parent family. *Journal of Social Issues,* 1965, **21,** 98–109.

Glick, P.G., & Norton, A. J. Marrying, divorcing and living together in the U.S. today. *Population Bulletin,* 1978, **32,** 3–38.

Glueck, S., & Glueck, E. *Unravelling juvenile delinquency.* Cambridge, Mass.: Harvard University Press, 1950.

Goode, W. Family disorganization. In R. K. Merton & R. A. Nisbet (Eds.), *Contemporary social problems.* New York: Harcourt, Brace, and World, 1961.

Green, R. *Sexual identity conflict in children and adults.* New York: Basic Books, 1974.

Greenstein, J. F. Father characteristics and sex-typing. *Journal of Personality and Social Psychology,* 1966, **3,** 271–277.

Gregory, I. Studies of parental deprivation in psychiatric patients. *American Journal of Psychiatry,* 1958, **115,** 432–442.

Gregory, I. Anterospective data following childhood loss of a parent: I. Delinquency and high school dropout. *Archives of General Psychiatry,* 1965, **13,** 99–109 (a).

Gregory, I. Anterospective data following childhood loss of a parent: II. Pathology, performance, and potential among college students. *Archives of General Psychiatry,* 1965, **13,** 110–120 (b).

Grief, J. B. Fathers, children and joint custody. *American Journal of Othopsychiatry,* 1979, **49,** 311–319.

Gronseth, E. The impact of father–absence in sailor families upon the personality structure and social adjustment of adult sailor sons, part I. In N. Andersen (Ed.), *Studies of the family, Vol 2.* Gottingen: Vandenhoeck and Ruprecht, 1957.

Hainline, L., & Feig, E. The correlates of childhood father absence in college-aged women. *Child Development,* 1978, **49,** 37–42.

Hall, P., & Tonge, W. L. Long standing continuous unemployment in male patients with psychiatric symptoms. *British Journal of Preventative and Social Medicine,* 1963, **17,** 191–196.

Hamilton, D. M., & Wahl, J. G. The hospital treatment of dementia praecox. *American Journal of Psychiatry,* 1948, **104,** 346–352.

Haworth, M. R. Parental loss in children as reflected in projective responses. *Journal of Projective Techniques,* 1964, **28,** 31–35.

Heckel, R. V. The effects of fatherlessness on the pre-adolescent female. *Mental Hygiene,* 1963, **47,** 69–73.

Hecksher, B. J. Household structure and achievement orientation in lower-class Barbadian families. *Journal of Marriage and the Family,* 1967, **29**, 521–526.

Herzog, E., & Sudia, C. E. Children *in fatherless families.* In B. M. Caldwell & H. N. Ricciuti (Eds.), *Review of child development research,* Vol. 3. Chicago: University of Chicago Press, 1973.

Hetherington, E. M. Effects of paternal absence on sex-typed behaviors in Negro and white preadolescent males. *Journal of Personality and Social Psychology,* 1966, **4**, 87–91.

Hetherington, E. M. Effects of father-absence on personality development in adolescent daughters. *Developmental Psychology,* 1972, **7**, 313–326.

Hetherington, E. M. Divorce: A child's perspective. *American Psychologist,* 1979, **34**, 851–858.

Hetherington, E. M., Cox, M., & Cox, R. Divorced fathers. *Family Coordinator,* 1976, **25**, 417–428.

Hetherington, E. M., Cox, M., & Cox, R. Family interaction and the social, emotional and cognitive development of children following divorce. Paper presented at the Johnson and Johnson Conference on the Family, Washington, D.C., May 1978.

Hetherington, E. M., & Deur, J. The effects of father absence on child development. *Young Children,* 1971, **26**, 233–248.

Hetherington, E. M., & Parke, R. D. *Child psychology: A contemporary viewpoint,* 2nd ed. New York: McGraw-Hill, 1979.

Hilgard, J. R., Neuman, M. F., & Fisk, F. Strength of adult ego following bereavement. *American Journal of Orthopsychiatry,* 1960, **30**, 788–798.

Hill, O. W., & Price, J. S. Childhood bereavement and adult depression. *British Journal of Psychiatry,* 1967, **113**, 743–751.

Hill, R. *Families under stress.* New York: Harper, 1949.

Hoffman, M. L. Father-absence and conscience development. *Child Development,* 1971, **4**, 400–406 (a).

Hoffman, M. L. Identification and conscience development. *Child Development,* 1971, **42**, 1071–1082 (b).

Hunt, L. L., & Hunt, J. G. Race and the father–son connection: The conditional relevance of father absence for the orientations and identities of adolescent boys. *Social Problems,* 1975, **23**, 35–52.

Hunt, J. G., & Hunt, L. L. Race, daughters and father-loss: Does absence make the girl grow stronger? *Social Problems,* 1977, **25**, 90–102.

Huttunen, M. O., & Niskanen, P. Prenatal loss of father and psychiatric disorders. *Archives of General Psychiatry,* 1978, **35**, 429–431.

Ingham, H. V. A statistical study of family relationships in psychoneurosis. *American Journal of Orthopsychiatry,* 1949, **106**, 91–98.

Jacobson, G., & Ryder, R. G. Parental loss and some characteristics of the early marriage relationship. *American Journal of Orthopsychiatry,* 1969, **39**, 779–787.

Jenkins, S. Children of divorce. In S. Chess & A. Thomas (Eds.), *Annual progress in child psychiatry and child development, 1979*. New York: Brunner/Mazel, 1979.

Jones, E. *Raising your child in a fatherless home*. New York: MacMillan, 1963.

Kagel, S. A., White, R. M., Coyne, J. C. Father–absent and father–present families of disturbed and nondisturbed adolescents. *American Journal or Orthopsychiatry*, 1978, **48**, 342–352.

Kellam, S. G., Ensminger, M. E., & Turner, R. J. Family structure and the mental health of children. *Archives of General Psychiatry*, 1977, **34**, 1012–1022.

Kelly, F. J., & Baer, D. J. Age of male delinquents when father left home and recidivism. *Psychological Reports*, 1969, **25**, 1010.

Kelly, J. B., & Wallerstein, J. S. The effects of parental divorce: Experiences of the child in early latency. *American Journal of Orthopsychiatry*, 1976, **46**, 20–32.

Keshet, J., & Rosenthal, R. Fathering after marital separation. *Social Work*, 1978, **25**, 14–18.

Klein, C. *The single parent experience:* New York: Avon, 1973.

Koch, M. B. Anxiety in preschool children from broken homes. *Merrill-Palmer Quarterly*, 1961, **1**, 225–231.

Kohn, H. L. Social class and parental values. *American Journal of Sociology*, 1959, **64**, 337–351.

Kopf, K. E. Family variables and school adjustment of eighth grade father–absent boys. *Family Coordinator*, 1970, **19**, 145–150.

Kriesberg, L. Rearing children for educational achievement in fatherless families. *Journal of Marriage and The Family*, 1967, **29**, 288–301.

Lamb, M. E. (Ed.) *The role of the father in child development*. New York: Wiley, 1976.

Lamb, M. E. Paternal influences and the father's role: A personal perspective. *American Psychologist*, 1979, **34**, 938–943.

Lamb, M. E., & Lamb, J. E. The nature and importance of the father–child relationship. *Family Coordinator*, 1976, **25**, 370–386.

Landis, J. I. A reexamination of the role of the father as an index of family integration. *Marriage and Family Living*, 1962, **24**, 122–128.

Landis, P. H. *Making the most of marriage*. New York: Appleton-Century-Crofts, 1965.

Landy, F., Rosenberg, B. G., & Sutton-Smith, B. The effect of limited father absence on the cognitive and emotional development of children. Paper presented at the meeting of the Midwestern Psychological Association, Chicago, May 1967.

Langner, T. S., & Michael, S. T. *Life stress and mental health*. New York: Free Press, 1963.

Lawton, M. J., & Sechrest, L. Figure drawings by young boys from father-absent and father-present homes. *Journal of Clinical Psychology*, 1962, **18**, 304–305.

LeCorgne, L. C., & Laosa, L. M. Father absence in low-income Mexican-American families; Childrens' social adjustment and conceptual differentiation of sex-role attitudes. *Developmental Psychology*, 1976, **12**, 439–448.

Lederer, W. Dragons, delinquents, and destiny. *Psychological Issues*, 1964, **4** (Whole No. 3).

Lee, P. C., & Wolinsky, A. L. Male teachers of young children: A preliminary empirical study. *Young Children*, 1973, **28**, 342–352.

Leichty, M. M. The effect of father-absence during early childhood upon the Oedipal situation as reflected in young adults, *Merrill-Palmer Quarterly*, 1960, **6**, 212–217.

Leiderman, G. F. Effect of parental relationships and child-training practices on boys' interactions with peers. *Acta Psychologica*, 1959, **15**, 469.

Leonard, M. R. Fathers and daughters. *International Journal of Psychoanalysis*, 1966, **47**, 325–333.

Lerner, S. H. Effect of desertion on family life. *Social Casework*, 1954, **35**, 3–8.

Lessing, E. E., Zagorin, S. W., & Nelson, D. WISC subtest and IQ score correlates of father absence. *Journal of Genetic Psychology*, 1970, **67**, 181–195.

Levy, D. M. *Maternal overprotection*. New York: Columbia University Press, 1943.

Longabaugh, R. Mother behavior as a variable moderating the effects of father absence. *Ethos*, 1973, **1**, 456–477.

Loeb, J. The personality factor in divorce. *Journal of Consulting Psychology*, 1966, **30**, 562.

Louden, K. H. Field dependence in college students as related to father absence during the latency period. Unpublished doctoral dissertation, Graduate School of Psychology, Fuller Theological Seminary, 1973.

Lynn, D. B. *Parental and sex-role identification*. Berkeley: McCutchan, 1969.

Lynn, D. B. *The father: His role in child development*. Belmont, Calif.: Brooks/Cole, 1974.

Lynn, D. B., & Sawrey, W. L. The effects of father-absence on Norwegian boys and girls. *Journal of Abnormal and Social Psychology*, 1959, **59**, 258–262.

Mächtlinger, V. Psychoanalytic theory: Preoedipal and oedipal phases with special reference to the father. In M. E. Lamb (Ed.), *The role of the father in child development*. New York: Wiley, 1976.

Madow, L., & Hardy, S. E. Incidence and analysis of the broken family in the background of neurosis. *American Journal of Orthopsychiatry*, 1947, **17**, 521–528.

Maxwell, A. E. Discrepancies between the pattern of abilities for normal and neurotic children. *Journal of Mental Science*, 1961, **107**, 300–307.

McCord J., McCord W., & Howard, A. Family interaction as an antecedent to the direction of male aggressiveness. *Journal of Abnormal and Social Psychology*, 1963, **63**, 239–224.

McCord, J., McCord, W., & Thurber, E. Some effects of paternal absence on male children. *Journal of Abnormal and Social Psychology*, 1962, **64**, 361–369.

McDermott, J. F. Parental divorce in early childhood. *American Journal of Psychiatry,* 1968, **124,** 1424–1432.

Meerloo, J. A. M. The father cuts the cord: The role of the father as initial transference figure. *American Journal of Psychotherapy,* 1956, **10,** 471–480.

Miller, B. Effects of father-absence and mother's evaluation of father on the socialization of adolescent boys. Unpublished doctoral dissertation, Columbia University, 1961.

Miller, W. B. Lower-class culture as a generating milieu of gang delinquency. *Journal of Social Issues,* 1958, **14** 5–19.

Mischel, W. Preference for delayed reinforcement: An experimental study of cultural observation. *Journal of Abnormal and Social Psychology,* 1958, **56,** 57–61.

Mischel, W. Preference for delayed reward and social responsibility. *Journal of Abnormal and Social Psychology,* 1961, **62,** 1–7 (a).

Mischel, W. Father-absence and delay of gratification. *Journal of Abnormal and Social Psychology,* 1961, **62,** 116–124 (b).

Mischel, W. Delay of gratification, need for achievement, and acquiescence in another culture. *Journal of Abnormal and Social Psychology,* 1961, **62,** 543–552 (c).

Mitchell, D., & Wilson, W. Relationship of father-absence to masculinity and popularity of delinquent boys. *Psychological Reports,* 1967, **20,** 1173–1174.

Monahan, T. P. Family status and the delinquent child. *Social Forces,* 1957, **35,** 250–258.

Moynihan, D. P. *The Negro family: The case for national action.* Washington, D.C.: U.S. Department of Labor, 1965.

Mueller, C., & Pope, H. Marital instability: A study of its transmission between generations. *Journal of Marriage and the Family,* 1977, **39,** 83–93.

Nash, J. The father in contemporary culture and current psychological literature. *Child Development,* 1965, **36,** 261–297.

Nelsen, E. A., & Maccoby, E. E. The relationship between social development and differential abilities on the scholastic aptitude test. *Merrill—Palmer Quarterly,* 1966, **12,** 269–289.

Nelsen, E. A., & Vangen, P. M. The impact of father absence upon heterosexual behaviors and social development of preadolescent girls in a ghetto environment. *Proceedings of the 79th Annual Convention of the American Psychological Association,* 1971, **6,** 165–166.

Neubauer, P. B. The one-parent child and his Oedipal development. *The Psychoanalytic Study of the Child,* 1960, **15,** 286–309.

Norton, A. Incidence of neurosis related to maternal age and birth order. *British Journal of Social Medicine,* 1952, **6,** 253–258.

Nye, F. I. Child adjustment in broken and unhappy homes. *Marriage and Family Living,* 1957, **19,** 356–361.

Oltman, J. E., & Friedman, S. Parental deprivation in psychiatric conditions: III. In personality disorders and other conditions. *Diseases of the Nervous System,* 1967, **28**, 298–303.

Oltman, J. E., McGarry, J. J., & Friedman, S. Parental deprivation and the broken home in dementia pracecox and other mental disorders. *American Journal of Psychiatry,* 1952, **108**, 685–694.

Parish, T. S., & Copeland, T. F. Locus of control and father loss. *Journal of Genetic Psychology,* 1980, **136**, 147–148.

Parke, R. D. Perspectives on father-infant interaction. In J. D. Osofsky (Ed.), *Handbook of infant development.* New York: Wiley, 1979.

Pedersen, F. A. Relationships between father-absence and emotional disturbance in male military dependents. *Merrill-Palmer Quarterly,* 1966, **12**, 321–331.

Pedersen, F. A. Does research on children reared in father-absent homes yield information on father influences? *Family Coordinator,* 1976, **25**, 458–464.

Pedersen, F. A., Rubenstein, J., & Yarrow, L. J. Infant development in father-absent families. *Journal of Genetic Psychology,* 1979, **135**, 51–61.

Pettigrew, T. F. *A profile of the Negro American.* Princeton, N.J.: Van Nostrand, 1964.

Phelan, H. M. The incidence and possible significance of the drawing of female figures by sixth-grade boys in response to the Draw-a-Person Test. *Psychiatric Quarterly,* 1954, **38**, 1–16.

Pollak, G. K. Sexual dynamics of parents without partners. *Social Work,* 1970, **15**, 79–85.

Pope, B. Socioeconomic contrasts in children's peer culture prestige values. *Genetic Psychology Monographs,* 1953, **48,** 157–200.

Radin, N. The role of the father in cognitive, academic, and intellectual development. In M. E. Lamb (Ed.), *The role of the father in child development,* New York: Wiley, 1976.

Reuter, M. W., & Biller, H. B. Perceived paternal nurturance-availability and personality adjustment among college males. *Journal of Consulting and Clinical Psychology,* 1973, **40**, 339–342.

Rexford, E. N. Antisocial young children and their families. In M. R. Haworth (Ed.), *Child psychotherapy.* New York: Basic Books, 1964.

Rogers, W. B., & Long, J. M. Male models and sexual identification: A case from the Out Island Bahamas. *Human Organization,* 1958, **27**, 326–331.

Rohrer, H. H., & Edmonson, M. S. *The eighth generation.* New York: Harper, 1960.

Roman, M., & Haddad, W. *The disposable parent.* New York: Holt, Rinehart, & Winston, 1978.

Rosenberg, M. *Society and the adolescent self-image.* Princeton: Princeton University Press, 1965.

Rosenthal, K., & Keshet, H. F. *Fathers without partners: A study of fathers and the family after marital separation.* Totowa, N.J.: Rowman & Littlefield, 1981.

Rubenstein, C. The children of divorce as adults. *Psychology Today,* 1980, **14**, 74–75.

Rutter, M. Parent-child separation: Psychological effects on children. *Journal of Child Psychology and Psychiatry,* 1971, **12**, 233–260.

Santrock, J. W. Paternal absence, sex-typing, and identification. *Developmental Psychology,* 1970, **2**, 264–272 (a).

Santrock, J. W. Influence of onset and type of paternal absence on the first four Eriksonian developmental crises. *Developmental Psychology,* 1970, **3**, 273–274 (b).

Santrock, J. W. Relation of type and onset of father-absence to cognitive development. *Child Development,* 1972, **43**, 455–469.

Santrock, J. W. Father absence, perceived maternal behavior, and moral development in boys. *Child Development,* 1975, **46**, 753–757.

Santrock, J. W. Effects of father absence on sex-typed behaviors in male children: Reason for the absence and age of onset of the absence. *Journal of Genetic Psychology,* 1977, **130**, 3–10.

Santrock, J. W., & Tracy, R. L. Effects of children's family structure status on the development of stereotypes by teachers. *Journal of Educational Psychology,* 1978, **70**, 754–757.

Santrock, J. W., & Warshak, R. A. Father custody and social development in boys and girls. *Journal of Social Issues,* 1979, **35**, 112–125.

Santrock, J. W., & Wohlford, P. Effects of father absence: Influences of reason for and onset of absence. *Proceedings of the 78th Annual Convention of the American Psychological Association,* 1970, **5**, 265–266.

Schlesinger, B. The one-parent family: An overview. *Family Life Coordinator,* 1966, **15**, 133–137.

Sears, P. S. Doll-play aggression in normal young children: Influence of sex, age, sibling status, father's absence. *Psychological Monographs,* 1951, **65** (Whole No. 6).

Sears, R. R., Pintler, M. H., & Sears, P. S. Effect of father-separation on pre-school children's doll-play aggression. *Child Development,* 1946, **17**, 219–243.

Seward, G. H. Cultural conflict and the feminine role: An experimental study. *Journal of Social Psychology,* 1945, **22**, 177–194.

Sexton, P. C. *The feminized male: Classrooms, white collars, and the decline of manliness.* New York: Random House, 1969.

Shinn, M. Father absence and children's cognitive development. *Psychological Bulletin,* 1978, **85**, 295–324.

Siegman, A. W. Father-absence during childhood and antisocial behavior. *Journal of Abnormal Psychology,* 1966, **71**, 71–74.

Stanfield, R. E. The interaction of family variables and gang variables in the aetiology of delinquency. *Social Problems,* 1966, **13**, 411–417.

Stendler, C. B. Critical periods in socialization and overdependency. *Child Development,* 1952, **23**, 3–12.

Stendler, C. B. Possible causes of overdependency in young children. *Child Development*, 1954, **25**, 125–146.

Stephens, W. N. Judgements by social workers on boys and mothers in fatherless families. *Journal of Genetic Psychology*, 1961, **99**, 59–64.

Stephens, W. N. *The Oedipus complex: Cross-cultural evidence.* Glencoe, Ill.: Free Press, 1962.

Stolz, L. M., et al. *Father relations of war-born children.* Stanford: Stanford University Press, 1954.

Suedfield, P. Paternal absence and overseas success of Peace Corps volunteers. *Journal of Consulting Psychology*, 1967, **31**, 424–425.

Sutton-Smith, B., Rosenberg, B. G., & Landy, F. Father–absence effects in families of different sibling compositions. *Child Development*, 1968, **38**, 1213–1221.

Sutherland, H. E. G. The relationship between IQ and size of family in the case of fatherless children. *Journal of Genetic Psychology*, 1930, **38**, 161–170.

Tasch, R. J. The role of the father in the family. *Journal of Experimental Education*, 1952, **20**, 319–361.

Tiller, P. O. Father-absence and personality development of children in sailor families. *Nordisk Psyckologi's Monograph Series*, 1958, **9**, 1–48.

Tiller, P. S. *Father separation and adolescence.* Oslo, Norway: Institute for Social Research, 1961.

Toby, J. The differential impact of family disorganization. *American Sociological Review*, 1957, **22**, 505–512.

Travis, J. Precipitating factors in manic-depressive psychoses. *Psychiatric Quarterly*, 1933, **8**, 411–418.

Trenaman, J. *Out of step.* London: Methuen, 1952.

Trunell, T. L. The absent father's children's emotional disturbances. *Archives of General Psychiatry*, 1968, **19**, 180–188.

Wahl, C. W. Antecedent factors in family histories of 392 schizophrenics. *American Journal of Psychiatry*, 1954, **110**, 668–676.

Wahl, C. W. Some antecedent factors in the family histories of 568 male schizophrenics of the U.S. Navy. *American Journal of Psychiatry*, 1956, **113**, 201–210.

Wallerstein, J. S., & Kelly, J. B. The effects of parental divorce: The adolescent experience. In E. J. Anthony & C. Koupernick (Eds.), *The child in his family: Children at psychiatric risk*, Vol. 3. New York: Wiley, 1974.

Wallerstein, J. S., & Kelly, J. B. The effects of parental divorce: Experiences of the preschool child. *Journal of the American Academy of Child Psychiatry*, 1975, **14**, 600–616.

Wallerstein, J. S., & Kelly, J. B. The effects of parental divorce: Experiences of the child in later latency. *American Journal of Orthopsychiatry*, 1976, **46**, 256–269.

Wallerstein, J. S., & Kelly, J. B. Divorce counseling: A community service for families in the midst of divorce. *American Journal of Orthopsychiatry*, 1977, **47**, 4–22.

Wallerstein, J. S., & Kelly, J. B. *Surviving the breakup: How children actually cope with divorce.* New York: Basic Books, 1980 (a).

Wallerstein, J. S., & Kelly, J. B. California's children of divorce. *Psychology Today,* 1980, **14,** 67–76 (b).

Walters, J. (Ed.), Fatherhood. *Family Coordinator,* 1976, **25,** 335–520 (Special issue).

Weiss, R. S. *Marital separation.* New York: Basic Books, 1975.

West, D. J. *Homosexuality.* Chicago: Aldine, 1967.

White, B. The relationship of self-concept and parental identification to women's vocational interests. *Journal of Consulting Psychology,* 1959, **6,** 202–206.

Whiting, J. W. M., Kluckhohn, R., & Anthony, A. The function of male initiation ceremonies at puberty. In E. E. Maccoby, T. M. Newcomb, & E. L. Hartley (Eds.), *Readings in social psychology.* New York: Holt, 1958.

Winch, R. F. The relation between loss of a parent and progress in courtship. *Journal of Social Psychology,* 1949, **29,** 51–56.

Winch, R. F. Some data bearing on the Oedipus hypothesis. *Journal of Abnormal and Social Psychology,* 1950, **45,** 481–489.

Wohlford, P., & Liberman, D. Effects of father absence on personal time, field independence, and anxiety. *Proceedings of the 78th Annual Convention of the American Psychological Association,* 1970, **5,** 263–264.

Wohlford, P., Santrock, J. W., Berger, S. E., & Liberman, D. Older brother influence on sex-typed, aggressive, and dependent behavior in father-absent children. *Developmental Psychology,* 1971, **4** 124–134.

Wood, H. P., & Duffy, E. L. Psychological factors in alcoholic women. *American Journal of Psychiatry,* 1966, **123,** 341–345.

Wylie, H. L., & Delgado, R. A. A pattern of mother-son relationship involving the absence of the father. *American Journal of Orthopsychiatry,* 1959, **29,** 644–649.

Author Index

Subject Index

Psychology and Psychiatry in Courts and Corrections: Controversy and Change
  by Ellsworth A. Fersch, Jr.
Restricted Environmental Stimulation: Research and Clinical Applications
  by Peter Suedfeld
Personal Construct Psychology: Psychotherapy and Personality
  edited by Alvin W. Landfield and Larry M. Leitner
Mothers, Grandmothers, and Daughters: Personality and Child Care in
Three-Generation Families
  by Bertram J. Cohler and Henry U. Grunebaum
Further Explorations in Personality
  edited by A. I. Rabin, Joel Aronoff, Andrew M. Barclay, and Robert A. Zucker
Hypnosis and Relaxation: Modern Verification of an Old Equation
  by William E. Edmonston, Jr.
Handbook of Clinical Behavior Therapy
  edited by Samuel M. Turner, Karen S. Calhoun, and Henry E. Adams
Handbook of Clinical Neuropsychology
  edited by Susan B. Filskov and Thomas J. Boll
The Course of Alcoholism: Four Years After Treatment
  by J. Michael Polich, David J. Armor, and Harriet B. Braiker
Handbook of Innovative Psychotherapies
  edited by Raymond J. Corsini
The Role of the Father in Child Development (Second Edition)
  edited by Michael E. Lamb